African Kingdoms

African Kingdoms

An Encyclopedia of Empires and Civilizations

Saheed Aderinto, Editor

ABC-CLIO™

An Imprint of ABC-CLIO, LLC
Santa Barbara, California • Denver, Colorado

Library of Congress Cataloging-in-Publication Data

Names: Aderinto, Saheed, editor.
Title: African kingdoms : an encyclopedia of empires and civilizations / Saheed Aderinto, editor.
Other titles: African kingdoms, an encyclopedia of empires and civilizations
Description: Santa Barbara, California : ABC-CLIO, LLC, [2017] | Includes bibliographical references and index.
Identifiers: LCCN 2017004700 (print) | LCCN 2017026779 (ebook) | ISBN 9781610695800 (ebook) | ISBN 9781610695794 (alk. paper)
Subjects: LCSH: Africa—History—To 1884—Encyclopedias. | Africa—Biography—Encyclopedias.
Classification: LCC DT25 (ebook) | LCC DT25 .A646 2017 (print) | DDC 960.03—dc23
LC record available at https://lccn.loc.gov/2017004700

ISBN: 978-1-61069-579-4
EISBN: 978-1-61069-580-0

21 20 19 18 17   1 2 3 4 5

This book is also available as an eBook.

ABC-CLIO
An Imprint of ABC-CLIO, LLC

ABC-CLIO, LLC
130 Cremona Drive, P.O. Box 1911
Santa Barbara, California 93116-1911
www.abc-clio.com

This book is printed on acid-free paper ∞
Manufactured in the United States of America

This book is dedicated to the Department of History, University of Ibadan (Nigeria), for its pioneering role in the academic study of Africa and its history.

Contents

List of Entries   ix

Preface   xi

Introduction: Uncovering Africa's Past   xiii

Timeline   xxvii

A–Z Entries   **1**

Primary Documents   295

Further Reading   323

About the Editor and the Contributors   331

Index   339

List of Entries

Adamawa
Aksum
Allada
Almohad
Almoravid
Alodia (Alwa)
Ankole (Nkore)
Arochukwu
Asante (Ashanti)
Badagry
Baguirmi
Bamum
Benin
Borno (Bornu, Kanem-Borno,
    Kanem-Bornu)
Buganda
Busoga
Carthage
Dahomey
Darfur
Denkyira
Dotawo
Egba (Abeokuta)
Egypt
Epe
Ethiopia
Fante
Fez
Funj (Sennar Sultanate)
Futa Jallon
Futa Toro
Ghana
Great Zimbabwe
Guiziga Bui Marva

Gyaman
Ibadan
Igala
Ijebu
Ile-Ife
Ilesa
Kaabu
Kano
Katsina
Kerma
Kilwa Kisiwani
Kitara
Kom
Kong
Kongo
Kuba
Kush
Lagos
Laimbwe
Lesotho
Loango
Luba
Lunda
Mahi
Mali
Malinke
Mandara
Mankessim
Mapungubwe
Maravi
Marinids
Meroë
Mutapa
Napata

Ndongo

Nobadia (Migi)

Nok

Nri

Numidia

Ogbomoso

Ohori

Ondo

Ouagadougou

Oyo (Old Oyo)

Rwanda

Sabé

Shambaa

Sokoto

Songhai

Takrur

Timbuktu

Toucouleur

Wanga

Weh *Fondom*

Whydah

Wolof (Jolof, Wollof, Ouolof)

Yatenga

Zulu

Preface

African Kingdoms: An Encyclopedia of Empires and Civilizations is a reference book on African civilization before the 1880s, when Europeans started to colonize much of Africa. States, kingdoms, and empires in precolonial Africa provide a clear window into the sophistication of African political, social, religious, and cultural institutions before the era of colonialism. Readers will encounter great men and women as well as notable events and achievements that ushered dramatic changes around the continent. Great scientific advancements, elaborate military and political institutions, intellectualism, and artistic prowess, among other achievements, were significant hallmarks of African precolonial civilization, which this encyclopedia highlights. The period covered reflects the change and continuity in African politics, which also informed the names of political entities, the vision of their leaders and "ordinary" people, their achievements and follies, and the pattern of their relations with the external world. While civilization such as that of Egypt emerged in ancient times, others such as the Ibadan Empire came into existence in the 19th century. The size of each kingdom was also shaped by the extent of human population or settlement, the environment, and other core physical or natural features. Thus, African civilizations functioned within the context of the opportunities and limitations imposed by the natural environment and humans' consistent attempts to transform it to meet their needs.

Regardless of when African empires, kingdoms, and states came into existence or the extent of their size and fame, one fact remains indisputable—Africa was a powerhouse of glorious civilizations. And as we shall see in the introduction, the term "civilization" needs to be rigorously contextualized to accommodate the diversity of ideas and practices among Africans from one era to another. The story of African civilization told from the perspectives of empires, kingdoms, and states validates the significance of a shared heritage of humanity across the world. From the history of warfare to the invention of writing and intellectualism, *African Kingdoms: An Encyclopedia of Empires and Civilizations* seeks to train a bright light on hidden historical treasures that validate the complex social, political, and religious institutions of the people of African past.

This encyclopedia contains a total of 91 alphabetically arranged entries covering the length and breadth of Africa. The entries attempt to trace the foundation of each kingdom, empire, and state to both internal and external political developments. The absence of written data in many parts of Africa in the precolonial period mean that it would be difficult to say in concrete terms when many African kingdoms emerged or ceased to exist. However, the approximate period given in the entries will help readers place historical development in time perspectives. The entries have been written in a language accessible to high school and college undergraduate students and nonspecialists interested in African history. Each entry ends with a "Further Reading" section, and the encyclopedia also includes a bibliography for readers interested in further research. The primary documents included in this encyclopedia will help students have direct engagement with the thoughts, ideas, and feelings of the people of the past. The authors of these documents varied from European travelers to Africans who documented their experiences of the communities where they lived or visited.

This project would not have come into existence without the contributors, who agreed with me that an encyclopedia focusing on African kingdoms and empires is necessary. I am grateful to them for attending to my numerous editorial demands at various stages of this project. I also thank the staff of the Western Carolina University library (especially Peter Johnson and Daniel Wendel) and research assistant Kyle Dreher for helping to search for and secure useful secondary and primary sources. My indebtedness goes to George Butler, my editor at ABC-CLIO, for allowing me to edit this encyclopedia. I am grateful to my wife, Olamide, and my children, Itandayo and Itandola, for supporting my career over the years.

Introduction
Uncovering Africa's Past
Saheed Aderinto

Every academic year, many high school and college students are introduced to African history for the first time. Some of the introductory lessons focus on the contributions of African kingdoms and states to world civilization. Instructors focus on kingdoms and empires for one main reason—they offer a critical window into African civilizations and the broader experiences of Africans over time, place, and space. Although textbooks on African history are legion, most of them treat African kingdoms cursorily and as part of a general survey of Africa, covering many centuries and thousands of ethnic groups. Some excellent academic monographs on specific kingdoms also exist. However, they are largely unsuitable for nonspecialist audiences and high school and college undergraduate students who need an accessible body of knowledge to fulfill general education requirement of the school curriculum or satisfy personal curiosity about non-Western societies.

African Kingdoms: An Encyclopedia of Empires and Civilizations addresses this deficiency and helps students learn more about several other kingdoms missing in most textbooks. More so, students and instructors will have core information on the exploits of each kingdom, state, and empire, comparing and contrasting how migration, geography, political processes, and other internal and external factors shaped popular history and consciousness. Students encountering African history for the first time and those taking world civilization courses will not have to scavenge through tons of library books to fully grasp the contributions of Africa to human civilization. *African Kingdoms: An Encyclopedia of Empires and Civilizations* offers a useful entry into researching broader African history by providing students with a handy source capable of initiating and sustaining critical thinking about comparative and cross-cultural civilizations. Materials in this encyclopedia include contemporary/modern reenactments of kingdoms in popular culture, movies, and arts. It is important to link the past with the present not just because this helps to emphasize the importance of historical events in shaping current thoughts but also because it is one of the best means of generating critical and culturally sensitive debate about the civilizations and achievements of the people of the past.

This encyclopedia draws on primary and secondary sources produced by both Africans and non-Africans. Contributors use popular oral traditions to corroborate and/or cross-examine documented information. Other useful bodies of material are derived from archaeology, arts, and written traveling accounts of European explorers, missionaries, and travelers who visited Africa. The life spans of the kingdoms and empires included in this encyclopedia vary widely. While some emerged thousands of years ago and survived until the European invasion of the 19th century, others came into prominence at the beginning of the 19th century and ceased to exist by the end of that century. Yet some have managed to survive up to the present day, undergoing significant cultural, political, and geographical changes wrought by colonialism and postcolonial quagmire. Regardless, the entries in this volume attempt to map out the changing geographies and cultural impacts of notable African kingdoms and states before European conquest of the 19th century. Some entries also detail the impact of colonial rule and postcolonial transformation within the context of the rise of modern states in Africa.

African Kingdoms: An Encyclopedia of Empires and Civilizations offers more than a critical insight into African politics, indigenous science and medicine, society, arts, customs, architecture, and military. This volume also renders a useful perspective on globalization. The entries situate the experiences of people of each kingdom, state, and community within regional and global histories of commerce, trade, and the exchange of ideas over several centuries. From ancient times, humans across time and place have shared customs ranging from food, language, and music to religion and spirituality. The massive movement of people across natural and artificial barriers permitted the flow of ideas, some of which have survived to today. This book thus sheds light on the foundations of modern globalization. The rise and fall and the expansion and contraction of kingdoms had strong implications for both internal and external African social structures. What is more, African kingdoms played a significant role in shaping Atlantic ideas before, during, and after the demise of the infamous transatlantic slave trade.

African Civilization in a Time Perspective: State and Empire Building in Africa

Until the second half of the 20th century, the study of African civilizations did not occupy a strategic position in academic discourse. The origins of this problem can be traced to the assumption that Africa did not have a civilization popularized by colonialists. European imperialists minimized (and in some cases completely denied) the contributions of Africans to the global history of humanity, science, technology, arts, literature, and leisure. The assumption that Africa did not have a civilization and or even a history was fueled in part by a Eurocentric conception of the term "civilization." The European colonialists who shaped the global perception toward the continent's history and culture tended to define civilization from their own prejudiced perspective. They believed that societies, which did not have their own historical artifacts, did not document the past in written form or conduct politics and organize society as the colonialists did and thus did not have a civilization. Slavery and the transatlantic slave trade contributed immensely to shaping a racialized perception of Africa. The dehumanization of Africans as objects of sale went hand in hand with the mischaracterization of the society that produced them as inferior, static, and unprogressive.

But from the early 1950s, significant archaeological discoveries and the works of local historians who documented their societies' histories in written form provided the fulcrum on which rested what I call the deracialization of African civilization. Archaeological research from the early 20th century has confirmed that Africa is the birthplace of humankind. Evidence from bone fragments and fossil skulls established that the earliest human ancestors probably lived in the high plains of Eastern Africa about 2 million years ago. In a site known as Olduvai Gorge in modern-day northern Tanzania, the earliest humans learned to make, shape, and use weapons and tools of stone to hunt a variety of game animals. Little is known about the daily lives of these first human inhabitants of the world. What is certain is that about 1 million years ago their population had increased. Remarkable differences in their body structure and shape were becoming apparent. It would appear that the core differences in bone structure, skin color, and other body and attitudinal features were formed about 30,000 years ago. Changes in the African climate, characterized by the shifting polar ice caps from wet to very dry, may have been responsible for the different looks that humans across Africa and beyond began to exhibit. Historians do not agree on the exact time that the earliest humans began to migrate out of Africa. What is certain is that they lived around well-watered areas and migrated eastwardly through the Middle East and India, into the various islands between the Indian Ocean and the Pacific Ocean, and eventually into Australia. As humans migrated outside Africa, they began to adapt to the natural environment of their new abode.

The history of the early human is patchy due to the absence of written records; however, it is certain that the first attempt by humans to transform the natural environment to meet their needs started in Africa. The basic needs of early Africans expanded from food and shelter to religion and spirituality, military expansion, music, architecture, and knowledge production. Indeed, the remarkable sophistication of African architecture and the African knowledge system, which both Africans and non-Africans began to document in written from the 12th century (or earlier), took several centuries of cultural, scientific, and artistic evolution. Some of the early European explorers of Africa from the 15th century accepted the truth about African civilization, which many others after them would deny. After sailing their ships down the South Atlantic and around the Cape of Good Hope in 1498, Vasco da Gama and his men were amazed by tall stone towns of wealth and comfort along the east coast of Africa. They then met people who knew about compasses and charts as they did. Similarly in 1518, Pope Leo X was surprised to learn from a captured Moor that the merchants and scholars of the legendary city of Timbuktu made greater profit from the sale of books than from other items of trade. This Moor was not merely trying to entertain the pope with fabricated stories about Africa; the incredibility of the intellectual life of Timbuktu was well known to many Africans of the region.

Yet, most of the early travelers of Africa could not fully comprehend the extent of the great African civilization they observed, because most of them did not penetrate into the hinterland. Many confined their activities along the coast and did not take time to associate with Africans in order to learn more about the historical and cultural contexts of what they observed. With time, early travelers discovered that reports on great African civilizations would not fascinate their European brethren and audience. So, they began to propagate falsehoods that satisfied the imagination of the European public, who fantasized about the remarkable racial and cultural difference of Africans and their alleged subhuman existence. The lurid details and misguided tales of Africans eating one another, living in trees, and having three eyes and a mouth on their foreheads aroused Europeans' curiosity about humans who were not lucky enough to have achieved the level of sophistication that existed in Europe. Indeed, much of the idea of Africa as a "dark" continent propagated until the 20th century was due to Europeans' lack of critical knowledge about the continent and a lot of misguided armchair comments.

One of the most significant achievements of African-centered scholarship that began to take firm root in the 1950s is a serious reconceptualization of what constitutes civilization in a cross-cultural and comparative sense. Pioneering Africanists have established that there is no universal criteria for measuring what constitutes civilization across societies and time. Each society developed cultural, social, and political institutions to serve its need. The peoples of these societies tamed the environment in order to maximize its numerous gains and delved into religion and spirituality in their endless quest to understand the complexity of the natural and supernatural world. African societies figured out ways to mobilize resources to address everyday challenges and responded to internal political changes as they emerged. What constitutes civilization must therefore be appreciated from local and indigenous perspectives, not from the viewpoint of the invaders of Africa.

If it is difficult to render a homogenous definition of civilization in global and periodic contexts, it is equally hard to say in absolute terms how big a society should be to qualify as an empire or a kingdom. Indeed, a simple contemporary English dictionary meaning of a kingdom as "a state or government having a king or queen as its head" and an empire as a "political unit having a territory of great extent or a number of territories or peoples under a single sovereign authority" cannot adequately explain the nature of political organization that existed in Africa before the European conquest of the 19th century. Information about the population and geographical stretch of precolonial African political entities is very sketchy. Thus, it would be difficult to use population and landmass to define kingdoms and empires within the African context. What is clear, however, is that many communities, such as the Igbo community in modern-day southeastern Nigeria, did not receive the appellation of a "kingdom" because it did not have a centralized political system ruled by a king. Yet, the Igbo community could have been as big or even bigger than societies ruled by kings and labeled "kingdoms." In another vein, communities defined as "empires" because they had many vassal states could be smaller than many societies designated as "kingdoms." However, a society does not have to be a kingdom or an empire to have civilization. While the nature of political organization is significant, the achievements of the society in art, music, architecture, law, philosophy, science and medicine, and education and intellectualism, among others elements of civilization, are the most vital.

The expansion and contraction of African societies due to state building, marriage and political agglomeration, and wars of expansion took place rapidly. A kingdom in one decade or century could later become an empire and vice versa. Many empires started as small autonomous communities blessed with visionary leaders and enabling natural and human resources. A kingdom or an empire could collapse, but its civilization may not. Indeed, when empires fall, their remains are absorbed into existing communities, where they can remain relevant for decades or even centuries. In other instances, a collapsed empire can be re-created elsewhere. Its lost glories, artifacts, and social and political institutions can be reinvented or reinstated in another location. This is particularly the case of the Old Oyo Empire. After its demise in the third decade of the 19th century, this most prosperous Yoruba empire ever known was reinvented in the mid-19th century in a completely different location. From the early 20th century, the Oyo Empire assumed an important position in colonial politics when the British gave the king enormous power, far beyond the one the empire had in the mid-19th century.

Thus, one of the major challenges of writing about African civilization from the perspectives of empires, states, and kingdoms is the need to trace their transformation over time. As some of the entries in this encyclopedia establish, some empires assume the names of ethnic groups and vice versa. Hence, Ijebu is both a Yoruba subethnic group and a territory consisting of kingdoms and towns of varying sizes, histories, and influence. If it is difficult to say in absolute terms when many kingdoms rose to power, it can be challenging to put a definite date on when they collapsed. With the exception of the African kingdoms that were sacked by European conquest in the 19th and early 20th centuries, pinpointing the exact year that many African empires ceased to exist is not an easy task. The reason for this is not far-fetched. The absence of written accounts in most African cultures until the 20th century means that historians have to rely on oral traditions, which rarely tell the exact dates when events took place. Moreover, naming and renaming of political entities due to wars, political agglomeration or disintegration, and change in leadership, to mention but a few, constitutes a great challenge for effectively tracking the transformation of societies. Be that as it may, what seems important is not just the nature of political systems but also the level of social, economic, and political activities that defined the activities of each society.

One of the obvious imbalances in the study of African kingdoms is the limited attention given to the role of women. A cursory reading of the massive documentation on empire and state building will lead one to conclude that only men were responsible for creating polities and political institutions. However, scholars of African women and gender have successfully proved that women were actively involved in virtually all stages of empire building as warriors, peacemakers, and suppliers of essential wartime materials. Indeed, economic activities such as farming and trading, which supplied the resources for war prosecution, were conducted by women across generations. Iyalode Afunsetan Aniwura, the head of the women and female chiefs in Ibadan, as Bolanle Awe and LaRay Denzer have shown, did not appear at the war front, as did her male counterparts. However, she supplied soldiers, arms, and other war supplies that strengthened Ibadan, Yoruba's most militarized state in the 19th century. Dahomey even had a regiment of women soldiers whose exploits have been successfully documented by historians, including

Edna Bay. It is on record that Mai Idris Aloma, the most famous Sefuwa ruler in Borno, received his knowledge of politics from his mother, Magira Aisa Kili.

Women's role in empire building went beyond serving as political advisers or suppliers of the human and material resources for waging wars. In some parts of the continent they were the main political and military leaders of their communities, making laws, leading armies, and organizing polities. Oral tradition affirmed that the rulers of Daura before the ninth century were women, the *magajiyas* (queens). If records of the exploits of these early female Daura rulers are unclear due to the absence of reliable sources, that of Amina, who became the queen of Zazzau around 1576, is clear. Before ascending the throne, Amina had distinguished herself on the battlefield and in military matters. The kingmakers had no other choice but to crown her as queen because she was the most qualified person to lead her community, which was under constant military attacks—like other states and empires in the central Sudan region.

What is more, the intersections of women, household, and statecraft has occupied the attention of Africanists, including Emily Lynn Osborn. Anyone familiar with the literature on African political and women's history would readily agree with Osborn in her study of the Bate society (present-day Guinea-Conakry) between the 17th and early 20th centuries that previous studies have paid limited attention to the relationship between statecraft and the household. They tend to focus largely on the activities of male elites and the public institutions they created at the expense of discourse on how the domestic sphere was structured and recognized as a site of political power. According to Osborn, "when men make states—and men consistently dominate state-making during the period under study—they also make households" (Osborn 2011, 1). She engages the shifting manner in which the past of the Bate society is narrated and its implication on how power was maintained, distributed, and transmitted across time and space. Her interesting story of how a household-centered statecraft in precolonial Bate gave way to a public and male-dominated one under French colonialism is important not only for the history of politics and gender relations but also for coming to terms with the origin of one of the core issues in postcolonial discourse of underdevelopment—women's lack of political and economic agency.

Social, Political, and Religious Institutions and Thought in Africa

Physical historical artifacts such as city walls, temples, shrines, and pyramids are not the only obvious evidence of the greatness of African civilizations. Others include complex religious, cultural, political, and philosophical and social thoughts and institutions. Africans, like other humans, attempted to understand their physical, natural, and supernatural environment and their place in it. This quest paved the way for creating ideas, knowledge, and practices that formed the bedrock of social and political institutions. Laws and customs, among other elements of traditions, were all invented to suit a particular purpose or set of ideals at a point in time. They were also regularly revised to accommodate changes in the political and social orders. Hence, the idea that precolonial Africa was culturally static until the colonial conquest of the 19th century is objectionable. Indeed, social change under colonial rule is part of a long history of transformation. Colonialism, as J. F. A. Ajayi has established, is an episode in African history of social change.

To start with, the diversity of the African myths of the origin of the universe challenge the homogenization of African experience—it compels us to rethink popular assumptions that African culture was/is the same across the continent. Yet, the common traits found in these myths validate the long history of cultural contact and sharing. Three main types of African creation myths are discernible. The first type, as seen among the Bushoong of Central Africa, credited the creation of the world to a primordial creator god. The myth contends that at the beginning of the world there were water, darkness, and Bumba, the creator god. One day Bumba experienced stomach pain, which caused him to vomit the sun. The intensity of the sun caused the water to dry out, leading to the creation of the land. Bumba later vomited the moon, the stars, and animals. Humans came last. The second category of myth posits that Earth was primordial and that the creator emerged from it. The Fulani of West Africa, for instance, believed that at first there was a drop of milk. Doondari, who made stone, then emerged from the milk. The stone then made iron, the iron created fire, fire made water, and water made air. Humans were created during Doondari's second trip to Earth. The third category of myths holds that both the gods and Earth were primordial. In the worldview of the Ijo of the Niger Delta of modern-day Nigeria, a field existed with a giant *iroko* tree. Suddenly a massive table descended, and on it were a big pile of dirt, a chair, and a large creation stone. Later a female deity, Woyengi, descended from heaven, rested her leg on the stone, and created humans from the dirt.

Regardless, African creation myths served multiple purposes across societies. Not only did the myths help in defining identity and forging sociocultural alliances across ethnicities, but they also served as the main fulcrum on which many religious ideologies rest. Religion reflected the complex relations that Africans established with nature and the physical environment. Natural features such as rivers, mountains and hills, and forests were the abode of the gods and goddesses, reminding people of the enormous power of nature. As sites/locations of historical events central to the life of the community, they connected people back to the realities of the past, directly or indirectly, consciously or unconsciously. The gods and goddesses were mostly former humans who made significant contributions to their society and were later deified and worshipped by the family and the community at large. Regular sacrifice and ritualistic veneration of the gods and goddesses were significant historical reenacstment that reminded people of the great men and women of the past. It was easy to invoke the achievement of the peoples of the past through rituals, because in most African societies physical death did not represent the end of life. When people die they simply transit to another world (the realm of the ancestors), where they moderate the affairs of the living. In other words, the human soul is indestructible. Sacrifices were important to ensure that the living continue to communicate with the ancestors, who still hold enormous power over the living. In most African religious cultures, the place of a supreme God was incontestable. The smaller gods, goddesses, ancestors, and deities served as a bridge to the supreme God. If contemporary culture and politics undermine the role of women, ancient African societies upheld it. Indeed, female and male deities complemented the power of each other in the maintenance of harmony between the living and the ancestors.

Yet, as Ali Mazrui has rightly observed, Africa is a continent of the triple heritage of traditional religion and spirituality, Islam, and Christianity. While cultural and social institutions centered on indigenous religions, they were complemented over time with Islamic thought, especially in the northern, western, and eastern parts of the continent. From the 12th century or earlier, Islam entered the main political structure of many African kingdoms and societies. Historians generally agree that Islam paved the way for the documentation of the history of many parts of the continent. In fact, the earliest written accounts of the history of modern-day Mali and northern Nigeria from the 14th century were written in Arabic. The linguistic culture of communities expanded as Arabic words, sayings, and proverbs entered and found a comfortable place in indigenous language and thought. Indeed, jihad (holy war), which led to the rise and demise of kingdoms, empires, and states, was inspired by Islamic revivalism. For example, the Sokoto Caliphate, the largest Islamic state in early 20th-century Africa, did not exist before the 19th century. Its rise and fall within a century testifies to the massive impact of Islam in Africa. Because politics had a strong influence on broader social processes, the Islamic jihad, which led to the creation and destruction of many political entities in 19th-century West Africa, also ushered in significant social change. Marriage, music, thought, and art all underwent massive transformations, drawing from local values and the imported Islamic culture. Thus, what constitutes "African" culture and civilization needs to be thoroughly contextualized and conceptualized within the framework of the interaction (and sometimes conflict) between indigenous and foreign cultural implantation.

What is true about Islam is equally correct about Christianity. Although Christianity did not begin to have a strong physical presence in Africa until the first half of the 19th century, its spread from that period would be speedy and steady. The divergence of the doctrine of the Christian missions that came to Africa in the 19th century meant that Africa would accommodate a multiplicity of Christian virtues. Thus, it is easy to differentiate between the Catholic Africa and the Methodist Africa. The European Christian missions were the first to introduce Western education to most parts of Africa from the 19th century as they struggled among one another for the African soul. The intersection of Western education and Christianity went beyond salvation and spirituality—it was also about cultural change. Significant social change was reflected in the rise of new educated elites (especially in West Africa), the majority of whom were also liberated slaves and their descendants. They introduced the first wave of modern entrepreneurship and intellectualism. They were also the first to revolt against the racial practices of the European churches by establishing African churches from the second half of the 19th century. The Africanization of Christianity was a direct testimony to the creativity of Africans in making a local expression of a foreign religion. Without this first generation of modern African intellectuals, nationalism and decolonization in 20th-century Anglophone West Africa would have taken a completely different turn.

Some, especially the Brazilian returnees, introduced Brazilian architecture and entrepreneurship in places such as Lagos and Ghana. The introduction of Brazilian architecture to West Africa validates how culture and place-belonging can shape artistry and architectural ingenuity. But more important, it demonstrates that African civilization was built not only by continental Africans but also by returnees from the diaspora who resettled among their long-lost brethren.

The discussion of the role of indigenous religion and Islam and Christianity in precolonial Africa leads to that of local conception of history and its transmission and documentation. A portion of the oral poem of Basorun Ogunmola, a distinguished warrior of 1860s Ibadan, reads:

Akokoluko ebo ti pa'gun le' rin
Opolopo ojo ti le'gun wo'le, keri, keri, keri
Okele akobu ti'ro gan gan di
Ina'ju ekun ti de'ru b'ode

[a massive sacrifice that amazes the vulture
the torrential rain that stops a masquerade from performing in public
the first morsel/bite of a solid food that worries the anus
the sight of a tiger that frightens the hunter]

This praise poem is a testimony to the creativity of the Yoruba in tapping into the natural, supernatural, physical, and even animal worlds in rendering an interesting profile of a distinguished personality. Significantly, it is about how a society generates knowledge and transmits it from one generation to another. Until the 20th century, when the imposition of colonial rule intensified the documentation of African history in written form, the pasts of most societies were stored in oral traditions. History was also a daily performance in that songs, sayings, proverbs, and statements connected people back to the realities of the past directly and indirectly, consciously and unconsciously. History manifested in the daily passage of time, in religious observances, and in social, political, and economic relations. Societies created historical narratives from observing everyday actions of communities, peoples, events, and circumstances. Some communities had special chieftaincy titles and persons (such as the griots of modern-day Mali) saddled with the responsibility of orally documenting and educating the community about history and indigenous practices. Moonlight stories told by elderly people to children were occasionally tied to the rite of passage and initiation into age grades and the transition from childhood to adulthood. Significant judicial decisions and collective responses to core challenges of state building served as markers of or reference points to a much bigger historical narrative. Oral traditions ensured that future generations had access to the achievements and follies of their ancestors. It is also dynamic because the indigenous mode of generating knowledge was rarely monopolized by any group of people or chieftaincy institution. The constant conflict over historical truth can partly be attributed to the diverse interpretation accorded to popular events of the past or the need to challenge the dominant version of a story promoted by powerful people.

Be that as it may, the dynamism of oral traditions, a significant element of African civilization, points to the value of history in precolonial African societies. Indeed, history was vital in every aspect of African life. It shaped decision making, guided actions, and molded attitudes and interpersonal and communal relations. History manifested in the daily veneration of the ancestors, in economic transaction, in marriage and career choices, and in life trajectories in general. The complexity of African oral traditions has led to a number of misconceptions about Africa. Indeed, until the 1950s Western academic culture did not believe that oral tradition is history. Academics, colonial administrators, and commentators thought that Africans who did not document their past in written form did not have history. They equated history with documented facts. This Euro-centric conception of the past equally shaped racial attitudes toward Africans. In fact, the European conquest of Africa was informed in part by the notion that Africa required colonialism because it lacked history. This attitude toward oral tradition clearly reveals that what constitutes an authentic past and the manner of transmission varies from one society to another. By the 1950s and 1960s, pioneering Africanist historians were able to successfully convince their counterparts working in Western historical tradition that oral tradition is history and that a large body of oral traditions could be collected, analyzed, and carefully synthesized to reconstruct the history of a society. Oral tradition has its own limitations (such as lack of dates and deliberate and nondeliberate distortion), which scholars and practitioners must contend with. However, these limitations do not override their importance as a useful source of history. One of the main arguments in favor of oral tradition is that the fact that a history is written does not mean it is authentic. All sources of history thus have their own shortcomings.

The mechanism for creating and transmitting oral tradition was definitely a component of indigenous African education, which focused on the training of the mind, body, hands, brain, and soul for the benefit of the family and the community at large. Thus, indigenous education was a total training that prepared an individual to assume social, economic, political, and military responsibilities in the community. Occupational training was central to indigenous education. Right from childhood, boys and girls learned the trade and craft of their parents and families to produce the economic and social capital for the larger community. The Asante would attach a small boy to an elder farmer and be given a small area of land to cultivate to ensure active participation. As he grew up, the boy was given a gun and gradually prepared to help defend the community. Girls would help their mothers with farmwork, food processing, domestic chores, and everyday running of the household. They would also learn simple arithmetic, as this helped them with trading and commercial transactions. The age grade system found in many parts of Africa was not just about rites of passage and festivals. It was a system carefully designed to educate children in the conundrum of the society. Children and youths learned from difference educators, which included parents and community leaders. Group learning fostered interpersonal communications, teamwork, the exchange of ideas, and self-expression, all of which helped communal harmony.

The introduction of Islam and Christianity expanded African education without killing preexisting educational norms. In addition to learning from home, children received additional training in European languages and Arabic. Indigenous education and Islamic and European education had a lot in common. For instance, they all involved memorization of information and facts. However, the distinct advantage of European and Islamic education was documentation. Some African Muslims and Christians began to document the history of their communities in Arabic and European languages centuries or decades before the imposition of colonial rule. Nana Asma'u, a princess, poet, and teacher and the daughter of Usman dan Fodio, the founder of the Sokoto Caliphate, is a good example of how Africans seized the opportunity of the introduction of Islam to expand the literary experience of their people. Over three dozens of Asma'u's surviving literary works, written in the 19th century, give an unusual insight into the history, politics, and culture of West Africa. Samuel Johnson of the Yoruba used his knowledge of English, which he acquired in Christian mission schools, to write the first detailed history of the Yoruba in the late 19th century. His book *The History of the Yorubas* has remained a classic and indispensable work for scholars across generations. In each case, we see how Africans combined their mastery of indigenous knowledge with European and Arabic literacy to produce works that affirm the brilliance of indigenous African thought.

The discussion of African education leads us to another form of knowledge system: divination. The central purpose of divination was to gain access to information or ideas not available through ordinary empirical means. Divination systems are poetic and philosophical statements and historical records on the societies that generated and used them for diverse purposes. The divination system was also used to diagnose diseases and misfortune, forecast the future, and provide the guidelines for peaceful inter- and intracommunal relations. Indeed, some divination system, especially that of the Yoruba (called Ifá), have been recognized as a treasure trove by UNESCO and studied in universities across the world. The sources of the information contained in divination systems were usually ancestors or god figures, relayed through a human medium. The methods of relaying information varied widely. Zulu mediums interpreted messages in dreams, while others, especially the Banem, Mambila, and Dogon, all used animal oracles. While the Banen and Mambila used spiders and land crabs, the Dogon used a fox, the animal that featured prominently in the people's creation story. The divination systems of many Islamic societies, including the Yoruba, made use of inanimate tools, such as the cowrie shell system and a random binary system using a tray covered with dust or sand. The Yoruba also used kola nuts.

Regardless of the methods of unlocking the unseen in the natural and supernatural worlds, acquiring the knowledge of divination required years of apprenticeship under superior diviners, who also served as cultural brokers in many societies. Like most professions in precolonial Africa, divination practice was usually monopolized by a family or community, who ensured that the art was transmitted from one generation to another. The regular sacrifices and rites of passage ceremonies conducted during divination training and after were all meant to initiate new practitioners into the mediumship realm, required for discerning and interpreting messages from the source of divination—the gods, goddesses, and ancestors.

Politics was central to African civilization. It ensured the distribution of social, economic, and political resources and goods across the community. Politics operated at diverse levels of African societies—home, community, town, and empire. But the most popular form of politics was the public type, which operated at the level of the community and the town or empire. The central purpose of public politics was peace and order, required for the society to grow. Indeed, all the evidence of African civilization—from the great pyramids of Egypt to the massive philosophies embedded in the divination system— flourished in the atmosphere of peace. It was also through politics that the society mobilized resources for collective growth, military recruitment and defense, and the administration of justice. One feature of politics in big empires is the delegation of power. The king or emperor allowed junior chiefs to coordinate politics in smaller towns and vassal states in order to ensure effective governance and retain loyalty. Each component/section of the society (military, religion, women, trade, public works, youths) had chiefs who oversaw them. Communities that did not have kings or centralized political cultures devised mechanisms to run their societies, using popular consensus among other methods, to make vital decisions.

The origins of political ideas and laws used for governing each society varied across time. But the similarities in the ways societies were governed is a clear indication that people shared ideas and borrowed practices, domesticating them to fit their needs. Many laws were definitely made by influential people, including kings and queens. The inevitable powers of the ancestors in African life made them a clear source of laws. Through their spirit medium, they could invoke orders and make laws, which everyone was expected to follow. In some cases, cultural practices were transformed into laws and used to mediate relations. African societies did learn from the mistakes of the past. In order to avoid repeating mistakes, laws could be made and enforced by the political and religious elites.

It is difficult to differentiate between law and custom, for they were closely intertwined. A contravention of customary practices invariably meant the breaking of laws. For instance, killing animals in the sacred forest or grove in most African societies was a taboo. Punishment for offenses depended on the severity and the individuals involved. Adultery was usually punished by banishment or presentation of sacrifice to the gods and goddesses, while capital punishment was inflicted for homicide and blasphemy. The introduction of Islam to Africa expanded the continent's legal system. In many parts of the continent, Islamic law coexisted with indigenous law, creating a lot of crisis of accommodation. In fact, many of the holy wars (jihad) were caused by the quest to entrench sharia, the Islamic legal system.

In sum, *African Kingdoms: An Encyclopedia of Empires and Civilizations* attempts to recover the glorious African past. The entries introduce readers to major empires and kingdoms, their political organization, and their achievement in arts, architecture, intellectualism, religion and spirituality, and science, to mention but a few.

Further Reading

Abimbola, Wande. *Sixteen Great Poems of Ifa*. Paris: UNESCO, 1975.

Abubakr, Sa'ad. "Queen Amina of Zaria." In *Nigerian Women in Historical Perspective*, edited by Bolanle Awe, 13–23. Lagos: Sankore, 1992.

Adediran, Biodun. *The Frontier States of Western Yorubaland, 1600–1889*. Ibadan: IFRA, 1994.

Adekunle, Julius. "Education." In *Africa*, Vol. 2, *African Cultures and Societies before 1885*, edited by Toyin Falola, 59–72. Durham, NC: Carolina Academic Press, 2000.

Adeleye, R. A. *Power and Diplomacy in Northern Nigeria, 1804–1906: The Sokoto Caliphate and Its Enemies*. Ibadan: Oxford University Press, 1971.

Aderinto, Saheed. "Crime and Punishment in Africa." In *Encyclopedia of Society and Culture in the Ancient World*, Vol. 1, edited by Peter Bogucki, 296–297. New York: Facts on File, 2008.

Aderinto, Saheed. "Law and Legal Codes in Africa." In *Encyclopedia of Society and Culture in the Ancient World*, Vol. 4, edited by Peter Bogucki, 621–622. New York: Facts on File, 2008.

Ajayi, J. F. A. *Christian Missions in Nigeria, 1841–1891: The Making of a New Elite*. Evanston, IL: Northwestern University Press, 1965.

Ajayi, J. F. A. "Colonialism: An Episode in African History." In *Colonialism in Africa, 1870–1960*, Vol. 1., edited by L. H. Gann and Peter Duignan, 497–509. Cambridge: Cambridge University Press, 1969.

Akinjogbin, A. I. *Dahomey and Its Neighbors, 1708–1818*. Cambridge: Cambridge University Press, 1967.

Atanda, J. A. *The New Oyo Empire: Indirect Rule and Change in Western Nigeria, 1894–1934*. London: Longman, 1973.

Awe, Bolanle. "The Iyalode in the Traditional Yoruba Political System." In *Sexual Stratification: A Cross Cultural View*, edited by Alice Schlegel, 144–160. New York: Columbia University Press, 1977.

Awolalu, J. Omosade, and P. Adelumo Dopamu. *West African Traditional Religion*. Ibadan: Onibonoje, 1979.

Bascom, William. *Ifa Divination: Communication between Gods and the Men in West Africa*. Bloomington: Indiana University Press, 1991.

Bay, Edna G. *Wives of the Leopard: Gender, Politics, and Culture in the Kingdom of Dahomey*. Charlottesville: University of Virginia Press, 1998.

Berman, Edward H. *African Reactions to Missionary Education*. New York: Teachers College Press, 1975.

Curtin, Philip. *The Image of Africa: British Ideas and Action, 1780–1850*. Madison: University of Wisconsin Press, 1964.

Davidson, Basil. *Africa in History: Themes and Outlines*. New York: Touchstone Books, 1966.

Davidson, Basil. *African Kingdoms*. New York: Time-Life Books, 1966.

Denzer, LaRay. "The Iyalode in Ibadan Politics and Society: A Preliminary Study." In *Ibadan: An Historical, Cultural, and Socio-Economic Study of an African City*, edited by G. O. Ogunremi, 201–234. Lagos: Cargo Press and Oluyole Club, 2000.

Fajana, Adewunmi. *Education in Nigeria, 1842–1939: An Historical Analysis*. London: Longman, 1978.

Falola, Toyin, ed. *Africa,* Vol. 1, *African History before 1885.* Durham, NC: Carolina Academic Press, 2000.

Falola, Toyin, ed. *Africa,* Vol. 2, *African Cultures and Societies before 1885.* Durham, NC: Carolina Academic Press, 2000.

Falola, Toyin, and Saheed Aderinto. *Nigeria, Nationalism, and Writing History.* Rochester: University of Rochester Press, 2010.

Griaule, Marcel. *Conversations with Ogotemmeli: An Introduction to Dogon Religious Ideas.* London: Oxford University Press, 1965.

Hamilton, Carolyn. *Terrific Majesty: The Powers of Shaka Zulu and the Limits of Historical Invention.* Cambridge, MA: Harvard University Press, 1998.

Idowu, E. Bolaji. *Olodumare: God in Yoruba Belief.* London: Longman, 1962.

Johnson, Samuel. *The History of the Yorubas: From the Earliest Times to the Beginning of the British Protectorate.* 1921; reprint, London: Routledge/Kegan Paul, 1966.

Kopytoff, Jean H. *Preface to Modern Nigeria: The "Sierra Leonians" in Yoruba, 1830–1890.* Madison: University of Wisconsin Press, 1965.

Kyles, Perry. "The African Origin of Humanity." In *Africa and the Wider World,* edited by Hakeem Ibikunle Tijani, Raphael Chijioke Njoku, and Tiffany Fawn Jones, 28–40. New York: Learning Solutions, 2010.

Last, D. M. *The Sokoto Caliphate.* New York: Humanities Press, 1967.

Mack, Beverly B., and Jean Boyd. *One Woman's Jihad: Nana Asma'u, Scholar and Scribe.* Bloomington: Indiana University Press, 2000.

Mair, Lucy. *African Kingdoms.* Oxford, UK: Clarendon, 1977.

Mazrui, Ali. *The Africans: A Triple Heritage.* Boston: Little, Brown, 1986.

Niane, D. T. *Sundiata: An Epic of Old Mali.* Translated by G. D. Pickett. London: Longman, 1965.

O'Connor, Kathleen. "Talking to Gods: Divination Systems." In *Africa,* Vol. 2, *African Cultures and Societies before 1885,* edited by Toyin Falola, 95–105. Durham, NC: Carolina Academic Press, 2000.

Olajubu, Oyeronke. *Women in the Yoruba Religious Sphere.* Albany: State University of New York Press, 2003.

Oloruntimehin, B. O. *The Segu Tukulor Empire.* London: Longman, 1972.

Osborn, Emily Lynn. *Our New Husbands Are Here: Households, Gender, and Politics in a West African State from the Slave Trade to Colonial Rule.* Athens: Ohio University Press, 2011.

Scanlon, David D., ed. *Church, State, and Education in Africa.* New York: Teachers College Press, 1966.

Shillington, Kevin, *History of Africa.* New York: Palgrave Macmillan, 2005.

Smaldone, Joseph P. *Warfare in the Sokoto Caliphate: Historical and Sociological Perspectives.* Cambridge: Cambridge University Press, 1977.

Tishken, Joel. "Indigenous Religions." In *Africa,* Vol. 2, *African Cultures and Societies before 1885,* edited by Toyin Falola, 73–94. Durham, NC: Carolina Academic Press, 2000.

Vansina, J. *Oral Tradition as History.* London. James Currey, 1985.

Webster, J. B. *The African Churches among the Yoruba, 1888–1922.* London: Clarendon, 1964.

Timeline

Ancient Period, Prehistoric Era to Circa 30 BCE

ca. 100,000 BCE   Humans migrate from Africa to other parts of the world.

ca. 5000 BCE   Farming begins in Egypt.

ca. 4000 BCE   Metalworking (copper) is practiced in Sinai.

ca. 3118 BCE   King Menes unites the kingdoms of Upper and Lower Egypt.

ca. 2600 BCE   The first pyramids are built in Egypt.

ca. 2000 BCE   Bantu-speaking people begin to migrate southward.

ca. 1700 BCE   The Kingdom of Kush emerges south of Egypt.

ca. 1000 BCE   The Barber civilization emerges in North Africa.

ca. 814 BCE   The city of Carthage is founded in Tunisia.

ca. 650 BCE   Ironworking spreads in North Africa.

ca. 30 BCE   Egypt becomes a province of the Roman Empire.

Precolonial Period, Circa 30 BCE–1880s

ca. 50 CE   The Kingdom of Aksum comes into existence in modern-day Ethiopia.

ca. 350 CE   Bantu-speaking people arrive in Zambia.

ca. 500 CE   Ironworking reaches Southern Africa.

ca. 642 CE   The Arabs conquer Egypt.

ca. 650 CE   Muslims travel across the Sahara on camels to trade and spread Islam.

ca. 698 CE   The Arabs capture Carthage.

ca. 800 CE   Trading towns are formed on the east coast of Africa.

ca. 1100 CE   The Kingdom of Ife in modern-day southwestern Nigeria becomes important.

ca. 1300 CE   The Kingdom of Benin in modern-day Nigeria becomes significant.

ca. 1315 CE   The Mossi kingdom is founded.

1324	Mansa Musa, the ruler of Mali, makes a pilgrimage to Mecca and displays his enormous wealth.
1325–1353	Ibn Battuta is traveling in different parts of Africa.
1327	Sankore University in Timbuktu is established.
1350	The Kingdom of Songhai arises in West Africa.
1375	The Adal kingdom is founded.
1415	The Portuguese conquer Ceuta in North Africa.
1434	The Portuguese reach the coast of West Africa.
1450s	The transatlantic slave trade begins.
1464–1491	Songhai under Sunni Ali conquers territories and expand.
1488	The Portuguese sail around the Cape of Good Hope.
1508	The Portuguese begin to settle in Mozambique.
1509	Bunyoro Kingdom is established.
1517	The Turks conquers Egypt.
1518	African captives are transported across the Atlantic by Europeans.
1525	The Turks take control of Algiers.
1530	Christianity is first established in the Benin kingdom.
1551	The Turks capture Tripoli.
1562	England joins the transatlantic slave trade.
1564	The Songhai Empire destroys the Mali Empire.
1571	The Portuguese begin to settle in Angola.
1590	Timbuktu is captured by the Moroccans.
1591	The Moroccans destroy the Songhai Empire.
1652	The Dutch found a colony in South Africa.
1700	Rise of the Asante kingdom in West Africa.
1722	French slaves and settlers arrive in Mauritius.
1723	A number of frontier wars begin between the Boers and the Bantu-speaking Xhosas of South Africa.
1725	The Imamate of Futa Jallon is founded.
1750	The Islamic revival movement spreads across western Sudan.
1791	The British found a colony for freed slaves in Sierra Leone.
1795–1797	Mungo Park explores the Niger River.
1804	The jihad of Usman dan Fodio begins.
1806	The Dutch colony in South Africa becomes a British colony.
1807	Sierra Leone and Gambia become British crown colonies. Britain abolishes the slave trade.

1811	Muhammad Ali attains power in Egypt.
1814	The first European school appears in West Africa.
1817	The Yoruba Civil War begins.
1819	Shaka founds the Zulu Empire.
1820s	Lesotho emerges as a powerful state in Southern Africa.
1822	The United States founds a colony for freed slaves in Liberia, West Africa.
1828	Shaka, king of the Zulus, is assassinated.
1830	The French invade Algeria.
1840s	The Ndebele state emerges in modern-day Zimbabwe.
1845	The first European high school is established in Sierra Leone.
1847	Liberia becomes independent.
1853	Botswana forces defeat Boer invaders.
1855	David Livingstone discovers Victoria Falls.
1858	John Speke discovers Lake Victoria.
1859–1869	The Suez Canal is built in Egypt.
1861	The British annex Lagos.
1873–1874	The Anglo-Asante War is fought.
1880–1881	War between the British and Boers in South Africa takes place.
1881	The Mahdist Revolt in Sudan begins.

Colonial Period, 1880s–1960s

1882	The British Army occupies Egypt and Sudan.
1884	The Germans take Cameroon, Togo, Namibia, and Tanzania.
	The Mahdis lead an anti-British uprising in Sudan.
1884–1885	The Berlin Africa conference takes place.
1885	The Mahdis capture Khartoum.
	King Leopold II annexes the Congo.
1886	Kenya becomes a British colony.
	Ethiopia defeats Italy in the Battle of Adowa.
	Gold is discovered in Transvaal.
1888–1889	The British take control of Rhodesia (Zimbabwe).
1891	Bishop Samuel Ajayi Crowther dies.
1893	The Yoruba Civil War ends.
1894	The British colonize Uganda.
1896	The Italians invade Ethiopia.

1898	The British defeat the Sudanese in the Battle of Omdurman.
1899–1902	The Boer War is fought in South Africa.
1908	The Congo formally becomes a Belgian colony.
1910	The Union of South Africa becomes independent from Britain.
1912	Italy conquers Libya.
1914	World War I begins.
1917–1919	The influenza pandemic occurs.
1920	The National Congress of British West Africa comes into existence.
1929	The Great Depression begins.
	The Women's War in modern-day southern Nigeria takes place.
1935–1936	Italy conquers Ethiopia.
1939	World War II begins.
1941	The British drive the Italians out of Ethiopia.
1942	The British defeat the Germans and Italians at El Alamein in Egypt.
1943	German and Italian forces in North Africa surrender.
1948	Apartheid is introduced in South Africa.
1951	Libya receives independence.
1952–1955	The Mau Mau Uprising takes place in Kenya.
1956	Morocco, Tunisia, and Sudan become independent.
	Oil is discovered in Nigeria.
1957	Ghana becomes an independent state.

Postcolonial Period, 1960s–Present

1960	Nigeria becomes independent.
	The Sharpeville Massacre in South Africa takes place.
1962	Uganda becomes independent.
1963	Kenya becomes independent.
1964	Zambia and Malawi become independent.
	The state of Tanzania is formed.
1965	Gambia becomes independent.
1966	Botswana becomes independent.
1967	Diamonds are discovered in Botswana.
1967–1970	Civil war occurs in Nigeria.

1969	Colonel Muammar Gaddafi takes power in Libya.
1971	Idi Amin seizes power in Uganda.
1973	Amilcar Cabral of Guinea-Bissau is assassinated.
1974	Emperor Haile Selassie of Ethiopia is deposed.
1975	Angola and Mozambique become independent.
	The Economic Community of West African States is formed.
1976	The Soweto Uprising takes place in South Africa.
1980	Robert Mugabe becomes the prime minister of Zimbabwe.
1981	The World Bank report on the recolonization of Africa is published.
1983–1985	The World Bank begins to impose structural adjustment programs on African countries.
1989	Civil war begins in Liberia.
1990	Namibia receives its independence.
1992	Civil war breaks out in Sierra Leone.
1993	Eritrea becomes independent.
1994	Nelson Mandela becomes the president of South Africa.
	Genocide occurs in Rwanda.
1997	Zaire is renamed the Democratic Republic of Congo.
1999	Thabo Mbeki becomes the president of South Africa.
	Presidential elections take place in Algeria and Nigeria.
2000	The African Union is created to replace the Organization of African Unity.
2010–2012	Civil wars, protests, and coups break out in Tunisia, Egypt, and Libya.
2013	Nelson Mandela dies.
2015	Muhammadu Buhari becomes the president of Nigeria.

A

Adamawa

Adamawa was the most eastern emirate created, in the aftermath of the jihad of Sokoto during the 19th century, by the Fulani living in the region south of the Lake Chad basin. Adamawa was delimitated by the Kingdom of Borno in the north and the equatorial forest in the south. The emirate's western border was the Hawal River, whereas in the east Adamawa was bounded by the Logone River and the southern limit of the plateau now known as the Adamawa Plateau.

Under the authority of Modibbo Adama, who had obtained a flag from Usman dan Fodio, a jihad began in Fombina in 1809 in order to establish an emirate on the model existing in the Hausa states or Borno. However, the jihad in Adamawa was rather different from its counterpart in Sokoto. First, most Muslims in the region were Fulani and constituted only a minority of the population. Indeed, numerous other ethnic groups populated the area, such as the Mbum, Tikar, Chamba, Bata, Kilba, Margi, Gudur, Gude, Chekke, and Fali. The aim of the jihad was thus not to reform lax Muslims, as in the Hausa regions, but instead to get rid of the political and economical domination of the non-Fulani populations in order to obtain more grazing lands. Second, the Fulani society was segmented and did not have a unique leader. As a result, the jihad united most Fulani populations under the leadership of one man, Moddibo Adama, who obtained the title of emir (*lamido* in Fulfulde) and gave his name to the region he dominated, Adamawa.

The spread of Islam came progressively in Adamawa with the consolidation of the power of Moddibo Adama, who had established his capital in Yola in 1841. From Yola, Moddibo Adama and his descendants ruled their emirate with the help of their subemirs, who controlled a series of strongholds surrounded by slave farms along the main trade routes of the emirate. Moddibo Adama's son, Muhammad

The City of Ngaoundéré

The city of Ngaoundéré, founded in 1835 by a Fulani leader (Ardo Djobdi) on the site of an older Mbum settlement, is now the capital of the Cameroonian region of Adamawa. Named after the eponymous mountain of Ngaoundéré, the city is the terminus of the railway from Yaoundé and is now a transport hub because of its location at the center of Cameroon.

Lawal, succeeded his father at his death in 1847 and led military expeditions to obtain more fertile lands. As a result, the Fulani managed to control a larger share of the wealth of the emirate, a phenomenon that attracted Hausa and Kanuri traders. The last decades of the 19th century were marked by the relative inactivity of Umaru Sanda, who had succeeded Muhammad Lawal in 1872, and the rise of Mahdism. It was under the influence of Hayat b. Sa'id, great-grandson of Usman dan Fodio, that many inhabitants of Adamawa chose to sever the links with Sokoto in order to recognize Muhammad Ahmed as the Mahdi.

The British, French, and Germans who arrived in the region in the last decade of the 19th century found a weakened emirate. Divided by a German and British border, Adamawa became a part of the British colony of Nigeria and the German protectorate of Cameroon. Yola, which was the political center of the emirate, was conquered by the British in 1901 and became a Nigerian border town. German rule in Adamawa was short-lived, and after World War I some sections of the German territory became administered by Nigeria. The rest of the German territory of Adamawa became part of the French League of Nations mandate of Cameroon.

British colonial Adamawa was characterized by the power given by the British colonial rulers to the Fulani minority. Quite uniquely, colonial agents in Adamawa were nearly always Fulani, because the colonizers thought that they were superior to the "pagan" inhabitants of the region. As they were Muslims and had migrated from West Africa, the Fulani supposedly had superior political skills. As they were also African, their domination would be considered more legitimate. This is how the British ruled the region by proxy, hoping that the Fulani would bring "civilization" to the non-Muslims. The *lamido* of Yola was thus given power over a territory that he did not control entirely before the British colonization. At a local scale in Chamba, for example, non-Muslim populations were given Fulani headsmen and found themselves at the bottom of a newly created hierarchy. This political situation is considered one of the origins of the tensions in present-day Adamawa.

Early French colonial administration was also marked by the same kind of indirect rule whereby the Fulani were given authority over other populations. In general, the French tried to achieve a rational organization of the territory based on what they perceived as precolonial ethnic identities. This principle became the basis for taxation, labor, and the creation of new villages along newly built roads. As in the case of British Adamawa, the relationship between the Muslim Fulani and the rest of the population became problematic, and after violent outbreaks at the end of the 1920s, the French administration chose to end the rule of the *lamido* of Nagoundere over the Mbere region. The Mbororo, even if nominally Fulani, also had to be separated administratively from other Fulani.

At the beginning of the 21st century, Adamawa is divided between the republics of Nigeria and Cameroon. Partly because of their peripheral situation, both the Nigerian state of Adamawa and the Cameroonian region of Adamawa have remained relatively poor. In the 2010s, because of the Boko Haram insurgency, thousands of displaced Nigerians from Borno had taken refuge in Adamawa.

Vincent Hiribarren

Further Reading

Abubakar, Sa'ad. *The Lāmībe of Fombina: A Political History of Adamawa, 1809–1901.* Zaria: Ahmadu Bello University Press, 1977.

Bobboyi, Hamid. *Adamawa Emirate 1901–1965: A Documentary Source Book.* Abuja, Nigeria: Centre for Regional Integration, 2009.

Burnham, Philip C. *The Politics of Cultural Difference in Northern Cameroon.* Washington, DC: Smithsonian Institution Press, 1996.

Kirk-Greene, Anthony. *Adamawa, Past and Present: An Historical Approach to the Development of a Northern Cameroons Province.* Oxford: Oxford University Press, 1958.

Aksum

The Kingdom of Aksum existed in what is today parts of Ethiopia, Eritrea, Djibouti, Somalia, Sudan, and Yemen from around 100–940 CE. Built on trade, Aksum was a major player in the routes connecting the Roman Empire to the polities of the ancient Indian subcontinent and features prominently in histories of both Christianity and Islam. Its capital, also called Aksum, is in present-day northern Ethiopia and is the purported home of the legendary Queen of Sheba and the resting place of the Ark of the Covenant. At its height in around 350 CE the Kingdom of Aksum spanned about 1.25 million square miles, from the subtropical Ethiopian highlands surrounding its capital to Meroë in the Middle Nile basin, the Mousa Ali Mountains, the Grand Bara Desert, and the coastal plains on the Red Sea and the Gulf of Aden. Aksum's strategic location between the Nile River and the Indian Ocean made it a prime location for an empire of trade. Aksum exported many agricultural products, including wheat and barley, but its main natural resources were gold, iron ore, and salt. It also increasingly became a post for slave trading, positioned as it was between the Indian Ocean and trans-Saharan trade routes.

Aksum had its own language and alphabet, Ge'ez. A southern Semitic language, Ge'ez continued as the main language of Aksum's successor, the Kingdom of Ethiopia, and remains the liturgical language of the Ethiopian and Eritrean Orthodox Churches, the Ethiopian Catholic Church, and the Beta Israel Jewish community. The origins of Ge'ez remain a matter of some debate among historical linguists, with some arguing that Ge'ez writing appeared as early as 2000 BCE and others placing it as late as the fifth to seventh centuries CE. Some early Ge'ez texts are translations of early Christian writings and include biblical literature that has been marginalized in other forms of Christianity.

The matter of the origins of the Aksumite kingdom has been the subject of significant historical debate. Earlier scholars argued that the civilization around Aksum originated with the Sabaeans, a group of Semitic-speaking people who crossed the Red Sea from the Arabian Peninsula in the 4th or 5th century BCE. However, more recent research has revealed that Sabaean influence was relatively short-lived and that a Semitic-speaking civilization was established as early as the 10th century BCE. Archaeological evidence, contextualized by ancient Greek and

Roman sources, indicates a long history of contact and exchange between the region that became Aksum and the cultures of the Arabian Peninsula.

This is further borne out by the *Kebra Negast* (Glory of Kings), an account of the meeting between the famed Queen of Sheba and King Solomon. In this story the queen, named Makeda, travels to Jerusalem to visit Solomon and, while she is there, conceives a child who will become Menelik I, the first king of Ethiopia. She takes Solomon's ring back to Ethiopia with her, and Menelik later uses it to identify himself to his father. After refusing Solomon's pleas to stay in Jerusalem and succeed him, Menelik travels back to Ethiopia, carrying with him the Ark of the Covenant. This document, which most scholars agree is a composite of much earlier oral traditions, establishes a link between the Semitic cultures of the eastern Mediterranean and the Arabian Peninsula and the pre-Aksumite culture in the Ethiopian highlands. The *Kebra Negast* formed the basis for claims that the post-Aksumite Ethiopian kingdom was descended from Solomon and that Aksum itself, with its long history of Christianity, was part of this legacy.

Though Christianity became the main religion of Aksum, this happened in the empire's middle years. According to an inscription translated in the early 20th century, King Ezana, who ruled from around the 320s to 350s CE, thanked the god Ares for his defeat of the rebellious Bega people. Ares, the Greek god of war, was identified with Mahrem, from whom the Aksumites believed their kings descended. This indicates that for its first few centuries Aksum was a predominantly pagan kingdom, much like the states that surrounded it.

The earliest references to Aksum are from the *Periplus of the Erythaean Sea* and Ptolemy's *Geography,* which date from the first and second centuries, respectively. The *Periplus* discusses Aksum the city, which suggests that the Aksumite civilization, like many ancient cultures, originated in an urban area and spread to the region around it. The first recorded king of Aksum was Zoskales, who is referred to in the *Periplus* as ruling over a state that included the Red Sea port of Adulis. However, this would mean that either Aksum was already a considerable polity by the mid-first century CE or that Zoskales was in fact king of a smaller state in what was soon to become Aksum.

By the second century, when Ptolemy wrote his *Geography,* Aksum the city was the settled capital of a growing regional power with a firmly established monarchy. Its power was based largely in trade from the Nile and the Red Sea as well as overland trade. Roman sources from the first century imply that there may have been conflict between the Kingdom of Meroë and Aksum over access to the Nile. This proved to be an ongoing conflict, especially as Aksum's power grew and Meroë's waned. Much of this early period, from the first to fourth centuries CE, was defined by conflict between Aksum and its Arabian neighbors, who vied for control on both sides of the Red Sea. While the Himyar, Saba, Hadhramawt, and Qataban kingdoms struggled against one another in southern Arabia, Aksum sought alliances between them that would ensure its autonomy and continued growth and prosperity. Aksum's power under King Gadarat (ca. 200–ca. 215 CE) extended into southern Arabia, providing a foundation for its growth into a major regional player by the reign of Endubis (ca. 270–ca. 310 CE).

Endubis ushered in a new era in Aksumite history with the creation of a new system of coinage. Aksum issued coins in gold, silver, and bronze, which helped portray it as a kingdom as powerful as its neighbors and solidified its place in the evolving system of trade between the Roman Empire and the Indian Ocean. These coins are also valuable historical sources that help outline the histories of the last pre-Christian kings of Aksum: Endubis, Aphilas, Wazeba, Ousanas, and Ezana. Some details from their reigns are also borne out in stelae from their tombs, though much of this remains to be excavated and translated.

Ezana, who ruled from the 320s to 350s CE, was the first Aksumite king to convert to Christianity, around 333 CE. His image on Aksumite coinage changes from the disk and crescent so popular with other ancient polities to the cross, which indicates his conversion. An inscription from a victorious campaign against the Noba people of the Kingdom of Kush may indicate why Ezana converted. As Aksum's power grew the kingdom increasingly looked west toward the Nile, which was controlled by the Kingdom of Kush. Kush was in a state of decline, and Aksum had been slowly encroaching on its territories. The Noba people fought back against the Aksumite people living on its borders, whom the inscription refers to as "the peoples of Mangurto, and Khasa, and Barya, and the blacks." In response to this, Ezana undertook a campaign against the Nobas and defeated them. Upon his victory, he left inscriptions in Ge'ez praising the Christian God for his favor in

Obelisks at Aksum, in present-day Ethiopia. The city was once the center of the kingdom of Aksum, which flourished from about 300–700 CE. After its decline in the 10th century, the emperors of Ethiopia continued to be crowned in Aksum. (Anton Ivanov/Dreamstime.com)

battle: "By the might of the Lord of Heaven, Who has made me Lord, Who to all eternity, the Perfect One, reigns, Who is invincible to the enemy, no enemy shall stand before, and after me no enemy shall follow."

Ezana's desire to control the trade routes of the Nile put him in direct contact with the Roman Empire, which by the mid-300s was becoming more Christian—particularly after Emperor Constantine's decriminalization and patronage of Christianity. Aksum was perfectly positioned between the Roman Empire and the Indian Ocean and would be at a significant advantage to control both the Nile and the Red Sea if Kush fell, and a shared religious tradition would only strengthen ties between Aksum and Constantinople. It was to Ezana's advantage to commemorate his victory with inscriptions giving praise to the Christian God instead of the old pagan gods.

The period between Ezana's reign and the reign of Kaleb (ca. 520–ca. 530) was a golden age for the kingdom. Trade flourished, and Aksum sat at the center of an increasingly Christian world. When Kaleb came to power he immediately invaded the Kingdom of Himyar, which was ruled at the time by the Jewish king Yusuf Asar Yathar. King Yusuf persecuted Christians in his kingdom, which provided an excellent justification for Kaleb's invasion. Several sources from both Arabia and Aksum itself indicate that Yusuf's predecessor had been an Aksumite appointee and that he had ascended the throne because the winter months made it impossible for the Aksumites to cross the Red Sea and appoint a new king. Kaleb handily defeated Yusuf and installed a new king, Sumyafa Ashwa, who was a vassal king to Aksum. A group of Himyars rebelled against Sumyafa, deposing him in about 525 and replacing him with Abreha, who was supported by a group of Aksumites left behind by Kaleb. Despite Kaleb's best efforts, Abreha retained the throne, ending Aksumite control of Himyar.

Kaleb's losses in southern Arabia did not doom the kingdom but did stretch its resources too far, beginning Aksum's very slow decline. The kingdom remained powerful for several more centuries until the growth of the Islamic empire forced it into isolation. Though Aksum remained a Christian kingdom, it became increasingly marginalized from the Christian states of Europe and was under continuous threat from the Muslim societies that surrounded it. By the seventh century CE, the people of Aksum were forced to abandoned their capital city and retreat farther into the mountains to defend themselves. Several theories exist relating to the end of the Aksumite kingdom, which all seem to center on a defeat by a powerful queen somewhere in the region.

Though Aksum was politically and militarily defeated, its culture remains influential in both the succeeding Agaw Zagwe dynasty and the Solomonic dynasty, which was established in 1270 and continued into the 20th century. Aksum's strong Christian orientation remained important to the developing Ethiopian civilization, and its history was adopted by the Solomonic dynasty as a means of solidifying its legitimacy and descent from Solomon and Makeda. Today, the city of Aksum remains part of Ethiopia. Most of its ancient foundations remain unexcavated, leaving rich possibilities for future archaeologists and historians of the region.

Sarah E. Watkins

Further Reading

Ayele, Bekerie. *Ethiopic, an African Writing System: Its History and Principles.* Lawrenceville, NJ: Red Sea, 1997.

Connah, Graham. *Forgotten Africa: An Introduction to Its Archaeology.* London: Routledge, 2004.

Henze, Paul B. *Layers of Time: A History of Ethiopia.* New York: Palgrave Macmillan, 2004.

Munro-Hay, S. C. *Aksum: An African Civilisation of Late Antiquity.* Edinburgh, UK: Edinburgh University Press, 1991.

Wolfgang, Hahn. "Askumite Numismatics: A Critical Survey of Recent Research." *Revue Numismatique* 6(155) (2000): 281–311.

Allada

At its political and economic peak in the 16th and 17th centuries, the coastal kingdom of Allada stretched from its port of Offra—now the suburb of Godomey in the current Republic of Benin's commercial capital of Cotonou—approximately 50 miles north into the hinterland beyond its capital city, also known as Allada. The state was flanked to its west by the politically independent Whydah (Ouidah). To its east, the state stretched approximately 40 miles, where it bordered the prominent Kingdom of Oyo. Immediately north was Dahomey, a state that would eventually grow into one of the more powerful regional empires in the early 18th century.

Referred to by various African and European sources as Adra, Ardra, and Arder, the kingdom lay in a subtropical coastal region that typically experienced two rainy seasons and two dry seasons each year. A longer rainy season generally lasted from April to July, with a much shorter and less intense season occurring again from late September to November. While it is difficult to gauge exact weather patterns of the past, rainfall in the area today averages approximately 50 inches per annum. Like a lot of the coastal area formerly referred to as the Slave Coast, most of Allada would have been hot and humid throughout the year, with levels of humidity reaching their zenith during rainier months.

The topography in the kingdom varied. The sandy coastal plain around Offra, which lay between the ocean and the large Nokoue lagoon, was oftentimes marshy, making travel by foot through sand and mud arduous. From here, elevation rose at a moderate rate of anywhere from 60 to 200 feet up to a forested plateau roughly 20 miles north. For those making the trek to the capital of Allada, conditions improved as they reached the series of routes and paths cut out of the dense forest mosaic. Shortly after reaching forested areas, travelers would then descend into the swampy Lama Valley, where Allada's kings occasionally kept prisoners and slaves, before rising again to a northern plateau where the capital lay.

Oral traditions indicate that the first settlers in the region were Aja speakers who arrived sometime in the 12th and 13th centuries from the area of Tado, which lay along the banks of the Mono River to the west. By the mid-15th century, the population of Allada had reached approximately 30,000 people. It seems likely that the collection of small settlements up to this time organized themselves politically along decentralized lines, meaning that they ruled by consensus rather than granting sovereignty to a leader or king. Demographic growth, however, likely necessitated a transition to political centralization. Legends suggest that three brothers who had descended from people in what is now the city of Allada split the region into three parts and administered rule as kings. The first, Kokpon, remained in the capital city and became the ruler of the Allada kingdom. His brothers Do-Aklin and Te-Agdanlin allegedly left the city to establish their own kingdoms of Dahomey and Little Ardra, respectively, in what is now the city of Porto Novo.

Of the three, Allada rose in political and economic prominence the earliest by engaging in the nascent phases of what eventually became a flourishing transatlantic slave trade. Although merchants in Allada also traded ivory and commodities such as cloth and cowrie shells, the transport and sale of humans soon took precedence. Warfare primarily with neighboring Yoruba-speaking communities to the east accounted for the majority of slaves, who upon capture would make the difficult journey through the marshy valley and coastal sand depicted above in reverse to Offra. At first the kingdom conducted trade with Portuguese, who sought laborers for their burgeoning sugar plantations in Brazil as early as 1553. When Dutch forces occupied the coastal Brazilian city of Pernambuco in the 1630s, however, traders from the Dutch West India Company displaced Portuguese traders and set up a slave "factory" at Offra. The company maintained preferential trading status with Allada's leaders for a few decades, but the king was able to dictate the terms of trade and engaged with English and French merchants as well, who likewise pursued slaves to work island plantations acquired in the Caribbean.

Allada sold approximately 125,000 slaves from 1640 to 1690, reaching a peak of roughly 55,000 in the 1680s. Increased demand for slaves, however, may have accounted in part for Allada's demise a few decades later. By the 1690s, the growing Dahomey kingdom effectively restricted Allada's supply from the north. In the interim, Whydah benefited from a more favorable supply chain, causing traders to turn to the western port to engage in trade. As a result, the coastal kingdom had displaced Allada as a primary source of slaves by the end of the 17th century. Although both Dahomey and Whydah had once paid tribute to the king of Allada, both wielded their combination of economic prosperity and military might to undermine Allada's power in the region. In 1724 Dahomean soldiers poured in from the north, easily overtaking the capital in three days and enslaving and transporting thousands of the kingdom's residents to the coast, where they were sold to European slavers and taken to New World plantations.

The Dahomean invasion effectively brought an end to the Kingdom of Allada. Once a trader of slaves, the polity quickly transitioned into becoming a source for slavers. Dahomean traders, backed by their empire's military strength, expanded their scope throughout the region. In spite of its past role as a regional and economic power, Allada is remembered more as a source of slaves rather than a trader of slaves. That sentiment is reflected in the collective conscious of Allada city's current residents, who remember their ancestors' past in relation to African and Atlantic world history as slaves who were uprooted from their home by Dahomean warriors and transported along the Middle Passage to various European colonies in the New World to toil on farms and in mines. Allada's favorite son, noted Haitian revolutionary Toussaint L'Ouverture, never even set foot on his kingdom's soil. Alleged to have been the son of an African prince enslaved after the sacking of Allada in 1724, L'Ouverture was born into slavery in what had been the French colony of Saint-Domingue. A statue of the first leader of the independent nation of former slaves in the Americas stands in the center of Allada, acting as a symbol of Allada's unique role in African and Atlantic world history.

Marcus Filippello

Further Reading

Akinjogbin, A. I. *Dahomey and Its Neighbors, 1708–1818.* Cambridge: Cambridge University Press, 1967.

Law, Robin. "Religion, Trade and Politics on the 'Slave Coast': Roman Catholic Missions in Allada and Whydah in the Seventeenth Century." *Journal of Religion in Africa* (1991): 42–77.

Law, Robin. *The Slave Coast of West Africa, 1550–1750: The Impact of the Atlantic Slave Trade on an African Society.* Oxford, UK: Clarendon, 1991.

Law, Robin. "The Slave Trade in Seventeenth-Century Allada: A Revision." *African Economic History* 22 (1994): 59–92.

Ross, David. "Robert Norris, Agaja, and the Dahomean Conquest of Allada and Whydah." *History in Africa* 16 (1989): 311–324.

Almohad

The Almohads (1121–1269 CE), or al-Muwahhidun, are known as the Unity Movement. The Almohads were one of a series of African empires on the northern shore of the African continent that controlled much of the economy of the Spanish peninsula between 711 CE and 1492 CE. The Almohad Empire began as a religious revival led by a charismatic African scholar named Muhammad Ibn Tumart.

As with many medieval Mediterranean Christian and Muslim empires, the line between religious identity, political structure, and economic order was blurred. For example, the name of the movement has different meanings in the English language. Many scholars suggest that "al-Muwahhidun" refers to a theological belief in the unity of God. However, in political and economic terms, Ibn Tumart led a counter-Almoravid insurgency designed to resubordinate the western Mediterranean economy and unify it under the leadership of eastern Mediterranean Islamic states. The pragmatic outcome of this revolution was the redirection of wealth from the Almoravid capital of Marrakesh toward Baghdad and Damascus, resurrecting the financial order of things as they were during the Eastern-influenced Abbadid dynasty that the Almoravids unseated. The money was needed in the East to finance the defensive wars against the Christian Crusaders.

Muhammad Ibn Tumart was born circa 1080 CE in Ijilliz in the Sūs Valley of the Atlas Mountains of Morocco and was a member of the agricultural Masmuda Berbers. As a youth he studied at Aghmet, an Almoravid center near Marrakesh. Then he went to the city of Almeira in Andalusia (Muslim Spain), where he studied Sufism with *qadis* (jurists) who were known to be anti-Almoravid. He then moved to Egypt, where he studied the Asharite approach to Islam, one that was more literal or fundamentalist, for it left little room for local customs. Ibn Tumart also studied another popular approach to Islamic theology that was promoted by al-Ghazali, who used Neoplatonism, a revival of ancient Greek philosophical style, to promote a more intellectual, emotive, and transcendental form of Islam. In circa 1103 CE al-Ghazali published his *Ihya 'Ulum al-Din,* a philosophical approach to Islam. Some of al-Ghazali's chapters suggest that women are inferior to men. Eastern intellectuals chose Ibn Tumart as a teacher most likely to convert feminist men in the Almoravid Empire to this exotic, patriarchal approach to Islam.

Ibn Tumart became a scholar of Islam at a time when Jews, Christians, and Muslims debated whether religion was political, intellectual, emotional, or really about economics. Part of the economic issue concerned women's rights to own and control wealth and property and their right to participate in government as protected under the sharia of Almoravid Maliki legalism. Al-Ghazali's tendencies toward misogyny may have been a reason for the public burning of his books in Córdoba around 1108, for such notions contradicted the values of the Almoravids, who believed in the equality of women and men.

Most historians agree on two turning points in the rise of the Almohads. First was the public burning of al-Ghazali's *Ihya 'Ulum al-Din.* Second, when Ibn Tumart returned to Marrakesh to preach this non-Maliki Islamic law, he gained notoriety by throwing stones at an African princess, the sister of the Almoravid emir, knocking her off her horse, because he disapproved of her appearing in public without a veil, as was local custom for all women, and in the company of her male bodyguards, whom he accused of being women because they wore veils after the desert Tuareg custom. Ibn Tumart had a reputation for physically beating men and women for socializing, even in public prayer areas, and also for destroying wine shops. His bold strictness attracted many students and followers, including Abd al-Mu'min Ibn Ali, who claimed to be a descendant of the founder of the Idrissid dynasty and a sharif, or blood relative, of Prophet Muhammad. So, in terms of ideology and in terms of genealogy, Abd al-Mu'min was the perfect candidate to become a future emir of the Almohad movement that ultimately redirected more of the profitability of the Maghrib away from feminist Zenaga Berbers and toward the patriarchal eastern Mediterranean states, where the gold of Ghana and the silver of Toledo would go far in financing the wars against the Christian Crusaders.

In 1121 Ibn Tumart proclaimed himself the Mahdi (a prophesied leader sent by God to lead the people in a time of turmoil). Ibn Tumart began a revolution against the Almoravids, moving his center of operations to the mountain fortress of Tinmel,

Koutoubia Mosque in Marrakesh, Morocco, 12th century. Almohad reconstruction of the structure, originally an Almoravid mosque, began about 1150 and was completed during the reign of al-Mansur (1184–1199). (Jupiterimages)

overlooking Marrakesh and Almoravid troop and caravan movements. Almoravid leader Ali Ibn Yusuf attempted to contain the Almohad revolution while he fought Alfonso, the king of Navarre and Aragon. In 1130 the Almohads tried to take Marrakesh, but this was a disastrous failure. Ibn Tumart died later that year.

Ibn Tumart had a succession plan, and his organization was pyramidal in structure rather than federated, as was a Saharan African custom. From 1130 to 1141 Abd al-Mu'min was in a stalemate. He changed tactics, turned north to Tlemcen, and then took Fez, followed by the port city of Sali, and finally conquered Marrakesh in 1147. Abd al-Mu'min ordered purges of Almoravid supporters while he built a new capital city at Rabat and demanded submission from Andalusi leaders who asked him to fight the Christian Crusaders in Spain. He created a centralized state, appointed his 14 sons as governors and excluded Ibn Tumart's brothers from power. A new aristocracy was formed from children of the first 10 or 50 followers. Abd al-Mu'min also installed a new elite military of Arab and Turkish soldiers who were paid monthly. He evicted Normans from Tunisia in 1160. After this campaign, he began fortifying Andalus. He died in 1163. After a brief succession struggle, Abu Yusuf Yaqub al-Mansur, the governor of Seville, was declared emir. While using his father's army to stabilize Andalus, Yusuf also supported intellectual activity in a new golden age that featured Ibn Tufayl, Ibn Rushd (Averroes), and Maimonides. Yusuf died in 1184.

Almohad caliph al-Mansur not only had to deal with the Christian Reconquista advancing from the north but also had to fight the Banu Ghaniya of Majorca (the remaining Almoravid leaders). In 1228 al-Mansur left Seville to the Christians and advanced to Marrakesh with 500 Christian knights, where he denounced Ibn Tumart, embraced Sunni Islam, and massacred the remaining followers of Ibn Tumart at Tinmel. The exotic, patriarchal insurrection initiated by Ibn Tumart was effectively over. The Almohads were then beleaguered by the Banu Marins until 1269, when a slave killed the last Almohad leader, Idriss II al-Wathiq. There are many architectural monuments to Almohad austerity in cities such as Fez, Marrakesh, Rabat, and Seville.

Marsha R. Robinson

Further Reading

Abdo-'l-Wahid al-Marrekoshi, Reinhart Dozy, ed. *The History of the Almohades.* Amsterdam: Oriental Press, 1968.

Bovill, E. W. *The Golden Trade of the Moors.* London: Oxford University Press, 1958.

Bovill, E. W. "North Africa in the Middle Ages." *Journal of the Royal African Society* 30(119) (April 1931): 129–141.

Cornell, Vincent J. "Understanding Is the Mother of Ability: Responsibility and Action in the Doctrine of Ibn Tumart." *Studia Islamica* 66 (1987): 71–103.

Ecker, Heather. "Great Mosque of Cordoba in the Twelfth and Thirteenth Centuries." *Muqarnas* 20 (2003): 113–141.

Fletcher, Madeleine. "The Almohad Tawhid: Theology Which Relies on Logic." *Numen* 38(1) (June 1991): 110–127.

Lagardere, Vincent. *Les Almoravides,* Paris: L'Harmattan, 1989.

Almoravid

The Almoravid Empire (1048–1142) can be seen as a medieval precedent of the African Union in that it promoted federalism, transparent regulation of taxation, infrastructure construction, scientific research, the humanities, women's rights, and international trade agreements. That said, it was an empire forged out of warfare and a degree of religious intolerance in an effort to impose economic stability in a region facing numerous external challenges. The empire weakened when its leadership strayed from the values that once made it a popular alternative to the waning Abbadid Empire that it replaced.

In the early 10th century CE, there was a thriving trade in northwestern Africa, one that connected the Niger and Senegal river economies to those of Spain, Italy, Egypt, Mesopotamia, and beyond. Goods that were traded included gold, sugar, copper, cotton, indigo, olive oil, honey, silk, coral, silver, and salt. They also traded in black, brown, and white slaves. People of many skin colors traveled across the Sahara desert, a sea of sand on which merchandise was transported from city to oasis to mountain fortress to seaside harbor.

By the 11th century the trans-Saharan trade, a source of growing wealth in Northwest Africa, destabilized when the Fatimid Empire in Egypt sent the no-madic Banu Hilal ethnic group to weaken North African polities such as that of the Zirid that were growing to be its economic rivals. Meanwhile, the Abbadid dynasty in Spain was losing control as Christian and Syrian and Arab rulers of ministates formed unstable and shifting alliances known as *taifa* states. Even Norwegian Vikings raided North African port cities. The result was a shift of trade routes from the Zenata, who operated in the coastal districts, toward the Zenaga and Tuareg ethnic groups, who transported West African gold to Europe, where it was needed to purchase spices from East Asia.

Diverse ethnic groups controlled portions of the Northwest African economic world system, including the Barghwata Federation on the Atlantic coast and the Sanhaja Confederation of the Lemtuna, Guddala, Massufa, Warit, Lamta, and other groups. Even though Islam predominated as a cultural system, there were many local variations that reflected social, economic, and legal values: Maliki, Shafi'i, Kharijite, Sunni, Shia, and Sufi groups. Some ethnicities practiced Judaism, and many people in this trading zone practiced religions that were not of the Judeo-Christian or Islamic tradition. Also, skin color did not predict social identity. Rather, language and cultural practices were the bases of personal identity. One of the culture ways that does not always appear in history texts is the Saharan African tendency to create federations. Another is the practice of identifying oneself by one's mother rather than one's father.

In 1039 Yahya Ibn Ibrahim, the leader of the Guddalas, made a pilgrimage to Mecca. After completing the hajj, he and his traveling companions stopped in Qayrawan on the Mediterranean coast to study Maliki Islamic law and social orga-nization. He asked for a teacher to go with him to the Guddalas. Abd Allah Ibn Yasin, a Sanhaja missionary, was selected from students at Sijilmasa, another mar-ket/religious center. Ibn Yasin's teachings were too strict for the Guddalas, and he was sent away. Ibn Yasin was reassigned to the Lemtunas, where he met Yahya Ibn Umar, a man with political aspirations who saw that Ibn Yasin's teachings could become a campaign ideology that he could use to unify the Zenaga into a confederation.

The name of the confederation was Almoravid, or al-Murabitun. Many schol-ars think this name refers to the ribats—the religious fortresses. However, Vincent Lagadere suggests that "Murabitun" means the people who are tied together, or a united federation.

Yahya Ibn Umar's confederation was forged in faith and in fierce battle. Beginning in Awdaghost, the confederation solidified its regional alliances. Yahya Ibn Umar died in 1057, and Ibn Yasin chose Ibn Umar's brother, Abu Bakr, who brought the Masmudas of Aghmat into the confederation. Meanwhile, Ibn Yasin set out to convert the Barghwatas to the Almoravid way, but he was killed in the process in 1059. In 1068 Abu Bakr turned north and married Zeineb bint Ishaq al-Nefzaoui al-Houari. Zeineb financed the northern expansion into Sijilmasa and Marrakesh. In 1071 after Abu Bakr divorced her prior to heading south on a dangerous military expedition to keep Guddala in the federation and to stabilize the gold flows from Ghana, Zeineb married Abu Bakr's cousin, Yusef Ibn Tachfin, whom Abu Bakr selected to become the commanding general of the successful northern campaign to control the Mediterranean intermodal trade hubs of Fez, Tlemcen, and Tangier. Economic order was restored to the western trans-Saharan trade roads.

The Almoravids were invited to Spain by several leaders of Muslim Andalus states to defend them against Alfonso VI and the Christians of Léon-Castile. After victory, Andalusis learned that Almoravid taxes were fairer than Abbadid taxes. Elite business and jurist families learned that the Almoravid federation could keep them in power in a transparent bureaucracy, promoting stable prosperity for many as opposed to the risky economy of the preceding *taifa* era. By 1098, the eastern Mediterranean Abbasid Empire recognized the efficient Almoravids as the rulers of Spain. By 1102 their effective economic sphere stretched from the Pyrenees to the Senegal River and from the Atlantic to Ifriqiyya.

Almoravid armies were formidable. They could put 30,000 uniformed camel and horse cavalry on the field in addition to lancers, javelin throwers, and swordsmen. After conquest the Almoravids imposed a colonial structure administered by *qadis,* who were experts in Maliki law and civil engineering. They also served as guardians of orphans, the poor, and the disabled and were fiscal managers of charitable trusts. These *qadis* had power over local governors and reported to the Almoravid leader, who kept a rotating court. The system worked because of Almoravid piety. Within two generations, Almoravid leaders were less pious, less admired, and less popular. Nonetheless, Almoravid success can be measured in their six mints for making gold coins. They taxed non-Muslims and reorganized agriculture so that more people lived in cities of 25,000 to 50,000 people, with Marrakesh and Fez boasting nearly 500,000 residents.

Almoravid silver *qirat*, Spain or North Africa, first half of the 12th century. (Los Angeles County Museum of Art)

Almoravid prosperity rested on keeping wealth within the empire and reinvesting it in economic expansion and in raising standards of living. In the eastern Mediterranean, such standards were threatened by the Christian Crusaders and the Latin states that they established in the Holy Land along the crucial trade routes connecting Constantinople and Cairo. The descendants of Zeineb and Ibn Tashfin, along with other Almoravid matriclans such as the Banu Ghaniya clan, would soon find themselves fighting Spanish Christians to the north and an eastern-influenced Islamic insurrection led by an African scholar named Muhammad Ibn Tumart, leader of the Almohads, who would eventually replace the Almoravids.

Marsha R. Robinson

Further Reading

Boone, James, J. Emlen Myers, and Charles L. Redman. "Archeological and Historical Approaches to Complex Societies: The Islamic States of Medieval Morocco." *American Anthropologists,* new series, 92(3) (September 1990): 630–646.

Bovill, E. W. "North Africa in the Middle Ages." *Journal of the Royal African Society* 30(119) (April 1931): 129–141.

Burns, Robert Ignatius. "Renegades, Adventurers, and Sharp Businessmen: The Thirteenth-Century Spaniard in the Cause of Islam." *Catholic Historical Review* 58(3) (October 1972): 341–366.

El Hour, Rachid. "The Andalusian Qadi in the Almoraivd Period: Political and Judicial Authority." *Studia Islamica* no. 90 (2000): 67–83.

Lagardere, Vincent. *Les Almoravides.* Paris: L'Harmattan, 1989.

Lagardere, Vincent. *Les Almoravides: Le Djihad Andalou (1106–1143).* Paris: L'Harmattan, 1998.

Alodia (Alwa)

Alwa was the southernmost of the three riverine kingdoms of medieval Nubia (the others were Nobadia and Makuria). Its northern border with Makuria was located between the fifth and sixth Nile cataracts, but its precise location has not been determined yet. The southern extent is not known due to the very limited archaeological research along the White and Blue Niles. Al-Yaqubi, an Arab historian, claimed that Alwa was more powerful than Makuria (Dotawo) and that it covered the territory of a three-month journey.

The origins and history of Alwa are very poorly known. It was formed in the heart of the Meroitic kingdom. The ethnicity of the founders of the new realm is obscure, but Alwa is considered a Nubian kingdom, as it was probably created by the Black Nobas. They are mentioned in the inscription of Ezana, the king of Aksum who invaded the Nile Valley in the 4th century CE. At that time they dwelled along the Takkaze and Atbara Rivers, eastern tributaries of the Nile. Certainly apart from the Black Nobas there were other ethnic groups living in Alwa, such as the Kursas. The capital city of Alwa, Soba, was excavated by Peter Shinnie and then

Derek Welsby. According to the Arab historian Ibn Selim, it had large monasteries and rich churches, and there was also a Muslim quarter in the city. Soba must have also been an important trade center, as is confirmed by archaeological finds of 12th- and 13th-century Chinese pottery, the presence of Muslim traders, and a stone mold for casting medallions bearing an Arabic inscription. There were probably two main trade routes leading north, one through the Eastern Desert from Wadi Allaqi directly to Alwa and the other one cutting the Bayuda Desert through Wadi Muqqaddam almost to Old Dongola, the capital of Makuria, and through Wadi Abu Dom to the fourth cataract region. Alwan buildings at Soba were almost completely dismantled, reportedly to build Khartum in the 1820s. There is no other Alwan settlement ever touched by an archaeologist's trowel, and at least several huge archaeological sites await excavation along the White and Blue Niles.

Alwa converted to Christianity circa 580 CE as a result of a mission sent by Byzantine empress Theodora. We do not know much more about Alwa until the 10th century, when there were close relations between Alwan and Makurian families, including intermarriages. There even might have been a personal union between the two kingdoms, as in 943 the king of Dongola ruled over Alwa. There is also a 12th-century inscription in the cathedral at Pachoras (Faras) stating that King Moses Georgios was the king of the Nobadians, Alwa, and Makuria. Alwa was the only medieval Nubian kingdom with rain-fed agriculture, and its wealth and prosperity, emphasized by the Arab geographers and historians, must have derived from the greater farming potential. According to zooarchaeological data, the husbandry in Alwa was mainly concentrated on sheep, but the Arab historian al-Aswani stresses that Alwans possessed vast herds of cattle and large plains for grazing. Archaeological evidence also suggests that domesticated chicken was a part of the diet of the inhabitants of Soba.

The Alwan society consisted of two groups relying on different sources for subsistence. The sedentary group depended on agriculture, while the nomads relied on herding. The organization of the kingdom was probably similar to that of Makuria, and even the system of succession (by the nephew of the king) was the same. We know of only six Alwan rulers: Giorgios (the dates of his reign are unknown), Asabiyus (ca. 935–955), Astanabus (ca. 955–?), David (999–1015), and Basil and Paul in the 12th century. The Alwan church hierarchy was subordinate to the patriarchate of Alexandria and consisted of six bishoprics at Borra, Gagara, Martin, Arodias, Banazi, and Menkesa, but their location is unknown. The Alwans used Greek and Old Nubian languages. We do not have confirmation of the use of Coptic, but it is likely that they used that language as well, since the Alwan church reported to the Alexandrian Monophysite patriarchate.

According to al-Harrani, the decline of the kingdom started at the end of the 13th century, when the capital was reportedly moved to Wajula. There is a record, dated to 1286, of an independent kingdom of Al-Abwab, formerly one of the districts of Alwa, but there is no mention of Alwa itself. Adur, the king of Al-Abwab, was a friend of the sultan and was hostile to Makuria. Mamluk emissaries to Nubia reported on the dissolution of Alwa into nine independent kingdoms. Yet the territories of Alwa were the last of the Nubian states to be converted to Islam, and

Christianity in organized form did not cease to exist there until the beginning of the 15th century. Alwa was conquered by the Funj kingdom in 1504.

Artur Obluski

Further Reading

Abdalla Zarroug, Mohi El-Din. *The Kingdom of Alwa.* Calgary: University of Calgary Press, 1991.

Adams, William Y. *Nubia: Corridor to Africa.* Princeton, NJ: Princeton University Press, 1977.

Welsby, Derek. *The Medieval Kingdoms of Nubia: Pagans, Christians and Muslims on the Middle Nile.* London: British Museum, 2002.

Welsby, Derek. *Soba: Archaeological Research at a Medieval Capital on the Blue Nile.* London: British Institute in Eastern Africa, 1991.

Welsby, Derek. *SOBA II: Renewed Excavations within the Metropolis of the Kingdom of Alwa in Central Sudan.* London: British Museum Press, 1998.

Ankole (Nkore)

Ankole, formerly Nkore, located in the interlacustrine region of East Africa, sits in the southwestern part of Uganda, a landlocked country in East-Central Africa. It is part of a long and narrow belt of savanna country stretching along the eastern side of the western Rift Valley from Lake Albert in the Sudan to Lake Kivu in Rwanda. Geographically Ankole typifies African savanna, with rolling grass-covered hills and little acacia scrub. To the west of the Ankole district is the ice-capped Mount Rwenzori, known as the fabled "Mountains of the Moon," and several lakes including Lake Albert and Lake Tanganyika. To the east is Lake Victoria. Part of an area encompassing 3 million hectares of highlands based on agroclimatologic criteria, Ankole constitutes land critical to Uganda's economic development. The Rwenzori Plateau, misty with cooler temperatures, favors tea cultivation. Lake Edward, Ankole's only lake, is its single source of water. Fertile soils in the Lake Victoria

King of All Cattle and Cattle of Kings

Sporting coats from light caramel-colored to chocolate brown with long horns exceeding 2.5 meters in length, Ankole cows populate Rwanda and southwestern Uganda and have existed since the Middle Ages. Their horns protect them against predators. From steaks to stews, they are tender and lowest in cholesterol of any cattle in the world. Their hides are used for drum coverings and clothing. They are closely connected to royalty. An owner's wealth is measured by the herd's size, color of the hides, and size of the horns. Trainers teach the cows to perform dancelike movements.

region support intensive cultivation. This region is a habitat for a variety of bird life. The lakes and rivers contain stocks of tilapia, Nile perch, catfish, lungfish, and elephant snout fish, among other species. The early kingdom bordered Bunyoro Kitara in the north, Karagwe and Buhaya in the south, Mpororo and Rwanda in the Southwest, and Buganda in the east.

Interlacustrine mythology identifies the first peoples in the region as the Tembuzis, followed by the Chwezis. Theorists date the Chwezi arrival in western Uganda from the north of the Nile to 500 CE. Chwezi bloodlines form the modern-day kingdom of Ankole. Evidence for the origin of the main interlacustrine kingdoms, based on royal genealogies of up to 30 reigns dating to the first half of the second millennium, discuss the pastoral Chwezis (or Abachwezis) who conquered the Bantus. The Chwezis may have entered Uganda from the north or northeast. These pastoralists were described as sportsmen and hunters who wore cowhide sandals and built grass huts. They were acknowledged for introducing the long-horned Ankole cows to the Nile region. Nkore emerged in the 14th century. Oral traditions of the population north of Lake Victoria suggest that the center of Kitara, a great kingdom ruled by the Chwezis, was located in Nkore. The Chwezis represent part of the oral histories and legends of most of the interlacustrine kingdoms. The Abachwezi dynasty collapsed around 1600 and was replaced by the Buganda, Bunyoro, Busoga, Toro, and Nkore kingdoms. The Abachwezis ruled Nkore. Tradition contends that Ruhinda, who established himself as ruler, founded the Abahinda dynasty that rules Ankole today.

The Chwezis were followed by the Luo Bitos, but the kingdom remained under Chwezi control. The Chwezis moved farther south, and Ruhinda, one of the few remaining rulers and the last Chwezi ruler, strengthened and consolidated territories into the state of Nkore. Early accounts describe Nkore as first occupied by the agricultural Irus and a few pastoral Himas, living in relative isolation and without a developed political organization. Later Hima migrations, a period of struggle, and final Hima subjugation of the Irus led to the establishment of a kingdom. Movements of small groups of farmers and herders occurred over centuries.

The Nkores made agricultural implements, including hoes, sickles, axes, and knives, along with weapons such as spears, bows and arrows, and clubs made of hardwood. They made pottery, wove mats and baskets, and used iron to make spears, knives, axes, and ankle bands and armbands. They used copper and brass to make jewelry. Carvers made milk pots, drums, wooden spoons, and decorations from wood, ivory, and bone. The Irus also practiced weaving, mat and basket making, and carving. The Himas and Irus established a relationship based on trade and symbolic recognition, but they were unequal partners. Nkore traded extensively with the Buganda, Bunyoro, and Toro kingdoms and with populations in neighboring countries. This system of trade has continued to the present day. Under Nkore law, the king controlled all land and livestock. Peasants cultivated designated portions of land. Millet was the main crop. Milk and meat were staples among the Himas, and grain and plantain were staples for the Irus.

Early Bantu settlers may have had an early Iron Age culture, and the Chwezis might have brought the later Iron Age culture with more developed tools and crops.

The Chwezis expanded to the south and east. They introduced iron and gold exca-vation, practiced iron smelting, and introduced coffee beans. The Chwezi and Bantu cultures merged, but the Chwezis dominated politically and socially. The Himas adopted the Iru language and other customs. Traditional rules prohibited intermar-riage. The Nkoles were divided into three major patrilineal clans: Abahindas (royal people), Abasambos, and Abagahes. The Abahindas included warriors, herdsmen, princes, guards, and others who performed services for the king. The patron-client contract served as a means for Hima subjugation of the Irus. Both groups spoke Runyankole, one of Uganda's Bantu languages. The Nkoles believed in a powerful creator named Ruhanga (God) who lived in Heaven. The cult of the drum Bagyendanwa played a significant role in Ankole's social and political life. The drum reportedly entered the kingdom with the dynasty's founder. The Bagyendanwa had its own shrine to which people brought offerings, and unlike other drums it was never played. The Nkoles believed that the drum could see and hear everything in the kingdom. Bagyendanwa helped people, punished those who wronged, avenged wrongs, induced fertility, favored marriages, and helped the needy. The drum cult's concern for the welfare of society as a whole culturally unified the Nkoles.

The roots of Nkore kingship date back 600 years. Subsequently, the Chwezis evolved into a centralized monarchy with administrative officials who formed the core of the Chwezi political system. The *mugabe* (king) headed this system with a network that included slave artisans, palace officials, and palace women. His power depended on the ownership and control of land. The *mugabe* exerted absolute rule. The drum cult of Bagyendanwa unified the kingdom politically. A direct connec-tion existed between the drum and the kingship, as both derived their power from the same source. Royal women (mothers and sisters) were second in power. Next in authority was the *enganzi,* the king's adviser. A chief administered each of the kingdom's 16 districts. Under the district chief was a junior chief. Succession and nomination of an heir to the throne were based on two requirements. The heir had to be a member of the royal line and the strongest of the king's sons. Contending sons engaged in combat until one emerged victorious and was entitled to claim the Bagyendanwa and the throne. In 1900, British colonizers continued the Hima-led political leadership structure.

When the British created Uganda as a protectorate in 1888, Nkore was a small kingdom ruled by a king. Under the Ankole Agreement of 1901, the British merged Nkore with smaller states (Mpororo, Igara, Buhweju, and Busongora) to form the Kingdom of Ankole, under the auspices of Britain's Uganda Protectorate. Ankole became a district in the southwest of the Uganda Protectorate. In 1906, British rule introduced new legal and political relationships. The *mugabe*'s power diminished, but he retained the titles and privileges attached to the office under the kingdom's traditional laws and customs. British rule dismantled the political system based on serfdom, slavery, and clientship. The caste structural differences between Himas and Irus continued. The authority of local kings required the British to rule using a federal system of semi-independent monarchies. In 1910, the kingdom lost its independence with British annexation but enjoyed more administrative autonomy than other parts of the colony. Commercial activities expanded with the availability of and demand for manufactured goods. Farming and herding continued, with ivory as the main export crop. In 1904, the British introduced cotton as a cash crop. The *mugabe* and the chiefs continued to control ownership, access, and use of land. With exploration for minerals came the discovery of tin. Following arrival of the British and other Europeans as well as Asians and Middle Easterners, many Nkoles embraced Christianity and Islam. In 1961, the British granted the Ankole ruler limited powers enforced in 1962 with Ugandan political independence. Milton Obote, founder of the Uganda People's Congress, headed the constitutional initiative. The first constitution granted considerable authority to Ankole. Obote's relationship with the kingdoms deteriorated, and in 1966 he ordered his army commander, Idi Amin, to topple the kingdoms. The Republic of Uganda's 1967 Constitution replaced the 1962 Independence Constitution and abolished Ankole and other kingdoms. While unrecognized legally under the state's constitution, the kingdoms, considered traditional cultural institutions, continued to be recognized by populations that demonstrated allegiance to the *mugabes*. The *mugabe* as traditional and cultural leader was restricted from joining or participating in partisan politics. Under the 1967 Constitution, the Uganda Land Commission assumed control and management of all land. Obote was ousted following a coup organized and perpetrated by Amin, who led Uganda from 1971 to 1979.

In 1971, the Nkole elders signed a memorandum requesting Amin not to restore the *mugabe*. Obote returned to power from 1980–1985. The majority of Nkoles rejected restoration of the *mugabe*. In 1981, Yoweri Museveni established the National Resistance Army. He campaigned in rural areas hostile to Obote's government, including the western regions of Ankole. Resistance among the southern Bantus of former kingdoms in the southwest led by Museveni, an ethnic Nkole, was followed by civil war. Museveni gained power in 1986. The 1995 Constitution restored the kingdoms as traditional institutions but stripped the kings of all administrative, legislative, and executive power. The restoration of monarchism in the Buganda, Bunyoro, and Toro kingdoms in 1993 did not include the Nkoles, who were divided on the issue of restoration. These differences continued unresolved into the 21st century. In 1985, Nkole nationalists declared independence from Uganda. The Ankole kingdom faced challenges, including access to water, a flow of Hutu and Tutsi immigrants escaping from genocide in Burundi and Rwanda, and increased Iru-Hima tensions, which erupted into civil conflict in early 1990. The quelling of Iru protesters followed by Ankole government reforms led to the creation of a more democratic system and the dismantling of the caste structure. Foreign aid in the 21st century has helped improve Ankole's economy. The current Ugandan government does not recognize the Ankole kingdom.

Many Nkoles believe that the Abachwezis did not die but instead disappeared and will return to rule. Today many sites and relics connected to the Abachwezis exist. They are sacred to the Nkoles and symbolize kingship. Nkole sentiment remains divided between those who support reinstatement of a monarchy and those against the restoration of a minority monarchy to rule the majority population. Contemporary Nkole settlements are scattered over the hills, slopes, and valleys of Ankole. Each family owns a plot of land used for livestock or subsistence farming.

The original inhabitants of Nkore, the forerunner of Ankole, constitute a minority population. Ankole is a constitutional monarchy with a king at the executive branch and a local elders' council in the legislative and judicial branches. Runyankole, the primary language, and English are the official languages. Ankole's economy still depends on agriculture and livestock. Under Idi Amin's reorganization, Ankole lost its designation as an administrative unit and was divided into six districts: Bushenyl, Ntungamo, Mbarara, Kiruhura, Ibanda, and Isingiro. Ongoing environmental concerns include the draining of wetlands for agricultural use, deforestation, overgrazing, soil erosion, water hyacinth infestation in Lake Victoria, and widespread poaching.

Maryalice Guilford

Further Reading

Harris, Joseph E. *Africans and Their History.* New York: Penguin Books, 1987.

Karugire, Samwiri R. *A History of the Kingdom of Nkore in Western Uganda to 1896.* Kampala, Uganda: Fountain Publishers, 2008.

Mair, Lucy. *African Kingdoms.* London: Oxford University Press, 1977.

Oliver, Roland, and Gervase Mathew, eds. *History of East Africa.* London: Oxford University Press, 1963.

Arochukwu

The Ibibio were arguably the first to occupy the area that is today known as Arochukwu, a place they occupied around 300 CE from the region of the Benue Valley in modern-day Nigeria. They established early states such as Obong Okon Ita and Ibom. After many years the Igbo immigrants surfaced, pressed into the Ibibio occupied territory, and established several states. The first of the Igbo group was known as the Ezeagwu, led by their leader Agwu Inobia. The Ibibio saw the establishment of states by the Igbo people as encroachment of their territory, and this led to the Aro-Ibibio wars, which ended in a stalemate.

Alvan Ikoku

Alvan Ikoku (1900–1971), the face on the Nigerian ten naira currency, is a native of Arochukwu. A respected political figure and educationist, Ikoku is credited for establishing the Aggrey Memorial College in Arochukwu in 1931. As a politician, he served on the Board of Education in the House of Assembly and in the Lagos Legislative Council representing the Eastern Region. He constantly pushed for educational development in Nigeria and demonstrated unwavering support for the Nigerian Union of Teachers.

As a response to the war situation, the Eze Agwu group employed the services of a priest named Nnachi, a native of Edda of northeastern Igboland, and the support of a group located at the east of the Cross River, the Akpa people. The Akpa people were led by Osim and Akuma and supported the Igbo people to gain control of the unclaimed area. This victory led to the formation of an alliance—the union of the old states and 19 new states to the Arochukwu kingdom between 1650 and 1700. The first king (*eze aro*) of a united Arochukwu was named Akuma, and after his demise Nnachi son's (the priest from Edda) Oke Nnachi became king, giving his descendants access to the throne up to the present time. The wars were of great significance, as it was during one such war that the leader of the Ibibio warriors was captured and killed in a village called Oro. This particular event gave the town a chieftaincy status.

Throughout the 19th century the violent activities of the Aro and the intrusive slave raiding undermined the *eze nri*'s influence in eastern Igboland. The success of the Aro was in the manipulation of an oracle that was used to advance the economic interest of the group; in addition to this was their use of mercenaries to obtain slaves and to compel observance of their will. The influence wielded by Aro led to the neighboring towns—Abam, Ohaffia, and Edda—hiring themselves out as mercenaries to the Aro. With this the Aro built a network of markets and trade routes around Igboland. The Aro controlled a great network of markets such as Bende and Uzuakoli, which brought together traders from different parts of southeastern Nigeria. In addition, the Aro bought supplies such as iron bars for the use of the smiths from the Cross River estuary and bought slaves from other trade areas such as Nkwerre, Ndizuogu, Uburu, and Nike.

Arochukwu was also one of the cities of the southern protectorate conquered by the British colonial government. Arochukwu housed the sacred Chukwu shrine, dedicated to the most dreaded oracle that was also known as Long Juju by the Europeans. The importance of the oracle lay in its position as judge, supreme deity, and recruiter of slaves for sale sent to the port of Bonny by Aro middlemen. The oracle at Arochukwu was more famous than any other and was referred to as "the voice of Chukwu," the high god. Arochukwu was on the edge of Igboland far from Igbo, which could make it impartial in settling disputes. Despite this, many people took their disputes to the oracle because its decisions final and were also enforced. The oracle was consulted not only by those in the Igboland but also by wealthy and powerful kings from the Niger Delta city-states, who forwarded their disputes to Chukwu.

An end was put to the shrine and the power of the oracle by the British during the campaigns against the people of Aro between 1900 and 1902. The influence of Aro over Igboland was so overwhelming that the British decided to attack the Aro oracle in 1902, but the first step to this was to conquer the hinterland, which gave the British the proof that Aro did not have any political control over the other Igbo groups. In the course of conquering the hinterland, it was discovered that Igboland was politically segmented and that the influence of Aro was merely spiritual, used for economic purposes. In addition, the economic influence of Aro was interrupted by the penetration of the British colonial officers. This penetration led to fierce battle that resulted in bloodshed and the outbreak of the Anglo-Aro War in 1901–1902. The Aro Confederation was defeated, and the British effectively occupied the area in Nigeria known today as the Eastern Region.

Apart from their oracle, one major concern of the Aro was the trading system. They had monopoly over the organization of the trade—the sale of slaves to the traders of delta city-states—and in return for this they procured firearms to equip their soldiers. The Aro also engaged in long-distance trade, and trade was organized on three major routes—from the north (here slaves were brought) to the central market (Bende) to the Bonny markets (the Imo River). The Aro employed mercenary soldiers from other clans to pull down any village that disobeyed the oracle. Any village found wanting was burned and its people taken as slaves. The Aro were instrumental in the organization of the palm oil trade that made Bonny the largest African exporter of palm oil. The attempt by the British to stop the export of slaves only led to slavery increasing internally for the harvesting and transportation of palm oil to market. The palm oil trade led to the establishment of colonies along the trade routes.

Morenikeji Asaaju

Further Reading

Afigbo, Adele Eberechukwu. *The Abolition of the Slave Trade in Southeastern Nigeria, 1885–1950.* Rochester, NY: University of Rochester Press, 2006.

Onwuke, S. O. *Rise and Fall of the Arochukwu Empire, 1400–1902.* Enugu: Fourth Dimension Publishing, 1995.

Asante (Ashanti)

The Asante (Ashanti) of modern-day Ghana are one of the famous ethnic groups in Africa, known for their rich culture and pride in their heritage. They belong to the Akan ethnic group and speak Asante Twi. The 2010 Ghana Population and Housing Census estimated the population of Asante to be 4,780,380, making up 19.4 percent of the total population of Ghana. The home country of the Asante is central southern Ghana, occupying a landmass area of 9,417 square miles. Asante shares borders with Brong-Ahafo in the north, the Central Region in the south, the Eastern Region in the east, and the Western Region in the southwest. Asante has two rainy seasons and a dry season that influence agricultural activities in the region. Asante geography consists of rain forest, savanna areas, and mountain scarps that all support animals such as apes, birds, reptiles, and butterflies. The drainage areas include Lake Bosomtwe and the Offin, Prah, Afram, Tano, Bia, and Owabi Rivers.

The Asante migrated into Adanse in the forest region of Ghana in the 15th century, from where they dispersed to found a confederation of towns. Osei Tutu, an Asante royal, with the assistance of his legendary fetish priest and friend, Okomfo Anokye, founded the Asante union in the 1670s by consolidating the petty

Otumfuo Nana Prempeh I

Otumfuo Nana Prempeh I (December 18, 1870–May 12, 1931) is the 13th *asantehene* of the Asante Empire. His ascension to the Asante throne threw the empire into a civil war because some states opposed him. With the help of the British Army, Prempeh I emerged victoriously and became the king in 1888. During his reign, he united all of the Asante and expanded Asante territories. He clashed with the British when he refused to surrender Asante authority to them. The ensuing result was the arrest of Nana Prempeh I, his parents, and some leading chiefs of Asante in 1896 and exile first to Freetown, Sierra Leone, and later to Seychelles Island in 1900. Nana Prempeh I and his entourage returned to Asante in November 1924, long after Asante had become part of the Gold Coast colony.

states and townships, defeating the Denkyira (Asante's overlord), and instituting the monarchy in 1701, with its center at Kumasi. Okomfo Anokye placed the fate of the Asante in the Golden Stool, the magico-religious symbol he conjured from the heavens. The stool represents the spirit, soul, and unity of the Asante union. Successive kings after Osei Tutu greatly expanded the boundaries of the union into an empire. At the height of the empire during the reign of Osei Bonsu (1801–1824), the borders extended to modern-day Ghana and parts of Togo, the Ivory Coast, and Burkina Faso.

The Asante monarchy is a constitutional one. The Oyoko clan is the royal clan. The king is the custodian of the Asante union and culture and the link between the living and the dead. A council of elders composed of chiefs and prominent members of the union assist the king. The council of elders serves as a check on the *asantehene* (king of the Asante), who has legislative, executive, and judicial powers. In the absence of the *asantehene,* the king of Mampong acts as a regent. The queen mother, in addition to catering to the womenfolk, works in consultation with the council to install a new king. The king is supposed to be without blemish in physical appearance and of the best of human character. He swears the oath of allegiance to the Golden Stool. The Asante Empire had a complex bureaucratic system and a powerful military. There were divisional chiefs, subchiefs, and village heads as well as several ministries of state, such as war and finance, which all played a significant role in the daily running of the empire.

The Asante are known for their resilience and fierce courage in warfare, epitomized in their adage "Asante porcupine, when thousands are decapitated, thousands shall rise!" The Asante's expansionist zeal brought them into several conflicts with their neighbors, such as the Akyem, Gyaman, Fante, and Assin. However, two groups stand out in Asante war history: the Fante and the British. Innovations in seafaring coupled with trade interests made it possible for Europeans to travel far to Africa in the 15th century. The Dutch, British, and Danes stationed at the Gold Coast conducted trade with the indigenes. The British replaced all the Europeans on the Gold Coast by the mid-19th century. Their interests in civilizing the indigenes, spreading literacy and Christianity, and encouraging trade in legitimate goods such as palm oil, gold, cotton, and rubber and later colonization brought them into conflict with Asante. The Fante, who inhabited the coast and so had direct access to the Europeans, monopolized their position as middlemen and often closed trade routes, thereby impeding trade between the states in the interior and the Europeans. Conquering the Fante always eluded the Asante. For these reasons, the Asante fought with the Fante and the British as allies in the 1824 Battle of Nsamankow, the 1826 Akatamanso War, and the 1874 Sagranti War. The wars and other internal factors saw Asante power diminishing during the reigns of Mensa Bonsu (1874–1883), Kweku Dua II (1884), and Agyeman Prempeh (1888–1931).

The tension between Asante and the British came to a climax in 1896 when the Asante refused British overlordship, resulting in the exiling of Asantehene Agyeman Prempeh and other important Asante royals first to Cape Coast, then to Sierra Leone, and later transferred to the Seychelles Islands. Asante then became a British protectorate. The final straw was Governor Frederick Hodgeson's demand for the Golden Stool to sit on to signify his authority as the representative of the British monarch on the Gold Coast. Asante response was the Yaa Asantewaa War of 1900–1901 led by the queen mother of Ejiso, Yaa Asantewaa (1850–1921). The defeat of Asante led to its integration into the British colony of the Gold Coast, thus ending the Asante Empire of some 300 years.

The basis of Asante economy was agriculture, trade, and mining. Farmers grew food crops for sustenance and later cocoa, which became the mainstay. They also partook in the trans-Saharan trade, which began in the first century BCE. Trade routes crisscrossed the interior of the African continent through the Sahara desert, linking Africa with the Mediterranean and Europe. The Asante exchanged slaves, kola nuts, gold, indigo, ivory, and other forest products with other African states such as Hausa, Wangara, and Mali. Following the introduction of the transatlantic trade, local, regional, and internal trade through the Sahara dwindled considerably. Asante attention diverted to the coast of the Gold Coast,

The queen mother of the Asante people, Yaa Asantewaa, holds court in Kumasi, ca. 1900. She was an important figure in the fight against British colonialism in modern Ghana. (Hulton-Deutsch Collection/Corbis via Getty Images)

which was lined up with forts and castles, such as those of Elmina and Cape Coast, to engage in the slave trade. Mining and craftwork—metalwork, woodcarving, sculpturing, and weaving of the colorful kente cloth—also gave Asante quite a name. Brass and gold casting, using an indigenous lost wax technique, created such beautiful ornaments and artistic objects. Religion was important in Asante. The Asante were mostly traditionalists. They venerated their ancestors, celebrated festivals such as Akwesidae Kesse and Odwira, and observed elaborate customs such as funerals. Islam was introduced by Muslim traders, scholars, travelers, and immigrants who traveled from North Africa and Hausaland to the empire beginning in the 11th century. The Asante court had many Muslim scholars working as scribes, administrators, and spiritualists assisting in warfare and spiritual protection. Christianity, introduced by Europeans, met with much hostility until the colonial era.

Lady Jane Acquah

Further Reading

Edgerton, Robert B. *The Fall of the Asante Empire: The Hundred-Year War for Africa's Gold Coast.* New York: Free Press, 1995.

Ghana Statistical Service. *2010 Population and Housing Census: National Analytical Report.* Accra: Ghana Statistical Service, May 2013.

Obeng, J. Pashington. *Asante Catholicism: Religious and Cultural Reproduction among the Akan of Ghana.* Leiden: Brill, 1996.

Wilks, Ivor. *Forests of Gold: Essays on the Akan and the Kingdom of Asante.* Athens: Ohio University Press, 1993.

B

Badagry

The historic city of Badagry is located in Lagos State, the economic capital of modern-day Nigeria. Badagry, located some 8 kilometers from metropolitan Lagos and covering approximately 172 kilometers, is situated on the Lagos western coastland near the international boundary along inland Badagry. The town is bounded on the north by the Yewa kingdom of Ilaro; to the west by the Republic of Benin (Dahomey); to the east by Ojo, an Awori town in the present-day Ojo local government of Lagos State; and on the south by the sea. The town is characterized by a network of waters, creeks, and swamps to the extent that very few people practiced agriculture. Mainly the people of Badagry engage in fishing, which has remained the chief occupation of the people since the precolonial period.

While the historical origin of Badagry has attracted a great deal of controversy, various scholars are of the opinion that the Ogu (Egun) and Awori people were the earliest settlers of the town. They were later joined by traders from the hinterland when the town came under European influence. The town was said to have been founded in the 1720s by the Ogu and Awori people, respectively, before they were joined by the Europeans and other migrants from the hinterland of the Yoruba kingdoms in the 19th and 20th centuries. The town at different times in its historical trajectory has come under different influences; the most noticeable and

---

Badagry Heritage Museum

Like many coastal West and Central African communities, Badagry participated in the transatlantic slave trade. The demise of the heinous crime took place in the 19th century, when the British used their naval power to stop African and other European nations trafficking Africans to the Americas. The Badagry Heritage Museum is one of the few surviving relics of the transatlantic slave trade. It has a total of eight galleries, namely Introductory, Capture, Transportation, Equipment, Resistance and Punishment, Industry, Integration, and Abolition, all of which explain the phases and process of enslavement and abolition. The original slave trade items displayed in the museum included the heavy metal used for containing enslaved people and photographs of leading abolitionist of the 19th century. Today, the museum is an important tourist attraction in southern Nigeria. Indeed, it is considered by many to be the most important physical relic of the transatlantic slave trade in the whole of Nigeria.

---

endurable are that of Lagos, its neighbor to the west, and Dahomey, to the east. While the influence of Badagry's neighbor to the east was limited to the realm of culture, Lagos's influence was more political and economic especially during the reign of Eleko Akinsemoyin (1760–1775) and Kosoko (1845–1851). These two monarchs exerted considerable influence on the town during their reigns as the king of Lagos. The town became independent of Lagos during colonial rule. Also, the activities of the Europeans, most especially the missionaries, placed the town on the historical atlas of the world in the 19th century. Being the first place where missionary activities was first recorded in the Bright of Benin in 1842 under the leadership of Thomas Freeman, Badagry eventually played a pivotal role in the spread of Christianity into other parts of Yorubaland.

Badagry recorded three waves of migration in its history. The town was first populated by the Ogu, Awori, and Aja people, respectively. The Yoruba who were part of the first wave of migration moved from Apa to join the earlier settlers. The third group to settle in Badagry, the Aja people, came in piecemeal. The Aja group that settled in Badagry includes the Allada, Setto, Tori, and Hwala. The Tori were essentially farmers who occupied the rural district of Avrankou in the coastal plain of Badagry. The Setto, who are best known for their fishing ability, occupied the lower delta areas, while the Hawalas built their fishing camps extending from Krake to the Seme beach. However, by the early 19th century, European merchants who were mainly slave dealers and missionaries also settled in Badagry as the town became a leading port for slave export and later the pioneer town for missionary activities in Yorubaland.

The people of Badagry were essentially farmers. The geographical location of Badagry is a major determinant of the occupations of its populace. This perhaps explains why fishing remains the chief occupation of the people. The infertility of the soil and the location of the town along the famous lagoon necessitated the people's occupation. The people exchanged their sea products with agricultural products they could not produce. Men are the principal actors in the fishing industry. However, some exceptionally gifted and brave women also join the menfolk in this process. Women are the actors when it comes to distribution. They also acted as middle women (*alarobo*). It is a common feature in Badagry markets for women to act as intermediaries between the producers and the final consumer. Various varieties of fishes are found in Badagry markets, including *epiya* (tilapia), *aro* (*Clarias genriepinus*), *igbakere* (*Lutjanus goreensis*), *sawa* (*Sadinella Aurita*), *obokun* (*Chrysichthys nigrodigitatus*), *kuta* (*Sphyreana piscatorum*), and *efolo* (*Ethmalosa fimbriata*). By the 1720s, Badagry had emerged as one of the leading ports for the external slave trade. Slaves coming from the Yoruba hinterland were transported to the New World through the port of Badagry. The Yoruba Empire of Oyo used Badagry to a very large extent for its external coastal trade. Goods coming from Oyo passed through Shaki, Iseyin, Igan, Ibese, Ijanna, Ilaro, Igbeji, Ihumbo, Ipokia, and Owo and on to Badagry.

The location of Badagry and its participation in the Atlantic trade transformed the community from a mere fishing village of disparate West African groups into a stable settlement. From the 18th century, the town had acquired a new status and wealth. With this wealth and status Badagry developed new sociopolitical institutions. The town was divided into eight administrative quarters for easy administration: Ahoviko, Awhanjigoh, Jegba, Boeko, Whrako, Asago, Posuko, and Ganho. However, Jegba was the royal quarter of the *akran* (king), while other quarters were administered by the white cap chiefs. For instance, the Ahovika quarter was administered by Wawu, the Awhanjigoh quarter by Jengen, the Boeko quarter by Mobee, the Whrako quarter by Finhento, the Asago quarter by Bala, the Posuko quarter by Possu, and the Ganho quarter by Agoloto. These chiefs were subjects to Akran authority.

The economic reality of Badagry in the early 19th century created a new elite. The chiefs, who were hitherto subject to the authority and control of Lagos, became independent and assertive. With their newfound wealth and the influence of Western education, Badagry chiefs began to see themselves as being equal to the *akran* until the advent colonialism, when the *akran* was recognized as the paramount ruler of the town. Also, Badagry became a reference point in the historical skyline of Lagos and indeed Nigeria. The first multistory building appeared in Badagry in 1845.

The history of this region and the significance of Badagry remain key to understanding the connection between the slave trade and the economic quagmire of Africa. A lot of the slaves that were transported to the New World were shipped from Badagry. The emergence of a slave market in Badagry not only stagnated the local agricultural and fishing economy but also undermined the production capacity of the local population. The Atlantic slave trade shaped the cultural evolution of Badagry and Lagos in particular. The study of this town could illuminate further our understanding on the cultural similarities between the Yoruba people of the Caribbean Islands and the Yoruba people in the coastal states of western Nigeria.

Mufutau Oluwasegun Jimoh

Further Reading

Dioka, L. C. *Lagos and Its Environs.* Lagos: First Academic Publishers, 2001.

Lawal, Kunle. "The 'Ogu-Awori' Peoples of Badagry before 1950: A General Historical Survey." In *Badagry: A Study in History, Culture and Traditions of an Ancient City,* edited by G. O. Ogunremi, M. O. Opeloye, and S. Oyeweso, 45–67. Ibadan: Rex Charles Publications, 1994.

Mann, Kristin. *Slavery and the Birth of an African City: Lagos, 1760–1900.* Bloomington: Indiana University Press, 2007.

Toyi, Wheno Aholu Menu. "Badagry in the Eyes of Time." In *Badagry: A Study in History and Culture of an Ancient City,* edited by G. O. Ogunremi, M. O. Opeloye, and Siyan Oyeweso, 10–25. Ibadan: Rex Charles Publications, 1994.

Baguirmi

The Kingdom of Baguirmi, also referred to as Bagirmi, was a Central African Islamic sultanate existing from circa 1480 until 1893 located east of the Chari

River, southeast of Lake Chad. This region is today part of the Republic of Chad. The kingdom stretched over more than 70,000 square miles, which included the capital city, its surroundings, and several tributary states. Baguirmi's population consisted of the Barma majority as well as Fulas, Kanuris, Shuwa Arabs, and neighboring groups. The name of the sultanate first appeared in written sources in a Bornu chronicle of 1578 was spelled "Bakarmi."

From the beginning, Baguirmi's rulers were addressed with the title *mbang*. This pre-Islamic custom was maintained even after the Islamization of Baguirmi's elite and political system under the reign of Abdullah (r. 1568–1608). According to different king lists, it was Mbang Birni Besse who founded the kingdom in 1522, while other sources trace the origin of the state to a leader called Abd al-Mahmud Begli (r. 1493–1503). The latter and his successor were responsible for the construction of a palace and a court building in the capital city of Massenya, located north of the Chari River and east of today's Cameroonian border. During its heyday, Massenya was the main economic center of the state. In 1850, about 15,000 inhabitants lived in this capital city protected by a seven-meter curtain wall. Except for the mosque and the palace, which were built of stone, all other houses were built of clay.

The history of Baguirmi had always been dependent on its powerful and larger neighbors, Kanem-Bornu to the northwest and Wadai to the northeast. Baguirmi's history has often been considered secondary to processes in the Bornu Empire, a perspective that may well be generated by the dominance of Bornu written sources. During the 15th century the Sefuwa dynasty ruling Kanem-Bornu had endeavored to expand the kingdom. Alongside Baguirmi, many smaller states had emerged at the southern Bornu frontier such as Mandara, Margi, and Kotoko. Intense trade was established between Bornu and its southern neighboring countries. Some of these were attacked and conquered militarily by Bornu, instancing Baguirmi, which was absorbed during the reign of the Bornu king Idris Alawoma (1564–1596), also called Alooma. By military and civil contact, Bornu culture and state systems influenced Baguirmi. Bornu was directly involved in the trans-Saharan trade (north-south) and pilgrimage networks to Arabia (west-east), and Baguirmi was located at the periphery of this entangled Sahelian-Saharan world. Thus, Bornu acted as a powerful middleman within this vast trade network. While Kanem-Bornu was competing against the late Songhai Empire in order to rule the favorite trans-Saharan trade routes, Baguirmi depended on Bornu for access to this trade.

The small sultanate traded animal skins, ivory, cotton, and slaves—including eunuchs—to Bornu in exchange for copper and cowrie shells used as currency. Many Baguirmi traders traveled far into the Hausa region, where they were considered to be Bornu merchants. Despite this homogenous outward appearance, many Baguirmi rulers rebelled against Bornu overrule. Due to the revolt of Abdullah (ca. 1561–1602), the Bornu king Idris Alawoma started a military expedition against him and was supposedly killed during this conflict. Reacting to Baguirmi expansionism, Bornu at least tolerated the foundation of the Wadai kingdom by a Muslim scholar in the early 17th century. Nevertheless, Bornu could not prevent Baguirmi from becoming independent. It was the Baguirmi king Muhammad al-Amin

(r. 1751–1785) who threw off Bornu dominance and threatened the former conqueror with a series of attacks on the eastern frontier.

Although remaining a tributary to Bornu, Baguirmi was raiding and conquering frontier regions autonomously. Whether the capture of many foreign slaves was the initial reason or an effect of these imperial ventures remains a controversial issue among historians. Alongside cotton, slaves were the most demanded tribute goods. They could be resold or forced to become soldiers. Especially non-Muslim neighboring political entities were raided regularly, and many of their inhabitants were captured and enslaved. Those raids and military expeditions could cause a constant political integration by smooth transition. In some sources, slavery appears more like a phase of life after which young men and women returned to their places of origin. Other sources, however, evaluate Baguirmi as the most important producer and exporter of eunuchs in precolonial Africa.

The Baguirmi military often cooperated with nomadic peoples in order to control smaller states. Those tributary regions accordingly delivered about 1,000 slaves every year as tribute for the Baguirmi palace. As a result of expanding diplomatic relations, neighboring societies soon adopted the Baguirmi title *mbang* for their own leaders. They also adopted Baguirmi elements of culture and lifestyle, such as Islamic practices, facial scarification, weaving, and the Barma language. This influence was often accepted voluntarily by tributary states that sent their young elites for education to the Massenya court. Those tributary regions under direct Baguirmi rule were governed by the *ngars,* the district rulers. Just like political power was organized by complex systems of title holders, professional guilds were represented by their own leaders—a scheme also existing in Hausa history. The highest rank of blacksmiths, for instance, was addressed as *milma.*

From the late 15th to the early 19th centuries, Baguirmi expanded far into the hinterland of the Chari River, including Muzgu, Gummai, and Kung. The Baguirmi rulers intermarried preferably with other regional elites, most notably with Busso, which gained a position as a favorite tributary among them. Both the Baguirmi and the Busso ruler were called *mbang* so that some travelers and researchers have considered it a dual monarchy. The Baguirmi king had many cowives from frontier regions, which led to the integration of a statewide entangled elite.

For the 19th century there is more detailed information about processes in Baguirmi, since European travelers and missionaries visited major African palaces and published those encounters. The Scotsman Hugh Clapperton reached the Lake Tchad region two times during the 1820s after having crossed the Sahara and yet again from the Atlantic coast. In 1850, the German traveler Heinrich Barth set out for another five-year journey across the Sahara desert, visiting Timbuktu, the Hausa region, and the Bornu Empire. The German traveler Gustav Nachtigal stayed in Bornu and Baguirmi from 1870 to 1872 and visited Massenya right after its destruction by Wadai forces. In the second half of the 19th century British, French, and German colonial officials generated sources about contemporary processes and historical accounts based on African informants.

By the turn of the 19th century, Baguirmi had lost many of its former dominions and eventually became a tributary of the expanding Wadai kingdom. In 1870

Massenya was besieged and partly destroyed by Wadai. Internal conflicts had further weakened the state when Rabih al-Zubayr invaded Baguirmi and burned down its capital, Massenya, in 1893. Rabih (or Rabah), born in Khartoum, served as a soldier in the Egyptian cavalry and then became a successful mercenary for slave traders. He became a powerful warlord and ruled his own state in today's Chad. Rabih attacked Darfur, conquered Baguirmi, and in this same year conquered also the Bornu Empire. Because of these catastrophes, the ruling Baguirmi sultan Abd al-Rahman Gwaranga accepted French colonial intervention, leading to protectorate status in 1897. After serious defeats, the French military together with Baguirmi soldiers killed Rabih in 1900, which led to a rapid disintegration of his whole state; Bornu fell into British hands, and all other territories of Rabih became French colonies. The Baguirmi Protectorate received French colonial status in 1902.

Stephanie Zehnle

Further Reading

Barkindo, B. M. "Kanem-Bornu: Its Relations with the Mediterranean Sea, Bagirmi and Other States in the Chad Basin." In *UNESCO General History of Africa V: Africa from the Sixteenth to the Eighteenth Century,* edited by Bethwell A. Ogot, 492–514. London: Heinemann, 1992.

Bjørkelo, Anders J. "State and Society in Three Central Sudanic Kingdoms, Kanem-Bornu, Bagirmi and Wadai." PhD dissertation, University of Bergen, 1976.

Forkl, Hermann. "Die Beziehungen der zentralsudanischen Reiche Bornu, Mandara und Bagirmi sowie der Kotoko-Staaten zu ihren südlichen Nachbarn unter besonderer Berücksichtigung des Sao-Problems." PhD dissertation, University of Munich, 1983.

Lebeuf, Annie M. D. "L'ancien Royaume du Baguirmi." *Mondes et Cultures* 38 (1978): 437–443.

N'Gare, Ahmed. "Le Royaume du Baguirmi (XVe–XXe Siècles)." *Hemispheres* 11 (1997): 27–31.

Palmer, H. R., trans. *Ahmed Ibn Fartua's History of the First Twelve Years of the Reign of Mai Idris Alooma of Bornu, 1571–1583.* Lagos: Government Printer, 1926.

Bamum

The Kingdom of Bamum, situated in the Western Region with its capital Foumban, head of the Noun Department, is one of the traditional states that constitute the Republic of Cameroon. Occupying the central part of the West African grassland's high plateau (altitude 700 meters), limited by mountains culminating at 2,200 meters to the north and the west and by Mbam River and Noun to the east and the southwest, the kingdom covers approximately 7,700 square kilometers and has more than 500,00 inhabitants of whom half speak the Bamum language, sharing common origins with the Bamileke traced back to their Tikar ancestry.

The grassland landscape is a savanna with few trees, regularly the victim of bushfires. Mountains and hills are covered by what remains of primary forest, still harboring wild fauna. The plateau is mainly used as pasture ground for bovines, and the millet and sorghum fields are richer in the floodplain of the rivers. Plantain raffia palm trees are cared for to extract what will make raffia wine. The region is of a tropical climate with a hot dry season, happily refreshed by the winds exchanged by mountains and the lower plains and a monsoon-like rain season that is as useful as it is sometimes destructive.

The Bamum polity has its origins in a group of exiled Tikar ethnic group led by Nchare from the Ngaoundere region to the West African grasslands in search of a settling land. This expedition from the south of the Adamawa Plateau, along the upper Mbam, to the first heights of the grassland plateau achieved the conquest of local polities centered on large villages more than on what could be called cities.

As Nchare was enthroned by the first Bamum king at Samba Nguo under the Sép tree, a first constitution was drafted by the king and his seven retainers (*koms*), who where in charge of maintaining the laws and customs of the state. These officials were to be autonomous of the authority of the king if they were apt to censor royal actions that could go against common law. To achieve the effective influence of the counselors, a ceremony called Nguon was devised. In this ritual celebration the king is formally deposed, opening the right to criticism by the *kom* officials, and then the monarch is reinstalled on his throne and addresses the nation with a speech. The political rite is accompanied with the gift of the goods due to the palace by the local chiefs of lineage villages and sumptuous feasts. Nguon, held every two years, was at the center of the Bamum calendar from the reign of Nchare until it was suspended by the colonial authority in 1923 as a way to diminish the power of Sultan Ibrahim Njoya, but his son and the actual sultan, Ibrahim Mbombo Njoya, reinstated it with much success in 1992, and the ceremony is regularly held to this day.

The new state elected Njimom as the first capital of the kingdom, a city still near to the river while protected by the ridge of the plateau. The success of the conquest of new lands to the south allowed the Bamum to quickly move to Foumban, at the center of the plateau. This enabled the successive kings of the Bamum to hold the conquests of Nchare under their control. A system of land tenure, acquainted with feudalism, gave the possibility to the dynasty of exacting taxes and military recruits to sustain the state. The wars held against the neighboring polities made slave capture activity prosperous, and the abundance of captives of the palace made their allowance to royal agricultural domains possible, boosting the production of those facilities and ending in the constitution of slave villages and lineages attached to land.

The institution of an extensive royal polygamy filled the palace with dynastical intrigues and feudal plots and was the reason for the creation of a large body of servants, officials, and dignitaries related to the royal wives. The court developed a complex protocol, and secret societies in charge of justice and war, housed in the palace, were constituted by princes and members of the different potent lineages that held formal political charges before the integration in the kingdom. In addition, different cults were allowed spaces to hold reunions and keep their ritual objects, such as dancing masks.

Around 1825 the king, Mbombouo, launched a series of conquests, achieving the occupation of new lands, increasing the state size by four, and doubling population to 50,000 inhabitants. During this turbulent reign, the king faced a Pulaar invasion, and Foumban fell to the first razzia wave. To escape further threats, a moat was dug that surrounded the city and gave it a defensive value, preventing the success of other expeditions.

Facing problems of succession, one of the king's sons and a regular claimant to the throne, prince Njoya looked for help from the Pulaar Lamido of Banyo. Assuring that he would become a Muslim if he was victorious, Njoya asked for guns and horses to train a cavalry like those of the Islamic polities of the north. He thus became sultan of the Bamum in 1896, converting only some of his major servants. After a short time, inspired by the potentialities of writing, Njoya began to create an alphabet adapted to the Bamum language, first intended for the secret use of palace officials.

Six years later, German missionaries arrived in Foumban and were allowed to establish trade and a church. The example of the missionary school made Njoya change his mind on the better use of his invention; he simplified the alphabet and began having it taught to children with their own language. He then converted to Christianity, and diplomatic gifts were exchanged with Berlin, consecrating the beginning of Bamum art collecting in Europe.

After World War I and an interlude under British rule associated with the Islamic states of northern Nigeria, King Njoya reverted to Islam. The Cameroon territories were assigned to the French in 1918, and thus the Bamum kingdom exerienced colonial power for a third time, with the policy of control not indirect or distant. Continual quarrels between the palace of Foumban and the French resident in the 1920s ended in the exile of the sultan in the capital of the newly founded country, Yaoundé.

The actual situation of the Noun Department is still that of an eccentric and neglected territory like it was at independence in 1960. This has led to problematic access to health infrastructures, while only 30 percent of the territory is electrified. The royal power had been in trouble in recent years, as the sultan became involved as a senator, creating great expectations around the palace. Before that turn of events, the major struggle for power in the grasslands was between the militants of the Union Démocratique du Cameroun, historically led by Adamou Ndam Njoya, and the Bamum opposed to the Bamileke of the Social Democratic Front of John Fru Ndi.

Jacob Durieux

Further Reading

Bosserdet, Jean. *Au palais des sultans de Foumban.* Paris: UNESCO, 1985.

Fowler, Ian, and David Zeitlyn. *African Crossroads: Intersections between History and Anthropology in Cameroon.* Oxford, UK: Berghahn Books, 1996.

Tardits, Claude. *Le royaume bamoum.* Paris: Armand Colin, 1980.

Benin

There is little clarity regarding the origins of the Benin people, although there have been many suggestions, including migration from outside of Nigeria. Archaeological and ethnographical studies suggest that the Edo (Benin people) may have been indigenous to the region. However, much more than other Nigerian peoples, Benin possessed a more reliable tradition in the form of a king list, folklore, and the survival of cultural practices. As a result, traces of that period and its history are found in popular myths and legends that have been distilled into traditions. Tradition suggests that there were two specific periods in the development of the Benin kingdom. Tradition points to the Ogiso period, placed at around 1000 CE, as probably occurring during the very early period of Benin history. The Benin kingdom was organized in small lineages that grew into villages and at best small towns, and the Ogisos are believed to have established monarchical traditions into the Benin political system.

The second period in Benin history is ascribed to a Yoruba influence on the kingdom. At a certain period, tradition recalls that the people of Benin were dissatisfied with their rulers and sent to Oduduwa in Ife for a ruler. He sent Oranmiyan, so the second period began at the inception of Oranmiyan's arrival. However, Oranmiyan is not usually recorded as the Benin *oba*. The dynasty is said to have started with his son, Eweka. By this time, the political history of the Benin kingdom became clearer. There were many rulers during the second period with attendant contributions. There was also political instability, which was consequent on the insurbodination and dominance of the Uzama chief. This may have contributed to the stunted growth of the kingdom until the reign of Oba Ewuare the Great.

It is important to note that the growth of the empire beyond its vicinity and attainment of its territorial height was through the effort of Oba Ewuare. None of the kings equaled the contributions of Ewuare the Great, who reigned around 1440 CE. He was a spirited leader and was also a magician, a physician, a traveler, and a warrior. It was under him that Benin expanded its territory and influence through several wars of conquest, and the result of this drive was a restructuring in the polity of the kingdom. Benin influence (economic and political) was definitely felt in the Niger Delta region as far as Onitsha, Agbor, and Auchi during this period. Similarly,

---

Invasion 1897

Invasion 1897, directed by Lancelot Oduwa Imasuen, is a historical movie on the deposing of Oba Ovonramwen Nogbaisi of the Benin Empire by the British colonialists in 1897. Nogbaisi ruled the Benin Empire between 1888 and 1897. This epic movie tells the tale of the punitive expedition that ravaged the ancient Benin Empire in 1897, how it was invaded by the British Empire and looted of its priceless ancient artifacts, including the famous commemorative head and pendant of ivory mask representing Queen Idia (from the court of Benin, 16th century), who was the mother of Esigie, the *oba* of Benin who ruled from 1504 to 1550.

Benin bronze sculpture of the head of an *oba* (king). It is thought to be a generalized portrayal of kingship rather than a representation of a particular *oba*. Such sculptures are used to commemorate the ancestral shrines of individual *oba*. (Multimedia Library)

the Urhobo and Itsekiri peoples were added to the Benin kingdom. Benin also expanded westward by conquering the Yoruba provinces of Akure and Owoh.

Upon contact with the Portuguese, Benin's economic influence reached a new level. By 1485, the Portuguese reached Benin and traded with the Edo at their port of Ughoton. By the mid-16th century, the Portuguese were already well established on the Nigerian coast and had regular trade links with the Edo, Ijebu, Ijaw, and Itsekiri people, with Benin serving as the middleman. They traded in pepper, ivory, and later slaves, with manila as a means of currency. The transatlantic slave trade at this time occurred on a low scale, but by the 17th century it was occurring on a large scale. It is significant to note that only a few Edo were sold as slaves. This is because Oba Esigie prohibited the sale of indigenes as slaves. However, the Atlantic slave trade expanded from the 18th century due to the fact that Benin lifted its embargo on the slave trade and began to sell captives taken during Benin's imperial wars. A number of adverse economic circumstances combined, such as political instability and the suppression of slave trade, undermined the economy of Benin in the first half of the 19th century.

The second half of the 19th century ushered in considerable developments in Benin, such as external attacks and the spread of British control. Vassal states took advantage of the political instability and an economic depression in Benin to claim their independence. As a result, Akure and some Ekiti towns rebelled, while states such as Ibadan, Ilorin, and Nupe launched various attacks on different part of Benin's empire. External aggression encouraged internal discord, and this was followed by succession disputes. Also, in 1897 Benin witnessed the British punitive expedition that led to the destruction of the city. Consequently, Benin lost its independence and was annexed to the Niger Coast Protectorate.

Various festivals are held in Benin yearly, but the most significant and popular is the Igue festival, which was instituted during the reign of Oba Ewuare the Great to celebrate the magical powers of the *oba* of Benin. Igue is usually celebrated between Christmas and New Year. Currently Benin city, apart from being the capital, is the largest city in Edo State. The present *oba* of Benin is Omo N'Oba N'Edo Uku Akpolokpolo, Erediauwa (CFR), who was crowned on March 23, 1979, as the 38th *oba* of Benin. In 2008, Comrade Adams Oshiomole emerged as the governor of Edo State, and since then Benin has witnessed infrastructural changes spanning the construction of new roads to beautification projects. Also, there has been an improvement in the economic prosperity of the Benin kingdom as well as political stability.

Damilola D. Fagite

Further Reading

Edo, V. O. "The Changing Phases of Power and Civil Administration in Benin: From Inception to 1987." *Nebula* 5(1–2) (2008): 164–173.

Egharevba, J. U. *A Short History of Benin.* Ibadan: Ibadan University Press, 1968.

Ryder, A. F. C. *Benin and the Europeans, 1485–1897.* London: Longman, 1977.

Stride, G. T., and Ifeka Caroline. *Peoples and Empires of West Africa.* Hong Kong: Thomas Nelson, 1971.

Borno (Bornu, Kanem-Borno, Kanem-Bornu)

Lasting nearly for a millennium, Kanem-Borno is the empire with the longest history in Africa (9th century–1893). Renowned for its trans-Saharan commercial links, the Kingdom of Kanem-Borno dominated the Lake Chad basin and was the first sub-Saharan political entity to adopt Islam during the 11th century.

The size of Kanem-Borno dramatically changed over the centuries. The kingdom was first created in the 9th century on the eastern shores of Lake Chad in Kanem (Chad) by the Kanembu (the inhabitants of Kanem), a population composed of agriculturalist and pastoralists who spoke a Nilo-Saharan language. The kingdom subsequently shifted to Borno (Nigeria) on the western shores of the lake

Muhammad al-Amin El-Kanemi

Muhammad al-Amin El-Kanemi (1776–1837) gradually became the leader of Borno during the Fulani jihad at the beginning of the 19th century. As a scholar and a gifted politician, he managed to resist the invasion of Borno and founded the dynasty of El-Kanemi. His name still evokes a certain pride in the glorious past of Borno.

during the 13th and 14th centuries mainly for climatic reasons. The Kanembu populations gradually migrated to Borno, and by mixing with the local Sao populations their language evolved into Kanuri. The center of gravity of the kingdom also moved, and Birni Ngazargamo (Borno) progressively replaced Njimi (Kanem) as the capital of the kingdom.

Because of its military successes, the empire reached its territorial apex at the beginning of the 18th century and dominated territories located in modern-day Libya (Fezzan), Niger (Bilma), Chad, Cameroon, and Nigeria, which explains why Kanuri became a lingua franca and is still spoken in some parts of the Sahara. The name "Kanem-Borno" thus refers to the historical period when the empire dominated the whole of the Lake Chad region. One of the main kings responsible for this expansion was Idris (known after his death as Idris Alooma) who, as a soldier himself, reorganized the army of Borno and made sure he benefited from his contacts from the other side of the Sahara in the 16th century. As king (*mai*), Idris was credited for temporarily introducing gunpowder weapons in Borno; reconquering Kanem, which had become autonomous; and pacifying Borno. The history of the 17th and 18th centuries is more often told in terms of consolidation, and the 19th century saw a decline of Bornoan authority under the pressure of the Tuaregs in the north and the Sokoto Caliphate in the west. Indeed, the jihad of Usman dan Fodio nearly put an end to the independence of Borno, as the capital of the kingdom was sacked, and the Borno authorities gradually lost their power over peripheral territories such as Zinder (Niger).

Kanem-Borno was ruled by three successive dynasties between the 9th and 19th centuries, and most of the names of the kings are known because of the existence of the *girgam* or *diwan,* a list of kings written down between the 13th and 19th centuries. The first dynasty was the Duguwas, an aristocracy who selected a king from within their ranks. Because of the scarcity of sources, not much is known about these early kings apart from the fact they may have converted to Ibadi Islam. During the 11th century, the Sunni Sayfawas replaced the Duguwas and reigned over Borno for nearly nine centuries. Because of the Sokoto invasion of 1808, the Kanemis finally took the place of the Sayfawas during the 19th century, and Kukawa (Borno) became the capital of the kingdom before being invaded by Rabah, a Sudanese warlord in 1893. After killing Rabah and his son, the British, French, and Germans chose to reinstall the Kanemis on the throne of Borno during the colonial period, which explains why the current *shehu* of Borno is a Kanemi.

Between the 9th and 14th centuries, the first empire of Kanem-Borno was a loose association of territories and populations ruled by the king. When the Sayfawas reorganized the kingdom in Borno during the 14th and 15th centuries partly to avoid internal wars, the structure of the country became more centralized. The second empire of Borno thus ruled its dependencies through tributary leaders who were often described as vassals by European outsiders. The relationship between the core territory of Borno and its peripheries was ensured by personal links between the different emirs and sultans but also repeated military operations in order to quell rebellions. The redistribution of wealth acquired via the trans-Saharan and trans-Sudanic trades was essential for the cohesion of the empire. The trade routes toward Tripoli and Egypt were those that ensured that Kanem and later Borno would sell slaves to the north of the Sahara. In exchange, Borno would acquire horses, weaponry, copper, and paper. Borno was more than a military power; it was also a commercial hub.

The trans-Saharan trade also connected Borno with Morocco, the Ottoman Empire via Tripoli, and Egypt at different periods. As a result, the kings of Borno were able to entertain a diplomatic correspondence with their northern neighbors. Borno was thus part of a wider Muslim world and became renowned for its Islamic culture. Its rulers adopted titles such as commanders of the faithful and caliph from the 14th century on. They built mosques, and some of them traveled to Mecca for their hajj. In the 13th century, a hostel in Cairo was kept for travelers from Borno. Books, mainly Korans and legal documents, widely circulated from the 15th century on, and Borno became a Sudanic center of religious education. The extent to which the whole of the population of Borno was Muslim is unclear, but it is very likely that Islam was not only an elite phenomenon. Borno thus became a center of Islamic culture in sub-Saharan Africa, with travelers choosing to undertake their studies in Borno.

After its conquest by Rabah in 1893 and nearly a decade of wars, Borno was colonized by the British and Germans. The largest part with a new capital, Maiduguri, became a province of the British colony of Nigeria, whereas the German section became part of Cameroon until World War I. Indirect rule was theorized in Nigeria, and Borno, along with Sokoto, became the archetypical African kingdom that the colonizers wanted to integrate within the colonial framework. Trans-Saharan links were mostly severed, slavery was slowly abolished, and Borno became an impoverished part of northern Nigeria far from the colonial capital of Lagos. Postcolonial Borno (since 1960) has remained a periphery of independent Nigeria; the level of poverty has remained high, while the level of education has remained low. The tendency of the federation of Nigeria to fragment was responsible in 1991 for the division of the state of Borno into two states, namely Yobe and Borno. At the beginning of the 21st century the corruption levels were very high, and Borno became infamous for harboring the religious sect Boko Haram.

Vincent Hiribarren

Further Reading

Barkindo, Bawuro. "The Early States of the Central Sudan: Kanem, Borno and Some of Their Neighbours to c. 1500 A.D." In *History of West Africa,* edited by Jacob Festus Ade Ajayi and Michael Crowder, I:225–254. 3rd ed. Harlow: Longman, 1985.

Dewière, Rémi. "Regards croisés entre deux ports de désert." *Hypothèses,* no. 1 (December 2013): 383–393.

Hiribarren, Vincent. *A History of Borno: Trans-Saharan African Empire to Failing Nigerian State.* London: Hurst and Oxford University Press, 2017.

Lange, Dierk. "Ethnogenesis from within the Chadic State: Some Thoughts on the History of Kanem-Borno." *Paideuma: Mitteilungen Zur Kulturkunde Paideuma/Frobenius-Institut,* no. 39 (1993): 261–277.

Lavers, John. "Islam in the Bornu Caliphate: A Survey." *Odu* 5 (1971): 27–53.

Buganda

The Kingdom of Buganda lies at the geographical and political heart of modern-day Uganda. A powerful precolonial state with a long history, the kingdom remains integral to Ugandan politics in the present day. Resting on the northwestern shore of Lake Victoria, the kingdom covers a wide area in central-southern Uganda. Its inhabitants (Ganda) constitute the largest ethnic group within the country, at around 5.5 million individuals in the 2002 census. Uganda takes its name from the Swahili-language form of the name Buganda. The Buganda kingdom lies astride the equator and has a largely temperate climate with significant annual rainfall as well as sunshine. Its dominant landscape is one of well-watered green hills and swamps, although certain areas, such as the southwestern region, are drier and less fertile. The kingdom has excellent soil for agriculture, and the dominant food staple of the Ganda and an integral part of Ganda history and culture is the cooking banana known locally as *matoke*. The kingdom also contains pastoralist communities inhabiting Buganda's section of Uganda's so-called cattle corridor, which runs from the northeast to the southwest of the country. Buganda also incorporates a number of island archipelagos, such as the Sese and Buvuma Islands. The inhabitants of these areas as well as those of the mainland lakeshore have historically engaged in both agriculture and fishing, ensuring that fish remains a key dietary component. During the colonial period Buganda became a major producer of cotton and coffee.

Buganda is also the most urbanized region in Uganda, incorporating the country's capital, Kampala. The kingdom was comparatively centralized with a well-developed system of roads prior to colonialism, and the 20th century witnessed a further growth in urban centers and urban migration. Including Kampala, with an estimated population of around 1.7 million inhabitants, Buganda contains eight of Uganda's twenty-five largest urban areas.

Politics in Postcolonial Buganda

Inequality of resource allocation coupled with increasing federalism within Buganda in the run-up to independence in 1962 led to a fraught relationship between kingdom leaders and Uganda's postindependence regime under Milton Obote. The kingdom was abolished by the national government in 1966. The period between the late 1960s and the mid-1980s was extremely difficult for Buganda's inhabitants. The brutal regimes of Milton Obote and Idi Amin were followed by a period of social breakdown and civil war during which Yoweri Museveni's National Resistance Army fought the national government controlled by Obote for a second time. Much of the destructive violence of this conflict played out in Buganda's heartlands. Following his victory in 1986 Museveni took control of Uganda, and in 1994 the Buganda Kingdom was restored as a cultural entity. In the years that have followed, Buganda's relationship with the Museveni regime has become increasingly strained, and tensions remain between Buganda's federalist instincts and national government control.

Ganda origin traditions recount the founding of the kingdom by the first *kabaka* (king), Kintu, a figure who also features in creation myths as the originator of humanity. The real or mythical nature of Kintu and his immediate successors has been contested, though most scholars understand Kintu and other of Buganda's first kings as legendary figures rather than real historical actors. Read carefully, however, the traditions concerning early Buganda do reveal broad historical patterns. It is clear that during the 15th century a number of communities based in the green hills and swamps of the northwest shore of Lake Victoria and organized into several clans and came together to form a kingdom. Initially the new polity was confined to a small geographical area, and the early kings were almost certainly only the first among equals in a society where clan leaders retained a powerful influence.

While the favorable climate and banana-growing culture of the Ganda facilitated the development of an increasingly complex and growing society, Buganda's power was initially circumscribed by the regional dominance of its northern neighbor, the Kingdom of Bunyoro-Kitara. In the 18th and 19th centuries, however, Buganda's power and influence began to grow. Increasingly centralized politically and culturally under the rule of the king, the kingdom developed strong military structures, maintained a network of roads and pathways, and had control over a

The Kasubi tombs, royal tombs of four Bugandan *kabakas* (kings) located outside of Kampala, Uganda, ca. 2000. It remains an important religious and spiritual site for many Ugandans. (Frank Vandenbergh/iStockphoto.com)

large fleet of canoes on Lake Victoria. As Bunyoro's power began to wane, Buganda was well placed to expand its territorial borders as well as its role in regional trade and geopolitics. As the size and population of the core kingdom expanded through raids, conquest, and migration, Buganda's increasing wealth and power allowed the kingdom to extend its influence over neighboring states, many of which became tributaries. The kingdom's wealth was largely derived from plunder, tribute, and the extensive taking of slaves through war, but its inhabitants also participated in regional trade in commodities, such as bark-cloth clothing (a special expertise of the Ganda), fish, and ivory.

In the mid-19th century, Arab traders reached Buganda on their trade routes inland from the Swahili coast, and the kingdom joined a wider sphere of commerce that saw ivory and slaves traded for cloth and guns, among other items. While increased firepower initially underscored Buganda's regional dominance, the growing preponderance of slaves and firearms within the kingdom undermined the binding ties of Buganda's society, which began to destabilize in the 1880s and 1890s. This process was also affected by the arrival of Europeans in the kingdom from the 1860s. One such visitor was the famous explorer Henry Morton Stanley, who arrived in the kingdom in 1875. Stanley was impressed with the power and order of Buganda's society and, following discussions with the king, wrote a famous letter printed in the British newspaper the *Daily Telegraph* calling for missionaries to go to Buganda and spread Christianity. The first Protestant missionaries arrived in 1877, and French Catholic orders soon followed. The spread of Christianity as well as of Islam through Arab merchants ensured that uniquely within the East African region, Buganda had a large number of adherents of world religions prior to the arrival of European colonialism. These new religious affiliations, however, fed simultaneously into underlying tensions, and in the 1880s a series of politico-religious wars broke out during which the king, Mwanga, was deposed, reinstated, and then later deposed once again. Into this tense situation arrived an expedition of the Imperial British East Africa Company under the command of Frederick Lugard—later the governor of Nigeria and the main proponent of the British colonial governing system of indirect rule. Lugard's intervention on the side of the Protestant faction was decisive and left a governing body of Protestant chiefs to negotiate the growing presence of British imperialism.

Buganda has strong cultural and social traditions that bind its inhabitants together. The growing role of the king in precolonial society has already been noted, but the Ganda were also linked by a common language, Luganda; the wearing of bark-cloth clothing; and cultural practices such as birth and marriage rites and religious beliefs. More recently, Ganda culture and popular royalism have experienced a renaissance. In addition, a number of Uganda's leading musicians, writers, and politicians have originated from within the kingdom.

From 1893 until 1962, Buganda existed under a system of British colonial rule. As elsewhere across colonial Africa, the kingdom's inhabitants experienced the imposition of an alien European power upon political, cultural, and economic life. Forms of labor, freedom of movement, and social ties were all affected by British rule; the Ganda experienced new taxes, new requirements to grow cash crops including cotton and coffee, and a changing social landscape through urban migration and significant immigration from beyond the kingdom. Nevertheless, Buganda's colonial history indicates the importance of highlighting continued African agency even under oppressive colonial systems. The kingdom retained a significant degree of autonomy under the new regime. Located at the heart of the British Uganda Protectorate, Buganda became the base for British governance. Moreover, early conversion to Christianity and the kingdom's centralized nature had convinced British administrators, imbued with notions of racial hierarchies, of the superiority of Ganda civilization in relation to neighboring peoples. As such, the Ganda were able to negotiate the retention of significant powers in the formal agreement of British rule in 1900. Leading chiefs, the king, and the Buganda parliament, the Lukiiko, continued to exert significant powers, and a new system of individual landownership placed the majority of the best land in the hands of the king and Ganda chiefs, with the British authorities receiving less fertile lands as well as wastelands. The British drew upon Ganda administrators to govern other areas of the protectorate, and the governmental system of the kingdom was imposed on a variety of other societies across Uganda. Buganda was also economically essential to the colonial government as a region in which both coffee and cotton could be grown for profit.

Buganda's political and economic importance as well as the unusual autonomy accorded the kingdom in the 1900 agreement ensured that the kingdom retained strong bargaining power within the colonial system. Indeed, while the British could impose their will on Buganda, as indicated by the deportation of the troublesome King Mutesa II in 1953, the public outcry that followed and the reinstating of the king in 1955 illustrate that they were often forced to curtail unpopular policies. Moreover, under British rule, Buganda became the wealthiest and best-educated region of Uganda.

Aidan Stonehouse

Further Reading

Hanson, H. *Landed Obligation: The Practice of Power in Buganda.* Portsmouth, NH: Heinemann, 2003.

Kagwa, A. *The Kings of Uganda.* Translated by M. S. M. Kiwanuka. Nairobi: East African Publishing House, 1971.

Kodesh, N. *Beyond the Royal Gaze: Clanship and Public Healing in Buganda.* Charlottesville: University of Virginia, 2010.

Reid, R. *Political Power in Pre-Colonial Buganda: Economy, Society and Welfare in the Nineteenth Century.* Oxford, UK: James Currey, 2002.

Stanley, H. M. *Through the Dark Continent: Or, the Sources of the Nile around the Great Lakes of Equatorial Africa and down the Livingstone River to the Atlantic Ocean.* 2 vols. 1878; reprint, New York: Dover, 1988.

Busoga

Busoga, located in the interlacustrine region of East Africa, sits in southeastern Uganda, a landlocked country. The population of 2.1 million occupies an area of 7,100 square miles bounded on the north by swampy Lake Kyoga, on the west by the Victoria Nile, on the south by Lake Victoria, and on the east by the Mpologoma River. This traditional Bantu kingdom, home of the Basoga, Uganda's second-largest linguistic group, lies east of Kampala, Uganda's capital. The name "Busoga" means "Land of the Soga" and includes 11 principalities of the Basoga/Soga (sing. Musoga) people. The kingdom's capital, Bugembe, was near Jinja, Uganda's second-largest city. The terrain of low flat-topped hills alternates with swampy valleys. Some hills are topped with weathered granite outcrops, but most are covered with heavy red earth and support vegetation. Relatively constant mean annual rainfall of 40–44 inches occurs throughout the region. Variations in the distribution of precipitation result in marked differences in natural vegetation and agricultural potential. The fertile soil on the right bank of the Nile River where it issues from Lake Victoria supports extensive banana cultivation. Northern Busoga has sandier soil less suited for agriculture. Natural forests represent Busoga's key natural resource.

Without the preservation of records or transmission of events from past to future generations, little written evidence exists to reconstruct Busoga's early history. Various traditional legends are used to explain the origins of the Basoga. The founder is generally identified as Mukama (also spelled Makuma), who came from the east side of Mount Elgon and with his wife, eight sons, two dogs, and other followers traveled through present-day Bugishu and Budama. Mukama is considered the creator of life in Basoga mythology. It is believed that he created the first hoes in Busoga, and its rivers are all believed to have originated with him. On arrival in Busoga he appointed his sons to rule over certain areas. Mukama continued on to Bunyoro, where he set up a kingdom. Other stories contend that Mukama was buried at Iganga, where his tomb magically transformed into a rock known today as Buswikara, the site of an important ancestral shrine.

Making a Difference: The Busoga Trust

The Busoga Trust, named after the Kingdom of Busoga, is removing the threat of disease and building healthy communities for Ugandans. The organization originates from a Busoga Diocese multisectored rural program established by Right Reverend Cyprian Bamwose, the bishop of Busoga in 1979. His efforts led to a UK-based nongovernmental organization funding and operating integrated water, sanitation, and hygiene development projects in Uganda. A dedicated Ugandan national and international staff encourages links between the United Kingdom and Uganda. Over 90,000 people throughout Uganda have benefited from initial or restored access to clean, safe water and improved sanitation.

The earliest inhabitants of Busoga traced their origin to the Katanga region of Central Africa. Busoga's first settlement may have been Kagulu Hill. Reportedly, the caves were discovered around 1686 and represent the first settlement and migration center in Busoga. The general opinion recounts that these kingdoms originated around the 16th century, and prior to that Bushmen occupied the area. Around 500 BCE Bantu peoples migrated from West Africa, traveling along the Niger River into the Great Lakes region, and occupied northern, central and western Uganda. Busoga emerged in the 14th century. The earliest inhabitants, the Langis, Itesos, and Bagisus, were later joined by other people from the Mount Elgon region and absorbed by migrants from Buganda. The Busoga population reflected the continuous movement and cultural intermingling of people within the region. As the Ganda expanded their territory in the 18th century, they assumed control of Busoga. Towns such as Jinja, Iganga, Kamuli, and Kaliro continue to face high levels of emigration. Key causes of these movements included famines, epidemics, and political conflicts.

The precolonial Busoga regional economy constituted a network of circulation, distribution, and redistribution, indicating a broad economic world beyond the village community. Before the arrival of European explorers, Arab and Swahili traders moved up and down the Lake Victoria region in the mid-19th century, trading guns and cloth for slaves and ivory. This part of East Africa was a cosmopolitan area with interethnic contact and mixture. Valuable goods and services circulated through many mechanisms. A mix of exchange institutions facilitated the survival and growth of communities far from the depots of regular trade routes and outside the economies of the growing but still small northern states. Trade and communication routes connected the states with each other and with the more powerful states of Buganda and Bunyoro. Busoga was endowed with fertile soil and a good climate to support cultivation. A pattern of subsistence agriculture guaranteeing peasants a steady and adequate food supply led to the stability of local community units. The rise of cash crop cultivation provided an additional source of income for acquiring Western goods and services. A division of labor based on gender existed in early Busoga. Each clan accessed land divided among its members by the clan head.

Busoga society consisted of several small kingdoms with no single leader. The community was organized around certain principles, the most important being descent traced through male ancestors, forming the patrilineage, which included an individual's closest relatives. The language of Basoga people was Soga or Lusoga. Early Basoga women played a major role in agriculture as laborers. Traditional Basoga wives in polygynous marriages controlled a portion of land for food crops. Lineage determined marriage choices, inheritance rights, and obligations to worship ancestors. A man's patrons also influenced his status in society. Warfare was uncommon but sometimes occurred between clans fighting over land. Basoga religion, a combination of polytheism, animism, and ancestral worship, involved prayers and offerings made to gods. The Basoga believed that certain trees and streams possessed spirits. They called their supreme being Lubaale. In the 1890s, Christian missionary groups attempted to establish permanent Christian missions in Busoga.

Busoga constituted 60–70 independent principalities, each ruled by hereditary chiefs who paid tribute first to the king of Bunyoro and then transferred allegiance to the king of Buganda by the end of the 19th century. There was no central authority. States were organized based on patrilineal kinship, ascribed rank, and the patron-client relationship. Busoga had 11 chiefdoms, but only 5 of these cultural units had traditional leaders (chiefs) with a constitutional mandate to elect a new *kyabazinga* (king).

In 1894, Uganda became a protectorate under colonial Britain. In 1895–1896, Busoga became an administrative district under the British protectorate government. In 1900, under the terms of an agreement between Buganda and the British government, the Bugandan king relinquished authority over Busoga, and a separate district administration was established. The traditional decentralized government was dismantled. The British divided Busoga into 14 larger principalities. In 1906, it was reshaped into one cohesive political entity. The British Empire controlled the region and implemented a European-style political system. The protectorate was divided into provinces and, within each province, into districts. Busoga was an administrative district within the Eastern Province. British policy recognized the indigenous state organization. The independent Basoga states were unified. In 1919, Britain created the title of *kyabazinga,* transforming Busoga into a centralized monarchy under a ruling king. An ordinance passed by the Ugandan colonial government in 1905 recognized the authority of the chiefs and rulers. In the early 20th century, the British recognized the traditional state systems as subordinate governments overseen by the protectorate government and established formal agreements with indigenous rulers. The British expanded Busoga-wide political institutions to form the Busoga African Local Government, strongly influenced by traditional beliefs and values. In 1949, the office of *kyabazinga* was made elective. By 1952, all hereditary rulers were replaced by individuals appointed based on personal qualifications. The British encouraged local councils. Basoga society continued with a traditional hierarchy of chiefs whose rule was based on indigenous customary law. The British used indigenous authorities to implement their policies. Colonial administrators introduced coffee and cotton as cash crops. Cotton initiated the conversion of peasants' tribute obligations into money payments. Rulers, chiefs, and headmen acquired cash incomes in addition to their income from tribute. A subsistence economy transitioned to the production of goods in demand by Europeans. In 1889, the British East Africa Company established trade routes, allowing communication between traders and chiefs. Trade routes facilitated the exchange of ivory and slaves. Scattered throughout Busoga were *duka* (shop) towns, small buying and selling centers featuring Indian- and Arab-owned businesses. Busoga transitioned from isolated subsistence cultivation to a global network of trade. Between 1920 and the 1970s, Jinja, Busoga's capital, grew in economic importance. Increased cotton production and completion of the Uganda Railway and the Owen Falls Dam transformed it into an agro-industrial center, attracting laborers from rural areas to work in factories. Many people also came from neighboring areas outside Busoga, among them Asian families looking to do business. Asians brought to Uganda from the Indian subcontinent by the

British helped establish Jinja as one of East Africa's most vibrant commercial centers. They also operated the area's sugarcane plantations. The colonial government created a Busoga railway in 1912, established regional schools and churches, and designated Luganda, the region's official language, as the language of the Ganda. The Anglican Missionary Society and the Catholic Mill Hill Fathers introduced Christianity. By political independence in 1962, Busoga was one of Uganda's most powerful regions. The regional capital, Jinja, was home to 70 percent of the country's industries. Following independence, the position of chief required merit and ability in addition to hereditary lineage. In 1961, the British granted traditional rulers limited powers enforced in 1962 with Ugandan political independence. Milton Obote, founder of the Uganda People's Congress, headed the constitutional initiative.

The first constitution granted considerable authority to rulers. In 1966, Obote ordered his army commander Idi Amin to topple the kingdoms. The Republic of Uganda's 1967 Constitution replaced the 1962 Independence Constitution and abolished all kingdoms. The kingdoms, considered traditional cultural institutions, continued to be recognized by populations with allegiance to traditional rulers. The Busoga king was restricted from joining or participating in partisan politics. Obote was ousted following a coup organized and perpetrated by Idi Amin, who led Uganda from 1971 to 1979. In 1969, the kingdoms were banned. Obote returned to power in 1980–1985. In 1981, Yoweri Museveni established the National Resistance Army. Resistance among the southern Bantus of former kingdoms in the southwest led by Museveni was followed by civil war. Museveni, who gained power in 1986, restored the kingdoms in 1993. The 1995 Constitution permitted the kingdoms to exist as traditional institutions. In 1996 Museveni won Uganda's first direct presidential elections, and Henry Wako Muloki, son of Busoga's first *kyabazinga,* was installed on the throne.

Today Bantu-language speakers comprise slightly over two-thirds of Uganda's population, including the eastern Lacustrine Bantu speakers of Busoga. Now home to people of six different origins due to patterns of migration and settlement, Busoga encompasses the following districts: Kamuli, Iganga, Bugiri, Mayuge, Jinja, Kaliro, and Busiki. Each district is headed by democratically elected chairpersons or a Local Council Five, with municipalities headed by an elected mayor. A 2005 amendment to the constitution reaffirmed the position of the *kyabazinga,* confirming his status in Ugandan society. Politically, the kingdom is a union of 11 chiefdoms. The *kyabazinga* is regarded as the overall leader supported by a council of 11 semiautonomous hereditary chiefs. Postindependence reforms, including the ending of state marketing of cash crops in the 1970s and 1980s, ended the incentive to produce cotton and coffee, placing greater emphasis on cultivating food crops. The primary economic activity in Jinja is manufacturing and trade. Local industries have been rebuilt since their collapse in the 1970s and 1980s. Financing remains a critical problem for cultural leaders. Although Uganda was the first country in sub-Saharan Africa to promote voluntary HIV counseling and testing clinics, Busoga continues to grapple with HIV/AIDS infection and poor hygiene and sanitation.

Maryalice Guilford

Further Reading

Cohen, David W. *The Historical Tradition of Busoga: Mukama and Kintu.* Oxford, UK: Clarendon, 1972.

Cohen, David W. *Womunafu's Bunafu: A Study of Authority in a Nineteenth-Century African Community.* Princeton, NJ: Princeton University Press, 1977.

Fallers, Lloyd A. *Bantu Bureaucracy: A Century of Political Evolution among the Basoga of Uganda.* Chicago: University of Chicago Press, 1965.

Fallers, Lloyd A. *Law without Precedent: Legal Ideas in Action in the Courts of Colonial Busoga.* Chicago: University of Chicago Press, 1969.

C

Carthage

Carthage is one of the earliest harbors of the southern Mediterranean shore still in activity. It has been a capital for the last three millennia, from the first Phoenician colonists to present-day Tunisia. The actual city of Tunis covers part of the ruins of the Antique settlement, covering approximately five square miles along the coast. The many destructions of Carthage (by the Romans, the Vandals, the Umayyads, etc.) never resulted in the abandonment of such a favorable site.

The first known inhabitants of the region are the North African Berber ethnic group, now mixed with the remnants of the different invaders and refugees. From 300,000 citizens at the height of the Roman Empire, its population regrouped in Tunis amounted only to a few thousand during the early Islamic period, while the present population is about three-quarters of a million. The historical importance of the site led to its designation as a UNESCO's World Heritage Site in 1979 and to an international campaign (1972–1992) to save the site from further destruction by the urbanization of Tunis.

The main features of Carthage—its commercial and military ports—lie at the northern edge of the Gulf of Tunis, dominated by the Byrsa Hill, center of the ritual life of the ancient colony and future forum of the Roman town. The town is protected from inland dangers by a chain of hills and dried lakes (*sebkha*), and potable water is provided by a nearby lake. Carthage has a Mediterranean climate, tempered by the sea, and relies on the agriculture of the plains constituting its hinterland and on the resources of the sea. There was a major shipyard there during antiquity, drawing its necessities from the woodlands of the nearby mountains.

Roman colonization transformed the economy of Carthage to make it one of the principal sources for grain and olive oil for Rome itself and the free distributions of food to Italian population. As a port, Carthage extracted from the sea a tinctorial mollusk (*murex*), giving a purplish-red dye known as purpureus, and as

Palace of Tunisian Presidents

The palace of the president of Tunisia is situated on the hill of Carthage, surrounded by the villas of high-ranking officials and well-off families. In this manner, the actual Republic of Tunisia still has its center at Carthage, perpetuating a multimillenial tradition.

an African port it has always been a market of particular importance for goods obtained from long-range trade with or through the Sahara (ostrich feathers, wild animals and their hides, ivory, and later on West African gold and slaves). Local African culture was deeply altered at contact with the Punic settlers. Literacy and the use of writing seem to have begun around that time, and the Berber alphabet currently known as Tifinagh may have a hypothetical origin in the imitation of the Punic script.

The city founded by the Phoenicians in Libyan lands as a place of trade, fortified to control the straits between the eastern and western Mediterranean, had a central role in the development of the Roman Empire. Seen as the nemesis of Rome, the two colonial power centers waged a war that endured for more than a century, from 264 to 146 BCE, and broke the might of Carthage forever, ending in the annihilation of the city and its reconstruction by the Latins. The main reason for this conflict was economical domination of the western Mediterranean trade and control of former Carthaginian colonies in Spain, North Africa, and the islands (the Balearic archipelago, Corsica, Sardinia, and Sicily).

At the collapse of the Roman Empire, Carthage was disputed between eastern and western factions in such a way that it fell into Hellenic influence, but the wandering of the Vandals through Europe from east to west found an end in the taking of North Africa at the hands of the Byzantines. The Vandal reign on Northern Africa lacks historical sources, and archaeology has not yet provided us with enough material ascribed to this period to be able to reconstruct its history. Soon after the Vandal reign, expeditions launched from Constantinople recovered Africa from the barbarians, but this was to be of short effect.

The conquest of the African province of the Byzantine Empire happened to be a complex task for the caliphate army, as the local population after much turmoil protected its land with fierce energy, and the Arab raiders were far from their bases. It took until 698 for an Islamic expedition coming from Egypt to take the declining city and put an end to its fame forever. For centuries afterward, the ruins of Carthage were used as a spolia ground from which hundreds of marble columns and tons of blocks of the antique monuments were extracted and scattered all around the Mediterranean. Overlooking the wasted capital now in ruins again, the village of Tunis became the center of power controlling the gulf that got its name from the city. It would take another couple of centuries for Tunis to reclaim its centrality in the Tunisian landscape and regain its position of capital city under the Almohads.

In 1270 French king Louis IX led a crusade to take Tunis from the Hafsid dynasty and put his camp on the hill of Byrsa. He died there from an epidemic and was buried in a chapel, where a part of his remains stayed until the 20th century, while the rest of his remains were repatriated in France at the king's basilica of Saint-Denis. Under the French protectorate and with the benediction of Cardinal Lavigerie of Algiers, Abbé Alfred-Louis Delattre led the first important archaeological excavations on the site (between 1874 and 1904). Lacking formal training but never sparing his efforts, he brought to light the structures of the Roman city built on the ruins of the Punic capital, the cemeteries of the different ages, and the major buildings of the late Roman metropolis, including its churches. These excavations were also the occasion of founding a museum on the site whose collections are the basis of the present one. The activity of Francis W. Kelsey around the Mediterranean and on the site was at the center of the collection of antiques that provided the University of Michigan in Ann Arbor with the core of its museum.

Jacob Durieux

Further Reading

Lancel, Serge. *Carthage: A History.* Oxford, UK: Blackwell, 1995.

Miles, Richard. *Carthage Must Be Destroyed: The Rise and Fall of an Ancient Civilization.* New York: Penguin, 2012.

D

Dahomey

Dahomey was located on the coast of West Africa. It was bounded in the south by the Atlantic Ocean and abutted in the west by the Asante kingdom and in the east by the Oyo Empire. Dahomey was adjoined in the southwest and the southeast by the small but formidable kingdoms of Popo and Badagry, respectively. To its northern fringe was Mahi. The topography of the kingdom varies from north to south. The flora of the region was predominantly savanna. The territory was dotted by plateaus, swamps, and rivers such as the Zou, Weme, and Mono. The definite map of the state may be difficult to determine, as the state continued to pursue an expansionist policy, but at its height Dahomey occupied an area of about 6,400 kilometers. It was about 80 kilometers from north to south and 45 kilometers wide from east to west but narrower toward the south. Thus, the structure of the boundaries of Dahomey was pyriform (pear-shaped).

Dahomey was a small state that was centered on the kingdom of Abomey. Abomey was founded around 1620 by the Fon, or Aja-speaking people. Their tradition of origin claims that the ancestors of the Aja people lived at Tado before migrating to settle in Allada toward the end of the 16th century, probably about 1575. Thus, the Aja migration from Tado formed a part of large waves of migration that included the westward movement of the Ewe to modern-day Togo and Ghana. Due to succession disputes, a group of Aja-speaking people migrated from Allada and settled on the Abomey Plateau, about 60 miles from the coast, probably in about 1620. The Aja founded a kingdom in Abomey and established the Aladaxonu dynasty.

The Amazons

Dahomey's Amazons are undoubtedly the most celebrated female soldiers in precolonial Africa. Their discipline and courage stood them out in the Dahomean Army. These Amazons were probably first used as the royal guards by King Agaja (1718–1740) and later as special fighting force in the Dahomean Army by King Gezo (1818–1858). By 1851 when Dahomey invaded Abeokuta, the fame and fear of the Amazons had already spread across West Africa and was noticed by some European visitors to the continent. It was estimated that about 700 to 800 Amazons were killed in the 1864 unsuccessful attack on Abeokuta by King Glele.

Dahomey possessed a well-organized system of government based on absolute monarchy. The king was semidivine and all-powerful and controlled all economic, political, and social affairs. He was assisted in his administration by a council of officials directly appointed and responsible to him. These officials were chosen among the commoner class based on meritorious contributions to the development of the state. They could be promoted, dismissed, degraded, or transferred by the king. Among the top officials were the *migan* (prime minister), the *meu* (finance minister), and the *yevogan* (provincial administrator of *ouidah/whydah* and overseas trade). Other important officials included the *tokpo* (minister of agriculture), the *to-no-num* (chief eunuch and protocol), the *agan* (general of the army), and *adjaho* (chief police officer and minister of the palace). The activities of the officials in the king's council were monitored by another group of officials called *nayes*.

The *nayes* were as powerful as the male officials. They were a group of exceptional and experienced older women past childbearing age assigned to watch and ascertain that the king's orders were honestly carried out by the male officials. They also ensured efficiency of the department they were assigned to. In order to ensure efficiency, they presented their own reports, committed to memory, that could either confirm or contradict the reports of male officials.

The state was divided into six provinces, and each was governed by a provincial governor. All conquered states were absorbed into Dahomey. This was done through the principle of Dahomenization, as their laws and customs were replaced by those of Dahomey. The principle also allowed the granting of Dahomean citizen to foreigners who so desired. To foster national unity and loyalty, it was believed that the national unity of Dahomey depended on every citizen of the state. Hence symbolically, the state was compared to a perforated calabash with water (the national unity), while the citizens were likened to fingers that supported every hole around the calabash. Thus, if any citizen removed his or her finger (i.e., support) from the calabash through disloyalty, the spirit of national unity would drain.

The greatness of Dahomey was not unconnected with the emergence of strong but brilliant kings. By the beginning of the 18th century, Dahomey had expanded from the small kingdom of Abomey to include the surrounding countryside. This was due to the activities of two courageous kings, Wegbaja (1650–1685) and Akaba (1685–1708), who ruled Abomey in the second half of 17th century. They were able to consolidate their firm hold on the conquered states. Perhaps the greatest of the 18th-century rulers of Dahomey was Agaja, who reigned between 1708 and 1740. Physically, Agaja was average in height with a full body and broad shoulders; what he lacked in height was compensated for in efficient administration, political astuteness, and military prowess. He laid the foundation of the future greatness of Dahomey. When he ascended the throne, the kingdom of Dahomey consisted of Abomey and about 42 to 62 villages. Agaja's foci were to annex the coastal states and bring all Aja kingdoms together under Dahomean suzerainty. To achieve his aims, he instituted a system of espionage called the Agbadjigbeto to spy on neighboring states. The Agbadjigbetos would present themselves as friendly merchants and learned the languages of the neighboring or enemy states. Their responsibility was to obtain vital information concerning the military strength and defense arrangements of the neighboring states and their protective gods and if possible enter friendship pacts with them. The Agbadjigbetos were also agents of propaganda within both Dahomey and the enemy states. They spread rumors and false information to destabilize the neighboring states. Oral traditions also credited Agaja as the initiator of an efficient military training scheme in Dahomey. His military school produced a highly efficient army. His soldiers were subjected to different rigorous exercises and military hardship.

Agaja subjugated states in the northwestern fringes and Weme in the northeast. Next were the coastal states whose monopoly of trade affected the prosperity of Dahomey. His attack on Allada, the ancient Aja kingdom to the south, on March 30, 1724, marked the beginning of the Dahomean domination of Aja and the effective collapse of the commonwealth system in the region. The fall of Allada meant that a new power had emerged in the region. Another important Aja kingdom that felt the might of the Dahomean forces was Whydah. On February 26, 1727, Agaja marched his army into Whydah. Within five days, the capital of Whydah and the outlying provinces were subjugated. The success of Agaja's military campaign could be attributed to two major factors. First, Agaja penetrated his neighboring states with spies who obtained vital information on military preparedness and strength of the enemies. These spies spread rumors and caused confusion in their areas of assignments. Thus, his strategy was to weaken the political fabric of the enemy states. Second, his campaigns against both Allada and Whydah were thoroughly planned and carefully carried out. Dahomean imperial mission soon attracted the attention of the Oyo Empire in the east. Between 1726 and 1740, Dahomey was invaded by Oyo cavalry. Despite the strength of Agaja's army, Dahomey became a tributary to Oyo in 1830.

Agaja was succeeded in 1740 by Tegbesu. Not much was added to the territory that Agaja left behind. With Allada, Whydah, and the outlying coastal states at his disposal, Tegbesu focused on improving the economy of Dahomey. Although initially the economy improved drastically, before the end of his reign in 1774 it began to decline. This economic misfortune was not unconnected to the withdrawal of the European trading posts from Whydah to Porto Novo. In addition, Oyo's influence and grip on Dahomey became more tightened. Neither Kpengla (1774–1789) nor Agonglo (1789–1797) could save Dahomey from Oyo's suzerainty. It was not until the reign of Gezo (1818–1858) that Dahomey breathed a sigh of relief from Oyo's invasions. During his reign, the regular army of Dahomey increased from about 6,000 to about 24,000. The women's corps, the famous Amazons, not only increased in number but also gained fame. In 1823, Gezo broke Dahomey free of its tributary status. With the Oyo Empire out of the way, Dahomey became the major power in the Aja region. In an attempt to remove Oyo's menace, Gezo launched different attacks against the western Yorubaland, especially Abeokuta. So frightening was the Dahomean threat against Abeokuta that the British had to support the latter militarily. Toward the north, a large part of Mahi was annexed to Dahomey. It is significant to note that despite his military campaign, Gezo did not neglect the economy of Dahomey. He encouraged agriculture, particularly palm oil plantation, to replace the unpopular slave trade.

Until the 1850s, Dahomey possessed a well-organized although unstable economy. The state was located in one of the poorest savanna and coastal regions of West Africa, and unlike its neighbors to the east, the land could not support large-scale farming. Neither was it blessed with natural resources, as were its neighbors to the west. Before 1807 when a British act of Parliament declared the slave trade illegal, the Dahomean economy largely depended on the slave trade. Slaves were either raided from Mahi republics to the north and Egbado to the east or acquired through wars. Thus, the European traders and visitors to West Africa before 1900 described the littoral from Popo to Lagos as the "Slave Coast." Besides trade in human cargo, the state also derived income from customs duties, tolls, taxes, and the monopoly of major trades such as the slave trade. The state imposed income taxes on individuals based on social and financial status. Livestock was not exempt from taxation. To ensure accurate figures of people and taxable livestock, the state regularly conducted population censuses. Initially the abolition of the slave trade nearly spelled economic doom for Dahomey, as there was no immediate replacement for the trade. Besides the lack of cultivable land, there was the fear that trade in palm oil could be profitable. By the 1850s, the port at Whydah had begun to export palm oil. By the 1870s, Dahomey had successfully shifted from the slave trade to the oil trade, although slave raiding particularly for farm labor continued. Thus, Dahomey emerged as the major exporter of palm oil in precolonial Africa.

The rise of Dahomey from a small kingdom on the Abomey Plateau to a large Aja state can be attributed to a number of factors. First, the state operated a highly centralized but efficient system of government headed by a semidivine king. The adoption of an absolute monarchy with a well-defined succession rule could not be divorced from the need to ensure a stable polity and to survive in the midst of militarily strong, spatially sprawling, and economically prosperous neighbors. Second, in order to survive economically, Dahomey raided its neighbors for slaves and waged wars to acquire fertile land for farming and access to trade ports on the coast. Thus, the involvement of Dahomey in the slave trade and later the palm oil trade bolstered its economy. From these two trades, duties were collected and taxes were imposed. Third, the complete integration of conquered states also reduced the incidence of revolts in Dahomey. Fourth, Dahomey also owed its rise to its strong and efficient army. Surrounded by militarily strong neighbors, Dahomey saw the need to build an invincibly formidable army that became thorns for its enemy. Finally, Dahomey was blessed with able rulers, such as Agaja and Gezo, who were determined to strengthen the state.

After different unsuccessful attempts by various European countries to infiltrate Dahomey, the French succeeded in 1894 after a series of campaigns in the Franco-Dahomean wars. The conquest was followed by the exile of Behanzin (1889–1894), the king of Dahomey. A new king, Agoli-agbo, was installed. Thus, this marked the beginning of French colonial rule in Dahomey. After its independence in 1960, Dahomey took the name Republic of Dahomey. This name was changed to Benin in 1975.

Shina Alimi

Further Reading

Akinjogbin, I. A. *Dahomey and Its Neighbours, 1708–1818.* Cambridge: Cambridge University Press, 1967.

Biobaku, S. *Egba and Their Neighbours.* Ibadan: University Press of Ibadan, 1991.

Boahen, A. A., with J. F. A. Ajayi and M. Tidy. *Topics in West African History.* London: Longman, 1986.

Webster, J. B., and A. A. Boahen, with M. Tidy. *The Revolutionary Years: West Africa since 1800.* London: Longman, 1980.

Darfur

The multiethnic Darfur Sultanate occupied a strategic location, straddling the Jebel Marra between the Libyan Desert and the Bahr al-Arab in the western region of modern-day North Sudan. The sultanate was about the size of modern-day Germany or France. Darfur featured arid regions in the north and a mineral-rich mountain range with peaks 10,000 feet high that were terraced over the centuries into fertile farmland and more verdant plains to the south. As such, a diversified agricultural and pastoral economy developed there that attracted merchants from all directions as part of the Sudanic network of empires stretching from the Atlantic Ocean to the Red Sea. The populations who have historically occupied the region include the Dajua, Tungurs, Bertis, Meidobs, Furs, Zaghawas, Birgids, and others. Nineteenth-century efforts by European ethnographers to classify the people of Darfur as either Negroid or Arab races reflect outsiders' ignorance in that century of the complex history of this region. Since then, numerous efforts have been made to collect oral histories of various ethnic groups.

The synthesis of these various ethnic histories is that the region featured three dynasties. In the 13th and 14th centuries, the pre-Islamic Daju dynasty, which had migrated to the southeastern region of Jabal Marra from the east, was founded by King Gitar, and his 6th of 12 successors in Darfur converted the lineage to Islam. During this dynasty, the Fur people paid tribute to the Daju rulers. The last Daju king in Darfur, Ahmad al-Daj, was such an oppressive tyrant that the people chased this ruler to the west, where a new Daju state was established in a region now incorporated into modern-day Chad.

The Tunjur dynasty followed in the early 16th century. There are several versions of the founding of this dynasty, but the consensus is that two brothers from Banu Hillal in the area of Tunis arrived in the greater Darfur region and that through them more trading connections were established with the Islamic world system of the Mediterranean. In one version, the brothers each wished to marry the daughter of King Kor of the western Daju kingdom. King Kor consented to the marriage of his daughter to Ahmad al-Ma'qur (crippled by a sliced hamstring), and the Tunjur dynasty that descended from the pair was forged of African and Arabian lineages. The Tungur dynasty built its administrative capital in the mountain town of Uri, where three trade routes intersected. The Tungurs' long-distance trade networks were so extensive that the dynasty maintained trade representatives in Medina (Arabian Peninsula) and in Cairo (Egypt), where their caravans brought elephant tusks, ostrich feathers, and slaves during a 40-day journey. Palaces in Uri and resort homes in nearby Ain Farah testify to the wealth of the Tungur dynasty of 13 kings. Their commercial success was noted in Arabic sources in the 16th century and in European sources in 1663.

Sources conflict about the decline of the Tungur dynasty. However, between 1535 and 1603, the western border of Darfur fell into such integration with the Bornu Empire that Bornu appointed a governor for the region named Dala Afnu or Dalil (a legal scholar who climbed the ranks of power as a eunuch slave and civil servant). He revised the legal code of the Tungurs along Maliki Islamic case law, reorganized the governing districts, and wrote the *Book of Dali,* which included a penal code. Some sources say that Dala Afnu is responsible for creating the next dynasty. Another source suggests that Dalil was asked to take over when his peer, the tyrannical and oppressive King Shau Dorshit, was chased from power around 1630. Neither source suggests any economic decline. Rather, the archaeological evidence is that Dalil was quite successful, for the remains of his compound at Jabal Foga measured 100 yards in diameter and included several round stone rooms. This evidence affirms the suggestion that Dalil may have had the power to launch the next dynasty.

The Keira dynasty replaced the Tungur dynasty around 1640. The dynastic family actually formed in 1625 through King Kuru, who was distantly related to the Tungur royal lineage. After Shau Dorshit was deposed around 1630 a civil war erupted, and the Keira line may have emerged as the more powerful faction, or if the Dalil story holds, the Keira line was selected by Dalil to take over the sultanate. In either case, the Keira sultans continued to follow the Maliki Islamic case law reform that Dalil initiated. During this time the capital shifted to Turra, where Keira sultans are buried.

Stories about the founding of the Keira dynasty vary. Some claim that Ahmad al-Ma'qur founded the Keira dynasty, and others say that the Keira sultans are descended from Ahmad al-Ma'qur. Both versions establish a lineage connection to Arabia. There is consensus that the first great Keira sultan was Sulayman Solongungu, who ruled from 1640 to 1660. He is remembered as a conqueror who enhanced Darfur's trade and elevated the Fur people to power. (The Fur people began to organize as a polity to defend themselves from slave raids by the Tungurs). When Sultan Sulayman took control, he equipped his slave raiders with armor, large war horses from Dongala on the Nile River, and weapons imported from Egypt. The Keiras were also known for allowing the royal women to practice a syncretic form of Islam in which traditional ideas of a semidivine king were restored. A semidivine king may have been more intimidating in the non-Muslim regions from which slaves were raided. Sultan Sulayman's power was such that he conquered the Sennar Sultanate of the Funj for a time. Nevertheless, the Keira Sultanate was known for a flourishing of Islamic teachings by scholars brought in from Egypt and Tunis, for construction of many mosques, and for the construction of many *fashirs*—unique palace compounds that at once were a residence, a warehouse, a bureaucratic center, a university for future civil servants, a treasury, and a parade ground for public ceremonies. This rational bureaucracy that supported the slave export trade fortified the Keira dynasty until 1874. The success of the governing style is remembered in the name of one of modern-day Darfur's largest cities, El Fashir.

Marsha R. Robinson

Further Reading

Arkell, A. J. "The History of Darfur 1200–1700." *Sudan Notes and Records* 32(1) (1951): 37–50.

Arkell, A. J. "The History of Darfur 1200–1700: Part 2." *Sudan Notes and Records* 32 (December 1951): 207–238.

Hasan, Y. F., and B. A. Ogot. "The Sudan, 1500–1800." In *Africa from the Sixteenth to the Eighteenth Century,* edited by B. A. Ogot, 70–91. London: Heinemann, 1992.

Lobban, Richard Andrew, Robert S. Kramer, and Carolyn Fluehr-Lobban. *Historical Dictionary of the Sudan.* Lanham, MD: Scarecrow, 2002.

O'Fahey, R. S. *The Darfur Sultanate: A History.* New York: Columbia University Press, 2008.

Denkyira

Denkyira origin stories suggest that climatic changes in the 14th century or earlier that resulted in drought and famine in the Volta region, south of the Niger Bend, forced the Denkyira people to migrate southward to settle at Nkyiraa in the ancient Bono State in present-day Ghana. The Denkyira people belong to the Akan ethnic group of southern Ghana but were originally called the Adawufos. According to their tradition, they stayed with the Nkyiraas for such a long time and became

---

The Battle of Feyiase

The Battle of Feyiase was an important historical event in the history of the Denkyira people, as it marked the beginning of their vassal status to the Asante kingdom in the 18th century. In 1701 the Asante kingdom, under King Osei Tutu, went to war with the Denkyira kingdom, which was the most powerful state in the hinterlands of the Gold Coast and controlled the gold trade with Europeans. Prior to the Battle of Feyiase, the two warring factions had been engaged in other battles in which the *denkyirahene* (king of Denkyira), Ntim Gyakari, believed that Denkyira would emerged victorious. However, in a surprise attack at Feyiase, the full force of the Asante army fell on the Denkyira forces, decisively defeating them and killing their king in the process. This battle allowed the Asante kingdom to replace the Denkyira kingdom as the most dominant and most powerful among the Akan people.

acculturated into Nkyiraa's culture and customs that people began to refer to them as Dan-Nkyiraas—that is, dependent on Nkyiraa, and hence their current name, Denkyira. Around the 16th century under the leadership of Nana Ayekraa Adeboa, their first female ruler, the Denkyira decided to move southward into the central forest region, perhaps due to conflicts or unfavorable climatic conditions.

The Denkyira settled at Tutumbe near Bonatifi, about two miles from Adanse Akorokyere in the present-day Ashanti region. Of the eight Akan clans/families (*abusua*), the Denkyira predominantly belong to the Agona (Anona) clan; hence, their newly established state became known as Agona State. Nana Ayekraa Adeboa reportedly had a very successful reign. Her eldest son, Annin Panyin, succeeded her after her death and was followed by his two brothers, Ahi and Aha. They were followed by Mumunumfi (1588–1624). During the later part of Mumunumfi's reign, Agona State became known as the Denkyira kingdom. By this time, they had developed effective political and military units. It has been asserted that Mumunumfi waged war against Adanse because of its wealth and power and succeeded in vanquishing the Adanses. The next *denkyirahene* (king), Wirempe Ampem (1624–1637), established their famous capital, Abankesieso.

Abankesieso was geographically located at 6°17′N 1°51′W within the general area of present-day Abuakwa, Aworansa, and Sudontoa in the Ashanti region and was about 20 miles to the east of the confluence of the Oda River with the Offin River in the Offin-Pra River basin. In spite of its general location, Denkyira did not have a well-defined territorial boundary. Instead, Abankesieso presided over groups of settlements and inhabitants who identified themselves as Denkyira either through marriage ties and lineage or may have migrated with the people of Abankesieso into the Offin-Pra River basin in the 16th century. Wirempe Ampem became known as the warrior king and was a cruel one. He had a very strong organized state army and used it to expand the territory of the Denkyira. It was during one of his campaigns that he died and was succeeded by an eight-year-old next of kin called Boa Amponsem Dakabere (1637–1695).

Until the late 1650s, Denkyira was sparsely populated. However, given its strategic location in the Offin-Pra basin, with an abundant water supply, good annual rainfall, and rich soil for agricultural production in addition to gold and diamond production, the population began to grow rapidly. The population increase and the prosperity derived from the gold from the Offin River allowed Boa Amponsem to develop a much more efficient military system than those of his predecessors. This enabled the Denkyira to continue with their territorial expansion and to wage war to their south to control the trade corridor to the Gulf of Guinea. With good agricultural production, trade with Europeans, and tributes from vassal states, Denkyira became the first Akan state to rise to the status of a large kingdom and the most dominant power in southern Ghana between the 1660s and 1690s. Denkyira became so rich that reportedly Boa Amponsem became the first king to appoint the first treasury head among the Akan people to keep account of the kingdom's gold stored in a house called Sikadan (Gold House).

Administratively, Denkyira was divided into metropolitan and provincial regions. Abankesieso and its environs were the metropolitan area. Besides the *denkyirahene,* who was at the top of the administrative structure, there were the trade minister (*batahene*), the treasury minister (*sanaahene*), the minister of home affairs (*gyaasehene*), the minister of foreign affairs and head linguist (*akyeamehene*), and the minister of religious affairs (*sumankwaahene*). The conquered territories formed the provincial region. It included states such as Asante, Twifo, Wasa Amenfi, and Assin. The kings of conquered territories were allowed to continue to rule their people; however, they were answerable to the *denkyirahene.* They were required to pay taxes (usually in gold and slaves) and to provide soldiers for the Denkyira Army in times of war. In terms of military organization, Denkyira's two regions also fell into three divisions: *akumatire* (advance guard), *kyeremfem* (leftwing), and *agona adontendom* (advance guard).

Economically, Denkyira in the mid-17th century was the most important supplier of gold and slaves to the Dutch at Elmina and the English at Cape Coast. Denkyira also imported European goods more than any other state, particularly European guns and ammunition. The monopoly of Denkyira over the trade with Europeans was the result of its control of the trade routes from the interior to the coast. Any vassal state that wanted to trade had to go through Denkyira by paying heavy taxes on their trade items. In addition, Denkyira held land title to the Elmina Castle of the Dutch, which gave Denkyira control over all trading activities that the castle conducted with others before losing this control to the Asante in 1701. Prior to 1701 Denkyira fought many wars, including wars with the Assin and Twifo in the 1690s, to keep its trading monopoly and its control of the 130-mile trading corridor from the interior to the coast. Controlling the trading corridor to the coast stretched Denkyira's financial and manpower resources to the brink and indeed proved very pricy in 1701.

Denkyira's apparent invincibility vanished in about 1694 when Boa Amponsem died after some 40 years of able leadership. He was succeeded by his nephew, Ntim Gyakari (ca. 1694–1701), whose first act as a ruler provoked resistance from a coalition of his northern vassal states led by Osei Tutu of Kwaman (Kumase). According to Kwaman traditions, Ntim Gyakari failed to walk the fine line of dealing with subjugated people by demanding that the Asante ruler fill a brass pan with gold to the brim and send this to him along with the precious *kyekyerekona* beads worn by Asante royal wives as a sign of obedience to their husbands; the Asante ruler and his provincial chiefs were also commanded to deliver to Ntim Gyakari their favorite wives and beloved children. Throughout the Denkyira-Asante relations, the Asante had always sent one royal member to the Denkyira court as a form of leverage, and Osei Tutu himself spent a considerable amount of time in his youth in Denkyira. Nonetheless, the Asante considered Ntim Gyakari's demands completely unacceptable.

Thus, the Asante confederacy refused to comply with Ntim Gyakari's demands, resulting in a hard-fought war between the two. The Denkyira became saddled with fighting on two fronts. That is, they had to conduct military operations in the north against the Asante coalition while holding down the south to keep their control of the trade route to the coast. This placed a great strain on Denkyira's resources and made the kingdom very vulnerable. In 1701 in the Battle of Feyiase, the Asante coalition defeated Denkyira, and Ntim Gyakari was killed. The fledging Asante kingdom acquired all Denkyira territories, effectively bringing the Denkyira kingdom to an end. The Asante ransacked Abankesieso and took all the Denkyira gold to Kumase. The defeated Denkyira did not immediately abandon Abankesieso. Many remained and became absorbed into the Asante kingdom. However, they continued to be dissatisfied under Asante rule and sought ways to rebel. From 1823 to 1824, the British took advantage of the Denkyira's animosity toward the Asante and used them in a campaign to defeat the Asante.

The campaign failed, forcing the *denkyirahene,* Kwadwo Tibo, to abandon Abankesieso and relocate with his people. According to oral tradition, Kwadwo Tibo and his people turned southward toward the Gulf of Guinea, but by the time they reached Dunkwa-on-Offin, many of the people were too exhausted to continue. Kwadwo Tibo thus sought and got the consent of the paramount chief (*omanhene*) of Wasa Amenfi to settle some of his people at Dunkwa-on-Offin. Oral tradition suggests that it was only the exhausted party that was left to settle at Dunkwa-on-Offin. Kwadwo Tibo and the rest of the party continued down the Twifo road to about 14 miles from the coast. From Dunkwa-on-Offin, it is believed that another group from the party settled at Odumase, which is about 7 miles north of the present-day town of Jukwa, the place where the final party with Kwadwo Tibo settled.

Prior to 1943, all Denkyira kings lived at Jukwa as the paramount seat. In 1943, the people of Dunkwa-on-Offin appealed to the British district commissioner and had their state capital moved to their town because the majority of the Denkyira people lived there and not at Jukwa. While the state capital may have moved from Jukwa to Dunkwa-on-Offin, the Denkyira traditional seat remained at Jukwa, for tradition has it that Nana Kufuo had declared it unmovable. As a result, many state functions still take place at Jukwa. Today, aside from oral traditions, old Denkyira has all but disappeared from the historical purview. While Abankesieso has not been geographically or archaeologically identified and although metropolitan Abankesieso was probably subsumed by Asante settlements, the Denkyira people continue to thrive in their new home in the Upper Denkyira and Twifo/Heman/Lower Denkyira Districts in the Central Region of Ghana.

Nana-Akua Amponsah

Further Reading

Daaku, K. Y. *Denkyira* (UNESCO Research Project on Oral Traditions). Legon, Accra: Organization of African Unity, Centre for Linguistic and Historical Studies by Oral Tradition, 1970.

Gordon, J. "Some Oral Traditions of Denkyira." *Transactions of the Gold Coast & Togoland Historical Society* 1(3) (1953): 27–33.

McCaskie, T. C. "Denkyira in the Making of Asante, 1660–1720." *Journal of African History* 48(1) (2007): 1–25.

Dotawo

Dotawo was a Nubian kingdom in the late medieval period. Nubian civilization in the medieval period stretched along the Nile Valley from the first cataract of the Nile in the north to the Gezira, the region between the White and Blue Niles, to the south of the sixth cataract in the south. After the end of Meroitic civilization in antiquity, this region was home to three independent kingdoms: Nobadia in the north, Makuria in the middle, and Alwa or Alodia in the south. While these kingdoms had contacts outside of the Nile Valley in the deserts to the east and west, nothing can be said with certainty about their political control over these regions. Nor does evidence permit us to estimate the population size of these kingdoms.

Archaeological excavations in Lower Nubia in the 20th century uncovered documents mentioning a Nubian kingdom named Dotawo. The texts from Qasr Ibrim naming kings of Dotawo date from the 1150s to the 1460s CE. One of these kings, Siti (r. 1330s), also appears in a graffito from Abu Negila (Kordofan) and in several inscriptions from Banganarti, but neither Dotawo nor any other name for his kingdom appears in these texts. The last of these kings, Joel, also appears in a graffito from Abu Hoda, an inscription from Tamit, and a legal text from Gebel Adda dating to the 1480s.

Several of these kings of Dotawo are known from external sources, particularly Arab historians and geographers, and are described as kings of the Nubians, of the Nuba, or as living in or ruling from Old Dongola, near modern Dongola, the current capital of Sudan's Northern State. The Nubian kingdom governed from Old Dongola and united the late antique and early Christian Nubian kingdoms of Nobadia, Makuria and Alwa and is itself described as Makuria in other sources. All of the texts mentioning Dotawo are in Old Nubian, the indigenous language of the Nubian people in the Christian period.

Thus, Dotawo was the indigenous name of a Nubian kingdom from at least the 12th to the 15th centuries CE, ruling all or parts of territory formerly known as Nobadia, Makuria, and Alwa. We have no evidence to suggest that the name "Dotawo" was used in earlier periods in Nubian history and no way of knowing what it means or why it came into use. The capital of Dotawo was Old Dongola until 1365, when ongoing wars and internal strife led to the city's abandonment. Some scholars argue that the court then moved to Daw (sometimes identified with the archaeological site of Gebel Adda) and that Daw remained the capital of Dotawo until its ultimate collapse at the end of the 15th century. Etymologically, Dotawo could mean "the area under Do" in Old Nubian, but it is not clear if this is a reference to Daw or some other place or if it has some other meaning entirely.

Compared to Egypt, Nubia was resource poor in the medieval period. The Nile Valley was more narrow in Dotawo than farther north in Egypt, and its banks were higher and more rocky. One consequence of this feature is that Dotawo had a lower agricultural output and a lower population than Egypt throughout its history. Another consequence of this feature was considerable reliance on the *saqiya* (a large hollow wheel with pottery jars attached to the perimeter that was used to bring up water) to irrigate its farmland. Although agriculture was fundamental to the Nubian economy, archaeological excavations have also uncovered major centers of cloth production and pottery manufacturing.

Nubia was a predominantly Christian culture from late antiquity through the medieval period. Ecclesiastical histories record that the united kingdoms of Nobadia and Makuria were home to seven bishops. Logically, this would be true of the kingdom of Dotawo as well, but not all seven are known with certainty. Major ecclesiastical centers and bishops are attested at Philae, Qasr Ibrim, Faras, Kourte, Sai, and Dongola. The bishop of the latter, as the bishop of the royal capital, was the archbishop, the highest ecclesiastical figure in Dotawo. Being under the authority of the Coptic patriarch of Alexandria, the Nubian church needed that patriarch's approval to appoint bishops, but these bishops appear to have been indigenous and appointed through local recommendation.

Dotawo's political system is poorly understood. We know that succession to the throne often took place matrilineally; the king was succeeded on the throne not by his son but instead by his sister's son. Thus, the *ngonnen,* or so-called queen mother, was a prominent figure in Nubian politics and society. At a regional level, government in the king's name was conducted by local governors. The best known of these and the most influential figure in northern Nubia was the *eparch* (lord of the mountain). He was responsible for border security and control of international travel and trade. External literary sources describe Nubia as ruled by 13 kings under the great king, presumably a reference to the *eparch* and other regional governors. Internal sources are in Coptic, Greek, Old Nubian, and Arabic. The majority of these sources remain unpublished and may reveal considerably more about Dotawo's political and religious systems.

Dotawo's greatest trading partner was also its greatest external threat. Relations between Egypt and Nubia had been generally stable throughout the Fatimid period (973–1171 CE). Those relations were governed by the so-called *baqt,* a treaty agreement perhaps dating back to the early days of the Muslim expansions in the seventh century CE. The terms of that treaty stipulated that the Nubians would give the Muslims several hundred slaves per year and that in exchange the Muslims would give the Nubians a specified amount of wheat, barley, clothing, and other trade goods. This treaty likely mirrors economic traffic across the Egyptian-Nubian border more generally. Slaves would have been one of Dotawo's largest exports north into Egypt.

Dotawo's relatively good relations with Egypt ended with Saladin's seizure of power there in 1171. A brief invasion by the Nubians was met with a massive response by Shams ed-Dawla, Saladin's brother. Although the Muslims soon left Nubian territory, good relations were never restored. In the 1270s and 1280s several Egyptian invasions succeeded in reaching Dongola, overthrowing the kings and installing more pliable candidates on the throne. In the 1300s, this pattern grew more complex as competing claimants for the Nubian throne turned to Egypt for help in ousting their rivals. This Egyptian influence led to the establishment of a mosque at Dongola in 1317, to the abandonment of Dongola as the capital in 1365, and to the slow decline and collapse of Dotawo in the 1400s.

The medieval territory of Dotawo is now divided between the modern nation-states of Egypt and Sudan. Large portions of Nobadia, the northernmost region of Dotawo, are now destroyed, flooded by the waters of Lake Nasser behind the Aswan High Dam in southern Egypt. Descendants of the Nubians of Dotawo still live in the Nile Valley. These people primarily speak the Nubian languages Dongolawi/Kenzi and Mahas/Fadijja. The latter language, also known as Nobiin, is the closest to Old Nubian, the written language found in the indigenous documents from the medieval period. Both groups of Nubians today are primarily Muslim, although their form of Islam is considered syncretistic, retaining traditional practices from the medieval period if not earlier.

Giovanni R. Ruffini

Further Reading

Adams, William Y. *Qasr Ibrim: The Late Mediaeval Period.* London: Egypt Exploration Society, 1996.

Browne, Gerald M. *Old Nubian Texts from Qasr Ibrim 3.* London: Egypt Exploration Society, 1991.

Ruffini, Giovanni R. *Medieval Nubia: A Social and Economic History.* New York: Oxford University Press, 2012.

Ruffini, Giovanni R. "Newer Light on the Kingdom of Dotawo." In *Qasr Ibrim, between Egypt and Africa: A Case Study of Cultural Exchange,* edited by Jacques van der Vliet and Joost Hagen, 179–191. Leiden: Peeters Publishers, 2013.

Welsby, Derek. *The Medieval Kingdoms of Nubia.* London: British Museum Press, 2002.

E

Egba (Abeokuta)

The city of Abeokuta, a historic Egba-Yoruba polity, is the capital of the present-day Ogun State in southwestern Nigeria. Abeokuta is located 48 miles from the coastal city of Lagos. Abeokuta has an elevation of 66 meters (217 feet) and is located in Nigeria's wooded savanna region, which possesses a surface area regularly covered in granite. The Olumo Rock is the most defining geological feature of this regional granite and is the icon for which the city was named Abeokuta (in Yoruba meaning "underneath the rock").

Abeokuta has a tropical climate that is typical of southwestern Nigeria. The climate consists of wet and dry seasonal patterns (also known in West Africa as the harmattan). The Egba people have historically farmed the lands on the periphery of Abeokuta. Farming has been a critical component of the city's history, for the people have long cultivated crops for international exchange as well as the domestic economy. Traditionally, the Egba people have cultivated typical items of the region such as cassava, shea butter, palm oil, yams, kola nuts, and rice. With growing British influence in the 19th century, the Egba people produced palm oil that greatly contributed to the Industrial Revolution and helped to shift Abeokuta's economy from one dependent on the slave trade to commerce in cash crops. In the 1850s, Anglican missionaries introduced cotton cultivation. That commercial legacy lives on today, as Abeokuta remains the center of an Egba economy built

Akinwande Oluwole Soyinka

Akinwande Oluwole Soyinka, better known as Wole Soyinka, was born in Abeokuta on July 13, 1934. At University College, Ibadan, Soyinka studied English, Greek, and history. He also studied at the University of Leeds, England (1954–1957), where he received a BA and an MA. In 1986, the Nigerian author received the Nobel Prize for Literature, the first black African author to earn that distinction. Primarily a playwright, the multifaceted Soyinka has also published poetry, fiction, literary criticism, memoirs, and translations of Yoruba-language classics. His autobiography, *Aké: The Years of Childhood* (1981), narrated his upbringing in colonial Abeokuta's important Aké Township.

around items such as indigo dye (which contributes to its world-famous Adire industry), rubber, timber, maize, and cotton.

Egba refugees from the Old Oyo Empire founded the city of Abeokuta in circa 1830. The Egba polity, prior to its 19th-century conquest of Abeokuta, inhabited a region of forests known as the Orile located around the modern-day city of Ibadan. The autochthonous peoples of Abeokuta continued to maintain some distinct institutions within the state. The Egba polity was historically governed by a triumvirate and later a quadripartite political structure in which each province maintained its own monarchy. The Egba polity's political economy was historically intertwined with the Atlantic economy during the slave trade and with the early 19th-century return of the emancipated Yoruba diaspora from Brazil, Cuba, and Sierra Leone to Abeokuta. In 1835, Abeokuta became the first interior Yoruba polity to invite Anglican Christian missionary evangelists. Abeokuta thus had the paradoxical position of being both a symbol of the slave trade and the iconic "Sunrise within the Tropics" for the English, which would help to disseminate abolitionist ideology and free market economics into the Nigerian interior.

Local historians of Abeokuta claim Egba monarchical descent from Ile-Ife, the mythological site of human creation, and the progenitor of the Yoruba commonwealth of states. In Yoruba cosmology, Odùduwà established the first Yoruba monarchy at Ife and sired 16 sons. Odùduwà's 16 sons migrated and established kingdoms in the neighboring regions over the course of the previous millennium (estimated to have begun in the eighth century CE). The direct descent from Ife is claimed by Egba historians for the state's leading monarchy, the Egba-Alake, who rules through the office of the *oba* or *alake* of Abeokuta. Abeokuta's four provincial dynasties were brought together due to various historical circumstances: the principal monarchy, Egba Alake (ruled by its Agbeyin dynasty); the Egba Gbagura; the Egba Oke-Ona; and the Egba Olowu. According to the main Egba narrative, the *alake* was brought to settle in Orile Egba by a Ketu farmer, Ako-Agbo, the offspring of whom became the *ikagbo* of Abeokuta. Furthermore, Odùduwà's wife, Omonide, was said to have moved with the *alake* to the Egba forest, where she died at Ake. Egba mythology lays out the state's constitution as a fundamental component of Yoruba cosmology in which the father of the Yoruba aristocracy, Odùduwà, was buried at the sacred city-state of Ile-Ife and the mother of the Ife dynasties remained buried at Orile Ake (the home of the Ake dynasty). Though the dominant royal lineage of Egba Ake, the *ajalake,* claimed descent from the House of Odùduwà, the Egba peoples likely resided in the forests for centuries before the state was constituted as such.

The Egba state, during its *longue durée* in the Orile, was presumably greatly decentralized. Oral traditions clearly establish that the state had been articulated, with a triumvirate federal structure, but that the monarchy was not yet centralized. Furthermore, the Egba polity was annexed into the Oyo Empire, the most powerful pre-19th-century Yoruba state. In Egba mythology, the subordination of the Egba state to the Oyo Empire was intertwined in the very Odùduwà cosmology. The *oloyo*, the progenitor of the Oyo, reputedly usurped the divine privileges of the Ife charter by demanding that its commonwealth "brothers" (the other Yoruba kingdoms) pay him tribute. Tradition holds that the Egba resented their subordination to the Oyos, and a man named Lisabi led a revolt against Oyo tyranny and liberated the Egba peoples. Egba resistance to Oyo coincided with a general fracturing of the empire. In 1754, the authority of the *alafin* itself became usurped by the takeover of the *basorun* Gaha; the *basorun* appropriated the imperial revenues to be circulated by the *oyo mesi,* the military, and the *alafin.* The Egba revolt on Oyo therefore came at a time in which the military junta became preeminent in Oyo politics—an era represented by the Egba-centric traditions as an absolutist perversion of the dynastic Ife constitution.

The 18th century was the apex of the transatlantic slave trade. In addition to dominating the interior commerce and trans-Saharan trade, Oyo aimed to dominate the external trade from the coast. Egba resistance to Oyo imperialism had as a consequence important implications for Atlantic history. The Egba state also itself became dominated by a new military aristocracy, which led to the erosion of an already decentralized and fluid political structure. Lisabi, an Itoku man by birth, was believed to have come to his political maturation in the Agbeyin township. Lisabi organized the leading men in the town, who by profession were farmers, and established a mutual aid society called the Egba Aro. The Egba Aro was a society that provided services for its members such as the construction of houses; the clearing of land, bush, or forest; the reroofing of homes; and agricultural help through the planting of seeds and the tilling of land. This self-help society evolved into the federal Egba military organization, the Egba Ologorun (military society), with its headquarters in a building called the Ile Olorogun (Military Chambers). While Egba organized a federal military apparatus to assert its sovereignty, estimated to have occurred in the late 18th century, the Oyo state also faced increasing resistance from the Fulani to the north. The Egba were the first subjects of Oyo to assert their independence from the southwestern provinces of the empire. Lisabi's Egba-wide revolt culminated in the Egba Olorogun leading a political assassination of 600 of the *alafin*'s *ilari* (imperial representatives) who had come to collect the imperial tribute.

The government of the Egba state remained decentralized, in contradistinction to the Yoruba city-states whose monarchies were highly centralized. In fact, the Egba state consisted of a federal structure, with diffuse provincial monarchical rule, and a foreign policy driven by its powerful military. The Ogboni Secret Society (the Egba Senate), the Olorogun Society, the Parakoyi Society (the Chamber of Commerce), and the Ode Society all constituted the functional basis of the Egba government. The Ogboni Secret Society, made up of wealthy Egba citizens, was said to derive from Ile-Ife but became a distinctive Egba institution. The society's membership consisted primarily of men who were initiated into a low grade with the meritocratic prospect of rising to the highest grade, which would enable one to sit on the powerful Iwarefa Council. Whereas the Old Oyo state was theoretically a society in which wealth was relatively closed, the dominance of the military in Egba affairs and the weakness of the hereditary titled aristocracy's civil chiefs presented a greater level of economic fluidity. Six senior chiefs constituted the Olorogun and the lesser Ologun; these men were the warlords. By the early 19th century, the power of the Ogboni in the Egba constitution was characteristically weaker than that of the Ologun. The Parakoyi was the trade guild, or chamber of commerce, and met every 17 days. The Ode was the hunters' guild, which provided protection for hunters from wild animals and robbers.

In addition to the township, the province was the most important political unit in the Egba state. In the Orile Egba, the Gbagura Province consisted of 144 towns. The province was split, with 72 towns holding allegiance to the *agura* and 72 to the *onigu,* with the consolidation vesting power in the *agura.* The historical process of subordinating the local nobles and chiefs into a centralized apparatus had occurred in the Oke-Ona Province in the Orile as well as in Ake's Egba Alake quarter. Whereas the Egba Alake had consolidated its authority, this authority was provincial, and yet it was constitutive of the Egba state as a whole. The Egba preferred federalism so as to prevent despotism and the centralization of power in the office of one man. Ake was the principal township, due to its ritual roots in Ife, but other towns, including Ijeun, Kemta, Iporo, and Itoku, had a significant vote in the election of the Egba Alake.

The last province, the Egba Olowu, refugees of Egbado (another regional Yoruba state), later joined the Egba at Abeokuta in the wake of the Owu War (1821–1826). The Egba participated in many of the great 19th-century Yoruba Wars. In the important Owu War, the Owu kingdom was devastated after the brutal invasion of an Ife-Ijebu coalition. Raiders from Ife and Ijebu besieged Owu from the north, seeking to exploit the instability caused by the northern Fulani (Islamic) penetration of Yorubaland. Egba, which was in the midst of its expansion and attempts to gain direct access to the coastal export trade, was under the assumption that neutrality would be the best policy in the Owu conflict. The Egba were soon engaged in the war, as they became great victims of the conflict and were sold away into slavery. Under the leadership of the *balogun* Sodeke (known as "the Lawgiver" of the Egba), the Egba settled at Abeokuta around 1830 and invited Ago-Owu to join the Egba confederacy, where the Owu Crown would be protected. At Abeokuta, Sodeke maintained a progressive open-door foreign policy. Because Egba faced incessant threats to its sovereignty by the Ijebu and the newly minted Ibadan Empire, Sodeke aimed to increase direct Egba relations with the coast in order to subvert the unending local Yoruba disputes.

Sodeke's administration of the Egba state was important, for he maintained good relations with King Adele of Lagos, an alliance that was instrumental in securing good firearms at good prices from trade with Europeans. Furthermore, Sodeke led a massive expansion of the Egba military, and towns that stood in their way, particularly Otta, were summarily conquered and forced to pay tribute to Abeokuta. King Adele expended great military resources that facilitated the Egba defeat of Ijebu and Otta, the primary threats to Egba supremacy in the region. Sodeke restored the legitimacy of Egba civil society by taking the Ogboni Secret Society, formerly a sectional institution, and made it into an all-Egba civic institution. Finally, Sodeke invited the emancipated Egba diaspora to return and settle at Abeokuta, where they were given sectional titles. Because he welcomed Anglican Christian missionaries by 1839, Sodeke is considered a harbinger for the great changes that would occur in Yorubaland throughout the century. These changes included the rise of Christianity, the standardization of the Yoruba language into a Latin script, and the introduction of missionary schools that would make Abeokuta a great center of learning during the era.

The rise of Christian evangelism in 19th-century Abeokuta was not a simple process. The perennial struggle between military (*ologorun*) and aristocratic (civil) wings of the state would be a defining feature in Abeokuta politics throughout the period. Egba experienced several invasions from Dahomey to the west (notably in 1851 and again in 1864). The new Egba Christian educated elite attempted to subvert the military and bring the polity in line with its vision of Abeokuta as a free market–abolitionist haven for the region. The vision of a bureaucratized civil society culminated in the constitution of the Egba United Board of Management (1865–1874). The sovereign Egba government streamlined the military and civil apparatus and was the first modern Egba bureaucracy. After the collapse of the Egba United Board of Management, a triumvirate of three military leaders governed Abeokuta: Ogundeyi Magaji, Nlado of Kemta, and Jaguna of Agbeyin. With the Anglo-Egba Treaty of 1893, Egba participation in the Yoruba Wars ceased, and the British recognized the Egba state as a sovereign state, under the regime of the Egba United Government (1893–1914). In 1914 the Treaty of 1893 was abrogated, ending the Egba state's sovereignty, which enabled the British to annex Abeokuta into the colony of Nigeria.

Abeokuta is today an important center of Yoruba history and culture. Many prominent Nigerians are from Abeokuta or of Egba descent, including Olusegun Obasanjo, former president of Nigeria (1999–2007); Fela Kuti, a prominent Nigerian musician; Funmilayo Ransome-Kuti, a Nigerian nationalist and women's rights activist; and Wole Soyinka, a Noble Prize–winning writer. Abeokuta has one university, the Federal University of Agriculture, Abeokuta, which opened in 1988.

Adrian M. Deese

Further Reading

Ajiṣafẹ, Ajayi Kọlawọlẹ. *History of Abẹokuta: With illustrations . . . and a Short Biography with Important Events during the Reign of Ọba Alaiyeluwa Ademọla II, Alake of Abẹokuta.* Lagos: Kash and Klare Bookshop, 1948.

Biobaku, Saburi Oladeni. *The Egba and Their Neighbors.* Oxford, UK: Clarendon, 1957.

Byfield, Judith A. *The Bluest Hands: A Social and Economic History of Women Dyers in Abeokuta (Nigeria), 1890–1940.* Portsmouth, NH: Heinemann, 2002.

Losi, John B. *History of Abeokuta.* Lagos: Bosere, 1924.

Pallinder-Law, Agneta. *Government in Abẹokuta, 1830–1914, with Special Reference to the Ẹgba United Government, 1898–1914.* Ann Arbor: University of Michigan Libraries, 1973.

Egypt

Egypt was home to one of the great civilizations in the world. Some scholars, however, have attributed Egypt's civilization to the Hamites. The Hamites, the so-called whites with black skins, were considered quicker witted than Africans.

Hosni Mubarak

Hosni Mubarak was born in 1928, ironically the year the Muslim Brotherhood was formed, a movement that was to have a lasting impact in forming his political career. A career officer in the Egyptian Air Force, Mubarak rose to become an air field marshal, and in 1975 President Anwar Sadat appointed him as his vice president. Upon Sadat's assassination, Mubarak became the president in 1981 and ruled until 2011, when his regime fell during the Tahir Square Uprising. Mubarak will be remembered for the establishment of enduring foreign relations with the Arab countries and Israel. He will also be remembered for his fight with the Islamic fundamentalists and their guerrilla warfare to force a return to multiparty democratic governance in Egypt.

Africans were thought to be static and agricultural, thus lacking the capacity to develop a civilization. However, recent scholarship has confirmed that Egypt was the homeland of humankind's civilization.

In 1974 Cheikh Anta Diop argued that this assertion was meant to deprive blacks of the moral advantage of Egypt's civilization. Martin Bernal also argued that the cradle of European civilization, ancient Greece, had its origins in Africa. Bernal blamed scholars for revising the roots of mankind's civilization with the intention of eliminating the critical role of Egypt.

Egypt owed much to the people who lived in the green savannas and moved around 5000 BCE northward to settle in the Nile Valley. Historians rely on Manetho's *History of Egypt* (1940) together with archaeological and anthropological sources to reconstruct its history. The Edfu text, found in the Temple of Horus at Edfu, has remained a crucial source. The Edfu text recounts that King Horus (the Hawk) led a band of followers from Somalia and the Great Lakes region to the Nile Valley through Nubia, where they came with a well-developed civilization.

Herodotus intimated that Egypt enjoyed the "gift of the Nile," which formed a narrow oasis thousands of miles long. Ibn Battuta, the Moroccan scholar-traveler, noted that the Nile River surpassed all in sweetness, length of course, and utility. Egypt occupied the broad floodplains, with abundant arable lands. The miracle of the Nile lays in its annual floods, which leave abundant silt that fertilizes the soils. This supported a productive agricultural economy capable of meeting the needs of a growing population. Plentiful food to feed a growing population freed others to devote their energies to crafts, trade, and embalming and to literature and the sciences. It was upon these conditions that the rulers of Egypt provided the able leadership to steer its development.

The kingdoms along the Nile vied for political superiority. They coalesced into Lower and Upper Egypt and by 4221 BCE introduced the 365-day calendar year. A united Egypt emerged in 3200 BCE with Menes, a conqueror from Upper Egypt who established his sway over the principalities and settled in Lower Egypt, making Memphis his capital. Menes united the principalities into Kemet (meaning "the black land"), later renamed Egypt, creating the first unified state in the world.

Menes's power came from the use of water resources, irrigation, and agricultural surpluses and the organization of the administrative structure.

Egypt achieved its peak of greatness during the archaic period (3100–2660 BCE) and the Old Kingdom (2660–2160 BCE). Memphis remained the seat of government, and Egypt witnessed continuity with four royal houses—the Third, Fourth, Fifth, and Sixth Dynasties—and ruled without interruption for 500 years, 2980–2475 BCE. The period marked the distinctiveness of Egyptian culture, religion, the arts, and language. It was also famed for the building of the greatest pyramids, the Djoser and Giza pyramids, and trade flourished. Trade with neighboring states increased. Egypt also captured Nubia to the south and control of its gold mines, a constant resource for the Egyptian treasury. Egypt kept trade routes to sub-Saharan Africa opened. The state also had a body of officials, including governors, a court of justice, a militia, and a host of scribes. The 500 years of continuity marked Egypt's most prosperous period.

Wars with Nubia together with internal upheavals weakened the Egyptian state. The Hyksos, a Semitic group from Asia, invaded much of Lower Egypt by 1650 BCE and ruled Egypt for a century. The rulers of the Eighteenth Dynasty—Sekenenre, King Kemsoe, and his son Ahmose I, assuming the leadership of the Theban House in 1580 BCE—eventually drove out the Hyksos and established the New Kingdom.

King Ahmose I, who ruled for 22 years, established a standing army with two divisions, appointed sons of pharaohs as generals, and introduced chariots in the army. Egypt recaptured Nubia and brought it under the governor of the city of Nekhen. Ahmose I divided the country into 27 administrative districts under governors with fiscal and judicial responsibilities. The most important were the vizier, the chief treasurer, and the judiciary, who met with the pharaoh every morning to discuss current business and make daily reports. Ahmose I laid the foundation for the Eighteenth Dynasty.

Egypt stood astride Africa and Asia and where the Mediterranean joins the Red Sea and the Indian Ocean. Egypt adopted sophisticated agricultural practices and built dikes to protect crops and receptacles for storing water for irrigation. This attracted sub-Saharan Africans, who brought watermelons, cattle, and donkeys into Egypt. Farming villages sprang up in the Nile Valley and enjoyed active trading relations from within and with Egypt's neighbors. From the Mediterranean came huge cargoes of cedar logs in exchange for gold, silver, dried foods, ivory resources, ebony, and leather products and textiles. These contacts ensured the fertilization of ideas that favored Egypt.

Tomb and pyramid paintings provide information on Egyptian artisanship. Workshops depicted in these paintings portray a great use of carpenters, who made cabinets, weapons, and mallets, and other artisans. As early as 3000 BCE Egyptians had knowledge of the working of copper tools and other metalworking such as forging, hammering, stamping, and casting. Evidence of larger statues found in Egypt dating back to 2300 BCE attest to Egyptian knowledge of ironworking. They also produced axes, chisels, and mallets designed for building and other industries as well as implements for war and agriculture. From 1500 BCE, Egyptian women engaged in hand-spinning and made linen and other fabrics for everyday use and for shrouds.

During the archaic period, Egyptians also invented a script, hieroglyphics, used in government and commercial transactions. The hieroglyphics, with their animal and human figures, were difficult for everyday use. From the third millennium, the priests began to rely on a simplified form, the hieratic, which received a boost with the use of papyrus and ink, and simplified the signs. Hieratic became significant for government and everyday use. The Berlin Museum published some of the recognizable parts of letters, legal proceedings, and memoranda from the period. However, the Greek alphabet later replaced the use of both hieratic and hieroglyphics. The Rosetta Stone, an inscribed stele, holds the key to our understanding of the ancient Egyptian methods of writing and society.

Vegetable fiber produced in Egypt supported a growing industry in textile and papyrus. Long bundles of reed were processed to form palm fiber, which was used to produce a variety of items as well as tough paper. Other methods existed, but the use of papyrus was the most practical. Papyrus became Egypt's principal export and was adopted by the Greeks, the Romans, the Byzantines, and later the Arabs.

Egyptian rulers were considered god-kings who ruled by divine ordinance and went to the grave with select royal servants. Egyptians believed that death was not an end to life but rather a transitional condition, and only the king and those sufficiently close to them survived the grave. They mummified the bodies of their kings and buried them in the pyramids in preparation for the eternal journey with large quantities of luxury items. The funeral practices changed from the Old Kingdom to the New Kingdom. During the New Kingdom, eternal life was extended to those who could afford it, and the "Books of the Dead" became a burial item. Whatever the status of the dead, relatives periodically visited the grave to offer prayers.

Egyptians worshipped deities and gods to whom temples were built and overseen by a class of priests. Protection depended on the offer of prayers and sacrifices to the gods, the most important being Amon and Re. While Amon was associated with creation, fertility, and production, Re was the sun god. Later in the New Kingdom, the deities were worshipped in unison and came to be known as Amon-Re, and a huge temple was constructed at Heliopolis in their honor. It was later believed that the two deities were God.

Egypt suffered a series of setbacks. Its prosperity attracted the envy of neighbors and dynastic struggles, which weakened the state. The civil strife that followed Queen Sebeknefrure's selection of a commoner from Lower Egypt as her spouse lasted 100 years and culminated in the Hyksos invasion of 1674 BCE, lasting 150 years. The Nubians, who had been suppressed following the Hyksos expulsion, reasserted their independence and subdued and ruled over Egypt for a century. The Assyrians later attacked Egypt, and in 525 it fell to the Persians.

Egypt left a legacy in science, technology, literature, architecture, philosophy, and religion. The Romans, who overran and ruled Egypt in 332 BCE, repatriated building materials to build Egyptian-style monuments in Rome, made the cult of Isis popular, and transformed Egypt into a seat of learning, with a huge library in Alexandria.

Abdulai Iddrisu

Further Reading

Bernal, Martin. *The Black Athena: The Afroasiatic Roots of Classical Civilization,* Vol. 1, *The Fabrication of Ancient Greece 1785–1985.* London: Free Association Books, 1987.

Breasted, James Henry. *A History of Egypt from the Earliest Times to the Persian Conquest.* Safety Harbor, FL: Simon Publications, 2001.

Burstein, Stanley. *Ancient Civilizations: Kush and Axum.* Princeton, NJ: Markus Publishers, 1998.

Diop, Cheikh Anta. *The African Origins of Civilization: Myth or Reality.* Translated by Mercer Cook. New York: Lawrence Hill, 1974.

Fage, J. D. *The Cambridge History of Africa,* Vol. 2, *From 500 BC to AD 1050.* Cambridge: Cambridge University Press, 1978.

Jackson, John G. *African Civilization.* New York: University Books, 1970.

Manetho. *History of Egypt and Other Works.* Translated by W. G. Waddell. Cambridge, MA: Harvard University Press, 1940.

Seligman, Charles Gabriel. *The Races of Africa.* Oxford: Oxford University Press, 1930.

Strouhal, Eugen. *Life in Ancient Egypt.* Norman: University of Oklahoma Press, 1989.

Epe

Epe is a riverine Ijebu settlement and part of the larger Ijebu kingdom under the jurisdiction of the *awujale* (king) of Ijebu and by implication a vassal state of Ijebu-Ode. Epe is located on the eastern shores of Lagos Lagoon. Epe town is situated within latitude 6.37°N and longitude 3.59°E. The town is nestled between the lagoon to the south and Iraye-Oke and Ketu-Ijebu to the east. The Ottin River separates the town from Digboloye to the north, where autonomous communities such as Odomola, Poka, Noforija, Ibowon, Odosiwola, and Odo-Iragunshin formed their own autonomous kingdom. This part of the town was mountainous. The land is suitable for agriculture and enjoyed abundant rainfall like other parts of southern Nigeria. The geographical location of the town along the lagoon aided the fishing

Shafi Lawal Edu (1911–2002)

Shafi Lawal Edu, a prominent businessman, politician, and conservationist, was born in Epe in 1911. After working as a primary school teacher from 1927 to 1930, Edu secured a job as a clerk with the Africa Oil and Nuts Company. He would later establish his own shipping and food supply business. Edu went into politics in the 1940s, supporting Jubril Martin of the Nigerian Youth Movement in the 1943 election. In 1951 Edu was elected as a member of the Western House of Assembly, and later he became a representative of Epe in the Federal House of Representatives in 1954. He was also a respected conservationist. In 1980 Edu founded the Nigerian Conservation Foundation, which works to preserve the country's biodiversity and natural resources.

activities of the people, while the forest provided them with the needed raw materials for boat building.

The town of Epe is largely inhabited by Ijebu-speaking people, who are directly linked to Huraka, a hunter whom the people regard as the founder of the town. There are, however, communities of migrants who have settled among the Ijebu-speaking people, especially the Awori settlers from Lagos, who have been incorporated into the community as the Eko Epe, Ijaw, Isoko, Itshekiri, and other ethnic groups, who are often categorized as "strangers." Like many other Yoruba towns, the historical origin of Epe is not devoid of controversy. There are two conflicting versions of Epe's tradition of origin. The first version is the Huraka tradition, while the second is the Alara tradition. The Huraka tradition, which was probably recorded in Epe itself and in Poka, a small town a few kilometers north of Epe, has it that Huraka, a hunter from Ile-Ife, was the first settler of Epe. According to this tradition, Huraka had founded Poka before coming to Epe. Huraka was said to have left Ile-Ife with a group of hunters on a hunting expedition. This expedition ultimately led Huraka and his group of hunters from Ile-Ife to Poka. While in Poka, his favorite hunting ground was a strip of forest along the lagoon that he called "Oko-Epe," from black ants that infested the forest. "Oko-Epe" has since been corrupted to "Epe." It was from Poka that Huraka was instructed by the Ifá oracle to cross the Otien River and settle down in Epe, according to Chief Olufowobi, an event dated probably to the 13th century. Thereafter Huraka left Poka to live in Epe, where at different times he was joined by other settlers, among whom were Alara, a prince who came with his royal attendant from Ile-Ife; Lugbesa; Agbaja; Ofuten; Ramepe; Ogunmude; and Oloja Sagbarafa, from Ijebu-Ode.

The second version of Epe's tradition of origin is the Alara tradition. This tradition is contained in a written account submitted by Oba Adesanya, the *alara* of Ilara, a town located a few kilometers northeast of Epe, to the colonial district officer of Ijebu-Ode in 1939. It claimed that the founder of Epe and many villages beyond the lagoon was Alara Adesowon, a prince from Ile-Ife. He migrated from Ile-Ife and traveled via Benin to Epe. On his way, he was said to have settled some of his followers in different places, which later developed into villages such as Abigi, Ilagbo, Igbogun, Ise, and Ibeju, among others. According to this tradition, the *alara* did not stay permanently in Epe, as he was later ordered by his oracle to leave Epe for Ilara. He left behind his four sons, whom he instructed to take charge of the town.

The political institution of Epe was not different from that of other Ijebu towns. Generally, the government of each of the subordinate towns of Ijebu-Ode was in the hands of the Osugbo chiefs. The council was closely supervised by the *awujale* through his special messenger, the *agurin,* who monitored and reported the Osugbo council to the *awujale* whenever the former exceeded its powers. Tradition has it that in some cases the Osugbo council overruled the king and could also take some action without any recourse to the *awujale.* The tradition of Epe was that the *oloja* ruled with the advice of the chiefs of the Osugbo council and the *balogun* (war captain), whom he had to consult before taking any decision on matters affecting the town.

Other members of Oloja's administrative council were the *otun balogun* (commander of the right wing of the army), the *osi balogun* (commander of the left wing), and the *seriki* (head of the vanguard). As with the *balogun,* these were the chief military Officers of the town. The *agbon* (the head of young men) was also a notable member of the Lotu council, Jagun Oba. He was the custodian of the drums used for summoning the town's meeting and rallies. Also, representing women are Erelu, Iyalode, and Iyaloja, representing the interest of market women. Paramount to the political institution of Epe is the role of *regberegbe* (age grade). This represents different segment of youths. Epe was divided into *itun* (wards). Each ward head was responsible for maintaining law and order in his ward. He settled minor cases and rendered the decision of his ward in any matters to the Oloja Council. Appeals were made from the ward court to the court of Oloja or the Osugbo council.

The town was first settled in the 13th century by the Ijebu people of the Ijebu kingdom of Ijebu-Ode. The second wave of migration was the Mahin people, who migrated to the town as a result of their fishing activities. However, they did not have a permanent settlement until 1933 because of their pastoral method of fishing. By 1851, the town received its largest wave of migration when the defeated forces of King (*eleko*) Kosoko moved away from Lagos to Epe. The Lagos migrants constituted the second largest settlement in the town. By the 1930s, other migrants came to the community. From the 1970s, when the government of the defunct western region opened the Epe plywood industry, other ethnic groups such as the Ijo, Isoko, Ishekiri, Hausa, and Igbo also migrated to the town. In other words, Epe is a motley community.

Owing to its strategic location on the lagoon, Epe became a veritable fishing emporium. There were two types of fishing activities, deep-sea fishing and lagoon fishing, which were practiced by both women and men including people from neighboring communities, especially the Mahin people of the Ondo riverine communities. Mostly the Mahin were not involved in the distribution process; Ijebu women of Epe extraction or women of their domiciled communities sold on their behalf and demanded some percentage of the sale from the final consumer. This percentage is generally referred to as *arobo* in Epe. Selling directly to final consumers was forbidden for the so-called strangers, who were thus compelled to go through the middlemen or middlewomen. Similar to the Baba-Isale system in metropolitan Lagos, these middlewomen, through their husbands, negotiated fishing permits from the paramount ruler of Epe, the *oloja,* who is a representative of the *awujale* of Ijebu-Ode or the *liken* of Iwopin, the king of Iwopin, depending on the side of the lagoon on which such a fisherman was based; in this case, the rule governing territorial space was strictly adhered to.

Mufutau Oluwasegun Jimoh

Further Reading

Jimoh, Mufutau Oluwasegun. "Independence: Through Grassroot Experience in the 1960s; A Case Study of Epe." In *Independence in Africa: The Event and Its Memories,*

1957/60–2010, edited by Odile Goerg, Jean-Luc Martineau, and Didier Natival, 273–294. Rennes: Rennes University Press, 2013.

Oguntomisin, G. O. *The Transformation of a Nigerian Lagoon Town: Epe, 1852–1942.* Ibadan: John Archer Publishers, 1999.

Oyeweso, Siyan. *S. L. Edu: My Journey from Epe.* Lagos: West Africa Book Publishers, 1996.

Ethiopia

Ethiopia is a state in Northeast Africa known for its fragmented mountainous plateau massifs. The rugged nature of Ethiopia's mountains and high plateau determined the course of the country's political and cultural history. Attempts by political leaders to unify the country as well as external invading forces found it very difficult to control. Additionally, the challenge harnessing Ethiopia's natural resources has proven insurmountable because of the topography. The spirit of relative independence influenced by geographic isolation has patterned the traditional lifestyles of many areas, where there is central government control.

Ethiopia's plateau extends over approximately two-thirds of the state and lies at an attitude of 6,000 to 10,000 feet above sea level. The Great Rift Valley, which runs north and south through East Africa, cuts the plateau into two large sections. Rivers and high mountains divide the two sections. Ras Dashen, a mountain of 15,158 feet, is the highest in Ethiopia. The plateau descends in different directions into low-lying areas. The plateau receives over 40 inches of rain annually, and average temperatures on the plateau range from 72 degrees Fahrenheit in areas below 8,000 feet to less than 60 degrees Fahrenheit at higher altitudes. Coffee originated from the forests that cover a large part of southwestern Ethiopia. Eucalyptus, imported from Australia in the 1890s, is the most common tree. Wildlife in the territory includes antelopes and simian foxes.

Aksum, centered on the northern part of the Amharas Plateau, was the first state in Ethiopia (now the region of modern-day Eritrea and northern Ethiopia). Aksum has flourished as an important trading place since classical times. The Aksumites were Kushites and Semites from southern Arabia. Aksumites were major players in the commerce between the Roman Empire and the Indian Ocean region. Askum developed into a productive urban center. Among its accomplishments are the region's own form of writing, Ge'ez (Ethiopic); coinage in gold and silver; a distinctive architectural style; unique monuments, indicative of quarrying and engineering skills; an extensive trading network beyond Africa; and Christianity of a distinctive type, introduced in the fourth century CE. Ancient Greeks, for instance, called the Aksumites "Ethiopia," meaning "burned faces." The name was intended to distinguish Egyptians from their southern neighbors, who were darker in skin.

The modern state of Ethiopia is the lineal successor of the Aksumite civilization. Ethiopia inherited a host of innovations from the Askumites, including famous granite monoliths (nearly 70 feet high) in southwestern Adowa, a unique practice of Christianity, and Ge'ez, the Askum writing style, when Askum declined as a civilization between the 7th and 11th centuries CE. Declining trade and religious wars marked the period of decline for Aksum. Descendants of Aksumites moved south to the center of the plateau. There, they subjugated and Christianized the Agaw-speaking people living in the region. A new society, constituting an amalgam of Aksumite and Kushites and referred to as Abyssinia, emerged.

The powerful Zagwe and Solomonic dynasties contributed variously to civilization. King Lalibela of the Zagwe dynasty constructed the monolithic churches at Lalibela between the 11th and 13th centuries. The Solomonic dynasty from Amhara ruled from 1270 to 1632, when interaction with the Middle East and Europe (especially Portugal) was intense. Missionary activities in the wake of European commercial exploration as well as military attacks launched by Muslims and Portuguese compelled the state to build the castle of Gondar as a permanent residence for the court. Menelik II moved the political core to Addis Ababa, now the country's capital.

The Solomonic kings were remarkable in their influence on the state and the church. Scholarship has deemed the skilled manner in which the Solomonic rulers dealt with local notables along traditional lines as feudal. On the ideological and institutional level, a clash of complex ideas and traditions shaped the status of the church. However, the Solomonic kings are known for their expansionist agenda in constructing the Ethiopian state. King Sahle Selassie of Shoa is known to have received more than 1,000 caches of firearms. Among these were 140 muskets purchased via a French representative, Rochet d'Hericourt. The British diplomatic mission of 1841–1843 presented him with 300 muskets. Tewodoros II was the first modern Ethiopian emperor to be crowned, which took place in 1855. His reign marked an intense period of imperial reconstruction. Yohannes IV continued this process after 1872. During this period, insurrection and repression, often resulting in bloody conflicts, accompanied succession struggles among the territorial magnates.

The reign of Menelik (1889–1914) of Shoa is remarkable for the defeat of Italian forces and the prevention of colonization during the European so-called scramble for Africa. Menelik's accumulation of weapons was determined by his imperial ambition and the internal dissensions that Ethiopia suffered in the wake of the Solomonic imperial agenda. Fifteen years of weapon stockpiling was a factor in his state's ability to beat back the Italian imperial forces at Adowa in 1896. Following the Treaty of Wichale (Ucciali) with Italy in 1889, which was interpreted differently by the signatories, the conflict among the two erupted at Adwa. Ethiopia enjoys a prestigious place in Africa's colonial history because of its defeat of Italy. As with the modern-day state of Liberia, Ethiopia preserved its independence throughout the period of European expansion into Africa as well as its political and religious institutions. Emperor Menelik is famous for renaming the Abyssinia's capital Addis Ababa, expanding its size, and constructing a railway between Addis Ababa and Djibouti. His reign was marked by the construction of modern infrastructure, such as schools and hospitals. In the 1930s, Emperor Haile Selassie I continued Menelik's modernizing efforts.

During the reign of Haile Selassie (1916–1974), the Italians who were based in Eritrea invaded Ethiopia in 1935 and occupied it until 1941. In 1952, Eritrea became part of Ethiopia. Although Haile Selassie promulgated a revised constitution in 1955 that delegated more powers to parliament, opposition against him and monarchical rule grew. Political violence in Eritrea and the Ogaden region in the southeast exacerbated this discontent. A military coup d'état in 1974 deposed Haile Selassie. The Provisional Military Administration Council, a Marxist-inspired regime, deposed the monarch and proclaimed Ethiopia a socialist state. In 1977, Mengistu Haile Mariam became the head of state and chairman of the Derg (meaning "committee" or "council"). The Derg was the coordinating committee of the armed forces, police, and territorial army, which ruled from 1974 to 1987.

The military government experienced its own share of problems during its rule of the state. Civil wars in Eritrea and Tigray and conflict between Ethiopia and Somalia over the Ogaden region compounded administrative problems. For instance, secessionists in Eritrea and militias in Tigray challenged the authority of the Derg, whose poorly planned land reform policies had generated popular discontent. Ethiopia's cyclical drought compounded the situation by causing famine and disease. Mengistu survived these internal problems until 1991. The fall of the Soviet Union and the combined efforts of rebel forces overthrew Mengistu's government. The government change came into existence with Eritrean independence on May 1993 and the promulgation of a federal constitution in 1995.

The Ethiopian government consists of the Federal Parliamentary Assembly and the offices of the prime minister and the president. The Federal Parliamentary Assembly is made up of the Council of the Federation and the Council of the People's Representatives. Ethiopia's states elect members of the Council of Federation, while the members of the Council of People's Representatives are selected by popular election. The Council of the People's Representatives chooses the prime minister. Both houses of the legislature elect the president, whose office is chiefly ceremonial. The country's nine states are ethnically based. In addition to the states, Ethiopia has two major cities, Addis Ababa and Dire Dawa. Local government in the states involves assembly elections, whereby individuals are selected for local parliaments. The Supreme Court is the highest in rank, followed by appeals courts. Below these courts, local associations adjudicate minor criminal and civil cases.

Agriculture employs around 85 percent of workers in Ethiopia and is mostly subsistence-based. Corn, sorghum, goats, sheep, and chickens are among the primary products. Some Ethiopians grow coffee, oilseeds, and sugarcane to sell. Textile production is the main manufactured item. Other manufactured goods include cement, processed food, and shoes. Ethiopia exports coffee, livestock, hides and skins, and oilseeds. Imports include chemicals, crude petroleum, and machinery. The Ethiopian government trades with the United States, Saudi Arabia, Germany, Italy, and Japan through Djibouti and its international airport at Addis Ababa. Ethiopia has had its share of environmental problems that have caused deaths and diseases. Major droughts, for instance, occurred periodically throughout the 1970s and 1980s.

Widely differing local religious systems, stories of origin, political histories and organizations, physical appearance, and dress make Ethiopian self-identification diverse and complex. About eighty languages are spoken in Ethiopia. Oromo is the largest linguistic and ethnic group. However, Amhara dominates in both political and cultural terms. The Tigrays follow the Amharas in terms of political and cultural influence. The Amharas and the Tigrays continue to occupy the highland provinces that have represented the core of the Ethiopian state over time. The Afari, Somali, Saho, and Agew are other ethnic groups in Ethiopia. The largest percentage of Ethiopians is either Muslim or Christian. Most Ethiopians who profess Christianity are members of the Ethiopian Orthodox Church. Few Ethiopians practice local religions.

Waseem-Ahmed Bin-Kasim

Further Reading

Adejumobi, Saheed A. "Ethiopia." In *Africa,* Vol. 1, *African History before 1885,* edited by Toyin Falola, 231–242. Durham, NC: Carolina Academic Press, 2000.

Connah, Graham. *African Civilizations: An Archaeological Perspective.* 2nd ed. Cambridge: Cambridge University Press, 2001.

Zewde, Bahru. *A History of Modern Ethiopia, 1855–1991.* 2nd ed. Athens: Ohio University Press, 2001.

F

Fante

The Fante Confederacy and its constitution are deeply rooted in the history of the coastal region of the Republic of Ghana. The Fante people historically occupied the region of the Gold Coast between the city of Accra and the twin cities of Sekondi-Takoradi. The Fante language constitutes a significant portion of the Akan linguistic family, a subset of the predominant Niger-Congo family of West African languages. During the precolonial era, Fante's social and political life were defined by its organization into a multitude of kingdoms, each subdivided into domestic compounds, with a city-state capital for each respective polity. Fante oral traditions claim descent from the inland Akan polity of Tekyiman. Fante history and its fortunes were shaped by its location at the heart of the wealthy Gold Coast of West Africa, and thus Fante had extensive relations with visiting European traders such as the Portuguese, the Dutch, the Danes, the Swedes, the Germans, the French, the British, and the powerful Akan-speaking Asante Empire, which dominated the interior. The location of the Fante states in this complex political geography enabled a long cosmopolitan cultural fluency and the unique experimentation with political forms that are significant achievements in the history of West Africa.

The location of Fante, on the Gold Coast, defines its climate and geography. The Ghanaian coast is located a few degrees north of the equator, giving the region a typical warm tropical climate. As a tropical climate, the Fante region has two main seasons: wet and dry (or West African harmattan) seasons. The coast of Ghana, on the Atlantic Ocean, stretches 560 kilometers (350 miles). The Fante-speaking region

---

John Evans Atta Mills

John Evans Atta Mills (July 21, 1944–July 24, 2012), a scholar and statesman, was born to a Fante family in Ghana in 1944. From 2009 to 2012, Mills served as the president of Ghana. After graduating from the Achimota School, he studied law at the University of Ghana, Legon, where he earned an LLB degree in 1967, and the London School of Economics, where he earned an LLM degree in 1968. In 1971 he earned his PhD at the School of Oriental and African Studies, London, where he submitted a thesis on taxation and economic development at the age of 27. Prior to becoming president, he served as Ghana's vice president from 1997 to 2001.

---

constitutes nearly 220 kilometers (136 miles) of that larger coastal region. Today, the Fante constitute about 3 million of Ghana's population of 27 million. This large population engages in agricultural and economic activities that are typical of the region, including fishing as well as the cultivation of yams, cassava, plantains, palm oil, and cocoa. In addition to abundant seafood, the people raise chickens, goats, and cattle for a diet that is rich in protein as well as in starch.

Around the 13th century the Fante, known as the Borbor Fante, migrated from Takyiman. The Fante migrated to the coast and established a settlement at Mankessim. Mankessim was the political and spiritual center for the articulation of the Fante state. At Mankessim, Fante political power coalesced in the Nananom Mpow (Grove of the Ancestors) shrine as temporal and ritual, linking the polity with the sacred. The Nananom Mpow shrine was conceptualized as the sacred heart of the Fante cosmological universe. Mankessim was also the subsequent location of the establishment of the Fante Confederation in 1868 and the enshrinement of its constitution. From their base at Mankessim in the 17th century, the Fante expanded to dominate most of the Gold Coast.

By the 18th century, the Fante had come to dominate the intermediary position in the vast transatlantic commerce in gold, cocoa, and human beings. Fante political ascendancy was articulated in terms of culture, however, for the Fante were characteristically a politically decentralized Akan civil society (in contrast to the more hierarchical and imperial Asante to the north). In classical Fante political theory, each *ohene* (head noble) of the disparate polities maintained a representative seat in the federal assembly at Mankessim. In that way, despite their decentralization, there was general continuity in coastal political and economic life. The *ohene* was in theory the father of the village, and his title to land and political rights in the *oman* (state) derived from the heredity descent of his ancestors who founded the polity. Under the *ohene,* different interest groups looked to him for guidance and power. These groups included his family, specifically wives and children; subordinate family groups that had branched off from the dominant landowning family; settlers; and subordinate family lineages in the same village. In addition to those dependents who were members of his family, other constituents under the protection of the *ohene* included slaves and people for whom loans had been given and had either gone into default or had not yet repaid their loans.

Whereas the *ohene* was essentially a sectional representative of the township, the *omanhene* was the national king and the embodiment of the general will of the state. The *omanhene* not only served as head of state but was also the arbiter of the judiciary and the head of the legislative body. The *supi* was the company captain, who maintained the polity's national flags and ammunition; he would also serve as a spokesman, rhetorician, and linguist for the *omanhene*. The *omanhene* appointed his *supi* who had to be confirmed by the national councilors, the *begwafus*. The *supi* was required to be bipartisan and was required to sever his connections to the state company so as to not present a conflict of interests. The councilor was viewed as a representative of the people; that is, he achieved the office without regard to inheritance. The *begwafus* were responsible for curtailing the power of the *omanhene* and therefore reflected the general will of the various villages and townships that constituted the state. These are all very general characteristics of the constitution of the indigenous Fante polity.

During the 18th century, the Fante *oman* became highly fractured due to the incessant wars with the Asante, Akuapem, and Ga polities. At its zenith, the Asante Empire had conquered a territory (nearly 250,000 square kilometers) larger than the Republic of Ghana. The Fante Confederacy established the *asafo* military company in order to effectively defend its borders and to maintain its sovereignty against Kumasi (Asante) and its Dutch allies. The *asafo* companies were paramilitary forces that provided defense and waged war in times of Fante expansion. The *asafo* companies provided young men, particularly slaves, an avenue for social mobility. The head of the various *asafo* companies were men known as *braffoes*. The *braffoes* could only be elected by the federal authorities based at Mankessim, where they received spiritual training and political apprenticeship and helped to structure Fante foreign policy.

Some Fante historians have argued that the decentralized structure of the old Fante Confederacy was not merely a response to political threats from its neighbors but instead represented a preference in Fante civil society for republican representative authority. Rather than coalescing into three general polities, in accordance with the three main Akan migrations from Takyiman, the Fante aristocracy established several core states along the Gold Coast littoral, including Asebu, Anomabu, Abora, Mankessim, Nkusukum, Ekumfi, Yan, and Gomoah. Under the administration of Asantehene (king) Osei Bonsu, Asante invaded and conquered the Fante Confederacy (1806–1824) in an attempt to break the Fante monopoly and gain direct access to foreign trade. The British Slave Trade Act of 1807, which abolished the human trafficking that had characterized commerce along the Gold Coast, further threatened the fortunes of the Fante Confederacy.

In 1831, the British representative at Cape Coast negotiated a peace treaty between the Fante and the Asante. The treaty guaranteed Fante protection from Asante's aggression and granted Asante access to external trade routes. Two great historical changes in the mid-19th century, however, led to great resentment for the British among the Fante. The Fante merchants, who since the abolition of the slave trade had relied on British capital loaned from London and Manchester trading houses, had grown to realize the precarious position of their debt. The establishment of the Gold Coast (Cape Coast) Protectorate in 1850 signaled increased British interference in Fante affairs. The British began to harbor fugitive slaves and imposed tolls and poll taxes; they also started to play a larger role in the installation of heads of royal families, overriding the basis of the legitimacy of the *oman*. These circumstances, increasing debt to European trading houses and encroaching British sovereignty on the coast, fostered the erosion of aristocratic authority and the decline of the Fante mercantile elite.

A Sierra Leonean, James Africanus Beale Horton, first publicized the idea that the Fante should draft a new federal constitution. Horton was a member of Sierra Leone's Creole community, the descendants of enslaved people who were resettled in the British colony following the abolition of the slave trade. Horton was of Igbo (southeast Nigerian) descent and had been educated at King's College, London, and the University of Edinburgh and was the surgeon major of the British Army in West Africa. In his *Political Economy of British Western Africa* (1865), Horton first articulated his plans for the development of different constitutions for West African states. He argued that the Gold Coast should be bureaucratized through the structure of its existing small republican governments. In his view, the British colonial state, with its interest in consolidating the entire colony, was problematic. He argued that the Fante king of Cape Coast and the Ga king of Accra should be allowed to sit on the Legislative Council, under the condition that they were Christian and English-educated.

In Horton's Gold Coast Constitution, all of the *ohenes* of the Fante *oman* must be allowed representation in the Congress of Kings that would be based at Cape Coast. Under Horton's schema, the government of the Gold Coast would consist of a diarchic regime, with a republican structure based on Ga federalism at Accra and a Fanti constitutional monarchy at Cape Coast. The Cape Coast government would be the headquarters for the Fante bureaucracy, which would reconstitute the states under one federal structure. In Horton's schema, the heads of the Fante states of Wassan, Dix Cove, Denera, Assen, Mansoo, Anamaboe, Abrah, Mankessim, Agimacoo, Western Akim, Essicoomah, and Akiufudie would constitute the Cape Coast government. Upon the establishment of the confederation, however, the key states of Cape Coast and Anomabu were absent. The absence of the Cape Coast polity was directly attributable to the fact that Cape Coast was the base for the British government, which disapproved of the constitutional movement.

The Fante Constitution was signed into power on November 18, 1871. The drafters of the constitution defined the aims of their state as being to advance the condition of their people and the promotion of industry. The first major feature of the constitution was that it established an executive council. This council, known as the Ministry, consisted of a vice president, a secretary of state, an undersecretary, a treasurer, and an assistant treasurer. The constitution called for a Representative Assembly responsible for the production of legislation and a National Assembly composed of the sectional kings and principal nobles who would meet to elect the king-president. King Ghartey IV (ca. 1820–1897) of Winneba was the first king-president. Whereas Horton subsequently advised the leaders to elect a president, over his earlier recommendation of a constitutional monarch, the constitution does not state anywhere Horton's theory that the president should be elected through a popular election. Instead, it maintained the tradition of the Fante *oman* that the councilors or sectional nobles would select the head of state. Moreover, the Representative Assembly would not be elected; instead, the kings and nobles of each section would choose its two legislators, one educated and one through the hereditary aristocracy. The king-president, the constitutional monarch, would be responsible for advising the Ministry and for sanctioning all laws passed by the Representative Assembly. In theory, this provision was no different from the indigenous Fante state, which united legislative and executive power in the will of one man. Scholars have argued that the constitution differed from classic Fante theory and Horton's recommendations only in terms of unifying the House of Nobles and the House of Commoners in order that they may sit together in the main legislative body, the Representative Assembly.

In fact, the Fante Constitution was silent on Horton's radical abolition of slavery and all forms of coercive civil subjecthood. Horton's political theory was inspired by European liberalism, which privileged the rights of man ideology in modern constitutionalism. The constitution embodied the principle of governance by consent, the electoral principle, and the legislative, judiciary, and executive aspects of modern constitutionalism. Horton argued for the legislative apparatus to be independent of the executive and for universal citizenship. The constitution sanctioned only merchants' and nobles' private property and fully reunified the executive and legislative branches. The Fante Constitution therefore was groundbreaking in that it embodied the virtues and the tensions of Fante political theory and European constitutional ideology. As a state, the Fante Confederation was weak, and in 1873 the Fante elite accepted an offer to come under British protection. After the British annexed it into the Gold Coast Crown Colony in 1874, the Fante Confederacy was immediately dissolved, and its constitution was abrogated.

Adrian M. Deese

Further Reading

Brown, James W. *The Fanti Confederation: A Reconsideration.* Sussex, UK: University of Sussex, 1967.

Horton, James Africanus Beale. *West African Countries and People, 1868.* Edinburgh, UK: Edinburgh University Press, 1969.

Kimble, David. *A Political History of Ghana: The Rise of Gold Coast Nationalism, 1850–1928.* Oxford, UK: Clarendon, 1963.

Limberg, Lennart. *The Fanti Confederation, 1868–1872.* Göteborg: University Thesis, 1974.

Fez

Fez, or Fes (Arabic, Fas), is a large city located in the northern part of Africa. It is bordered to the north by the Strait of Gibraltar, to the east by Algiers, to the south by Morocco, and to the west by the Atlantic Ocean. Fez is now part of Morocco and forms the most valuable portion of the country. Fez was founded around CE 793 by Idris ibn Abd Allah, a descendant of the Umayyad dynasty from Damascus who had fled to Morocco to escape persecution by the Abbasids. The name "Fez" is reputedly derived from the pickax of silver and gold (*fas*) that was used by Idris to trace the outlines of the city. Leo Africanus described Fez in the 12th century CE as containing 700 temples and mosques. This was in recognition of the importance of the city at the time, which was considered almost as sacred as Mecca.

Fez al-Bali

Fez al-Bali, also known as Madinah and Old Fez, is a unique architectural and urban center. Awareness of its historical value began early during the French protectorate when arrangements were put in place to protect the medieval structures against modern development. The national authorities and the United Nations Educational, Scientific and Cultural Organization (UNESCO) became aware that the old city of Fez had a unique cultural heritage. Much of the pattern of residence and daily life continues as it has done for many hundreds of years. Since 1967 Fez al-Bali has been closed to cars and protected by UNESCO as a World Heritage Site. An agency for slum clearance and renovation, Ader-Fez, was established and charged with the renovation of housing, the restoration of monuments, and the training of supervisors and specialized craftsmen. Currently, despite a population of close to 1 million, Fez's importance as a primary national city has diminished. Rabat has displaced it as the capital and administrative center, and Casablanca had become the nation's commercial center. Nevertheless, the leading families of Fez make up a fair portion of the Moroccan political elite, and the city itself remains an important national historical and religious center.

The development of Fez owes much to its natural resources. There is the Fez River, which flows through the city, and there are other numerous springs and tributaries. In the immediate vicinity, there are quarries that traditionally have provided building stones, sand, and lime. In addition, the Middle Atlas mountain range is close by, and its oak and cedar forests provide timber and wood of very good quality for construction and decoration. The economy of Fez was based on textile and flour mills, oil processing, tanneries, soap factories, and other crafts. The fez, a brimless cylindrical felt hat, takes its name from the city. The area surrounding Fez produces cereals, beans, olives, and grapes, and it is a market town for sheep, goats, and cattle raised in the region.

Idris II, the son of Idris ibn Abd Allah, the first ruler, began the real development of the city in 809 and built the celebrated mosque of Mulai Idris. Fez received its Arab-Andalusian character from waves of immigrants from Córdoba in 818 and from Kairouan in present-day Tunisia between 824 and 826, who settled on either side of the city's river. Thus, two distinctly different districts emerged in Fez al-Bali. The right bank of the wadi has its roots in the Andalusian culture its original inhabitants brought with them. The left bank was settled by immigrants from Kairouan and brings a distinct Maghrebi culture to the quarter. The Kairouan and Andalus mosques built in 859 and 862, respectively, and the university that developed in association with them helped give Fez its stature as a prominent Islamic center of learning that rivaled al-Azhar University in Cairo for many years. The famous Kairouan University has for 11 centuries been a religious and intellectual center whose influence has spread far beyond the confines of the region. Its numerous disciplines attracted students from all the Muslim kingdoms of Spain and Africa.

Between 980 and 1012 CE, Fez came under the protection of the Umayyads in Córdoba (Cordova) and enjoyed increasing prosperity and fame. In 1069 when the Almoravids arrived, the twin cities were united within one external wall and made into a major military base of the Almoravids in northern Morocco. The Almohades came after the Almoravids and made Marrakesh their capital. In 1248 under the Marinids, Fez became the capital of Morocco for almost three centuries. The Marinids founded the new palace city of Fez Jdid and became the patrons of a series of outstanding mosques and madrassas, bringing the urban culture of Fez to its height and enhancing Fez's position as a major commercial center linking the Mediterranean with sub-Saharan Africa. Mosques, houses, shops, flour mills, public baths, and *funduqs* (two-story lodging houses for visiting merchants) were built in such number that by the late 13th century, no more space remained within the city walls. As a result, a new royal and administrative town to the west of the ancient one was founded in 1276. This new urban center was first named the White City (al-Madina al-Bayda) and is now known as Fas al-Djadid (New Fez). It consists essentially of the palace, administrative buildings, and a mosque to which were added other sanctuaries, barracks, homes of dignitaries, and in the 15th century a Jewish quarter known as al-Mellah, with its own unique forms of architecture, was established.

The importance of Fez as a Moroccan city declined under the Saadids (1517–1666), who chose Marrakesh as their capital. Under the Alawids Fez fared better, and its political status was revived. For example, Sultan Mawlay al-Hasan (r. 1873–1894)

View of the Fez al-Bali, the old section of Fez, Morocco, 2013. (Edwardje/Dreamstime.com)

undertook important public works in Fez and connected the two urban areas of Fas al-Djadid and Fas al-Bali, the Madinah, which had until this time remained separated by two long walls. Fez suffered both politically and economically under French rule (1912–1956) and by the modernization and absorption into the world economic system that came in its wake. Protest against the French first manifested itself along religious lines. As the traditional religious center and former capital of Morocco, Fez was the place where the religious protest of the Salafiyyah movement and Moroccan nationalist agitation converged. The French also left their mark on Fez in the construction of a third urban area, the *ville nouvelle,* which housed the administration and the military.

In terms of cultural continuity, Fez benefited from its peripheral location. It was shielded from major geopolitical conflicts in the Fertile Crescent and Egypt, such as the Christian Crusades and the Mongol invasions. Thus, although exposed to regional power struggles, Fez was able to build up a strong local tradition, undisrupted by the external shocks that befell other cities such as Baghdad, Damascus, and Cairo. The relatively good physical preservation of the old city is also due to the fact that Western influences became active at a later stage than in most other Islamic cities. In Morocco, the colonial age started around the time of World War I, and its impact on Fez was mitigated by the fact that most of the modern development pressures were focused on the coastal cities. While Fez remained the acknowledged "spiritual capital," economic and political primacy shifted to Casablanca and Rabat.

Aribidesi Usman

Further Reading

Dumper, Michael. "Fez." In *Cities of the Middle East and North Africa: A Historical Encyclopedia,* edited by Michael R. T. Dumper and Bruce E. Stanley, 151–157. Oxford, UK: ABC-CLIO, 2007.

Morse, Jedidiah, and Richard Morse. *A New Universal Gazetteer: Or Geographical Dictionary, 4th edition, Revised, and Corrected.* New Haven, CT: S. Converse, 1823.

Stefano, Bianca. *Urban Form in the Arab World: Past and Present.* New York: Thames and Hudson, 2000.

Funj (Sennar Sultanate)

The Sennar Sultanate, located between Abyssinia and Ottoman Egypt along both the Blue and White Nile Rivers, was a multiethnic empire respected for its economic diversity and its administrative systems. It was also known for its fusion of Nile Valley and southern Arabian Peninsula values. One of the ethnic groups is the Funjs, who claim descent from two Umayyad men exiled from a place called Lulu by the Abbasids. One of these men married the daughter of a Nubian king, creating the Unsab dynasty. According to Peter M. Holt's record, all future kings were married to a daughter of this woman's lineage. In terms of matrilineal culture, these princesses were known as "the daughter of the sun's eye," a title that echoes Barbara S. Lesko's research on ancient Egyptian "god-wives" who were the mothers of pharaohs. In terms of patrilineal culture, Sennar sultan Amara Dunqas forestalled an invasion by the Ottoman Empire because of his patrilineal descent from a sharif, meaning that he descended from Prophet Muhammad's family.

In 1504, Makk Amara Dunqas brought his people to the Nubian lowlands owned by a woman named Sinn Nar, and there he plotted the future capital city of Sennar. From this city, he announced his stabilization of Nile River trade by sending canoes downriver to establish tributary relationships. Sultan Amara Abu Sikaykain (1544–1545) encouraged education. King Dakin B. Nayil (1562/1563–1577/1578) enhanced the rational bureaucracy of the empire. Badi II Abu Diqn (1642/1643–1687/1688) extended the sultanate southward into the Shilluk and Nuba territories, creating an army of captured people housed in royal villages surrounding Sennar city. He also built the mosque at Sennar and a palace that was five stories high. This palace was both residential and administrative. The wall that surrounded it contained nine gates, each leading to different administrative divisions. Sennar became a cosmopolitan center with resident Abyssinians, Arabs, Jews, Portuguese, Greeks, Armenians, and others. The presence of international merchants and scholars testified to Sennar's effective management of international and intercontinental trade with Mediterranean and Indian Ocean world systems. Exports included gold, gum arabic, ivory, camels, and slaves who were captured in the annual royal slave raids to the south.

Sennar's decline was gradual but noticeable during the reign of Badi IV Aba Shullukh (1721–1762), who alienated some of the nobility to the point that he was deposed. The aristocracy seated Abu Likaylik and instituted an era of relatively decentralized power that lasted until 1821, when Turco-Egyptian forces conquered the Sennar Sultanate.

Marsha R. Robinson

Further Reading

Arkell, A. J. "Fung Origins." *Sudan Notes and Records* 15(2) (1992): 201–250.

Holt, Peter Malcolm. "Funj Origins: A Critique and New Evidence." *Journal of African History* 4(1) (1963): 39–55.

Holt, Peter Malcolm, ed. *The Sudan of the Three Niles: The Funj Chronicle.* Boston: Brill, 1999.

Jedrej, M. C. "Indessana and the Legacy of the Funj Sultanate: The Consequences of Turkish Conquest on the Blue Nile." *Africa: Journal of the International African Institute* 70(2) (2000): 278–297.

Lesko, Barbara S. "Women's Monumental Mark on Ancient Egypt." *Biblical Archaeologist* 54(1) (March 1991): 4–15.

Spaulding, Jay. "The Funj: A Reconsideration." *Journal of African History* 13(1) (1972): 39–53.

Futa Jallon

Futa Jallon (Fouta Djallon, Foutah Djallon, Futa Djalon, Futa Jalon), one of four areas in the modern-day state of the Republic of Guinea, is a mountainous region stretching into Sierra Leone and Liberia. With an average height of 3,000 feet, the Futa Jallon highlands form the second-highest land area in West Africa. Labé is the largest city, and the town of Timbo was the region's capital in the precolonial era. The dominant population of Fula or Fulani, who call themselves Fulbes and are also referred to as Peuls, speak the Pulaar language. The Fulani constitute 40 percent of Guinea's total population. Futa Jallon is also home to smaller ethnic groups including the Jallonkes, from whom the region gets its name, and the Jahankes.

The highlands, called the "water tower of West Africa," host the sources of several of the region's major rivers, including two of West Africa's great rivers, the Senegal and the Niger. Along the plateaus of Futa Jallon are grassy plains and fields of millet. The mountainous region, which cuts north to south across West-Central Guinea, is home to sandstone plateaus from which sprawling trenches and gorges are carved. Futa Jallon covers a total area of 384,300 kilometers and encompasses parts of five countries: Guinea, Guinea-Bissau, Mali, Senegal, and Sierra Leone. Ecologically homogeneous and climatically diverse, Futa Jallon receives abundant rainfall and cool temperatures. Gum, kola, and fruit trees grow well. Lions, panthers, leopards, hyenas, and wildcats prevail in northern Futa Jallon.

Hunter-gatherers first occupied the region that is now Guinea. In 900 CE the Malinke and Susu people entered the region, and around 1250 CE what is now Upper Guinea became part of the Mali Empire. The Susus migrated from the banks of the Falama River, a southern tributary of the Senegal. Their arrival dates to about 1400. The Susu were part of the Soninke kingdom, itself part of the Kingdom of Ghana until 1076, when the Almoravids overran the Soninke capital. The Fulani, cattle-herding nomads, had been moving south searching for pasture and watering holes since the 13th century. In the early 15th century they spread eastward through the middle Niger region and south, settling in Futa Jallon. By 1500 CE, the Fulani had claimed Futa Jallon. From about the first quarter of the 18th century a series of new states emerged under the leadership of the Fulani, who traded and settled

---

Ecosystem

The Futa Jallon Highlands, a mountain ecosystem, encompasses the Republic of Guinea, Guinea-Bissau, Senegal, Mali, Côte d'Ivoire, Liberia, and Sierra Leone. As the source of several of West Africa's most important rivers, the highlands sustain life for populations in Senegal, Mauritania, Gambia, Mali, Nigeria, and Niger, providing irrigation, drinking water, and hydroelectric power. The Futa Jallon is facing degradation due to land use, causing deforestation, soil infertility, and loss of biodiversity. Few mechanisms exist to reward conservation practices. Futa Jallon countries plan to develop reward schemes for environmental services to create a foundation for addressing degradation.

down in towns. As traders, they encountered and accepted Islam and played a major role in the Islamic revival of the 18th and 19th centuries. Dominant among the people of Futa Jallon, they established unity and led revolutionary movements to revive and restore the power and law of Islam throughout much of western Sudan. By 1700, small communities of Muslim Fula settlers resided in Futa Jallon. The Muslim pastoral Fulani, educated and politically sophisticated, generally tolerated non-Muslims. In the late 18th and early 19th centuries Fulbe Muslims led a succession of Islamic jihads (holy wars), which swept West Africa and coincided with a broader movement of spiritual renewal and religious reform and revival.

In 1725, Muslim Fulani declared a holy war against the non-Muslim Malinke and Fulani. The Muslim Fulani rebelled against their rulers and, supported by Muslim traders, waged holy war against settled agriculturalists whom they considered pagans. Ultimately successful, the Muslim Fulani won Futa Jallon independence and established a theocratic kingdom under Almamy Karamoka Alfa of Timbo. They brought the region under Islamic law and created a Fulbe-dominated state. By the end of the 18th century, Futa Jallon had become a stronghold of Islam and an Islamic state. The 19th-century golden age of Islam was the century of great scholars and the growth of Islamic culture. All the disciplines of the Koran were known and taught. Intellectual and religious activity made Futa Jallon a leading religious center in West Africa. The Fulbe of Futa Jallon spearheaded the expansion of Islam in Guinea. The state of Futa Jallon became known for high levels of scholarship practiced by local Fulani. Aspiring students of Islam from across West Africa traveled to study in the kingdom. Koranic schools taught the Arabic language, literature, and Muslim law. Futa Jallon emerged as a center for Islamic learning, attracting students from neighboring regions. The establishment of law and order along the trade routes and at the marketplace further enhanced Futa's influence. Futa Jallon was a major center of Fulfulde composition. Fulbe Muslim scholars developed an indigenous literature using the Arabic alphabet known as Ajamiyya. Futa Jallon attracted students from Kankan to Gambia, featuring Jakhanke clerics at Tuba and Fulbe teachers. A wave of Islamic poetic texts and historical narratives written in Fulfulde by Futa Jallon's Fulani scholars later appeared in present-day Guinea. The 19th-century jihad movement gave birth to a unique idiom and expression of mosque architecture.

Eighteenth-century Futa Jallon was a hierarchical society. At the top was the aristocracy of the Great Fulbe, descendants of families who had participated in the holy war. They depended on slave labor, rents collected in the territories they administered, and booty from raids conducted over their frontiers and within their borders. Muslims enjoyed the full rights of free people. Non-Muslims were subjected to slavery. This distinction led to the division of society into two main groups: the *rimbhès,* free individuals, and the *jiyabhès,* the slave class. Members of the aristocracy concentrated on the administration of political power and religion. People in the lower class (ordinary free men, artisans, and slaves) performed manual labor and services. On the margins of society were foreigners. The parish (*misîde*) was a political and religious district in which all inhabitants joined together for prayer every Friday. Within the parish large families were grouped in quarters. One family occupied the position of leader, with one to four subordinate families around it. Polygyny allowed Muslim men a limit of four wives. The 19th century consolidated the transition from a patriarchal, egalitarian society to a hierarchical one dominated by the aristocracy that emerged from Islamic conquests.

The early Futa Jallon subsistence economy was based on farming, animal husbandry, gathering forest products, hunting, fishing, and trading. Staple crops included millet, rice, and peanuts. Foreign trade with Sudan and the Atlantic coast as well as the tax system benefited the ruling class. In exchange for slaves and gold brought down from the Bouré, the Futa-Jalonkés received imported goods from Europe, mainly gunpowder and firearms.

Futa Jallon, a Muslim theocracy, extended from Côte d'Ivoire to Mauritania and Mali. Following the Muslim victory in the Battle of Talanson, one ruler, or *almamy,* with eight *almamys* ruling nine provinces, controlled the Futa Jallon Empire. The Peuls constructed a centralized theocratic Muslim state, with two families, the Soriyas and the Alfayas, heading the government. Male members of those families occupied the position of *almamy* for alternating terms of two years. The basic political unit was the village administered by a headman, assisted by an advisory council. The next unit embraced a number of villages under the authority of a district leader appointed by the provincial governor, who headed the next higher unit, the province. At the head of this hierarchy were the *almamy* and his advisers. At the end of the 18th century and into the first half of the 19th century, succession crises weakened the central power. By the last quarter of the 19th century, decline set in. Factionalism between ruling families continued. Most of the 19th century involved wars between the two sides. In 1895, the Futa regional chiefs rebelled against the central authority. Meanwhile, the French had been signing treaties with various *almamys.* In 1881, the French signed a friendship and protection treaty with Futa Jallon and annexed the state in 1888. French Guinea became a colony with its own governor in 1893. In 1896, the French Army, using military force, defeated the last *almamy* in the Battle of Poredaka.

In 1897, the French signed a protectorate treaty with Futa Jallon, reduced the state to three provinces, and proclaimed the others independent. In 1899, this region was incorporated into French Guinea. In 1906, the French further partitioned the state with provincial chiefs. The French established a bureaucracy to administer the colony, collected taxes, and requisitioned forced labor. They built schools, courts, and medical clinics and relied on local chiefs and institutions to administer the colony. The French colonial administration's anti-Catholic policies in the region during the 20th century accelerated the acceptance of Islam. The colony was divided into administrative units called circles. Africans were used as intermediaries serving as chefs de canto (a new administrative position) and as village headmen. Former chiefs loyal to French authority retained power. Their duties included collecting taxes, recruiting manpower for forced labor or military service, carrying out judicial responsibilities, and implementing economic policy at the local level. Cattle from Futa Jallon were traded for firearms on the coast. Goods from Futa Jallon flowed into the region around the mouth of the Senegal River. Agriculture (mainly cash crops) remained the basis of the economy and the main source of revenue until the 1950s, when large quantities of mineral ores were exported.

The first product to be exported on a large scale, and one of the motives behind the colonization of the interior, was wild rubber from Central and Upper Guinea. The rubber cycle was followed by a long economic depression until the colony started to export bananas from Lower Guinea in the 1930s. Futa Jallon in French Guinée remained a major center of Fulfulde religious writing. Domestic slavery, although formally abolished in Futa Jallon in 1905, continued under colonial rule. Slaves were estimated at more than 50 percent of the population. Colonization introduced changes in the relationships between elders and family members of lower social status. The *indigenat,* a system introduced in 1887 and modified in 1888 and 1924, authorized French officials to summarily punish Africans for certain offenses. Formal political activity was restricted until 1946, when political parties, labor unions, and cultural groups were authorized. Representatives from Guinea helped found the Rassemblement Démocratique Africain party in Bamako, and the following year the Guinean branch was started and renamed the Parti Démocratique de Guinée in 1950. The party grew under the leadership of Sekou Touré, who became secretary-general in 1952. He led the nation's independence movement in the 1950s, and Guinea gained political freedom from France in 1958.

The Fulbe in Futa Jallon are sedentary and practice animal husbandry. The main crop cultivated is fonio, although rice is grown in richer soils. Fonio is particularly important as a subsistence crop in rural areas. It is widely grown and highly valued for its nutrition and place in traditional cuisine. Most of the area's soils degrade quickly and are highly acidic with aluminum toxicity, which limits the kind of crops that can be cultivated. The region's main cash crops are bananas and other fruits. The farming and cattle herding sectors of Futa Jallon support 40 percent of the population. A rural-urban divide affects land access and ownership. In rural areas land is abundant, with ownership dictated by local custom and complex traditional laws. Efforts by the government and nongovernmental organizations to streamline property rights have had little success.

Maryalice Guilford

Further Reading

Austen, Ralph A. *Trans-Saharan Africa in World History.* New York: Oxford University Press, 2010.

Carney, Judith A., and Richard Nicholas Rosomoff. *In the Shadow of Slavery: Africa's Botanical Legacy in the Atlantic World.* Berkeley: University of California Press, 2009.

Northrup, David. *Africa's Discovery of Europe, 1450–1850.* New York: Oxford University Press, 2002.

Reynolds, Jonathan T., and Erik Gilbert. *Africa in World History: From Prehistory to the Present.* Upper Saddle River, NJ: Pearson, 2004.

Shillington, Kevin. *History of Africa.* New York: Palgrave Macmillan, 2012.

Futa Toro

Futa Toro has been influenced strongly by Islam and has had an important role in shaping regional Islam dating back to the 11th century CE. The Fulbe, a social group in West Africa that has often influenced 19th-century Islamic reforms in West Africa, is from Futa Toro. The name "Futa Toro" refers to the area around the middle valley of the Senegal River, now Senegal and southern Mauritania. Early Arabic sources refer to the region as Takrur, but the Fulbe called it Futa Toro. The inhabitants of Futa are the Futankoobe, who live on both sides of the river. Futa Toro has been a melting pot for the diverse group of people drawn to it. A splinter of ethnic groups from the Soninke in the east, the Wolof in the west, the Moors to the north, and the Fulbe in the south sought shelter in the region. The interaction of the diverse ethnicities, along with the Sere and Mandinka in Futa Toro, produced a group known as the Tokolor. The Tokolor constitute the majority of the Futankoobe and dominate other groups in the region. In West African linguistic terms, the Tokolor are speakers of Pular, a language of the Fulbe. The Tokolor are a subdivision of the Fulbe.

The Senegal River begins to rise from the far mountains of Guinea, southeast of Futa Toro. By August, the river floods the Futa region, depositing rich soil onto the floodplain. The Futankoobe begin planting when the flood recedes from November to December. Futa Toro is a very rich agricultural region in Senegambia and Mauritania due to its two growing seasons annually. The locals grow millet in the highlands with the summer rainfall in the first season, and in the dry season they farm sorghum (or large millet) in the moist floodplain of the Senegal River. The region supports a larger population than other parts of the Senegambia and Mauritania region due to the degree of food production. The Futankoobe even export grains to surrounding regions in Senegambia and Mauritania. Fishing and animals are another pillar of the Futankoobe lifestyle. Fishermen form a separate group and live along the river. Besides fishing, their location by the river and its tributaries provide the added advantage of monopolizing water transportation. All fishermen and farmers keep some livestock.

Futa's ethnic diversity made it extremely difficult to govern. Additionally, factors that made governance problematic include the river's long and slender shape and raids from nomadic neighbors. Islamic principles played a part in ordering society, as the rulers considered themselves Muslims and sought to fulfill Islamic obligations. However, rulers did not abandon traditional religious elements that were still part of court practices. Moreover, Islam even extended beyond the court and was part of the customs of the local communities well before the 18th century, when the activities of Islamic reformers began to grow intensely. Some local Muslim families relocated to other parts of Senegambia and turned to prominent Islamic elites. The influence of these led to the preeminence of the Tokolor culture in Islam in the 19th century. The Tokolor practice of Islam, with elements of indigenous customs, helps to explain Islamic reforms in Senegambia.

Beginning with the reformist movement of Nasir al-Din in the late 17th century, leaders of the movement sought ways to establish legitimacy among the locals. They criticized current Islamic practices, instituted sharia (Islamic law), demonstrated supernatural abilities, and indicated some connection to Prophet Muhammad and other Islamic authorities. Thierno Brahim, for instance, took advantage of his ties to a renowned teacher, Sidiyya al-Kabir, to establish his credibility. Seku Umar and Mamadu Lamin Drama's pilgrimage made them undisputed authorities. Additionally, the reformers patterned their early works on their understanding of the example of Prophet Muhammad, which included preaching, opposition, and *hijra* to a new place with a following of core disciples, then gaining a wider audience, and finally taking a militant stance.

The Toorodbe (singular, Tooroodo), Muslims from diverse classes and ethnicities, established an imamate (Islamic regime) in 18th-century Futa Toro after the Denyankes abdicated the responsibility of ruling the region. The Denyanke ruled Futa Toro for 250 years beginning in the 16th century. The Denyanke dynasty neither practiced Islam nor fulfilled its obligations to maintain clerics at the court. In the 17th century, external pressure from Mauritania mounted on the Denyanke kings because of the dynasty's indifference to Islam. Intensifying pressure on the Denyanke through raids of the Mauritanian and Moroccan armies in the 1720s and 1730s resulted in the surrender of Denyanke's ruling family. Sultan Mulay Ismail of Morocco collaborated with Hassani warriors to capture slaves in the Futa Toro area. The Toorodbe took advantage of the abdication of the Denyanke rulers, created a reform movement, and began to provide for their own defense.

The Toorodbe, under the cleric Sulayman Bal, transformed into a ruling class with inherited status. When Sulayman died in battle, the new ruling class chose Abdul Kader Kan as *almamy* (from the Arabic term *imām,* meaning "prayer leader"). The new imamate regime lasted from the appointment of Abdul Kader in the 1770s until the French conquest of 1891. A learned man governed the imamate with a class of the Toorodbe. Sheku Umar, the Islamic reformist, made a far greater impact on Futa Toro and indeed Senegambia due to the theocratic nature of the state he created. Sheku Amadu ruled through provincial governors, who were mostly his relatives, as well as a central council of elders. The performance of Islamic law was rigid in Umar's state. During this time, these development led to widespread conversion to Islam in the region. Sheku Umar was successful due to his intellectual and religious authority, the latter of which he based on his pilgrimage to Mecca and his demonstration of a connection to the holy city and to Prophet Muhammad as well as the founder of Tijaniyya, a Sufi brotherhood.

It is undeniable that Islam introduced and integrated different ethnicities and classes and also introduced a charter in Futa, but wars fought in the name of jihad disrupted trade in the region. The wars of Sheku Umar especially weakened the imamate, making it easy for the French to conquer and colonize Futa Toro.

Waseem-Ahmed Bin-Kasim

Further Reading

Gomez, Michael A. *Pragmatisms in the Age of Jihad: The Precolonial State of Bundu.* Cambridge: Cambridge University Press, 1992.

Robinson, David. *Chiefs and Clerics: Abdul Bokan Kan and Futa Toro, 1853–1891.* London: Oxford University Press, 1975.

Robinson, David, Philip Curtin, and James Johnson. "A Tentative Chronology of Futa Toro from the Sixteenth through the Nineteenth Centuries." *Cahiers d'Études Africaines* 12(48) (1972): 555–592.

G

Ghana

Ghana is one of the earliest African polities south of the Sahara to be mentioned in written sources. The period of its foundation remains unclear, possibly the fifth or sixth century CE. After the conquest of North Africa by Arab Muslims and the subsequent remodeling of trans-Saharan exchanges, Ghana appears as one of the main actors on the African side of the trade. Al-Fazari, a geographer who lived in the second half of the eighth century, is the first author to mention the polity Ghana in a work now lost but quoted by al-Masudi (ca. 896–956) in his description of the world titled *The Meadows of Gold and Mines of Gems.* In all the early Arabic texts Ghana is presented as rich in gold, although it was a gateway for metal produced in distant areas rather than a gold-producing center itself.

The location of Ghana has been a subject of debates in Europe, particularly after the second half of the 19th century as more Arabic medieval and early modern manuscripts mentioning Ghana came to light and as Europeans developed a better understanding of the geography of the interior of Africa. For instance, the 17th-century chronicle known as the *Tarikh al-Sudan* became central to the discussion after it was made known in Europe by the German explorer and scholar Heinrich Barth, who had read it at Timbuktu in 1853.

By the beginning of the 20th century, most of western Sudan had been incorporated into the French colonial empire. Colonial administrators, anxious to legitimate the new imperial rule, developed narratives presenting it as a continuation of former African political traditions. This resulted in a new scholarly effort to reconstruct the history of Ghana, Mali, and Songhai, as exemplified by the publications of Maurice Delafosse, an ethnographer and colonial officer commissioned to establish scientific foundations to such a political fiction. Under his penmanship, Ghana, Mali, and Songhai, which had previously been mentioned as "kingdoms," became "empires," a terminology that has proven enduring. In the same vein, exploratory missions aimed at locating ancient Ghana and its capital were launched in the western Sahel in the 1910s in order to locate its capital. In 1914, local guides recruited from nomadic groups active around Walata, in southeastern Mauritania, took the French colonial administrator Albert Bonnel de Mézières to the site of Koumbi Saleh, which soon entered the colonial narrative as the capital of Ghana.

Today, the site of Koumbi Saleh is located in the Islamic Republic of Mauritania, a few kilometers north of the Malian border, 1,200 kilometers west of Nouakchott, in the southeastern part of Hodh ech Chargui Province, at the southern edge of the

Aouker depression. The presence of impressive ruins of stone houses and mosques convinced the influential Delafosse that he had found the lost capital of Ghana. In fact, this identification was also informed by the *Tarikh al-fattash,* a 17th-chronicle written at Timbuktu that referred to the capital of the Kayamagna dynasty as Koumbi. It was assumed that Kayamagna, presented as the predecessor of the Mali Empire, was a reference to Ghana. Yet to date, despite several archaeological campaigns, no inscription or clear evidence was recovered from Koumbi Saleh to support this claim. The identification of this site as the capital of Ghana remains debatable but is often presented as an established fact in the historiography.

The geographic association between the polity Ghana mentioned in Arabic sources with the southeastern part of modern-day Mauritania seems credible. Its core might have been the Tagant Plateau and the arid Aouker depression, characterized today by a succession of valleys and plains made up of steppes and savanna grasslands, rocky ridges, and dunes of wind-swept sand covered with scrub grasses. The southern part is dominated by thorny bushes and a declining number of acacia trees. This seems to be confirmed by al-Bakri who, in the mid-11th century wrote of Ghana as the title of the king of a country called Awkar. Such a location would have been ideal to control the southern outlets of trans-Saharan trade routes linking North Africa and sub-Saharan West Africa. Climatic change, however, gradually turned Awkar into an increasingly difficult environment for settled life and a large population. Archaeological data from Koumbi Saleh suggest a long period of urban decline in relation to climatic change, leading to the total abandonment of the area, probably in the 17th century.

We have limited historical sources on Ghana. Attempts at reconstructing fragments of its history rely on three major types of sources: texts written in Arabic, late oral traditions, and the archaeological record. Correspondences between these different sources can be elusive, but early French colonial historians undertook to fuse them into a seamless narrative. To date, all or parts of this narrative are still uncritically accepted and reproduced in most textbooks and scholarly publications. From the late 1990s, however, historians and archaeologists have stressed the need to challenge this dominant narrative. They endeavored to uncover the fragile nature of the evidence underlying it and to expose its anchorage in the political design of the French colonial empire in the early 20th century. The present entry attempts to stay away from a romanticized perspective of Ghana.

When the name of Ghana appeared in Arabic texts in the 8th century CE, it was already associated with the trade in West African gold across the Sahara. In his *Book of Highways and of Kingdoms* (1068), al-Bakri provided a snapshot of mid-11th-century Ghana from reports he had collected from merchants and travelers. He provided the name of two kings, Basi and his successor Tunka Manin/Tankaminin, whose reign reportedly had begun in 1062/1063. Al-Bakri suggested that Muslims were welcome and well treated in Ghana. Although the king had not converted to Islam, Muslims had a distinct quarter in the capital that was said to include 12 mosques. Muslims were reported to play an important role in the administration of the kingdom. The king had his own distinct quarter, surrounded by a wall, that included guarded sacred groves—shrines and the burial place of his ancestors—as well as a palace, a mosque for visiting Muslims, a prison, and a court of justice. Houses were built of stone and acacia. Textiles were said to indicate status. Besides Muslims, only the king and his would-be successor could wear sewn garments. Al-Bakri's description focuses on the riches of the king, particularly gold, which is said to have been lavishly displayed at the royal court. Taxes were collected on the trade in salt, copper, and gold. The latter was said to originate from the faraway town of Ghiyaru. Ghana was said to have a great army, including archers and horsemen. Beyond its own territory, Ghana controlled several tributaries. One of them, Sama, was said to be a four-day journey from Ghana. In al-Bakri's text, the regional political landscape appears highly fragmented, and polities gravitate around urban centers. In fact, Ghana seems to have been among many rather small polities asserting their authority on a number of neighboring entities reduced to the rank of tributaries. Al-Bakri reported hostilities between Ghana and Anbara, a neighboring polity and probably a competitor for the control of regional trade routes.

After al-Bakri, Ghana appears again in the writings of al-Zuhri, author of a pamphlet probably written after the first third of the 12th century. It signals the conversion of the country to Islam, possibly in 1076/1077, in the context of the expansion of the new Almoravid Islamic power over Andalus, the western Maghreb and the Western Sahara, now controlling the major trans-Saharan roads between Ghana and Sijilmasa. One of the most debated aspects of the history of Ghana is the context of this conversion: was Ghana military conquered by the Almoravids and Islam imposed over its population? Although most scholars agree that there is no strong evidence for a military intervention of the Almoravids against Ghana, the influence of the zealous Berbers in control of the northern part of the western trans-Saharan trade routes probably played a role in the spread of Sunni Islam in sub-Saharan Africa. In fact, instead of a conquest, al-Zuhri's text suggests that Ghana and the Almoravids might have formed alliances in the 1080s against some of their competitors, including the Sahara town of Tadmekka in modern-day northern Mali.

The next most detailed description of Ghana is included in the works of al-Idrisi, whose unique geographical work was compiled from written sources and oral accounts at the court of Roger II of Sicily before 1154. Like with all Arabic sources of the time, al-Idrisi's account of Ghana must be taken with a grain of salt. Nevertheless, updates he made to the account of al-Bakri point to changes that likely occurred between the mid-11th and mid-12th centuries. One such important change was the Islamization of Ghana, a confirmation of al-Zuhri's text. The king of Ghana is presented as a Sunni Muslim and a descendant of Prophet Muhammad, a prestigious claim frequent among West African ruling elites. Another major difference between the accounts of al-Bakri and al-Idrisi is mention by the latter of a capital of Ghana divided into two towns located on each side of the "Nile." This was a generic term used to designate all major bodies of water flowing in Africa and, in the Ptolemaic tradition, thought to be connected to the Nile River. Some historians have glossed on this aspect of al-Idrisi's account to suggest that the location of the capital of Ghana might have shifted southward since the 11th century, but this remains to be demonstrated. In al-Idrisi's work, the regional political geography around Ghana is quite different from that described by al-Bakri. If the northern border is still marked by the Sahara, new toponyms appear such as Makzara in the west, Wankara in the east, and Lamlam in the south. While "Makzara"—a generic name applied to the people established around the Senegal River, including Takrur—seems to have been autonomous from Ghana, different provinces that formed the Wankara country, the country of gold, were said to be tributaries of Ghana. In the south, the Lamlam country was said to be a source of slaves. If the accounts provided by the early Arabic geographers are reliable, this would indicate that as Ghana became Islamized by the mid-11th century, it also extended its political rule over a larger area, including parts of the northern and southern banks of the Niger River, farther south from its central territory. The political tributary model, however, seems to have remained the same, the king of Ghana being at the apex of a network of tributaries that provided the gold and slaves in exchange for salt and copper, all goods that made Ghana a crucial broker of the trans-Saharan trade.

In a few surviving pages written in the early 1300s, al-Sarakhsi made mention of a letter sent by the Almohad governor of Sijilmasa to the king of Ghana stating that the two were not of the same faith. Such a mention has sometimes been interpreted as evidence that by the turn of the 13th century, the king of Ghana was no more a Muslim, possibly as a result of the conquest of Ghana by Sosso/Susu, an expanding polity located at its southeastern border, as mentioned in later sources and in some oral traditions. This, however, remains a point of conjecture, as the difference in religion mentioned in the letter could have referred to some sectarian differences within Islam. The Almohads were adherents of the Zahirite school of law, while the Almoravids they had succeeded—and probably Ghana—followed the Malikiyya tradition.

The last important Arabic source for Ghana is Ibn Khaldun's work, dating from the last quarter of the 14th century. According to Ibn Khaldun, Ghana was overcome by Sosso/Susu, which in turn was conquered by Mari Jata, ruler of the Mali polity. The standardized chronology of early Mali—relying heavily on Ibn Khaldun's unique genealogy of the Malian's rulers—suggests that the rise of Mali occurred at some point during the first third of the 13th century. Mali would then have eclipsed Ghana as the dominating regional power, incorporating it as one of its tributaries/provinces. Although the details of the chronology of early Mali need to be handled with caution, the general time frame and the political shift in power from Ghana to Mali remain largely accepted by modern-day scholars.

Ghana's history was last echoed in the *Tawarikh,* written in the 17th century in Timbuktu. The memory of this polity may also survive in Soninke's oral traditions in the form of the legend of Wagadu.

Gérard L. Chouin

Further Reading

Masonen, P. *The Negroland Revisited: Discovery and Invention of Sudanese Middle Ages.* Helsinki: Finnish Academy of Science and Letters, 2000.

Triaud, J. L. "Le nom de Ghana, mémoire en exil, mémoire importée, mémoire appropriée." In *Histoire d'Afrique: Les enjeux de Mémoire,* edited by J. P. Chrétien and J. L. Triaud, 235–280. Paris: Karthala, 1999.

Van Doosselaere, B. *Le Roi et le Potier: Etude technologique de l'assemblage céramique de Koumbi Saleh, Mauritanie (5e/6e–17e siècles AD).* Frankfurt am Main: African Magna Verlag, 2014.

Great Zimbabwe

Great Zimbabwe was the most famous of a series of dry-stone walled kingdoms located in Southeast Africa that flourished between the 12th and 16th centuries. It was both a large African metropolis and the capital of a larger kingdom, with subsidiaries linked through alliance, marriage, and tribute to its leaders. The historic kingdom's monumental stone architecture made it the center of controversy in the colonial era and later a famous UNESCO World Heritage Site. Research into Great Zimbabwe's history has faced the major challenges of colonial-era looting and site destruction. What is now known about Great Zimbabwe is a testament to the persistence and ingenuity of multiple generations of researchers who skillfully worked with the available archaeology, oral traditions, and travelers' descriptions.

Great Zimbabwe was located in the southeast of the country of Zimbabwe, approximately 27 kilometers from the present-day town of Masvingo. The historic kingdom's capital was a stone-walled city that covered 1,779 acres (approximately 800 hectares) at its largest. The historic kingdom lay in the southern section of the large Zimbabwe Plateau, which was the watershed between the Zambezi and Limpopo Rivers. The plateau varied in elevation and was marked by rocky outcroppings and granite kopjes (isolated rocky hills). The general plateau environment supported a variety of microenvironments and, most important, had ideal vegetation for livestock rearing. The plateau lacked the tsetse fly, which carried the sleeping sickness disease (*trypanosomiasis*) that could devastate herds. Large gold deposits were also found on the plateau. This factor and the plateau's relative proximity to the East African coast became pivotal for long-distance trade.

Great Zimbabwe in the Classroom

The civilization of Great Zimbabwe is an ideal topic for history courses that examine early Africa from the K–12 to the advanced college level. One wonderful teaching resource is the episode "Great Zimbabwe" from the series *Lost Kingdoms of Africa* (IWC Media Limited, 2009). Presented by art historian Dr. Gus Casely-Hayford, the episode emphasizes the trade connections between Great Zimbabwe, the Swahili coast, and the Indian Ocean world. The approximately hour-long episode also introduces students to the controversy of Great Zimbabwe when some attempted to deny the African origins of this famous kingdom.

The word *zimbabwe* has been variously translated as "house of stone" or "sacred house." More generally it refers to the widespread tradition of constructing granite stone walls without mortar in Southeast Africa. This was a tradition developed by the distant Iron Age ancestors of current Shona-language speakers, who used the original stone enclosures for protection and cattle keeping. In the area that became Great Zimbabwe, early settlements by cattle keepers and agriculturalists were dated at around 500 CE. Many consider these early inhabitants the Gokomere culture, a distant cultural and linguistic ancestor to the present-day Shona. Over time local leaders emerged, forming alliances and attracting followers with cattle and agricultural resources. Often called the Gumanye, these later inhabitants began to build substantially at Great Zimbabwe, creating pole and *dhaka* homes. They also began importing glass beads around 800 CE.

The rise of large hierarchical kingdoms such as Great Zimbabwe continues to be a subject of scholarly debate. Earlier views on Great Zimbabwe's formation searched for single-factor explanations. In particular, many credited its rise to control of the long-distance gold trade with the Indian Ocean commercial world. Others offered structural explanations and suggested that the kingdom functioned as a religious center with different monuments, each having ritual roles. Political explanations were also popular where Great Zimbabwe was the capital of a royal family whose leaders through charisma or management of regional specialists (such as ironworkers) gained power.

The Great Enclosure at Great Zimbabwe, most likely built by Bantu-speaking Shona. Great Zimbabwe, which comprises 100 acres of stone buildings, was the center of a thriving trade region up until the 15th century. (Corel)

Recent research reveals that Great Zimbabwe was in fact among 300 other stone walled sites on the Zimbabwe Plateau. Its rise came significantly after the earliest signs of commercial ties with the Indian Ocean world. The latest chronological research also showed that Great Zimbabwe overlapped with the other independent large states of Mapungubwe and Khami (once believed to be Great Zimbabwe's predecessor and successor states, respectively). These insights complicate theories that credit trade or Great Zimbabwe's role as the dominant plateau empire as causes. Currently scholars favor instead a complex-causal view where growing elite control over cattle and trade was important, as were other factors relating to leadership, resource management, and ritual. Future research at previously neglected stone walled sites outside Great Zimbabwe's capital itself may bring new understandings.

Great Zimbabwe began to grow around 1000 CE as cattle keeping (and likely alliances and local hierarchies) intensified. By about 1290 Great Zimbabwe had emerged as a large-scale settlement, and its earliest stone buildings appeared. The hill complex was the oldest of these, built atop a hill 262 feet high. Scholars have suggested that its initial location was chosen for defensive or religious reasons. The complex grew to become an oval enclosure surrounded by stone walls with an outer wall height of 37 feet. Building and expansion continued over the next century and a half. By 1400, Great Zimbabwe's metropolis featured elaborate stoneworks on the highest hill and five smaller stone enclosures in the nearby valley. At its largest, this capital covered almost 800 hectares and was home to a population estimated at between 11,000 and 18,000 people. The stonework throughout was built from rectangular granite blocks taken from nearby rocky outcroppings. The walls and structures were built in layers without mortar and often featured the site's trademark chevron decoration. The site's most iconic structure was arguably the massive Great Enclosure, an elliptical building with an enclosing wall that is approximately 800 feet long and stands in places 32 feet high. It is the largest stone structure in Southern Africa. Although multiple theories were (and continue to be) proposed as to the purpose of each monumental building, the growing consensus is that these structures reflected successive rulers' choices for their royal residences.

Great Zimbabwe's strategic position allowed rulers to use long-distance trade as an additional source of wealth. The kingdom's location between the goldfields along the Limpopo River and the coastal trading city of Sofala gave these elites (like their relative contemporaries in the independent states of Mapungubwe and Khami) a chance to control and tax parts of the gold trade. Later, Great Zimbabwe's inland networks expanded to send ivory and copper to the coast. Such trade brought cloth, glass beads, and Asian ceramics in turn. However, elites did not have an entire monopoly on trade profits. Various trade goods are found with frequency among the nonelite parts of the city. The strategic location of the whole plateau also meant that other kingdoms (large and small) also participated in this long-distance trade.

Nonetheless, Great Zimbabwe's capital and kingdom had clear sociopolitical hierarchies. The power and luxury living of the rulers was reinforced by their locations within monumental stone dwellings. Luxuries from the Indian Ocean world were only one source of wealth for the kingdom. Managing cattle and agricultural surplus continued to be others. In addition, Great Zimbabwe's metropolis supported a variety of craft and artisanal specialists. They worked iron, gold, and copper, and other specialists were active in cotton cloth manufacture. The regionally valuable metals, copper and iron, arrived via the kingdom's broad inland trade networks that extended to Ingombe Ilede in present-day Zambia and beyond. Artisanal work provided more than merely additional luxury goods. Craft experts also appear to have produced the large soapstone birds found on-site, which became perhaps some of the most famous (and debated) symbols of Great Zimbabwe. One prevailing view is that the soapstone birds, like the monumental architecture and spatial demarcation of the whole site, were meant to represent the mediating political and ritual roles of the leaders.

By the 1450s, the site of Great Zimbabwe was abandoned. Some argue that the shifting gold trade, which moved west as local goldfields were depleted, was the cause. Others point to a theory of resource exhaustion. The large urban population depended on shifting-field agriculture in addition to cattle for much of their basic livelihood. Yet this form of agriculture required gradual rotations of cultivated land to be sustainable over the long term. Because the land was exhausted or due to possible political or economic motives, Great Zimbabwe's residents dispersed. Soon after other prominent similar kingdoms emerged, including Torwa and Mutapa.

In later historical eras, the legacy and memory of Great Zimbabwe exerted powerful symbolism. Early European explorers, such as the German explorer Karl Mauch who discovered the site, had difficulty believing that indigenous Africans could have built such a majestic stone city. Instead, influenced by the scientific racism of the day, a variety of alterative theories were proposed, suggesting that the site was the long-lost location of King Solomon's mines, the work of Egyptians, Phoenicians, or other non-Africans. Widespread looting of key artifacts from the site have complicated the archaeological record. Misguided efforts to remove artifacts that appeared indigenous further compounded the challenges facing scholars.

Thankfully for the historical record, the work of scholars David Randall-MacIver and Gertrude Caton-Thompson in the early 1900s confronted these views and confirmed the indigenous African creation of the kingdom. However, the colonial government of Rhodesia heavily censored their findings, as the example of a monumental and powerful African kingdom strongly undermined their ideology of colonial rule. Only at Rhodesia's independence did the situation change for the better. Renamed Zimbabwe, after Great Zimbabwe, the new country also added a soapstone bird to its flag, remembering one of the impressive artistic achievements of its namesake kingdom. UNESCO named Great Zimbabwe a World Heritage Site in 1986. Nonetheless, concern remains today that the site is underfunded for adequate preservation, and in popular Western culture myths persist portraying this historic African kingdom as an "unsolved riddle."

Andrea Felber Seligman

Further Reading

Caton-Thompson, Gertrude. *The Zimbabwe Culture: Ruins and Reactions.* Oxford, UK: Clarendon, 1931.

Chirikure, Shadreck, Munyaradzi Manyanga, Innocent Pikirayi, and Mark Pollard. "New Pathways of Sociopolitical Complexity in Southern Africa." *African Archaeological Review* 30 (2013): 339–366.

Chirikure, Shadreck, and Innocent Pikirayi. "Inside and Outside the Dry Stone Walls: Revisiting the Material Culture of Great Zimbabwe." *Antiquity* 82(318) (December 2008): 976–993.

"Great Zimbabwe." Episode 3 of *Lost Kingdoms of Africa*. DVD. Directed by David Wilson, Ishbell Hall, Michael Simkin, and Ross Harper. IWC Media Production for BBC, London, 2009.

McIntosh, Roderick J., and David Coulson. "Riddle of Great Zimbabwe." *Archaeology* 51(4) (July–August 1998): 44–49.

Ndoro, Webber. "Great Zimbabwe." *Scientific American* (1997): 94–99.

Pikirayi, Innocent. *The Zimbabwe Culture: Origins and Decline in Southern Zambezian States.* Walnut Creek, CA: AltaMira, 2001.

UNESCO. "Great Zimbabwe National Monument." UNESCO World Heritage Centre, 1992–2016, http://whc.unesco.org/en/list/364/.

Guiziga Bui Marva

The Guiziga Bui Marva kingdom was established in the beginning of the 17th century and straddles the Diamare Plain and the Mandara Mountains' piedmonts. The kingdom made the village of Masfaye its capital, which was already populated since the 16th century by the Sao people from the banks of the Chari River in the east; the Movos from Dulo in the north, beyond Mora; the Dogoys, a group claiming to be from the Baguirmi kingdom; and a group of paleo-Mofus, who fled from the Guiziga Bui Marva into the surrounding massifs. The latter arrived at the end of the 17th century from the Mundang country in the south, around Lere (current-day Chad), to settle in Masfaye, which they renamed Marva, a place where they

Contemporary Guiziga Bui Marva

Today, some descendants of the former Guiziga Bui Marva kingdom reside in Maroua, capital of the province of Extreme North. But most of them are still living in the villages that made up the Guiziga Bui Marva kingdom, scattered in the foothills of the Mandara Mountains, included today in the district of Meri. These villages are all now ruled by Fulani chiefs, vassals themselves of the great Fulani chief of Maroua. Since 2012 because of their location in the Mandara Mountains close to the Nigerian border, these villages are particularly affected by the abuses and the violence perpetrated by the Boko Haram jihadist movement.

united numerous clans under their command. However, from the 18th century onward, the Guiziga Bui Marva kingdom fell under the control of the great Muslim Wandala Empire, farther north, of which it became a vassal together with the Zumaya kingdom, with which it was sharing control of the Diamare Plain.

The territorial organization of the Guiziga Bui Marva kingdom was based on the village capital that constituted its center, following the model of the fortified cities along the Logone River. The Bui king resided within it in a vast compound, surrounded by his numerous wives and his many offspring, his slaves, and an assembly of notables (*gaola bui ay*) and officiants (*miki kuli*) of the local religion, Kuli. Prominent among them, the *massa ay,* considered as the owner of the land based on descent from an autochthonous clan, was conducting most of the important rituals, such as the enthronement of new *Bui* who were conceived as the descendants of a clan of migrant hunters in the region. The Guiziga Bui Marva architecture was characterized by its vegetal and modular aspects, with numerous removable components making up several units of huts facing each other. The king's palace was distinguishable by a high fence made of dried sorghum stalks, reinforced by a green hedge of *Commifora Africana.* Incidentally, this system of vegetation hedges, made also of euphorbias, encircled each neighborhood with the double function of protecting the gardens from the small cattle and defending the capital against the attacks of the horsemen coming from the neighboring kingdoms.

The village capital, Marva, was at the center of the kingdom, which extended for many hundreds of kilometers and included numerous villages. At the head of those on the borders of the kingdom, the *Bui* named his male kin, brothers, sons, or nephews (who could be dismissed at the end of his reign). The control and expansion of the vast territory of this predatory kingdom, which did not hesitate to conduct frequent raids in the Mofu country, within the Mandara Mountains, and also later under the Wandala command in the Diamare Plain, was ensured by a caparisoned cavalry of ponies and barb horses. These numerous raid campaigns, supplying slaves and booty of grains, cattle, iron weapons, etc., thus supported the economy of the Guiziga Bui Marva kingdom. The kingdom was located within a semiarid ecosystem, and its economy was mainly based on small livestock farming and sorghum cultivation.

Eventually, the Guiziga Bui Marva kingdom was characterized by a very special recourse to waste for ostentatious purposes, to mark its territory, and as an instrument of power. A great trash heap called *Kitikil a Bui* (the King's Trash Heap) was indeed erected in front of the king's palace, and its big size was maintained by his slaves. Several smaller trash heaps were also made in the villages on the kingdom's borders. The first objective of these waste accumulation was to mark the center and limits of the Guiziga territory and to signify in the meantime the length of their presence in it and, consequently, their legitimacy to rule it. The second goal of the erection of a big garbage dump in front of the *Bui* palace was to display ostensibly his wealth in goods, using the important quantities of trash produced by his household. He also requested his notables, vassals, and subjects to come at least once a year to dispose waste on his great trash heap as a sign of allegiance. Finally, several elements charged with specific "forces" (the blood from an adulterous couple executed at the foot of the trash heap, the skull of somebody dead by smallpox, the heads of sacred animals such as panthers, etc.) were buried inside the great garbage dump. This made it a point on the kingdom's territory of the concentration of Kuli, the power addressed by the local religion, but also served to attract invisible and ambivalent entities, *setenes,* or "spirits of the place," on it. Each successive sovereign was consequently not only identified with the great trash heap at the heart of the kingdom but was also physically associated with it, notably through several rituals of contact during the enthronement.

The *Bui* could in return mobilize the *kuli* and the *setene* of his great garbage dump to protect the kingdom against external attacks, such as those led by the cavalries of the neighboring kingdoms. Internal aggressions, notably with witchcraft, were also addressed by ordeals realized directly on the great trash heap. The powers of the king's garbage dump finally lured good rains upon the kingdom, thus ensuring the reproduction of its crops, its livestock, and its subjects. This great trash heap can also be identified as the true support of the kingdom and as the repository of the sacred kingship principle incorporated and embodied by each successive king. This ultimately depended on the great accumulation of waste erected in front of his palace. This case constitutes an original form of sacred kingship, a political and religious system developed in a great number of areas on the African continent before the 19th century (for instance, in modern-day Nigeria, Chad, Cameroon, and the Democratic Republic of Congo).

The king's great trash heap represents today the last vestige of the Guiziga Bui Marva kingdom. Besides, it is not located in Maroua, the former Marva, anymore, but instead in Kaliao, a village farther west on the Mandara Mountains' piedmonts. Around 1795, Fulani and Muslim horsemen descended from the northwest (notably through the Hausa States and the Bornu Empire), conquered the Guiziga capital, and chased away its occupants. Several members of the Guiziga chieftainship (some of whom were accused of having helped the Fulani take Marva) fled to Kaliao and tried to rebuild the kingdom's capital there, particularly by erecting another great garbage dump in front of the new palace of the king in exile. As for the great trash heap in front of the *Bui* of Marva's former palace, it was covered by a mosque built by the new Fulani and Muslim masters of the city. This was to place their mark on it and also to fight against the "pagan" forces coming from the Guiziga Bui Marva great garbage dump. The new chieftainship of Kaliao managed to remain independent for the whole 19th century until the installation of the German colonial administration during the first half of the 20th century, which reinforced Fulani hegemony over the area. The Germans demanded that the Guiziga chief of Kaliao at the time, the *Bui* Zum Biko, submit to the authority of the Lamidat of Maroua, ruled then by the *Laamiid'o* Hamadu Koyranga (1908–1909, 1914), adopt the Fulani title, and finally convert to Islam.

Nowadays, few people in the Diamare Plain remember the prestigious past of the Guiziga Bui Marva kingdom, obliterated by two centuries of Fulani domination, a century of European colonial administration, and the introduction of new administrative structures since the independence of Cameroon in 1960. Only the

Bui big trash heap still remains at the center of Kaliao village, and only a handful of elders, including the last officiants serving the *kuli,* still remember its greatness and power during the time when the Guiziga Bui Marva kingdom reigned from the Mandara Mountain piedmonts to the heart of the Diamare Plain. It is thanks to the richness and accuracy of their testimony that their history can today feature in this encyclopedia.

Emilie Guitard

Further Reading

Boutrais, Jean, ed. *Le Nord du Cameroun: Des hommes, une région.* Paris: ORSTOM, 1984.

Feeley-Harnick, Gillian. "Issues in Divine Kingship." *Annual Review of Anthropology* 14 (1985): 273–313.

Guitard, Emilie. "The Sacred King as a Waste Heap in Northern Cameroon." *Journal of Material Culture* (forthcoming 2017).

Seignobos, Christian. "Les migrations anciennes dans le bassin du lac Tchad: Temps et codes." In *Migrations et mobilités dans le bassin du lac Tchad,* edited by Henry Tourneux and Noé Woïn, 135–162. Marseille: IRD Editions 2009.

Seignobos, Christian, and Olivier Iyebi-Mandjek, eds. *Atlas de la province Extrême-Nord Cameroun.* Paris: IRD/MINREST, 2004.

Gyaman

The Gyaman (Gyaaman) state, currently situated in two countries—northeastern Ghana and northwestern Ivory Coast—is a legacy of colonial machinations in Africa. Drained by the Komoe and Black Volta Rivers, the area has two vegetative covers, savanna and forest, that support a rich array of plant and animal life such as cocoa, coffee, cotton, indigo, grains, roots crops, elephants, tigers, primates, and livestock. Gyaman has a long rainy season and a dry season that influence economic activities such as farming and gold mining.

The aboriginal Gyaman, Abron, were part of the Akan who settled in Akani, Kwaman, and Tafo. Tan Date, the first Gyaman king, founded the state in 1690. The Asante under Osei Tutu constantly fought them in their own state-building process in the early 16th and 17th centuries. These wars resulted in a series of Abron migrations northwest to Abassim, where Abron founded towns such as Bondoukou and intermixed with other ethnicities such as the Nafanas and Kulongos.

In all of Gyaman history, the Asante were their sworn enemy. In 1740, the Asante under Opoku Ware I conquered them and turned them into a tributary state, stopping only in 1875. The war was so devastating that it dispersed the Brong, many of whom fled to Kong and beyond. The intermixing of the Brong with other ethnicities created the Anyi and Baule subgroups of the Akan found mainly in the

Ivory Coast. Gyaman became "the wife of the Asante" through this tributary relationship with Asante. The tribute, often exacted in gold and slaves, was not fixed, but depended on the circumstances of the sitting Asante king. The Gyamans rebelled on several occasions—in 1750, 1764, 1802, and 1818—against the Asante but failed in all instances, often with calamitous results such as paying heavy indemnities and expensive ransom prices, as in the case of the queen mother, Ama Tamia, for whom they paid 400 ounces of gold. Besides the Asante, the Gyaman also clashed with the Bunas in 1805, capturing many people among whom was the famous Abu Bakr al-Siddiq, whom they sold into slavery.

The economy of the Gyaman state was vibrant and relied on agriculture (food crops, cash crops, and animal husbandry), gold mining, crafts (metalworking, cloth and basket weaving, sculpturing, cotton spinning and dying), and trade centered at Bondoukou. Gyaman was famous for its abundance in gold, which it traded. In addition, some towns specialized in certain crafts such as ironworking (the Numus), Motiamo Degha women specialized in pottery, the Hausa stationed at Bondoukou were master dyers, and the Abron and Dyula were weavers. The economy also depended heavily on the labor of slaves to do menial and laborious tasks such as farming, gold mining, and carting goods. Often slaves were incorporated into the society if they showed good behavior, but they remained at the bottom of the social ladder.

The Gyaman state had traits of a confederacy even though it was not. The state consisted of five provinces (Penongo, Achedom, Anenefy, Fumasa, and Ciagni) with a central state capital, Bondoukou, headed by the *gyamanhene*. Provincial chiefs saw to the daily running of the provinces. However, the *gyamanhene*'s court served as a court of appeal to all of the provinces. A council constituted by the *gyamanhene* and the provincial chiefs handled foreign affairs, diplomatic issues, and matters of peace and war. The council also shared in the costs and booty of war. Although Gyaman did not have an elaborate bureaucratic system like those of Asante and Akwamu, the offices available were all inherited, making it easy to create new classes of officeholders such as the *safohene* (paramilitary leaders granted land by the *gyamanhene*). The village and immigrant communities had their own chiefs, who enjoyed much autonomy in governing their people.

The internal politics and relations between the Gyaman and the Asante led the former to seek the protection of the British in 1875 after the British defeated Asante in the Sagranti War of 1874. In 1888 the Gyaman king, Agyeman, sought the protection of the French by signing a treaty of friendship. However, this friendship did not translate into any tangible benefit, leaving the Gyamans vulnerable to Almami Samore Toure and his army, who invaded Gyaman in 1895 and occupied it until 1897, when the French succeeded in driving away Samore's forces and established their own authority in Gyaman.

Coincidentally, the scramble for Africa split Gyaman into two factions between the French in the east and the British in the west in 1897. French Ivory Coast received the majority of the Gyaman territory, while some remained in the Jaaman district in the Gold Coast. The French colonial machinery undermined the authority of the Gyaman aristocracy by ending slavery, customary levies, and tributes exacted from the various sections of the state and replaced it with forced labor in 1898, excise duties and trading license in 1893, and a head tax in 1901. With these came the end of the autonomy of Gyaman chiefs and subsequently the state.

Gyaman society and culture are not very different from those of the Akan. The Gyaman state celebrates the Odwira, Adae, and Fofie festivals annually. Cultural similarities exist in the naming patterns of the Gyaman and the Akan. Babies are named after the day of the week they are born. Gyaman fertility statues/sculptures received much attention, as they were believed to make barren women fertile. The people worshipped the god of the Tano River and made sacrifices to it during the annual yam festival for goodwill. They consulted the god in time of war and epidemics as well. There were Muslims who lived in Kong, Barabo, and Bondoukou. The Marabouts offered spiritual services during war and assistance for life in general by producing magic-induced amulets for protection to anyone who sought after them. In the later part of the 19th century, Europeans introduced Christianity to the Gyaman.

In 1942, World War II politics led the *gyamanhene* Kwadwo Agyeman, his son Kofi Adingra, some important chiefs, members of the aristocracy, and a great following to migrate to Sunyani, northwest of Asante in Ghana (Gold Coast), in support of Charles de Gaulle. The migrants left behind their houses, farms, and possessions. All attempts by the French to get the fleeing Gyaman to return proved futile; instead, more people fled to the Gold Coast. Under threat and coercion with gifts, the French succeeded in having the remaining Gyaman install a new king. Within weeks of the fall of Vichy France, the migrants returned to Ivory Coast to resume their former positions. From this period on, the Gyaman chiefs of both countries have often interfered in each other's affairs. The most important affair has been border-related issues, leading to several government interventions and repositioning of the boundaries on both sides in 1976, 1984, and 1988.

Political instability in Ivory Coast in April 2010 affected the Museum of Civilization in Abidjan, which exhibited centuries-old historical artifacts. Several priceless Baule artifacts were stolen or destroyed, robbing the Gyaman of an important aspect of their history.

Lady Jane Acquah

Further Reading

Lawler, Nancy. "The Crossing of the Gyaman to the Cross of Lorraine: Wartime Politics in West Africa, 1941–1942." *African Affairs* 96(382) (1997): 53–71.

Wilks, Ivor. *Asante in the Nineteenth Century: The Structure and Evolution of a Political Order.* Cambridge: Cambridge University Press, 1975.

I

Ibadan

Ibadan is a major city in southwestern Nigeria spanning 1,190 square miles, situated just 128 kilometers north of Lagos. It is currently the capital of Oyo State and has over 3 million residents, making it the third most populous city in Nigeria. While Ibadan is no longer the most populous city in sub-Saharan Africa, it currently holds the distinction of being the largest city in sub-Saharan Africa in terms of landmass. Another point of fame is the University of Ibadan, the country's first university, established in 1948. Much of what we know today about Nigerian history can be credited to the early generation of scholars produced by this university, who are collectively referred to as the Ibadan School.

Ibadan is located in the tropical forest zone, close to the savanna border. Like most of Nigeria, Ibadan experiences a rainy season from April to October with a slight pause in August, while the dry season runs from November to March. The start of the dry season is marked by the arrival of the harmattan winds, which come from the Sahara desert, and lower temperatures at night, while the day remains hot.

While most of its residents identify as Yoruba, a sizable minority population of the Hausa reside here. Since the Hausa first arrived in large number from the late 19th century, they have controlled the cattle and kola trade with northern Nigeria. A major center of trade in the colonial period, Ibadan remains a city of sizable commercial activity. The farmland once found inside the city during the precolonial period has since been urbanized, but the highly fertile farmland located on the outskirts of town provides another important facet of the city's economy. Producing, trading, and processing agricultural products has long been vital to the urban economy.

Taiwo Akinkunmi and the Nigerian Flag

Born in 1936 and a lifelong civil servant of Ibadan, Akinkunmi is easily most famous for designing the Nigerian national flag. Only 23 years old at the time and studying abroad in London, Akinkunmi was prompted by a newspaper advertisement to enter the competition. His winning design earned him £100 and the nickname "Mr. Flag Man." The green and white stripes of his design serve as the inspiration for the color scheme of his house in Ibadan, where Akinkunmi currently lives with his son.

View of Ibadan, Nigeria, in 2012. Some architecture from the colonial period remains, scattered among newer construction and tin-roofed homes. The majority of Ibadan's residents identify as Yoruba. (AP Photo/Jon Gambrell)

Historical reports provide conflicting dates for the origins of Ibadan, with some tracing evidence of a settlement as far back as the 16th century. However, the first settlement about which oral traditions agree dates from the 18th century and is referred to as the "first" Ibadan, then called Eba-Odan. According to these traditions, Jagun Lagelu, a military commander from nearby Ile-Ife, founded this small town of mostly Egba Gbagura people. For some time afterward, residents lived peacefully surrounded by other Egba settlements.

The cause for conflict that led to the downfall and destruction of the first Ibadan is tied to an important institution in Yoruba political culture: the Egungun masquerade. Still practiced today, the Egungun masquerade is similar to other West African masquerades, where young men in "secret societies" adorn costumes and parade about, making visits to the compounds of important men in town. Masquerades are often linked to political power, and the Egungun masquerade is no exception. According to Yoruba tradition, the Egungun masquerade represents the ancestral spirit of past rulers and is thus a symbol of political continuity. It is therefore understandable why it was a serious affair when some residents disrobed an Egungun masquerader. The fact that women participated in his humiliation made the incident all the more offensive, since women were forbidden to see the masquerade even when properly masked. When the news spread to the powerful ruler of nearby Oyo, he ordered the town to be razed.

Though the Oyo armies razed the infrastructure of the first Ibadan, several residents, including an elderly Lagelu, survived the attack by fleeing to a nearby hill. Eventually the survivors ventured back down the hill to found the "second" Ibadan, which they called Eba Odan. Before long the city grew with an influx of a variety of Yoruba ethnic groups, becoming an important commercial center in the region. One of these migrant ethnic groups was the Owu. The downfall of this second city started when the ruler who came after Lagelu sought to strengthen ties between the Ibadan and the Owu by allowing the Owu leader to marry his daughter. Tragedy struck when the Owu leader sacrificed his new wife to appease the goddess of the Osun River. The resulting conflicts embroiled the town, and eventually the second Ibadan disintegrated.

In the 1820s the town of Ibadan repopulated again, and this "third" Ibadan is the origin of the contemporary megacity we know today. The 19th century was the period of the so-called Yoruba Wars, and this series of events proved critical to the formation of modern-day Ibadan. This complex series of battles and conflicts made the region of Yorubaland unstable and eventually brought down the Oyo Empire. These conflicts quickly swelled the population of Ibadan as a war camp where a diverse array of peoples and armies sought refuge, including the Ijebu, Egba, Ife, and Oyo. Based on oral traditions, it appears that around 1829 a handful of war chiefs from the Yoruba Wars made Ibadan their official base. The war chiefs considered Ibadan's location at the southern outskirts of the Old Oyo Empire and the hilly terrain to be ideal protection against the Fulani armies from the north.

Tense conflict marked the early years of Ibadan. Though the initial city boasted a diverse population, the different Yoruba ethnicities did not mix freely and instead settled in distinct districts. Not surprisingly, the war chiefs affiliated with these sub-ethnic groups could not peacefully agree on a political structure. It was only after years of violence that the Oyo chiefs emerged as the recognized leaders of Ibadan in 1833. Though relative stability followed, the political and economic landscape during the first decades of Ibadan reflected its militant origin and environment. In stark contrast to the standard political organization in Yorubaland based on the inherited title of *oba* (king), Ibadan adopted military rule. Bravery, not birth, determined titled appointments. Only one title was a civil position, and even this usually fell to an ex-warrior. One benefit of the strong military rule was that by the late 1830s slave raiding by roving outside bands came to an end.

The continued conflict in the broader region initially stymied long-distance trade and encouraged self-sufficiency among Ibadan residents. The fertile land made this possible, and most family compounds contained a small farm. This produced the quick sprawl of the city; rather than agricultural land kept on the outskirts of town, it was contained within the town's center. By the 1840s Ibadan managed to maintain a temporary peace, and trade and craft production became vital to Ibadan's economy. This trend only increased in the 1850s, when Ibadan emerged as a large city of over 100,000 residents. Besides economic prosperity, the openness of the city to outsiders and its relative abundance of land encouraged its rapid growth.

Despite these great advancements, the trajectory of Ibadan continued to fall victim to regional insecurities. The Ibadan-Ijaye War of 1860–1861 was followed by the war with Egba and Ijebu in 1877. That same year also saw the start of the devastating 16-year war with Ijesa and Ekiti in 1878. By the time the conflict ended, the weakened Ibadan proved vulnerable to another outside power: the British. The British government in the nearby Lagos colony, along with the Church Missionary Society, got involved in Yoruba hinterland politics in 1884, in large part because the continued conflicts proved disadvantageous to British trade interests. One consequence of the British-engineered treaties that ended the Yoruba Wars was that they made the region, Ibadan included, a British protectorate in 1893.

Sara Katz

Further Reading

Falola, Toyin. "From Hospitality to Hostility: Ibadan and Strangers, 1830–1904." *Journal of African History* 26(1) (1985): 51–68.

Falola, Toyin. *Ibadan: Foundation, Growth, and Change, 1830–1960.* Ibadan: Bookcraft, 2012.

Lloyd, P. C., A. L. Mabogunje, and B. Awe, eds. *The City of Ibadan.* Cambridge: Cambridge University Press, 1967.

Watson, R. *"Civil Disorder Is the Disease of Ibadan": Chieftaincy and Civic Culture in a Yoruba City.* Athens: Ohio University Press, 2003.

Igala

Igala is located in the Niger-Benue confluence in the present-day Kogi state of Nigeria. The community is bounded on the east by the Idoma people of Otukpa, Ugbokolo, Okpogu, and Awokpe, on the west by the Yoruba and Benin peoples, on the south by the northern Igbo of Nsukka and Onitsha, and on the north by Nupe. The terrain facilitates different atmospheric conditions in Igalaland. The northern part is characterized by high plains, hills, rocks, and valleys. Few rivers and streams support adequate grassland. The southern part features low plains, valleys, table-lands, few hills, and numerous lakes, streams, rivers, tributaries of the Niger River, and thus encouraged thick forests. Precolonial Igala people lived in an area of mixed forest and savanna between the wet high forest of the south and the dry savanna of the north. Thus, the region enjoyed the geographical features of both northern and southern Nigeria. This enhanced a variety of occupational activities, such as fishing, farming, hunting, lumbering, mining, and animal rearing. Igalaland was highly endowed with adequate natural resources in both its northern and southern parts.

The Igala before the 19th century inhabited the entire triangular tract of territory on the banks of the Benue and Niger Rivers about 100 kilometers above and below their confluence. The Igala-speaking peoples could also be found on the right bank of the Niger below the confluence, opposite Etobe. Over the course of time, some villages lost their original settlements to water erosion as a result of the strong current of the Niger River. They lived in a clustered settlement, and as their population increased they began to scatter to distant spaces. The history of the Igala people refers to Yorubaland, Benin, and Jukun as likely homes of origin, representing likely waves of migration. However, the Yoruba influence is the most dominant. The center of Igala civilization is Idah. An archaeological excavation at Ojuwo in Idah has since proved that Igala must have started around 1495 CE. The last major waves of migration from Idah led to the founding of many villages throughout Igalaland. There are Igala communities in the Anambra, Benue, Delta, Edo, and Enugu states of Nigeria.

The earliest political structure at Idah was based on clans and gerontocracy. Each clan was presided over by a chief (usually the eldest). By 1470, the Igala council became the highest political authority in Igalaland. This involved the division of Igala society into nine administrative districts (*igalamelas*) headed by an *etemahi,* who was the most senior district head. The nine district heads met usually at Idah to resolve state issues before the rise of the *attah* system. In about the 15th century, the institution of *attah* emerged in the form of a divine kingship system of government. The kingship system in Igala was said to have been established by a breakaway Jukun group led by Ebuluejeonu, the daughter of Ebutu-Eje, a noble king of Jukun, who moved westward between 1595 and 1625 along the southern bank of the Benue River and came to a temporary halt in the vicinity of Amagede (now in the Omala local government area), where he died. His daughter stepped into her father's shoes and led her people from Amagede to Idah, where she was installed as the first *attah* Igala. Her brother, Agana-Poje, succeeded her. Idoko succeeded his father, Agana-Poje, as *attah* and also begat Atiyele and Ayegba, who later became the fourth *attah* of the Igala kingdom.

The government was controlled principally by the *igala mela* with the *achadu* as the president, whereas the *attah* had veto power. The *igala mela* selected and installed a new *attah* and served as check to royal excesses and autocracy. The chief justice of the kingdom was the *ogbe,* who presided over the traditional court at Idah. He was assisted by four judges who ruled on his behalf and forwarded their decisions to him for approval. He in turn sought the approval of the central government headed by the *attah* for the execution of court verdicts, especially in the case of death sentences, banishment, slavery, and maiming. By the close of the 18th century, Igala had certainly become a powerful state and had in all probability reached its zenith. At the peak of the Igala kingdom, it extended up to Ajaokuta and Lokoja. Other Igala communities on the bank of the river included Ifeku, Owoli, Okpatawo, and Ilushi in the Edo and Delta states.

War ensued between the Igalas under Aji Attah and Benin under Oba Esigie in 1515–1516. It was a struggle for control of trade along the banks of the Niger River. This was later followed by the war with Jukun. Igala was a tributary state to the Jukun or Kwararafa Empire until the rise of Attah Ayegba in the 17th century, the fourth *attah* of Igala, during which the Jukun kingdom went to war against the Igalas because Ayegba refused to pay royalties to the *aku* of Wukari. Igala warriors drove out the Jukun and secured Igala's independence. Ayegba's successor, Akumabi, also fought the Nupe. In the reign of Okoliko, the 16th *attah,* the people of Bassa Komo invaded the area of Onu Ife in traditional Igala society in the late 1800s.

The precolonial Igala kingdom had a subsistence economy dominated by peasant agriculture. Yams, corn, millet, maize, cotton, groundnuts, beans, and tobacco were grown. The Igala also engaged in maritime occupations such as fishing and salt and canoe production. Craft industries such as weaving and broom and basket making as well as blacksmithing, pottery, and cloth dyeing were extensively practiced in certain areas of Igalaland. There existed an exchange among various households and between Igala and its neighbors. There is evidence of trade in salt, dry fish, canoes, *ona* (locally manufactured cloth), and red pepper before 1600. There was also a flourishing trade in horses that passed through Lafia and Doma and across the Benue to Amagede in Igala. Groundnuts, palm oil, and cotton were exported from Igalaland during the colonial period.

Islam spread in the western Sudan into Igala through trade. A traditional belief system also existed. Most of the people in Igala believed in the worship of the river deities. There was also ancestral worship. Christianity spread later following the Niger Expedition of 1841, during which treaties were signed with Attah Amochje, thus giving the British a foothold in Igalaland. The expedition was followed by commerce, culminating in the opening of trade posts in Idah and other coastal communities on the Niger by the Royal Niger Company. At Lokoja in January 1900, Lord Lugard hoisted the Union Jack and declared a protectorate over northern Nigeria, signaling the end of independent existence of all hitherto existing kingdoms and empires in the region. Igala became part of the Benue Province. Due to state creations in postcolonial Nigeria, the Igala people are now in Kogi State.

Olisa Godson Muojama

Further Reading

Boston, J. S. *The Igala Kingdom.* Ibadan: Oxford University Press, 1968.

Clifford, M. "A Nigerian Chiefdom: Some Notes on Igala Tribes in Nigeria and Their Divine-King." *Journal of Royal Anthropological Institute* 66 (1936): 393–436.

Ford, D., ed. *Peoples of the Niger-Benue Confluence.* London: Lowe and Brydone, 1970.

Okwoli, P. E. *A Short History of Igala.* Ilorin: Matanmi, 1973.

Ukwedeh, J. N. *History of Igala Kingdom, 1534–1854.* Zaria: Ahmadu Bello University Press, 2003.

Ijebu

Similar to other Yoruba kingdoms, there are different accounts of the origin of the Ijebu people. Some scholars are of the opinion that the Ijebu are descendants of Ajibota, a son of Noah. Ajibota was said to have migrated from Benin and settled at Ijebu-Ode. Another tradition of origin is that of Obanta. According to this version, which was popularized by Samuel Johnson, Obanita was said to have escaped from a powerful ruler, Olowo, who attempted to kill Obanta for human sacrifice before he

Adeola Odutola (1902–1995)

One of the greatest characters to dominate the sociopolitical and cultural landscape of Ijebu-Ode in the 20th century was Chief Adeola Odutola. He was born on June 16, 1902, into the family of Sanni Odutola Seyindemi, a prince of the Molodas of the Odogbolu dynasty, a Muslim who was married to a converted Christian, Sabinah Otubajo Odutola Seyindemi. Odutola was 13 years old when he lost his father. The death of his father at this tender age forced him to acquire skills that would make him independent and fired in him a driving spirit for self-development, which encouraged him to unlock his potentials. By the 1930s Odutola had successfully transformed from a mere subaltern to a foremost aristocrat within and outside Ijebu-Ode. Chief Odutola not only made his mark in business but also became one of the major financial backers of the Action Group of Nigeria, a Pan-Yoruba political party formed by Chief Obafemi Awolowo, whose request for a loan to study law in London Odutola had earlier turned down. Chief Odutola was arguably the richest Ijebu-Ode man during his era.

escaped from his captors. Obanta moved out of his domain and settled in Ijebu-Ode. However, this tradition acknowledged the existence of thriving settlements in Ijebu-Ode before the arrival of Obanta. Oral tradition collected from the palace of the paramount ruler of Ijebu-Ode claimed that the Ijebu people came from Wadai in the present-day Republic of Sudan. The migration was led by Olu-Iwa, who first settled at Ile-Ife before moving to Ijebu-Ode.

Modern traditions trace large population movements into the region to about 1000 BCE. The kingdom profited from a series of migrations from other kingdoms. At different times, different war leaders, princes, and other notables led migration movements to the kingdom. However, the largest migration was said to have been led by Olu-Iwa around 100 BCE. Going by different traditions of origin, one can safely argue that the peopling of the Ijebu geographical space was the result of series of migration led by different peoples at different times.

Ijebu people of Ogun State in Nigeria are famous for the production of *gari*. Among the forest people of Nigeria, cassava production remains the most enduring occupation; in fact, the Ijebu people are noted for their peculiar skills in the production of suitable cassava flour. In other words, agriculture remains the major occupation of the people. Apart from cassava production, other cash crops such as cocoa, kola nut, rubber, and palm oil are also produced by the people. Food crops were also produced on a commercial scale. These included plantain, maize, and vegetables. The riverine areas of Ijebu, such as Iwopin, Oni, Imakun, Ode-Omi, Ikeran, Emina, and other Ijebu fishing villages, engage in extensive fishing activities throughout the year. During the colonial period, rubber plantations were introduced to the people as part of the colonial policy of encouraging Africans to produce raw materials for the survival of their industries in the metropolitan cities.

Ijebu women work in a cassava grinding mill in the Oru-Ijebu community, southwestern Nigeria, November 19, 2009. (Reuters/Alamy Stock Photo)

Similar to other Yoruba societies, the Ijebu political system was essentially monarchical. At the top of the political pyramid of the Ijebu people is the *oba*. In theory, the *oba* exercised absolute power. Practically, there are a number of checks and balances that limit the power of the *oba*. In Ijebuland, four societies are central to the day-to-day administration of the kingdom: the Osugbo, Ilamuren, Pampa, and Odi societies. The Ilamuren is the supreme ruling council of the kingdom and also performs legislative functions for the kingdom. In addition to their legislative duties, the *awujale* delegates duties to the Ilamuren from time to time. Members of the council were the principal members of the *awujale* cabinet. They are the *olisa, egbo, ogbeni-oja, olotu-ifore, jagirin,* and *apebi.*

The Osugbo society is the most important judicial organ of the Ijebu kingdom. All criminal cases are referred to the court for adjudication. Deliberations of cases are not open to members of the public except for its initiates. The *awujale* sent representatives to the court of Osugbo. An *erelu* (female member) represents the interests of the *awujale.* The *oluwo* is the head of the Osugbo. The *apena, olurin,* and *akonoran* are other members of the highest decision-making body. Another organ of government of the Ijebu kingdom is the Pampa. The principal function of the society is the supervision of markets across Ijebuland. They ensure that markets are in order, settle disputes, and ensure fair trade. The *agbon, lapoekun,* and *kankanfo* are the three heads of the society. In Ijebu-Ode, they represent the three most important quarters: Isale-Iwade, Oke-Iwade, and Porogun.

The Odi society completes the administrative arm of the kingdom. Odi members are basically the messengers of the *awujale;* they run diplomatic and political errands for the monarch. They also serve as an important link between the *awujale* and the other societies and between the *awujale* and the people. Within the Ijebu kingdom, towns are divided into quarters (*ituns*) for administrative conveniences. The head of an *itun* is called the *olori itun.* He is responsible to the king and appoints representatives to act on behalf of the king. The age grades (*regberegbe*) also perform important sociopolitical functions within the Ijebu kingdom. Occasionally, representatives of the age grades are invited to attend the council of state meetings. It is important to note that women are not marginalized in the sociopolitical arrangement of the Ijebu kingdom. *Erelus* represent the interest of the women in the council of states and other decision-making bodies.

The Ijebu culture witnessed much transformation in the 19th and 20th centuries as a result of European incursion. The Ijebu people are very industrious and are famous for their hard work. They are also famous for being financially prudent and are noted for a high taste for social life. Since the 19th century, the Ojude Oba festival remains the high point of their Sallah celebration. Ijebu was the last kingdom to be conquered by the colonial government in 1892 after the famous Imagbon War. The Anglo-Ijebu war opened the kingdom to colonialism. Understandably, the people also participated in the decolonization process. Notable Ijebu people participated actively in the independence movement. Chief Obafemi Awolowo (founder of the Action Group and the first premier of the Western Region) hailed from Ikenne, a town located a few kilometers away from Ijebu-Ode. Other notable Ijebu are Adeola Odutola; Oba Akisanya, an active participant in the Nigerian Youth Movement and a stalwart of the National Council of Nigeria and the Cameroons; S. O. Gbadamosi; Joseph Odumosu; and T. O. S. Benson.

Mufutau Oluwasegun Jimoh

Further Reading

Alao, F. O., and G. O. Oguntomisin. "The Peopling of Ijebuland." In *Studies in Ijebu History and Culture,* edited by G. O. Oguntomisin, 1–15. Ibadan: John Achers Publisher, 2002.

Ayantuga, Femi. "Ijebu and Its Neighbour, 1851–1914." PhD dissertation, University of London, 1965.

Ile-Ife

Located in the margin of the forest belt of West Africa, Ile-Ife is the cradle of the Yoruba people and is situated in Osun State in southwestern Nigeria. Administratively, the city is divided into four local government areas: Ife East, Ife North, Ife South, and Ife Central. The close proximity of Ife to other commercially viable cities of southwestern Nigeria, such as Lagos and Ibadan, has influenced Ife to assume a much more cosmopolitan configuration in the last two decades or so,

Olojo Festival

Among the several festivals celebrated in Ile-Ife, Olojo appears to be the most popular, drawing participants from far and wide. Thus, Ooni Okunade Sijuwade Olubuse II described Olojo as the festival of all festivals and the festival of all Yoruba. The Olojo festival is annually celebrated to worship Ogun, the Yoruba god of war and iron in the sacred city of Ile-Ife. Ogun plays a significant role in the Yoruba myth and pantheon, and thus the Olojo festival represents a ritual of peace, unification, and reenactment of Ile-Ife's myth and tradition through sacrifices to Ogun. Once the Ogun priest (Chief Eredunmi) announces the date of Olojo, preparation takes 40 days, and the festival itself spans 4 days. The Ooni is a major player in the festival. During 3 out of the 4 days of the Olojo festival, the Ooni embarks on a pilgrimage to Oke M'ogun (Ogun Shrine) for ritual performance and sacrifice in the company of priests, chiefs, and large crowd of the Ife people, associates, and well-wishers. The performances and the sacrifices are to appease Ogun for peace and tranquility in Ile-Ife and for the successful reign of the Ooni. Beyond the ritual performances and processions, the Olojo festival is also characterized by merriment, excitement, and social gathering. In fact, it is a time of unification of all religions. Olojo is a period of family reconnection whereby many Ife indigenes in diaspora return home. It has also become an avenue for ambitious politicians to publicly show their interest by supporting aspects of the festivity and congratulating the Ooni in newspapers and on posters. Beyond the ritual and sacrifices, the Olojo festival holds the social, economic, religion, and political fabric of the Yoruba people and Yoruba descendants across the Caribbean and the Americas.

The Olojo festival in Ile-Ife, Nigeria, October 15, 2016. The Olojo festival is an annual celebration of Ogun—the Yoruba god of war and iron. (Reuters/Alamy Stock Photo)

although archaeological evidence has shown that this process was already in place as far back as the 12th–15th centuries CE. While archaeological evidence estimated the population of ancient Ife to about 150,000 in the 14th–15th centuries, contemporary record shows that the current population of the city is about 650,000 in the four local government areas combined.

The topography of Ile-Ife is characterized by many hills. However, the ancient city occupies a plain approximately 275 meters above sea level that is surrounded by seven prominent hills: Oke-Ora, Oke-Araromi, Oke-Owu, Oke-Pao, Oke-Ijugbe, Oke-Onigbin, and Oke-Obagbile. Thus, these hills make Ile-Ife appear in a bowl-like layout. The location of the city was an advantage for the ancient inhabitants because of the area's suitability for farming. This would have been one of the factors that attracted the early occupants to this area dating back to about 500 BCE, although the historical narrative of the development of the ancient kingdom is only known for the last 1,000 years.

According to oral traditions, the Kingdom of Ife started as scattered villages and hamlets. The inhabitants were mostly farmers with perhaps a few artisans. These scattered villages consisted of 13 settlements, namely Ido, Ideta Oko, Ilora, Iloromu, Ijugbe, Imojubi, Iraye, Iwinrin, Odun, Oke Awo, Oke-Oja, Omologun, and Parakin. Each settlement was further divided into quarters, with a priest king or chief priest as its ruler. The settlements contained different lineages, and the ruling system was flexible, lacking centralization, but fostered mutual cooperation among clans. Therefore, the system of government was a confederacy that can be described as a loose political alliance short of political integration, with no central chieftaincy hierarchy, powerful royal dynasties, centralized governments, or urban capital.

Oral traditions and archaeological evidence have shown that complex sociopolitical structures began to emerge between the 10th and 11th centuries CE at Ile-Ife. Oral tradition has it that Oduduwa, who became the first *ooni* (supreme ruler, king) of Ile-Ife, laid the foundation for the social complexity in Yorubaland. The reign of Oduduwa was characterized as the period of state formation and political upheaval in Ile-Ife. Conversely, this epoch marked the beginning of a new dynasty and a new political culture that reaffirmed the religious cult and brought a total transformation to the economic base of Ile-Ife from agriculturist to craft specialist. The archaeological excavation by Frank Willett at the Orun Oba Ado site in Ile-Ife yielded a radiocarbon date of the 10th century associated with beads. This date suggests the presence of craft specialists in the later part of this phase of Ife occupation. Similarly, the foundation of complex urban planning was laid at the same time, with evidence of a concentric city wall system.

This emerging complexity that began in the late 10th century or the 11th century set the foundation for much more social complexity, or the classical era, in the second millennium CE, which was centered on new social, political, religious, and economic ideology and urban conglomeration.

Archaeological, anthropological, historical, and oral tradition evidence have confirmed the 12th–15th centuries as the era when Ile-Ife flourished, which ushered in a sociopolitical and economic transformations that began in the late first millennium CE. These transformations were amplified, with evidence of complex craft specialization in glass beads, terra-cotta, bronze, pottery, and potsherd pavement. This period also witnessed settlement expansion and domination of the politically or religiously weaker settlements as well as a tightening of Ile-Ife's security. During this era, the sociopolitical structure of Ile-Ife became totally federated and centralized, with the political and religious leaders in control of all aspects of life in Ile-Ife.

The political system and the religious power of Ile-Ife are directly readable from its material culture. For example, the technology of bronze casting proliferated in Ile-Ife between the 12th and 15th centuries. These bronze figures often depict the political rulers in their royal regalia and their paraphernalia of office. Similarly, Ile-Ife developed a monopoly of intensive production of glass beads, as glass beads became a status symbol of political power and authority. Ife also sold and distributed glass beads to other parts of the Yoruba region for consumption as objects of paraphernalia of political and religious office. For example, no legitimate king can be enthroned in the Yoruba-Edo–speaking region without a beaded crown. This political ideology was enforced by Ile-Ife for two reasons: first for reverence as a prime spiritual center and second for patronage of its production of glass beads. The power and importance of the *ooni* of Ile-Ife was described in historical records. The Moroccan explorer Ibn Battuta described Ife in the mid-14th century as one of the biggest countries of Sudan and described the *ooni* as one of the greatest sultans. Pereira Pacheco, the Portuguese sailor, soldier, and explorer, also remarked in the late 15th century, comparing the power of the *ooni* to that of the pope of his time.

By the 15th century, Ile-Ife had developed intercontinental contact through long-distance trade and an exchange network. Ife traded cash crops such as kola nuts and valuable materials such as glass beads. These goods were perhaps at the same time exchanged for copper alloy materials, which were used in bronze casting. Lead isotope analysis of Ile-Ife bronze revealed that the copper alloys used would have been sourced from across the Mediterranean in Northern Europe through the trans-Saharan trade route sometime in the second millennium. This external contact and participation in the trans-Saharan commerce revolutionized the economy of Ile-Ife, which made the ancient city much more prosperous than other African kingdoms of its time. The location of Ile-Ife at the northern bulge of the forest and its proximity to the Niger River allowed the city to participate in the early north-south trade network.

By the end of the 15th century, and the early 16th century, Ile-Ife had become a center of strong politico-religious power centered on sacred kinship, with the elite in control of the major economic entrepôt. Ile-Ife's complexity during this period spread beyond its geographical boundaries. Its politico-religious influence was mirrored in the material culture recovered in other settlements outside Ile-Ife's core area, where Ile-Ife artistic and ceramic traditions occurred dating to between the 13th and 15th centuries.

By the 16th and 17th centuries the flourishing city of Ile-Ife began to wane, and its strong polity and industries started to go under. Unlike many ancient kingdoms, Ile-Ife was not sacked or abandoned at this time. The waning of Ile-Ife, which was mainly attributable to a loss of political influence, was due to the forma-tion of new polities such as the Oyo Empire farther north and Benin to the south with different political ideologies centered around militarism and economies de-rived from coastal commerce.

This formation of new polities led to a population drift out of Ilc-Ifc. Many of the skilled specialists at Ife also migrated, which resulted in a drastic decline in the production of materials of power and authority. Although there was continuity in pottery tradition, particularly in morphology and decoration attributes, from the 10th century through the 16th century the fabrication of humanistic terra-cotta and bronze figures were completely lost. Hence, this industry proliferated among the newly formed polities in Yorubaland (e.g., the Owo, Ilesa, and Ijesa polities) and the Edo region. The center of bronze/brass casting shifted to Benin. By the end of the 17th century, according to James Africanus Beale Horton, Ile-Ife was one of the smaller political units in the Yoruba region without great wealth or military power.

In the 19th century, the aged unbroken record of the kingdom of Ile-Ife as a city that was never sacked nor abandoned was broken. The political turmoil that raged in the entire Yoruba nation in the 19th century swept through Ile-Ife. Between the 1850s and the 1880s conflict arose between Ile-Ife and its neighbor, Modakeke. Modakeke had the upper hand in these wars and sacked Ife first in 1853 and later in 1882. Ife remained in ruins for over a decade but began to be reoccupied in 1893.

Despite the destruction of Ile-Ife in the 19th century and its loss of military and economic power, the city remains the religious headquarter of the Yoruba up the present day. The sacred kingship established in the earlier centuries still exists, and Ife is known as a city of many gods. The gods are said to number up to 201 or 401. Hence, there is a belief that gods/deities are worshipped in Ife every day of the year except one day that is unknown to the public. This further emphasizes the religious significance of Ife.

Abidemi Babatunde Babalola

Further Reading

Akinjogbin, I. A., ed. *The Cradle of a Race: Ile-Ife from the Beginning to 1980.* Port Harcourt, Nigeria: Sunray Publications, 1992.

Drewal, H. J. "Ile-Ife: Origins of Art and Civilization." In *Yoruba: Nine Centuries of African Art and Thought,* edited by H. J. Drewal and J. Pemberton III, 45–76. New York: Center for African Art, 1989.

Drewal, H. J., and E. Schildkrout. *Dynasty and Divinity: Ile-Ife Art in Ancient Nigeria.* New York: Museum for African Arts, 2009.

Horton, R. "Ancient Ife: A Re-Assessment." *Journal of the Historical Society of Nigeria* 9(4) (1979): 151–186.

Ogundiran, A. O. "Chronology, Material Culture and Pathway of the Cultural History of Yoruba-Edo Region, 500 BC–AD 1800." In *Sources and Methods in African History:*

Spoken, Written and Unearthed, edited by T. Falola and C. Jennings, 33–79. Rochester: University of Rochester Press, 2003.

Willett, F. *Ile-Ife in the History of West African Sculpture.* London: Thames and Hudson, 1967.

Ilesa

Ijesa is the name of a subethnic group among the Yoruba people of West Africa. Ijesa is also the dialect spoken by its people; this language is a subdialect of the larger tonal Yoruba dialects, with similar orthography and closer linguistic link with Ekiti and Akure dialects. The Ijesa kingdom could be described as a commonwealth of several constituent kingdoms nucleated around the nodal town of Ilesa in Osun, Nigeria. This chief town is generally regarded as the economic and political capital of the Ijesa people; the other satellite towns converge almost conically around this capital territory. Ilesa is located at latitude 7.63°N longitude 4.72°E at an altitude of 462 meters above sea level and is situated in the deciduous rain forest belt adjacent to the savanna region of Nigeria. The forest canopies and carpets harbor several trees, shrubs, and climbers that spread over the region and are home to several wild life animals and birds. It is situated east of the major Yoruba towns of Oshogbo and Ile-Ife and is bordered by Akure and Ekiti to the east, Ijebu and Ondo to the south, and Igbomina to the north.

The Osun, Oni, Owena, and Sasha Rivers course through the general Ijesa nation, watering the largely hilly geographical formations of the country. The popular Olumirin waterfalls are located within Ijesa territory. The soil feature is largely red laterite, which sits atop the Precambrian basement complex, and other subterranean features such as folded peltic schists, quartzites, hornblende gneisses, and

Festivals in Modern Ilesa

A unique feature of Ijesa is the annual festivals that include the Ogun, Uyi Arere, and Iwude festivals, among many others. These sociocultural events have as their central theme the unity and solidarity of the general Ijesa communities. Iwude (the assembly of the people) seems paramount of all the other festivals because it epitomizes the unity and the coming together of Ijesa people at home and abroad annually to celebrate achievements and fraternal cooperations. It is an age-old tradition of the Ijesa, who are known for their mercantile system of trade; these traders usually come home around the Iwude festival to remember their war heroes, celebrate success, and also organize for communal development. Uyi Arere and Ogun are religious festivals, with the former led by the *owa obokun* (the king of Ilesa) and with his chiefs offering prayers for the peace of the Ijesa people in the various shrines around the community. All of these festivals are moments for celebrating unity, cooperation, success, and achievements.

amphibolites. The last two mafic and intermediate rocks are common in southwestern Nigeria, which is the homeland of the Yoruba people. The location of Ilesa and some parts of the larger Ijesa commonwealth on the schist and amphibolite belts explains the large gold deposits that the area is known for. The Ijesa commonwealth includes hundreds of towns and settlements, prominent among which are Esa-Oke, Ibokun, Ipetu-Ijesa, Esa-Odo, Erin-Ijesa, Osu, Iloko, Iwara, Erinmo, Ilerin, Ilase, Igangan, Imo, Iperindo, Ibodi, Itamerin, Ijebu-Ijesa, Ifewara, Ipole, Idominasi, and Alakowe.

As common with precolonial societies, most of the genesis accounts of the Ijesa people are intertwined in legends and oral traditions passed down over the years. The Yoruba, however, have something in common: their familial ties with Ile-Ife, which is regarded as their ancestral home. Ilesa's close proximity to Ile-Ife lends credence to this account; however, the traditional account of the origin of Ijesa is traced to Oduduwa Olofin Aiye, who is regarded as the progenitor of the Yoruba. Like most Yoruba towns, the history of Ilesa is tied to a powerful founding leader, Owa Ajibogun Ajaka (meaning "ubiquitous warrior"). Also known as Owa Obokun Onida Arara, Ajibogun is the last-born son of Oduduwa Olofin. According to oral tradition, it was to Ajibogun's credit that their father, Oduduwa Olofin, regained his sight when Ajibogun went on a perilous mission to fetch the mythical *omi okun* (brine) that was used as part of the ingredients prescribed by the Ifá oracle for curing Olofin's old-age blindness. The Ijesa are known as Omo Owa Obokun (meaning "descendants of the *owa* [king] who fetched the brine"); this significant marker is derived from the chivalrous exploit of Owa Ajibogun.

On Ajibogun's return from the errand, his elder brothers had distributed their father's inheritance, including the revered beaded crowns, among themselves, leaving nothing for their brother. A grateful Olofin, upon regaining his sight, placated his cheated son with the *ida ajase* (victory sword) and bequeathed his own beaded crown (without frontal beaded fringes) and a staff of authority to Ajibogun. Olofin instructed his son to pursue his brothers and regain his dues from them; the other instruction was that no battle would be lost if prosecuted with the *ida ajase*. Ajibogun's patrimony is believed to have extended from the entrance of the palace of the Ooni of Ife, which is referred to today as Enuwa and Enu Owa (Owa's court or gate). He migrated with his followers to settle in several towns such as Igadaye, Ilowa (from "Ilu Owa," meaning "Owa's town"), Ilemure (which they renamed Ibokun), Ilare, and Ilaje (later renamed Ipole Ijesa) before finally settling in Ilesa. Another account claims that Owa Ajibogun died, leaving his son Owa Oke Okile and grandson Owari to continue the journey.

The site of present-day Ilesa was chosen by Owari's son, Owa Oge. It was originally built and ruled by a king known by the title *onila* (king of the Okro planters). The name Ilesa (from "Ile Isa," meaning "the town of water pots") probably came from the famous pottery skills for which the women of the town were known. Other traditions claim that Ilesa means "Ile Orisa" (town of the gods). Onila abdicated the throne for Owa Oge and agreed to be second-in-command to the new *owa;* his descendants hold the title *obala,* which is considered a second rank next to the *owa* of Ilesa today. Some Ijesa towns such as Imesi-ile, Esa-Oke, and Ipetu-Ijesa, however, trace their ancestry directly to Ile-Ife, but the common Ijesa language accentuates a primordial, protofamilial connection. The word "Ijesa" is believed to have been derived from the Yoruba expression "Awon enia ti a sa," which means "chosen people," as denotative of their uniqueness.

Around the beginning of the 19th century Ilesa became renowned as a town of kola nuts, with several merchants moving into the town for trade and commerce; these settlers include non-Yoruba traders and those from surrounding Yoruba towns. The Yoruba internecine wars of the 19th century caused great population dispersals in northern Yoruba towns, including Ilesa. Before the expiration of the Kiriji Wars (Ekiti Parapo Wars of 1877–1893) between Ibadan and Ekiti-Ijesa armies led by Ogedengbe, the town's population was estimated to be between 20,000 and 40,000—a significant population for a big city around that period.

The economy of Ilesa in the 19th century was largely agrarian. The forests provided opportunities for farming; itinerant farmers and farmhands from outside of Ilesa were employed on plantations. Nonlandowners, mostly migrants, were sometimes granted land leases through the *isakole* system—a land tenure system to pay tributes from their yields at agreed time intervals and terms. The large migration of people from northern Nigeria became prominent around this time. There was also massive trade in cocoa, kola nut, cocoyam, palm oil, etc. Trade and commerce were transacted with neighboring Yoruba towns and other towns outside of Yoruba, including Hausa and Nupe to the north and Benin to the south; there was also trade in slaves before the abolition campaigns of the British. The medium of exchange was through trade by barter and cowries (*monetraia moneta*) until the later part of the century, when paper money was introduced as legal tender through colonial intervention in southern Nigeria. Aside from agriculture, there was also skilled craftsmanship in pottery, textile designs, woodwork and metalwork for decorative art, ceremonial artifacts, farm implements, warfare implements, and household items.

Yoruba states of the 18th and 19th centuries were under the rule of monarchs; many of them were under the authority of the Oyo Empire. Ilesa was a monarchical state headed by the *owa* as the king with several other *ijoyes* (chiefs) presiding over matters of state. Ibadan grew from a camp settlement for Oyo warriors into a highly militaristic city and a miniempire with influence over towns that were under the Old Oyo Empire. The waning power of Oyo led to the emergence of Ibadan as a new political power among the Yoruba. Ibadan conquered or inherited some of these states, appointing *ajeles* (governors) over these territories, including the larger Ijesa, Ekiti, and Igbomina countries. These Ibadan governors became despotic, and their overbearing rules led to the revolt of Yoruba states under the leadership of Ekiti and Ijesa, which culminated in the civil war of 1877–1893 known as the Ekitiparapo War.

The Ekitiparapo confederate army was led by Ogedengbe Agbogungboro, assisted by Fabunmi Oraralada of Okemesi; their camp was at Imesi-Ile. The Ibadan army, camped at Igbajo, was led by Obadoke Latoosa. Other Yoruba towns joined the Ekitiparapo confederate army against the Ibadan army. The Ibadan army was fighting on five different fronts against the Egba, Ijebu, Ilorin, Ile-Ife, and Ekitiparapo armies. The war ended in 1893 through the intervention of the Church

Missionary Society, represented by Samuel Johnson and Charles Philips. A treaty was signed around Igbajo under the supervision of Governor Gilbert T. Carter. Ogedengbe. the confederate war general, was honored by the Ijesa with the title *obanla*. The Kiriji War defines the political significance of Ijesa because the war brought the creativity and military strategic capabilities of the people to the fore. The end of the war later culminated in the Britain exercising its dominion over northern and southern Nigeria with the capitulation of Oyo in 1895 and the defeat of Ilorin by the Royal Niger Company in 1897; these events heralded the effective presence of British colonialism in Nigeria.

The Ijesa of the 19th century practiced the indigenous religion until the turn of the century, when Christianity made an inroad into the land; Islam came into Ilesa through peripatetic northern Yoruba Islamic scholars and Hausa-Fulani traders. Festivals such as Uyi Arere and Iwude Ogun and the Ladeoko festival of the people of Isona Ward in Ilesa were periods of celebrations, with some of them featuring music, dance, masquerades, and drums of several shapes and sizes. All Yoruba sub-ethnic divisions such as the Oyo, Ekiti, Ijebu, Akoko, and Igbomina have distinctive identification marks. The Ijesa are known by the *pele* Ijesa facial mark, which consists of four lines about a quarter of an inch long inscribed on both cheeks.

Toward the end of the Ekitiparapo War, most of the towns in Yoruba territories including Ilesa were incorporated into the Southern Nigeria Protectorate. Areas south of Lokoja were merged with the Niger Coast Protectorate to form the Southern Protectorate in 1900. Ilesa was made the capital of the Ijesa/Ekiti Parapo Council by the British colonial administration on June 21, 1900, making the town the first local council headquarters in Nigeria. In 1914, the Southern and Northern Protectorates were unified to form the Nigeria Protectorate under a governor-general, Sir Federick Lugard. Nationalist movements featured some Ijesa-educated elites, among whom were Christopher Alexander Sapara-Williams, James Johnson and Philip Jose Meffre, who were leading members of the Ijesa Association, an Ijesa pro-independence group formed at the Lagos Breadfruit Church in 1852.

The political and economic situation of Ijesa is tied to the experiences of other Yoruba communities in southwestern Nigeria. There are presently increasing agitation for the creation of Ijesa State; this call became prominent after the creation of Ekiti State, a province that was part of the old Ijesa/Eikiti Parapo Local Council. The Ijesa people are asking for the Ijesa State to be created out of the current Osun State because of what they perceive as political marginalization; they believe that the capital of the current Osun State should have been situated in Ilesa and not Osogbo, because Ijesa is the largest ethnic group in Osun State. On the whole, Ijesa politicians and technocrats have held and are still holding offices in Nigeria.

Peter Damilola Adegoke

Further Reading

Akintoye, S. A. "The North-Eastern Yoruba Districts and the Benin Kingdom." *Journal of the Historical Society of Nigeria* (1969): 539–553.

Atayero, Samuel O. S. *A Short History of Oba Owa of Ijesha-Land, and Oni of Ife.* Lagos: Ijesha Royal Press, 1948.

Awe, Bolanle. "The Ajele System: A Study of Ibadan Imperialism in the Nineteenth Century." *Journal of the Historical Society of Nigeria* 3(1) (1964): 47–60.

Familusi, M. M. *Royal Ambassador: The God-Guarded and God-Guided Life of Sir Adedokun Abiodun Haastrup.* Ibadan: Heinemann Educational Books, 2004.

Peel, J. D. Y. *Ijeshas and Nigerians: The Incorporation of a Yoruba Kingdom, 1890s–1970s.* Cambridge: Cambridge University Press, 1983.

Smith, Robert S. *Kingdoms of the Yoruba.* London: Methuen, 1969.

K

Kaabu

Kaabu (also spelled Kabu, Gabu, and Gabou) was a polity located in the hinterland of Upper Guinea that probably emerged in the 13th century and controlled an important area of territory, especially during the period of the transatlantic trade. Because of its Mande roots, the history of Kaabu has often been interpreted as that of a western province of the Mali Empire, which became autonomous before the 16th century. It collapsed definitively in 1867, defeated by the Fula of the Imamate of Futa Jallon in the Battle of Kansala. Its territory was later shared among French, English, and Portuguese colonies at the end of the 19th century.

At its period of maximum expansion, Kaabu extended from the southern shores of the Gambia River in the north to beyond the Grande River in the south and from the foothills of the Futa Jallon in the east to the creeks and forests on the coasts in the west. The latter remained outside its direct control. Today, the core of Kaabu is shared between southeastern Gambia, eastern Casamance, and a large part of eastern Guinea-Bissau. Kaabu's environment belongs to the ecoregion usually referred to as the Guinean forest-savanna mosaic. The area is characterized by grassland studded with trees and by patches of forests often to be found on hills and along waterways. This landscape is the result of fires that make it difficult for trees to colonize the open country in spite of its hot and humid climate.

Kaabu is mentioned in early modern European documents related to trade in Upper Guinea as a powerful hinterland polity and a provider of slaves, especially in the 16th and early 17th centuries. For the most part, however, the memory of Kaabu survives in the form of oral traditions to be found among the Mandinka populations of the Gambia, Casamance, and Guinea-Bissau peoples, who consider themselves as originating from the Mande world. In such oral traditions there is no specific word that designates Kaabu as a political entity, and the term "Kaabuland" is usually used. Nevertheless, Kaabu is clearly understood as a very complex and dynamic construction, including a centralized power controlling a confederation composed of a large number of lineage-based territories.

Oral traditions have been used as a major source to retrace the history of Kaabu. Overall, however, many gaps and uncertainties remain concerning the origins of this polity, its warrior elite group, and its king lists as well as its political and administrative organization. Oral traditions and chronicles recording oral material usually discuss the myth of the origins of Kaabu and then skip to the 19th century to provide details on the fall of the kingdom and its annexation by the

Imamate of Futa Jallon. Unless new sources are revealed or archaeological data are collected and analyzed, the details of Kaabu's history will remain fragmentary. Five periods of the history of Kaabu can be used, with caution, as a working chronological framework.

During the first period, the pre-Mandinka period, presumably corresponding to the first few centuries of the second millennium CE, Kaabuland was occupied by a number of self-governing matrilineal communities claiming different identities and speaking a variety of languages. These communities hosted the first generations of Muslims, mainly traders and farmers, migrating from various part of the western part of the Mandingo world. Power, however, seems to have changed hands when a leading Mandinka warrior—the founding father of Kaabu—and his followers conquered the area, perhaps in the 13th century during the period of expansion of the Mali Empire. According to this tradition, the sons of the conqueror were said to have been settled in different conquered provinces, where they formed a military aristocracy. Other existing traditions do not make reference to a unique founding father but instead suggest several military conquests of different areas by distinct Mandingo groups. This second phase of Kaabu's history was characterized by the conquest of preexisting communities by a Mandingo military elite who divided Kaabuland into provinces. Members of this military elite bore the title *koring*.

The period of military conquest and division of the spoils of war between patrilineal heirs of the conquerors was followed by a period of reorganization of Kaabu into a centralized kingdom, with Kansala as the capital and a system of three dominant provinces controlled by a new elite, known as *nanco*. This period possibly began by the turn of the 15th century. The legend of the three daughters of the founder of the royal matrilineage of Kaabu marrying princes from three provinces illustrates the process of political construction of Kaabu. The fact that access to the throne of Kaabu rotated among three lineages anchored in different provinces illustrates the essence of the political constitution of Kaabu: a confederation of provinces providing heirs to a shared royal matrilineage that exercised central authority. In fact, Kaabu rested on a complex network of alliances between a variety of territorial elite groups, with multilayered and fluid identities serving as shared references and with an ideology of power rooted in a variety of sources—including the Mandingo imperial experience, Islam, and the long-established autochthonous communities.

The three core provinces of Kaabu were Pajaana (where the fortified capital of Kansala was located), Jimara, and Saama. Succession to the throne of Kaabu rotated between the *nanco* groups of these three territories. Other provinces were attached to Pajaana, Jimara, or Sama through a complex system of alliances between their *koring* and *nanco* aristocracies. Relations with the core of the Mandingo world probably weakened after 1600 following the fall of the Songhai Empire.

We do not have any account describing Kansala before its fall in 1867, and there has been no archaeological work conducted in the area. The location is known, however, and remains a place of memory. Traditions agreeing that Kansala was not the first capital of Kaabu—although the location of this even earlier capital is disputed—may be a sign that several capitals succeeded each other. Kaabu had limited direct access to the coast and did not extensively engage directly in trade with Europeans and their representatives in Upper Guinea. Coastal populations were much more directly involved, and although they were often loosely dependent on Kaabu, they were never integrated into the confederation. Nevertheless, the armies of Kaabu were actively involved in the capture of slaves in the hinterland for export to the Atlantic world, and this occurred as early as the 16th century. Unfortunately, sources are lacking to clearly outline the nature of this involvement and how it impacted the regional sociopolitical landscape. It probably entailed raids and military expansion of Kaabu into its hinterland, which ultimately resulted in a confrontation with the Fulas, who had formed a theocratic state in neighboring Futa Jallon in 1735.

Control over access to the Atlantic trade and strategic and religious motives would have fueled tensions between wealthy Kaabu and its Fula neighbors throughout the 18th and 19th centuries. This period of tension leading to the fall of Kaabu forms the last period of its history. It began in the last decade of the 18th century with an increasing number of raids against Kaabu. By 1850, European travelers reported that its territory had already dwindled significantly. Several battles in the second half of the 19th century are remembered in Kaabu's tradition as having taken place at Sankolla Berekolong (1851), Kanjongs (1854), and Tabajan (1858). Meanwhile, Kaabu seems to have been torn apart by internal divisions, although the details of the roles played by the different provinces and their aristocracies in the disintegration of the polity remain little documented. During the last stand at the siege of Kansala in 1867, only a few among the provinces of the confederation remained faithful to the central authority and provided troops in support of the last king, Jankee Wali. After a heroic resistance, the siege ended with the collective suicide of Kansala's inhabitants, and the gates of the city were opened to the Fula army. Unbeknownst to them, the king had ordered that the gunpowder stores of the fortress be set afire, and both the defendants and a party of the assailants perished in the explosion that blasted the settlement. Although some resistance, particularly in the south of the territory, continued until about 1880, the Battle of Kansala sealed the effective end of Kaabu as an independent polity. By the end of the 19th century as Futa Jallon fell in turn to French rule, the old territory of Kaabu had become divided among colonial powers.

Gérard L. Chouin

Further Reading

Giesing, C., and V. F. Vydrin. *Ta:rikh Mandinka de Bijini (Guinée-Bissau): La mémoire des Mandinka et des Sòoninkee du Kaabu.* Leiden: Brill, 2007.

Green, T. *The Rise of the Trans-Atlantic Slave Trade in Western Africa, 1300–1589.* Cambridge: Cambridge University Press, 2011.

Niane, D. T. *Histoire des Mandingues de l'Ouest: Le royaume du Gabou.* Paris: Karthala Editions, 1989.

Kano

Kano, an ancient city in northern Nigeria, is situated on the west of Hausaland between Zaria to the south and Katsina to the north. Kano lies between latitude 13°N and 10.30°N and between longitude 8°W and 10°E. Kano, with a landmass of about 20,740 square kilometers, occupies the central position of northern Nigeria. Geographically, Kano falls mostly within the Sudan vegetation zone and consists mostly of flat, undulating plains sloping to the northeast. In spite of its uniform landscape it has special features, as the area is characterized by plains, rivers, and hills. Kano is underlain by granites, schist, and gneiss. It is made up of 40 local government areas and has a population of 9,401,288 based on the official result of the 2006 Nigerian population count, which makes Kano the third-largest city in Nigeria. The climate of Kano is usually severe, and the area is mostly dry. However, the rainy season lasts from May to October and between July and September reaches its peak, which is normally characterized by violent dust storms and tornadoes. The vegetation of Kano is semiarid savanna, which makes it an ideal zone for human accomplishment. Its well-off vegetation makes Kano a seemly area for rearing livestock and cultivating cereals.

According to the Bayajidda legends of the precolonial Hausa states, Kano is one of the seven Hausa Bakwai (legitimate) states, founded by one of the children of Bayajidda. Another tradition has it that Kano was founded by the Abagawa migrants who came seeking iron ore, a mineral needed for farm implements that was abundant at the Dala Hill, where they eventually settled. Due to the high demand for iron ore, they decided to settle there permanently. Soon this attracted people from other places and subsequently led to a settlement pattern. By the 10th century the population in Kano had become large enough to form a political structure, which evolved under a Daura migrant known as Bagauda. Bagauda became the first king of Kano (999–1063), and the city walls for which Kano is so famous were started in the reign of Bagauda's son, Gayamusa. Gayamusa located his capital to the south of Dala Hill (present-day Kano) and started the construction of the famous Kano Walls in order to protect Kano against external attacks. The walls were completed during the reign of Sarkin Yusa. However, the greatest of the kings who ruled Kano was Sarkin Mohammed Rumfa, who ruled at the end of the 15th century.

During Rumfa's reign, the Kano city walls were extended to accommodate the many migrants, especially those from Bornu and North Africa, who came to Kano because of its economic and later religious importance. Kano's first contact with

The Durbar Festival

The most popular annual festival celebrated in Kano is the Durbar Festival. It is usually celebrated at the culmination of the Muslim festivals Eid al-Fitr and Eid al-Adha. The Durbar Festival begins with prayers, followed by a parade of the emir and his entourage on horses, accompanied by music players, and ending at the emir's palace.

Islam dates to the 14th century during the reign of Sarkin Yaji (1349–1385) and was said to have been introduced by the Wangarawa Muslim clerics and merchants from the Mali Empire. Islam was made the official religion during the reign of Yaji and then was reemphasized during the reign of Rumfa. However, the fact that Islam was made the official religion did not mean that everybody accepted it. That is, Islam existed in Kano alongside traditional religions. Al-Maghili, a North African scholar from Tlemcen who visited Kano during the reign of Rumfa, and wielded very strong influence such that the practice of Islam in Kano was radicalized. As a result of his continued activities as well as that of other Arab scholars, Kano evolved into a city with features that showed profuse influence from the Arab world. Islam became the main religion, while other aspects of the society such as architecture, social, economic, and politics bore the features of Islamic centers in North Africa and the Middle East.

Economic development in Kano can be traced to around the 15th century, a period during which Kano became one of the important and famous routes of the long-distance trans-Saharan trade. The connection with the trade route invariably meant a link with many cities in North Africa and certain cities in Europe. Slaves as well as items such as Moroccan leather and grains were exported from Kano to North Africa during the trans-Saharan trade. The production as well as the export of these goods from Kano to North Africa made Kano merchants famous in West Africa. Thus, Kano assumed an imposing economic stature that drew migratory waves of people to the city, eventually swelling it into an urban center.

Around 1500, Kano was the most powerful of the precolonial Hausa states. Although Kano subjected both Katsina and Zaria to tributary states in the first decade of the 16th century, Kano's position was not secure. Kano faced regular attacks from the Borno forces, Kororofa raids, and the rising power of Katsina. Nevertheless, through its position on a major trans-Saharan trade route and the economic acitivity of the commercial and artisan class that resided within the emirate, Kano managed to maintain a regional power after over a century of prolonged hostility. By the mid-17th century Kano and Katsina proclaimed peace, partly out of the need to present a united front against the Kororofa attacks that hampered them. It is possible that the Kororofa threats brought an end to the Kano-Katsina wars, but even then neither was able to stem the invasions.

By 1807, the Sokoto Caliphate had established control over Kano during the Fulani jihad led by Shehu Usman dan Fodio. It should be noted that before the British conquest of Kano there was no centralized authority exercising political power over Kano, and in 1903 Kano was conquered by the British and submitted peacefully to the authorities of the British colonial administration. The major cultural practice in Kano is the Durbar festival, which represents the foundation of the Hausa society. The Durbar festival takes place normally twice in a year during the Muslim Eid-al-Mubarak and Eid al-Fitr celebrations.

In 1967, Kano State was created from the ancient Kano emirate by the federal military government headed by Major Yakubu Gowon. As a result, investors began to concentrate on metropolitan Kano. The year 1980 marked the incidence of religiously motivated riots led by Mohammed Marwa Maitatsine. Riots occurred again in 2000 following the reintroduction of sharia, which caused many Christians to leave the city. In November 2007, political violence broke out as a result of the alleged rigging of the 2007 general elections. Also, in 2012 a series of bomb attacks rocked the city for which Jamā'a Ahl al-sunnah li-da'wa wa al-jihād, an Islamic sect better known by its Hausa name, Boko Haram, claimed responsibility.

Damilola D. Fagite

Further Reading

Albert, I. O. "Violence in Metropolitan Kano: A Historical Perspective." In *Urban Violence in Africa: Pilot Studies,* edited by Eghosa E. Osaghae et al., 14–24. Ibadan: IFRA, 1994.

Falola, Toyin, et al., eds. *History of Nigeria,* Vol. 1. Lagos: Longman, 1991.

Paden, J. N. *Religion and Political Culture in Kano.* Berkeley: University of California Press, 1973.

Katsina

Katsina, which was a historic kingdom, is at present a state and an emirate in northern Nigeria. Katsina is located between latitude 12°15′ North and longitude 7°30′ East. With a landmass of 24,193 square kilometers, it shares an international border with the Republic of Niger to the north, while to the south it borders Kaduna State to the east. Katsina shares borders with Kano and Jigawa State, whereas Zamfara State lies on its western frontiers; Katsina shapes part of the big plains referred to as the High Plains of Hausaland. The town is surrounded by city walls built in the mid-16th century that are 21 kilometers (13 miles) in length.

Mamman Shata (1923–1999)

Mamman Shata, a famous Hausa griot/musician whose vocals were often followed by talking drums, was from Katsina. He performed mostly among the people of northern Nigeria. Well versed in the Hausa Muslim oral tradition, Shata chose the music profession over farming despite not receiving the necessary support from his father. Shata started his music career by singing for fun in the marketplace and the local playground. He was a highly respected folklorist, active for about 60 years, but the number of songs he produced is unknown. Shata was widely traveled, and his songs covered a wide range of issues affecting Hausaland, from politics and agriculture to culture and religion. His contributions to Hausa literature earned him an honorary degree from Ahmadu Bello University. Shata entered politics in the 1970s and served as councilor and chairman of his local government at various times.

The first inhabitants of Katsina were foreigners from East Berber who arrived about the 10th century. Although a dynasty was not discovered until late into the 12th century, these Berbers were originally from Durbi ta Kusheyi and Bugaje. Katsina started as a meeting point that was midway between the two Durbi ta Kusheyi and Bugaje settlements where the Berbers met for their annual feast and display. This place is believed to be Ambuttai, which was a ward of Katsina town where the mosque is located. Before the establishment of a dynasty, the head of Katsina was a semidivine ruler known as a *sarki* who was sentenced to death if found to display incompetency in his ruling style. The first Katsina dynasty was founded by Kumayo, a grandson of the legendary Bayajida of Daura fame.

The name "Katsina" was derived from a princess of Daura who married Janzama, a king of Durbawa who ruled at Durbi ta Kusheyi, about 18 miles southeast of the present-day town of Katsina. The memory of the king is preserved in the name of a rock very close to Mani. It is assumed that Janzama was conquered by Kumayo, as early kings were at first rotated between the house of Kumayo and the descendants of Janzama, but this changed with the killing of Sanau, the last of the Kumayo dynasty, by Korau-a malam, of western extraction, by the mid-13th century. His emergence also led to the establishment of a new dynasty.

The process of selecting a new king revolved around certain rites connected with a sacred snake or by throwing a spear into the ground. The upright position of the spear at the mention of the name of the candidate when it was thrown confirmed the new king. There were other important rites such as those involving the king's period of reign, rainfall, and the fruitfulness of land. The irregularities in these periods point to the failure of the king's physical powers, which was an indication to have him eliminated. Katsina is mostly a Hausa-Fulani community, as most of if not all of its people speak only the Hausa language.

Bornu invaders held sway in Katsina from 1250 to 1468. In 1512 Katsina also witnessed the temporary overlordship of Songhai when it became a fiefdom of Gao. This position was changed in 1554 in the Battle of Karfata during the reign of King Askia Daud of Gao, when Katsina regained its freedom. The influence of Gao over Katsina was great especially right after the war. This was reflected in the diversity of interests, activities, and names of its quarters. When the Songhai Empire was broken up at the end of the 16th century, Katsina transferred its allegiance to Bornu, as every king of Katsina was required to send tribute in the form of 100 slaves to the *mai* of Ngazargamu (Bornu). This continued until the reign of Agwaragi in 1784, when Katsina came under Bornu as the protector.

Katsina was engaged in a rivalry with Kano for about 200 years over control of the western Sudan region of trans-Saharan trade. A war spanning 11 years between Kano and Katsina came to an end with the defeat of Katsina by Abdullahi, who was Mohamman Rumfa's (1463–1499) son and successor. In 1570 Katsina defeated Kano, with the destruction of the city up to the gates of Kano. Kano's reprisal attack on Katsina was a success, as Kano made away with many prisoners, but Katsina's attempt to retaliate was a total failure. Not much later in Katsina there emerged Muhammadu Wari, a strong and fearful leader whose might cannot be rivaled. His ascension to the throne led to the signing of a treaty of alliance with

Kano against common enemies—the non-Muslim people of Hausaland. The treaty was a way of courting the friendship of the king of Katsina, thus preventing him from killing the king of Kano because of the long rivalry between the two states.

The 18th century began with Katsina as one of the leading states in the western and central regions of Sudan. With the defeat of the Songhai Empire in western Sudan and of Bornu in central Sudan, Katsina reached its peak of prosperity and power, as the old wealth and traditions of Songhai also came its way. This new status attracted Islamic scholars to Katsina rather than Timbuktu (a city in the Songhai Empire), which was once a scholarly center. These scholars and the extensive trading network made the place very important. Other attractions that were diverted to Katsina from Timbuktu included the leather-working trade, the courtesy and manners of citizens, administrative style, and the judiciary.

The 19th century started with the Fulani jihad of Shehu Usman dan Fodio, which was followed by a change of regime. Before then Katsina was ruled by traditionalists who were only Muslims in name, as they mixed traditionalism and Islam. Islam was introduced in the 1450s, but by 1809 the Shehu flag bearers gained control of Katsina, leaving the Hausa nobility and other people with the option of fleeing into exile. Their going into exile led to the establishment of new settlements such as Tassawa and Maradi. The Fulani herdsmen played a predominant role in the jihad led by Shehu Usman dan Fodio against Gobir, the traditional enemy of Katsina, and their zeal further spread the revolt. The Fulani herdsmen settled in Katsina around the 15th century. The wars with Gobir marked the start of Katsina's decline.

Katsina was also the main commercial center before the Fulani regime and was the center of an agricultural region producing groundnuts, cotton, hides, millet, and guinea corn. Unfortunately, however, Katsina was not able to recover from the wars of the Fulani jihad; as a result, the position as agricultural center was taken over by Kano from about 1815. Katsina was also an important junction of the trans-Saharan trade, with the crossing of camel caravans from the Sahara to Ghademes, Tripoli, and Tunis southward to Katsina, and this brought great prosperity to the state. Katsina's power and status kept it in constant battle with its neighbor, Gobir. The two states were great rivals for the caravan trade of western Hausaland. Katsina also waged war against Kano in 1649, which was worn down by Katsina. In 1750 Katsina faced bold raids from Tuaregs, who were established near Gao on the Middle Niger. Katsina's eminence among the Hausa Bakwais and its history of active resistance to encroachment did not prevent British colonial authority for another 30 years. In 1903 Katsina's emir pledged allegiance to the British rulers of northern Nigeria. The setting up of the Niger-Nigeria boundary in 1904 reduced the size of Katsina, making part of it a Kano province. In 1926 Katsina was transformed to Zaria; Katsina Province was not formed until August 1934.

Agriculture is important to Katsina, and from time immemorial hides and skins have been produced, for which Katsina is known throughout Africa. Cattle provide milk and are of great value to the fertility of the soil and are also killed or sold for meat. Katsina is one of the states in Nigeria where crops are grown year-round; this is so because of the numerous dams in existence, as dry-season farming is done along riverbanks. A great number of crops are cultivated in the state. Also of great importance are the traditional crafts of weaving, cotton dyeing, leatherworking and metalworking, and embroidery, pottery, and calabash design form, which are important occupations in the state. Katsina achieved the status of a state on September 23, 1987, and was carved out of the former Kaduna State, which was part of the old Katsina Province in the old Northern Region.

Morenikeji Asaaju

Further Reading

Burdon, J. A. *Northern Nigeria: Historical Notes on Certain Emirates and Tribes.* London: Gregg International Publishers, 1972.

Hogben, S. J., and A. H. M. Kirk-Greene. *The Emirates of Northern Nigeria: A Preliminary Survey of Their Historical Traditions.* London: Oxford University Press, 1966.

Meek, C. K. *The Northern Tribes of Nigeria.* London: Frank Cass, 1971.

Kerma

Kerma was a Nubian (Kush) kingdom established at least 5,500 years ago in present-day southern Egypt and North Sudan. The kingdom is known as Kerma because the remains of its capital now lie within the modern-day Sudanese town of Kerma. This early Nubian civilization is contemporary with the Egyptian Middle Kingdom and Second Intermediate Period (ca. 2055–1550 BCE). Kerma grew from a small chiefdom society into a state with a social complexity comparable with that of Egypt. Kerma is one of the most powerful states in the history of Nubia. The Kerma kings ruled much of what is presently North Sudan and parts of southern Egypt. Kerma exercised power over the first to fourth cataracts, a territory as expansive as ancient Egypt.

The long history of Egyptian military activities in northern (lower) Nubia indicates that Kerma was seen as a threat to pharaonic Egypt at different times. The Egyptians built walls in the Middle Nile Valley during the Middle Kingdom to protect the upper Egyptian border against raids from Kerma and protect the important trade routes between the two regions. Egyptian records also described Kerma as very rich in resources, with fertile land for agriculture. Gold, cattle, milk products, ebony, incense, and ivory that the Egyptian elites sought after were plentiful in the region.

The wealth of the Kerma kingdom is demonstrated in the construction of a large palace and the extravagant royal burials of the kings. In the early Kerma period, the body was placed on a tanned ox hide, and another hide was laid over the body. Burials are marked by a low circular superstructure of slabs of black sandstone, stuck into the ground in concentric circles. In later Kerma, royal graves

Ruins of the ancient Nubian city of Kerma in present-day Sudan. First excavated in the 1920s, Kerma remains a significant archaeological site in Africa today. (Lassi Hu)

included massive earth and gravel tumuli on top of the burial pit. The size of their tumuli and their rich grave goods demonstrate the power and wealth of these early Kushite rulers. A whole herd of cattle was sacrificed at each royal burial, and hundreds of their skulls were arranged around the rim of the earthen tomb. The rulers' bodies were not mummified and were dressed in leather garments, sandals, and jewelry and laid in a natural position on gold-covered beds with their weapons placed nearby. During this later period of Kerma, human sacrifice was introduced in burials. The bodies of men, women, and children, possibly servants and wives, were found on the corridors leading to the burial chambers of the royal tomb. The kings of Kerma also built their own temple, called the Deffufa (modern-day Nubian word for "mud-brick ruin"). Besides numerous statues that decorated the temple, the Deffufa was also surrounded by workshops, bakeries, and warehouses.

The highest achievement of Kerma art was its distinctive pottery. The pottery showed sophistication of the manufacturing technique in the form of thin-walled, black-topped, red-polished vessels. The black-topped pottery tradition was taken to the greatest peak of development by the Kerma culture. The shallow bowls of the early Kerma civilization later developed into bell-shaped cups with remarkably thin walls and flaring rims. Although they were products of a court, they were nevertheless produced as prestige objects in large quantity. Being widely distributed, the fine Kerma pottery wares provide an example of the cultural influence of a court art exerted through the medium of artifacts of general domestic use.

Kerma is one of the largest archaeological sites in ancient Nubia. Decades of extensive archaeological excavations and other research have produced thousands of graves and tombs and the residential quarters of the main city surrounding the Western/Lower Deffufa. Early archaeological work at Kerma started with George Reisner, an American with joint appointments at Harvard University and the Museum of Fine Arts in Boston. Reisner worked in Egypt and Sudan for 25 years (1907–1932). Kerma was one of the earliest sites to be excavated in this Nubian region, and Reisner's contributions to the region's archaeology are significant. A basic chronology of Kerman culture was established, which provided context for all other findings in the region.

When Kerma was first excavated in the 1920s, Reisner believed that the site was the base for an Egyptian governor and that these Egyptian rulers evolved into the independent kings of Kerma. Reisner's interpretation was anchored on the presence of inscribed Egyptian statues in the large burials, which he thought belonged to those named individuals. For decades after Reisner's excavations, his dismissal of the site as an Egyptian satellite fortified city was accepted. In later decades, scholars began to think that Kerma was a trading outpost of the Egyptians, being too small and far away from the known borders of ancient Egypt to be more directly linked to it. In the past 10 to 15 years, archaeological excavations have revealed that Kerma was much larger and more complex than previously assumed. It was also believed that the material culture and burial practices here are overwhelmingly of indigenous Kerman origin rather than Egyptian. From 1977 to 2003, Charles Bonnet and an international field crew excavated at Kerma. They uncovered a large independent, complex society that ruled most of the third cataract for centuries. The excavations revealed the foundations of numerous houses, workshops, and palaces, suggesting that as early as 2000 BCE Kerma was a large urban center, presumably the capital city and a burial ground of the kings of Kush.

Bonnet's Swiss team has excavated different types of sites at Kerma, including an ancient town, a princely tomb, a temple, residence/administrative buildings, a potter's workshop, Meroitic cemeteries, fortifications, Neolithic grain pits and huts, and bronze forge, among other sites. In 2003 Bonnet, excavating near Kerma, discovered black granite statues of the pharaohs of the Twenty-Fifth Dynasty of Egypt, particularly ones belonging to the dynasty's last two pharaohs, Taharqa and Tanoutamon. Different from those of ancient Egypt in theme and composition, Kerma's artifacts are characterized by extensive amounts of blue faience, techniques that the Kermans developed independently of Egypt.

At the zenith of its power, Kerma formed an alliance with the kings from the eastern Mediterranean called Hyksos and attempted to crush Egypt. The Hyksos are best known for bringing horses and chariots to Egypt. By 1600 BCE the Kerma people, together with the Hyksos, controlled most of southern and northern Egypt, while the Egyptian kings were ruling only a small district centered at Thebes. In about 1550 the Hyksos were forced out of northern Egypt. Egypt then turned its army south and began a war against the kingdom of Kush that lasted about 50 years. Kerma, the capital city of Kush, was destroyed, and the rest of the kingdom fell. Egyptian forces ruled Nubia as part of Egypt for more than 400 years. After the conquest, the Egyptians brought their administrators and priests into Nubia (Kush) territory. Egyptian kings built colossal pyramid temples in Nubia during the period of their domination, and Kerma culture was increasingly Egyptianized. During the New Kingdom, Kerma became a key province of the Egyptian Empire—economically, politically, and spiritually.

Aribidesi Usman

Further Reading

Bonnet, Charles. "Excavations at the Nubian Royal Town of Kerma, 1975–1991." *Antiquity* 66(252) (1992): 611–625.

Bonnet, Charles, and Dominique Valbelle. *The Nubian Pharaohs: Black Kings on the Nile.* New York: American University in Cairo Press, 2007.

Edwards, David N. *The Nubian Past: An Archaeology of the Sudan.* London: Routledge, 2004.

Kendall, T. *Kerma and the Kingdom of Kush, 2500–1500 B.C.: The Archaeological Discovery of an Ancient Nubian Empire.* Washington, DC: National Museum of African Art, Smithsonian Institution, 1996.

Török, Lásló. "Nubia." In *Africa: The Art of a Continent,* edited by Tom Phillips, 46–51. London: Prestel, 1999.

Kilwa Kisiwani

Kilwa Kisiwani (literally "Kilwa on the Island") was a famous and powerful commercial center and city-state on the East African coast during the 12th through 15th centuries. Kilwa's elites dwelled in an elaborate coral stone city, and its rulers directed much of the East African gold trade that supplied demands in medieval Europe and the Middle East. The history of Kilwa demonstrates the wide-reaching connections of the East African coast and the cosmopolitan yet distinctly East African Swahili culture of its inhabitants.

Located about 300 kilometers south of Dar es Salaam, Tanzania, Kilwa is a small island with a tropical climate about three kilometers off the East African mainland. Other prominent Swahili settlements nearby include Sanje ya Kati, Songo Mnara, and, farther to the north, Mafia Island. As with all coastal East African city-states, the nature of the Indian Ocean's monsoon climates played a key role in Kilwa's historic commercial importance. Kilwa was located at the southernmost point from which sailors could reliably expect to use the monsoon winds to sail back and forth between East Africa and the Middle East, India, and East Asia.

Thanks to detailed archaeology, linguistics, travelers' accounts, and Swahili oral traditions, a great deal is known about Kilwa's inhabitants. Archaeological records indicate an early settlement on the island by the fourth century CE. Like many East African communities, these early residents practiced a mixture of

---

Kilwa Today: New Research and Discoveries

Kilwa and its neighboring island, Songo Mnara, continue to be sites of ongoing research and discovery. Project directors Dr. Stephanie Wynne-Jones (University of York, UK) and Dr. Jeffrey Fleisher (Rice University, USA) have led an interdisciplinary team of researchers for a multiyear project exploring urban space, social memory, and materiality at Songo Mnara and surrounding islands. Their detailed project website makes available a rich array of images, interactive maps, and new publications of interest to advanced students, educators, and researchers alike.

---

farming, fishing, and hunting, with maritime resources playing a major role. By about 800 CE coastal Swahili culture and language began emerging on the East African coast, spanning from parts of present-day Somalia through Mozambique in the south. Although unified by common language and culture, Swahili settlements and towns remained locally ruled and characterized by a variety of regional differences. Before the 13th century, the most prominent trading Swahili towns were on the northern coast. At Kilwa, archaeology indicates some commercial ties (in the form of imported ceramics and other trade goods), yet the more significant early long-distance connections may have been religious and cultural. Around the eighth century, the first mosque was built on the island. For the next several centuries Kilwa's residents lived in small wattle-and-daub homes on the island, while trade appeared to be only one of many endeavors. The major changes in these foundational eras appeared to be social, not political, as the local and regional Swahili culture developed and an interest in commerce grew.

In the 12th century, Kilwa's situation changed, as first commercial and then political expansion gave the island its famous trading role. Oral traditions, often called the Kilwa Chronicle, offer varied accounts of Kilwa's founders. One version explains that the first sultan, Ali bin al-Hasan, was a *shirazi* (namely of Persian descent) who arrived and married the local ruler's daughter, thus beginning the ruling dynasty. This claim emphasized the prestige of connections to key centers in the Islamic and commercial worlds. Other accounts relate that he was a migrant of African origin from farther north on the coast. In the past, much scholarly ink was spilled debating whether Swahili origins were predominantly African or the result of widespread intermarriage with migrants from the Middle East. Today most scholars view Kilwa's residents, and Swahilis generally, as East African with a culture and worldview that emphasized cosmopolitanism with the Indian Ocean world. Some intermarriage took place between elites and traders (a common way to solidify commercial alliances). Yet, extensive migration from the Middle East to East Africa only occurred in later eras.

One of the key 12th-century changes at Kilwa was the development of a ruling dynasty that directed much of the island's trade. The concentration of commercial power with the ruling dynasty was famously described in oral traditions as being the result of the founder Ali bin al-Hasan's purchase of the island from the local African ruler using a large amount of cloth. One popular version related that the island had to be completely covered in cloth. The archaeological record also underscores the expansion of commerce and imported prestige goods. Many of the island's famous coral stone buildings began in the 12th century and were significantly expanded in the next two centuries. In the 1300s the new Mahdali dynasty came to rule Kilwa, and the city-state entered one of its most luxurious phases. The famous world traveler Ibn Battuta visited Kilwa in 1331, and travel by members of Kilwa's elites to and from the Middle East was common. By the 1400s Kilwa emerged as arguably the most powerful Swahili state, replacing earlier hubs of power, including Mogadishu and Lamu to the north.

A key feature of Kilwa's rise to prominence was its direction of the East African gold trade that began in the 12th century. This gold from the Zimbabwe Plateau was brought overland to the Swahili town of Sofala. Close ties between this town and Kilwa meant that the gold was then shipped directly to Kilwa. Highly coveted in external markets, this gold helped supply the soaring demand for gold in Renaissance Europe as well as parts of the Middle East and Asia. Merchants from around the Indian Ocean region followed the monsoon seasons to buy gold along with other trade items from the African mainland, including ivory, tortoiseshell, wax, animal skins, and enslaved people. Kilwa's rulers and merchants imported fine silk and cotton cloth, cowrie shells, and decorated and glazed ceramics. The local manufacture of cotton cloth and pottery provided additional trade options. All of these goods flowed throughout a variety of coastal, mainland, and Indian Ocean trade networks. Many goods functioned as both luxuries and currencies. In addition, Kilwa's rulers manufactured their own coins, which have been found far afield.

Political authority in the Kilwa city-state was closely tied to trade, but the power of rulers was never absolute. Rather, power was tied to a delicate dance of redistributing enough wealth and trade goods to maintain social and political alliances on the island and among allies in other (potentially rival) Swahili cities. Because of the option for many to enter trade, rulers such as the Kilwa sultan had to work to reinforce their authority and attract followers. One sultan, Abu al-Mawahib, who met the world traveler Ibn Battuta, was remembered as "the father of gifts," a testament to his generosity and savvy use of gift giving to form alliances and cultivate his supporters.

Kilwa's commercial ties and luxury imports also fulfilled additional roles beyond being the literal (and metaphorical) currency of wealth and power. These luxury imports became part of a broader cosmopolitan culture, as Kilwa's residents (from elites to commoners) imagined their identities as active participants in the broader Indian Ocean and Muslim worlds. Kilwa's coral stone architecture closely reflected these intersections. Many imported ceramics, for instance, were displayed on household and palace walls in special niches. One of the largest surviving 14th-century buildings, Husuni Kubwa, functioned as both a royal palace and a large warehouse to strategically store trade goods awaiting the optimum market time. Other elaborate buildings fulfilled a mixture of public and private functions, such as

The Great Mosque of Kilwa in present-day Tanzania. Built in the late 12th to early 13th century, it is the earliest extant mosque structure on the East African coast. (Elene Blossfeld/ Dreamstime.com)

Kilwa's Great Mosque as well as multiple smaller mosques. The Great Mosque is considered the oldest mosque still standing in East Africa. Before the 16th century, it was also the largest mosque in East Africa. It has 16 domes and vaulted bays and originally dates from the 11th century. In the 15th century, the large enclosed area of Makutani was built. It contained a royal palace and several smaller coral stone homes, one with an adjoining mosque. In the next century, a cemetery was added on the island. It had a number of decorated tombs, some with elaborate plasterwork, others with ceramic plates. Among the many other coral stone structures were multiple wells providing vital access to freshwater (as the island has none at surface level) and also providing nearby water sources for religious ablutions. Some of these wells are still in use today by the island's current residents.

Kilwa's prosperity came to an abrupt decline when the kingdom was attacked and sacked by Francisco d'Almeida in 1505. This was part of a wider series of attacks by Portuguese ships as they sought to gain control over the lucrative trade networks in the Indian Ocean world. Initial Portuguese admiration for Kilwa's architecture and luxuries, which they likened to the beauty of Lisbon, was not enough to spare the city. In addition to the violence and destruction in 1505, Portuguese efforts to intercept and confiscate goods from traders they deemed nonofficial (e.g., ones not officially sanctioned by them) further hastened Kilwa's decline. Kilwa's surviving elites and the island itself did not regain their former hegemony. In later centuries, the island's strategic location was utilized by a variety of outside powers. The Portuguese built a fort on the island in 1505; however, after 1512 they switched to using other locations. In the early 19th century, the Omani Sultanate (based on Zanzibar) also used and expanded the original Portuguese fort. The nearby mainland towns of Kilwa Kivinje and Kilwa Masoko also became regional bases for the German and British colonial administrations, respectively.

In the colonial era, Kilwa's prosperity and elaborate coral stone houses made it, like other African kingdoms, subject to controversy, as European officials and academics doubted that Africans could have built such an impressive city-state. Instead, one popular view proposed that migrants from the Middle East founded Kilwa and introduced the natives to Islam. The British archaeologist Neville Chittick first challenged this outsider origin hypothesis with his detailed excavations at Kilwa in the 1960s. Such views gained acceptance, particularly after Tanzania's independence. Kilwa was named a UNESCO World Heritage Site in 1981. Kilwa's monuments were considered endangered in the 1990s and early 2000s. More recent preservation efforts have been successful, and in 2014 the site was removed from UNESCO's List of World Heritage in Danger.

In Tanzania and abroad, Kilwa is considered to be a key example of a powerful and influential commercial city-state that flourished prior to European contact. More recently, there has been some hope that Kilwa will take on a new role and encourage historical tourism to the region, which could offer benefits to the island's current residents. Ongoing research at nearby Songo Mnara, an affluent Swahili town that flourished in the 14th through 16th centuries, also promises renewed interest in preserving and studying the history of these Swahili commercial centers.

Andrea Felber Seligman

Further Reading

Chittick, H. Neville. *Kilwa: An Islamic Trading City on the East African Coast.* Nairobi, Kenya: British Institute in Eastern Africa, 1974.

Fleisher, Jeffrey. "Performance, Monumentality and the 'Built' Exterior on the East African Coast." *Azania: Archaeological Research in Africa* 48(2) (2013): 263–281.

Horton, Mark, and John Middleton. *The Swahili: The Social Landscape of a Mercantile Society.* Oxford, UK: Blackwell, 2000.

LaViolette, Adria. "Swahili Cosmopolitanism in Africa and the Indian Ocean World, A.D. 600–1500." *Archaeologies: Journal of the World Archaeological Congress* 4(1) (2008): 24–48.

Moon, Karen. *Kilwa Kisiwani: Ancient Port City of the East African Coast.* Dar es Salaam: Tanzania Printers, Ministry of Natural Resources and Tourism, Tanzania, 2005.

Nurse, Derek, and Thomas Spear. *The Swahili: Reconstructing the History and Language of an African Society, 800–1500.* Philadelphia: University of Pennsylvania Press, 1985.

UNESCO. "Ruins of Kilwa Kisiwani and Ruins of Songo Mnara." UNESCO World Heritage Centre, 1992–2016, http://whc.unesco.org/en/list/144/.

Wynne-Jones, Stephanie. "Creating Urban Communities at Kilwa Kisiwani, Tanzania, AD 800–1300." *Antiquity* 81 (2007): 368–380.

Kitara

The Kitara Empire, sometimes also known as the Bacwezi Empire and the Kingdom of Bunyoro-Kitara, has existed in various forms since at least the 13th century CE. Today known as the Kingdom of Bunyoro, it spans part of western Uganda in the Bulisa, Masindi, Hoime, Kiryandongo, and Kibale districts, a little over 3,200 square miles. The approximately 1.4 million Banyoro (people of Bunyoro) are primarily agriculturalists, and most practice Christianity. Bunyoro is a constitutional monarchy, currently ruled by the *omukama* (king) Solomon Iguru I (r. 1994–present) and Prime Minister Jackson Kasozi Nsamba, who was appointed by the *omukama* in 2012.

Present-day Bunyoro-Kitara was restored from exile in 1993 and was recognized along with the Buganda, Busoga, and Toro kingdoms in the 1995 constitution. Bunyoro sits on expansive forests, making its timber industry an important part of the economy. But these forests are also being cleared at a rapid rate in order to allow for more farming of cash crops. There are also deposits of iron ore, oil, and gas that have the potential for greater economic exploitation. Still, the vast majority of Banyoro are rural dwellers who rely on subsistence farming for most of their day-to-day needs.

At its height, around the 16th century, the Kitara Empire encompassed most of present-day Uganda, parts of western Tanzania and Kenya, the eastern Democratic Republic of Congo, most of Rwanda, and parts of northern Burundi. But the empire's origins in or around the 13th century remain shrouded in mystery. The so-called Batembuzi and Bacwezi dynasties allegedly founded the kingdom, yet the rulers of these dynasties are largely considered to be mythological demigods descended directly from the heavens. The religion centered around Cwezi-Kubandwa worship is widespread in the region and had a significant impact on the development of ritual kingship in Toro, Ankole, Rwanda, and Karagwe.

Kitara had some sort of political centralization prior to the 16th century, though it is not clear because of the nature of the oral sources precisely what this organization looked like. Like many societies in the region, centralization seems to have been developed from an increasingly complex system of cattle clientship. Indeed, it is likely that the long-horned cattle that became so prized through the Great Lakes region were introduced from Bunyoro-Kitara. Through long-term climatic change between 1000 and 1450, forests slowly gave way to more pastoral land, increasing the ability of people who owned cattle to claim land and enrich themselves. This led to increased political power for herders and an entrenchment of forms of spirituality that emphasized the relationship between kingship, chiefship, and cattle.

The most important and lasting element of Kitaran culture was the worship of the Cwezi-Kubandwa spirits. The Kubandwa spirits were both good (*ezera,* meaning "white") and bad (*eziragura,* meaning "black") and could possess people, cause illness or dreams, or be prayed to in order to intercede on people's behalf. While the Cwezi "kings" found their way into many regional origin myths and helped later migrations of elites legitimize their conquests, the Kubandwas remained independent from state control, and Iris Berger argues that the Kubandwa cults created space for social protest, particularly by women.

The Kitara Empire broke into several kingdoms by the late 16th century, most notably Bunyoro. The Babito dynasty was established in Bunyoro by invaders from the east, probably Luo from western Kenya. We can somewhat accurately pinpoint the dates of these invasions based on eclipses recorded in regional oral traditions. Most notable was the invasion of 1520, which likely marks the beginning of the Babito dynasty and its first ruler, Isingoma Mpuga Rukidi I. The dynastic chronology names 27 Babito kings (*omukamas*), though there is reason to approach royal chronologies with a healthy skepticism given that they were most often used to legitimize the person currently in power and could be manipulated. Still, the *omukama* who reigns in Bunyoro today claims descent from this dynasty, meaning that there is still political power to be gained by declaring oneself part of this ancient legacy.

Though Bunyoro is not identical to the Kitara Empire, the latter's history is an integral part of Bunyoro's culture, since Kitara's foundations lie in what became Bunyoro. When Milton Obote came to power in 1967 following Ugandan independence in 1962, he moved to abolish the remaining kingdoms, including Buganda, Busoga, and Bunyoro. Many royal officials went into exile and remained there through the reigns of Obote and Idi Amin. After Yoweri Museveni's successful overthrow of Obote's second stint in power in 1986, negotiations went on for years until the adoption of a new constitution in 1995, which officially recognized four of the kingdoms that had been banned under Obote (Ankole remains unofficial). According to the 1995 constitution, the *omukama* is recognized as a cultural leader whose role in politics is limited.

Sarah E. Watkins

Further Reading

Berger, Iris. *Religion and Resistance: East African Kingdoms in the Precolonial Period.* Tervuren, Belgique: Musée royal de l'Afrique centrale 1981.
Bonte, Pierre. "'To Increase Cows, God Created the King': The Function of Cattle in Intralacustrine Societies." In *Herders, Warriors, and Traders: Pastoralism in Africa,* edited by John G. Galaty and Pierre Bonte, 82–86. Boulder, CO: Westview, 1991.
Doyle, Shane. *Crisis and Decline in Bunyoro: Population and Environment in Western Uganda, 1860–1955.* London: British Institute in Eastern Africa, 2006.
Karugire, Samwiri Rubaraza. *A Political History of Uganda.* Nairobi: Heinemann Educational Books, 1980.
Rennie, J. K. *The Banyoro Invasions and Interlacustrine Chronology.* Los Angeles: African Studies Center, University of California, 1973.
Robertshaw, Peter. "Seeking and Keeping Power in Bunyoro-Kitara, Uganda." In *Beyond Chiefdoms: Pathways to Complexity in Africa,* edited by Susan Keech McIntosh, 124–135. Cambridge: Cambridge University Press, 1999.
Schoenbrun, David Lee. *A Green Place, A Good Place: Agrarian Change, Gender, and Social Identity in the Great Lakes Region to the 15th Century.* Portsmouth, NH: Heinemann, 1998.

Vidal, Claudine. "Le Rwanda des anthropologues ou le fétichisme de la vache." *Cahiers d'Etudes Africaines* 9(3) (1969): 384–401.

Kom

Kom is one of the largest kingdoms (*fondoms*) or chiefdoms in northwest Cameroon in West Africa. Kom covers 280 square miles and shares its eastern boundary with the Kingdom of Oku and Nso and its southern frontier with Kedjom Keku (also known as Big Babanki) and the Ndop Plain. Bafut is on the western border, while to the north are Bum and Mmen. Kom is located in the heart of the savanna that the Germans named the Bamenda Grassfields and has an ecology that is grassy and interspersed with trees in the valleys.

The ancestors of Kom migrated from Ndobo in northern Cameroon with other Tikar groups to Babessi, where they settled temporarily. A popular legend recounts their movement from Babessi to their present settlement and states that while the Kom people were at Babessi, their presence was seen as threatening. The king of Babessi therefore devised a trick to eliminate them. One day the king of Babessi told the king of Kom that some of their people were becoming obstinate and might cause a war between the two groups. He therefore proposed that they should each build a house in which the troublemakers would be burned. The king of Kom, Muni, agreed to the plan, and the houses were constructed accordingly. But while the king of Babessi constructed his house with two doors, the naive Muni built his own house according to what was agreed, with only one door. After locking the front doors, the houses were set ablaze. Oral tradition states that in his anger and frustration, Muni promised his remnant wives and sisters that he would avenge the death of his people. He told them that he would hang himself on a tree in a nearby forest and on that spot a lake would emerge and all the maggots from his decomposing body would turn into fish there. The lake was discovered by a Babessi hunter and immediately reported to the palace. A royal fishing expedition was organized. At the peak of the fishing the lake somersaulted, and all the Babessi people present drowned. Following Muni's instructions, a python's track, believed to be the incarnated king, led the Kom people from Babessi to Nkar and Idien in the present-day Bui division of the northwestern region of Cameroon. At Idien they settled near a stream beside a raffia bush. There the queen mother, Tih, bore a son who was to be the next king. That son was called Jingjua, meaning "suffering." She also gave birth to Nange Tih, the future mother of the Ikui clan; Nakhinti Tih, the future mother of Itinalah and Ndzitewa Tih, the future mother of the Achaff clan. Once the python trail reappeared, the Kom people left Idien for Ajung, where the python's trail disappeared again. At Ajung the king of Ajung married Nangeh Tih and bore Jinabo, Nangebo, Nyanga, and Bi. After a while the python's track reappeared, and the Kom people left for Laikom. From Idien, the trekkers moved through the Ijim forest and reached Laikom, where they finally settled.

The first *fon* (king) of Kom was Jinabo I, son of Nandong. At Laikom, also known as Kom country, three compounds were constructed that gave rise to three other clans: namely the upper compound, which gave birth to the Ekwu clan; the lower compound, which gave birth to the Intinalah clan; and the marshland compound, which gave birth to the Achaf clan. These compounds formed the nucleus of the Kom kingdom, which was later expanded. According to Kom traditions, some royals migrated out of Laikom and founded new settlements at Abuh, Njinikom, Yang, and Alim. The possible reasons for this early expansion by the mid-18th century were population growth and the desire for farmland and hunting grounds. Witches, wizards, and other people who were ostracized from the settlement at Laikom also founded new settlements. Njinikom, which means "on the other side of Komland," was one such settlement and is still considered a refuge for dissident exiles from Laikom. These early settlers at Laikom had displaced the aboriginal Ndonaliis, who later took refuge at Achain. Their first challenge came from an attack by the Mejang people. They had planned to attack and occupy Laikom when Kom men were on a hunting expedition at Akeh but failed because Kom women disguised and dressed like men repulsed them. That victory was later followed up by the men who attacked the Mejangs at Mbam and displaced them. Thereafter, Fon Kumambong (ca. 1785–ca. 1805), the successor of Jinabo I, occupied Mbam.

The 19th century was the height of Kom power, as Kom fought with and displaced most of its neighbors. In the Belo Valley the first group to be displaced was the Nkwens, who were evicted out of Dzie-Nkwen. In circa 1845 the Kedjom people were expelled from Belo and took refuge in the southern part of the Kom kingdom. Farther south, smaller kingdoms were subjugated and brought under Kom control. These areas became vassals to the Kom kingdom and included Baiso, Mbengkas, Mbueni, and Mejang. Besides their rich soils, suitable especially for oil palms and palm oil, the area also abounded with game, which constituted part of the menu of the Kom palace. The animals included elephants, leopards, and lions. In return, Kom gave protection to these satellite groups against Bafut, which also had an interest in conquering these areas.

By the end of the 19th century, the Kom kingdom had 42 villages and 10 vassal states. The population of these villages increased in the second decade of the 20th century from 5,570 in 1921 to 13,454 in 1928, recording a marked increase of 7,884. That increase seemed to have been caused by the Fulani raids that were unleashed by the jihadists from the north of Cameroon. They terrorized many groups in the Ndop Plain, causing them to flee for safety into Kom. Security, unity, and peace also attracted many people from neighboring groups into Kom who distinguished themselves in the Ambena, Ndowum, Ndokang, Ndo-Egayn, No-Wambong, Mejang, and Ndo Nambang clans.

The territorial and demographic expansion of Kom was finally achieved by Fon Yuh I (1865–1912), who not only gave military protection to Mejang, Mejung, Baiso, Baicham, and Mbengkas against Bafut harassment but also raided Bafut for slaves. In that venture, Kom became the main provider of slaves from the Bamenda Grassfields to the middlemen trading with the coastal area. After strengthening Kom hegemony in the south, Yuh turned to the northern part of Kom and attacked Din, which is located today in the Bui division. Its ruler was captured and taken to the royal compound of Fuli, and some of his people were handed over to the ruler of Mbesinaku. Din was temporarily placed under Akeh, one of the vassal states of Kom.

The main economic activities of Kom were agriculture, local industry, and trade. Agricultural production was mainly in the hands of the women, who produced enough food for local needs. Men helped in the clearing of the farms. Crops cultivated included cocoyams (*Colocasia antiquorum*), yams (*Dioscorea dumetorum*), native carrot (*Coleus dazo*), sweet potatoes (*Ipomoea batatas*), cassava (*Manihot utilissima*), native spinach (*Solanum nodiflorum*), okra (*Hibiscus esculentus*), egusi (*Lagenaria vulgaris*), and groundnuts (*Arachis hypogea*). Maize was the staple Kom diet food and has remained the only crop that is cultivated twice a year. These various crops suggest that Kom was never an island and indicate the entanglement of Kom with other parts of the globe through mobility.

Industry included the manufacturing of local crafts, carvings, and mats. Specialized skills or talents were required for one to become a carver, an important profession in precolonial Kom. Carvers produced chairs, stools, door posts, masks, wooden bowls, mortars, pestles, staffs, camwood, mixing bowls, and a wide range of local needs. Kom was prominent in carving and is noted for a carving school. One of the most famous of these schools was founded and directed by King Yuh. This school produced the *Afo-a-Kom,* a wooden statue the size and height of a normal human being, one of the finest pieces of art in the Bamenda Grassfields.

The political organization of the Kom kingdom was very hierarchical. At the apex of the kingdom's sociopolitical and economic affairs was the king, whose powers were sacred. He ruled the kingdom with the help and respect of his people. His compound housed his wives, children, pages, guards, and advisers. He was respected with many praise and honorific names, including *mbai* (lord), *lum nyam* (greatest creature), *cha-mufor* (great man), and *nyamabo* (leopard). Diviners of the kingdom who were in constant contact with the spirit world were expected to initiate the new

Kom mask, wood and pigment, Cameroon, early 20th century. (Yale University Art Gallery)

king into his new role. His authority over all the vassal states was unquestionable. He was closely guided by the *nkwifoyn,* the executive arm of the traditional government. The *nkwifoyn* checked the excesses of the king, and the king also checked the excesses of *nkwifoyn.* This promoted checks and balances in government. In the villages, 42 in number, the king was assisted in the discharge of his duties by the village heads (*ibonteh;* sing. *bonteh*), who were the founders of the villages. The village heads were representatives of the king and reported anything that could threaten the peace. They also executed the orders of the king and the *nkwifoyn* in their villages and maintained law and order. Although most village heads did not owe their office to the king, all were required to present themselves and pay allegiance to him as soon as they were installed as heads by the *nkwifoyn.*

The Kom encounter with colonialism ruptured Kom society more profoundly. Kom fell under German and British colonial administration. The precolonial period, with its commercial and political hierarchies in trade and other activities, was shaken. For example, in the colonial situation the old hierarchies—which included the king, the *nkwifoyn,* and quarter heads—were reinforced, and the structures that were put in place, such as the wider roads and missionary schools, accelerated geographical mobility patterns. The king, who was at the summit of power before the arrival of the Germans and was checked only by the *nkwifoyn,* was now under colonial control, answerable to the colonial authorities. The British took over one-fifth of the Cameroons from the Germans in 1916. The rest was taken over by the French. In 1922 the British created Native Authorities in the most densely populated areas of the Cameroons Province, and Kom was one of them. In 1927 Christianity was introduced into Kom, although with some resistance by the Kom people. In September 1939, World War II broke out in Europe. Many Kom people were recruited into the British Army. In the mid-1950s, the so-called winds of change—decolonization and the idea of independence for African colonies—were already blowing across Africa. The demand for independence became more intense. Kom elites strongly participated in the demand for independence through their membership of political parties in Kom. One such party, the Kamerun National Democratic Party, which won the 1959 election, had a strong stronghold in Kom. Cameroon gained independence from colonial rule in 1961. Following the new administrative decentralization of Cameroon in 1992, the Boyo division was created out of the Kom kingdom by Decree No. 92/186 of January 9, 1992, and was further divided into three subdivisions: Belo, with Belo as the capital; Njinikom, with its capital in Njinikom; and Fundong, which doubled as the capital of the Boyo division and the Fundong subdivisions.

In 1993, the reconstruction of the Bamenda-Fundong road began. This time it was a bituminous road. The construction was completed in 1998, and this greatly facilitated movement in and out of Kom and further transformation. The completion of the road also coincided with the introduction of cell phones in 2000. The interconnections developed between a wider tarred road, and cell phones led to significant social change in Kom hitherto unknown in its history.

Walter Gam Nkwi

Further Reading

Chilver, E. M. "The Kingdom of Kom in West Cameroon." In *West African Kingdoms in the Nineteenth Century,* edited by Daryll Forde and P. M. Kaberry, 123–151. Oxford: Oxford University Press, 1967.

Chilver, E. M. *Zintgraff's Exploration in Bamenda, Adamawa and the Benue Lands, 1889– 1892.* Buea, Cameroon: Ministry of Primary Education and Social Welfare and West Cameroon Antiquities Commission, 1966.

Nkwi, Paul Nchoji. *Traditional Government and Social Change: A Study of the Political Institutions among the Kom of the Cameroon Grassfields.* Fribourg: University of Fribourg Press, 1976.

Nkwi, Paul Nchoji, and Jean Pierre Warnier. *Elements for History of the Western Grassfields.* Yaounde, Cameroon: Publication of the Department of Sociology, University of Yaounde, 1982.

Nkwi, Walter Gam. *African Modernities and Mobilities: An Ethnographic History of Kom, Cameroon, c. 1800–2008.* Mankon, Bamenda: Langaa RCIPG, 2015.

Nkwi, Walter Gam. *Kfaang with Its Technologies: Towards a Social History of Mobility in Kom, Cameroon, 1928–1998.* Leiden: ASC Publication, 2011.

Kong

The town of Kong, with a current population of about 29,000 (2014), is located in the northeast of the contemporary country of Côte d'Ivoire (Ivory Coast). Kong's place in the historical literature and oral traditions is due to the two politically and economically dominant immigrant groups of the region—the Jula (Dyula) and Sonongui peoples, who settled in the ethnically complex region of predominantly Gur-speaking farming and hunting groups. These are Mandekan-speaking groups who became clearly differentiated by their value systems, occupations, appearance (with and without patronymic-specific facial scarification), and residences. Kong was a Jula town and an economic center, while the politically dominant Sonongui lived in various surrounding and widely dispersed villages. The Jula had moved into the area at least by the 16th century and were well known for their success in trade and cotton weaving and dyeing as well as for Islamic scholarship. The Mandekan-speaking Sonongui cavalry warriors followed them in the mid to late 17th century. These two groups made Kong famous among West Africans and also among some Europeans searching for the nonexistent "mountains of Kong," which appear in numerous European maps to the end of the 19th century. In 1888, the first European to enter the town, Louis Binger, remarked that these elusive mountains did not exist. And so the mountains disappeared from the maps.

Kong is situated in the southern savanna climate zone, with one rainy season from June to October and one dry season from November to May. Rainfall averages 53 inches a year, with 41 percent of the rains falling in August and September. Historical climate studies are not rich for this region, so much of these data come from 20th-century studies. The average temperature is 80 degrees Fahrenheit, but in December and January temperatures in the upper 40 degrees Fahrenheit can occur. The Komoé River and its tributaries provide the main river system, but many of the streams are dry for part of the year. Transport was done primarily through headloading, though donkeys were used by long-distance traders passing through.

Vegetation in the region is that of a boundary zone between the savanna and the forest. Trees do not grow to great heights, and most of the groundcover consists of grasses, with a wide seasonal variety in grass height and thickness. As in much of West Africa, the soils are laterite with low silica and high iron content. Farmers used shifting cultivation, which means that farming village sites did move throughout history, often keeping their original place-names while changing their physical sites. Primary food crops before the introduction of American crops (such as corn/maize, peanuts, tomatoes, potatoes, and beans) were yams, millet, sorghum, fonio, and okra. All of these Old World crops continue to be cultivated in the region along with the more recently introduced American and Asian crops, including mangos from Asia. The Jula introduced cotton from the north, and it became an important revenue-producing crop for the Jula cotton industry. The Gur/Senoufo groups welcomed the introduction of cotton cloth, as oral traditions make clear, and prized it in burial customs.

There is much wild game in the region, and hunting is important in the traditions of all peoples resident there, though it is currently illegal in the country. The ivory from the elephants that used to be numerous, killed by Sonongui and Gur hunters, was an important trade item for the Jula in the past. The Sonongui leadership demanded one tusk from each elephant killed. Goats, sheep, chickens, and guinea hens were also raised by most families. Cattle herding was difficult due to the presence of the trypanosomiasis-carrying tsetse fly. The Sonongui warrior group was a horse-mounted cavalry force. Maintaining a horse in the current tsetse environment of Kong would be impossible without now-available inoculations. In all likelihood, tsetse flies have advanced in the region in the 20th century due to ecological changes. In addition, the Sonongui moved their horses out of danger to the north or into enclosed structures during the rainy season. Also, boys were given the task of brushing flies off the horses and pack animals.

Kong is well situated to be a trading point between two ecological zones, savanna and forest, and is close to both the Akan and Black Volta or "Lobi" goldfields. In addition to its location close to gold deposits, Kong is northwest and north of two rich kola-producing zones. Kola is important as a permissible stimulant (high in caffeine and theobromine) for Muslim peoples and is of great importance in trade. Kong thus developed as a major trade point linking these southern gold and kola areas to the Niger River trading ports, such as Jenne and Timbuktu. The Jula also were known for their trade in salt, which was not available in the region from local sources. Oral traditions indicate the desire for salt of the farming groups in this southern savanna zone and their allowance of Jula settlement due to the Jula access to salt obtained from the well-known Saharan rock salt deposits of Taghaza and Taodeni. The Jula are also well remembered as slave traders in the region, trading slaves obtained by the raiding of the Sonongui both to the Akan of the contemporary nation of Ghana and north to other slave-using and -trading peoples. The Jula also used slave labor extensively in the 19th century as domestic, farming, and trade-assistant labor. As with many areas of West Africa, when the Europeans outlawed the transatlantic slave trade, domestic slavery increased. Kong is approximately 400 miles from the Atlantic coast. This distance is the reason for the lack of direct slave-trading contact with European slave traders in the historical sources. Undoubtedly, the people raided by the Sonongui warriors did make their way into the transatlantic slave trade.

The founder of the Kong state is given the name Seku Watara by oral traditions and more recently produced Arabic manuscripts. Seku's descendants, then, became the inheritors of the political leadership of the state. In a patrilineal succession system, the founder's heirs were known as the *jamanatigi,* chief (*tigi*) of the *jamana* (land/state). The French colonists, beginning at the start of the 20th century, continued to use the state structures of the Kong state or empire, allowing the maintenance of the *jamanatigi* position, which was continued by the independent country of Côte d'Ivoire. Many of the conquered peoples in the Kong hegemony adopted the Watara patronym. The Watara leadership was said to rule because of *fanga* (physical force). This leadership headed cavalry warring groups, which incorporated people from various groups who made their living through raids, hunting, and slave trading and protection of Jula trade caravans. A clear distinction was made between the two groups, and the Sonongui were frequently described in traditions as not being Muslim, since they were hard drinkers and engaged in war without religious sanctions. A strong effort is made now to undo this non-Islamic past in oral traditions.

The Jula were ethnically related traders, weavers, and Islamic scholars. Kong was part of a well-developed Islamic scholarship network in West Africa, and students traveled far to study there with resident scholars, as they did in Jenne, Timbuktu, and other centers in the West African savanna areas. The Sonongui protected the pilgrims even as slave trading continued to grow, making travel in the 19th century sometimes quite dangerous. The textile art of the Jula is well known, and their woven pieces appear in museums throughout the world. In addition, the Jula were known for distinctive mud architecture for their mosques.

In the late 18th and early 19th centuries there was a clear division of the Watara family, with a competing sister polity developing around Bobo Dioulasso, the trading and Islamic scholarship center to the north in contemporary Burkina Faso. Family and scholarship ties remained, but political disputes often interrupted trade and discourse.

Samori Toure, a Malinke warrior and resistance leader against the French, settled to the south of Kong in about 1895 and then in 1897 destroyed the town, killing hundreds among the Jula families who had taken refuge in the mosque. The Sonongui did not live in Kong and were therefore saved from this attack. Samori Toure, who is vaunted in resistance literature for West Africa, is thus not fondly remembered by the people of Kong. Anger over the lack of protection afforded the Jula by the Sonongui in this instance is also related in oral traditions.

The period of French rule in this region was short, lasting only about 60 years. In that time a railroad was built linking the coastal capital of Abidjan with the Burkina Faso cities of Bobo Dioulasso and Ouagadougou. The Islamic leadership of Kong, fearing non-Muslim forces controlling the state, elected to refuse to have the railroad pass through the town. It thus was built to pass through a Senufo town, Ferkessedougou, about 100 kilometers to the west. Ferkessedougou has since grown exponentially. Tourists sometimes visit the mosque, which they are not normally allowed to enter, and continue on their way. There are no hotels or restaurants to receive them, maintaining the tradition of Islamic separatism, which is not embraced by the younger generations without political authority. This leads to great out-migration and a continued dwindling of the population.

Kathryn L. Green

Further Reading

Bassett, Thomas J., and Philip W. Porter. "'From the Best Authorities': The Mountains of Kong in the Cartography of West Africa." *Journal of African History* 32 (1991): 367–413.

Bernus, Edmond. "Kong et sa région." *Etudes éburnéennes* 8 (1960): 239–324.

Binger, Louis-Gustave. *Du Niger au golfe de Guinée par le pays de Kong et le Mossi.* 2 vols. Paris: Hachette, 1892.

Green, Kathryn L. "Dyula and Sonongui Roles in the Islamization of the Region of Kong." *Asian and African Studies* 20 (1986): 103–123.

Green, Kathryn L. "The Foundation of Kong: A Study in Dyula and Sonongui Ethnic Identity." PhD dissertation, Indiana University, 1984.

Şaul, Mahir. "The War Houses of the Watara in West Africa." *International Journal of African Historical Studies* 31(8) (1998): 537–570.

Wilks, Ivor. "A Medieval Trade-Route from the Niger to the Gulf of Guinea." *Journal of African History* 3 (1962): 337–341.

Kongo

The history of the Kingdom of Kongo is very important because it offers a remarkable and valuable insight into the early encounter and relationship between Europe and Africa. Founded by Lukeni Lua Nimi in the 14th century, the Kongo kingdom became one of the largest and most powerful states in Central Africa during the 15th and 16th centuries. It was located on the western coast of Central Africa, specifically in portions of the modern-day African states of Angola, the Republic of Congo, and the Democratic Republic of Congo. The kingdom was divided into six important provinces: Soyo, Mbata, Nsundi, Mpangu, Mbamba, and Mpemba. Most of the population lived in villages around the capital city, Mbanza Kongo. The first Portuguese travelers who arrived in Mbanza Kongo described the capital not only as a large and densely populated city surrounded by rain forests but also as an

Nkisi N'Kondi/Mangaaka

Nkisi N'Kondi, or Mangaaka, power figures are considered one of the most distinctive landmarks in Kongo culture. In response to incursions by colonial traders, Kongo chiefs developed an impressive set of power figures as defense mechanisms along the Central African coast. These sculptural creations, made out of wood, iron, resin, ceramic, plant fibers, and textiles, were meant to intimidate and inspire great fear. Sculptors and ritual specialists worked together to create these magical charms that, for the most part, were studded with nails or blades to indicate how often they have been used.

important popular place for trade among all the people who lived in the various parts of the Congo River's huge basin.

The economic structure of the kingdom was primarily defined by a centralized system of taxation characterized by a hierarchy of collectors. Village chiefs collected taxes from people in villages and brought them to provincial governors. These governors were instructed to gather all the resources that were collected in villages and bring them to the king, who rewarded the governors with gifts. Within the kingdom, agriculture was the basis of production. The whole community in each village owned lands, and each harvest was divided among families, with a portion set aside for the payment of taxes.

The Kingdom of Kongo was ruled by kings called *mani-kongos*. When Lukeni Lua Nimi, the hero-founder of the kingdom, died, his brother Mbokani Mavinga took over the throne, conquered new territories, and expanded the kingdom to include the neighboring state of Loango. The kingdom was characterized by a rigid social class system that included the aristocracy, free people, and slaves. Unlike the slaves in Western civilizations who labored for their masters while being housed and fed, slaves in the Kongo kingdom, mostly obtained by wars of conquest, fed themselves and their families on land that they planted on their own account.

In 1483 the Portuguese explorer Diogo Cão was the first European to enter the Congo River and encounter the Kingdom of Kongo. After landing in the Congo estuary near a city called Mbanza Sonyo, Diogo Cão sent messengers and gifts to the king, Nzinga Nkuwu, who lived in the capital, Mbanza Kongo. After several weeks as his messengers were not returning, Diogo Cão decided to continue his journey and traveled 700 miles south. He later on returned to the mouth of the Congo, seized four Kongo nobles, and sailed for Portugal. In 1485 Diogo Cão set off again from Lisbon and returned to the Kongo kingdom with the four African nobles who, after spending nearly two years in Portugal, had been converted to Christianity and taught to speak some Portuguese. This time Diogo Cão traveled inland to Mbanza Kongo, where he met the king, who was greatly impressed not only by all the gifts the explorer brought from Portugal but also by the change that occurred in the lives of the four Kongo nobles.

The contact between the Kongo king and the Europeans had important and long-lasting consequences for the African kingdom. Diogo Cão returned to the Kongo capital city in 1491 and brought along with him Portuguese missionaries, monks, armed soldiers, masons, carpenters, peasants, and some women who had to instruct the Kongo people in Portuguese housekeeping. Soon the missionaries converted thousands of Kongo people to Christianity and baptized them, including King Nzinga Nkuwu, who decided to take the name João I in honor of Portugal's king at the time, João II. João I ruled over the Kongo kingdom until 1506 and at his death was succeeded by his son Afonso Mvemba a Nzinga (famously known as Afonso I). The new king, Mani-Kongo Afonso I, who was raised as a Christian, worked hard to convert the whole kingdom to Christianity and European ways. As he was able to write and speak Portuguese, between 1509 and 1541 Afonso I sent several letters to kings, government officials, and church leaders in Lisbon, Rome, and the Vatican. All of those letters have been crucial in offering great insight into the social and political life of the Kingdom of Kongo.

Establishing Christianity as the state religion, Afonso I renamed the capital city São Salvador and made important arrangements for the creation of Kongo schools, where children of nobles received religious instruction. He sent Henrique, his own son, to be educated in Europe, and in 1518 Henrique became an ordained priest and, later on, the first Kongo bishop. By the end of his rule, Afonso I had successfully created a new version of the Roman Catholic Church in his kingdom.

Because of the strong links that Afonso I was able to forge with Portugal, the relationships between the Portuguese and the Kongo people continued to be those of mutual respect for many decades. However, toward the end of the reign of Afonso I because of the high demands of the slave trade, the links between Portugal and the Kongo kingdom began to deteriorate. Portuguese were no longer willing to send to Kongo priests, doctors, or guns as gifts. Instead, they demanded slaves in exchange for anything that King Afonso I requested from Portugal. To meet the demands, the Kongo king undertook raids into neighboring territories to capture people and sell them into slavery. A greater instability was created within the Kingdom of Kongo when Portuguese traders, mostly interested in increasing their private fortunes, began to bypass the king in Mbanza Kongo and trade directly with provincial nobles and local officials. Consequently, the coastal province of Soyo became the most important point of purchase, sale, and embarkation for slaves. Receiving African captives from several sources, Portuguese traders were able to increase the number of slaves they sent to the New World to work the plantations. It is estimated that the Kingdom of Kongo alone in the 16th and 17th centuries was sending about 15,000 slaves annually.

Afonso I wrote several long letters to the king of Portugal to complain about the harsh treatment that his people received at the hands of Portuguese traders but received for the most part dismissive responses from Europe. Despite several restrictions that he introduced on the slave trade in his kingdom, thousands of captives continued to be illegally exported annually, causing severe destruction of the social structure of the kingdom and weakening the authority of the king.

Afonso's death in late 1542 or early 1543 was followed by fierce competition over succession to the throne, since all the successors faced serious problems with factional rivals from various family clans. The Kingdom of Kongo eventually suffered several major civil wars and declined rapidly. Following the battles between rival provinces, the capital city São Salvador was burned to the ground in 1678. All the villages around the capital were depopulated as people, seeking refuge from the conflicts, dispersed into the forests and mountains. By the end of the 17th century the Kingdom of Kongo suffered several other invasions and interventions by Portuguese forces, causing the kingdom to disintegrate into a number of less powerful small states, all controlled to varying degrees by Portugal. Eventually the territory of the Kingdom of Kongo was incorporated mostly into Angola and the independent state of Congo.

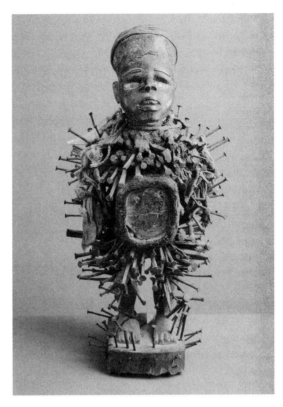

Kongo power figure (*Nkisi Nkondi*), wood, iron, cloth, mirror, leopard tooth, fiber, and porcelain, 18th–19th century. (Yale University Art Gallery)

Daniel Kahozi

Further Reading

Hilton, Anne. *The Kingdom of Kongo*. Oxford, UK: Clarendon, 1985.

Pigafetta, Filippo. *A Report of the Kingdom of Kongo and the Surrounding Countries*. London: Frank Cass, 1881.

Thornton, K. John. *The Kingdom of Kongo: Civil War and Transition 1641–1718*. Madison: University of Wisconsin Press, 1983.

Kuba

The Kuba kingdom is located in the present-day Democratic Republic of Congo, between the Lulua, Kasai, and Sankuru Rivers. A multiethnic kingdom, it emerged as a confederation of smaller kingdoms and chiefdoms in the 17th century and grew in power until it was colonized by the Belgians in the late 19th century. Most Bakuba (people of Kuba) are Bashongo speakers, though others in the kingdom including groups of Twa Pygmies speak other languages. The current ruler of Kuba, known as the *nyim,* is Kot-a-Bweeky III, who ascended the throne in 1969.

Kuba lies in a tropical zone between three rivers. It is a heavily forested region, with many types of palm trees from which the famous Kuba textiles are manufactured. Today, Bakuba cultivate corn and oil palms as cash crops and also grow crops such as cassava, millet, groundnuts, and beans as subsistence staples. Historically Kuba was heavily involved in trade, being strategically located on river routes. Bakuba traded raffia cloth and other textiles, cowrie shells, and wooden cups and boxes that were ornate and much sought after. In return they incorporated new agricultural products into their communities, including New World crops such as manioc (cassava), tobacco, and corn. The savannas in Kuba's territory were ideal for growing these crops as well as for mining iron ore and for pottery clay for the art that would make Kuba famous.

The name "Kuba" was given by the Bakuba's southern neighbors, the Luba. The name was also used by Europeans but not by the Bakuba themselves. They referred to themselves merely as "people of the king," but not by one unifying moniker. This is likely because as a confederation of smaller groups, Kuba shared a unified political system but not a single culture. The Bashongo and most of the other Kuba groups—excluding the Cwa, Coofa, and Mbeengi—practiced matrilineal descent, and families were patrilocal. This meant that inheritance was passed through the mother's line but that men lived with their fathers until the father died and then moved to the mother's brother's village.

The Kuba kingdom emerged from a loose confederation around 1625, when Shyaam aMbul aNgoong, from the Bashong ethnic group, began the process of centralization. The history of Kuba took the form of oral literature, including narratives, poetry, and songs, and was meticulously remembered and taught through generations. In addition to the oral literature of the kingdom, each chiefdom, village, and clan had its own literature and its own people designated to preserve them. For the kingdom, the main figures in maintaining the transmission of the oral literature were the king himself; the *muyum,* or chief ritual practitioner; the *mwaddy,* or eldest living son of the king; and the woman who taught all the king's wives the royal songs relating to nature spirits and the list of queen mothers. As Jan Vansina argues, these types of royal rituals—especially lists of kings and queen mothers—were methods of legitimation: by presenting the history of the kingdom as an unbroken chain of hereditary rulers, these traditions stabilized the rule of the current king and made it more difficult for him to be challenged or overthrown.

Shyaam aMbul aNgoong was said to be the adoptive son of a Bashong queen mother. The queen mother was a regular feature of many African monarchies, though she was not always the biological mother of the king; in Asante, for example, the queen mother (*asantehemaa*) was a woman from the king's matrilineage, often an aunt or cousin. Shyaam was born to Mbul aNgoong, who was an enslaved woman. He traveled extensively during his youth to the surrounding cultures of

Pende, Leele, Ding, and Mbuun. Shyaam learned many things from these peoples that he brought back to Bashong and implemented there, including how to make palm wine, a stick used as a mnemonic device to remember fines, many charms that would help bolster his claim to the kingship, and seeds to grow maize, tobacco, millet, sorghum, and cassava.

As Vansina rightly points out, much of the mythology surrounding Shyaam is crafted specifically to legitimize his overthrow of the previous political order and the establishment of Kuba. But Shyaam was also clearly a transformational figure who brought with him the fruits of his extensive travels: new crops, new artistic and agricultural techniques, and trade contacts that would create wealth within his new kingdom. The two kings who came after Shyaam, Mboong aLeeng and MboMboosh, expanded the boundaries of the new kingdom through warfare, trade, and marriage and ruled cumulatively until 1680, when Kuba entered what Vansina calls the "Classical Period." The kings of this period are not well remembered beyond their names and the names of the capitals they founded throughout the kingdom.

Like many African kings, the king of Kuba was first and foremost a priest, or ritual practitioner. He was considered the highest of the priests in the kingdom and sometimes more—Shyaam was thought of as a spirit, just like those with which he communed. Kingship itself was the crucial element of Bakuba identity—there was, in fact, no unifying identity outside of allegiance to the office of the king. Through the two and a half centuries it existed prior to colonization in the 1880s, the rituals associated with kingship in Kuba became more and more elaborate. Vansina demonstrates this through his description of the burial rituals following a king's death. These ceremonies took a year and involved every segment of the population.

The investment of the people in the institution of kingship stemmed from regional understandings of what the king represented, all of which can be traced back to official histories of Shyaam. This loyalty to the king produced long-term political stability, and this can be credited with the incredible profusion of Kuba artistic innovation that endured throughout this period. Kuba artwork is one of the most ubiquitous and recognizable forms of African art and is featured prominently in some of the world's most important collections, including New York's Metropolitan Museum of Art. This artwork includes intricate woven textiles, wooden cups and containers, and most especially a red basket decorated with cowrie shells and beads, which is meant to signify the basket of knowledge from the Kuba origin story.

Unlike its Atlantic neighbors Kongo and Ndongo, Kuba was not affected significantly by the Atlantic slave trade and continued to flourish up until European contact in the 1880s. However, after this Kuba went into decline, which was compounded by the massacres during the invasion by the Nsapo people, or Zappo Zaps, a group from the Kasai region who worked for King Leopold II's Congo Free State. In 1899 the Zappo Zaps under the leadership of Mulumba Nkusu invaded Kuba, demanding tribute in the form of rubber. The chiefs in the Pyang region refused to pay what they saw as an unreasonable tribute, and in September 1899 the Zappo

Zaps looted and burned their way through the region. In a story that ran in the *New York Times* in January 1900, Reverend William Henry Sheppard described seeing evidence of cannibalism, mutilation, and at least 60 women confined to a pen. According to Adam Hochschild, this type of abuse was a regular occurrence during Leopold's rule in the Congo Free State, of which Kuba became a part during this period.

Kuba remained a recognized kingdom under Belgian rule after 1908, after its population was severely depleted due to the depredations of Leopold's Congo Free State. Kuba was semiautonomous during the Belgian period, which lasted until Congo's independence in 1960. The Kuba kings impressed the Belgian administration with their internal unity, artistic innovation, and resourcefulness. They were able to use these qualities to negotiate some concessions under indirect rule, especially as the political and economic climate changed with the coming of the Kasai railroad to Bakuba territory, the Great Depression, and the realignment of European priorities following World War II. Urban dwellers in the Kuba capital of Nsheng lived relatively comfortable lives, as they surrounded the royal court and administration. But the compulsory colonial labor that built up the commercial infrastructure and connected Kuba to the rest of Congo fell harshly on its rural subjects.

Though the kingdom continued to exist through the end of colonialism and into the independence era, its autonomy was increasingly weakened under Mobutu Sese Seko's Zairean state. Though attempts were made, particularly during the Conférance Nationale Souverain in 1991, to restore some level of authority to indigenous polities, these ultimately failed. Kuba today is a fully incorporated part of the Democratic Republic of Congo and works with regional partners in Kasai to support economic policies that will modernize its infrastructure and administration.

Sarah E. Watkins

Further Reading

Hochschild, Adam. *King Leopold's Ghost: A Story of Greed, Terror, and Heroism in Colonial Africa.* Boston: Houghton Mifflin, 1998.

Josefsson, Claes. *Politics of Chaos: Essays on Kuba Myth, Development and Death.* Goteborg: Socialantropologiska institutionen Goteborgs Universitet, 1994.

Vansina, Jan. *Being Colonized: The Kuba Experience in Rural Congo, 1880–1960.* Madison: University of Wisconsin Press, 2010.

Vansina, Jan. *The Children of Woot: A History of the Kuba Peoples.* Madison: University of Wisconsin Press, 1978.

Kush

The origin of the term "Kush" is unknown. However, the name "Kush" was referenced in Middle Egyptian in an Egyptian text written from 2000 BCE to 1300 BCE as *küsi*. Mentuhotep II, the Egyptian pharaoh who founded the Middle Kingdom in the 24th century BCE, waged military campaigns against the Kushites. "Kush" is used in a geographical sense to refer to inhabitants called the Nehesys—that is, the people who inhabited the river valley—as opposed to the Mejays, who occupied the wadis in the Eastern Desert. "Kush" also referred to the region south of the first cataract. Kushites are mentioned in the Bible and were well known to the Romans at early period. The Kush people are an indigenous African population and one of the earliest civilizations to develop in the Nile River Valley. They are located in what is today North Sudan. Kush peoples have occupied the middle portion of the Nile Valley since at least 6000 BCE and likely much longer. At least one Egyptian inscription refers to Kush by the old Egyptian term for the area south of the frontier, Ta Sety, meaning "the Land of the Bow."

Kushite tradition is one of the oldest in the world. Most of what we know about the history of Kush comes from archaeology, especially the pioneer work of George Reisner and Charles Bonnet. The Kushites founded a number of kingdoms in the Nile River Valley, which at times ruled independent of Egypt. The civilization of Kush represented an indigenous culture that also incorporated elements borrowed from its northern neighbor, Egypt, and from deeper into the south of the African continent. The Kushites buried their kings along with their possessions, servants, family members, and courtiers. A burial practice common to the people is what archaeologists refer to as "pan-grave culture." This involved digging pits and placing stones around them in a circle. Kushites also built burial mounds and pyramids and shared some of the same gods worshipped in Egypt, especially Amun and Isis. The Kush rulers were regarded as guardians of the state religion and were responsible for maintaining the temples.

Around 727 BCE, the Kushite king Piye (also known as Piankhy) invaded Egypt and seized control of Thebes and eventually the Delta. This is the Twenty-Fifth Dynasty of Egypt or the period of the "Black Pharaoh," that continued until about 671 BCE, when the Kushites were defeated by the Neo-Assyrian Empire. Following the defeat the Twenty-Fifth Dynasty was moved to Napata, in Nubia, which is now Sudan. The Kushite kingdom reached the apex of its glory during the reigns of Piye and his successor, Taharka (Taharqa), the two early pharaohs of the Twenty-Fifth Dynasty. This dynasty ushered in the renaissance period of ancient Egypt. Religion, the arts, and architecture were restored to their old glory. For example, Taharka built or restored temples and pyramids throughout the Nile Valley, including in places such as Memphis, Karnak, Kawa, Jebel Barkal, etc. Writing was introduced to Kush through Egyptian influence in about 700–600 BCE, although this was mostly confined to the royal court and major temples. By 700 BCE, war between Kush and the Assyrians erupted. Between 674 and 671 BCE the Assyrians succeeded in driving Taharka from power; he fled to Napata, where he died a few years later. One of the famous descendants of Taharka was his great-grandson, Aspelta, who ruled from 600 to 580 BCE. About 591 BCE the Egyptians invaded Nubia, and Aspelta's armies were defeated. His new palace in Napata was destroyed, and he was forced to relocate south to Meroë.

Far from the reach of enemy forces and unable to return to Egypt, the Kushites established a royal court in Meroë. It is possible that Meroë had always been the Kushite capital or a royal center of some sort. But it is also believed that the Kushite rulers may have chosen Meroë as their political center because it had enough wood to provide fuel for ironworking. Furthermore, Kush no longer needed the Nile for trading with the outside world, as most goods were being transported from Meroë to the Red Sea, where Greek merchants were available in large numbers. In about 300 BCE the move to Meroë was made more complete when the monarchs began to be buried there instead of at Napata. One theory is that this represents the monarchs breaking away from the power of the priests at Napata. At that time, King Arkamani was said to have received an order from the gods to commit suicide. But Arkamani instead marched on the temple and killed the priests. During this same period, Kushite authority extended some 1,500 kilometers along the Nile River Valley from the Egyptian frontier in the north to areas far south of modern-day Khartoum and probably also substantial territories to the east and west.

Women held very high status in the Kushite culture and played a key role in the governance of the kingdom. They determined who was going to be the next king or queen. Customarily, the throne was passed on from the ruler to the child of a sister. However, in some caes, one brother might be chosen to succeed another on the throne, as was the case with King Aspelta and King Anlamani. Women could also be rulers themselves, and many queens ruled the Kushite kingdom. One well-known queen was Amanitore, who reigned at about the time of Jesus. She was the daughter of a queen and became queen herself. The mother of the king and the sisters of the king also held very prominent positions in society. During the Twenty-Fifth Dynasty they placed the Theban area under the control of a royal Kushite princess. She was given the title "God's Wife of Amun."

In the Napatan period Egyptian hieroglyphs were used, and writing seems to have been restricted to the court and temples. From the second century BCE there was a separate Kush writing system. The Meroitic alphabet is composed of 23 symbols, written in both a hieroglyphic and a shorthand, or cursive, form. Some of the signs were adapted from Egyptian hieroglyphs, though the Meroitic language itself appears to be much different than Egyptian. To date, the Meroitic writing system remains one of the great ancient mysteries.

The Kushites were defeated in a war with Roman Egypt in the first century BCE, and Napata was sacked. Not discouraged, in 22 BCE a large Kushite army again moved northward against the Romans with the intention of attacking Qasr Ibrim. The Romans quickly organized counterattacks. The Kushites, probably sensing another defeat, sent ambassadors to negotiate a peace settlement with the Romans. The peace treaty, which was negotiated on favorable terms, increased trade between the two nations. Kush began to gradually disappear as a power by the first or second century CE, weakened by the war with the Roman province of Egypt and the decline of trade. There was also the arrival of Christianity and its impact on the indigenous Egyptian religion. By the mid-sixth century the Kingdom of Kush finally ended.

Aribidesi Usman

Further Reading

Bonnet, Charles, and Dominique Valbelle. *The Nubian Pharaohs: Black Kings on the Nile.* New York: American University in Cairo Press, 2007.

Diop, Cheikh Anta. *The African Origin of Civilization.* Chicago: Lawrence Hill Books, 1974.

Friedman, R. "Nubians at Hierakonpolis: Excavations in the Nubian Cemeteries." *Sudan and Nubia* 5 (2001): 29–38.

Jackson, Robert B. *At Empire's Edge: Exploring Rome's Egyptian Frontier.* New Haven, CT: Yale University Press, 2002.

Reisner, G. A. *Excavations at Kerma.* Cambridge, MA: Harvard University Press, 1923.

Török, László. *The Kingdom of Kush: Handbook of the Napatan-Meroitic Civilization.* Leiden: Brill, 1997.

Welsby, Derek A. *The Kingdom of Kush: The Napatan and Meroitic Empires.* Princeton, NJ: Markus Wiener, 1998.

L

Lagos

Though Lagos is no longer the political capital of Nigeria, it still remains the cultural and economic hub of Nigeria. Recent estimates put the city at 999.6 square kilometers and roughly 21 million residents, making it the most populous city in all of Africa. Contemporary Lagos consists of a handful of islands and several ever-sprawling neighborhoods along the mainland. Three major bridges connect Lagos Island to the mainland. A landfill connects the eastside of Lagos Island to Ikoyi. A bridge links the south of Lagos Island to Victoria Island, which is connected by land to the Lekki Peninsula. Though all of Lagos borders bodies of water, only Victoria Island and the Lekki Peninsula touch the Atlantic Ocean. The other major bodies of water are Lagos Harbor and Lagos Lagoon.

The climate of Lagos is tropical, and its proximity to the monsoon zone ensures a significant wet season that spans from April to October, with precipitation in June topping 12 inches. The dry season, from November to March, is accompanied by the harmattan winds that descend from the Sahara desert. The first known history of Lagos dates to the 14th century, when the Awori people, a Yoruba ethnic group, populated the area then known as Oko, meaning "farm." Before long other Yoruba groups arrived and lived peacefully under the Awori ruler. Oral tradition suggests that these migrants were fleeing disturbances in the hinterland. Yet the population in this early period remained small, perhaps because the sandy soil prevented substantial agriculture.

Herbert Macaulay (1864–1946)

Born in Lagos to Sierra Leonean parents in 1864, Herbert Macaulay would become a key figure in modern-day Nigerian history. A sharp critic of the British colonial state, Macaulay aggressively used the press and electoral politics to protest colonial rule. His Nigerian National Democratic Party (NNDP), founded in 1923, remained dominant in Lagos until 1938. After this loss Macaulay harbored national ambitions, and he merged the NNDP with Nnamdi Azikiwe's party, the National Council of Nigeria and the Cameroons, in 1944. Though Macaulay died in 1946, Nigeria's achievement of independence in 1960 owes much to his efforts. Today, the University of Ibadan library houses the Herbert Macaulay Collection.

View of Broad Street in Lagos, 1940s. Broad Street was an important site of colonial modernity in Lagos, featuring many businesses such as bookstores and hotels. (National Archives, Ibadan)

The first significant political change in Eko resulted from the nearby powerful Benin Empire. The *oba* (king) of Benin first became aware of the settlement in the 15th century. On their return they informed him that they had experienced mistreatment by the Awori people. The *oba* of Benin sent forces to subdue Eko, and they succeeded. The Benin Empire faced other security threats at the time and decided to use its new settlement as a base for military operations, changing the name to Eko, meaning "war camp."

The arrival of the Benin did more than change the political structure of Lagos. Up to that point residents only lived on the mainland; Lagos Island was empty except for a pepper farm and fishing posts. This changed when the first king of Lagos, Oba Ado, built his palace on the island, and several Benin warriors and local people joined him in building homes. Before long, explorers from a land much farther than the Benin Empire drastically changed the political, economic, and social dynamics of Eko and in so doing transformed the town to a major commercial city. The Portuguese first arrived in the 1470s, naming the town Lagos, which in Portuguese means "lakes." Initially brass, copper, pepper, cloth, and beads dominated the trade between Lagosians and the Portuguese. A few slaves were taken back to Europe but no more than the normal internal West African trade produced. The event that changed this was the discovery and conquest of the Americas by the Portuguese followed by the Spanish, French, and British. By the 16th century large labor-intensive sugar plantations in the Americas fueled the demand for cheap workers and the subsequent exploitation of Africa.

In the case of Lagos, the start of the slave trade was gradual. Initially traders from the formidable Oyo Empire preferred the slave ports of Ouidah and Allada. Though located farther away, the fact that these ports rested directly on the Atlantic Ocean made them preferable for large ships. This arrangement came to a close in the 1720s when control of both ports fell to the Kingdom of Dahomey. This spurred the quest for new ports and pushed some of the trade east to Porto Novo and Badagry. The *oba* of Lagos encouraged the trade to move even farther east when he established a slave port in the 1760s. The eastern ports continued to dominate the slave trade until Dahomey enacted strict regulations that ultimately deterred traders, preferring the relative laxity of Lagos.

The devastation that the slave trade caused to the region around Lagos cannot be underestimated. It is no coincidence that the highly destructive Yoruba Wars, which enveloped most of Yorubaland in violence, commenced shortly after Lagos became an important slave port. It is true that the jihad launched by Usman dan Fodio of the Sokoto Caliphate in 1804, in what is now northern Nigeria, contributed much to the instability of the region. However, it was the demand for slaves and access to gunpowder from Europe that spurred the continuation of conflict, weakening regional chiefs and governments.

The slave trade influenced the growth and culture of Lagos. Most of the slave ships that left Lagos sailed to the slave port of Bahia, Brazil. Yoruba Lagos traders traveled to and from Brazil, and Brazilian traders traveled to and from Lagos, bringing with them their culture and commercial goods. The result of this human exchange is still felt. Today much of Yoruba culture and religion are found in Brazil, while in the Brazilian quarter on Lagos Island you can still find residents who trace their roots to Brazil. Moreover, the neighborhood carnival colors are yellow and green—the same colors of the Brazilian flag.

The vital importance of trade alliances inspired many interethnic and interracial marriages in Lagos, adding to the port city's cosmopolitan feel. The Lagosian elites mixed freely at social events with European elites; both sides initially benefited from the slave trade and wished to nourish their relationship. Given the great wealth produced from the slave trade, the parties that took place at its height were quite lavish, with Yoruba musicians, palm wine, and culinary delicacies. Evidence of this elite culture built on the profits of slavery remains in Lagos today. Tinubu Square, which today bustles with commerce, takes its name from Madam Tinubu, a major slave dealer from the 19th century. Additionally, the Lagosian elite often commissioned homes built in the Portuguese style, several of which still stand. Though the Europeans ultimately exploited Lagos as occurred in the rest of Africa, it is important to note that the local political elite maintained power over the terms of the trade. Europeans had to court their friendship and abide by their rules, such as not venturing any farther than the coastal regions.

Despite the initial profit afforded to the Lagosian elites, by the time Britain officially abolished the slave trade in 1807 the city and surrounding polities were greatly weakened. And despite the formal end to the trade, the flood of slaves passing through Lagos continued until 1851, when the British set up a consular authority in Lagos to combat the trade. This would prove to be the first step of Britain's colonization of Lagos followed by the rest of what is now modern-day Nigeria, a process made all the easier by the destabilizing destruction wrought by the slave trade. In the decade between the formation of the consulate and the formal colonization of Lagos in 1861, the chief export from the docks of Lagos shifted from slaves to palm kernels and palm oil. The enhanced stability and ethnic inclusiveness of Lagos attracted refugees from the Yoruba Wars, and the second half of the 19th century witnessed a population boom that continues today.

Sara Katz

Further Reading

Echeruo, Michael. *Victorian Lagos: Aspects of Nineteenth Century Lagos Life.* London: Macmillan, 1977.

Law, Robin. "Trade and Politics behind the Slave Coast: The Lagoon Traffic and the Rise of Lagos, 1500–1800." *Journal of African History* 24(3) (1983): 321–348.

Mann, Kristin. *Slavery and the Birth of an African City: Lagos, 1760–1900.* Bloomington: Indiana University Press, 2007.

Smith, Robert. "The Lagos Consulate, 1851–1861: An Outline." *Journal of African History* 15(3) (1974): 393–416.

Laimbwe

Laimbwe, a cluster of three small kingdoms, was founded in the mid-18th century in the present-day Menchum and Boyo divisions of the Northwest Region of Cameroon. Laimbwe as a language is spoken in the Baisso, Bu, and Mbengkas kingdoms. Satellite and neighboring settlements such as Mbongkesso, Teitengem, Mughom, and Aguli also speak Laimbwe in addition to other languages. Much of Laimbwe territory is located within and around the Kom-Wum Forest Reserve, one of the few montane forest reserves announced in 1951 for the grasslands of Cameroon by the British colonial administration. In this forest reserve and other secondary forests were animal species such as monkeys, gorillas, porcupines, elephants, and deer, among others. The forest is also rich in rare species of birds of the montane forest in Cameroon. The territory is also well served with rivers and streams which include the Mughom, Meteh, Tschu'akooghe, Anzhieh, Mezele, Meveh, and Menchum, where fishing and the cultivation of crops such as rice, maize, groundnuts, cocoyams, plantains, and cassava took place.

There are two principal versions about the origin of the Laimbwe. One version states that they were part of a migratory wave of ethnic groups from Ndobo in the present-day Adamawa region of Cameroon when Usman dan Fodio launched the jihads to establish an Islamic caliphate in the early 19th century. The other version holds that the Laimbwe migrated from Ndewum, a plateau settlement in

Bafmeng in the Fungom subdivision of the Menchum division. Oral narratives are, however, persistent that the Laimbwe and other kingdoms of Fungom subdivision left Ndewum in the 18th century and eventually broke up into three related kingdoms: Baisso, Bu, and Mbengkas. They had settled in the Ndewum Plateau to escape the Kom raids to expand the boundary of the Kom kingdom, among other factors.

The migration of the Laimbwe from Ndewum to their final settlement was due to a harsh climate and the need for fishing and for hunting game and occurred in several stages. The first stop from Ndewum with Kuk and Bafmeng people was Esei (Ise). From Esei, the Laimbwe and Kuk peoples moved together and settled at Ipalim but only temporarily. From Ipalim the Laimbwe and Kuk peoples separated, with the Laimbwe people moving into the Kom/Wum Forest Reserve within the Meteh Valley, where there was an abundance of exploitable natural resources. They settled at Mbuhndum and then at Mba-ahzih and Fufuam. Mbuhndum was a crossroad, with many people from other kingdoms such as Kom passing through it for trade in oil and iron implements with the Menchum Valley kingdoms. Within the Kom/Wum Forest Reserve, the Laimbwe people eventually separated into the three Baisso, Bu, and Mbengkas kingdoms. One of the groups found a valley of edible wild vegetables called *tesso,* migrated, and settled permanently there. The name "Baisso" is therefore a derivative of *tesso,* meaning "valley of vegetables." The Mbengkas branched off from Mba-ahzih to Uuzoi and then to their present settlement. The branching off is where they derived their name *bengka,* meaning "our branching off." The Bu (Eh'bouh, meaning "we are tired") people crossed the Meteh River to settle at Kulinaiwile (Old Town Hill) and from there migrated to their present settlement. One reason that the Bu people were forced to relocate from Kulinaiwile was Bafut and Kom raids for slaves.

Farming, gathering, trading, hunting, and fishing were main activities of the economy of precolonial Laimbwe. The people cultivated different crops such as maize, cocoyams, cassava, and plantains in the rich fertile valley served by the Meteh, Menchum, and Mughom Rivers. The Laimbwe gathered fruits and hunted game in the Kom/Wum Forest Reserve. Fishing took place in the Meteh, Tschu'akooghe, Menchum, and Mughom Rivers as well as in streams. The people traded with the Menchum Valley kingdoms Aghem and Kom. They were also long-distance traders in commodities such as palm kernels and mats, which took them to Bafut, Bande (Mankon), Widekum, Mamfe, Kumba, Nkongsamba, and Victoria. Trade with the coastal region intensified during the colonial period with the additional opening up of the hinterlands to global trade.

The Laimbwe kingdoms have a centralized consensual administration, typical of Tikar kingdoms of Cameroon's western grasslands. The *fon* is the executive head, and the regulatory societies of *Kuiifuai* and *Mukuum* for men and *Kefa'a* for women form the legislative branch of administration. The Council of Elders, made up of family heads and quarter heads, dispensed justice according to local customs and tradition. Women also exercised political power as a group when they were dissatisfied. This explains why between 1957 and 1959 the Laimbwe *kelu* women rose against the colonial administration. Succession to the throne or to the headship of the family is matrilineal. When a family head or *fon* died, he was succeeded by the brother or sister's son. The Laimbwe kingdom is one of the few kingdoms in the western grasslands of Cameroon that is matrilineal. The other kingdoms include Kom, Kuk, Aghem, and Bafmeng.

A powerful socioeconomic class emerged from trading in palm oil, kernels, pots, and mats in the 19th and 20th centuries. At the beginning the Laimbwe people settled into closely knit matrilineal groups, and over time the trend changed. Leaders of matrilineal groups were involved in the decision-making processes for community stability. In the early period of the German colonial administration, the people constructed roads and supplied food to the Germans regularly. The people were guided by the communal philosophy of "all for one and one for all."

The Germano-Douala Treaty of July 14, 1884, eventually brought the Laimbwe region under German administration. When the Germans were defeated after World War I, Laimbwe territory fell under the British-administered part of southern Cameroons. The Basel mission was brought into Laimbweland in 1926, and eventually the Catholic and Baptist missions also founded stations in the Laimbwe kingdoms. In the struggle for the independence and reunification of Cameroon in 1961, Laimbwe people voted for integration into Nigeria. The significance of the Laimbwe is that to understand the history of precolonial movements in the northwestern part of the western grasslands, one needs to appreciate the role they played. The history of German incursions into the area is incomplete without discussing the role of the Laimbwe. Laimbwe was the gateway into Menchum during the German colonial administration, and many people from Aghem and the Fungom areas spent nights there on their way to and from markets in Bafut, Bande (Mankon), and other distant places toward Nigeria. The British maintained a rest house in Bu village for administrative reasons. The site is now host to the Presbyterian Church Bu.

Henry Kam Kah

Further Reading

Kah, Elvis Fang. "The Role of Kom-Wum Forest Reserve in the Laimbwe Clan of the North West Province." MA thesis, University of Yaounde I, 2001.

Kah, Henry Kam. *The Sacred Forest: Gender and Matriliny in Laimbwe History (Cameroon).* Berlin: Lit Verlag, 2015.

Muam, Ndo. *Traditional Structures and Political Evolution: A Case Study of Bu Chiefdom.* Bamenda: Quality Printers, 2001.

Wakai, Nyo. "Reflections: The Church and Society." In *Journey in Faith: The Story of the Presbyterian Church in Cameroon,* edited by Nyansako-ni-Nku, 147–151. Yaounde: Buma Kor, 1982.

Lesotho

Lesotho, with an area of 11,720 square miles, is a landlocked country in Southern Africa that is completely surrounded by the Republic of South Africa. Known as

Contemporary Life in Lesotho

Contemporary life in Lesotho offers numerous events and activities featuring visual and performing arts. Perhaps the most notable event is the Morija Arts and Cultural Festival, which
features nationwide cultural competitions among area schools, exhibitions of fine arts, poetry
and performing arts, film screenings, and the renowned Mohlomi Memorial Lecture series.
Although this annual event has been temporarily suspended since 2014, when an alleged military coup forced former prime minister Motsoahae Thomas Thabane to briefly flee to South
Africa, the mantle has been taken up by the Morija Museum and Archives, which hosts these
events and activities throughout the year.

the "mountain kingdom," Lesotho's geographic height ranges from 1,400 meters
(4,600 feet) to 3,482 meters (11,424 feet), making it the country with the highest
starting elevation in the world. Today approximately 2.1 million people live in the
Kingdom of Lesotho, the majority of whom consider themselves Basotho, a broad
cultural designation linking one to any number of southern Sotho-speaking clans
from across the region. The Kingdom of Lesotho, formerly known as Basutoland,
was historically the heartland of various southern Sotho populations, and today
there are approximately 3 million Basotho who are citizens of the Republic of
South Africa. The majority of Basotho in South Africa reside in the Free State
Province, which borders the Kingdom of Lesotho.

Lesotho is largely made up of mountain plateaus, which cover nearly two-
thirds of the kingdom throughout the eastern and southernmost regions. Toward
the northwest one finds a small area of fertile lowlands and rolling foothills where
the tributaries of the Orange and Caledon Rivers flow. The kingdom has a temperate climate, with cold, dry winters and hot, wet summers, and an annual rainfall of
approximately 30 inches a year.

Lesotho maintains a wide variety of flora, with plants from the daisy and sun-
flower families found on many of the mountain slopes. These hardy, fast-growing,
and generally frost-resistant plants are perfectly suited to the climate of Lesotho and
have been used to produce a wide variety of South Sotho visual arts for centuries.
One also finds flowers from the lily family as well as the rare spiral aloe, which is
unique to the Kingdom of Lesotho and does not naturally grow anywhere else across
the globe. In addition, one can find numerous tree species along the riverbanks, such
as willows, wild olive, and other medium-sized deciduous species. Lesotho also has
large quantities of grasses, of which over 100 species have been recognized, and
these grasses have been used for feeding livestock as well as thatching, plaiting
household items, and creating baskets and hats.

Although South Sotho oral histories as well as the written accounts of numerous 19th-century travelers and missionaries note the presence of animals such as
buffalo, eland, zebra, hippopotamus, hyena, and lion, the Kingdom of Lesotho currently hosts a limited variety of antelope species, such as the mountain reedbuck.

Smaller animals found across the country include baboon and jackal as well as mongoose and rock hyrax, which are well suited to the rocky terrain. One can also find several species of snake, including the berg adder, as well as nearly 300 species of birds such as the southern bald ibis, the bearded vulture, and the sentinel rock-thrush.

Lesotho is also home to a number of important natural resources, including diamonds, sand, clay, and building stone, although soil erosion has increasingly become a concern across the country as a result of such industries. However, its most critical resource is water, which is used to produce hydroelectric power through the largest water transfer project on the African continent. Known as the Lesotho Highlands Water Project, Lesotho's water resources are used to supply neighboring South Africa with this important resource and generates enough power to supply electricity for nearly the entire kingdom. There are several large dams across the country, with the Katse Dam and the Mohale Dam being the most notable.

Culturally speaking, the Basotho nation was founded in the early 19th century and originated under Morena (King) Moshoeshoe. During this time, numerous events were taking place across Southern Africa involving multiple cultures—both African and Western—that historians have labeled as the *lifiqane* (scattering). Although numerous studies have been undertaken to determine the catalysts of these events, it is generally accepted that non-Sotho cultures from the eastern part of Southern Africa began subjugating neighboring peoples, resulting in the disruption, migration, and extermination of many cultures throughout the region. Because South Sotho populations were separated from the eastern lowlands of Southern Africa by the immense Drakensburg mountain range, Basutoland served as a natural refuge for disenfranchised peoples who were fleeing from the chaos of the east. During this period, Moshoeshoe (who was then known as Lepoqo and later Tlaputle) was a minor South Sotho chief residing in his father's village of Menkhoaneng in the northwest region of present-day Lesotho. Oral history suggests that the young Moshoeshoe was taken by his grandfather to see the renowned South Sotho healer and sage Mohlomi, who professed greatness over the young chief, symbolically electing him as his successor. Moshoeshoe took this meeting to heart and soon thereafter began to distinguish himself as a just and powerful diplomat.

As the events in the east continued to unfold, various disenfranchised groups of Sotho- and non-Sotho-speaking peoples were driven toward the central interior of Southern Africa, subjecting the residents of Basutoland to waves of attacks. This climate eventually led Moshoeshoe to relocate toward a new region of Basutoland that was better suited for defense, and he eventually settled at Thaba Bosiu, a mountain near the present-day city of Maseru, making it his new capital. After relocating, Moshoeshoe continued to consolidate his power and grow his supporters by allowing any disparate peoples to settle under his protection and oversight. At this point the strength and authority of Moshoeshoe was being recognized throughout the region of present-day Lesotho, and other established chiefs began to submit to his rule. Nonetheless, the climate of the day continued to bring the threat of neighboring peoples such as the amaNgwanes of Matuoane, the amaHlubis of Mpangazitha, and Moselekatse, a chief of the Nguni-speaking kwaKhumalos.

In order to protect his own standing throughout the Caledon River Valley, Moshoeshoe undertook numerous acts of diplomacy that displayed the farsighted wisdom that he soon became famous for. By 1831 Basutoland was released from the grip of fear brought on by the *lifiqane,* and Moshoeshoe became the primary authority throughout the region, accepting numerous refugees under his protection and establishing the Basotho polity under his leadership. Yet during this time of relative peace there came another force from the west, which again challenged Moshoeshoe's authority over Basutoland. History refers to this group as the Korannas, and they were a culturally mixed community originating from the southern reaches of present-day South Africa, which had moved inland. Due to their extended contact with peoples of European descent, the Korannas had early access to guns and horses, which gave them military superiority over many of their Sotho-speaking and Khoi-San (indigenous peoples of Southern Africa, or the so-called Bushmen) neighbors. The Korannas took advantage of this and maintained a strong presence throughout the present-day Western Free State of South Africa, continually raiding those peoples within their surrounds. It was in this state of stress that the first people of European descent were invited by Moshoeshoe to settle among the Basotho. Thus, in June 1833 missionaries of the Paris Evangelical Missionary Society—Eugene Casalis, Thomas Arbousset, and Constant Gosselin—made the journey to the Basotho king to establish a mission station in Basutoland. In the 50 years following the arrival of the French missionaries, who proved to be important allies to King Moshoeshoe, interactions with African and non-African peoples resulted in sociopolitical consolidation throughout the Caledon Valley.

For example, between 1830 and 1870 Basutoland increasingly became an area of dispute, as Moshoeshoe I claimed it for his South Sotho polity, while emigrant Boers—descendants of the Dutch-speaking settlers who first arrived in the southeast portion of South Africa in the 17th and 18th centuries—proceeded to settle inland as though it were unclaimed and empty territory, largely ignoring the king's warnings of trespass. Because there was no British interest in expanding authority into the interior at this time, the lands possessed by Africans largely relied on treaties to protect their claims. Thus, between 1843 and 1870 Moshoeshoe's polity was subjected to six treaties at the hands of both the British-controlled Cape Colony and the newly formed Orange River Sovereignty (which later became the Orange Free State, an independent Boer sovereign republic), each of which resulted in the reduction of South Sotho territory and arable land. When the military proceedings of 1865 between Basutoland and the Orange Free State reached a point of urgency, Moshoeshoe signed the Treaty of Thaba Bosiu, which reduced Basutoland to approximately one-fifth of its former size and called for an immediate evacuation of the newly annexed land. When Moshoeshoe later renounced the treaty, a final settlement was reached on March 12, 1868, when it was announced that the British government had taken Basutoland as a crown protectorate, placing it under the direct authority of the British-run Cape Colony. In the end the two sides came to an agreement, resulting in the national border that one finds today. Thus, by 1869

Moshoeshoe had lost all of the land to the north and west of the Caledon River, and nearly half of Basutoland had been signed away. The treaty was ratified on March 19, 1870, eight days after the death of Moshoeshoe.

If one reviews the details of the aforementioned events regarding land, mapping, and ownership, there is no doubt that the inhabitants of present-day Lesotho were fighting for their very existence, with Moshoeshoe consolidating the various cultures within his territory in order to maintain a foothold. This act of consolidation gains increasing speed as one approaches the mid-19th century, with representatives of both the Boer Republic and the British Empire recognizing the authority of Moshoeshoe over Basutoland and maintaining contact with the South Sotho king when negotiating topics of landownership. Even those non-Sotho populations residing in the upper Orange River drainage system in southern Basutoland, such as the Baphuthis, the Thembus, the Vundles of Tyhali, and the Hlapos—who were non-Sotho speakers—were consolidated under Moshoeshoe's authority. It is notable to mention that throughout the latter decades of the 19th century Moshoeshoe's Basotho polity was subjected to numerous military attacks and sieges, including those by the Orange Free State and the British Cape Colony, but was never defeated. Thus, only through the centralized military strategy of Moshoeshoe was Basutoland able to withstand the pressure of outside forces, and only through his foresight and diplomacy was he able to negotiate for the whole of the region, which eventually became the saving grace of present-day Lesotho.

As the 20th century arrived, the Basotho would find these past issues brought to the forefront once again. Although Britain eventually won the struggle against the independent Boer Republics for control of the central interior of Southern Africa through the Anglo-Boer wars (1880–1902), the Afrikaner Nationalist Party would eventually come to power in the surrounding Republic of South Africa in 1948, with its philosophy of apartheid. This system of government, which sharpened ethnic boundaries through political, social, and economic discrimination and segregation against nonwhites, continued on for nearly half a century and established exploitative state-sanctioned labor conditions that directly impacted Lesotho, whose migrant workers made up 77 percent of the population in the Orange Free State, until the end of white minority rule of South Africa in 1994.

On October 4, 1966, Basutoland gained independence from Britain and was renamed Lesotho. During the first two decades following independence the country was governed by the Basuto National Party, although the following decades were fraught with political unrest—sometimes violent—until constitutional reforms were established in the late 1990s. Peaceful but contested parliamentary and National Assembly elections were held in both 2002 and 2007, and in May 2012 competitive elections involving 18 parties resulted in the victory of Motsoahae Thomas Thabane and his coalition government. Currently, the political system of Lesotho is a parliamentary constitutional monarchy and includes a representative from the royal family (King Letsie III), a prime minister (Pakalitha Mosisili), and a Parliament composed of elected representatives and customary chiefs.

David M. M. Riep

Further Reading

Casalis, Eugene. *The Basutos.* 1861; reprint, Morija: Morija Museum and Archives, 1997.

Gill, Stephen J. *A Short History of Lesotho.* Roma: National University of Lesotho, Institute of Southern African Studies, 1993.

Riep, David. "House of the Crocodile: South Sotho Art and History in Southern Africa." PhD dissertation, University of Iowa, 2011.

Smith, Edwin W. *The Mabilles of Basutoland.* 1939; reprint, Morija: Morija Museum and Archives, 1996.

Thompson, Leonard. *Survival in Two Worlds: Moshoeshoe of Lesotho, 1786–1870.* New York: Oxford University Press, 1976.

Loango

Loango, one of a cluster of small kingdoms, existed from the 15th to the 19th centuries and covered areas within what are now the nations of Gabon, the Republic of Congo, Angola (Cabinda Enclave), and the Democratic Republic of Congo. The Loango coast stretches 460 miles between Cape Lopez in the north and the Congo River in the south. The name "Loango" refers to a specific settlement at Loango Bay consisting of four provinces: Loangiri (also Loango or Longo), Loangomongo (hilly Loango), Pili, and Chilongo. At the time of European contact, the Loango coast included tributary polities such as Gobby, Sette, and Bukkameale to the north and Kakongo and Ngoyo to the south. Known for its great surf and underwater earthquakes, the Loango coast posed high risks for sailors. A significant portion of the Loango coastal region included primeval forest with trees rising to 150–200 feet in addition to a diverse environment of open lagoons, mangrove swamps, scattered clusters of trees, parklike reaches, dense walls of tangled undergrowth along the rivers, prairies of tall grass, and patches of cultivation. Vegetation consisted of baobabs, silk cotton trees, screw pines, and palms. Farmers cultivated manioc, bananas, groundnuts, tobacco, and vegetables. Loango, home to a variety of animal life, hosted the crocodile, the hippopotamus, and several types of apes. Fauna life

Avenue of Mango Trees

The planting of mango trees along the Loango coast memorializes the transatlantic slave trade by tracing the path on which slaves walked to the coast. Loango Bay was a major port for 17th-century European traders. Nearly half of the slaves shipped from Africa between 1501 and 1866 probably originated from West-Central Africa. Many traversed Loango Bay. Tradition describes slaves dropping mango seeds along the path. The trees that grew from those seeds signified their last African meal. Another story tells how people left behind planted a mango tree symbolizing the loss of an individual life.

prevailed, with gray parrots, shrikes, flycatchers, rhinoceros birds, weaver birds, ice birds, butterfly finches, hehnet birds, doves, and snipes.

The Portuguese noted the Kongo Empire as early as the 14th century but did not reference Loango, an emerging kingdom north of Kongo. Some historians view Loango as an offshoot province of Kongo in the late 16th century. Traditions held in the 17th century also connect its origin to Kongo, which dates back to the 14th century. The nature of that connection remains obscure. One conjecture, based on a 17th-century account, suggests that if the kingdom was founded through conquest originating from the small state of Nzari on the Zaire River and if the king of that small state in 1624 ruled for 60 years as estimated by written accounts of his death, he may have been the founder of Loango.

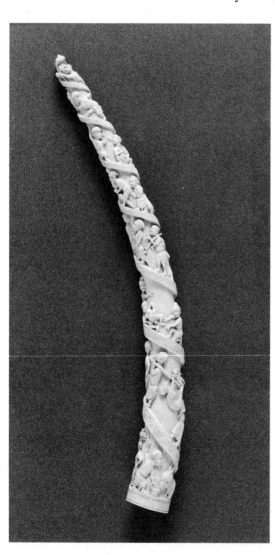

Carved tusk, ivory, Vili culture, late 19th–early 20th centuries. (Yale University Art Gallery)

Modern traditions trace large population movements into the region with no specific dates attached. Three groups populated Loango. The first, the Vilis (Bavilis) or Fiotis, a Kongo people who migrated to the coastal region in the 1300s, lived in Loango in the mid-15th century and traded with Europeans at Loango Bay. The second, the Kotchis, belonged to the Kakongo polity and traded at Malemba. The third, the Woyos, belonged to the Ngoyo polity and traded at Cabinda Bay. The Vilis, portrayed as farmers who broke away from the Congo groups because of a land shortage in the interior, dominated Loango. They passed through the Mayombe region and settled in the coastal plain between the Kwilu and Chiloango Rivers in the 13th or 14th centuries. Initial contact between the Vilis and the Portuguese transpired in the late 15th century. Loango became an independent state under Vili rule in the late 1300s or early 1400s. Over the next 100 years, the Vilis dominated the Loango coast. The Dutch appeared in 1593. The coastal population resisted the permanent settlement of Europeans. Loango was one of the region's oldest and largest kingdoms. At the height of its power, the chief Mani-Congo extended his rule over modern-day Angola as far east as the Kasai and Upper Zambesi Rivers. In the 1830s, the French on the fringes of western equatorial Africa established several trading stations and missionary centers on the Gabon coast.

Farming was the basis of the Vili precolonial economy. By the end of the 16th century, Loango advanced from a subsistence economy to commerce. The Vilis established trading networks to Mayumba in the north, Stanley (Malebo) Pool in the east, and Luanda in the south. They operated independently of Europeans and focused on forming permanent contacts in other communities through settlement, which facilitated a flow of merchants and caravaners between localities. The Vilis developed a distinct and unique interconnected trading network. Trading routes to the interior excluded the Portuguese *pombeiros* (African agents representing European merchants). Routes extended from the Atlantic coast to Stanley Pool to the Teke town of Monsol, where the Vilis traded for slaves, ivory, and copper. On routes to the northeast the Vilis sold European goods and salt from Mayombe to the Jagas in exchange for slaves, copper, and ivory. As middlemen, the Vilis imposed tributes on the coastal polities of Ngoyo and Kakongo. Through long-distance trade within West-Central Africa, Loango exported to the north, east, and south. In Loango, coastal estuaries, creeks, and lagoons formed an interconnected protected system of waterways facilitating the large-scale movement of goods. These coastal waterways allowed easy communication between the mouths of the Senegal and Gambia Rivers. Winds and ocean currents created a natural barrier at the Congo River. The market at Stanley Pool, the crucial transit point where boat transportation toward the coast was blocked by the long stretch of the Congo Rapids, was the heart of the Kongo trade. The rapids divided the Kongo trade into an upper or waterborne segment and a lower or overland segment linking Stanley Pool with a series of ports along the coast both north and south of the estuary. Between the ports and Stanley Pool, a series of subsidiary inland markets were transit points for a change of bearers, and each had its own middlemen serving the larger trade. Most of these markets drew on the caravan trade to Stanley Pool. The Vilis functioned as specialists in caravan operations north of Kongo. During the 16th century the Vilis gained a reputation as astute traders, and Vili became one of the region's most important trading states. The Vili coastal population received copper, palm cloth, skins, redwood, ivory, and elephant tails from the interior.

By the 1660s, mining, smelting, and transporting of copper for sale at Loango was a highly organized business in Vili hands. They sold to African consumers and Europeans on the coast. After the 1570s a regular trade in copper and ivory developed between Angola, the newly established Portuguese colony, and Loango. The European demand for ivory, the most important Portuguese export from Loango, precipitated the growth of Vili external trade. The Portuguese secured goods such as raffia cloths and redwood from the Vilis to trade in Luanda for slaves. The arrival of the Dutch in the late 16th century expanded Loango's external trading. The Dutch established factories at Loango Bay and Mayumba, the kingdom's two principal ports, in the first decade of the 17th century. In the 1620s, slaves were among Loango's exports. Vili merchants traveled long distances to reach markets first pioneered in the copper trade. The practices and organization of the copper trade prepared Loango to participate in the long-distance slave trade. Loango's slave trade grew in volume. By the 1660s, Vili traders found it more profitable to trade in slaves than in ivory. From the 1670s, Loango's slave trade expanded. Loango's source for slaves was distant inland kingdoms such as the Mpumbo region, Kongo, and Angola. Loango merchants traveled in caravans, established bases in distant places, and delivered slaves from those areas to Dutch, English, and French merchants stationed in Loango and in its two southern neighbors, Ngoyo and Kakongo.

During the late 17th century, Loango increased its export of slaves. Guns were exchanged for every slave sold. The slave trade was maintained in Loango longer than anywhere else on the West African seaboard. The majority of slaves exported to Brazil originated from the South Atlantic seaboard states such as Loango. At the end of the 17th century, Loango dominated the southern trade routes. By the second half of the 18th century, Loango lost its place in the slave trade to its rivals, Kakongo and Ngoyo. Geographical features facilitated a triangular shipping pattern on the Loango coast, allowing Europeans to ship textiles, guns, and alcohol from Europe in exchange for slaves in Africa. The kingdom's ruler imposed his own conditions on European traders. All trade regulations imposed by the king and the *mafouk* (chief port official) had to be obeyed. African merchants could not trade directly with Europeans and could trade only through *mafouk*-appointed brokers. Loango's coastal population stands out as the region's most effective at engaging European trade without compromising indigenous cultural values.

Loango separated from Kongo in the late 16th century and was a powerful centralized state divided into four large provinces, several central districts, and villages. Each province, district, and village had chiefs and a hierarchical system. Succession to royal office was rotational, so the ruler of each province in turn assumed the kingship. Succession was based on heredity. When the king died, his sister's son succeeded him. By the 18th century, power was fragmented, and the administration was decentralized. By the end of the 18th century, the system deteriorated. The Regency Council of chief ministers took power. The emergence of wealthy brokers and officials who bought their offices compromised the central power. The political impact of Loango's role in the Atlantic slave trade weakened central authority. The trade created a class of rich nobles whose wealth did not depend on the king, resulting in the collapse of centralized authority and the eventual lapse of the kingship.

A powerful Vili class emerged in the late 17th century. Members owed their status to commercial wealth. Participation in the slave trade created new opportunities for advancement independent of the traditional system. The base of political, economic, and social power broadened as Vili society became more open and men outside the nobility sought opportunities to advance. The system that evolved to operate the slave trade required more people—brokers, merchants, caravan leaders, interpreters, surf boatmen, water carriers, and personal servants for

Europeans—than previous trading conditions. Power, measured less in terms of traditional rights, depended more on a man's place in the slave-trading system and the wealth amassed from his position.

Under the Treaties of 1885, Loango became part of the French Congo. Pierre Savorgnan de Brazza explored the area in 1879 and 1880 and signed treaties with local rulers, placing the territory under French protection. The region became known as the Middle Congo, which in 1910 became one of the colonies federated into French Equatorial Africa. In the early 20th century, there were 24 European missionaries in the area. Loango, at the head of the Niari-Kwilou portage route and the starting point of the caravan route to Brazzavile, was the most important. In 1960, the Middle Congo became the independent Republic of Congo.

The history of this region and the significance of Loango remains key to understanding the connection between the African American diaspora and West Central Africa. An estimated 69 percent of all Africans transported in the transatlantic slave trade between 1517 and 1700 were from West-Central Africa. Between 1701 and 1800, people from that region of Africa represented about 38 percent of all Africans brought to the West for enslavement. By 1730, most of the African slaves in South Carolina were from West-Central Africa, with many native-born African Americans descendant from that region. The interconnections developed between Europe, Africa, and the Americas during the Atlantic slave trade shaped subsequent patterns of trade, migrations (forced and free), and cultural exchange.

Maryalice Guilford

Further Reading

Gilbert, Erik, et al. *Africa in World History: From Prehistory to the Present.* Upper Saddle River. NJ: Pearson, 2004.

Martin, Phyllis. "The Trade of Loango in the Seventeenth and Eighteenth Centuries." In *Forced Migration: The Impact of the Export Slave Trade on African Societies,* edited by J. E. Imikori, 102–130. New York: African Publishing, 1982.

Oliver, Roland, and J. D. Fage. *A Short History of Africa.* New York: Penguin, 1995.

Shillington, Kevin. *History of Africa.* New York: Palgrave Macmillan, 2012.

Thornton, John. *Africa and Africans in the Making of the Atlantic World, 1400–1680.* New York: Cambridge University Press, 1992.

Luba

The name "Luba" refers to a variety of groups of people who share a common political history based on the origins and decline of the Luba empires. Although no one knows for sure the exact time when the centralized empire emerged, scholars believed that the empire could be traced as far back as the early 15th century or the 16th century. Oral traditions reveal the existence of the first Luba Empire, which was established by Nkongolo Mukulu in the middle of the 17th century, and the

---

Luba

For over three years now, the Luba have been in conflict with the Twas, a Pygmy people who inhabit the northern part of Katanga Province in the Democratic Republic of Congo. Both opposing forces have organized into militias that are armed with machetes and bows and arrows. Since large-scale fighting started in May 2013, hundreds of civilians have been killed, dozens of villages have been burned, and tens of thousands of people have been displaced from their homes. Violence between the two groups is mainly driven by social inequalities, unfair working conditions, and a lack of access to basic services and land resources.

---

second empire, which was founded by Kalala Ilunga. Most rulers of the Luba Empire traced their ancestry to Kalala Ilunga, who was praised as the great mythic hunter who succeeded in overthrowing the despotic King Nkongolo.

The Luba Empire was located in the middle of Central Africa, stretching from the shores of Lake Tanganyika in the east, the Lomami River in the north, the Luembe River in the west, and the southern region of the present-day Democratic Republic of Congo. At its peak, more than 1 million belonged to the empire, and they all expressed their political loyalty by paying tribute to the king. The payment or exchange of tribute constituted one of the major characteristics of the empire. The king and his subjects were said to be mutually dependent. The subjects paid tribute to the king, who in return offered gifts of equal value to his subordinates. Refusal to pay tribute was considered a serious act of political insubordination that could pave the way to actions of retaliation. Special members of the Luba royal court were appointed to supervise the tribute payments of specified villages or states. As the empire grew in size, the royal court became an important center where goods produced by all villages and states were consumed, allocated, and redistributed.

It is important to understand that the Luba ruler was actually a king over many other sacral kings who were independently invested. The centralized empire was under the authority of the *mulopwe,* the traditional king of the Luba people. Because of the size of the empire, the *mulopwe* had at his disposal a powerful and large army that could wage war hundreds of kilometers from the capital. His authority, however, was less effective outside his capital town. A local ruler who was also called a *mulopwe* governed each territory beyond the capital, or chiefdom. The imperial court was a large residential center where the number of the population was augmented by a constant flow of official visitors from all over the empire. These visitors often stayed on for days or weeks at a time, being fed on the foods that were brought in as tribute payments from distant areas.

The incorporation of kingdoms within the Luba Empire played a crucial role in not only its expansion but also its disintegration. As more and more kingdoms and lineages were incorporated into the empire, the number of royal male children eligible to rule over the centralized empire multiplied. Consequently, serious problems of lineage politics arose at the capital. The death of the *mulopwe* was then usually followed by major succession crises that weakened both the empire and the chiefdoms.

Luba rulers had a divine status. Upon their deaths they were worshipped as gods, and the villages from which they ruled were transformed into sacred living shrines. The new king had to relocate to a different village and establish a new capital city. To preserve the history of the kings and their sacred shrines, a secret society, the Bambudye, was created, and its members had primarily the responsibility of learning, maintaining, and teaching the oral histories of Luba kings and ancestors. These ancestors, whose spirits were venerated, were the ones who provided a spiritual link between Luba villages.

Members of the Bambudye, also called "men of memory," were more than simple storytellers. They played the roles of historian, librarian, and educator. But above all they were instrumental in keeping order and continuity in the political regime from one generation to the next. The most important element in the training of these men of memory was the recitation of dynastic and local lineage histories. When they were asked to provide oral testimony about any Luba royal dynasty, the men of memory could spend up to 60 minutes reciting genealogies, naming places, and recounting important events that occurred during the lifetime of elders.

Each time the king made a trip to a different village, he was always accompanied by several members of the Bambudye, who were in charge of giving public dances, singing the king's praises, and proclaiming his exploits and those of his ancestors. The Bambudye was able to survive the decline of the Luba Empire. It is reported that the last generation of initiates disappeared toward the end of the 1960s. Today, the extensive information that the Bambudye collected throughout the centuries has become public knowledge.

Ilunga Kabale happened to be the last king to rule the Luba Empire when it was intact and the first king whose death date can be established with any precision. Scholars believe that he died sometime between late 1868 and late 1870. However, the first ruler of the empire to have been mentioned in contemporary written records is Kumwimbe Ngombe. It is reported that Kumwimbe Ngombe sent special envoys to the court of the Kingdom of Kazembe in late January and early February 1832.

Trade throughout Lubaland involved journeys by foot of hundreds of kilometers. Villagers sold raffia cloth, charms, zebra hides, iron, cord, baskets, pottery, musical instruments, beads, ornamental feathers, copper, and food products such as oils, salt, and smoked fish. Iron was used primarily as a utilitarian metal for hoes, axes, and weapons, while copper was traded exclusively as a royal or prestige good. Beads were also used as prestige goods that were often brought to the royal court as payment of the tribute to the king.

It is believed that the disintegration of the Luba Empire occurred between the 1860s and 1891. Like many other kingdoms in Central Africa, the Luba Empire was seriously affected by the demands of the slave trade. However, the decline of the empire took place in a different and unique way. Since the Luba Empire was located so far in the interior, it took much more time for the international trade to influence the development of the empire than it did for coastal kingdoms. Power relationships within the Luba Empire were primarily destabilized by the intrusion of Arab and Swahili slave and ivory traders who, from the early 1860s, entered the territories of the empire from the East African coast and the southwest. It was almost impossible for the Luba warriors, who did not use any guns, to organize any resistance to these intrusions, since the use of firearms gave slave traders a greater advantage. Msiri, a trader from Tanzania, conquered the southern border of the empire, while slave and ivory traders from Angola—called *ovimbundus*—occupied the southwestern region. Tippu Tip, the most famous of the Arab Swahili traders, raided several regions of the Luba Empire, disrupting local political regimes and expanding his slave and ivory trade in a very significant way. By the end of the 19th century, the Luba Empire was split in two by a succession dispute and was eventually dismembered and incorporated into the Belgian Congo Free State.

Daniel Kahozi

Further Reading

Reefe, Q. Thomas. *The Rainbow and the Kings: A History of the Luba Empire to 1891.* Berkeley: University of California Press, 1981.

Vansina, Jan. *Kingdoms of the Savanna: A History of Central African States until European Occupation.* Madison: University of Wisconsin Press, 1968.

Verhulpen, Edmund. *Baluba et Balubaisés du Katanga.* Anvers: L'Avenir Belge, 1936.

Lunda

The Kingdom of Lunda, also known as the Lunda Empire, existed between 1665 and 1887. Located within the present-day borders of northeastern Angola, northwestern Zambia, and the Katanga Province of the Democratic Republic of Congo, the Lunda kingdom expanded by the absorption of the chiefs of neighboring villages. Absorbing these chiefs into the empire proved to be more effective than deposing them. For more than two centuries, the Lunda kingdom experienced peace and prosperity, thanks not only to the consolidation of the centralized state by the adoption of an orderly system of succession but also to control over the slave trade within the empire. The Lunda Empire is known as one of the precolonial African confederations that provided the largest number of slave captives to the Portuguese. The Lunda were able to trade directly with the Portuguese because they subdued intermediary chiefs and kingdoms.

According to oral tradition, Chibunda Ilunga, a famous hunter, came in 1450 from the Luba Empire, where his brother ruled, and founded the new Lunda dynasty by marrying a princess from an area in the south of Katanga Province. Chibunda Ilunga and his wife founded the first Lunda village, called Gaaand in the KiLunda language. Later on, their son was able to unify the Lunda people from remote territories and expand the empire. He gave himself the title *mwanta yaav*

Hugh Tracey and the International Library of African Music

In 1957 Hugh Tracey, founder of the International Library of African Music, traveled to Zambia and the Democratic Republic of Congo to create a collection of Lunda songs and dances. He visited several mining regions in both countries and recorded what experts believe are among the most popular songs and dances from the Lunda culture. These songs and dances, performed by Lunda men and women who went to mining zones to find work, celebrate life and the heritage of ancestors, recount the stories of Lunda heroes, and highlight important family values.

(supreme lord). Between the 1600s and 1700s, the Kingdom of Lunda reached its peak, controlling more than 150,000 square kilometers. With more than 175,000 inhabitants, the Lunda kingdom became powerful economically and militarily. And to further increase their influence within the region, Lunda kings (*mwata yamvos*), married descendants of the Luba kings, creating political ties that proved useful in times of conflict. By the end of the 18th century, the Lunda kingdom became a confederation of hundreds of chieftainships that paid their tribute to the supreme lord while enjoying considerable local autonomy. For scholars the study of the Lunda system of governance is very important, as it sheds light on the high level of social, political, and economic organization that existed in Africa before European colonization.

A council of royal dignitaries advised the supreme lord of Lunda. At first power was passed down through the male line, but because of the influence conquered chieftainships had on the centralized state, succession became eventually matrilineal. Some of the kings who ruled over the Lunda Empire were Mbala I Yaav (1690–1720), Muteba I Kat Kateng (1720–1750), Mukaz Waranankong (1750–1767), Nawej Mufa Muchimbunj (1767–1775), Cikombe Yaava (1775–1800), Nawej II Ditend (1800–1852), Mulaj a Namwan (1852–1857), Muteba II a Cikombe (1857–1873), Mbumb I Muteba Kat (1874–1883), and Cimbindu a Kasang (1883–1884).

The Lunda kingdom featured what many considered one of the first police forces in Africa. Members of these forces had the responsibility of enforcing the king's orders in the capital and its neighboring villages. Another similar group consisted of traveling chiefs (*kawattas*), whose main responsibility was the collection of tribute. *Kawattas* had the power to stop and check caravans, determine what was appropriate to give to the supreme lord, and give warnings to chiefs who paid their tribute late or paid insufficient tribute. Lunda tribute collection significantly assisted the growth and prosperity of the centralized state. However, the supreme lord redistributed several goods that were collected to his aristocrats, remote chiefs, and many disadvantaged groups. This system of redistribution of wealth gave the king maximum loyalty from his people.

The economy of the Lunda kingdom was based not only on the slave, copper, salt, and ivory trades but also on hunting, agriculture, and fishing. It is known that the Lunda people lived in an area rich in swamps, rivers, streams, and lagoons. After cassava was introduced to Lunda, it quickly became the staple food for all the people. They also used cassava and millet to make a special beer called *katubi*. The first trading partners were the Arab Swahili traders coming from East Africa, but from the beginning of the 17th century the Portuguese took over. In return, Lunda traders received from them firearms and textiles.

Lunda people lived in small villages that were more permanent than those of neighboring people. Lunda houses were small huts built of tall grass and wood, and the roofs were hatched. The Lunda abandoned the use of grass when they acquired the knowledge of building mud houses. Within the regions of Central Africa, the Lunda were recognized as famous artists, as they were skilled at making bangles and ornaments with thin copper wire that were used both for decoration and as currency. Because of their cultural, political, and economic ties with neighboring kingdoms, the Lunda shared similar art traditions with the Luba and the Kuba. It is believed that Lunda kings emulated and adopted the insignia and most of the sumptuary articles of Luba royalty. For example, to convey political prestige and spiritual powers, all Lunda kings adopted Luba thrones.

The Kingdom of Lunda declined toward the end of the 19th century after the Chokwe, who were armed with more powerful guns, invaded it. Although Lunda chiefs and people continued to live within the borders of the empire, the Chokwe imposed their language and customs on them, causing a rapid disintegration of the Lunda culture. At the beginning of European colonization, the Lundaland was divided between Portuguese Angola, King Leopold II's Congo Free State, and the British in Rhodesia.

Daniel Kahozi

Further Reading

Bustin, Edouard. *Lunda under Belgian Rule: The Politics of Ethnicity.* Cambridge, MA: Harvard University Press, 1975.

Thomas, Hugh. *The Slave Trade: The Story of the Atlantic Slave Trade, 1440–1870.* New York: Simon and Schuster, 1997.

Thornton, John K. *Africa and Africans in the Making of the Atlantic World, 1400–1680.* Cambridge: Cambridge University Press, 1992.

M

Mahi

Although it may not be considered a kingdom in a traditional sense, Mahi in what is now the middle region of Benin and Togo consisted of a quasi-centralized polity and a cultural linguistic community insofar as it was a confederation of otherwise decentralized groups of people and small regional states that assimilated with one another on the interstices of larger regional empires such as Dahomey and Oyo during the transatlantic slave trade in the 18th and 19th centuries. Situated north of Ouidah and sandwiched between the Volta River to the west and the Ouémé River to the east, the territory of Agonli-Cové marked the region's geographical and cultural center. Sixty miles north of the coast and equidistant from Abomey and Kétu, Agonli-Cové served as a junction for those who migrated between Fon- and Yoruba-speaking areas.

The center of the Mahi region rested in a higher elevation area with scattered hills in what is now central Benin. Often identified by European explorers as the Kong Mountains, the region north of Abomey experienced intense heat that could reach up to 40 degrees Celsius during dry seasons. The rainier months from May to June and October to November brought cooler temperatures but much more concentrated humidity, which would have made traveling along the networks of roads and rivers leading into and out of the area more daunting for traders and slave captives en route to the coast. A geography that boasted numerous rivers and small hills, however, served the region's residents well. The rivers supported agricultural and fishing economies, while the hills helped many of the smaller communities find refuge from bands of warriors seeking slaves.

Gbe-speaking peoples (Ewe, Fon, Adja, Gun, and Yoruba) who migrated from various areas throughout what is now Ghana, Togo, Benin, and Nigeria established the foundation for Mahi culture from the early 11th century onward. Its people did not share a common cultural-linguistic or ethnic identity at this time, but similar languages, religious beliefs, and forms of political organization allowed communities to assimilate and forge a social connection over time.

The arrival of Europeans on the coast and the onset of the transatlantic slave trade in particular had a notable impact on what eventually became a Mahi polity from the late 17th century onward. The confluence of the large Zou and Ouémé Rivers in the area and established road networks made the region easily accessible for the militaries of powerful neighboring empires that sought a consistent supply of captives. A primary source of slaves, the area likely provided a significant portion of the 400,000 Africans sold and transported to the Americas as the trade reached its zenith in the first quarter of the 18th century.

People in the region, once a fluid assortment of small states and communities, forged a more established political bond starting in the early 18th century. In addition to being targets of slavers, people in Agonli-Cové found themselves at the crossroads of fighting between Dahomey and Oyo in the 1720s. Their collective Mahi identity emerged as they countered the powerful Dahomean kingdom in the early 18th century. They did so by uniting to resist the empire's growing military might. The word *mahi,* which roughly translated means "revolutionaries," derived from a term Dahomey's leaders used to describe the people who lived between their kingdom and Oyo. The name became synonymous with the formation of a common cultural-linguistic and political identity, however, as refugees displaced from the area following Dahomean raids in the early 1730s convened in the Jagun dynasty.

It is important to note that identity formation constitutes a fluid process. While some may have categorized themselves as Mahi by the mid-1700s, others certainly would have also described themselves as belonging to a range of smaller ethnic groups that made up a broader multiethnic Mahi culture and polity. Regardless, its residents' unified stance and proclamations of autonomy complicated Dahomean authority. A confederation between the small regional kingdoms of Gbowèlé, Tchahounka, and Houndjroto constituted one of the more cohesive challenges to Dahomean supremacy. In response to their unified struggles, Dahomey's leaders often targeted Mahi's Sakpata religious leaders for enslavement, hoping that their capture and deportation would unravel the fabric of the region's rebellious activities. Devotees of the god of smallpox, Sakpata leaders were often healers and wielded considerable power in building a sense of cohesive identity. Narratives of slaves performing Sakpata-related healing practices in Brazil abound, suggesting that many who either held religious and political power in Mahi or at least had some exposure to healing practices were captured.

Mahi resistance persisted in waves for nearly a century, with short-lived periods of calm. The Dahomean king, Kpingla, for example, forged a brief diplomatic connection by marrying a Mahi woman during his reign in the late 18th century. In spite of the occasional thaw in relations, Dahomey's leaders continued to seize the area by force in hopes that they could control access to rivers and trade networks leading to the coast. Later, the Dahomean kings Adandozan and Gezo continued annual onslaughts on Mahi into the 19th century. Gezo's troops suffered a humiliating defeat in 1823 but retaliated by sacking Houndjroto in 1832, which effectively brought parts of Mahi more formally under direct Dahomean rule.

Marcus Filippello

Further Reading

Akinjogbin, A. I. *Dahomey and Its Neighbors, 1708–1818.* Cambridge: Cambridge University Press, 1967.

Anigkin, Sylvain C. "A History of the Mahi Populations: On the Controversy about the 'Mahi' Ethnonym and Toponym." *Cahiers d'Études Africaines* (2001): 243–265.

Law, Robin. *The Slave Coast of West Africa, 1550–1750: The Impact of the Atlantic Slave Trade on an African Society*. Oxford, UK: Clarendon, 1991.

Mulira, J. G. "A History of the Mahi Peoples from 1774 to 1920." PhD dissertation, UCLA, 1984.

Sweet, James H. *Domingos Álvares, African Healing, and the Intellectual History of the Atlantic World*. Chapel Hill: University of North Carolina Press, 2011.

Mali

The present-day state known as Mali is one of the old West African kingdoms that played a crucial role in the trans-Saharan trade of which the articles of trade were salt, gold, and other priceless products. It must be pointed out that before the formation of the Malian Empire under the headship of Sundiata, the state had a series of quality leaders who contributed to its growth. According to archaeological finds, it was established that the old Malian state of Jenne-Jeno had been in existence

Mansa Musa, king of Mali, holding a gold orb, detail from a map of North Africa attributed to Abraham Cresques, 1375. (Fotosearch/Getty Images)

since 200 BCE. The Mandinka (Malinke) were instrumental in the formation of the empire. These Malinke developed various chiefdoms out of which the Kangaba emerged as the most influential in the beginning of the 13th century. By the 16th century, however, the state started losing its authority and control.

The leader of the Soso kingdom, Sumanguru Kante, subjugated the Malinke and succeeded in bringing them under his authority in 1224. Given his oppressive style of leadership, there was a rebellion during his reign. Sundiata, a Kangaba prince who had been in exile for some time, spearheaded the rebellion. Having returned from exile in 1230, he brought under his leadership the various chiefdoms of the Malinke. In 1235 with the support of the united force of the Malinke, which he led, he succeeded in overcoming Sumanguru in the War of Kirina. Subsequently, he brought the Soso territory under his control. He then commenced the process of forming a new state among the Malinke. A new capital thus emerged at Niani, which can be located in the current borders of both Mali and Guinea. In 1255 Sundiata died, but prior to his demise he had laid the foundation for the change of the state into an empire. For example, Mali, with his triumph over the Soso, became larger in terms of territorial expansion to the northern part, which was hitherto an area formerly under the influence of the Ghana Empire. In the western part, the control of Mali covered Senegal as well as the Gambia River. Interestingly, the gold-rich areas of Bure and Bambuk in the south became incorporated into the Mali Empire.

During the reign of Mansa Ulli (1255–1270), Sundiata's son, the frontiers of the empire became more expanded. It was during Mansa Ulli's reign that Walata, Timbuktu, and Gao were integrated into the empire. Bewteen 1270 and 1285 there were three different leaders who ruled the empire. But in 1285 Sakura, one of the leading officials in the state, took the throne through a coup d'état. Sakura further transformed Mali and set it on the path of glory when he died in 1300. The climax of the power and prosperity of Mali was under the leadership of Mansa Kankan Musa (1312–1337). A number of factors were responsible for the greatness of Mali during his reign. First was his ability to have effective control over every part of the state. Second, he had a functional administrative system that saw to good governance. Third, there was a deep sense of appreciation for hard work and merit, while no room was left for oppression and injustice given the efficiency of the law guiding crime and punishment in the land. In view of all this, trading and commercial activities came to a promising stage and expanded against the backdrop of the tight security in the several trade routes and centers.

The religion of Islam was another contributing factor to making the empire a great one. Mansa Musa promoted the religion to the advantage of the empire such that it became known to the outside world and thus became connected with the Muslim world. In 1324 Mansa Musa went on a pilgrimage to the Holy Land, Mecca, through Egypt. On this journey he had a large quantity of gold. He showed his act of benevolence by giving out the gold to people as gifts. This to a large extent adversely affected the economy of Egypt in which case the value and price of the commodity crashed. The activities of Mansa Musa became so popular that the news reached Europe, hence the appearance of the Mali Empire on different world maps in the 14th century.

Interestingly, while on pilgrimage Mansa Musa secured property in both Mecca and Cairo to provide shelter for worshippers from western Sudan. Given the wonderful impression he had of the architectural designs of great places that he found in Cairo, he decided to have the services of al-Sahili, a renowned poet and architect whom he took to Mali with him. Al-Sahili took time out to design unique and beautiful mosques in Gao and Timbuktu. Amazing palaces were equally developed at Niani and Timbuktu for the use of the emperor. In view of all the great things he witnessed in the Holy Land, Musa sought to maintain a link with the Islamic world and formed a diplomatic association with the sultan of Fez in Morocco.

On his return to Mali, Musa made Islam the state religion and made it mandatory for everyone in the state to uphold the Islamic creed. Koranic academies were set up, while students were given support to acquire more knowledge in Morocco. This gave Timbuktu the privilege of becoming a leading academic and trading center in West Africa. By the time Mansa Musa finished his reign, the frontiers of the state had become more grand. For instance, the Mali Empire had reached the Atlantic coast in the west to Tadmekka and Gao in the east by 1337. Toward the north the empire succeeded in incorporating Walata and the regions of the Upper Niger in the south. Mansa Suleyman succeeded Mansa Musa between 1341 and 1360. However, the shining glory of the empire began to fade with the exit of Suleyman. Thus, within a space of 40 years Mali had as many as six different rulers. This points to the fact that the empire suffered from power tussles and political instability, which did not augur well for the empire as it began to lose a grip of its hitherto conquered territories.

Furthermore, the decline did not abate until the 15th century; hence, the ruler of the newly emerging state of Songhai invaded Niani around 1420 and ransacked the city. The implication of the disintegration of the empire was disheartening to the extent that Mali found it difficult to take charge of Timbuktu, given the deluge of attacks from both the Mossis and the Tuaregs. In the end, Walata capitulated to the pressure of the Tuaregs in 1434, while more feudal states freed themselves of Mali's encumbrance. For example, Mema freed itself from Mali but was later forced to become a part of the Songhai Empire in the 1450s. Against the backdrop of these crises, Mali reduced in size to its initial Malinke territories and stopped existing around the 17th century.

Ola-Oluwa A. Folami

Further Reading

Davidson, Basil. *The Growth of African Civilisation: A History of West Africa, 1000–1800.* London: Longman, 1965.

Stearns, P. N., ed. *The Encyclopedia of World History.* 6th ed. New York: Houghton Mifflin, 2001.

Stride, G. T., and C. Ifeka. *Peoples and Empires of West Africa.* Ontario: Thomas Nelson and Sons, 1971.

Malinke

The Malinke people—often referred to as Mandinka, Mandinko, and Mandingo—reside in West Africa in regions that were previously part of the Mali Empire (ca. 1230–ca. 1600). The Malinke were one of the two kingdoms that joined to create the empire, along with the Bambara. Though one of the largest ethnic groups in West Africa, the Malinke are a minority in every country in which they live with the exception of Gambia. Most Malinke practice Islam as a result of both the conversion of leaders of the Mali Empire—such as Mansa Musa—and the Fula jihads of the early 19th century. A substantial number of Malinke were captured and sold as slaves during wars in the 17th and 18th centuries, and many ended up in the Americas.

Because the Malinke live across several countries in West Africa—including Mali, Gambia, Guinea-Conakry, Sierra Leone, Liberia, Côte d'Ivoire, Senegal, Burkina Faso, Mauritania, and Niger—the climate and livelihoods vary widely. Malinke people live in both urban and rural environments, though like the majority of Africans most Malinke are rural dwellers. Most of West Africa exists on a low plateau buffeted by coastal plains in the west on the Atlantic Ocean, with isolated highlands throughout. The landscape is divided by five main river systems, two of which—the Senegal and the Niger—flow through areas inhabited by the Malinke.

Malinke people today are both farmers and herders, many of whom live in settled villages throughout West Africa. Like many other African herders, Malinke familial compounds are built to protect both families and cattle, with fields for subsistence farming and, increasingly, cash crops built around the living areas. Politically, the Malinke are part of many different states, meaning that traditional authorities have varying amounts of power in everyday life. In many cases these traditional authorities are tied to decisions over land tenure and resource use, such as in Senegal.

The Malinke are perhaps best known for their songs, poetry, and other forms of oral literature passed down through generations through teachers called griots. This literature contains not only the histories of the Malinke but also poetry, songs, and other types of knowledge. Because this knowledge was generational and proprietary, the recipients and guardians of it developed into a hierarchical caste system, which helped to keep it within specific lineages. Griots, leather workers, blacksmiths, praise poets, and weavers were known collectively as *nyamakala* and served as politically important advisers to rulers and throughout the empire.

Malinke history is ancient and rich. Malinke was part of the Ghana Empire (ca. 300–ca. 1230), which was the first of the great empires of West Africa. Though there is some scholarly debate, the current consensus is that the Ghana Empire rose in response to increasing trade with Berbers and Arab merchants from North Africa via the Sahara. A great deal of information about this ancient kingdom comes from the Andalusian Muslim geographer and historian al-Bakri, whose writings condense and synthesize information from travelers (and who lived in Iberia for most of his life and never traveled to Africa). He wrote extensively about the economic foundations of Ghana. Salt, copper, textiles, and gold were some of the most important goods traded from the Ghana Empire.

The Malinke lived mostly around Wagadou (present-day Ouagadougou) during the time of the Ghana Empire. Known as the Mande people, they slowly formed a confederation of smaller groups that challenged the central authority of Ghana. They were finally unified by Sundiata Keita, who became the first Mali emperor. The *Epic of Sundiata* chronicles his life and reign and is considered part of the national mythology of Mali, Gambia, Senegal, and Guinea-Conakry. This epic poem is still performed by griots in masked performances and contains cultural elements that remain central to Malinke life today, including ideas about familial relationships, lineage, hierarchy, and spirituality. Like many national origin stories, the *Sundiata* epic includes a prophecy fulfilled, an heir in exile who returns to claim his throne from evil forces, and overcoming adversity.

Though much of the Sundiata epic is mythological, what is true is that Sundiata Keita unified the Malinke (Mande) under his rule and created an empire larger than any that had come before it in West Africa. That the subsequent Keita dynasty (and its successors) all claimed to trace their lineage back to Bilal, the muezzin of Prophet Muhammad, demonstrates not that this was historically accurate but that Islam became a central defining element of the ruling class of the Mali Empire. Sundiata's dynasty existed for only three generations, until 1275. Ouali (sometimes Ali) Keita I seized the throne after Sundiata's death, usurping Sundiata's son and half brother, who should have succeeded according to law. Ouali was an effective ruler, expanding the empire farther west into the Senegambia and enacting agricultural reforms that put many former soldiers to work in the newly conquered areas, helping them to be assimilated more fully. Ouali's reign lasted until 1270, and after his death the empire went through years of instability due to fighting between two of Sundiata's adopted sons.

The empire came under the administration of court officials with ties to Sundiata from 1275 to 1300, at which point Sundiata's sister's line reclaimed control. Known as the Kolonkan Keita dynasty (from the name of Sundiata's sister, Kolonkan), these *mansas* (kings) ruled in a less military style than their predecessors and brought stability and prosperity to the empire. The last ruler of the Kolonkans, Abubakari Keita II, abdicated the throne in 1312 and ceded it to the son of Abubakari Keita I, one of Sundiata's advisers who had ruled during the previous dynasty. This new lineage, named the Faba Laye Keita for its progenitor, ruled until 1389, producing some of the most important rulers of the empire. The first of these was the famous Mansa Musa Keita I, usually known simply as Mansa Musa.

Mansa Musa is one of the most famous precolonial African leaders to ever live. Musa was a devout Muslim and expanded the faith within the empire, making it the religion of the nobility. He peaceably annexed the scholar city of Timbuktu and transformed the university from a small center of Islamic learning into one of the most important educational sites in the entire Muslim world, Sankore. He expanded the kingdom, including accepting the submission of the king of Gao. Most famously, Musa went on hajj from 1324 to 1326, spending such a large amount of gold that he caused its value to decline in Egypt for the better part of two years.

This extravagance caught the attention of both the Christian and large Muslim worlds, and Mali appeared on many global maps beginning in the 14th century. Musa also brought back to Mali with him famous scholars and architects, adding to the prestige of Sankore and creating some of the most recognizable architecture in the world.

Musa's son, Maghan I, was not as efficient a ruler as his father and lived more extravagantly than his means allowed. However, his rule was not long, and his brother, Suleiman, became ruler in 1341. Suleiman ruled until 1360 and brought fiscal discipline back to the empire. He also hosted the Muslim traveler Ibn Battuta, who recorded his impressions of the empire during his stay in the 1350s. Suleiman was succeeded by his son Camba Keita, but Camba was overthrown within a few months by one of Maghan I's sons, and the empire was run for several years by an administrator descended from a slave lineage. By the end of the dynasty in 1389 the empire had lost some territory and prestige but remained on solid footing.

Over the next 150 years the Malinke Empire lost increasing territory to the growing Songhai Empire to its north as internal disputes and mismanagement brought about its slow decline. The trans-Saharan trade routes that had made the empire great were gradually diverted to the coast, giving Songhai and the emerging kingdoms to the south the advantage. In 1537 a new Malinke kingdom emerged in the south, called Kaabu. A province of Mali since its conquest by Sundiata in the 1230s, Kaabu broke away from Mali as the empire was broken up by raids from the Mossis to the south and the Songhai Empire to the north. The culture of the Mali Empire, which was largely based in Malinke traditions, lived on within Kaabu. Its ruling structure was less centralized, and the *mansa* was accountable to a council of chiefs from around the kingdom.

By the beginning of the 19th century with the decline of both Mali and Songhai, a new religious fervor swept West Africa in the form of jihads carried out by Fula from the Niger basin. These jihads would eventually overtake Kaabu, ending Malinke power there and leaving it under the control of the Fula until European colonization later in the 19th century. By the 20th century, the Malinke were dispersed throughout West Africa and did not hold power in any of the countries they inhabited. They emerged again into the consciousness of the African diaspora in the United States with Alex Haley's *Roots,* in which the main character, Haley's purported ancestor Kunta Kinte, was Malinke (Mandinka). Though historians and genealogists have remained skeptical of the veracity of these claims, the Malinke have become an indelible part of the diasporic imagination.

Sarah E. Watkins

Further Reading

Diagne, Khady. "Governance and Natural Disasters: Addressing Flooding in St. Louis, Senegal." *Environment and Urbanization* 19(2) (2007): 1–11.

Jansen, Jan. "Masking Sunjata: A Hermeneutical Critique." *History in Africa* 27(2000): 131–141.

Levtzion, Nehemia. *Ancient Ghana and Mali.* London: Methuen, 1973.

Masonen, Pekka. *The Negroland Revisited: Discovery and Invention of the Sudanese Middle Ages.* Helsinki: Finnish Academy of Science and Letters, 2000.

Niane, Djibril Tamsir. *Sundiata: An Epic of Old Mali.* London: Longmans, 1965.

Mandara

Mandara can be referred to as both a region and a state. As a region, it is located within the mountainous range of northern Cameroon and northeastern Nigeria. Thus, the inhabitants of Mandara are called Mantognards, a French name meaning "hill dweller." The Mandara region also includes the plains surrounding this mountainous range; therefore, the region's boundaries are not clearly defined. The Manadara region is inhabited by different ethnic groups and can be classified as a region or zone of high linguistic diversity in West-Central Africa. This ethnic-linguistic diversity in part has significantly contributed to the history of the region. As a state, the Mandara kingdom emerged between the 15th and 16th centuries CE, known as the dynasty period. Not much is known about Mandara prior to the 16th century, but the available albeit meager historical sources indicate that the predynasty period was relatively peaceful, with somewhat mutual interaction among groups. The political structure was centered on the sacred kinship system whereby the craftsmen and hunters were major political-religious figures. In most cases, they were chiefs over several autochthonous communities.

Mandara Mountains

The Mandara Mountains are a chain/cluster of rugged volcanic mountains extending to approximately 125 miles across the international boarders of Nigeria and Cameroon in the countries' northeastern and northwestern regions, respectively. The mountains are of low altitude characteristically, but the highest elevation above sea level is 4,900 feet. Both the hilltops and the surrounding valleys/lowlands are of great significance to the development of centralized states and the occupation of diverse ethnic groups in the region. The formation of the mountains makes them suitable for hiking. The inhabitants create terraces in the slopes of the mountains for suitable agricultural practices to support the local economy of the settlers and the surrounding communities. For almost a decade Judy Sterner and Nicholas David have advocated harnessing the tourism potentials of the Mandara Mountains, particularly to economically support the impoverished communities on and around the mountains. Among other things, Sterner and David have proposed an international peace park and other national and local initiatives to develop an ecocultural tourism package for the region of the Mandara Mountains. Unfortunately, the outbreak of the Boko Haram insurgency in northeastern Nigeria and northern Cameroon has significantly halt the campaign to develop the Mandara Mountains as a tourist destination. In fact, the British and other international authorities have declared this region unsafe for Western tourists, who represent the target of the tourism initiative.

By the late 16th century the Mandara state had fully emerged, and the political structure became quasi-centralized. The drive for expansion and conquering neighboring communities became the rule of the land. This expansionist ideology of Mandara was initiated by the dynasty of Sankre, who was a warrior. Sankre waged war and conquered Dulo toward the end of the 16th century, and he made Dulo the capital of Mandara state. This seizure of Dulo marked an era of political contestation and intense suspicion between the Mandara kingdom and its neighbors. For example, Idris Alaoma, emperor of the Bornu Empire, instigated the process of installing another dynasty in Mandara. This process culminated in the enthronement of Nanda in the early 17th century as the new Mandara dynasty. The implication of the alliance with the Bornu Empire was the Islamization of Mandara and the protection of Bornu's political and economic interests; thus, Mandara became a sultanate. However, the subordination of Mandara to Bornu did not last long. A stronger Mandara emerged in late 18th century, defeated Bornu, and had several other kingdoms and chiefdoms under its jurisdiction.

During the heyday of the Mandara state, the kingdom was a major partner in subcontinental trade. The richness of the region in iron ore opened the trade opportunity in iron, and Mandara was a center for great iron production. The state was a major supplier of iron in the region. Although there is sketchy evidence on whether this industry was in the control of the political elites, the role of the elites in slave raiding and trading in the region raises some degree of certainty affirming that the elites would have been in charge of iron production and distribution. According to Scott MacEachern, during the precolonial period of Mandara, the slave trade was a social and economic cornerstone for the maintenance of local elite status, which allowed the elites to demonstrate their control over the bodies of common people and to buy horses, armor, weapons, and imported goods that signified and enhanced elite status. Horse breeding, as one of the major occupations in Mandara, was instrumental in its activities in slave raiding and trading in long-distance commerce.

At the dawn of the 19th century, Mandara hegemony was threatened by the increasing presence of the Fulani pastoralists who had previously enjoyed a mutual relationship with Mandara in cattle husbandry in the region. The Fulani, Adamawa jihadist, and Mahdist coalition with the weaker Borno Empire launched fierce attacks on Mandara within the last two decades of the 19th century. As a consequence of these attacks, toward the end of the century the capital of Mandara, Dulo, was finally devastated, leading to the eventual downfall and loss of power, authority, and influence of Mandara in the region.

However, unlike many African kingdoms, the fall of Mandara was not the end of its existence. Mandara still remains not as the vibrant and indomitable kingdom of the 16th–18th centuries but rather as a region. The Mandara region witnessed a series of unpleasant experiences with different colonial administrations, which further weakened the power of the sultan and reduced the office to a mere level of existence. Shortly after the fall of the Mandara kingdom, the region was conquered by Germany in 1902. The Germans then handed colonial administration of this region to the French in 1918. Also, the British administration in Nigeria was in charge of the part of the region that falls within Nigerian territory. Although modern-day Mandara lies in the northern part of Cameroon, its fragmented portion in northeastern Nigeria is still historically and culturally connected with the great Mandara kingdom.

Abidemi Babatunde Babalola

Further Reading

Asiwaju, Anthony Ijaola. *Partitioned Africans: Ethnic Relations across Africa's International Boundaries, 1884–1984.* Lagos, Nigeria: University of Lagos Press, 1994.

MacEachern, Scott. "Residuals and Resistance: Languages and History in the Mandara Mountains." In *When Languages Collide: Perspectives on Language Conflict, Language Competition and Language Coexistence,* edited by Brian D. Joseph and Johanna Destafano, 21–44. Columbus: Ohio State University Press, 2002.

MacEachern, Scott. "Selling the Iron for Their Shackles: Wandala-Montagnard Interactions in Northern Cameroon." *Journal of African History* 34(2) (1993): 247–270.

Mankessim

Mankessim derives its name from *oman kese,* meaning "big town." It is the ancestral home of the Fante people of Ghana and is located along the Atlantic coastline in the Central Region of Ghana. Mankessim is a low-lying area with dense scrub and grassland and scattered trees, which grow to an average of five meters. The climate is mild, with temperatures ranging from 24 to 28 degrees Celsius due to its contiguity to the Atlantic Ocean. Double-digit rainfall figures are recorded from May to a peak in June, with drier conditions dominating from July to early September. These physical features enable the Fante people to engage in agriculture, namely farming and fishing.

The history of Mankessim dates from the precolonial era, when the Fante were initially part of the Asante kingdom, which extended as far as Bono-Manso in the Brong Ahafo region of Ghana. According to their traditions, the Fante people

Borbor Mfantse Festival

Annually, the people of Mankessim celebrate the Borbor Mfantse festival. This festival marks the beginning of food harvesting and the remembrance of revered ancestors. During the festival, ritual offerings are divided into private and public ceremonies. Private rituals include sacrifices to divinities and ancestors, ritual libations, and incantations. Public celebrations commence with a grand durbar of chiefs, where people pledge allegiance to their leaders. Other programs organized during the festival include procreation rites for mothers of twins, food bazaars, street carnivals, and sports competitions.

separated from their Akan kin as a result of population pressure. This separation led the Fante to being referred to as "Fa-Atsew," meaning the "half that succeeded." This Akan community migrated south under the leadership of three warriors known as Obrumankoma (meaning "the whale"), Odapagyan (meaning "the eagle"), and Osono (meaning "the elephant"). Obrumankoma and Odapagyan died during the migration, and Osono led the Fante people to the Central Region, where they met autochthonous peoples such as the Asebus, Etsiis, and Morees. The Fante occupied the Etsii capital Adowegyir in 1252 and renamed it Mankessim. The chief religious leader, Komfo Amono, planted a spear in the ground at Mankessim. The location of the spear became the site of an important shrine (Nananom Mpow) and hallowed ground where traditional celebrations and the installation of chiefs took place. The Fante people thus became a distinct nation.

In 1650, various Fante groups began to spread out from Mankessim to found a number of settlements that evolved into independent city-states, such as Abora, Anomabu, Gomoa, and Komenda. This migration was due to population pressure, the growth of the Atlantic trade, and political rivalry among the various groups that made up the state at Mankessim. The Fante structured themselves into quarters, each with its own political head (braffo). However, there was one head braffo who led the various heads of quarters. The heads of the quarters also doubled as war-lords (asafohene). Thus, they were responsible for ensuring the material welfare of their people, undertaking communal and social work, and being military leaders in times of war.

As European trade became more important and British and Dutch forts littered the Gold Coast, many Fante states founded outposts and settlements along the coast to participate actively in the trade both as middlemen and as traders in their own right. In this commercial capacity Fante relations with Asante waned, leading to several Asante invasions in the 18th and 19th centuries. The Fante monopolized the coastal trade, especially the import of firearms, and controlled the trade route to the interior, effectively excluding the Asante from direct trade with Europeans. Regrettably, these invasions proved inimical to British interests and coastal trade. Britain allied with the Fante, preferring to practice a strategy of divide and rule among small states rather than be at the mercy of a powerful one.

The Fante-Asante wars had far-reaching effects on the history of the Gold Coast (Ghana). On the Asante side, the wars led to the breakup of the great Asante Empire and the British conquest of Asante in 1874 and its annexation into the British colony of the Gold Coast in 1901. The wars also solidified Fante unity. With respect to Britain, its alliance with the Fante led to the steady growth of British influence, resulting in the Bond of 1844 that legalized the jurisdiction that Britain had exercised unofficially over the people of the coastal states.

Traditional Fante reaction to this steady growth of British power and jurisdiction crystallized in 1868 in the formation of the Fante Confederation, which despite its name included non-Fante states such as Denkyira, Twifu, Wassa, and Assin. The drive toward this confederation was due to a host of factors, including the Select Committee report of 1865 that advocated eventual British withdrawal from the Gold Coast. The Fante began to organize themselves for defense against future Asante invasions and for taking over the administration from the British in the event of their proposed withdrawal. Another reason was the Fante resistance to the Anglo-Dutch exchange of forts in 1867. The exchange was unacceptable to the Fante because they were not consulted, and they regarded the Dutch as the traditional ally of the Asante; thus, the exchange of forts would lead to their states being overrun by the Asante.

The Fante Confederation as constituted in 1868 succeeded in establishing governmental machinery in Mankessim. It was headed by a king-president and had an army and a civil service. In 1869, the confederation asserted its sovereign status by declaring itself independent of the British, setting up its own Supreme Court at Mankessim, and imposing a poll tax to raise revenue for administration. On October 16, 1871, the Fante states drew up a constitution. Unfortunately, the Mankessim Constitution never came into effect. The British administration arrested and imprisoned its leaders for treason. Though they were freed a month later, the confederation never recovered from the shock, and by 1873 it was no more. Having silenced the confederation, the British formally annexed the Fante states and all other states of southern Ghana as the Gold Coast Colony and Protectorate in 1874. Until then the autonomy of the indigenous states had suffered little encroachment.

Mankessim today remains the homeland of the Fante, an affable people who took an active part in the destabilization of colonial rule. Citizens of the Fante state such as Kobina Sekyi, Kwegyir Aggrey, Casely Hayford, and Mensah Sarbah questioned the basis of racial inequality and criticized colonial rule, shattering the veneer of the British colonial government and ultimately contributing to Ghana's independence in 1957.

Cyrelene Amoah-Boampong

Further Reading

Adu-Boahen, Robert. *Ghana: Evolution and Change in the Nineteenth and Twentieth Centuries.* London: Longman, 1975.

Amenumey, D. E. K. *Ghana: A Concise History from Pre-Colonial Times to the Twentieth Century.* Accra, Ghana: Woeli Publishing Services, 2008.

Crayner, John. *Borbor Kukumfi.* Accra, Ghana: Bureau of Ghana Languages, 1969.

Gocking, Roger. *The History of Ghana.* Westport, CT: Greenwood, 2005.

Shumway, Rebecca. *The Fante and the Transatlantic Slave Trade.* Rochester: University of Rochester Press, 2011.

Mapungubwe

Mapungubwe is a settlement site located in Limpopo Province at the northern border of South Africa with Zimbabwe and Botswana and at the confluence of the Limpopo River (the second-largest river in East Africa) and the Shashe River.

Mapungubwe is thought to have been the last capital of a polity—sometimes referred to as the Kingdom of Mapungubwe or as Southern Africa's first state—that controlled the area in the 13th century. The site and its surroundings, extending over an area of about 300 square kilometers, form the Mapungubwe Cultural Landscape, which was classified by UNESCO as a World Heritage Site in 2003 and is part of the Mapungubwe National Park, established in 1995. In 2009 the park became part of the Limpopo-Shashe Transfrontier Conservation Area, which covers 5,900 square kilometers spread between South Africa, Botswana, and Zimbabwe.

Mapungubwe's current landscape is characterized by dry savanna woodland dominated by shrubby *C. Mopane* (butterfly tree) and a number of baobabs. The climate is semiarid and marked by recurrent drought and much variability in rainfall from one year to the next. Wildlife includes a number of large African game species, such as elephant, rhinoceros, lion, leopard, giraffe, and antelope, and a large variety of birds and reptiles.

The area is dotted with sandstone hills and ridges rising to approximately 60 meters high. One of these, Mapungubwe Hill is elongated in shape and was the site of an important settlement usually interpreted as the capital of the kingdom bearing the same name. Its flattened hilltop is defended by steep cliffs and could be ascended only from its southwestern side. It formed an elite area inhabited by a leader and his family, while the rest of his followers lived in a settlement located at the foot of the hill.

Mapungubwe emerged from a process of political consolidation that took place in the area around 900–1300 CE. The first communities of farmers moved into the Limpopo-Shashe Confluence area in the 10th century. They established their main settlement at the site of Shroda, where they interacted with hunter-gatherers and manufactured a type of pottery known as Zhizo. In about 1000 a group of newcomers entered the area and established a new central settlement at another site, known as K2. On the basis of their material culture, archaeologists have established that they were related to an archaeological complex in southwestern Zimbabwe called the Leopard's Kopje culture. Archaeologists have often referred to the K2 site as the capital of this new polity established by migrants from Zimbabwe. With an estimated population of 1,500 inhabitants, K2 was a settlement about three times as large as Shroda, and cattle seem to have occupied a central place in the political economy of this community. By about 1220, after roughly 200 years of occupation, K2 seems to have been abandoned for the nearby Mapungubwe site. This abandonment has been interpreted by archaeologists as resulting from an internal process of social change characterized by a growing distinction between commoners and an elite group. At Mapungubwe, the latter became physically separated from the rest of their communities when they settled on the top of the hill and inscribed in the landscape the importance they granted to social stratification. The settlement, with an estimated population of 5,000, was abandoned by the end of the 13th century after less than a century of occupation.

The ruling elite status of the inhabitants of the Mapungubwe hilltop, possibly associated with the control of rainmaking rituals, was theorized on the basis of a number of shallow burials, with unique sets of grave goods discovered at the center of the hilltop. These included a number of exotic glass beads imported through the Indian Ocean trade as well as an astonishing assemblage of gold objects, which have contributed to the celebrity of the site. The gold was hammered into thin sheets that were then applied on a wooden core and maintained in place by gold tacks. The largest collection of gold foil fragments was recovered in 1933 from a burial known as the Original Gold Burial M1, A620. These fragments are all that is left of animal figurines—including the famous Golden Rhinoceros and bovine, crocodile, elephant, and feline figurines—which may have been part of a divining bowl. Unfortunately, the site was first discovered in 1933 by a group of hunters, who began pillaging the graves and compromised the ability of later scholars to perfectly record the context of these finds. Trained archaeologists first arrived on the site in 1934, and there were no fewer than seven annual or multiannual excavation campaigns at Mapungubwe and K2 from then until 1999.

The gold at Mapungubwe was an import, possibly from northeastern Botswana and southwestern Zimbabwe. Evidence also suggests that iron products were imported. Traces of copper smelting on the hilltop suggest the import of copper ore, as there is no known local source of this metal. Copper was mixed locally with imported tin to make bronze. Elephants were abundant, and ivory probably constituted a large part of the area's exports. On the face of the material evidence, it has been suggested that Mapungubwe was a regional power center that stood at the crossroads of a number of regional long-distance trade routes. The control of long-distance trade combined with demographic growth has often been seen as central in driving the process of state formation at Mapungubwe.

Mapungubwe was occupied for only a short period before its abandonment in about 1300. Climatic changes and especially aridification of the area, combined with demographic growth, have often been seen as factors explaining the departure of its population. Some scholars view the Mapungubwe polity as a possible model for the Great Zimbabwe society that seems to have reached its florescence by the first half of the 14th century (period IV). Great Zimbabwe, located about 300 kilometers north of Mapungubwe, was also characterized in the 13th century by class distinction and sacred authority, and there are examples of dry-stone walls at the latter site, prefiguring the stone architecture that made Great Zimbabwe one of the most remarkable urban sites in Africa.

Gérard L. Chouin

Further Reading

Chirikure, S., P. Delius, A. Esterhuysen, and S. Hall. *Mapungubwe Reconsidered: A Living Legacy; Exploring beyond the Rise and Decline of the Mapungubwe State.* Johannesburg: Real African Publishers, 2016.

Duffey, A. E. "Mapungubwe: Interpretation of the Gold Content of the Original Gold Burial M1, A620." *Journal of African Archaeology* 10(2) (2012): 175–187.

Huffman, T. N. "Mapungubwe and Great Zimbabwe: The Origin and Spread of Social Complexity in Southern Africa." *Journal of Anthropological Archaeology* 28(1) (2009): 37–54.

Steyn, M. "The Mapungubwe Gold Graves Revisited." *South African Archaeological Bulletin* 62(186) (2007): 140–146.

Woodborne, S., M. Pienaar, and S. Tiley-Nel. "Dating the Mapungubwe Hill Gold." *Journal of African Archaeology* 7(1) (2009): 99–105.

Maravi

The name "Maravi" was given to a number of East African territorial states located in central and southern Malawi. From their origins as small states in the 16th century, Maravi states became key commercial players in the 17th century. At their height they were active in the international ivory trade and served at varying times as allies and rivals to the Portuguese. Historians have debated aspects of Maravi state formation, especially the chronology of the states' emergence and the role of the ivory trade. Past and current scholarship has faced the limitations of relatively sparse documentary accounts from the Portuguese and a corpus of oral traditions compiled only in later centuries. Recent archaeological work at Mankhamba, the site of one major Maravi capital, offers useful new evidence.

Maravi states developed near the shores of Lake Malawi. The area generally had good rainfall for farming and abundant wildlife that could sustain relatively large populations. In early times it was home to inhabitants who were mixed farmers, fishers, and frequent hunters. Pre-Maravi communities were remembered in oral tradition as autochthonous populations known as Batwa. Later migrants (considered proto-Chewa-language speakers) were called Banda and Kalimanjira. Some oral traditions consider proto-Chewa communities as migrants from Central Africa; however, linguistically speaking, their language was more closely linked to East African ones. Historical linguistic evidence offers an approximate date of the start of the first millennium CE for the arrival of ancestors to proto-Chewa speakers. Whether actual or metaphorical, oral traditions of external origins here and elsewhere reveal deeper understandings about power sharing between newcomers and autochthons.

Pre-Maravi communities were small-scale matrilineal societies who shared widespread regional participation in rain cults and secret mask societies. Their local rulers were spiritual authorities, seen as guardians of the local lands responsible for crop fertility and wider communal well-being. Some oral traditions remember them as predominantly female figures called *mangadzi* (later *makewana*, meaning "mother of children"). Also influential were *nyau* groups (men's dance societies) that provided another form of horizontal network between communities. Both forms of ritual authority played important roles in later Maravi states. In some cases, ritual specialists and shrines were co-opted (with varying degrees of success) into partnerships with Maravi rulers. In others, conflicts developed.

Most scholars agree that the founders of the early Maravi states arrived in the Zambezi region as part of a series of gradual migrations. Oral traditions described their origin in the Luba region of Central Africa. At sites such as Mankhamba (later a key Maravi capital), the archaeological record indicates new communities arriving in the 1300s. One of the significant migrant groups was the Phiri clan that became, at times, synonymous with the Maravi state. In the 1400s, leaders of the Phiri clan began using the royal title *kalonga*. Kalonga Chidzonzi was considered the founder of the first Maravi state. It began on the western side of Lake Malawi, with its capital at Manthimba (also frequently called Maravi in records). The Phiri clan is also credited with introducing the new religious rituals that gave Maravi states their name (often glossed as "people of the fire"). In varying ways, these rituals attempted to merge preexisting rain shrine practices with veneration for forces that supported Maravi leaders. This new ritual celebrated Mlira, the spirit of the *kalonga,* who took the physical form of a snake. The ceremony culminated with burning the Marimba bush (found throughout this region) as a sacrificial offering.

Maravi rulers claimed to be "owners of the land" but in practice had to rule through agreements with local authorities. This synthesis of hierarchical authority (of Maravi territorial states) with horizontal ritual authority (with ritual specialists serving rain shrines) became a successful political innovation. Subordinates of existing rulers (or ambitious individuals) soon created their own small territorial states. Often likened to a confederacy, the Maravi states were at varying times independent of each other or linked by hierarchies of tribute and conquest. New Maravi states were often known by the names of their founders, while the original Maravi state was called Kalonga. In the 16th century, Kalonga grew to include areas around Lake Malombe, the upper valley of the Shire River, and the Kirk mountain range. In the southern Shire Valley, two more Maravi states followed, Kaphwiti and Lundu. In the early 17th century, the ruler Muzura created a powerful Maravi state that eventually conquered Lundu. Later, the Undi state developed between the Shire and Zambezi Rivers. By the 18th century, Maravi states declined in scale and power as powerful other states and ivory and slave trading groups threatened their autonomy.

Lundu was the most centralized of the Maravi states. Around the start of the 17th century, the Lundu state expanded into parts of contemporary central Mozambique to include areas inhabited by Lolo and Makhuwa societies. Portuguese contemporaries called this state Bororo. Lundu leaders worked with the famous (or infamous) Zimba warriors. Much debate has centered on the Zimbas' origins as well as their relationship to this Maravi state. Called lawless marauders and even cannibals by the Portuguese after the Zimbas attacked the coast in the 1580s, some scholars suggest that the Zimbas were a specialized army created within the Lundu state. Others argue that the Zimbas were a migrant group from the southern Zambezi region who banded together to serve as mercenaries. Lundu expansion was politically as well as militarily different from other Maravi states. Lundu leaders, unlike other Maravi rulers, attempted to fulfill roles as leaders of the state's rain cult. Preexisting rain shrines and other mask societies were destroyed. After Lundu's incorporation into Muzura's state, rain shrines were reestablished. Their religious purpose was reimagined with the growth of the Mbona territorial cult that became a powerful force in subsequent centuries.

Muzura (also called Masula) created a prominent Maravi state in the early 1600s. Most sources indicate that he was a newcomer, not a Maravi elite, who successfully created a Maravi-style state. Portuguese contemporaries believed that he was an ex-slave or a former foreman from a Portuguese settlement in the south. Reported as a charismatic military leader, he was able to expand and unify the Maravi states south of Lake Malawi to create a confederacy that stretched to the East African coast near Angoche and Mozambique Island. In 1622, he allied with the Portuguese and successfully attacked the Lundu kingdom and added their territory to his rule. Earlier cooperation with the Portuguese, however, did not mean a lasting alliance. Later, Muzura allied with African kingdoms to the south (Karangaland and later Mutapa) to oppose Portuguese inland expansion. After a failed attack on Quelimane, Muzura's state declined in power as that of Kalonga grew.

Despite Portuguese attempts to settle and control more inland regions along the Zambezi, Maravi states maintained their influence and autonomy into the next century. At the close of the 1600s, the Portuguese described the "Empire of the Maravi" as controlling regions along the northern bank of the Zambezi River, while the Portuguese remained on the southern bank. Most Maravi states lasted until the 19th century, although their central authority weakened as professional ivory hunters and slave raiders began targeting the region.

Throughout their rise and decline, Maravi states' growth and expansion was closely linked to long-distance trade. Maravi elites, traders, and artisans were active in commerce with both East Africa's coast and copper-producing regions of inland Africa. Although scholars originally credited the ivory trade for the rise and fall of the Maravi states, recent views advocate for a broader commercial picture. Maravi states were traders as well as producers of a variety of valued trade items. At sites such as Mankhamba, a wide variety of imported items were found, including Khami glass beads, Chinese porcelain and other glazed ceramics from the coast, and large amounts of copper as wire, ingots, and jewelry. Site debris indicates a high volume of local ivory working, as both raw and worked ivory (into bangles) was exported regionally and to the coast. Maravi craftsmen also produced and worked iron and cotton cloth.

Today, many consider the historic Maravi states as the inspiration for the name of Malawi. The rain shrine at Mankhamba still exists (although it is not in use) and is considered an important Maravi site.

Andrea Felber Seligman

Further Reading

Alpers, Edward. *Ivory and Slaves: Changing Pattern of International Trade in Central East Africa to the Later Nineteenth Century.* Berkeley: University of California Press, 1975.

Ehret, Christopher. *An African Classical Age: Eastern & Southern Africa in World History, 1000 B.C. to A.D. 400.* Oxford, UK: James Currey, 1998.

Juwayeyi, Yusuf M. "Archaeological Excavations at Mankhamba, Malawi: An Early Settlement of the Maravi." *Azania: Archaeological Research in Africa* 45(2) (2010): 175–202.

Newitt, Malyn D. D. "The Early History of the Maravi." *Journal of African History* 23(2) (1982): 145–162.

Ntara, Samuel Josia. *The History of the Chewa (Mbiri ya Achewa)*. Translated by W. S. Kamphandira Jere and edited by Beatrix Hintze. Wiesbaden: Franz Steiner Verlag, 1973.

Phiri, Kings M. "Northern Zambezia: From 1500 to 1800." *Society of Malawi Journal* 32(1) (January 1979): 6–22.

Phiri, Kings M. "Pre-Colonial States of Central Malawi: Towards a Reconstruction of Their History." *Society of Malawi Journal* 41(1) (1988): 1–29.

Schoffeleers, J. Matthew. "The Zimba and the Lundu State in the Late Sixteenth and Early Seventeenth Century." *Journal of African History* 28(3) (1987): 337–355.

Marinids

Beginning in the 11th century, Arab nomads started attacking the northern region of Africa. Eventually they took over and established control over the Maghrib region. During this period of occupation, great social, economic, political, and cultural changes took place, including the creation of the two greatest Islamic empires ever built in the Islamic world: the empires of the Almoravids and Almohads. Before the demise of the two Islamic empires, they succeeded in unifying the whole of the Maghrib region into one single entity, a feat that has not been repeated in that part of the world since the 13th century, not even by leaders of the contemporary Maghrib region. After the Almohad Empire disintegrated in the 13th century, it was succeeded by three different Zenata Berber dynasties of Hafsids, Zayyanids, and Marinids, which sought without much success to replicate the achievements and successes of the Almoravids and Almohads, especially in the tasks of constructing regional unity and forging a distinct racial and regional identity. In fact, during the Marinids' rule the Maghrib experienced a general decline when compared to the eras of the Almoravids and Almohads.

From the foregoing it is clear that the Marinid state was established by nomadic Berbers and started to grow and spread from the east of modern-day Morocco until covering almost the entire country. At height of its growth and glory, the Marinid Empire therefore must have been within latitude 32 degrees north and 5 degrees west. The Marinids were both pastoral and nomadic people, and some of them were professional soldiers who for many years were fully engaged in bitter battles with the Almohads. In 1248 these soldiers, under the able leadership of Abu Yahya, comprehensively defeated the Almohads. And once it became obvious that they were going to have their own state, the Marinids declared themselves jihadists against Christians in Spain. Further, some Marinids were actively engaged in privateering. Finally, through the coastal cities, which were near the Mediterranean Sea, the Marinids were involved in extensive maritime trade activities and networks. Thus, they supplied gold, ivory, and slaves from West Africa to the Middle East and Europe. The Marinid leaders in an effort to consolidate their power and authority not only took very keen interest in cultural matters, Islamic learning, and education but also patronized them. The capital of the empire was developed into a center of Islamic learning and scholarship. In addition to building a new city—New Fez—from scratch, they also built schools, mosques, and madrassas in New Fez and in other towns and cities.

Prior to 1248, the Marinids had been consistently defeated in battle by the Almohads. However, in late 1248 in yet another war with the Almohads, their leader was killed. This development must have given the Marinids the needed courage and rare opportunity to rebuild their army and to restrategize and launch attacks against their neighbors and enemies. In that last major battle with the Almohads they took Fez, which they made the capital of the new Marinid dynasty. From Fez, they attacked and captured Marrakesh, the former capital of the Almohad state, in 1269. With this development the Marinids were thus able to achieve the rare feat of occupying the whole of modern-day Morocco. In addition to that feat, during this period of unimpeded success they occupied Algeria and part of Tunisia.

Also, as part of their strategy of further expand their spheres of control and influence, the Marinid leaders entered into an alliance with Granada. This was with a view to defending the latter in Andalus against encroachments from Christians. Consequently, the Maranids took over Granada but failed in capturing other Andalusian territories. However, the Marinids did not always have things their own way. For many years in the 10th century, they came under constant barrage from Castile. Then in 1267 Castile invaded Morocco. The Castilians were, however, beaten back by the Marinidian ruler, Abu Yusuf, who turned the tide and repeatedly tried to invade Spain, which he eventually occupied in 1285. Later in the same year, he signed a peace agreement with the king of Spain.

Under Abul-Hassan Ali and his successor and son, Abu Inan, the Marinid state expanded farther into Tunisia and captured Tlemcen. Ali built a new city, Mansura, with its own mosque. Similarly, he built some mosques in Sharabliyyin and Abul-Hassan in Fez and a madrassa in Rabat. In 1339, Ali completed the construction of the al-Ubbad Mosque in Tlemcen. He was overthrown by his own son, who quickly took over as the real leader of the Marinid state in 1348. However, he continued his late father's imperial policy of capturing other territories and annexing them, where possible, to the Marinid state. Like his father, he also built madrassas in Fez and Mekness.

By the second half of the 14th century, the Marinid state had started to fall and decline. Earlier in 1340, it had been defeated by a joint Portuguese and Castile army in the Battle of Rio Salad and was forced out of Andalusia. The state's decline was further accelerated in 1358 when Abu Inan was assassinated by his own vizier, one of the Wattasids, who came to dominate the political leadership of the empire until its final collapse. In this general confusion, the Bedouins and Berbers decided to secede from the empire. On the other hand, the Marabouts, professional spiritual advisers to the great and powerful in the Marinid state, withdrew their support from the leaders. This was due to the reduction in their personal allowances, which were being paid to them by the Marinid government. The reduction was actually necessitated by weaknesses and crises in the empire's economy. In 1415, Portuguese soldiers captured Ceuta, and by 1513 they had taken over all of the important ports along Morocco's Atlantic coast, sources of much revenue and channels through which imports and exports moved in and out of the empire. The final blow to the empire's existence was dealt by the Wattasids, who in 1465 overthrew the Marinid dynasty and then ruled in their stead for another century.

So many factors were responsible for the eventual collapse of the Marinid state. First, it relied very heavily on foreign mercenary soldiers, including Christians and Jews. These soldiers of fortune had no abiding interest in the empire, and as soon as they had satisfied their financial interests they simply moved on to other states and wars. Thus, in such circumstances the Marinids were left to their own devices. Second, the administration of other key activities of the Marinid state were concentrated in the northern cities, which were very close to or along the Mediterranean Sea and were dependent on maritime activities dominated by Europeans. The implication of this reality was that the southern parts of the state were marginalized from governance and development and were at the mercy of the Arab pastoralists and spiritualists. Third, there were many internal rebellions that weakened the dynasty and the empire. Fourth, succession to the throne of the empire was never systematized, and therefore there were many crippling succession disputes that destroyed the empire.

Tokunbo A. Ayoola

Further Reading

Abun-Nasr, Jamil M. *A History of the Maghrib in the Islam Period.* Cambridge: Cambridge University Press, 1987.

Brett, Michael, and Elizabeth Fentress. *The Berbers.* Oxford, UK: Blackwell, 1997.

Hallett, Robin. *Africa to 1875: A Modern History.* Ann Arbor: University of Michigan Press, 1970.

Illiffe, John. *Africans: The History of a Continent.* Cambridge: Cambridge University Press, 2007.

Naylor, Phillip C. *North Africa: A History from Antiquity to the Present.* Austin: University of Texas Press, 2009.

Meroë

Meroë (ancient Bedawe/Medewe) is located approximately 120 kilometers north of Khartoum in Sudan. Meroë was one of the most significant administrative, religious, and artistic centers of the Kingdom of Kush between approximately the 7th century BCE and the 4th century CE, although these dates are far from certain. It seems that Meroë was a substantial town under Nubia's Napatan rulers (ca. 760–270 BCE) and rose in status as to become the capital of the Meroitic kingdom (ca. 270 BCE–350 CE). Meroë is regarded as one of the oldest and most significant urban settlements in Africa outside of Egypt.

Meroë is situated on the east bank of the Nile in a strategic location for agricultural, craft, and trade purposes. The environment surrounding Meroë experiences rainfall and possessed substantial agricultural and grazing lands. Other natural resources included varieties of sandstone for building, iron ore for the smelting industry, and clays for ceramic production. These meroitic trade goods appear to have been exchanged with goods from Egypt and the Mediterranean, the Gezira (the region between the Blue and White Niles), Aksum (Ethiopia), and the Red Sea.

Although Herodotus and other ancient writers mentioned Meroë, little was known about it until the age of European exploration. The Scottish traveler James Bruce (1730–1794) first tentatively identified Meroë in 1772 on the basis of the Temple of Amun (M260–280), broken pieces of obelisks, and statue fragments. Remarkably, Bruce did not mention the Meroë pyramids, which have commanded most antiquarian and modern-day interest in Meroë. Other significant explorers included Frédéric Cailliaud (1821), Linant de Bellefonds (1821), and Karl Richard Lepsius (1842–1845).

Collectors and antiquarians followed the explorers to Meroë. Giuseppe Ferlini (1800–1870) is one of the most notorious of these historical figures because he initiated a destructive search for treasure in Meroë's pyramids. Ferlini claimed that he found jewelry and other items in the pyramid belonging to Amanishakheto. At the request of Lepsius, Berlin acquired the majority of these jewels. Sir Earnest Alfred Wallace Budge (1857–1934) excavated at Meroë in order to collect antiquities for the British Museum. Troops furnished by Sir Reginal Wingate made paths to and between the pyramids and sank shafts into the site. Little is known of the results of

Pyramids of the Kushite kings at Meroë in present-day Sudan, ca. 800–280 BCE. Meroë was an ancient Ethiopian city-state that served as the capital of the Kushite kingdom for several centuries. (Mike63/iStockphoto.com)

these explorations, although there are finds housed in the National Museum in Khartoum that may derive from this work.

John Garstang's expedition (1910–1914) was the first formal excavation at Meroë and the first positive identification of the site as Meroë. The Amun Temple excavations revealed correspondences with historical descriptions. Further proof was provided by the fragments of a hieroglyphic stele that mentions of the city of Meroë. This stele was dedicated by King Aspelta (late seventh–early sixth century BCE) and found in Temple M250. Garstang's few publications emphasized the importance of Egyptian and Hellenistic influences and imports on Meroë. World War I interrupted Garstang's fieldwork, and the results were not published in final form until László Török's multivolume publication in 1997. This pattern of delayed publication was repeated by George Reisner, who excavated Meroë's royal cemeteries, located east of the city (1920–1923). Dows Dunham published Reisner's excavations decades later.

The most large-scale excavations in Meroë city were those directed by Peter Lewis Shinnie. Shinnie's excavations (1965–1984, intermittent) exposed domestic houses, industrial areas, and components of the urban layout in addition to the site's many temples. Although the results of these extensive excavations were inconclusive, they corroborated the suggestions that Meroë was densely occupied for a long period of time and that iron production was a significant industry.

Meroë city occupied a large area that was approximately 2.6 square kilometers. To the extreme west are constructions that scholars have assumed to be quay structures. The dominant component of the western portion is a walled enclosure known as the Royal City, which is roughly rectangular in shape and measuring approximately 275 by 137 meters. A labyrinth of buildings slumbers within these walls, many of which are monumental in size and ornamentation. Most of the buildings are composed of mud brick with exterior baked brick faces. A few buildings are built of stone. The buildings in the Royal City were repaired and rebuilt innumerable times. As a result, the original ground topography is difficult to interpret, and the settlement phases are understood poorly. Large square buildings, nearly identical in size, are located near the center of the walled enclosure and are believed to be palaces. Other buildings have been interpreted as storage magazines, audience chambers, and domestic quarters for the palace staff. One of the most distinctive buildings in the Royal City is the so-called Royal Bath, which is situated against the west wall. Originally excavated and named by Garstang, current research reinterprets the baths as a Roman-style water feature complemented with Hellenistic-influenced sculpture and a garden.

The Temple of Amun adjoins the Royal City enclosure on the eastern side and served as the southern equivalent of the great Temple of Amun at Jebel Barkal. The Temple of Amun is large (137 meters long) and included a colonnaded court, columned halls, and a sanctuary on top of a platform. A processional route led east from the Temple of Amun to the so-called Temple of the Sun outside of the city. The Temple of the Sun was an enclosed area with a single-chambered cult building surrounded by a colonnade and standing on a platform. Additional temples line the processional street through Meroë and in its vicinity in this eastern portion of the site. The decoration of these temples appears to have included faience tiles, plaques, and medallions, which were probably inlaid in the floors and the walls. There are also numerous plaques and objects in the round provided with suspension rings, which were possibly hung from the ceiling or from some kind of temple furniture. Some of these objects represent small shrines, feathers, and crowns.

Extensive superimposed residential and industrial zones were located to the east and northeast of the Royal City. The houses are poorly understood, as none of them were excavated in their entirety, and they were superimposed on top of one another or were leveled to make way for later temple construction. The ceramics assemblage includes a distinctive white fabric ware made from locally sourced kaolin. Other ceramics include handmade black wares and a wheel-made brown ware as well as imported fabrics. Additional material includes handmade figurines (predominately of quadrupeds), terra-cottas, weaving implements, weights and measures, jar seals, stamps, beads, lip/ear/nose plugs, metals, and numerous other objects relating to the social, economic, and material life of ancient Meroë. Slag heaps, derived from iron smelting, are located at the eastern edge of the city, marking the craft quarter. The location of smelting along the edges of the city may have been to protect inhabitants from the fumes and heat produced during manufacture.

Farther to the north and east are the spacious cemeteries, including a field of pyramids belonging to the relatives of rulers. Immediately to the east of the city are three discrete cemeteries, which provide an enormous source of information. The northernmost of these cemeteries dates to circa 100 BCE–200 CE. The other two cemeteries appear to have been active later. Most graves were marked with a mound of sand or gravel and appear to be those of the elite.

The pyramids of the kings and *kandakes* (queens) are located still farther to the east and are arranged in a triangle. The western pyramid tombs are those of lesser royals. The northern and southern tombs include nearly all of the known rulers of Meroë. Early pyramids were built of stone masonry, and later ones were built of brick and rubble. These Meroitic pyramids differed from their Egyptian counterparts; they were steeper and often had an attached chapel, and it seems that those of the kings had a pylon. Chapels had scenes and texts, which often repeated between the various tombs. Burial mounds and mastabas that appear to have been for queens, princes, and the elite are distributed among these pyramids.

Meroë had connections to the Roman Empire since Rome first occupied Egypt, although the nature of these connections is contested. Cornelius Gallus, the first prefect of Egypt, established the Egyptian border at the first cataract in about 29 BCE. Subsequently, this border was pushed south by 70 miles to Hiera Sycaminos (Maharraqa) to include the Dodekaschoinos, a region of much-disputed control for this and the Ptolemaic era. During the prefecture of Gaius Petronius (25–21 BCE), the Meroites attacked Syene, Elephantine, and Philae at the first cataract. They were taking advantage of the transfer of troops from this area to Arabia Felix for Aelius Gallus's campaign there. This attack is thought to be the one that resulted in Augustus's statue head being placed beneath the threshold of one of the temples at Meroë.

Petronius advanced to Primis (Qasr Ibrim) in revenge. A Roman presence in this area is clear, although the nature and duration of this occupation are far from resolved. Likewise, the nature of Nero's interest in Meroë is also unclear. It does seem, however, that the relationship between Rome and Meroë were times of peace and trade between the two powers during the first three centuries CE. The movement of trade goods between Meroë and the Roman Empire (and particularly Roman Egypt) seems to corroborate this picture. Aksum (along with some incursions by the Nobas) has often been credited with destroying Meroë toward the middle of the fourth century CE. The evidence for Aksumite destruction levels at Meroë is minimal. Additional connections with other areas in Africa are certain, but additional study of the material culture is required to identify locales with greater confidence.

Despite its national and international importance, research at Meroë has often lagged behind the peripheral regions of Kush. The UNESCO Salvage Campaigns in the 1960s and 1970s, followed by the present concerns over dam building in Sudan, have refocused archaeological attention to peripheral areas instead of Meroë itself. Moreover, excavations within Meroë have experienced significant time lags between excavation and final publication, which has hindered more thorough archaeological interpretations of the material. The declaration of Meroë as a UNESCO World Heritage Site in January 2011 has refocused attention to this significant urban site.

Anna Lucille Boozer

Further Reading

Boozer, A. L. "A Historiography of Archaeological Research at Meroë, Sudan." *Ancient West & East* 16 (2017).

Bruce, J. *An Interesting Narrative of the Travels of James Bruce Esq. Into Abyssinia, to Discover the Source of the Nile: Abridged from the Original Work by Samuel Shaw, Esq.* London: H. D. Symonds, 1790.

Dunham, Dows. *The Royal Cemeteries of Kush*, Vol. 4, *Royal Tombs at Meroë and Barkal*. Boston: Museum of Fine Arts, Harvard University Press, 1957.

Dunham, Dows. *The Royal Cemetaries of Kush*, Vol. 5, *The West and South Cemeteries at Meroë*. Boston: Museum of Fine Arts, Harvard University Press, 1963.

Ferlini, G. *Cenno sugli scavi operati nella Nubia*. Bologna: Nobili, 1937.

Grzymski, K. A. "Recent Research at the Palaces and Temples of Meroe: A Contribution to the Study of Meroitic Civilization." In *Between the Cataracts, Part I,* edited by W. Godlewski and A. Lajtar, 227–238. Warsaw: Wydawnictwa Uniwersytetu Warszawskiego, 2008.

Humphris, J. "Post Meroitic Iron Production: Initial Results and Interpretations." *Sudan & Nubia* 18 (2014): 121–129.

Kirwan, L. P. "Rome beyond the Southern Egyptian Frontier." *Geographical Journal* 123(1) (1957): 13–19.

Lepsius, K. R. *Briefe aus Aegypten, Aethiopien und der halbinsel des Sinai, geschrieben in den jahren 1842–1845, während der auf befehl sr. majestät des königs Friedrich Wilhelm IV von Preussen ausgeführten wissenschaftlichen expedition, von Richard Lepsius*. Berlin: W. Hertz, 1852.

Priese, K. H. *The Gold of Meroe: Exhibition Catalogue.* New York and Mainz am Rhein: Verlag Philipp von Zabern, 1992.

Shinnie, P. L. *Meroe: A Civilization of the Sudan.* London: Thames and Hudson, 1967.

Mutapa

The Kingdom of Mutapa (ca. 1425–1917) was a Shona kingdom in present-day Zambia, Zimbabwe, and Mozambique. Its people were descendents of the people who built Great Zimbabwe. Its founder, Nyatsimba Mutota, supposedly came from the more southern Shona kingdom of Torwa and established the Mutapa capital at Zvongombe, about 215 miles north of Great Zimbabwe. The kingdom expanded from the Zambezi River to the Indian Ocean and began trading with the Portuguese in the 16th century, making it the largest and most prosperous of the Shona kingdoms.

Stretching between the Zambezi River and the Indian Ocean, Mutapa was a resource-rich kingdom and exploited those resources in order to grow and sustain itself. Allegedly Mutota, the founder of the kingdom, went north from Great Zimbabwe searching for a new source of salt. When he found it in what is today northern Zimbabwe, he settled there and conquered the Shona peoples of the area, creating a new kingdom that would overtake Great Zimbabwe as the main inland source of trade to the coast. Using the Zambezi to connect with the Indian Ocean, Mutapa quickly grew into an important trading partner for the Portuguese.

Portuguese sources are some of the most detailed in describing the Mutapa kingdom and help contextualize oral traditions and archaeological evidence found in northern Zimbabwe. The Portuguese conquered much of the trade in the Indian Ocean beginning in 1505, and this included the gold trade in East Africa from Sofala. Given that Sofala's goldfields were almost completely exhausted by the time the Portuguese took them, they looked for other sources of trade and found Mutapa, rich with gold, copper, and ivory. Mutapa was further inland than the Swahili states that were mostly conquered by the Portuguese by the late 16th century but was still a site of multicultural trade and exchange. Muslim traders from the coast had been traveling inland for many years and had established a foothold in the Mutapa capital, Zvongombe. Though the Portuguese attempted to subvert the Swahili traders, they were unsuccessful.

In 1561, a Portuguese Jesuit missionary named Gonçalo da Silveira traveled to Zvongombe and was granted an audience with the *mwenemutapa* (king). The king converted to Christianity, which did not sit well with his Swahili trading partners, who urged the king to kill the missionary. And thus, only a few days after his conversion the king had Silveira put to death. This provided all the justification the Portuguese needed for an invasion, which they undertook in subsequent years. They were never able to capture any significant part of Mutapa territory and continued trading with Mutapa. The Portuguese king, Sebastian, even gave the *mwenemutapa* a ceremonial coat of arms in 1569, recognizing their trade partnership. Still, the

Portuguese continued their military campaign until 1572, though their forces were decimated by disease, and eventually returned to the coast, where they massacred the Swahili. This created the beginnings of the *prazeiro* culture in coastal Portuguese Mozambique.

Internal disputes in the 17th century threatened Mutapa's stability and continued existence, as factions within the kingdom sought to overthrow the *mwenemutapa* using Portuguese aid. This helped the Portuguese gain a foothold, and in 1629 they were able to put one of their own clients on the throne, Mavura Mhande Felipe. With Mutapa as a client state, the Portuguese moved farther into the interior of Southeast Africa and increased their share of the trade in gold, copper, ivory, and slaves.

This was complicated by Butwa invasions from the southwest. The Butwa kingdom had been taken over by a group of Rozvi pastoralists in the 1680s, who used their wealth from trading with Arabs and Portuguese on the coast to fund their expansion. When the *mwenemutapa* died in 1692, this produced the first in a series of succession crises, giving the Rozvis opportunities to claim territory and wealth from Mutapa. Mutapa became a vassal state for the next several decades, with successive kings inviting either Butwa or Portuguese dominion in return for their rule. The Rozvis could only maintain their hold on Mutapa for a short amount of time, however, because they were much more concerned with building their empire in the south, around the former Great Zimbabwe. Having lost much of its territory by 1723, the new *mwenemutapa*, Nyamhandi, moved his capital closer to Portuguese settlements in the east, which brought the kingdom further under the influence of the growing Portuguese colonial presence.

When the *mwenemutapa* Dehwe Mapunzagutu died in 1759, this began yet another brutal civil war, and Mutapa ceded even more land to the surrounding kingdoms. Though it limped ahead with relative autonomy throughout the 19th century, Mutapa was no longer a regional power. The final *mwenemutapa*, Mambo Chioko, was killed in battle with the Portuguese in 1917.

Sarah E. Watkins

Further Reading

Axelson, Eric. *Portuguese in South-East Africa, 1488–1600*. Johannesburg: C. Struik, 1973.

Beach, D. N. *The Shona and Their Neighbours*. Oxford, UK: Blackwell, 1994.

Isaacman, Allen F. *Mozambique: The Africanization of a European Institution: The Zambesi Prazos, 1750–1902*. Madison: University of Wisconsin Press, 1972.

Mudenge, S. I. G. "The Role of Foreign Trade in the Rozvi Empire: A Reappraisal." *Journal of African History* 15(3) (1974): 373–391.

Oliver, Roland, and Anthony Atmore. *Medieval Africa, 1250–1800*. Cambridge: Cambridge University Press, 2001.

Peel, J. D. Y., and T. O. Ranger. *Past and Present in Zimbabwe*. Manchester, UK: Manchester University Press, 1983.

Pikirayi, Innocent. *The Zimbabwe Culture: Origins and Decline of Southern Zambezian States*. Walnut Creek, CA: AltaMira, 2001.

N

Napata

Napata was the chief religious center of the ancient Kingdom of Kush and its capital from 750 to 590 BCE. The Kushites, inhabitants of Napata, buried their kings in pyramid tombs in this capital. Napata was located near Kuraymah in North Sudan, downstream from the fourth cataract of the Nile River, an area extending from Nuri Kuuru to the east and south of Kuraymah in Nubia. Nubian civilization is one of the oldest in the world and shares an economic, political, and social past with ancient Egypt.

Ancient Nubia lay in the modern-day countries of Egypt, Sudan, and Ethiopia. The northern border of Nubia began approximately at the town of Aswan in Egypt, extending to the southern border of Khartoum in Sudan. Ancient Nubia was made up of Lower Nubia in the north and Upper Nubia in the south, nearly corresponding to the modern-day boundary between Egypt and Sudan. Ninety-six percent of Nubia is desert. The smooth-flowing Nile River is broken from Aswan southward by huge granite boulders, which turn the river into rapids called cataracts. There are six of these cataracts that make navigation very difficult and sometimes impossible in Nubia.

In the ancient period, people could not survive the harsh conditions of the desert areas of Nubia without living near the Nile for their water supply. They fished and hunted ducks and other waterfowl living along the Nile. Farming was done along the banks of the Nile. During the summer the Nile flooded its banks and deposited rich soil called silt. When the water receded, farmers grew fruits and vegetables, which the desert climate favored. For many centuries, Nubia's Nile Valley was a dependable point of crossing for travelers between Africa and the Mediterranean Sea.

A shared past of conquering and being conquered characterized Egyptian and Nubian relations. When one state was politically and militarily weak, the other dominated. Egypt emerged as a major imperial power during the New Kingdom (ca. 1560–1087 BCE). During this period, Egyptian kings from Thebes fought and expelled the Hyksos from northern Egypt in 1550. The Egyptian rulers turned south and conquered most of Nubia around 1500. The rest of the Nubia fell when Kerma, the Kushite capital, collapsed. Egypt dominated Nubia as far south as the fourth cataract. Egyptian forces occupied the second cataract and ruled Nubia effectively as part of Egypt. The "Kings Son of Kush" was the high-ranking official, heading a court of administrators and priests in Nubia. Egyptian occupation of

Nubia for 400 years witnessed progressive Egyptianization of Kushite religion, language, and writings skills. The Egyptian ruling class built temples where Kushites worshipped Egyptian deities. Nevertheless, the Nubians did not abandon their gods and instead worshipped them.

The decline of Egypt from 1000 BCE had given the Kushites the opportunity to assert their independence. They emerged as a new dominating power, controlling the Nile confluence from Napata, but maintained trade relations with Egypt. By 730, the Kushites were strong enough to invade and conquer Egypt. It has been speculated that some priests of Amun at Thebes who were on voluntary exiled in Napata inspired the rulers to invade Egypt. In 724 King Piye (Pee-yeh), also known as Piankhy (meaning "Living One") conquered Egypt and declared himself pharaoh of all of Egypt and Nubia. He moved his capital to the great Egyptian city of Thebes. Piye built a granite tablet of stone at Jebel Barkal, close to Napata, on which the details of his conquest are inscribed. Alara, a descendant of Piye, established the Twenty-Fifth Dynasty, or the Ethiopian dynasty, at Thebes.

Kushite domination of Egypt was, however, short-lived, lasting for about 60 years. Emerging from the region in modern-day Iraq, iron-using Assyrians dislodged the Nubians in 670 BCE after battling the combined forces of Kushites and Egyptians. The Kushite dynasty relocated to Napata, but continued tensions between Napata and Egypt led to an attack on the Napatas in 590. The rulers migrated farther south and established a new state and an administrative center on the "island of Merowe" (Meroë), just north of the sixth cataract and at the confluence of the Nile and its Atbarah tributary. Under Nubian influence, a distinctive civilization emerged and flourished for 700 years in Meroë. The ruins of this civilization are 100 miles north of modern-day Khartoum. The Greeks called the civilization Ethiopian erroneously.

At the time of their occupation of Egypt, the Kushite conquerors did not effect much change in Egypt because they had assimilated Egyptian cultural elements. They wore the double crowns of Upper and Lower Egypt and worshipped Egyptian deities. The Nubian kings constructed Egyptian-style temples and tombs, and their arts and crafts bore marks of Egyptian royal traditions. The Kushite dynasty has made its mark for restoring to Egypt its ancient customs and beliefs. For instance, the dynasty revived literature and arts.

The culture of the people of Napata was Egyptian in character at the time. Its architecture, paintings, writing script, and other artistic styles were Egyptian. Egyptian pyramid building for burying royals was also practiced in Napata. The ruling dynasties built the first pyramids that the Nile Valley had seen since the Middle Kingdom. People of Napata worshipped several Egyptian gods, but the most important to them was Amun, a Theban deity. Amun's temple was located at Jebel Barkel. However, Nubians retained some aspects of their own distinctive characteristics, as evidenced in their symbols of kingship, art, costume, jewelry, hairstyle, pottery, dwellings, styles of burials, and gods. A huge part of this distinctive Nubian culture reflects a blend of traditions of Africa and the Mediterranean. The Nubian region was a meeting place for travelers from the interior of Africa as well as from the Mediterranean world trading their wares.

Throughout the ancient world, Nubia was known as an important trade route. The name "Nubia" is a derivative of the Egyptian term *nub,* meaning "precious metals." The most important mineral deposit was gold. Additionally, Nubia was an important region to the pharaohs of ancient Egypt because of the Nile River. The Nile, the lifeline of ancient Egypt, traversed Nubia. Two major sources of the river, the Blue and White Niles, joined in the region (now in Khartoum). Trade relations between Egyptians and their southern neighbors developed very early. Trading items that were brought into Egypt included exotic animals skins, ostrich eggs and feathers, ivory, ebony, and, most important, gold bought from Nubia. Traders from the interior of Africa brought some of these commodities, and acting as Middlemen, Nubians traded the items in Egypt and other parts of the Near East. Sometimes they charged taxes for the trade passing through their region. Besides the Egyptians, Nubia was familiar to Greeks and Romans due to Nubia's popularity as a trading region.

Napata emerged as the center of power and controlled the Nile region and trade in Nubia when Egypt had grown weak politically and militarily. Rulers of Napata conquered and occupied Egypt. The rulers restored Egyptian customs and beliefs before the Assyrians dislodged them.

Waseem-Ahmed Bin-Kasim

Further Reading

Connah, Graham. *African Civilizations: An Archaeological Perspective.* 2nd ed. Cambridge University Press, 2001.

Davison, Basil. *The African Past: Chronicles from Antiquity to Modern Times.* New York: Universal Library, 1967.

Hayness, Joyce L. *Nubia: Ancient Kingdoms of Africa.* Boston: Museum of Fine Arts, 1992.

Ndongo

Ndongo was a centralized polity on the southwest coast of Africa founded by Bantu-speaking Mbundus. The capital of Ndongo was Kabasa. Ndongo emerged as a kingdom in the second decade of the 16th century. Kongo, to the north of Ndongo, was more centralized and controlled the Mbundu region prior to the emergence of the Kingdom of Ndongo. The Mbundus speak Kimbundu, which was one of the major languages in the region. The core of the Ndongo state is today's Republic of Angola. Angola is bordered to the north by the Republic of Congo (Congo Brazzaville) and Congo (Kinshasa), to the southeast by Zambia, to the south by Namibia, and to the west by the Atlantic Ocean. Ndongo was ethnically defined and lay to the east and south of the modern-day city of Luanda. The Kwanza River drains the Ndongo area.

The Ndongo area was an open grassland dotted by occasional wooded savanna. This topography was extensive in the 16th century, but the wooded savanna receded over the years due to increasing hunting and the cutting down of trees. Besides the grassland, a dense forest covers the mountains along the western end of the Luanda Plateau, and spots of forest around the lower course of the river characterized the region. Rains are moderate and fall in an uneven seasonal pattern. Toward the end of the year, the region experiences light and irregular rainfall followed by dry conditions, and then between February and March the heaviest precipitation occur. Successful agriculture depends on the rainy season.

Sixteenth-century Mbundu farm products were millets and sorghum, which lasted through the dry season from May to September. Dietary supplements were wild vegetables and fruits, collected at the forest along the river especially. In contrast to the ridge, the Mbundus settled around river bottoms and mountain valleys because the ground moisture lasted longer. Additionally, they domesticated scores of animals such as chickens and goats and also hunted wild game with bows and arrows and traps to supplement their food. During the dry months, lowered water levels confined fishes to areas that were easily accessible for fishing activities. The Mbundus had an Iron Age technology, which enabled them to produce implements from the ore deposits found in the north and south of the river.

Sobas (rulers) governed 736 independent Mbundu *murindas* (territories) during the 16th century. Portuguese sources identify the *sobas* as *fidalgos* (or lesser nobles). Each *murinda* covered a number of villages. Sometimes *sobas* warred against each other or allied when jurisdictional disputes occurred. Through alliance or wars, larger territories formed known in Kimbundu as *kandas* (provinces). There were between 4 and 12 dominating *kandas,* including Ilamba, Lumbo, Hari, Kisama, Haku, and Museke.

Ngola Kiluanje (ca. 1515–1556), the *soba* whom Angola was named after, dominated a number of *murindas* and founded a dynasty named after him. The extent of Ngola's territory was beyond Kisama, Libolo, and Tunda by 1518. By the mid-16th century, Ndongo's claims included about half the territory and population that Kongo ruled directly. The conquered *sobas* continued to govern their *murinda* but paid taxes and provided military service in return. Members of the king's family, officials, and nobles who controlled land and people in the different territories assisted the king in ruling. Various categories of authorities were bonded to the kingdom by administrative ties and kinship links, including intermarriages. These ties were critical in holding the structure of the kingdom in place. A slave class, referred to as *mubikas,* was in Ndongo. People were enslaved because they were war captives, were purchased, or were adjudicated guilty of some sort of offense. The Mbundus had both elite and non-elite armies. The non-elites were hordes of archers who were recruited hurriedly from villages when an attack was eminent. The non-elites started battles with arrow strikes but fled when this task was done, giving way to elite fighters. The elite army fought with bladed battle-axes as principal weapons. During battles, elite forces depended on personal maneuvers to dodge enemy blows, a skill developed from consistent training. The Mbundus did not always have infantry. The army obtained supplies from human porterage during battles.

The Ngola dynasty ruled the kingdom of "Angola," the largest consolidation the Portuguese knew in 1518 on their arrival. Ndongo was integrated into the Atlantic economy when the ruling dynasty initiated contact with Lisbon and requested a missionary in 1518. Missionary activities began in Ndongo following the request. Additionally, tens of thousands of captives were exported as slaves after 1605 due to local disputes and Portuguese meddling in local politics. Violent confrontations between Portugal and Ndongo were the result of former interference in the internal affairs of the latter. In 1590, for instance, allied forces of Ndongo and Matamba crushed a Portuguese force sent against Ndongo. In 1617, a Portuguese alliance with Imbangala mercenaries sacked the capital of Ndongo and forced King Ngola Mbandi to flee. Many Mbundus were taken prisoners following the defeat of Ndongo. Portuguese failure to honor a truce with Ndongo and several other events led to the rise of Queen Nzinga, whom the Portuguese defeated in 1628. Nzinga had to flee. The slaves from these wars who entered the Atlantic system shaped a uniquely Afro-Atlantic culture. However, Portuguese monopoly of commerce was altered when Dutch and English merchants began to visit the region in the early 17th century.

Increasing Portuguese involvement in the slave trade in the Ndongo region turned into colonization. The slave trade flourished so well that by the early 17th century, the Portuguese exported about 5,000 to 10,000 enslaved people annually from Luanda. By the 1890s the boundaries of modern-day Angola began to take shape, but it was in 1926 that it took its present borderline shape in the aftermath of a dispute with South West Africa (now Namibia). Under Portuguese colonialism, economic opportunity for the Mbundus was limited, and forced labor was a means of exploiting the resources of the territory for the benefit of Portugal. The Mbundis reacted to Portuguese exploitation and forced labor with armed resistance. Militant activities of locals against Portuguese colonial authorities intensified in the 1960s and 1970s.

Nationalist movements that led to Angolan independence from colonialism started in the 1950s. The Mbundus dominated the fight for independence with a Marxist-oriented party, the Popular Liberation Movement of Angola (MPLA). The MPLA's support base was Luanda. Other nationalist groups were organized along ethnic, regional, and ideological lines. The Portuguese colonial authorities, along with a large portion of the white population numbering up to 300,000, withdrew from Angola in 1975. After independence from colonialism, a civil war occurred due to interparty struggles. the National Union for Total Independence (UNITA), a guerrilla-Ovimbundu party, challenged the MPLA for control of the country. Many Angolans relocated from the cities to rural areas because of the civil war. The belligerent parties got support from opposing Cold War countries. The Soviet Union and Cuba assisted the MPLA, and the Western countries backed UNITA. Angolans reached a peace accord that ended hostilities in 1991, and both parties competed for elections in 1992.

Waseem-Ahmed Bin-Kasim

Further Reading

Birmingham, David. *Trade and Conflict in Angola: The Mbundu and Their Neighbours under the Influence of the Portuguese, 1483–1790.* Oxford, UK: Clarendon, 1966.

Heywood, Linda M., and John K. Thornton. *Central Africans, Atlantic Creoles, and the Foundation of the Americas, 1585–1660.* Cambridge: Cambridge University Press, 2007.

Miller, Joseph C. *Kings and Kinsmen: Early Mbundu States in Angola.* London: Oxford University Press, 1976.

Nobadia (Migi)

Nubia is a historical territory that today is North Sudan and the southern part of Egypt. Generally it is assumed that Nubia covered the area along the Nile between the first and sixth Nile cataracts. Nubia formed a corridor along the Nile River, linking continental Africa and the Mediterranean. The fourth century CE brought the fall of Meroë and witnessed the birth of three kingdoms: Nobadia, Makuria, and Alwa.

Nobadia is the northernmost kingdom of this triad and spread from the first to the third Nile cataracts in its heyday. The landscape in its southern part is typical cataract scenery: barren rocky terrain almost devoid of vegetation. It was a sparsely populated area passable for river transport only at the time of high water on the Nile. The valley widened around Soleb, Wawa, Abria, and Amara, providing a considerable amount of farmland. Farther downstream, down to the second cataract, was a region called the Belly of the Rock (Batn el-Hajar), the most inhospitable part of the Nile Valley. From Wadi Halfa down to Faras lay vast agricultural lands, particularly on the western bank. Further, enclaves of farmland surrounded Arminna and Toshka. The zone between Masmas, ed-Derr, and Tumas was the most fertile and densely settled area in Nobadia. There are hardly any patches of agricultural land on both sides of the river down to Korosko, which was the point of departure for caravans traveling through the Eastern Desert to Napata, Old Dongola, and farther downstream to Abu Hamad. The next wide fertile plain suitable for extensive agriculture in Nobadia lay around Dakka, where the valley was about a mile wide. Farther to the north the valley was again inhospitable, its width tapering down to about 220 yards at Bab el-Kalabsha.

Nubia

Nubia found its way into the movie *Star Wars*. It is one of the planets in the Nubus system, which was considered a part of the Core World. Nubia was the home of T'chooka D'oon, a human male Jedi master assaulted by General Grievous. Senator Padmé Amidala piloted an H-Type Nubian yacht in the Clone Wars, and in episode one the Royal Naboo Starship was referred to as "Nubian."

The dawn of Nobadia dates back to the end of the fourth century and coincides with the decline of the Meroitic Empire. The fall of Nobadia brought to life two competing chiefdoms: Blemmyan in the Dodekaschoinos (Dodekaschoinos is a name derived from the Greek *dodekas choinos,* meaning "12 miles," that is, about 75 miles south of Aswan) and Nobadian grouped around the second Nile cataract. In circa 420, Olympiodorus of Thebes, a Roman historian, visited the Blemmyes. According to his account, despite controlling the Nile Valley, the Blemmyan king preferred to remain in the desert. At the same time the Nobades, whose royal cemeteries have been found in Qustul and Ballana, started an expansion to the north. As a result, the Nobades subdued the Dodekaschoinos and settled relations with the Byzantine Empire, which allowed for an increase in the volume of trade and an influx of new political and religious ideas. The conflict between the Blemmyes and the Nobades is attested in an inscription of Silko, the victorious Nobadian ruler, in the temple of Mandulis in Kalabsha, located at the heart of the Blemmyan territory, and in the correspondence between Aburni, one of his heirs, and the Blemmyan ruler Phonen found in Phrim (Qasr Ibrim). In the middle of the fifth century Nobades controlled the whole territory between the first and second Nile cataracts, which is called Lower Nubia. Then they directed their military expansion to the south, and in the sixth century they held sway as far south as the third cataract. The capital of Nobadia was located at Pachoras (Faras). At the beginning of the sixth century, the Nobadian elites strengthened their position within the multiethnic society, searched for effective forms for integration of the state and the people, and reached for the Christian religion. The king of Nobadia converted officially in 543.

In the so-called Nobadian period (end of the fourth century through the beginning of the eighth century CE), Nobadian territory was inhabited by various ethnic and cultural groups: the autochthonous peoples who lived in the Nile Valley in the Meroitic period (third century BCE–fourth century CE), Egyptians, settled Blemmyes, and Nobades. In the early stages of the Nobadian state formation, the official titles had ethnic epithets. Then at the beginning of the sixth century they began to be territorial, clearly indicating a transition in the state organization from ethnic to territorial. The officials recruited from the ranks of the extended royal family and local elites.

The old Meroitic religion lasted to at least the middle of the fifth century but was practiced by the local Meroitic population. We know nothing about the religion of the Nobades before they accepted Christianity in the Monophysite rite. Christianization of the peoples in Nubia did not happen overnight. It extended over time, and churches did not start to be an important element of the Nobadian landscape until about a century later. Church hierarchy developed gradually, and at the beginning there was only one bishop of the Nobades, indicating a lack of regional dioceses. Three factors spurred the economy of Nobadia in the early stages: long-distance trade of luxury goods from the African interior, widespread use of the camel, and the *saqiya* (a large hollow wheel with pottery jars attached to the perimeter that was used to bring up water). The camel increased the volume of trade in roadless Nubia because the weight of commodities carried by one animal was greater; the *saqiya* enlarged the area of land available for cultivation.

There is ambiguity about when Nobadia came to an end. The Arabic sources on the Arab incursion in Nubia in 643 and 652 do not mention Nobadia, yet other sources, such as *History of the Patriarchs,* cite an ongoing war between Nobadia and Makuria in the second half of the seventh century. It is certain that the two states merged into one before 707, when an inscription mentioning Merkurius, the king of Makuria, was placed in the cathedral of Pachoras.

Artur Obluski

Further Reading

Adams, William Y. *Nubia: Corridor to Africa.* Princeton, NJ: Princeton University Press, 1977.

Ibn al-Mukaffa, Severus. *History of the Patriarchs of the Egyptian Church: Known as the History of the Holy Church.* Le Caire: Imprimerie de l'Institut francais d'archeologie orientale, 1948–1959.

Török, László. *Between Two Worlds: The Frontier Region between Ancient Nubia and Egypt, 3700 BC–AD 500.* Leiden: Brill, 2009.

Welsby, Derek. *Soba: Archaeological Research at a Medieval Capital on the Blue Nile.* London: British Institute in Eastern Africa, 1991.

Williams, Bruce Beyer. *Noubadian X-Group Remains from Royal Complexes in Cemeteries Q and 219 and from Private Cemeteries Q, R, V, W, B, J, and M at Qustul and Ballana.* Chicago: Oriental Institute of the University of Chicago, 1991.

Nok

Nok is an archaeological complex—also referred to as Nok culture—in central Nigeria that evolved between 1500 and the end of the first century BCE, first described by colonial administrative officer and archaeologist Bernard Fagg in the mid-1940s. It takes its name from a tin-mining village located in the south of the modern-day Kaduna State in Nigeria, where the first clay figurines representing animals and humans that would become synonymous with this complex were recovered.

Today, the Nok region stretches from the Benue River Valley in the south to beyond Kaduna in the north. The majority of the sites have been identified in the foothills of the Jos Plateau to the northeast of Abuja, the federal capital of Nigeria. The area falls in the Guinea zone and can be characterized as a relatively wet savanna with annual rainfall of about 1,200 millimeters. The hilly landscape is dominated by a mosaic of patches of perennial grasses and relatively densely wooded areas, with forest galleries along watercourses. The savanna is a man-made landscape resulting from a complex arrangement of cultivated plots and older parcels left fallow. During the Nok period, the landscape seems to have been comparable to that of today, although possibly wetter.

The archaeological complex was first defined with reference to a unique set of terra-cotta sculptures representing people or animals and sometimes a combination of both. Recent research shows that the complex can also be defined by its pottery, its early association with iron smelting, and its cultivation of pearl millet and cowpeas as well as by a number of discrete archaeological features such as refuse pits, stone pavements, and stone circles. The societies that produced the Nok complex have also been shown to be much older than previously thought. They developed by the middle of the second millennium BCE, probably declined after 400 BCE, and disappeared from our records by the beginning of the first millennium CE.

Although Nok is defined mainly by a subset of the material culture of small-scale agrarian communities and is only sparsely documented, it remains important as one of the few archaeological complexes in the Guinea zone that spanned the first millennium BCE, a period of exten-

Nok culture terra-cotta figure, Nigeria, ca. 900–300 BCE. (Yale University Art Gallery)

sive changes that paved the way to later complex societal dynamics. The growth of iron metallurgy, for instance, had a strong impact on the interaction between people and their social and natural environments and contributed to the concentration of power in elite groups. The people of Nok may have played a central role in this transition. Dates establishing the development of iron metallurgy in the Nok region (800–500 BCE) are among the earliest documented for smelting sites in sub-Saharan Africa.

The Nok communities also left behind a very rich iconography in the form of a collection of fired clay sculptures, the oldest found in sub-Saharan Africa. These sculptures seem to have been characteristic of the Nok complex only from about 900 to 400 BCE, contemporary with archaic and classical Greece and with the Zhou dynasty in China. The terra-cottas are characterized by large semicircular or crescent-shaped eyes in which a cutout hole represents the iris. The majority of these sculptures show male and female figures with elaborate hairdressing and finery and sometimes with clear signs of disease, including tumors and possible cirrhosis. The size of the head is usually disproportionally large. Other terra-cottas represent animals and human-animal hybrids. How the sculptures were perceived by the people who used them, their meaning, and the role they played in Nok society cannot be retraced, but they seem to have been used in ritual contexts, as implied by their impressive stylistic resemblance over time and the fact that many were deliberately broken before being deposited, a fact well established by archaeologists. The uniformity of style across a period of approximately 500 years implies the existence of a limited number of centralized workshops, where the makers of the terra-cottas established and transmitted strict standards from one generation to the next. This also implies the existence of a form of centralized ritual order, capable of controlling the production and meaning of the sculptures and their later deposition. As such, the Nok terra-cottas may represent an early example of a cult exercising social control over numerous communities covering a large area. Although we do not know how the Nok people were organized socially and politically, there is little doubt that regionally uniform ritual practices were a structuring part of their social fabric.

Gérard L. Chouin

Further Reading

Breunig, P., ed. *Nok: African Sculpture in Archaeological Context.* Frankfurt am Main: Africa Magna Verlag, 2014.

Fagg, B. *Nok Terracottas.* London: Ethnographica for the Nigerian Museum, 1977.

Jemkur, J. F. *Aspects of the Nok Culture.* Zaria: Ahmadu Bello University Press, 1992.

Nri

Nri, the ancient city-state of the Nri-Igbo subgroup of the Igbo people in north-central Igboland, is located in the present-day local government area of Anaocha in Anambra State, Nigeria. Anaocha is bordered to the north by Awka, to the south by Idemili, to the east by Aguata, and to the west by Njikoka local government areas. Anaocha has a land area of about 171.62 square kilometers with a population of about 300,000. Present-day Anambra State is a cluster of numerous populated villages and small towns, which gives the area an estimated average density of 1,500–2,000 persons per square kilometer. The state is rich in crude gas and oil, bauxite, and ceramic, and has arable soil advantageous for agro-based activities such as farming, pasturing, and animal husbandry. Among the precolonial West African

Eze Nri Ènweleána II Obidiegwu Onyeso

His Highness Eze Nri Ènweleána II Obidiegwu Onyeso is the present monarch of what remains of the Kingdom of Nri. He ascended the throne in 1988. Onyeso was honored with a national award, Member of the Order of the Federal Republic of Nigeria, on December 16, 2003, by the then president of Nigeria, Chief Olusegun Obasanjo, in Abuja.

kingdoms, Nri is regarded as the earliest Igbo city-state, reputable for spirituality, learning, and trade. As Greece is identified as the cradle of Western civilization, Nri is remarkable for Igbo customs and civilization.

Nri, founded in about 900 CE in north-central Igboland, flourished from the 11th to 17th centuries and declined in the 19th century. The kingdom has diverse traditions of origin, which make its origin a subject of speculation. One of the traditions of Nri origin suggests that Nri, who was the founder of the Nri clan, migrated to present-day Nri from the Ama-Mbala River Valley in northern Igboland, Anambra. The tradition also believes that Nri inherited spiritual powers from his father, Eri, the founder of Aguleri, whose history is surrounded with myth. Eri is described as a sky being who was sent by Chukwu (God) to make peace by settling disputes, cleansing abominations, and providing Igbo people with food ranging from yams to cocoyams. Another version is known as the Igbo mythology. Igbo mythology speculates that Eri may have migrated to Anambra from the Igala dynasty located in central Nigeria. This claim is questionable, however, as historians have gathered contradictory evidence and established that Onoja Oboli, who founded the Igala dynasty, was another son of Eri. In the face of diverse traditions of origin, the Nri people generally trace their origins to Eri, with other Igbo groups and cultures joining in the 13th century.

The state system of Nri was remarkable in the history of African politics, as it developed to be a theocratic one in which its state system was sustained by divine authority and ritual power rather than military power. Nri had at its helm of political structure a divine ruler (*eze nri*) who possessed both ritual and mystic powers other than those of a precolonial African king. According to Nri traditions, Nri-Ifikwuanim is said to have taken after his progenitor, Eri. Usually, *ezeship* candidates were not expected to possess any supernatural powers until they had been installed by electors after a period of interregnum. The new *eze* is installed after he has symbolically journeyed to Aguleri on the Anambra River. In the course of his journey, the *eze* was expected to undergo symbolic burial and exhumation by means of mysterious influence to accumulate pebbles beneath the water. After the successful completion of the rites, the *eze* was anointed with white clay, which symbolizes purity. The *eze nri* was responsible for the management of trade and markets as well as diplomatic relations, and at death he was buried seated in a chamber lined with wood. However, *eze* kingship titles as we have in contemporary Igbo societies originated from Nri.

Nri's hegemony developed as a result of its ritual powers, diplomatic skills, market and trading networks, and administration and management expertise. The *eze nri* established four market days with spirit names—*eke, oye, afor,* and *nkwo*—for the purpose of exchanging commodities and knowledge. Markets were structured in a way that stationed *alusis* (deities) at the market square, and at the hosting communities were representatives of the *eze nri* responsible for guarding and collecting tributes. Other features of Nri's economy included hunting and farming in yam and cocoyam. A sophisticated system of using cowrie (*ego ayo*) as a medium of exchange and valuation was developed and used until the beginning of the 19th century, when the British introduced the pound, shilling, and pence currency system. Also within

Nri's economy, a rudimentary local banking system developed. Individuals with strong and secured harbors kept the cowries of successful business merchants in return for commission. These individuals later rose to become rich and capable of offering capital loans to individuals in need of setting up business ventures. One striking difference that Nri had compared to many traditional Nigerian economies of the period was its nonpractice of slave possession and trading. It was not only a sanctuary where *osus,* people rejected in their localities, seek asylum but also where slaves were granted freedom.

The significant influence of religious authority and control over commercial routes on the expansion of Nri cannot be overemphasized. While the local kings in the areas of Nri's influence were vested with religious authority, the powers to manage agriculture and judiciary rested with the *mburichis,* ritualized *ozo* traders who represented the *eze nri.* As great travelers, Nri people were also businesspeople involved in the long-distance trans-Saharan trade. Colonies' loyalties were maintained through ritual oath rather than through military force. Nri maintained relative peace with and within its subjugated communities through its regard of internal strife and violence as abominations that tainted the world. For hundreds of years, the people under Nri's influence were devoted to peace and harmony based on religious pacifism. The peace maintained and enforced by the ritualized *ozo* traders had a consequential effect on the economy, as it allowed trade to thrive.

While Nri people lived under formal theocratic administration, they were at the same time devoted to the religious rites and traditions and obeyed their agent on Earth. The people of Nri believed in deities, and their day-to-day living depended on religious ethics. Nris believed that Anyanwu (meaning "the light") was a deity who lived in the sun and represented perfection that all humans must seek. Agbala, the deity for fertility, was the combined spirit of all sacred beings, both human and nonhuman. Agbala was believed to be Chukwu's agent on Earth, whose agents are chosen based on merit. This belief had an implication on Nri tradition, based on the idea of peace, truth, and harmony. Ritual scarification known as *ichi,* whereby repeated scare lines were drawn from the center of the temple to the chin to obtain a pattern meant to imitate the rays of the sun, was Nri's way of honoring the sun and was also a form of ritual cleansing.

The spirituality of Nri was characterized with the use of taboos and symbols. Of the religious symbols, *omu*—a tender palm branch—was prominent. It was used to sacralize travel delegates and restrain intruders from certain objects. The symbol was so popularly acknowledged within and outside Nri that anyone or any object carrying the twig was considered secured. There was also an established taboo metaphoric code that was divided into six components: twin, speech, temporal, animal, behavioral and place. The interpretations of the code were employed in educating and governing subjects. In essence, the acknowledgment of symbols and institutions made possible the consolidation of Nri's sociopolitical powers over its subjugated communities. More so, central to Nri were the earth cults. Oral tradition suggests that Nri's power and abundant harvests were the rewards for the *eze nri*'s blessing, as subjects exchanged enormous tubers of yam and cocoyam for consent.

Socioreligious influence of Nri at the height of its power developed into what historians have acknowledged as a holy land and compared to the religious cities of ancient Rome and Mecca. Nri rose to become the center of a dominant and imperial city-state whose influence was felt in most precolonial Igbo communities of Awka, Onitsha, Efik, Ibibio, Ijaw, Nsukka, southern Igala, Asaba, and Anioma. Nri hosted people as pilgrims who seek forgiveness for their sins, as it was believed that one could be cleansed of sins and taboos by entering the holy city. The significance of Nri was not limited to being a sacred land; it was also regarded as a healing haven where people brought their abnormal children for ritual cleansing rather than killing them, as required by local traditions to kill dwarfs and children who cut an upper tooth before the lower tooth. Nri also hosted people from other communities whose reason for visiting was to receive the knowledge of yam medicine known as *ogwuji* in exchange for annual tributes.

Among the institutions established to maintain Nri's power and influence over its subjects, the Igu Aro festival—during which the *eze nri* proclaims the beginning of the lunar calendar—was the most prominent. It was a regular event when the *eze nri* met and communicated openly with his subjects. Each community under Nri's sphere of influence was represented in the payment of homage and tribute to the *eze nri,* thereby demonstrating their allegiance and loyalty. In exchange for their allegiance and pledge of loyalty, the *eze nri* gave out *ogwuji* and blessings of fertility for abundant harvest. Igu Aro day was observed as a day of peace when it was an abomination to plant crops before the day, split wood, and carry out certain other activities. Igu Aro was a regular event that gave the *eze* an opportunity to speak directly to all the communities under him.

Nri's influence over many communities in Igboland was felt from the reign of the 4th *eze nri* to the reign of the 9th *eze nri*. It was after the reign of the 9th *eze nri* that patterns of conflict emerged in the sociopolitical and religious history of Nri. The pattern of conflict that started from the reign of the 10th *eze nri* to the reign of the 14th *eze nri* may have been implicated by the economic importance of the slave trade. The power and domination of Nri started to decline in the early 18th century. With a declining relevance and influence, Nri survived until 1911, when British troop ended the political power once enjoyed by forcing the reigning *eze nri* to surrender the ritual power of the religious cult known as the *ikenga*. The Atlantic slave trade and British colonialism have been attributed as contributory factors to the decline of Nri. Nevertheless, the power and influence of Nri's civilization is manifested in Igbo-Ukwu bronze items, iron technologies, and copper and pottery works.

Modern Igbo societies acknowledge the ancient kingdom of Nri as the oldest area of Igbo settlement, homeland of the Igbo people and the cradle of Igbo culture. The present *eze* of Nri is Obidiegwu Onyesoh, who ascended the throne in 1988 as Nrienwelana II. The present-day Nri kingdom, though still a consolidation of the existed sociopolitical organization, has lost its religious influence to Christianity as a result of missionary activities during the colonial rule. The community has a town union, Nri Progress Union (NPU), that is responsible for securing and addressing developmental issues affecting the community. The NPU hosts government schools, a primary health center, and the Odinani Museum, a store of archaeological cultural heritage of Igboland.

Tosin Akinjobi-Babatunde

Further Reading

Anunobi, Chikodi. *Nri Warriors of Peace.* Ibadan: Zenith Publishers, 2006.
Ikime, Obaro, ed. *Groundwork of Nigerian History.* Ibadan: Heinemann, 2004.
Isichei, Elizabeth. *A History of the Igbo People.* New York: Palgrave Macmillan, 1976.
Onwuejeogwu, M. Angulu. *The Social Anthropology of Africa: An Introduction.* Ibadan: Heinemann, 1975.

Numidia

Numidia (202 BCE–46 CE) was an ancient Berber kingdom in North Africa on the Mediterranean. Spanning parts of present-day Algeria and Tunisia, Numidia existed as an independent kingdom, a Roman client state, and a Roman province. Its capital was Cirta (present-day Constantine), which had a large Mediterranean port called Russicada. Its city of Hippo Regius would later produce Saint Augustine, one of the most important theologians of the Catholic Church.

Numidia lay between the Mediterranean to the north and the Sahara desert to the south. According to ancient sources, Numidia traded extensively with its neighbor, Carthage, and this is especially evident from pottery and numismatic evidence. Ancient writers such as Livy and Polybius describe the relationship as vacillating between alliances and conflict. Numidia traded with Ibiza, Iberia, the Sahel, Ionia, and Pergamon, giving them supplies of wine, honey, anchovies, fish sauces, and tablewares. Their position in the Sahara gave the Numidians access to salt and gold, which helped develop their trading economy. Most Numidians, however, were nomadic herders, which is where their Latin name, "Numidae," derived.

Though its early history is difficult to trace, the Numidian kingdom was originally two separate but related kingdoms: the Massylii in eastern Numidia and the Masaesyli in the west. These kingdoms interacted with one another but had separate administrative structures and separate alliances. During the Second Punic War (218–201 BCE), the Massyliis initially allied with Carthage, and the western Masaesylis under King Syphax allied with Rome.

Syphax used his alliance with the Romans to attack the eastern Massyliis, who were ruled by King Gala, and take more of their territory. This campaign lasted from early in the Second Punic War until around 206 BCE, when Gala died. His sons, Masinissa and Oezalces, fought over who would succeed, further weakening the Massylii kingdom and allowing Syphax to take over more territory. According to Livy, who recorded the history of this conflict, Syphax attempted to play both the Roman general Scipio and the Carthaginian Hasdrubal in order to obtain for himself the best possible position. He became engaged to Hasdrubal's daughter Sophonisba in order to seal their alliance. Meanwhile, Masinissa triumphed over his brother and switched his allegiance to Rome, which he determined would emerge victorious from the war. He and Scipio eventually were able to defeat Syphax, whom Scipio took back to Tibur with him, where Syphax died around 202. Masinissa meanwhile sought to reassert an alliance with Carthage by marrying Sophonisba. Scipio did not trust this alliance and, instead of attempting to subvert Masinissa, requested that Sophonisba travel to Rome for the triumph that marked Rome's victory in the war. Masinissa did not want to see his bride humiliated, nor did he wish to damage his relationship with Rome, so he gave poison to Sophonisba with which she killed herself in 203.

Masinissa's victory and alliances with Rome and Carthage marked the beginning of the unified Numidian kingdom, which emerged toward the end of the Second Punic War in 206. His rule was a long one, extending until his death in 148. During this time he was able to stabilize his kingdom and strengthen its ties with Rome. His grandson Micipsa succeeded him and ruled for another 30 years. When Micipsa died in 118 the throne went to his sons, Hiempsa I and Adherbal, as well as to Jugurtha, Massinisa's illegitimate grandson. The three fought over the succession, with Jugurtha having Hiempsa killed and fomenting a civil war between Adherbal and Jugurtha's factions.

Jugurtha's power was short-lived, however; he came into conflict with the Romans after he had some Roman agents working for Adherbal killed. Though initially Jugurtha successfully settled for peace with the neighboring Roman governor, the governor was accused of bribery, and both he and Jugurtha were brought to Rome to testify. Jugurtha lost all credibility once the Romans learned of his murder of Hiempsa, and the Romans went to war to remove him. The campaign took several years, but Jugurtha was finally defeated by the quaestor Lucius Cornelius Sulla and was brought back to Rome to be executed as part of Sulla's triumph in 104.

As a client state of Rome, western Numidia was intitally ceded to the Kingdom of Mauretania, which continued until the war between Julius Caesar and Pompey (49–45 BCE). The Numidian king Juba I allied himself with Pompey and specifically with Pompey's ally Cato the Younger, who fled to Utica from Caesar. When Caesar defeated Juba I at Thapsus in 46, Cato committed suicide, and Caesar made Numidia a Roman province, renamed Africa Nova. It remained thus until Augustus returned Numidia to native rule under Juba II, to whom he married Cleopatra Selene, the daughter of Cleopatra and Mark Antony. Juba II was the son of Juba I and assisted Augustus during a campaign in Spain.

Augustus also named Juba II and Cleopatra Selene the monarchs of neighboring Mauretania. They renamed the capital Caesaria, where art and architecture from around the Mediterranean flourished. Juba II ruled together with his son, Ptolemy, from 21 CE, and died in 23, leaving Ptolemy the sole ruler of both Numidia and Mauretania. During his rule, Numidia was divided between Mauretania and the new province, Africa Vetus, and was put under direct imperial control in 25. Numidia continued to be absorbed into surrounding client states and provinces until 46, when it ceased to exist in any meaningful form.

Sarah E. Watkins

Further Reading

Biroux, Virginie. "Numidia and the Punic World." In *The Punic Mediterranean Identities and Identification from Phoenician Settlement to Roman Rule,* edited by Josephine Crawley Quinn and Fentress, Elizabeth W. B. *Numidia and the Roman Army: Social, Military and Economic Aspects of the Frontier Zone.* Oxford, UK: BAR, 1979.

Roller, Duane W. *The World of Juba II and Kleopatra Selene: Royal Scholarship on Rome's African Frontier.* New York: Routledge, 2003.

O

Ogbomoso

The city of Ogbomoso, one of Nigeria's largest cities (estimated population 1.2 million), is located in the present-day Oyo State. Ogbomoso is a Yoruba polity of historical significance, for it was founded as a military outpost of the Oyo Empire (1400–1896). Unlike many Yoruba city-states that claimed direct descent from Ile-Ife, a warrior from the Oyo kingdom founded the ruling *soun* dynasty of Ogbomoso. The establishment of Ogbomoso dates back to the 17th century, estimated to have occurred during the reign of Oyo's *alafin* (king) Ajagbo circa 1600–1650, and there are many rival local traditions that contest the history of how the *soun* dynasty became established over the city-state. The coronation of the current monarch, or the *soun* of Ogbomoso, Oba Jimoh Oladunni Oyewumi, Ajagungbade III, occurred on October 24, 1973.

Situated on a high plateau in Yorubaland at an elevation of nearly 1,200 feet, Ogbomoso benefits from the highly fertile soils of Nigeria's savanna region. Characteristic of Yoruba urban settlements, Ogbomoso is a town whose citizens engage extensively in farming in the agrarian plains adjacent to the city. The important cash crops produced by the Ogbomoso people include many staple items of this region of West Africa: yams, cassava, maize, and tobacco. Ogbomoso has a tropical savanna climate, with a wet and dry (harmattan) seasonal division, though leaning more to arid. Ogbomoso's central location, at the heart of transport networks to important cities such as Oyo, Ilorin, Osogbo, and Ikoyi, has helped to shape the contours of its history and its present.

Samuel Ladoke Akintola (1910–1966)

Samuel Ladoke Akintola was a Nigerian nationalist. He held the aristocratic title Aare Ona Kakanfo. Akintola was educated at the Church Missionary Society School in Minna and at Ogbomoso's Baptist College. While teaching at the Baptist Academy (1930–1942), he became active in the Baptist Teachers' Union and the Nigerian Youth Movement. After studying law in England, he served as the legal adviser to Nigeria's Action Group party. In 1959, he was appointed the premier of the Western Region. In 1965, Akintola led the Nigerian National Democratic Party; he was assassinated in Nigeria's coup of 1966.

The Ogbomoso polity was among the frontier Yoruba polities, whose strategic location helped to buttress the Old Oyo state from its northern rivals. In contrast to the other important Yoruba frontier state to the northeast, Ilorin, Ogbomoso defeated the invading Fulani in the early 19th century. The Ogbomoso Army checked the expansionary Fulani incursion, fortified its ruling dynasty, and helped to bring equilibrium to 19th-century Fulani-Yoruba relations in the savanna border zone. Whereas the Fulani onslaught resulted in regime change for Ilorin and a fracturing of the Oyo Empire, the Ogbomoso dynasty managed the political changes of the 19th century by shifting its allegiance from Oyo to the Ibadan Empire following Ibadan's triumphant defeat of the Fulani at Osogbo in 1840.

As with many of West Africa's kingdoms, the precise chronology of the Ogbomoso state's early formation is shrouded in the myths of oral tradition, which function as both a historical narrative and an ideological charter of the civic community. Archaeology, however, clearly affirms the antiquity of human settlement in the region. What is undisputed is that the town's political structures and its monarchy were well established by the mid-17th century. The Ogbomoso region was likely peopled in several waves. The successive waves of human migration are reflected in the complexity of the state's political structure.

The Ogbomoso state maintains an official tradition that four people settled the region before Soun Ogunlola, the progenitor of the Soun dynasty. In the first wave, a Nupe (a people inhabiting the region north of Yorubaland) hunter of elephants named Aale established a settlement astride a hill that provided strategic access to the Afon stream used by the elephants. In Ogbomoso, that settlement is today referred to as Oke Elerin (Elephant Hill). Ohunsile, the second settler of Ogbomoso, was an unsuccessful claimant to a title in his hometown of Awori, located outside of Lagos. Ohunsile was the first Ogbomoso settler to make his distinction as a warrior in the Old Oyo military. For his service to the Oyo army, Alafin Abipa granted Ohunsile a homestead in the region of Ogbomoso. That area is today known as Oke Ijeru (Ijeru Hill). The third settler, Orisatolu, was a Borgu man. Orisatolu was an Ifá *babalawo* (priest/diviner), a renegade farmer who settled and cultivated the Yoruba vegetable *isapa* (*Hibiscus sabdariffa*). Akande, another Borgu man, was the final pre-Soun dynastic settler at Ogbomoso; he was also a renegade, a Sango devotee from Old Oyo. The predynastic Ogbomoso settlers established provincial lineage quarters within the polity that continue to be governed by a respective *baale*: the Oke Elerin, Oke Ijeru, Isapa, and Akande quarters (though the *baale* title of Akandie quarter is now defunct).

The founder of Ogbomoso's dynasty, *soun*, was also a man of Borgu descent. Soun's parents served in the government of Old Oyo's Ibolo Province: his father was a soldier of the Olugbon, the leader of the province and third-in-command of the *alafin,* and his mother was the daughter of the *aresa,* an Ibolo leader who was second-in-command of the *alafin*. The official tradition of Soun is significant, for it symbolically details the way in which *soun* gained ascendancy over the prior settlers and inhabitants of Ogbomoso. Soun established a warrior band at Ogbomoso from which he rallied the population to engage in military pursuits. In this period, he committed a crime by killing a man after a quarrel. Soun was taken before the courts of Old Oyo, where his case was to be seen before the *alafin* himself. While he was awaiting his trial, the Oyo Army invaded an enemy town, and Soun volunteered to participate in the campaign. He successfully defeated the enemy combatant and delivered his head to Alafin Ajagbo at Oyo. As a consolation, the *alafin* issued Soun a state pardon and decorated him with the *ogbo,* the Oyo state cutlass that symbolized unity of power and justice. Soun's receipt of the state cutlass conferred on his descendants the authority to govern the royal *ilu* (town). Tradition states that in honor of Soun's military victory the settlement was named Ogbori Elemaso (meaning "the settlement of he who decapitated the marksman"), which was shortened to Ogbomoso.

While Soun was responsible for introducing the Soun dynasty to Ogbomoso, it was his descendant Kumoyede who fully established the monarchy and articulated its rules of succession. Each of Kumoyede's sons achieved the *baale* title: first Toyeje and then his brothers Oluwusi, Baiyewuwon, Bolanta, and Odunaro. Each of Kumoyede's sons became the progenitor of a royal house. It is from these five principal lineages, or royal houses, that ascension to the Ogbomoso monarchy is selected today.

The origins of Ogbomoso as a military post for Oyo meant that for much of its history, warfare was a defining feature of its economy and external relations. The 19th century was a time of great internecine wars between the Yoruba-speaking states and massive demographic upheavals. The Oyo Empire suffered major defeats in the first half of the century, first among the Egba and then among the Hausa-Fulani at Ilorin (1824). After these major losses to the empire, Oyo moved its capital to the new Oyo city. The Ibadan Empire arose as the dominant successor to Oyo in Yorubaland. After the collapse of Oyo, Ogbomoso shifted its allegiance to Ibadan. Of the many wars of the period, Ogbomoso allied with Ibadan in the Ijesa War of 1869. The battle was noteworthy, for the *balogun* Ibikunle of Ibadan, himself an Ogbomoso man, helped to restore the proper monarchical succession during the temporary interregnum. Many people migrated or were displaced throughout the century, and Ogbomoso served as a haven for migrants from other parts of Yorubaland. Ogbomoso produced many noted figures in this period, including Opeagbe, the *baale* of Ibadan in 1850–1851.

Whereas Islam has a very old history in Ogbomoso, Christian missionaries such as the Anglican Church Missionary Society and the American Baptist Mission (ca. 1870s) became active only in the late 19th century. After the signing of the Anglo-Ibadan Treaty of 1893, Britain gradually elaborated its indirect rule system in which Ogbomoso was subordinated administratively to Ibadan, with power vested in the *alafin* of Oyo. Ogbomoso thinkers, who argued that the British misinterpreted the bilateral nature of Ibadan-Ogbomoso relations, resented the British subordination of Ogbomoso to Ibadan (and the *alafin*).

Today Ogbomoso is a large Yoruba market town and an educational center for the region. It is home to the Ladoke Akintola University of Technology, named after its famous citizen Samuel Ládòkè Akíntolá, the former premier of Nigeria's old Western Region. The Baptist Church of Nigeria maintains its Baptist Seminary in Ogbomoso.

Adrian M. Deese

Further Reading

Agiri, B. A. "Chief N. D. Oyerinde and the Political, Social and Economic Development of Ogbomoso, 1916–1951." *Journal of the Historical Society of Nigeria* 10(1) (1979): 86–112.

Agiri, B. A. "When Was Ogbomoso Founded?" *Transafrican Journal of History* 5(1) (1976): 32–51.

Agiri, Babatunde. "A Reconsideration of the Chronology of Ogbomoso History before the Colonial Period." *Odu* 15 (1977): 19–29.

Akinyele, I. B. *The Outlines of Ibadan History.* Lagos: Printed at Alebiosu Printing Press, 1946.

Oyerinde, N. D. *Iwe Itan Ogbomoso.* Jos, Nigeria: Niger Press, 1934.

Ohori

Ohori, perhaps one of the least well-known kingdoms of West Africa, lies in the once densely forested eastern portion of the expansive Lama Valley that crosses the entirety of the southern Republic of Benin. The kingdom's center, Ohori-Ije, consists of an archipelago of 17 villages that rest in the deepest recesses of the valley, approximately 10 miles from the southern plateau town of Pobé and 15 miles from Kétu, a prominent Yoruba kingdom that overlooks the basin from the north. Consisting of Yoruba-speaking peoples, the people who founded the Ohori state arrived in the area from numerous neighboring regions throughout the 17th, 18th, and 19th centuries. When French colonial officials first visited Ohori-Ije in 1890, they estimated its population at 5,000 to 10,000.

A linear rift created by geological fault-line activity several millennia ago, the Lama Valley stretches the roughly 30 miles from south to north and another 70 miles along a west-to-east axis, ranging from the far eastern reaches of what is now Togo and traversing southern Benin to the southwestern edge of Nigeria. A black cotton soil, or vertisol, dominates a land rich in humus, meaning that carbon and important nutrients have drained into the basin from higher elevations. Thousands of years of carbon buildup lend the pliable clay soil of Ohori-Ije a dark color and provide an uncharacteristic amount of agricultural stability relative to the rest of the region.

Climate in the Ohori kingdom is marked by seasonal extremes. Dry seasons arrive in late December or early January as harmattan winds from the north carry sands from the Sahara desert through the Sahelian region and into subtropical West Africa. Along with the dusty haze that descends on the valley, the dry air soaks up the moisture of the previous season's rains before giving way to two or three months of intense heat that can reach up to 35 degrees Celsius. Higher temperatures and limited rainfall cause the clay surface of the valley to crack. The area often experiences two periods of rain during the course of a year, ranging from March to August and then October to November. It is not uncharacteristic, however, for showers to persist up to nine months, beginning in March and continuing through December. The region generally receives its heaviest rainfall from May to July, when a northerly shift in wind patterns causes the airstream to reroute, driving tropical moisture farther into the hinterland.

Like much of what now makes up southern Benin, the Ohori kingdom rests in an area that experiences a unique sub-Guinean weather pattern that accounts for more rainfall than other areas along the interior of the Bight of Benin. The area of the kingdom today receives an average of 50 inches of rainfall per year, compared to the 25 or 30 inches that parts of Togo and Nigeria receive each year. The landscape takes on a dramatically different character during these months. The dark clay soil captures water spilling into the basin from the plateau to the south and from higher elevations in the north. In its first few centuries, rainy season marshes constituted the only vital sources of water for the community. Because the eastern section of the valley has no rivers, lakes, or reservoirs, residents up to the latter half of the 20th century established their homes around ponds or areas with larger depressions where rainwater could collect. A tributary from the Ouémé River had once trickled its way into the heart of the basin north of the Ohori country, but the stream likely dried up before the first settlers appeared.

Most Ohoris claim that their descendants traveled to the valley from either Oyo or Ile-Ife, two important Yoruba cities in Nigeria, anywhere from the 16th century to the 19th century. It seems likely, however, that many people who settled the valley were refugees from all over the region who sought protection from transatlantic slaving activities in the dense forest that dominated the valley's landscape. The timing of the arrival of the first settlers is difficult to know with certainty, but oral traditions place the appearance of the first settlers, a hunter named Ahoua (oftentimes recorded as Ahura) and his wife Kouoka, at some point in the 16th century. Regardless of their veracity, local legends indicate that by clearing a small plot out of the valley's dense brush, striking their hoes firmly into the basin's dark clay soil, and planting new crops, Ahoua and Kouoka sowed the seeds from which the Ohori kingdom eventually sprang.

Residents attribute the kingdom's name to the discovery by Ahoua of a Sohori tree one day as he was hunting near the farm he and his wife carved out the forested landscape. Ahoua believed that the leaves of the tree had medicinal properties that would allow his wife to bear numerous children. After collecting a few of the leaves, he kneaded them together and gave them to Kouoka to consume. Legends indicate that Kouoka bore 16 children in all, 8 boys and 8 girls, each of whom left their natal village to settle elsewhere, thus symbolically laying the foundations for 16 of Ohori-Ije's villages.

Leaders in Oyo installed Ahoua and Kouoka's third son, Alafèka, as the first Ohori monarch, thereby marking the establishment of the kingdom. In the interim, members of the community expanded their population at a gradual pace and surrounded themselves within the confines of a forest they called Igbó Ilú, which means "forest home" or "forest state." Shortly after the turn of the 19th century, however, population growth sparked intensive political centralization and a split from the larger empire. Oyo's collapse generated significant political and demographic upheaval throughout the region. The population of Ohori-Ije grew rapidly as a result, as refugees fearing political instability and increased slaving activities learned of Igbó Ilú's protective capacity.

Although the dense forest and difficult traveling conditions through thick mud and swampy conditions during rainy seasons likely precluded slave raiders from entering the kingdom, rumors persisted that Igbó Ilú possessed a cosmological energy that prevented foes from crossing its boundary safely. Oral traditions explain the transition to a more centralized kingship through the tale of a man named Aromokoukomoulèkè, meaning "the war has captured everyone but him," who arrived at the Ohori border at some point in what may have been the early to mid-19th century. Legends indicate that the traveler surprised many Ohori residents by crossing through the forest without incident, whereupon he requested that people install him as a new king. His ascent to the position suggests the development of a more refined political structure that occurred as refugees engaged and assimilated with Ohori-Ije's population. Unlike many other kingdoms in the region, however, Ohori favored choosing new leaders via a revolving kingship rather than opting for a hereditary model whereby a son of a leader assumed the position upon the death of his predecessor. Instead, prominent religious figures developed a rotating succession structure whereby they chose new leaders from four different villages.

Like other kingdoms throughout the region, Ohori remains intact today. Throughout the colonial era, many residents never considered themselves as colonized. Even after independence, many in the kingdom claimed that they have political autonomy. Perhaps what is most unique about Ohori, though, was its residents' disaggregation from the transatlantic slave trade during a precolonial epoch. Inhabitants of other kingdoms often engaged in slave trading or were captured, or both. Ohoris clearly developed trading relationships with outside communities but appeared to have eschewed slave trading while also using their location to protect themselves from being enslaved.

Marcus Filippello

Further Reading

Asiwaju, A. I. "Anti-French Resistance Movement in Ọhọri-Ije (Dahomey), 1895–1960." *Journal of the Historical Society of Nigeria* 7, no. 2 (1974): 255–269.

D'Almeida-Topor, Héléne. "Une société paysanne devant la colonisation: La résistance des Holli du Dahomey (1894–1923)." In *Sociétés Paysannes du du Tiers Monde,* edited by Catherine Coquery-Vidrovitch, 81–89. Lille: Presses Universitaire de Lille, 1980.

Garcia, Luc. "Les mouvements de résistances au Dahomey (1914–1917)." *Cahiers d'Études Africaines* 37 (1970): 144–178.

Ondo

The Kingdom of Ondo, founded circa 1510, is a historical Yoruba city-state in southwestern Nigeria. The capital of Ondo, Ondo City, has a current population of

Sunday Adeniyi (1946–)

Sunday Adeniyi, popularly known as King Sunny Ade, was born on September 1, 1946, in Oshogbo. Born into the royal family of Ondo, he studied at the grammar school in Ondo and moved to Lagos to pursue a music career. In the 1970s Sunny Ade was proclaimed the "King of Juju," a genre that originated in 20th-century Nigeria. Juju music utilized elements such as the talking drum, polyrhythms, and call-and-response. His albums include *Sound Vibration* (1977), *The Royal Sound* (1979), and *Juju Music* (1982), which propelled him to international stardom. In 1999, Sunny Ade was nominated for a Grammy Award for *Odu* (1998).

nearly 300,000 and is the second-largest city in Nigeria's Ondo State. Nigeria's Ondo State has a geographical area of 15,500 square kilometers (6,000 square miles), while the historical Ondo state occupied a significantly smaller though varying component of this territory. The Ondo kingdom is located in the eastern area of the Yoruba-speaking region. The eastern region of Yorubaland include the important centers of the Akure kingdom—Ijebu-Ode, Ode Ondo, Idanre, Ile Oluji, Ode Itsekiri—and the Kingdom of Owo to the northeast. The eastern region of Yorubaland is also located to the immediate west of the Edo-speaking region, centralized around the Benin kingdom, which historically influenced the heterogeneous composition of the Ondo kingdom's diverse population. The king (*oba*) of the Ondo monarchy is known as the *osemawe*. The reigning *osemawe*, Oba Adesimbo Victor Kiladejo of the Osemawe dynasty's Okuta ruling house, ascended the throne on December 29, 2008.

The Ondo state historically shared with the other Yoruba polities a monarchical governmental structure, myths of Ile-Ife dynastic origins, an urban marketplace culture, and a rural agricultural economy. The location of Ondo, in a complex hilly terrain, helped to shape its history. The region's system of hills provided some degree of protection from the expansionary Old Oyo Empire (ca. 1400–1835) to the northeast and the Benin kingdom to the south, allowing for a high degree of continuous political autonomy. The warm climate of the Ondo region has helped to shape the type of cultivable agricultural products grown in the region. Ondo, along with the rest of southwestern Nigeria, possess a tropical rainy-dry seasonal pattern. As is common in the region, Ondo produces various agricultural products such as tobacco, yams, cassava, pumpkins, and cotton. By the early 20th century, Ondo's chief export commodities were cocoa and timber products. Characteristic of Yoruba culture, Ondo is also a center of textile production.

The predominant mode of Yoruba government is monarchical. In Yoruba mythology, the sacred city-state of Ile-Ife is considered to be the site of human creation. The main Yoruba dynasties all trace their origins to Ile-Ife, its divine founder Odùduwà, and his progeny who were believed to have settled there. Historical evidence and archaeology also suggest that prior to the establishment of the Ife dynasties throughout the region, other political forms existed and continue to function, as they belonged to the autochthonous peoples of the region. The autochthonous groups typically were constituted under a republican structure, which consisted of a gerontocracy; they were organized by age sets, governing village elders, and political power was decentralized and representative. The political heritage of these complex forms is visible in the history of the Ondo state and continues to play an important role in contemporary Nigeria.

The founding of the Ondo kingdom in circa 1510 drew on elements of these various traditions of governance. The exact origin of Ondo's Osemawe dynasty is contested. The Ile-Ife version, the view that many Ondo thinkers accept, holds that the Osemawe dynasty had its origins at Ile-Ife. The mythical wife of Odùduwà gave birth to twins—then considered unlucky for the Yoruba—and was thus forced into exile to the south. Ultimately she reached the area that would now be Ondo, where each child established a new monarchy: the son established a kingdom at the village of Epe, 10 miles northwest of Ondo, and the daughter, Pupupu, founded the city-state of Ondo. Although the Ondo kingdom surpassed Epe in size, ultimately engulfing it, upon installation of each new *osemawe,* Ondo customary ritual mandates a visit to Epe's Jegun monarch in order to acknowledge its seniority.

Ondo scholar Jerome Ojo characterized the Ondo state as possessing a pyramidal structure. At the apex of the state is its monarch, the *osemawe.* A cabinet-like council of six titled individuals, referred to as the Iwarefa, historically supported the office of the *osemawe.* In order of primacy, the six individuals of Iwarefa council, after the *oba,* are the *lisa,* the *jomu,* the *odongho,* the *sasere,* and the *adaja.* The *lisa* is the second in authority in the Iwarefa, for he is the representative of all the people of the Ondo kingdom with the exception of the Ondo royal family, the Otunba. In precolonial times, the Iwarefa would have been responsible for the executive, judiciary, and legislative elements of the state's governing apparatus.

The second stratum of the Ondo state consists of the Ekule chiefs, who rank second-in-command after the Iwarefa. The Ekule has seven members, and four of its offices correspond to the Iwarefa in a deputy formation. The seven Ekule titleholders include the *odofin,* the *arobo,* the *logbosere,* the *odofindi,* the *sagwe,* the *sara,* and the *lotomoba.* The *odofin* is the deputy to the *lisa* and maintains a residence at Okelisa. The Ekule deputies to the Iwarefa include the *arogbo* to the *odongho,* with a residence at Igele; the *logbosere* to the *sasere,* with a residence at Oreretu; and the *odofindi* to the *adaja,* with a residence at Iparuku. The other three nondeputized offices in the Ekule cabinet includes the *sagwe,* resident at Odosida; the *sara,* resident at Igunrin; and the *lotomoba,* resident at Oke-Otunba. The *sagwe* served as the royal messenger for the king and executed the chiefly roll call at the king's festivals.

The next important titleholders in the Ondo kingdom's governing hierarchy were the members of the Elegbe. The Elegbe is particularly important because its members were responsible for the management of the provincial bureaucracy in the different town quarters. The Ondo city-state was divided into 15 provincial districts, or *oiles,* in which each *oile* corresponded to the original 15 quarters founded by the Osemawe dynasty in its early history. The first quarter, Oke Ayadi, was founded during the reign of Oba Airo, and the last quarters, Ogbontitun and Oke-Sarowo, were founded during the reign of Oba Ulikolasi. Power was further decentralized at the provincial level, as each Elegbe titleholder had underneath him an extensive hierarchy of chiefs who executed policy and public works at the municipal level. In addition, each street contained councils that were accountable to the larger Elegbe governing structure. Within each bureaucratic structure there were theoretically elements of juridical, legislative, and executive power upon which the office's jurisdiction rested.

The offices were also gendered, with women having their own titles that corresponded to the *iwarefa* and *ekule* titles for men. The most important women's titles have existed since the founding of the Ondo kingdom: *lobon, lisa lobon, omo lobon, orangun lobon, sasere lobon,* and *adafin.* The other important Ondo titleholders included the Alaghoro, or the priestly class, responsible for executing the state's ritual ceremonies. The senior figure of the Ondo priestly class, the *sumo,* was the *osemawe*'s chief diviner and maintained his residence directly adjacent to the king's palace (*afin*), as he needed to be in great proximity to consult the oracles whenever the king needed to. Most of the titles within Ondo's hierarchy were theoretically meritocratic. The titles could be earned or granted through appointment. At the base of the Ondo state, however, is an aristocratic core that consisted of the primary titles of state: *oba, jomu, sora, akunara,* the *eki* at Ifore, the *oloja* of Idoko, *lobon, lotu agbede,* and the now defunct *ayunna* (former bell ringer).

The legend of Pupupu's founding of the Ondo state, though embellished over time for various political reasons, was likely rooted in historical events. The Ondo monarchy was unique in that a woman who reigned as king founded it. Pupupu's reign likely ended around the year 1530, after which her son Airo was enthroned as the *oba* of Ondo. Airo's reign was most important in the consolidation of the Osemawe dynasty and the formation of the current composition of the Ondo kingship institution. As *oba,* Airo was a reformer who made the office of the *ayadi* the highest ranking among the Elegbe cabinet instead of the *egbedi.* Airo made the position of the *lisa* second-in-command of the *osemawe,* demoting the position of the *odofin.* He also replaced the *ologbosere* with the *sasere.* In addition to cementing the Ondo constitutional hierarchy, Airo was committed to the undertaking of public works projects that would stabilize the Ondo kingdom. He helped to clearly define the composition of the Ondo royal family, as each one of his sons would establish a royal lineage from which the selection of a monarch would alternate. The most historically significant Ondo deity, Oramfe, was introduced during Airo's reign. The public works undertaken under his reign included the massive renovation of the Ondo *afin* (palace) and the construction of the city-state's ramparts in order to help fortify the state from external threats.

Osemawe Luju, who reigned from circa 1561 to 1590, succeeded Oba Airo. Luju furthered the public works projects that began under the previous monarch. He attempted to clearly demarcate the state's boundaries through the extensive digging of trenches that fully enclosed and fortified the city. To strengthen the polity, he furthermore advocated that all Ondo citizens construct their homesteads within the city's boundaries. Luju introduced the cultivation of silk cotton trees in the town and the worship of the Osanyin deity. During Luju's reign, Ondo would expand yet maintain good relations with the more powerful expansionary Oyo

Empire. Luju's state visit to Alafin Ajiboyede was an important highlight of Ondo-Oyo relations during this period. Luju studied the blueprint of the *alafin*'s palace and brought it back to Ondo in an attempt to reform the *osemawe*'s palace in accord with the Oyo model. This era was a highlight of Ondo-Oyo relations.

Oba Kuta was enthroned as the Ondo monarch in circa 1590. The previous monarch, Luju, was dethroned in a popular revolt against his rule. Upon his ascension, Oba Kuta led an Ondo territorial expansion, annexing new lands to create the state's Oke Augwa quarter, over which he selected the *augwa* as the senior Elegbe titleholder. The name of this new quarter, Augwa ("a ri owa," meaning "we have found a king") commemorated the political circumstances of Kuta's reign and the people's desire for political change.

Many kings reigned in the Ondo kingdom from its foundation to the British annexation. Oba Luyare, enthroned in circa 1614, introduced the worship of the Babaji deity. Oba Liyen came to the Ondo throne in 1685. Liyen (it is said) introduced the Ifá divination and devotion to its Orunmila deity of wisdom into the Ondo kingdom. Liyen also incorporated the important Agemo masquerade during his reign. As in many West African states during this era, the Ondo fought wars, both defensive and expansionary, in a growing economy dependent on the transatlantic slave trade. This political economy presented the opportunity for the acquisition of wealth by some but a climate of uncertainty and interstate predation for most. Ondo participated in the important Yoruba Wars at Omu in circa 1716. During the reign of the seventh *osemawe,* Leyo, the Ondo kingdom engaged in military conflicts with the Oyo on the northwest frontier. The deterioration of Ondo-Oyo relations was partly a consequence of Oyo's great ambitions to expand into eastern Yorubaland and partly a reflection of Leyo's military ambitions in the region. Regardless of the hostility's origin, the Ondo military was successful in defeating the Oyo military and repelling its attempted annexation of Ondoland into the Oyo Empire.

Another noteworthy administration in the long history of the Ondo monarchy would include Oba Aganmede, who led successful campaigns against the Akure and Ijebu. In addition to defeating Ondo's enemies, Aganmede annexed new territories, creating the provincial districts of Oke-Sare and Idimi Sokoti. During the reign of Oba Terere (ca. 1770), the important Eku festival was introduced into Ondo. In the Owu War of 1809, the Ondo defeated the encroaching Owu invaders. The 19th century is known as the era of the Yoruba Civil War in Yoruba historiography. The Ondo state was no exception to the incessant belligerence of the century. Perhaps the most decisive Ondo conflict was its participation in the Irele War of 1870. The strain of the conflict helped to engender uncertainty within Ondo, resulting in civil unrest throughout the state's primary villages: Ajue, Igbado, Erinla, Oke-Opa, Oboto, Ateu, Ilnla, and Aisa. This conflict culminated in the forced exile of the state's aristocracy for 11 years, during which they established an interregnum governing structure at the village of Oke-Opa (Okopa). The instability of this period coincided with a greater interest on the part of the British in controlling the internal trade of the Yoruba region. The British governor at the Lagos crown colony, John Glover, aimed to create an alternate road into the interior through Ondo. Concurrently, an Ife-Ijesa military coalition led an invasion of Ondo and attempted to take Ode Ondo, which sparked an Ondo insurrection. The warfare ultimately culminated in a peace treaty, spearheaded by Governor Glover and signed by representatives of Ondo and Ife in 1872. Christian missionary evangelism began in 1873 but was halted until the Anglicans returned in 1875. The *osemawe* of Ondo signed a free trade treaty with the British in 1899, and the Ondo kingdom was incorporated into the Lagos Protectorate and thereafter the colony of southern Nigeria.

Adrian M. Deese

Further Reading

Akintoye, Stephen Adebanji. "The Ondo Road Eastwards of Lagos, C. 1870–95." *Journal of African History* 10(4) (1969): 581–598.

Law, Robin. *The Oyo Empire, c. 1600–c. 1836: A West African Imperialism in the Era of the Atlantic Slave Trade.* Oxford, UK: Clarendon, 1977.

Ojo, Jerome O., and Valentine Ojo. *Yoruba Customs from Ondo.* Wien: Acta Ethnologica et Linguistica, 1976.

Ojo, Olatunji. "Slavery and Human Sacrifice in Yorubaland: Ondo, C. 1870–94." *Journal of African History* 46(3) (2005): 379–404.

Olupona, Jacob Kehinde. *Kingship, Religion, and Rituals in a Nigerian Community: A Phenomenological Study of Ondo Yoruba Festivals.* Stockholm, Sweden: Almqvist and Wiksell International, 1991.

Ouagadougou

Ouagadougou is the capital city of the West African country Burkina Faso, formerly known as Upper Volta. Burkina Faso's largest town, with a population of about 1.5 million people, Ouagadougou is situated strategically between the Saharan bends of the Niger River and the forest zone of West Africa. The relatively flat terrain of the region and the sufficient rainfall made the area attractive to early human habitation.

Ouagadougou developed as a result of the expansion of the Dagomba people of the Gold Coast (modern-day Ghana) into the Volta region and their conquest and partial absorption of the autochthonous inhabitants such as the Ninisis. The emerging population, the Mossis, established a number of polities headed by rulers called *nabas.* According to one historical account, the Mossis under Naba Oubri arrived in the Ouagadougou area in about the 12th century CE. Ouagadougou reached its zenith as the capital of the Oubri dynasty during the reign of Mogho Naba Ouaraga (ca. 1661–1681). Early travelers reported that precolonial Ouagadougou consisted of a complex of villages spread over 12 square kilometers and linked by footpaths to Na'Tenga and to the marketplace. The entire complex inhabited by the people had no wall. Each homestead within the villages and hamlets was surrounded by its own gardens, or village farms. The pre-Islamic traditional religion of the Mossis included belief in an otiose god called Winnam. This religion revolved around a female deity known as Tenga.

Ouagadougou was an important trade and market center in western Sudan. Sultan Muhammed Bello of Sokoto claimed that the Hausa merchants established extensive trade with the Mossis before the arrival of the Europeans. German traveler in western Sudan Henry Barth mentioned Ouagadougou as a major travel point of caravans moving between Timbuktu and Salaga in northern Ghana and between the areas of the present Republic of Niger and Kong in northern Ivory Coast.

The French conquest of Ouagadougou on September 5, 1896, ushered in a new era in the history of the town. The French were interested in territory and in trade, and when the ruler Mogho Naba Wobogo refused to surrender his authority, the French used force. Wobogo's army was defeated, and the king fled, never to return to his capital. The French installed Sighiri, Wobogo's brother, as Mogho Naba. The French used Ouagadougou as a military camp from where they staged the conquest of the remaining Volta region. By 1899 the base became the headquarters of the Second (Volta) Military Territory, and its resident officers were empowered with establishing peace and order.

The commercial activities of the French in the Upper Volta transformed the traditional economic life of Ouagadougou. The Ouagadougou market was relocated from its traditional site in front of Mogho Naba's palace to an area about one kilometer southeast of the palace. European trading companies sent African representatives to establish trading centers in the area. This lured many more traditional African merchant groups such as the Dioulas and Hausa to Ouagadougou. On June 25, 1901, Father Guillame Templier and three other white priests set up a Christian mission in Ouagadougou. The presence of missionaries increased the number of Europeans in the capital.

In 1904, the French created the colony Haut-Senegal et Niger, with Ouagadougou as the *chef-lieu* (chief town) of a *cercle* (a French administrative unit) also called Ouagadougou. The creation of the Haut-Senegal et Niger colony increased the town's population and European and African commercial activity in the region. The Compagnie Francaise de la Côte d'Ivoire established a presence in Ouagadougou through its African representatives. In 1907–1908, many more Hausa, who traded kola nuts and salt between Salaga and Timbuktu, arrived and settled in the Hausa quarter called Zanguettin. They were later joined by Yoruba traders from Salaga who moved to Ouagadougou to trade in cloth and kola nuts.

In 1919 the Upper Volta became a separate colony in French West Africa, and Ouagadougou was made the capital. Ouagadougou was transformed into a *commune mixte* by the decree of December 4, 1926, and officially recognized as a town. A French official was appointed as *administrateur-maire* (administrator-mayor) to work closely with the *cercle* commander, the governor, and the traditional officials in the town. However, the Great Depression (1929–1939) denied early achievements in the physical, municipal, and demographic growth of Ouagadougou. The economy of the colony was based on cotton, and with the collapse of the world cotton market, the economy became comatose. Because of financial bankruptcy and the exodus of the Mossi labor to the Ivory Coast, Upper Volta was discontinued as a colony on September 5, 1932, and Ouagadougou lost its status and role as a colonial capital.

On September 4, 1947, the French government decided to re-create the Upper Volta colony and redesignate Ouagadougou as its capital. French and African civil servants arrived to staff the new administrative services. Other people came to the town to seek employment with the government or with private companies. Postwar Ouagadougou also attracted a large number of Mossis who had earlier fled to the Gold Coast and the Ivory Coast to avoid forced labor. The Mossi population of the town increased with the departure in 1960 of many non-Volta civil servants who had previously dominated many of the institutions. A new law of November 18, 1955, further made Ouagadougou a *commune de plein exercice* and gave it the right to elect a municipal government. One year later the Ouagadougous held elections for their municipal council. Most of the political parties in Upper Volta and some independent candidates contested the municipal council election on November 18, 1956.

Upper Volta became independence from France on August 5, 1960. The Voltaic Democratic Union-African Democratic Rally emerged as the victorious party in Upper Volta, and its leader, Maurice Yemeogo, became president of the republic. Less than one month after the Ouagadougou municipal election of December 5, 1965, was concluded, the people of Ouagadougou revolted against the national

View of Maurice Yameogo Avenue, the commercial center of Ouagadougou, Burkina Faso. (MT Curado/iStockphoto.com)

government. The event that led to the revolt was the adoption by the National Assembly of a proposal to reduce the salaries and perquisites of the civil servants, most of whom lived in Ouagadougou. The introduction of austerity measures was the result of a decline in external aid, particularly from France, and the heavy strain of paying the salaries of civil servants and temporary technical personnel. A nationwide strike protest was organized by the labor union. On January 3, 1966, the government declared a state of emergency, but protests and the workers' strike continued. The people insisted that the president, Maurice Yemeogo, must go and that the army should take over power. Finally, Colonel Aboubakar Sangoulé Lamizana, the army chief of staff, announced to the crowd that the army "has assumed its responsibilities." The people of Ouagadougou had brought down the government of the republic through bloodless mass uprising.

Instability and unrest continued to mark much of the history of Upper Volta. In 1983 Captain Thomas Sankara, a member of the army, became president and introduced widespread reforms such as literacy and gender equality. Also, Sankara changed the name of the country from Upper Volta to Burkina Faso in 1984. Sankara was assassinated in 1987, and Blaise Compaoré, also a member of the military, became president. Unrest continued throughout Compaoré's administration both for economic issues and his attempt to extend his 27 years of rule. In October 2014, thousands of protestors gathered in Ouagadougou to demand that Compaoré resign the presidency. He consequently gave in to the pressure and resigned as president of Burkina Faso on October 31, 2014.

Aribidesi Usman

Further Reading

Barth, Henry. *Travels and Discoveries in North and Central Africa.* New York: Harper and Brothers, 1859.

Clapperton, Hugh. *Second Voyage dans L'interieur de L'Afrique,* Vol. 2. Translated by M. M. Eyries and de la Renaudiere. Paris: Arthus Bertrand Libraire, 1829.

Skinner, Elliot P. *African Urban Life: The Transformation of Ouagadougou.* Princeton, NJ: Princeton University Press, 1974.

Skinner, Elliot P. *The Mossi of Upper Volta.* Stanford, CA: Stanford University Press, 1964.

Oyo (Old Oyo)

The Old Oyo Empire, located north of the modern-day town of Oyo in southwestern Nigeria, rose to prominence in the 17th century and reached its peak in the 18th century. When the empire finally collapsed in 1835, it was territorially the largest and the most politically powerful Yoruba kingdom ever. Scholars do not agree on the extent of the size of the Old Oyo Empire. However, what is certain is that at the height of its power in the 18th century, the eastern end of the empire extended from the coast near Badagry northward along the western boundary of Ijebu territories,

The Oyo Crisis of 1954

From the early 1950s, administrative reforms at the local government level across Nigeria introduced new conflicts between and among different classes of elites, political parties, and the colonial government. In Oyo, local government reforms by the Action Group, the ruling political party in the Western Region, and the central Nigerian government drastically curtailed the power of the *alaafin* (king), Adeniran Adeyemi II, who had previously amassed enormous political and economic resources under the indirect rule system that flourished until the early 1950s. The new reforms prevented Adeyemi from collecting taxes, introduced new levies, and elected councilors, who vied for political power with the king. In response to the unfavorable actions of the ruling party, the king allied with the National Council of Nigeria and the Cameroons, the opposition party in the Western Region. The uneasy situation between the Action Group and Adeyemi led to serious violence, culminating in the exile of Adeyemi in 1954.

covering such places as Apomu, Osogbo, and Ede. Oyo was bounded in the north by the Niger and Moshi Rivers. Oyo's western and southern borders reached Dahomey in the present-day Republic of Benin, and its capital was approximately 40 miles northwest of Ilorin. The oval-shaped town wall built for the defense of the capital was about 15 miles in circumference and about 4 miles in diameter one way and 6 miles in diameter the other way. The palace of the empire itself was protected by a 1-square-mile wall.

One of the most intriguing aspects of Oyo civilization was its elaborate political institution centered on the monarchical system of government headed by the king (*alaafin*). In theory, the *alaafin* was an absolute and divine king. He was the second-in-command or deputy of the gods who could do as he wished—thus the praise name *iku baba yeye, alase ekeji orisa* (the almighty, the ruler and companion of the gods). However, his power was regulated by a council of chiefs called the Oyo Mesi, composed of the eight most senior chiefs in the capital city. Headed by the *basorun*, the Oyo Mesi advised the king on domestic and foreign economic and political matters. They were required to assemble at the palace on the first day of every Yoruba week, which consisted of only four days. This weekly meeting also allowed the *alaafin* and the Oyo Mesi to collectively worship Sango (the Yoruba god of thunder), one of the empire's most important gods. Thus, like many Yoruba societies, rituals and spirituality fused with politics. In all senses, Oyo was a theocratic society. In the advent of interpersonal or popular conflict, the Oyo Mesi also had the power to compel the king to commit suicide by uttering the statement "The gods reject you, the people reject you, earth rejects you." Another group of highly important title holders (*omo obas*) moderated relations between the *alaafin* and the Oyo Mesi, ensuring that divisive political opinions did not degenerate into a massive crisis that could threaten public peace and the political process. But on several occasions, this group could not successfully resolve conflict between the *alaafin* and the Oyo Mesi. For instance, all the *alaafins* who reigned between circa 1658 and 1754 were compelled to commit suicide by the Oyo Mesi. Popular Yoruba history and oral tradition established that this unusual situation was made possible by the autocracy of a particular *basorun* called Gaa.

The effective governance of provincial towns was central to the preservation of the power of the king and the stability of the region. There were two main types of provincial towns, namely royal towns and ordinary towns. The royal towns were administered by princes from the ruling house in the metropolis of Oyo, who were given the title of king (*oba*) and the opportunity to wear a crown and build their palace to resemble that of the metropolis. The ordinary towns, however, had loose or distant relations with the Oyo metropolis. Their head (*baale*) was of a lower status than the *oba*; a *baale* could not build his palace to resemble that of the Oyo capital or wear a crown, even though his function was exactly that of the *oba*. In short, the symbolisms of power and authority between the Oyo metropolis and the provincial towns (both the royal and ordinary) were meant to define social status, which also influenced social privilege among communities and peoples. To ensure that provincial towns continued to respect the sacred power of the metropolis, the appointment of their rulers was usually ratified by the *alaafin*. Provincial towns were also required to send representatives to the Oyo metropolis during important festivals. Similarly, the *alaafin* would appoint a local representative (*ajele*) to monitor and oversee the affairs of provincial towns in order to maintain his interest.

Information about Oyo's economic activities is scanty, but like other Yoruba towns, historians generally agree that the people practiced agriculture to produce food to feed the ever-expanding population. Craft work and ironworking were vital domestic industries that supplied the materials needed for diverse social, economic, and aesthetic purposes. Like many West African states of the 18th century, the Oyo Empire also engaged in the transatlantic slave trade. Its sources of slaves included captives of wars of military expansion.

A combination of internal and external factors was responsible for the decline of Oyo after the death of King Abiodun in 1789. One notable external factor was the increasing power of its provincial and vassals states, which began to break away because the central government could not effectively administer the expanding empire. Provincial chiefs and warriors who were required to respect the order of the *alaafin* began to carve out part of the empire for themselves. The most consequential of these secessionist projects was that of Ilorin under Are Ona Kakanfo Afonja, the highest-ranked of the military chiefs. After carving Ilorin for himself, Afonja invited the Hausa-Fulani jihadist from the north to help populate his new territory. With time the Muslim jihadist, inspired by the teachings of Usman dan Fodio, a respected Islamic scholar based in Sokoto, the capital of the Islamic caliphate that covered much of present-day northern Nigeria, took over the town from him and launched an onslaught on the Oyo capital. The final end to a once glorious Yoruba empire came around 1835 in the Eleduwe War, when the capital of Oyo fell to the jihadist. It was completely sacked, with the entire population dispersed over other Yoruba territories. Historians of Yoruba agree that the collapse of the Old Oyo Empire left a political vacuum in the region and paved the way for a series of wars and revolutions that did not come to an end until the last decade of the 19th century, when the British imposed colonial rule on much of Yorubaland.

Saheed Aderinto

Further Reading

Atanda, J. A. *The New Oyo Empire: Indirect Rule and Change in Western Nigeria, 1894–1934.* London: Longman, 1973.

Johnson, Samuel. *The History of the Yorubas: From the Earliest Times to the Beginning of the British Protectorate.* 1921; London: Routledge/Kegan Paul, 1966.

Law, Robin. *The Oyo Empire, c. 1600–c. 1836: A West African Imperialism in the Era of the Atlantic Slave Trade.* Oxford, UK: Clarendon, 1977.

R

Rwanda

The terrain of Rwanda, known as the "land of a thousand hills," is mostly grassy uplands with mountains in the west, tropical savanna in the east, and numerous lakes and rivers throughout the country. The country lies 75 miles south of the equator in the Tropic of Capricorn, 880 miles west of the Indian Ocean, and 1,250 miles east of the Atlantic Ocean. Temperatures average 70°F in Kigali, with a temperate to subtropical climate range, and there are two dry seasons and two rainy seasons per year. Average annual rainfall is approximately 45 inches, concentrated during the rainy seasons. Rwanda's natural resources include gold, cassiterite, wolframite, methane, hydropower, and arable land, with chief exports being coffee and tea. Rwanda's national parks include the Akagera and Virunga Volcanoes National Parks. Rwanda is known for its mountain gorillas as well as its buffaloes, zebras, impalas, baboons, warthogs, lions, hippopotamuses, and giant pangolin anteaters.

Archaeological evidence has pointed to settlement by hunter-gatherers in the late Stone Age, followed by a larger population of early Iron Age settlers who produced pottery and iron tools. These early inhabitants were ancestors of the Twa aboriginal Pygmy group. The historical origin of ethnic identity in Rwanda remains a topic of controversy. One theory developed during the colonial period held that Rwanda's ethnic groups emerged from waves of conquest and immigration. It was thought that Bantu groups migrated to Rwanda from West Africa and cleared forestland for

---

Rwanda in Films and Documentaries

Rwanda has appeared as the central focus of movies such as *Gorillas in the Mist* (1988) and, more recently, in films about the genocide, such as *100 Days* (2001), *Shooting Dogs* (2005), *Sometimes in April* (2005), and *Shake Hands with the Devil* (2007), as well as in songs such as "Million Voices" by Wyclef Jean and "In All Rwanda's Glory" by the Rx Bandits. The Academy Award–nominated film *Hotel Rwanda* (2004) told the story of Paul Rusesabagina, acting manager of the Hôtel des Mille Collines in Kigali, during the 1994 genocide. The historic hotel appears in *Sometimes in April* and *Shake Hands with the Devil*. Rusesabagina published his memoir *An Ordinary Man* in 2006. Other films and documentaries such as *In the Tall Grass* (2006), *Flower in the Gun Barrel* (2008), *My Neighbor, My Killer* (2009), and *Coexist* (2014) have depicted the reconciliation process in Rwanda.

agriculture. Hutu agriculturalists are believed to have descended from the Bantus. This theory posits that the pastoralist Tutsi cattle herders were partially descended from Caucasoid migrants from the Horn of Africa and North Africa and were thought to have subsequently conquered the territory and established their authority.

Another theory argues that the Hutus and Tutsis belonged to the same Bantu population and were artificially divided by German and Belgian colonists for the Tutsi minority to serve as overseers for the colonial powers. This theory suggests that the designations held little social significance and that the groups shared a common language and culture, living together throughout the territory. As a result of colonial policies, these categories became transformed into ethnic identities. A third theory suggests that the Hutus and Tutsis were related but not identical and that the differences between the groups were exacerbated by colonial powers. It is thought that Belgian colonists designated people as Tutsi or Hutu based on their cattle ownership and church records and installed a Tutsi elite class to represent colonial interests. This theory holds that the development of Tutsi dominance began in the late precolonial period and was accelerated by colonial rule, transforming identity through Western ideas of race and discrimination based on ethnicity and giving greater meaning to the designations than was previously held.

The Kingdom of Rwanda occupied approximately the territory of the modern-day Republic of Rwanda. Oral history tells that the Kingdom of Rwanda was founded by Tutsi pastoralists. The king ruled through cattle chiefs, land chiefs, and military chiefs. As the king centralized power, he distributed land among individuals rather than through lineage groups. The Hutus, Tutsis, and Twas maintained a symbiotic relationship through the exchange of labor in a system known as *ubuhake*. The centralized land distribution implemented by the Tutsi monarchy was known as *uburetwa*. Under this system, Hutu farmers were entitled to use Tutsi cattle and land in exchange for personal or military service. Eventually this system became a class system whereby land and cattle were consolidated into power for the Tutsis, similar to the European feudal system. The *mwami,* or Tutsi king, sat at the top of the feudal pyramid and was thought to have divine ancestry. The system was supported by European colonists in order to maintain control through the Tutsi aristocracy and indigenous power structure but was phased out in the 1950s due to increasing pressure for independence within colonial Africa.

In 1899, the independent Kingdom of Rwanda, along with neighboring Burundi, became a German colony known as Ruanda-Urundi following the 1885 Berlin Conference. After the defeat of Germany during World War 1, under the Treaty of Versailles, Rwanda became a League of Nations protectorate administered by Belgium. Once the League of Nations was dissolved, the area became a United Nations trust territory in 1946, with the promise that the Belgians would prepare the area for independence. Economic profits from the cultivation of the land were sent to Belgium and utilized for development in the colony. In 1935, the Belgian colonial administration issued identity cards to all Rwandans that named their ethnicity and instituted a policy that ethnicity was inherited from one's father, eliminating any fluidity of identity. Those who possessed 10 or more cows were registered as Tutsis, and those with fewer than 10 cows were registered as Hutus.

In 1959, a group of disenfranchised Hutus organized to form an uprising to drive Tutsis from their positions of power and into exile. Rwanda gained its independence from Belgium in 1962, and Gregoire Kayibanda was elected Rwanda's first president. Using ethnic appeals to build support, Kayibanda's Hutu government and military troops, the Rwandan Armed Forces (FAR) retaliated against attacks by exiled Tutsi rebel groups in the 1960s. Violence erupted again in response to the 1972 genocide of Hutus in Burundi, where Tutsis regained political control. In July 1973, a coup d'état installed Hutu major general Juvenal Habyarimana as president. Ethnic tensions initially diminished but rose again in the mid-1980s due to economic decline. In 1982, persecution of Tutsis by President Milton Obote's government in Uganda caused thousands of Rwandan Tutsis to attempt to return to Rwanda, only to be turned away at the border by Rwandan troops. Many Tutsis joined the rebel movement in Uganda that brought President Yoweri Museveni to power in 1986. Tutsis within Museveni's National Resistance Army founded the Rwandese Patriotic Front (RPF).

In October 1990, the RPF invaded Rwanda, moving Habyarimana to retake political control, beginning the Rwandan Civil War. The military began to organize massacres of Tutsis under the guise of responding to the RPF attack. Public opinion shifted against the RPF due to rumors of civilian massacres in areas controlled by the RPF. Although the Arusha Accords were signed in 1993 to promote peace in Rwanda, it was perceived that the agreement ceded too much power to the RPF. This galvanized the movement for Hutu power. Anti-Tutsi ideologies promoted by the Hutu Power movement were spread through the radio station Radio Television Libre Mille-Collines. The 1993 assassination of Burundi's Hutu president Melchior Ndadaye also contributed to distrust of the Tutsis, causing an eruption of interethnic violence in Burundi that drove Hutu refugees into Rwanda. Rwandan military personnel began to provide paramilitary training to youth wings of Hutu Power parties, such as the Interahamwe militia. The United Nations Assistance Mission for Rwanda (UNAMIR) was established in 1993 as a peacekeeping force to aid in the implementation of the Arusha Accords. UNAMIR initially withdrew troops and nationals as violence erupted again in 1994.

On April 6, 1994, the plane carrying President Habyarimana and Burundi president Cyprien Ntaryamira was shot down in Kigali. The RPF was initially blamed for the assassination, although others believed that troops close to Habyarimana planned the attack. This assassination set the plans for genocide in motion, with members of the presidential guard and elite troops spreading lists of RPF sympathizers throughout Kigali within hours of the assassination. Initially, the attacks were focused in Kigali on prominent Tutsis and moderate Hutus perceived to be opponents of the regime but eventually spread across the country to target Tutsis in the name of self-defense and security as a result of careful planning and coordination by military and government officials. Between 500,000 and 1 million people were killed during the genocide of 1994.

The RPF's armed wing, the Rwandese Patriotic Army, subdued FAR troops beginning in the eastern part of Rwanda in May 1994, eventually reaching the capital of Kigali on July 4. Many refugees fled into Tanzania and Zaire (now the

Democratic Republic of Congo), including organizers of the genocide and armed forces. The RPF declared victory and established an interim government. The RPF arrested and executed hundreds of people suspected of involvement in the genocide. Refugee camps comprising former FAR and citizen militias in Zaire remained a security threat to the RPF government. Following the genocide, the government worked to rebuild infrastructure and the society by establishing accountability through judicial proceedings in *gacaca* courts. The United Nations Security Council created the International Criminal Tribunal for Rwanda to try those responsible for the genocide and other violations of international law. The government has implemented reforms to maintain peace in the country, promoting a unified national identity, establishing memorials and commemorations, changing the national anthem and the flag, and decentralizing the political structure.

In 2003, Rwanda adopted a new constitution after a political transition following the genocide. Presidential elections were held in 2003 and 2010, with Paul Kagame winning both elections. Rwanda is the only country in the world in which women outnumber men in government, with 45 out of 80 seats of parliament won by women. In 2006, Rwanda was admitted into the East African Community to promote trade with Kenya, Tanzania, Uganda, and Burundi. The government has been pursuing an agenda of economic development through the program Vision 2020. The program includes a list of goals the government hopes to achieve by the year 2020, including developments in infrastructure and transportation, good governance, agricultural production, the private sector, reconstruction, health, and education. The government is also working to improve the quality of universal health insurance coverage and challenges posed by the HIV/AIDS pandemic.

Carla De Ycaza

Further Reading

Clark, Phil, and Zachary D. Kaufman, eds. *After Genocide: Transitional Justice, Post-Conflict Reconstruction and Reconciliation in Rwanda and Beyond.* New York: Columbia University Press, 2009.

Dallaire, Romeo. *Shake Hands with the Devil: The Failure of Humanity in Rwanda.* New York: Random House Canada, 2003.

des Forges, Alison. *Leave None to Tell the Story: Genocide in Rwanda.* New York: Human Rights Watch, 1999.

Mamdani, Mahmood. *When Victims Become Killers: Colonialism, Nativism, and the Genocide in Rwanda.* Princeton, NJ: Princeton University Press, 2001.

S

Sabé

The area that made up the Kingdom of Sabé (pronounced Sha-bay) is beside what is now the Republic of Benin's eastern border with Nigeria and extended from the Oyan River west to the Ouémé River. A relatively small Yoruba polity, Sabé (also commonly referred to as Savé) served as a major nodal point for people who traveled through western Yoruba-speaking regions throughout the precolonial era. As a result, Sabé has been considered by many scholars to be influenced by the various cultures of passersby who often crossed through its space.

In spite of its relatively small size, Sabé boasted a diverse environment. Large hills and boulders dominate much of its space approximately 120 miles north of coastal Benin. Alluvial soils in riverine areas and consistent rainfall of approximately 25 to 30 inches per year also accounted for stable agricultural production. Produce ranged from vegetables grown on the banks of the area's rivers to yams, tobacco, and palm oil harvested for local consumption and export to neighboring communities. The kingdom also had enough open space to grow cotton and raise cattle. Sabé was known throughout the area for its cloth production, and its herders constituted the primary suppliers of meat to Oyo's residents during the great regional power's imperial zenith in the 17th and 18th centuries. Sabé's center was in what is now the town of Savé, or Ile-Sabé. Its location near rivers and established east-west trade networks made it a veritable crossroads for traders, travelers, and competing regional kingdoms' leaders. The numerous hills that dotted the region, however, also offered refuge for residents and refugees from neighboring polities who fled political instability throughout the broader region from the 16th century onward.

The ease in which outside communities reached what became Sabé had a tremendous historical impact on the region. It is unclear when the first settlers arrived from Popo areas in what is now the coastal area of eastern Togo, but it is likely that their descendants had been there for many generations, if not centuries, before Yoruba-speaking migrants reached Sabé's hills in the late 15th to early 16th centuries and established a series of small city-states. In the late 16th century, people from a Yoruba subgroup called Amusu descended on the region from the Sahelian area of Borgu in what is now northern Nigeria and Benin after upheaval there in the wake of the Songhai Empire's collapse. Many Amusus claimed original descent from Ile-Ife, the historical cradle of Yoruba civilization and culture.

With so many different cultural and linguistic groups having settled the area over time, oral traditions are often murky or contradictory. Regardless of whether

Amusu descended from Ile-Ife or merely made the claim as a means to assimilate with the more established Yoruba-speaking city-states, their leaders certainly tried to impose their power over Sabé's diverse collection of towns and villages, whose inhabitants engaged in prolonged conflicts in resisting Amusu hegemony. The area experienced a brief spell of peace during the early 17th century when an Amusu leader, Ola Musu, sacrificed two sons to local gods in order to convince residents that his leadership was legitimate. The calm was short-lived, however. Rival groups contested the third Amusu leader, Ola Yonge, which paved the way for many years of subsequent conflict.

Indeed, Sabé did not become a kingdom until around 1750, when a leader of the Babagidai group named Yai consolidated power among many of the area's prominent city-states. Yai centralized power and organized a sovereign polity whose people recognized him as *oba* (king or "owner") of Sabé. Although the Babagadais had not descended from any of the Yoruba groups who by that time dominated the area around Ile-Sabé, they had ostensibly become Yoruba through processes of assimilation. That many Babagadais spoke a local dialect of the language and shared cultural practices accounted for part of the reason why Yai was able to centralize power with people in the region and become the first king of Sabé.

In spite of Yai's diplomacy, sustaining political stability proved difficult. The king tried to reconcile with the Amusu people, for example, but they resisted Babagidai leadership and fought to return Ile-Sabé to its former position as an independent city-state. Amusu soldiers challenged Yai's forces in three major battles before the Babagadais finally suppressed Amusu rebellion for good. Throughout the conflicts, Yai convinced many lineage heads of the region to join him in an alliance. The fighting nonetheless destabilized the region, and hostilities toward Babagidai leadership persisted for generations. Both Yai and his successor, a younger brother named Sabi, died mysteriously, leaving power vacuums that later leaders tried unsuccessfully to fill for generations. It was not until the reign of the fifth king, Akinkanju, that the kingdom maintained a sense of calm. A savvier politician and notable diplomat, Akinkanju consolidated his leadership by accumulating a group of lineage heads into a permanent council of advisers who, combined, were able to expand their influence in the flourishing slave trade with Porto Novo.

Much like his predecessors, however, Akinkanju suffered in part due to Sabé's relatively easy access to neighboring communities. Sporadic raids from the north in the mid-19th century by Fulani jihadists started a long process of political unraveling that eventually spelled the end for the kingdom. The attacks destabilized the region, but the ascent to the throne of a woman named Ina Mego in 1835 brought hope that Sabé could survive the political instability. In particular, Ina Mego erected numerous defensive walls around the capital. Sabé, however, was a conservative patrilineal society, and Ina Mego faced constant attempts by male family members to unseat her. Their efforts did little to promote political strength. By the time a cousin usurped her position in 1845, the cracks in the deeply fragmented polity were exposed, and rival groups descended en masse in hopes of taking control of the region.

Sabé experienced far more intense raids at this time from people coming from what is now west-central Nigeria who were vying for power in the wake of Oyo's demise in the early 19th century. Compounding that were frequent onslaughts by Dahomean troops intent on expanding their empire. Troops from Sabé's powerful neighbor to the west sacked and destroyed Sabé's capital on two occasions: first in 1848 and then again in 1855 as the city's residents were engaging in the process of rebuilding. Raids on Ile-Sabé and other notable settlements in the area persisted throughout the 19th century. The razing of the capital by Dahomean troops once again in 1885 effectively put an end to the kingdom.

Today, the town of Savé is one of the main cities of the Republic of Benin's Collines administrative department. The French term *collines* means "hills." The hills and boulders that people in the area once looked to as refuge for what at times must have seemed like constant onslaughts now attract rock-climbing tourists from around the world who visit the region by the thousands each year.

Marcus Filippello

Further Reading

Adediran, Biodun. *The Frontier States of Western Yorubaland, 1600–1889*. Ibadan: IFRA, 1994.
Asiwaju, A. I. *Western Yorubaland under European Rule, 1889–1945*. London: Longman, 1976.
Moulero, T. *Histoire et legend de Shabe (Savé)*. Cotonou: Études dahoméennes, Gouvernement du Dahomey, 1969.

Shambaa

The Shambaa kingdom was located in the northeastern corridor of modern-day Tanzania. Popular legend attributed the founding of the kingdom to a hunter named Mbegha, who was welcomed by the community and made king. The story of Mbegha is that of the humanization of a wild creature. Before he became the protector of the community, Mbegha was said to be a dangerous and obscene man who lived in the wilderness.

Vugha, the capital of the kingdom, was built like a typical Shambaa village on the hilltop encircled by a banana garden. The distribution of political power also influenced architecture—the king's houses, located at the center of the capital, could only be thatched with dried banana sheaths, while the houses of ordinary people could only be thatched with wild grass. In addition, the architectural practices were metaphoric—the king owned the kingdom, just like the elders of the community owned the territory of their banana farms, not the wild areas of grass. Apparently bananas and their sheaths were more highly valued than the wild grass. Much of the materials for building the homes of the kingdom were sourced locally, thereby enhancing the power of the elites to shape consumption across social class.

The imaginary north-south line that divided Vugha into two was figuratively seen as the Zimui River that divided Shambaa into halves, west and east. This division of the capital also reflected the distribution of political power among the elites. The kingdom's official who resided in the eastern half of the capital administered that section, while western officials were the king's representative west of the river. The administration of vassal territories such as Gare, Shembekeza, and Bumbuli was carried out by the sons of the kings. All chiefs and elites were considered sons of the kings.

Agriculture was the mainstay of the precolonial Shambaa economy. Each lineage produced enough to eat and keep during the dry season—thus, the people practiced subsistent agriculture. Each lineage was required to pay tribute in the form of agricultural produce to the kings and political elites. The lineage involved in regular litigation paid higher tribute to the king than the ones with fewer cases. In addition, during such periods of adversity as famine, the political establishment imposed higher tributes on the community. Much of the tribute collected went into maintaining the king's courtiers and guests. In order to increase tributes paid by each farmer, the political elites could increase the population of their subjects. War booty also supplemented the resources of the kingdom. Each fighter had his own spear, shield, and bow and arrow. War drums were used to mobilize all men for military purposes. Other sources of tribute included hunters, who killed wild animals. The early Shambaa kings collected one tusk of each elephant killed by hunters. Trade was not so significant to the political economy of early Shambaa. The kings used tribute wealth to acquire trade goods for direct personal consumption rather than to build political following. In addition, they expended large resources for purchasing charms and magic used for appeasing the god of rain and fortifying the army.

Saheed Aderinto

Further Reading

Feierman, Steven. *The Shambaa Kingdom.* Madison: University of Wisconsin Press, 1974.

Sokoto

The Sokoto Caliphate was an outcome of a political revolution that started in the first decade of the 19th century and culminated in the establishment of centralized political administration of the Hausa states by Shehu Usman dan Fodio. The length and breadth of the Sokoto kingdom has metamorphosed since the takeover by the British by the beginning of the 20th century. The topography of Sokoto has an overbearing influence on the occupation of the people. Over 85 percent of the population is engaged in agriculture. The main crops are millet, guinea corn, sugarcane, beans, and cereals. The natural livestock survey showed that Sokoto has a

Usmanu Danfodiyo University

Established in 1975, Usmanu Danfodiyo University is one of the federal universities in Nigeria. It is named for Usman dan Fodio, the leader of the Sokoto jihad that swept across modern-day northern Nigeria and beyond in the 19th century. About 90 students commenced classes at its temporary sites (now called City Campus) in October 1977. In 1980, the institution produced its first graduating class of 73. They all earned bachelor degrees in arts, science, and education. Since the early 1980s the university has grown exponentially. It awarded its first PhD in 1986. Today the university has 10 colleges focusing on agriculture, arts, and Islamic studies; health sciences; education and extension services; law; management sciences; pharmaceutical sciences; and veterinary medicine. The vision of the university is "To be a centre of excellence in terms of teaching, research and community service in all fields of human endeavour[,] i.e. Arts, Humanities, Pure and Applied Sciences."

livestock population of nearly 1.18 million cattle, nearly 2.9 million goats, 1.98 million sheep, 2 million chickens, 45,000 camels, 34,532 horses, and 51,388 donkeys. In fact, Sokoto is popular for its Gudale cattle in addition to large deposits of clay and limestone formations all over the state.

Historically, by end of the 18th century the various states of Hausaland had reached important stages of development. The *sarauta* (kingship) system had reached its peak of maturity in terms of laws of succession to the throne and appointment to offices, protocols, administrative centralization, and structured institutions. However, by the middle of the 18th century, the states in Hausaland began to experience dynastic conflicts and succession disputes in addition to religion sycretism and corruption among the rulers and the ulemas. These threats to the socioeconomic and political stability of the Hausa states reached a climax with the emergence of Usman dan Fodio, who in 1804 embarked on a jihad in order to rescue the states from all forms of impurities.

The jihad brought about many changes that had both long- and short-term effects on the history of what later became a large part of Nigeria. The first and immediate impact relates to political changes. The jihad resulted in the collapse of the Hausa states and other polities and communities. These were incorporated into a single political unit known as the Sokoto Caliphate. The jihad also led to the collapse of the 1,000-year-old Sayfawa dynasty and the emergence of a new dynasty, the al-Kanemi dynasty in Borno. Demographically, the jihad had a tremendous effect on the demography of the Nigerian area. The wars led to the dislocation and displacement of the population and the sedentarization of the Fulani and other nomadic groups. These and the establishment of *ribats* (fortresses) all over the caliphate resulted in the emergence of settlements, towns, and cities and the expansion of the old ones. Many of the towns found in the northern part of Nigeria today, such as Gombe, Yola, Bauchi, Kontagora, and Sokoto, date back to the time of the jihad.

On the economic front, the jihad recorded remarkable expansion through the efforts of the flag bearers in their jurisdictions, especially Caliph Muhammed Bello.

He encouraged the administrators of the areas covered by the caliphate to take special interest in economic development ranging from provision of security on the trade routes and the construction of markets to regulating business transactions. In addition, there was a remarkable increase in the degree of integration between the agricultural and industrial sectors of the economy. Raw materials were produced to be consumed directly in the industrial establishments. This pattern of production fostered specialization, which enhanced the quality and quantity of a variety of goods that were produced. This expansion in the agricultural and industrial sectors was made possible by the tremendous increase in internal and long-distance trade. Indeed, many factors favored this expansion in trade and commerce, but the most important is the fact that the caliphate was a large market that stimulated exchange.

In regard to the spread of Islam and the accompanied sociocultural changes in the established caliphate in the 19th century, it is on record that the emergence of towns with substantial cosmopolitan populations under the control of Muslim emirs had helped to spread Islam. As more and more non-Muslims came into peaceful contact with Muslims from the emirates, especially through trade, Islam was better understood and eventually embraced. In most emirates, scholars who moved about and enlightened the public on their duties and obligations were patronized by the emirs. In some other emirates such as Ilorin, in spite of the stoppage in territorial expansion, religious and cultural expansion continued to the end of the 19th century.

Culturally, the jihad had a tremendous impact on the societies. There was a remarkable increase in scholarship and other forms of intellectual activities. These showed in the writings of the jihad leaders: Usman dan Fodio, Abdullah, and Muhammed Bello. Conservatively, they are said to have produced 258 books and pamphlets, and this is probably not a complete list. Besides, the spread of Islamic religion affected all spheres of life of the society, including the mode of dressing, marriages, manners, and economic transactions.

The Sokoto Caliphate, in spite of its organized political centralization, was never free from internal threats. The caliph and the emirs faced serious internal crises and external threats, and these tended to undermine the normal functioning of government. The instability arising from these internal crises and external threats weakened the empire considerably, such that by the end of the 19th century the British had no problem in the conquest of the caliphate. This was how Sokoto formed part of the new northern protectorate of the British colonial administration in the 20th century.

Monsuru Muritala

Further Reading

Adeleye, Roland. *Power and Diplomacy in Northern Nigeria, 1804–1900.* Lagos: Longman, 1971.

Balogun, Ismail. *The Life and Works of Uthman dan Fodio.* Sokoto: Islamic Publication Bureau, 1975.

Last, Murray. *The Sokoto Caliphate.* Lagos: Longman, 1967.

Saa'd, Abubakar. "The Established Caliphate: Sokoto, the Emirates and Their Neighbours." In *Groundwork of Nigerian History,* edited by Obaro Ikime, 301–326. Ibadan: Heinemann Educational Books, 1980.

Songhai

The ancient Songhai Empire had its base in the neighborhood of present-day Mali, precisely the city of Gao in the heart of the Sahara desert. The desert of the Sahara in West Africa is the largest in the world, covering about 3.5 million square miles (9.065 million square kilometers). The open nature of the area encouraged a thriving trade across the Sahara, which significantly increased contact between the people of West Africa and Muslim North Africa. Many caravans moved in and out of trade centers across the desert, with high volumes of goods and services exchanged between the Arab traders and people of the West African region. Indeed, the availability of some trade articles, such as gold, salt, and slaves, made trans-Saharan trade a major factor in the socioeconomic and political development of the precolonial West African kingdoms. The scheming to hold on to or secure control of the lucrative trade across the Sahara, especially at the various trade centers, became the essential preoccupation of existing and emerging kingdoms in Sudan. Hence, the various African kingdoms scrambled to dominate and rule over the trading centers within their environs and harness their territorial hegemony through wars and conquests.

The Songhai Empire occupied the whole of the Niger River Bend. The empire shared boundaries with Tripoli in the north, Timbuktu in the west, Kumbi Saleh to the south, and Lake Chad to the east. The Songhai Empire was thus located in the northern plains of the Sahara. It has a hot temperature with swirling winds and shifting sand dunes. The people engaged in fishing and trading activities. Hans Vischer, an explorer, described the Saharan route connecting the West African region to the coast of the Mediterranean Sea as a "death road." This covers more than 1,500 miles, representing 2,414 square kilometers of the Sahara. The desert therefore represents the domain of the Songhai Empire, which succeeded the ancient Ghana and Mali Empires. Essentially, Songhais were predominantly nomads and traders depending on trade routes and finding oases for living.

In the region of the Sahara desert where Songhai was located, there were animals such as donkeys, horses, and camels, which aided the sociopolitical and economic activities of the people. Initially, Berber traders from North Africa carried goods on donkeys and horses in the hot climate, which often killed them. Consequently, the use of camels, also nicknamed "ships of the desert," was introduced by the Romans to revolutionize the trans-Sahara trade between North and West Africa. Some records stated that the caravans to cross the desert going to and from West Africa used about 12,000 camels. Indeed, the location of the Songhai Empire close to the Niger River and the Mediterranean Sea created an enabling environment for the caravans and the camels to thrive.

The Songhai Empire was the largest empire and became the last of the three major empires in West Africa. The empire existed from circa 1375 to 1591. It was one of the largest Muslim-populated empires in history. The rise of Songhai was due to the decline of the Mali Empire after the death of its last and strongest king, Mansa Musa, in 1337. The decline was traced to the period when Emperor Mansa Musa embarked on an extravagant pilgrimage to the holy city of Mecca. The king also failed to stop the invasion of Berber conquerors, who ruled Timbuktu for some time. Subsequently, Sunni Ali in 1468 became the leader of Songhai, invaded Timbuktu, and conquered the Berbers. He began a campaign of conquest and established the capital of the empire at Gao on the Niger River.

Sunni Ali made use of the Songhai location along the Niger River maximally to his advantage. He ordered a fleet of war canoes to seize control of the river trade. His troops moved inward to the Sahara, where they eventually overtook the Berber salt mines. Songhai became the largest empire in West Africa during his reign. Shortly after the death of Sunni Ali in 1492, his son Sunni Baru, who reigned for 14 months, was conquered in a battle and deposed by a powerful rebel known as Mohammed Ture, who became Askia the Great.

The empire reached its peak during Askia's reign (1493–1528). The merchant caravans from North Africa came to trade goods such as salt, cloth, and horses for gold and slaves. In Songhai at this time, the market cities witnessed more wealth and importance. The empire entered a new stage in its political life. Most of the leaders in the towns were Muslims by this time, and Islam began to make progress among the people of Songhai and other parts of the region. Although Askia ruled strictly as a Muslim, many traditional customs and practices were still observed at his court. Moreover, he developed the political administration and built up a machination of central government beyond Sunni Ali's system and even stronger and more detailed than other empires in western Sudan.

Songhai, having existed for almost two centuries, in 1591 was stormed by armies from Morocco in North Africa who then crossed the entire Sahara. The Arab kingdom soldiers came with more sophisticated weapons, which include cannons, guns, and gunpowder, that were used against and cut down the armies of Songhai soldiers, who were armed with swords, spears, and bows and arrows. Moroccan soldiers eventually destroyed and conquered the Songhai Empire. The Tomb of Askia the Great and evidently the most important of all the emperors of the West African ancient empires was built in Songhai. The mosque in Gao is one of the most notable in West Africa. The empire gained more recognition and importance through the control of the trade routes and the trade in slaves. Songhai eventually took control of Timbuktu and Jenne.

Kabir Abdulkareem

Tomb of Muhammad Ture (who took the name Askia), ruler of the Songhai Empire from 1493 to 1528, at Gao in present-day Mali. (Werner Forman/Universal Images Group/Getty Images)

Further Reading

Boahen, Adu. *Topics in West African History.* London: Longman, 1997.

Davidson, B., and F. K. Buah. *The Growth of African Civilisation: A History of West Africa, 1000–1800.* London: Longman, 1975.

Davidson, Basil. *West Africa before the Colonial Era: A History to 1850.* London: Longman, 1998.

Niane D. T., ed. *General History of Africa,* Vol. 4, *Africa from the Twelfth to the Sixteenth Century.* Berkeley, CA: UNESCO, 2000.

T

Takrur

Located in the Middle Senegal Valley at the border between Senegal and Mauritania, Takrur is one the earliest historically known West African kingdom. The earliest historical evidence about Takrur comes from the 1068 account by the Arab chronicler al-Bakri, who mentioned two cities: Takrur and Silla. He also stated that people of both cities were Islamized by the king of Takrur. This made Takrur the first West African kingdom to accept Islam.

The Middle Senegal Valley is a reasonably fertile floodplain located at the core of the African semiarid climate zone known as the Sahel. The climate is characterized by high interannual variability and by major climate fluctuations at the scale of decades, centuries, or millennia. In the Sahel, the existence of permanent water resources is critical for subsistence activities such as agriculture, pastoralism, and fishing. A lateral cross-section of the Middle Senegal Valley shows the existence of three major human exploitation zones that are defined by the topography of the floodplain: the floodplain (*walo*), the noninundated area outside the floodplain (*jeri*), and the transition zone between the two (*jejeengol*). Each exploitation zone is defined based on its topography, pedology, and historical experience with subsistence and settlement activities.

Areas such as the Middle Senegal Valley are highly advantageous for populations in search of wet ecological zones suitable to their subsistence activities. Indeed, contrary to its surrounding areas that offer only one season of cultivation, the Middle Senegal Valley offers two cultivation seasons: one during the rainy season and the other during the progressive retreat of the flood. This is why the Middle Senegal Valley became an economic and cultural contact zone between the Sahara and the savanna. This strategic position had made Takrur an important center during the trans-Saharan trade era. The economy of the kingdom was mostly based on the cultivation of millet and on the trade in sorghum, salt, cotton, copper, gold, and slaves (obtained from the raiding of non-Muslims living farther south). Archaeological data show that metallurgy and fishing were very important during that time. Takrur took advantage of the expansion of Islam and the trans-Saharan trade to become at one point a rival of the Ghana Empire. Takrur's privileged position later hastened its domination by the Ghana Empire (11th century) and the Mali Empire (13th century).

Takrur was a pioneer in the Islamization process in West Africa. The king of Takrur, War Jabi ibn Rabis, who died in 1040–1041, was the first West African king to wage holy war. He converted to Islam, established Islamic law, forced his people to convert to Islam, and used Islam as the justification for his expansion southward. Takrur also played an important role in the rise and expansion of the Almoravid movement, an 11th–12th-century militant Islamic movement that went on to conquer the Maghreb and parts of Spain and Portugal. War Jabi's son, Labi ibn War Jabi, was an ally of the Almoravids.

Information about the population makeup and the social organization is scanty because Arab sources and oral record focus on the elites. However, a lot of Senegal ethnic groups state that they come from the Middle Senegal Valley. This is the case for the Serers who, according to oral history, refused to convert and fled the Middle Senegal to settle in their present locations in central Senegal. Even though it is mute on the social organization, oral tradition states that Takrur was ruled through time by five dynasties: Jaa-Ogo, Manna, Tonjong, Lamtaga, and Lamtermes.

The Jaa-Ogo dynasty founded Takrur. The dynasty is estimated to have lasted between 130 and 300 years. Oral tradition also states that it was the Jaa-Ogos who introduced metallurgy in the area. Archaeological data from the site of Walalde show that the Middle Senegal Valley started to be occupied around 800–550 BCE by iron-using agropastoralists. The occupation continued throughout the first millennium CE in other areas of the Middle Senegal Valley, where archaeological data show population growth, sporadic settlement clustering, political and economic integration, and new settlement locations during Phase III, dated to 550–1000 CE.

The Manna dynasty ruled the Middle Senegal Valley for another 150 to 300 years. The dynasty nominated local leaders (*faris*). One of these local leaders was probably War Jabi.

There is a general agreement about the order of succession the Tonjong, Lamtaga, and Lamtermes dynasties. However, there is wide disagreement about their origins, the duration of their tenure, and the extent of their territorial domination. But the fact that both *taga* and *termes* refer to localities located in the Chemama (the Mauritanian side of the valley) is a probable indicator of political relations between the two sides of the Middle Senegal Valley. Moreover, this profusion of rulers undoubtedly illustrates a turbulent period that lasted until the middle of the 16th century, when the leader of the Dénianké dynasty, Koly Tenguella, seized the Tékrur that latter became Fouta Tooro.

Alioune Dème

Further Reading

Al Naqar, U. "Takrur: The History of a Name." *Journal of African History* 10(3) (1969): 365–374.

Dème, A. "Archaeological Investigation of Settlement Evolution and Emerging Complexity in the Middle Senegal Valley." PhD dissertation, Rice University, 2003.

McIntosh, R. J., S. K. McIntosh, and H. Bocoum. 2016. *The Search for Takrur: Archaeological Reconnaissance along the Middle Senegal Valley.* New Haven, CT: Yale University Press.

Timbuktu

The city of Timbuktu is located at the intersection of the Southern Sahara and the Sahel near the Niger River Bend. The ancient Timbuktu was reputed as an active player in the trans-Saharan trade, a city of scholarly elites, and a religious center. Although in existence as far back as the last few decades of the fist millennium BCE, Timbuktu emerged as a significant trade city in the 12th century that facilitated trade between the tropical African population and the northern Berber group as well as the Mediterranean traders. The Azawad basin (although now dried up), which retained water during flooding that allowed navigation, and the location near the Niger River trade terminus were great contributors to the ascension of Timbuktu to trade center and significant city status. The location of Timbuktu also defines the salt and gold caravan routes that connect the southern and northern trade centers. This trade corridor that defines Timbuktu made it an enviable city that every dynasty wanted to have. As a result, the historic Timbuktu played a major role in the development of great empires such as the Mali, Songhai, and Ghana Empires. Thus, rulers of these powerful empires had some political influence over Timbuktu.

One of the characteristics that earned Timbuktu its greatest significance in African history, which is still accorded the city today, is its viable participation in early trade networks, which was the major source of its wealth. But this did not just start in the 12th century. Geomorphological and archaeological evidences have revealed an earlier Timbuktu in an area that supported urban clusters and long-distance commercial activity. By the 12th and 13th centuries, Timbuktu was controlling the southern trans-Saharan trade lining western Sudan in the commercial network. Salt was one of the most important trading products at this time. Copious numbers of camels were loaded with rock salt for transportation to Timbuktu, an entrepôt for the trans-Saharan trade. Timbuktu grew to surpass other commercial centers such as Walata and Gao by the 15th century and became the principal

Ali Ibrahim "Farke" Touré

Ali Farke Touré (1939–2006) was an internationally acclaimed Malian musician and was born in the region of Timbuktu. Although known as a guitarist, Touré was also a multi-instrumentalist. The distinctive style of Touré's music earned him the nickname "bluesman of Africa," which led many to liken him to the American blues legends John Lee Hooker and Otis Redding. Touré's music is believed to have been influenced by Arabic, yet Touré generally promoted his Malian (African) heritage, cultural, tradition, and history. His music often exemplifies the notions of African authenticity, locality, and global music. For example, Touré lived most of his life in a rural community of Mali, where he often sang from and also sang about. He titled his 1994 album *Talking Timbuktu* and repeatedly narrated the locality of Timbuktu as being in the center of the world, as opposed to the illusionary notion of Timbuktu in the Western view. Although Touré resided in a rural African village, his music made it into the global music platform, and he was a two-time Grammy Award winner.

exporter of gold. Gold was transported from the goldfield farther south to Timbuktu enroute to the trans-Saharan commerce. In addition to salt and gold, Timbuktu also traded kola nuts, horses, and grains (particularly African rice and sorghum) as well as slaves, all of which formed the basis of the economic power of Timbuktu.

As Timbuktu grew in wealth and domination of this significant trade corridor leading the south termini to the trans-Saharan commerce, it became an object of imperial attack. Early Timbuktu had been under the jurisdiction of the great Mali Empire. The ascension of Mansa Musa as the ruler of Mali bolstered Timbuktu's wealth, making it a target of Mali's enemies. Thus, the Mossis took advantage of an ailing Mali and invaded and possessed Timbuktu around the early 14th century. But this short-lived, as Mali rebounded and reclaimed the city. However, the Tuaregs took over Timbuktu for a period of 35 years in the 15th century. During the Tuareg period, Timbuktu witnessed economical transformation and political stability, which broadened the commercial base of the city. The Tuaregs were able to achieve this simply by embracing the merchant community and fostering a good relationship with all the parties important to the running of affairs in Timbuktu. For example, Muhammad Naddi, belonging to a merchant family, was named the Timbuktu *koi* (governor), who oversaw the commercial activity in the city and maintained cordial relationship with the Tuareg imperial office.

The prosperity of Timbuktu soon attracted the Songhai authorities who had conquered Mema and a few other trade entrepôts in the south. Thus, Sunni Ali Ber led several assaults against Timbuktu and finally captured it around 1469. With the

The Sankore Mosque was at the center of the great Islamic scholarly community at Timbuktu during the 15th century CE. (David Kerkhoff/iStockphoto.com)

seat of power situated in Gao, the Songhai Sunni Ali's rule in Timbuktu was faced with a low commercial yield. This was due to the fact that his trade policies were considered detrimental by the elite and merchant families of Timbuktu who fled the city and refused to trade with Sunni Ali's regime. Sunni Ali was also hostile to Islam and deposed the Sankore scholars. All of this contributed greatly to Sunni Ali's failure. While Sunni Ali's administration failed in Timbuktu, the trade entrepôt remained under Songhai hegemony for several decades. Askia Muhammad, who came to power in the early 16th century, brought back the lost glory of Timbuktu. He vehemently embraced Islam, restored the Sankore scholars, expanded the commercial network, and revitalized the depleted economy of the empire. Askia also stroked power balance between his administration and the Timbuktu authorities. Although Timbuktu had no imperial authority, power was vested in the hands of the local *qadis,* yet tax collectors and military commanders were appointed from Gao. Michael Gomez in his article "Timbuktu under Imperial Songhay: A Reconsideration of Autonomy" referred to this system of ruling at Timbuktu as "a dual administration" whereby there is an imperial authority leading directly from Askia in Gao to a municipal government of the *qadi.* Songhai continued the domination of Timbuktu with Askia after the *qadis* began to rebel against Askia's authority over revenue remittance and taxation. The Gao-Timbuktu relationship grew sour during the reign of Askia Ishaq and Askia Dawud. This created another opportunity for another imperial authority to weigh in on conquering the flourishing Timbuktu.

Change in the ideology of Timbuktu and the imposition of contrary regulations contributed to the decline of the prosperity of the empire. Toward the end of the 16th century, the Moroccan Army invaded Timbuktu, obviously for economic reasons, and other outlier towns and cities of great influence in trans-Saharan commerce. The Timbuktu governing system was restructured dramatically in such a way that it completely negated the established norm that helped the previous administrations to succeed. This change set the stage for the decline of Timbuktu as an important trade empire. It is not surprising the Timbuktu was a prime target during the European scramble for Africa. The reports of Timbuktu's trade in gold and salt and its location on an admirable trade corridor were incentives for the France conquest of Timbuktu in the late 19th century. By this time, the image of Timbuktu as an El Dorado began to give way, and a colonization scheme took place. Unlike many ancient empires that collapsed following their heydays, Timbuktu remains a town in today's Mali but without the degree of prosperity seen between the 13th and 17th centuries. However, Timbuktu maintains its status quo as a religious and intellectual city.

Throughout the 13th and the 17th centuries, Timbuktu was a center of Islamic learning and a seat of great scholars. The building of the Great Mosque by Mansa Musa in the 14th century and the Sankore mosque established an institution of the scholarly elites, as the mosque became an intellectual resident. Both of these mosques are still standing today in Timbuktu. The imam of the mosque was also the *qadi.* Among the famous Timbuktu scholars of the 16th and 17th centuries were Muhammad Aqit; Ahmad Baba; Mahmud Ka'ti, who was of Spanish descent;

and Abu 'lA 'raf, of Moroccan origin. The scholars taught and wrote on diverse issues and subjects including jurisprudence, Islamic religion, Islamic science, history, grammar and syntax, and the Arabic language. The notion of slavery and enslavement also featured prominently in their writing, which incited the jihadist movement on the basis of enslavement of unbelievers—non-Muslims. Copious Timbuktu manuscripts have been collated and conserved in libraries and educational research facilities within Mali and all over the world. The manuscripts are major sources of the histories of the ancient Timbuktu Empire and western Sudan.

Abidemi Babatunde Babalola

Further Reading

Gomez, M. A. "Timbuktu under Imperial Songhay: A Reconsideration of Autonomy." *Journal of African History* 31(1) (1990): 5–24.

Hunwick, J. O. ed. *Timbuktu and the Songhay Empire: Al-Sa'di's Ta'rīkh Al-Sūdān Down to 1613, and Other Contemporary Documents,* Vol. 27. Leiden: Brill, 2003.

Shamil, J., and B. D. Souleymane. *The Meaning of Timbuktu.* Cape Town: HSRC Press, 2008.

Toucouleur

The Toucouleur Empire was a Muslim theocratic state that was established by al-Hajj Umar Tall (1794–1864) in the mid-19th century during the religious revolutions, or jihads, that were taking place across the West African region. At the peak of its power and glory, the empire extended from Medine, at the eastern border of modern Senegal, in the east to Timbuktu in the west, a distance of 1,500 miles, and from Futa Jallon and Dinguiray (in modern-day Guinea) in the south to Nioro in the north. Thus, at its apogee the empire occupied almost the entire landmass of modern-day Mali.

Since the empire was completely contained in modern-day Mali, it must have been situated between latitudes 10 degrees south and 25 degrees north and between longitudes 13 degrees west and 5 degrees east. Furthermore, the Muslim empire was south of the famous Sahara desert and in the savanna region. Its climate ranged from tropical in the south to arid in the northern part. As a result, the people of the empire were sedentary farmers, cattle rearers, fishermen, and traders. Among the important commodities they traded in as part of the network of the all-important trans-Saharan trade, which had some of its termini in the empire, were salt and rice.

The empire owed its development and expansion to al-Hajj Umar. He was born in Futa Toro, in modern-day Senegal. In the second decade of the 19th century he embarked on an elaborate pilgrimage to Mecca, where he was formally initiated into the more populist Tijaniyya Muslim Brotherhood. On his return journey home he made it a point of duty to visit major Islamic empires in West Africa, particularly Bornu, where he remained for some time and consulted widely with the revered leader and great Islamic scholar El-Kanemi. From Bornu Umar crossed over to the famous Sokoto Caliphate, where he lived from 1830 to 1837; wrote *Suyuf al-Said,* which contained his religious thoughts and teachings; and established a close personal relationship with Muhammed Bello, the son of Usman dan Fodio, the founder of the caliphate. Before leaving Sokoto for home, Umar married one of Bello's daughters. This development must have cemented the brotherly Muslim relationship between the two leaders.

In 1839, Umar and his followers and supporters settled in Jugunko in Futa Jallon (in the modern-day Republic of Guinea), close to his town of birth, Futa Toro. Here he built a strong standing army, the *talaba,* whose members were schooled by Umar in the doctrines and moral ethics of the Tijaniyya Brotherhood. Furthermore, he started purchasing firearms from European merchants who were settled along the Atlantic coast of West Africa. Having thus fortified himself, his base, and his supporters, he started preparing for a jihad (holy war) against those he perceived as unbelievers. In 1848 he went on a *hijra* (holy flight)—in the same manner and tradition as did Prophet Muhammad from Mecca to Medina before launching his own jihad—from Futa Jallon to Dinguiray, which became the capital of the Toucouleur Empire. In 1852, Umar formally launched a jihad against those who were labeled infidels, starting from his hometown of Futa Toro. However, the people of Futa Toro, who must have seen Umar as an ingrate and a traitor to the fatherland, fought back ferociously and succeeded in flushing him and his army out of the town. Ironically, the strongest support for Umar's jihad and empire-building process came from his own people, the Toucouleurs.

Four years after Umar formally declared his jihad, his army invaded Nyoro, where the influence of the French had already been entrenched. Then in 1857 after enduring many months of military ambush by the Toucouleur Army, the French took Medine. This capture had the effect of inserting the French and their African supporters between two territories, Kaarta and Dinguiray, that were parts of the Toucouleur Empire. Having lost to the French in the west, Umar turned eastward. In 1861, he captured the Bambara kingdom of Segu. Then in 1862–1863 his soldiers and jihadists conquered the Futa states Hamdullahi and Masina and the commercial town of Timbuktu. Umar justified the attacks on and capture of Masina, an ostensibly Muslim state, on the fact that its leaders were religious hypocrites who were in an unholy alliance with the pagan leaders of Segu. Umar, however, met a tragic end when he tried to impose the Tijaniyya Brotherhood's doctrines on a largely Quadriyya Brotherhood of believers and supporters. In the ensuing backlash, Umar was killed by Fulani Muslims led by Ba Lobbo.

Umar was succeeded by his chosen successor, his son Shehu Ahmad, who, however, lacked the charisma, charm, strength of character, and political authority of his father. Ahmad's problems were further compounded when his own cousin, Tijani, contested the position of successor to the leadership of the empire. Thus, as a result of personal leadership weakness and confusion, in the 1870s and 1880s many provinces under the empire unilaterally declared their independence from the Toucouleur Empire. In addition to these internal crises were external attacks, particularly from the French, who started invading the empire's land from the east.

In 1891, the French captured Nioro. Thereafter they besieged Bandiaga, where Seku Ahmad had fled to. When eventually the French entered Bandiaga, Ahmad again fled eastward and died in 1897. With this development, it was a matter of time before the French would take over the entire Toucouleur Empire. This was achieved in the late 1890s when they succeeded in occupying what was left of the empire.

The Toucouleur Empire was a theocratic and military state that was governed according to the tenets of the Koran. Its grand norm was sharia law, which was applied to all aspects of citizens' lives. In the area of governance, the power and authority of the political leaders were clearly separated from those of the military top brass, whose primary responsibility was to defend and expand the empire. Sitting on top of this political structure was the spiritual leader—first al-Hajj Umar and later Seku Ahmadu—who was assisted by the Council of Elders, whose members were very knowledgeable in Islamic laws and faith.

Compared with other Islamic states in the West African subregion, the Toucouleur Empire did not last very long. This could be attributed to the fact that even though its leaders stated that their aim was to build a strong Islamic state, they were nonetheless primarily preoccupied with imperialistic agendas of capturing and annexing other territories, including those belonging to fellow Muslims who were branded as pagans and infidels. However, the Toucouleur leaders' imperial ambitions were matched by those of the French, who ultimately defeated their Muslim state and incorporated it into the French empire in Africa.

Tokunbo A. Ayoola

Further Reading

Ajayi, J. F., and I. Espie. *A Thousand Years of West African History.* Ibadan: Ibadan University Press and Thomas Nelson, 1976.

Conrad, D. C. *Empires of Medieval West Africa: Ghana, Mali and Songhai.* New York: Facts on File, 2005.

Hiskett, M. *The Development of Islam in West Africa.* London: Longman, 1984.

Oloruntimehin, B. O. *The Segu Tukulor Empire.* London: Longman, 1972.

Trimingham, J. S. *History of Islam in West Africa.* Oxford: Oxford University Press, 1962.

Webster, J. B., and A. A. Boahen, with H. O. Idowu. *The Growth of Africa Civilisation: The Revolutionary Years: West Africa since 1800.* London: Longmans Green, 1967.

Wanga

The Wangas, also known as Abawangas (translated as "Wanga's people" after the legendary founder of the kindgom), are among the 19 subethnic groups of the Luyia-speaking people of western Kenya. According to Luyia folklore, the kingdom derived its royal vestiges and patterns of central authority from the interlacustrine Bunyoro, Kitara, and Buganda kingdoms. The Wanga kingdom came into existence between 1598 and 1625 when the founders of the present-day Hima, Mulembwa, Nashieni, and Leka clans moved and settled at Imanga Hill, located four miles south of the town of Mumias in Kakamega County, Kenya.

At its apogee the Wanga kingdom had absorbed numerous neighboring clans, making them subjects of the king (*nabongo*). Different narratives abound pointing to the establishment of the kingdom during the 16th century. Popular folklore, however, posits that on arrival in the area between 1544 and 1652, Wanga (the founder of the dynasty) bequeathed his name to the kingdom. Prior to Wanga's rise to power and assumption of leadership, the kingdom was under the reign of Nabongo Muhima. Wanga took leadership by overthrowing Muhima and installing himself as the next powerful leader of the ruling Abashitsetse clan at a place called Imanga. The ambitious Wanga established hegemony further over the adjoining areas and the neighboring clans in an effort to expand and make his kingdom powerful. Under Wanga's leadership the kingdom enjoyed relative stability derived from a well-established but centralized authority under the king as the ultimate ruler, who fully controlled his subjects' resources. It is little wonder, then, that his style of leadership and big appetite for more power led him to expand the kingdom's boundaries to adjoining centers. This included important fertile areas south of Musanda and north to Matungu in present-day Kakamega County.

While Wanga's tight grip on the apparatuses of power and authority helped stabilize the kingdom, the absorption of newly arrived immigrants to the region added the much-needed human capital and economic resources for territorial prosperity. The king collected tribute and goods from the neighboring people under his authority to ensure that he had the resources needed for the kingdom's expansion and stability. The king relied on social capital for political and economic development. Clearly, therefore, the kingdom's history is largely the story of migration, absorption, settlement, and consolidation of power rooted in the ancestral pedigree of the Abashitsetse clan. Over time the king established a tributary form of economy within the region to enhance his power and authority.

The large population served the kingdom quite well in the latter period of the 18th century, when the king sought further territorial expansion. Nevertheless, the population also brought with it an awkward but burdensome baggage that escalated court jostling for power as well as aristocratic rivalry over who should inherit the throne, creating crises of governance for the king. Consequently, the kingdom experienced cantankerous succession disputes that resulted in civil wars, intrigues, and threats largely from disgruntled royalty and the courtiers, who wanted to break away and establish autonomous centers of power. One of the disgruntled royalty was Wanga's son, Wabala, who moved out and established a small state at a place called Ekhatola. But despite intermittent rivalries between the new state and the old center of power, Wabala's authority would last into the 18th century, when Wamukoya Netya unified the kingdom in his quest to centralize power again.

The unification of Netya's reign, lasting from 1760 to 1787, notwithstanding, the kingdom continued to experience crises, being dogged by frequent attacks and skirmishes pitting the Wangas against the neighboring polities of Iteso, Jo-Ugenya, Bukusu, Idakho, and Banyala. Paradoxically, however, the raids from these neighboring communities solidified the kingdom's resolve to maintain unity. Evidently, the presence of the skilled Uasin Gishu Maasai warriors who had settled in the area during Netya's rule lent a hand in his effort to fight off the stubborn but hostile invaders. Netya also used the Maasai militia to raid the neighboring clans for cattle, thus providing them a free hand and a significant role in matters of governance at the king's court. Folklore has it that in his bid to dodge paying the Maasai warriors for the military services they had rendered him, Netya arranged to get them drunk and proceeded to murder them in cold blood. Not long afterward the Maasai leaders discovered the evil deed, leading to the overthrow and killing of Netya in revenge. Netya's treachery and deception of the Maasai notwithstanding, his deed was aimed at getting rid of the Maasai influence at the court and placing power directly in his hands.

Netya was succeeded in 1787 by his son Osundwa, who was aware of the military prowess and the general combat skills of the Maasai at his court and was keen on winning back their friendship when he ascended the throne. However, between 1814 and 1841 the court appeared to be dogged by incessant dynastic feuds that threatened the kingdom's own existence if not disintegration. In an act of diplomacy Osundwa established a friendship with the neighboring Batsotsos, whom he deftly used to check the military incursions of Jo-Ugenyas into his territory. He also tried to eradicate witchcraft from his kingdom.

Whereas the kingdom appeared to prosper under Osundwa, it soon experienced some trying moments underscored by the cutthroat rivalry of his sons Kweyu and Wamukoya over who should succeed to the throne after the king's demise. Frail and approaching his deathbed, Osundwa summoned his two sons to try to create a balance in sharing power. Folklore has it that he gave his eldest son, Kweyu, a spear to symbolize ultimate authority and handed the younger son, Wamukoya, a rope to signify that he would be the former's deputy. But when Osundwa died in 1710 events took a different turn, with rivalry playing out in an ugly drama that witnessed Wamukoya trick his elder brother Kweyu in a plan to succeed his father. The deception led to Kweyu's protest and secession to establish a separate state of his own, known as Wanga Mukulu (Upper Wanga). Wamukoya ruled Wanga Elureko (Lower Wanga). While the two states coexisted, it was Wanga Elureko that flourished and enjoyed prominence. Wamukoya ruled from 1841 to 1882, establishing central and effective authority.

On another level, rivalry and intermittent civil war continued between Kweyu and Wamukoya. When Wamukoya died he was succeeded by Shiundu, while his cousin Sakwa ascended the throne at Kweyu's demise. Forging an alliance with Marama, Shiundu was able to conquer Kisa and Buholo, establishing centralized authority that witnessed the kingdom flourish and reach what some scholars regard as its peak. Meanwhile, the Jo-Ugenyas regrouped and defeated the allies of Shiundu, becoming a threat to his reign and kingdom. Keen to achieve prosperity and benefit from the 19th-century mercantile commerce, Shiundu welcomed the coastal Swahili traders in ivory and slaves who built their headquarters at Elureko (present-day Mumias). On Shiundu's death in 1882, Mumia ascended the throne to become perhaps the most well-known king to rule the Wanga. Mumia's fame rode on the accommodation of Christian missionaries at his court and helping British administrators establish colonial rule in western Kenya. In return the British made paramount the chiefs of the Abaluyia, Iteso, Jo-Ugenya, Buholo, Jo-Alego, and Jo-Gem peoples. Mumia died in 1949 and was succeeded by Shitawa. Shitawa's reign came at a time when the political climate in Kenya was not favorable to monarchies, thus making his succession to the throne of mere ceremonial value. In 1974 Peter Mumia became the next king of Wanga after the death of his father.

Hannington Ochwada

Further Reading

Bulimo, Shadrack Amakoye. *Luyia Nation: Origins, Clans and Taboos.* Bloomington, IN: Trafford Publishing, 2013.

Kenyanchui, Simon. *Nabongo Mumia.* Nairobi: Heinemann, 1992.

Owino, Meshack. "The Impact of Colonialism on Indigenous African Military Institutions: The Case of the Jo-Ugenya to c. 1914." *Journal of Eastern African Studies* 5(1) (February 2011): 70–84.

Were, Gideon S., and Derek A. Wilson. *East Africa through a Thousand Years.* New York: Africana Publishing, 1987.

Weh *Fondom*

Founded around 1750 and brought under German colonialism in the first quarter of the 20th century, the Weh *fondom* was/is one of the numerous polities that sprang up in the northwestern Bamenda Grassfields in the Northwest Region of present-day Cameroon. The polity lies about 1,000 meters above sea level and shares boundaries with Esu on the northwest, Aghem on the southwest, Kuk on the south, and Zhoa on the northeast. This precolonial *fondom* demonstrates further evidence for the existence of nations in Africa, contrary to biased Western theories of nationhood.

This Tikar *fondom* has a diversified geography comprising rivers, hills, rich soils, valleys, plains, and a varied vegetation of trees, grasses, and raffia palms. Weh's dominant geographical feature is the grassy plateau that covers most of the *fondom*. Prior to the peopling of the area by the Weh, there were patches of high forest spread across most of the low-lying areas. The polity is well watered, as streams such as the Ngbi, Unung, and Wai, among others, flow in various directions across the polity. There are alternating dry and rainy seasons. While the wet season commences in mid-March and terminates in November, the dry season spans from December through March. Like other polities in the northwest of Cameroon, the soils in Weh are fertile, offering great potentialities for agricultural development. There is also a variety of fauna ranging from reptiles, birds, and apes to insects of numerous sorts. This rich diversified natural environment was instrumental in attracting the settlement of Weh as well as shaping the civilization that accrued from their intellectual acumen.

The peopling of the area that eventually emerged into the precolonial Weh polity dates to about the mid-18th century. By this time the first waves of migration into the area were unfolding, and Weh was on the path to emergence in the northwestern Bamenda Grassfields. The pioneer settlers constituted part of the Tikar migration from the north of Cameroon. The Wehs are said to have migrated from the Bamun country and finally arrived in their present site circa 1750 under the leadership of Tshumbeiseng. These first migrants into the area began interacting with the natural environment as they struggled to sedentarize and craft the *fondom*. Tshumbeiseng therefore started the first family in Weh and became the pioneer *bahtum* (*fon*). He is seen by the Wehs as a charismatic leader who founded the dynasty of chiefs. As he was establishing governance institutions, some of the Ukpwas took up settlement in Weh, as they were coerced by the Aghems who had just migrated into present-day Wum. Indeed, the migration of the Ukpwas into this area resulted in the growth of the Weh *fondom* in terms of population and territory. The Ukpwas who were pushed by the Aghems were instrumental in constituting the Kefum quarter in Weh. In the early 19th century, the Zhoas, who were still moving in search of an appropriate homeland, temporarily settled among the Wehs in the present-day Azoh quarter before moving to their current site. Notwithstanding the migratory waves that accompanied the settlement of the various people in Weh, everyone recognized themselves as Wehs.

Weh's path to emergence as a nation was tortuous, as it was engulfed by power crisis, fought wars with neighboring kingdoms, and faced repeated raids from the Chambas, who had a huge appetite for slaves. In about the first quarter of the 19th century the *bahtum*, Tukuu, died, leaving behind a son who was too young to ascend the throne. Tukuu's daughter, who acted as regent, was killed by her husband, Fento'. Fento' later appropriated the symbol of power *sou ina'* (communal horn) she kept and imposed himself as *bahtum*. This forceful takeover of power weakened the *bahtum*'s authority and sowed the seeds of conflict between the Wehs and their rulers. Other trying moments came from the wars the Wehs fought with the Aghems to the southwest and Kuk to the south. Christraud Geary observes that the Wehs were involved in numerous small-scale fights with these neighbors. But the Aghems were the archenemies of the Wehs, with whom they fought throughout the polity's history. Around 1830, the Wehs were raided severally by the Chambas for slaves. These three events (power crisis, wars, and raids) caused some of the Wehs to migrate and thus delayed the growth of the kingdom. In 1840, calm returned to Weh under the leadership of Mounyi. It was from this moment that Weh became better organized politically, with a foundation of governance based on the conception that the king and institutions ruled at the pleasure of the people.

The polity consisted of five quarters: Azoh, Kefuum, Keghe, Mbaukusu, and Uwert (the seat of government). There existed a well-organized political system of government, and the process of succession was hereditary and patrilineal. The Weh system of administration, like elsewhere in the region, centered around the person of the *fon*. The *fon* was mostly a priest chief, given that his ritual functions were the most important aspect of his chieftaincy. However, as elsewhere there existed mechanisms that acted as checks and balances on the power of the *fon*. The powers of the traditional ruler in Weh were constrained by the Traditional Council (Ndau-Tse). The latter consisted of elders (lineage heads), each representing one of the influential patrilineages (*kobi*). Before taking any decision, the *fon* consulted the Ndau-Tse to ensure that the will of the people was sought. In addition to the lineage heads, the five quarter heads were also members of the Ndau-Tse as representatives of their quarters. Contrary to the central role of the Kweifo in the dispensation of power in most Bamenda Grassfields *fondoms* in Cameroon, the Kweifo in Weh lacked judicial and executive power. This is because the secret society was owned by quarters and not the entire *fondom*. In numerous instances, Weh *fons* attempted to appropriate the Kweifo from quarter heads and give it the status of a palace institution. In 1885 and 1919, respectively, Ndze Ika and Mou Sei Ndoudzu were deposed and assassinated because they were cruel and subversive in the manner in which they broadcast power. This became a deterrent to rulers who wanted to override the customs and traditions of the Wehs.

The precolonial Weh economy was centered on agriculture, trade, livestock rearing, and local crafts. The people depended on land for farming, and their ideas about the proper use and ownership of land were often expressed in terms of religion. This justifies the traditional religious belief that land is the ownership of the supreme being. The Wehs cultivated sorghum, corn, cocoyams, yams, and many other food crops. Iron smelting was also an important feature of the Weh economy, as blacksmiths produced household utensils and farming tools such as hoes and cutlasses. Other craft works included the weaving of baskets, bags, and caps, among other articles. Regarding trade, some individuals were involved in long-distance trade through which they used what they had to acquire goods they could not produce. The advanced nature of the iron smelting industry enabled the Wehs to export iron hoes, cutlasses, axes, and spears that were greatly needed in neighboring and far-off communities. Long-distance trade permitted the Wehs to import palm oil and salt, which were integral parts of their diet. Trade was carried out by small groups of Wehs, carrying iron tools and kola, who walked through Esu, Kuk, Mmen, Kom, and other places. Broadly, the Wehs were part of an extensive network of trade through which they benefited as middlemen.

Religion played an important role in precolonial Weh. The Wehs were notoriously religious, as there was hardly any aspect of societal life in which religion was absent, such as farming, hunting, warfare, marriage, birth, and death. Religious ritual ceremonies rooted in the traditional beliefs of the people were quite often established to address these aspects of societal life. This was the spiritual duty of ritual priests, who possessed powers circumscribed by the will of the gods and ancestral spirits. The Weh religion centered on the belief in a supreme being called Keze (God). Besides Keze, the Wehs venerated ancestral spirits to whom they offered prayers and sacrifices. There existed a plethora of cult societies that performed specialized religious rituals. They included the Ndau Keum (House of Cleansing and Protection), the Ndau Ifá (House of Ifá), the Ndau Kenyi, the Ndau Keze (House of God), and the Ndau Asang (House of Guinea Corn). The last three were meant for the purification of the farmlands. Generally, the Wehs had a priestly elite group that kept the people's religion alive and guaranteed their well-being through appeal to ritual practices.

Prestige was attained through membership in special societies that were of economic and social importance. Among the associations for men, Djitisem, Okum, Kweifo, and Ndau Ibaam took a key position because they provided a unique opportunity for the individual to achieve prestige. While most men gained membership into Djitisem and Kweifo due to affordable conditions, only a few economically potent ones could complete payments in order to achieve the Okum and Ndau Ibaam grades. New members fed the entire *fondom* and demonstrated their riches and generosity to heighten their prestige. There were also female societies through which women gained prestige, such as Fumbwi and Kefab, that were understood as female counterparts for the men's Djitisem and Okum. These associations defined the status of females in the community and amounted to prestige for its members. To these prestigious societies should be added the numerous recreational associations that existed, such as Ndong, Kesem, Ufeng, Fundzubang, Feukum, and Kenung, among others.

What emerges from the foregoing is that Weh was a composite structure that started to expand in the 18th century, attaining full nationhood status in the mid-19th century. In the first decade of the 20th century the Germans, who had annexed the coast of Cameroon in 1884 and began pushing inland, arrived in Weh to impose their colonialism. But it was only in 1912 that the Germans succeeded in bringing the Weh polity under their protection. Three years later during World War I they were forced out of Weh by British military operations in Cameroon. From 1922 to 1961, Weh was administered as part of British Cameroon, a League of Nations mandate, by Britain.

By the time the colonialists got to Weh, the Wehs were already a single people traditionally fixed on a well-defined territory, speaking the same language, possessing governance institutions, and shaped to a common mold by many generations of historical experience. The successive German and British colonial governments alongside the heavy presence of Catholic and Protestant missionaries helped in transforming the Weh *fondom* in ways not known during the precolonial era. Since 1961, Weh has been part of the Cameroon state and is presently found in the Menchum division of the Northwest Region. And in spite of being caught in Western influences, the institutions and culture of Weh to a marked degree have survived to this day, though modified.

Michael Kpughe Lang

Further Reading

Chilver, E. M., and P. M. Kaberry. *Traditional Bamenda: The Pre-Colonial History and Ethnography of the Bamenda Grassfields.* Buea, Cameroon: National Government Publication, 1967.

Geary, Christraud. "Traditional Societies and Associations in Weh (North West Province, Cameroon)." *Paideuma* 25 (1979): 53–72.

Lang, M. K. "The Role of Local Communities in Self-Help Development: The Case of the Weh Water Supply Project in Northwest Cameroon." *Global South SEPHIS e-magazine* 9(1) (2013): 15–24.

Lang, M. K. "Traditional Religious Purification Rituals among the Weh in North West Cameroon since the Pre-Colonial Period." *Pan-Tikar Journal of History* 2(1) (2015): 24–41.

Lang, M. K., and M. B. Funteh. "Poor Governance, Dethronements and Execution of Fons in the Bamenda Grassfields (Cameroon): The Case of Fon Mou of Weh." In *Indigenous Political Hierarchy and Sustainable Collective Meaning in the Changing Cameroon Grassfields,* edited by Mark Bolak Funteh, 23–25. London: Dignity Publishing, 2015.

Whydah

Whydah, also known in the precolonial era as Hueda, rests along what has been called the Slave Coast of West Africa in what is now the Republic of Benin. The port town of Ouidah, the namesake of the former state, lies approximately halfway from the borders of Togo to the west and Nigeria to east. A small kingdom relative to neighboring communities such as Dahomey, Asante, and Oyo, Whydah constituted an important and bustling hub during the height of the transatlantic slave trade in the 18th and 19th centuries.

Whydah received considerably more rainfall per annum than the towns and kingdoms that lay roughly 20 to 30 miles in either direction. The region of Whydah rested in a unique area where sub-Guinean weather patterns resulted in upwards of 50 inches of rain each year, compared to 30 to 35 inches for nearby communities. Although some of the northern outskirts of Whydah were in forested regions with slightly higher elevations, much of the kingdom lay in the sandy coastal plain, making travel by foot extremely difficult.

The Whydah kingdom's origins are unclear. Its formation may have involved the merging of two separate political groups settled nearby on the littoral: the

Huedas, who likely descended from nearby Savi, and a similar cultural-linguistic people called the Hulas, who hailed from the smaller port town of Glehue. Accounts of Savi's and Glehue's foundations vary, but oral traditions suggest that the first people arrived to settle the coast from Tado, a village on the Mono River in what is now near the eastern boundary of Togo. The exact timing is obscure, but Savi's founder and first king, Hahalo, migrated to the coast probably in the 12th or 13th century. His successor, Kpase, established Glehue shortly thereafter.

The importance of Whydah, once a vassal of the larger Allada kingdom, as a commercial hub waned in comparison to Allada's main port in nearby Offra up to the mid-17th century. Following a revolt against Allada, Whydah became a primary supplier of slaves starting in the 1670s. While it maintained diplomatic relations with Allada, Whydah nonetheless displaced its former imperial ruler as the dominant middleman in what by that time had become a booming transatlantic trade. By this time, it is likely that Whydah had become a monarchy. The kingship was hereditary, with successors drawn from one patrilineal family. Custom dictated, however, that kings remain within the palace. Exceptions were made once or twice a year for important religious ceremonies.

By the early 18th century, heads of the leading family had sought to centralize power to control the active and profitable slave trade. The limitations on a king's mobility may have restricted his capacity to enact sovereignty. Driven in part by the heightening slave trade, the region's population had swelled, and power was displaced among leading slave traders called *caboceers*. Men in these ranks constituted a type of nobility who often engaged with and profited from their dealings with European slave traders. Bitter internal disputes within all social and economic strata provided little more than a shaky political foundation for the kingdom.

A king's main function was to serve as a judicial authority. To that end, upwards of several hundred women of the palace, often referred to as the king's wives, traveled throughout the land to enforce the king's legal power. Their roles as judges who operated on the king's behalf granted the wives a great deal of power. Their status was likewise highly regarded. Subjects who even touched them could face capital punishment. On occasion, they also played roles as peacemakers when leading traders and people in their districts clashed. Although the wives often steered members of the community away from civil war, there was at least one occasion when warfare among groups competing for dominance in the slave trade erupted, causing tremendous instability.

Whydah's demise as a regional power can be traced to the reign of its last king, Huffon, in the early 18th century. The unexpected death of his predecessor, Aysan, in 1708 thrust the 14-year-old Huffon into the position during a tenuous era. Given his youth, he was never quite prepared to rule, particularly with more savvy and experienced traders and politicians using the situation to undermine his position. As he grew older Huffon tried to assert power, but his sovereignty remained limited, in part because while he maintained to adjudicate throughout the region, he did not hold hereditary rights to land. As a result, *caboceers* could simply ignore his demands.

The unraveling of Whydah's political framework in this tense environment paved the way for Dahomey's king, Agaja, to send forces into the northern reaches of Whydah in March 1727. Later that year, the better-trained and -equipped Dahomean soldiers ransacked the port town, driving much of Whydah's population into exile. The onslaught effectively ended the existence of the kingdom of Whydah.

Today, many people in Ouidah derive their income from tourist activities. The Temple of Serpents, a notable vodun site of worship, attracts thousands of Benin's visitors to the coast every year. The temple and other attractions lie in the heart of the town approximately two miles from the sandy beach, where hundreds of thousands of Africans last stepped on African soil before being shipped across the Atlantic as slaves. From the center of town, tourists often trek along a path known as *la route des esclaves* (the slave road). Regardless of the season, many find the hike through the loose sand a tedious one, and they welcome the sound of waves crashing on the beach and the otherwise cooling breeze that greets them as they near the coastline. Among the first sites people taking this path see as they reach the coast is the massive structure, The Door of No Return, that commemorates the millions of Africans who left the continent during the period of the transatlantic slave trade. Like other "gates" or "doors of no return" that have been built along

The Door of No Return at the old slave fort on Goree Island, Senegal, is an infamous remnant of the African slave trade. (Shutterstock)

the West African littoral, the monument acts a stark reminder of how the trade impacted most if not all people who came from and lived in the region.

Marcus Filippello

Further Reading

Akinjogbin, A. I. *Dahomey and Its Neighbors, 1708–1818.* Cambridge: Cambridge University Press, 1967.

Law, Robin. "'The Common People Were Divided': Monarchy, Aristocracy and Political Factionalism in the Kingdom of Whydah, 1671–1727." *International Journal of African Historical Studies* 23, no. 2 (1990): 201–229.

Law, Robin. *Ouidah: The Social History of a West African Slaving Port, 1727–1892.* Athens: Ohio University Press, 2004.

Wolof (Jolof, Wollof, Ouolof)

The Wolof Empire, a medieval West African state, ruled parts of present-day Senegal and Gambia from 1360 to 1890 during the early period of European contact with West Africa. The Wolofs constituted the largest ethnic group in Senegal and one of the major groups in Gambia. This region, called Senegambia, a term used by the British as early as 1765, referred to Wolof settlements on Saint-Louis and the island of Goree in Senegal and James Island in Gambia. The term was used until 1783 when the Treaty of Versailles returned Saint-Louis to France. Senegal, a mainly low-lying country, includes a semidesert area in the north and northeast and forests in the southwest. The country's largest rivers are the Senegal in the north and the Casamance in the south. Gambia, the smallest country on the African mainland, borders the North Atlantic Ocean and Senegal, surrounding it on three sides following the path of the Gambia River, one of the continent's major rivers. Natural resources include fish, clay, silica sand, titanium, tin, and zircon. Gambia's terrain is a grassy floodplain.

Benjamin Banneker

Benjamin Banneker (1731–1806), an African American scientist, mathematician, urban planner, and astronomer, authored six almanacs. Biographer Silvio Bedini's color-blind assessment of Banneker's scientific and mathematical accomplishments points to African and specifically Wolof ancestry as the source of Banneker's innate intelligence. His name, phonetically traced to Senegal and possibly derived from a Wolof mother and the Wolof name Banakas, originates from the royalty of Walo, a Wolof kingdom. Possible African cultural influences in Banneker's mathematical thinking include numerology, evidenced in a mathematical puzzle-poem he wrote, and geometry, as illustrated in his journal passage describing a dream.

Wolof existed first as an empire, which rose after the decline of ancient Ghana in the 13th century. In the mid-16th century, the empire splintered into several separate kingdoms. The Wolof language and people originated from Mali after the fall of ancient Ghana. Wolof traditions trace their origins to the lower Senegal and the Jolof Empire, circa 1200–1500. Traditional accounts agree that the founder of the state and later the empire was Ndyadyane Ndyaye who lived in the 13th century. Several small states beginning with Waalo in the north established the empire's foundations. Before the empire's formation, Waalo was divided into villages ruled by separate kings using the Serer title *laman*. Later the ruler of Sine suggested that all rulers between the Senegal and Gambia Rivers voluntarily submit to one king, which they did. The new state of Djolof, named for the central province where the king resided, was a vassal of the Mali Empire for much of its early history. Djolof remained within that sphere until the late 14th century. During a succession dispute between two rival lineages within the Mali Empire's royal bloodline in 1360, Wolof gained independence.

The west coast of Africa was exclusively occupied by populations speaking languages of the West Atlantic family (Wolof and Fulani). The Wolofs occupied the savanna and agricultural regions south of the Senegal River. By the mid-14th century the Wolofs occupied a large area near the coast between the Senegal and Gambia Rivers and organized powerful states that resisted the forces of Mali. The Wolofs rebelled against Mali and built a confederation of strong states. By 1400, the Mali Empire, which ruled Senegal, lost control over the area. At the end of the 15th century, Wolof was the dominant state in the Senegambia region. In the 1480s, Prince Bemoi ruled the empire in the name of his brother, Burba Birao. The Wolof Empire dominated the Senegambia region for several centuries. The empire's territories included the Wolof provinces of Jolof, Waalo, Kajoor, and Bawol and the Sereer provinces of Siin and Saalum, all of which later became independent kingdoms. Jolof was considered the senior of all the provinces, and its king had precedence over the other territories. In 1549, the empire split into five coastal kingdoms—Waalo, Kayor, Baol, Sine, and Saloum—from north to south. Wolof traditions date the end of the empire to the Battle of Danki (1549), when the ruler of Kajoor led a rebellion that dismantled the empire and created the successor Wolof kingdoms. By 1600, the Wolof Empire ended. Jolof became one among several independent Wolof states. At this time the Wolofs were at the height of their power and extended authority over the Malinke states on the northern bank of the Gambia River. The Portuguese had some stations on the banks of the Senegal River in the 15th century, and the first French settlement appeared at Saint-Louis in 1659. By 1800, the five kingdoms with large Wolof populations controlled the northern bank of the Gambia River.

Peaceful trade relations were established between the Wolof Empire and Portugal. Agriculture was the main economic activity. Farmers cultivated millet and sorghum and also integrated cattle keeping with agriculture. After 1840, Wolof farmers started growing peanuts as a new export crop. Because French merchants dominated the gum trade, the peanut trade represented a new opportunity. Wolof cultivators, including the aristocracy and peasants, welcomed the new trade. Wolof and Sereer peasants were strategically located in relation to the railways and

Atlantic ports. The peanut basin coincided with the territory of the Wolof and Sereer kingdoms including the frontier zones in the east, where many migrants settled in underpopulated lands. Wolof and Sereer populations migrated over short distances within the peanut basin in search of new land as well as seasonal wage labor in the cities. Cash from peanuts became the major source of wealth for social transactions.

Wolof elites engaged in slave raiding as a means of accumulating wealth and expanding their territory. Slaves were captured in war or enslaved as punishment for rebellion or failure to pay tribute. Wolof slaves labored as personal servants, soldiers, and administrators. They produced surplus crops for royal courts and for export to coastal trading towns. Slaves were exchanged for horses, saddles, and other equipment needed to maintain cavalry forces. The Wolof kingdoms maintained an active trade with the Saharan region to the north, exporting slaves and grain in exchange for horses and other livestock. The gold of Bambuhu, a major source of wealth for the Wolof Empire, was tied to the trans-Saharan trade.

In 1455, the Portuguese established commercial relations with the Wolofs south of the Senegal River. In the 17th and 18th centuries, the Wolof kingdoms traded in food and slaves with the Atlantic coastal region. Later rather than flowing north across the Sahara, gold moved south to European coastal trade centers at Saint-Louis and Goree Island. The Wolof kingdoms maintained an active trade in foodstuffs and other provisions with European forts on the coast. Five kingdoms with large Wolof populations controlled the northern bank of the river. The African merchant communities of Goree and Saint-Louis played a key role in the 18th-century river and coastal trade. The Wolof kingdoms traded grain, fresh produce, cattle, and other provisions with French merchants based in Saint-Louis and Goree. Wolof participants in this trade became well established in the coastal towns. The intermediary role played by Wolof merchants between the coast and the riverine hinterland compelled farmers and slaveholding landowners of the interior to raise produce for the new urban markets.

The Wolof states were the main source of slaves for the New World. Slaves were exchanged for guns, textiles, iron bars, alcohol, and manufactured goods. Goree Island became a major center for the Atlantic slave trade through the 1700s, with millions of Africans shipped from there to the New World. The Atlantic trade created a thriving market for food to feed the slaves held at Goree Island and Saint-Louis awaiting export by European, mainly French, merchants. These communities supplied French merchants with slaves, gold, ivory, gum arabic, grain, and other goods. Wolof kings taxed Europeans for the right to trade. A large proportion of slaves originated from the area between Senegal and southern Angola. At times Wolofs were the majority of Africans abducted. The Senegambia slave trade peaked at the beginning of the 18th century. By the second half of the 18th century, the French trade on the Senegal had fallen into the hands of the Saint-Louisians—men generally Wolof in language and culture and formally Muslim. The African ethnic groups brought to the Americas closely correspond to the regions of heaviest activity in the slave trade. Over 45 distinct ethnic groups were taken to the Americas during the trade. Of that number, the 10 most prominent, according to slave documentation of the era, included the Wolofs of Senegal. By 1800, the Wolofs played a leading role in the trade between northern Senegambia and the Atlantic world. The Wolofs also played a role in the smuggling trade of the Cape Verde Islands. Smugglers used *panos* (trade cloths) as currency (two *panos* were equal to one iron bar) to undermine the Portuguese Crown's trading monopoly. Wolof spinners and weavers made *panos* from cotton, which was then dyed using both orchil and urzella. As the Senegambia slave trade declined, the number of slaves originating from the Wolof states dwindled.

The languages of Senegambia were Wolof and Serer. Wolof, closely related to Fulani, was spoken throughout Senegambia. Wolof society was highly stratified. Several castes existed below the monarchy, including a landed aristocracy, a hereditary military class, members of craft guilds, free peasants, hereditary house servants, and slaves. Blacksmiths were important for their ability to make weapons. Griots, employed by important families as advisers and chroniclers, recorded early Wolof history. Although Wolof nobility were Muslim, Islam did not fully penetrate Wolof society. Polygyny was customary. Society was also divided by age.

During the 18th century, the European trading settlements on Goree Island and Saint-Louis, at the mouth of the Senegal River, developed as important urban commercial communities. These African merchant communities included important families of mixed African and European ancestry. The majority of inhabitants were slaves who worked in the river trade or provided domestic labor to maintain European trading operations and feed the slaves held in transit on the coast. Slave owners were free women from the mainland called *signares* by French merchants. Male children of the *signares* and male merchants were referred to as habitants. Because most of the free migrants to the European settlements were Wolof speakers from Kajoor and Waalo, Wolof became the dominant language and culture in the new coastal cities. The pattern of urbanization that emerged, with Wolof urban language and culture dominating and with Wolof speakers serving as intermediaries between Europeans and Africans, continued in later centuries.

Islam played an important role in the dynastic traditions of Wolof society. The Wolof populations living near the Senegal River in Waalo and northern Kajoor were initial converts to Islam. Those residing in southern Kajoor and Bawol lived interspersed with Sereer communities that resisted Islam until the contemporary era. In the 16th century, Islam was confined as a court religion represented by leaders (marabouts), often foreigners living under the protection of the king. In 1670, Muslim clerics from Mauritania stirred up a rebellion against the Wolof ruler, invading and killing the rulers of Waalo and Kayor. The Wolofs restored their rulers. The Mauritanians continued their raids. By 1700 the monarchy in Kajoor and Bawol ceded local autonomy to Muslim communities, giving land grants and titles to Muslim marabouts. Within their domains, marabouts distributed land, collected taxes and rents, and served as religious councilors, judges, and educators. They assisted the monarchy in defending the kingdom and served as intermediaries between their followers and the state. Lesser Muslim scholars served as teachers, judges, and prayer leaders in Muslim villages. In the 1790s, marabouts in the Kajoor kingdom led a major rebellion against the monarchy. Wolof Muslims condemned the monarchy for enslaving fellow Muslims and consuming alcohol. Pious farmers resented the immorality of their ruling families. This continued into the 19th century, when Islam fully penetrated Wolof society. Conflicts between the traditional Wolof kingdom and Muslim reform leaders began in the 1850s and lasted until about 1900. These conflicts, part of Muslim reform movements that swept across the Senegambia region in the second half of the 19th century, destroyed traditional African ethnic polities and established new Islamic states.

Each one of the Wolof Empire's five coastal kingdoms (Waalo, Kayor, Baol, Sine, and Saloum) was governed by a chief appointed from the descendants of the founder. Governing chiefs possessed attributes of a divine king. These kingdoms were tributaries to the dominant landlocked Wolof kingdom, whose ruler was Burba Wolof. He ruled from the capital of Linguere. Each ruler was autonomous and cooperated with the *burba* on matters of defense, trade, and provision of imperial revenue. Women played a key role in government. The queen mother was the head of all Wolof women and was influential in politics. She owned a number of villages, which cultivated farms and paid tribute to her. In the empire's most northern kingdom, Walo, women served as rulers. Matrilineal dynasties monopolized political power.

The British took parts of Senegal at various times, but the French gained possession in 1840 and incorporated it into French West Africa in 1895. Muslim reformers resisted French conquest. In 1818, France established the first government schools in Senegal. Initially, Wolof was used as the language of instruction. Precolonial writing systems and literacy continued and expanded in the colonial period. The Murid and Tiani Sufi brotherhoods produced new religious literature using Arabic and Roman scripts. In 1946, Senegal became an overseas territory of France and then in 1960 gained political independence. In 1965, Gambia achieved political independence from the British.

Today Senegambia refers to the combined area of the Republic of Gambia and the Republic of Senegal and the region surrounding the Senegal and Gambia Rivers. In 1981, the two countries merged, forming the Senegambia Confederation. Each country maintained its independence. The confederation dissolved in 1989. Wolof remains one of the main ethnic groups of Senegambia. Wolofs reside anywhere from the Sahara desert area to the rain forests. The Wolof language is spoken and understood in all parts of Gambia, Senegal, and Mauritania. Islam, the predominant religion among Senegambians, united African ethnic groups. Wolof rice, originally from the Wolof kingdom in Senegal, spread to the Wolof population in Gambia and is now enjoyed throughout West Africa and Western civilizations.

Maryalice Guilford

Further Reading

Austen, Ralph A. *Trans-Saharan Africa in World History.* New York: Oxford University Press, 2010.

Barry, Boubacar. *Senegambia and the African Slave Trade.* New York: Cambridge University Press, 1998.

Carney, Judith A., and Richard Nicholas Rosomoff. *In the Shadow of Slavery: Africa's Botanical Legacy in the Atlantic World.* Berkeley: University of California Press, 2009.

Gilbert, Erik, and Jonathan T. Reynolds. *Africa in World History: From Prehistory to the Present.* Upper Saddle River, NJ: Pearson Prentice Hall, 2004.

Shillington, Kevin. *History of Africa.* New York: Palgrave Macmillan, 2012.

Y

Yatenga

Located in the Upper Volta region of present-day Burkina Faso, West Africa, the Yatenga kingdom gained prominence in the 14th century but reached its peak in the 15th and 16th centuries. Originally founded as one of the Mossi states in the northwest of the territory of the Mossi kingdom, Yatenga grew powerful with a very intimidating military force in the form of cavalry army and shook the whole region for several centuries. Yatenga held on to its hegemony for so long that it gained the status of the longest centralized kingdom in West Africa. The vibrant Yatenga kingdom waned in political power and prominence in the 19th century, but it still exists today in the Nord region of Burkina Faso, with its administrative capital in Ouahigouya. The title of the traditional head of the contemporary Yatenga is *naaba*—drawing from the title of the ruler of the ancient kingdom of Yatenga. Between the 14th century and the dawn of the 20th century, about 23 *naabas* had ruled other Yatenga. One characteristic unified all the Yatenga *naabas:* the drive for warfare. No Yatenga *naaba* would hesitate to engage any kingdom perceived to be an enemy or of potential benefit to Yatenga's existence.

Yatenga was popular for its fierceness and quickness to go to war with any kingdom or empire, despite its coexistence with the mightier Islamic Mali and Songhai Empires. Soon after the founding of Yatenga among other Mossi states, it began to rebel against the Mossi authority. Yatenga launched assaults on many Mossi states in several years-long wars and eventually took over some Mossi states, including the southern Mossi territory of Zondoma. The victory of Yatenga in these prolonged wars and the overtaking of Mossi kingdoms was an impetus for more attacks on other kingdoms, including the larger and more powerful empires. The Songhai Empire became Yatenga's next target, with special interest in taking over Timbuktu.

The location of Timbuktu in the transition zone of the Niger Bend and the Sahara desert allowed its control of the trade corridor connecting the south with the north in the trans-Saharan trade. Timbuktu was a major player in the trade of luxurious items such as gold and ivory. It also traded kola nuts, salt, and slaves. This trade made Timbuktu one of the most prosperous African empires of the 13th through 17th centuries and thus an envy of other empires. Between the 14th and 15th centuries during the reigns of Naaba Yadega, Yolomfaogoma, and Kourita, Yatenga invaded many trade posts under the control of the Songhai Empire. Yatenga sacked Timbuktu twice in the 14th century and took over the trade capital of the kingdoms in western Sudan. The takeover of Timbuktu significantly boosted the political power of Yatenga but posed an unbearable affront to the Songhai hegemony. The Songhai Empire's loss of Timbuktu to Yatenga and the Yatenga Empire's rise as a formidable power in the region made military campaigns against Yatenga a major political ambition of Songhai rulers. Hence, Sonni Ali led a series of attacks on Yatenga in the late 15th century. In all of these assaults, Sonni Ali lost badly to Yatenga to the point that he died in one of the battles. Ascending the throne as the Songhai ruler, Askia Muhammad launched an attack on Yatenga in 1498. Askia Muhammad's invasion was a big blow to the Yatenga Empire that Ousman Murzik Kobo describes in his book *Unveiling Modernity in 20th Century West African Islamic Reforms* as the "most decisive defeat in Yatenga history" (Kobo 2012, 57).

Another distinctive characteristic of the Yatenga kingdom was its overt hostility to Islam. Islam was already a popular religion in West Africa by the 8th century and was adopted by some important kingdoms and states, including the Mali and Songhai Empires. Since Yatenga was founded and remained a non-Muslim kingdom, it was a target for Islamic jihadists. It is remarkable that although Askia Muhammad defeated Yatenga in the 15th-century, Yatenga resisted conversion to Islam and adhered to its traditional beliefs. In the 19th century when several states and kingdom embraced Islam in West Africa, leading to the rise of the Massina Empire and the Sokoto Caliphate, the Fulbe and Ba Lobbo jihads attempted to capture Yatenga and force it to convert to Islam. The weaker Yatenga defeated both jihadist movements and again resisted conversion to Islam. Yatenga did not adopt Islam until later in the 19th century. The circumstances that led to Yatenga's conversion to Islam are unclear.

The decline of the Yatenga kingdom was connected to its obsession to expansionist ideology, which created a fracas in its military camp. As a result of internal unrest that created fractions in the military, Yatenga lost badly in major battles in the 19th century. Naaba Wobgho I was defeated in one of the battles and retreated to exile. In addition, Yatenga lost in succession to the Yako, Jelgoji, and Riziam kingdoms. These successive defeats set the stage for Yatenga's decline in military power, which created a loophole and a weaker kingdom. By the time of the French invasion later in the 19th century, Yatenga was a microcosm of itself in terms of power and territorial control. Yatenga thus became a French protectorate and then a province after independence.

Odunyemi Oluseyi Agbelusi

Further Reading

Arhin, K., and J. Ki-Zerbo. "States and Peoples of the Niger Bend and the Volta." In *General History of Africa,* Vol. 6, *Africa in the Nineteenth Century until the 1880s,* edited by J. F. Ade Ajayi, 662–698. Oakland: University of California Press, 1989.

Kobo, O. *Unveiling Modernity in Twentieth-Century West African Islamic Reforms.* Leiden: Brill, 2012.

Skinner, E. P. "The Mossi and Traditional Sudanese History." *Journal of Negro History* 43(2) (1958): 121–131.

Z

Zulu

The well-known and fabled Kingdom of the Zulus lasted an impressive 81 years, from 1816 to 1897. This warrior nation rose to prominence during King Shaka's reign. As one of the most revered leaders of his time, Shaka built an impressive African state. In fact, he used the geopolitical terrain to his savvy advantage. With his permanent standing army (*amabutho*) of able-bodied Zulu men he organized into age regiments, Shaka invaded and incorporated conquered peoples into his fold. Seeking grazing lands, cattle, and the ivory trade routes, Shaka's empire consisted of dispossessed and defeated rivals and also less threatening and powerful neighbors. At its height, the once powerful Zulu kingdom stretched approximately 11,500 square miles from the flowing waters of the Pongola River in the north to the Tukela River in the south. In today's geographical parlance, the kingdom covered the present-day rolling hills and coastal plains of KwaZulu/Natal to the car manufacturing city of East London on the Indian Ocean. Shaka rose from relatively humble beginnings and complete obscurity to claim legendary and iconic stature. Much of the Zulus' success was built on Shaka's conquering back. He was an ingenious leader. As with all legends, Shaka had his critics and his faults. He has long been vilified in academic texts and oral accounts, and people continue to malign his image and character even on the star-studded silver screen. Others such as apartheid proponents used his alleged treachery and cruelty and the wave of unrest his expansion caused (known as the Mfecane) to justify why their ancestors had claimed "uninhabited" lands. Shaka was undoubtedly a multidimensional historical figure: a starved crazy despot on the one hand and a fabled military leader on the other. His reputation not only reverberated throughout the African continent

Zulu (Film)

In 1964, American screenwriter Cy Endfield directed the film *Zulu*. The film captures the historic battle between the British and the Zulus that took place at Rorke's Drift on January 22, 1879. After its stunning defeat of the British at Isandhlwana, a Zulu regiment launched another attack against the British at Rorke's Drift. This time, as the film graphically depicts, the British handily defeated the Zulus. Like its predecessor, this battle became part of the lore that defined and characterized the Anglo-Zulu War, which finally ended in July 1879.

and the far corners of his native country but also reached the shores of foreign lands. Even today the name Shaka still has currency, as his descendants far and wide hold this military tactician in high esteem.

Born the illegitimate son of Senzangakona and Nandi around 1787, Shaka grew up in his mother's kraal. His father, fearing backlash from an out-of-wedlock pregnancy, decided to banish Nandi and the future king. This impacted Shaka in a profound way. According to oral accounts, Senzangakona's rejection weighed heavily on Shaka, who compensated for his father's cruelty by excelling at militarism. Resolved to be a leader to rival them all, the physically chiseled Shaka also took advantage of unique résumé-building opportunities. Following the assassination of his mentor and fatherlike figure Dingiswayo, who had ruled the Mthethwa Confederacy, Shaka found the opening he had long awaited. After internal succession battles and organizing a small Zulu army, Shaka rose in the ranks and became the king of the Zulus.

During his 11-year reign from 1817 to 1828, Shaka ushered in new military innovations and even adopted some of his predecessor's ingenuities. Traditionally, the Zulus wore sandals during battle. Shaka ended this by requiring that all armed soldiers tackle the terrain's harshness with bare unprotected feet. No longer encumbered by shoes, Shaka's men could enhance their mobility and their agility. Greater mobility was required for the type of military operations that Shaka commanded and the strategies he drew up. Instead of only attacking enemies frontally, Shaka proposed and implemented the bull flank formation. Along with a column of soldiers coming from the middle, two other regiments skirted the right and left sides. This enabled the Zulus to surround the enemy completely. Once the Zulu soldiers sequestered their political, geographical, demographic, and military threat, they attacked their enemies with short stabbing spears. Known as assegais, these deadly weapons replaced the longer ones that the Zulus used to hurl at opponents. Shaka saw the original weaponry as a disadvantage for one primary reason. When they launched their spears, his soldiers only had their shields to protect them. Shorter spears also enabled Shaka's troops to fight intimately. They could mortally wound opponents by sticking their assegais deep into their enemies' bodily crevices. Shaka not only enhanced his geopolitical positions but also, as historian Iris Berger suggests, controlled direct threats to his rule. Perhaps Shaka viewed a takeover as a personal defeat or a sign of crippling weakness. It was clear by Shaka's actions that he refused to renounce the throne he painstakingly attained. Only death ensured a regime change.

Before Shaka's half brother Dingane successfully executed his assassination in 1828, Shaka went to great lengths to build his diverse nation. With the innovations he incorporated, he also instituted a code of moral conduct. Soldiers married after completing service. With their mentality set on defeating enemies, the dominoes fell one by one. Shaka's *amabutho* defeated King Zwide's army. Zwide had longed eyed power as he clutched onto an amalgamated empire he created after ordering Dingiswayo's death in 1817. Skilled in the art of Zulu fighting tactics, the Ndwandwes put up a good fight. But in the end, Shaka gained a decisive advantage by engaging in guerrilla warfare and defeating the Ndwandwes at the Battle of

Mhlatuze River in 1819. Now splintered, various groups broke off into subsections, going in all directions. Some went to Swaziland and Mozambique, while others fled to Malawi and Zambia. With women detailing the military installations and his armed units poised for battle, Shaka and his forces left countless others who dared to cross their conquering paths. By 1826, Shaka had silenced all rival groups by either killing their leaders or incorporating their people into his ever-growing kingdom.

Shaka's land- and people-grabbing spree, however, had its demographic repercussions. During the 1820s and 1830s, Nguni rulers responded in several ways. Fearing Shaka's wrath and wanting to start his own kingdom, his longtime consultant Mzilikazi took his refuges and escaped to present-day Zimbabwe. His state and the people he commanded became known as the Ndebeles. While Mzilikazi chose flight, King Sobhuza's successor Mswati encouraged intermarriage. Although people spoke mutually intelligible languages, customs differed. In order to create a national identity, Mswati tried to homogenize his kingdom. State building, as Mswati's actions further showed, entailed more than assuming landownership. Leaders sought to solidify their territories around commonalities. For the Zulu nation this meant military prowess. Shaka's successor, Dingane, cultivated unity by killing the leader, Piet Retief, and his diplomatic party in 1838. Mpande's successor, Cetshawayo, brought the Zulus back to iconic lore when he orchestrated

Zulu warriors pose with shields and weapons, South Africa, ca. 1875. (Private Collection/The Stapleton Collection/The Bridgeman Art Library)

the British defeat in the Battle of Isandlwana in 1879. And finally, Dinuzulu kaCetshawayo faced banishment for his alleged complicity in the 1906 Bambatha Rebellion (a tax revolt).

While militarism defined Zulu identity, so did diplomacy. Solomon kaDinuzulu ascended to the throne in 1913. During his 20-year reign, which ended with his death in 1933, he opposed the 1920 Natives Affairs Bills. With his newly formed Inkatha kaZulu, the son of the exiled Dinuzulu sought change through his political body. At the time of Inkatha kaZulu's incarnation, then segregation leader and war veteran Jan Smuts sought to group Africans into distinct "tribal" districts. His policy foreshadowed the apartheid Bantustan policy. Under the 1970 Bantu Homelands Citizenship Act, the government created 10 ethnolinguistic territories for Africans to inhabit. In these areas only recognized by the South African government as countries, Africans faced uncertain economic futures on inhabitable and infertile lands. Chief Mangosuthu Buthelezi was not only a former prime minister of one of these homelands, KwaZulu, but was also a major cultural revivalist. His lineage was also regal and possibly prepared him for his cultural embracement. His mother, Princess Magogo kaDinuzulu, was a well-known vocalist. On top of that he dabbled in acting, starring as his maternal great-grandfather Cetshawayo kaMpande in the miniseries *Zulu*. Buthelezi was also a historian, reviving Inkatha into a cultural and political party in 1975. He championed Zulu dress, song, culture, and dance and other identity markers that had made this great nation proud. Buthelezi single-handedly fortified Zulu ethnicity in the modern era.

Zulu leaders used different identity markers to nation building. Shaka paved the way for Chief Buthelezi and his people to even embrace the spiritual, political, and cultural meanings of Zuluness. While such films as *Zulu* mythologized Shaka and his people as savages, actor Henry Cele's deep baritone voice adds a lyrical tenor to the film. Not only does his voice command the audience's attention, but his chiseled physique also adds authority to his portrayal. Rather than focusing on Shaka's redeeming qualities such as his mother's undying love, viewers see the inherent racial prejudices. When many missionaries and colonial powers had "invaded" Africa and had begun to "civilize" them, they focused on cultural differences rather than obvious commonalities. Had they done the latter, the African continent and its scramble and partition may have never occurred. Instead, Shaka's vilification tainted the glorious history that he created. He commanded allegiance, professed spirituality, and demanded honor. Shaka's build embodied the Zulu nation: strong, fortified, resilient, and commanding. This was not only the legacy of an illegitimate warrior but was also the Zulu peoples' enduring heritage, their timely present, and their hopeful future.

Dawne Y. Curry

Further Reading

Berger, Iris. *South Africa in World History.* Oxford: Oxford University Press, 2009.

Goplan, Daphne. *Inventing Shaka: Using History in the Construction of Zulu Nationalism.* Boulder, CO: Lynne Rienner, 1998.

Hamilton, Carolyn. *Terrific Majesty: The Powers of Shaka Zulu and the Limits of Historical Invention.* Cambridge, MA: Harvard University Press, 1998.

MacKinnon, Aran S. *The Making of South Africa.* 2nd ed. Upper Saddle River, NJ: Pearson, 2012.

Thompson, Leonard. *A History of South Africa.* New Haven, CT: Yale University Press, 2001.

Primary Documents

DUARTE BARBOSA

The East Coast of Africa at the Beginning of the 16th Century, 1540

Duarte Barbosa was a Portuguese royal commercial agent who traveled the East African coast documenting his experience and the sociocultural and political life of the people he encountered.

Sofola

Having passed the Little Veiques, for the Indies, at xvill leagues from them there is a river which is not very large, whereon is a town of the Mooors called Sofala, close to which town the king of Portugal has a fort. These Moors established themselves there a long time ago on account of the great trade in gold which they carry on with the Gentiles of the mainland: these speak somewhat of bad Arabic (garabia), and have got a king over them, who is at present subject to the king of Portugal. And the mode of their trade is that they come by sea in small barks which they call zanbuces (sambuk), from the kingdoms of Quiloa, and Mombaza, and melindi and they bring much cotton cloth of many colours, and white and blue and some of silk; and grey, and red, and yellow beads, which come to the said kingdoms in other larger ships from the great kingdom of Cambay (India), which merchandise these Moors buy and collect from other Moors who bring them there, and they pay for them in gold weight, and for a price which satisfies them and the said Moors keep them and sell these clothes to the Gentiles of the kingdom of Benamatapa (Munhumutapa) who come there laden with gold, which gold they give in exchange for the before mentioned cloths without weighting, and so much in quantity that these Moors usually gain one hundred for one. They also collect a large quantity of ivory, which is found all round Sofala, which they likewise sell in the great kingdom of Gambay at five or six ducats the hundred weight, and so also some amber, which these Moors of Sofala bring them from the Veiques. They are black men, and men of colour—some speak Arabic, and the rest make use of the language of the Gentiles of the country. They wrap themselves from the waist downwards with cloths of cotton and silk, and they wear other silk cloths above named, such as cloaks and wraps for the head, and some of them wear hoods of scarlet and of other coloured woolen stuffs and camelets, and of other silks. And their victuals are millet, and rice, and meat, and fish. In this river near to the sea there are many sea horses (hippopotamus) which go in the sea, and come out on land at times to feed. These have teeth like small elephants, and it is better ivory than that of the elephant. And whiter and harder, and of greater durability of colour. In the country all round Sofala there are many elephants, which are very large and wild and the people of the country do not know how to tame them: there are also many lions, ounces, mountain panthers. Wild asses and many other animals. It is country of plains and mountains, and well watered. The Moors have not recently begun to produce much fine cotton in this country, and they weave it into white stuff because they do not know how to dye it, or because they have not got any colours; and they take the blue or coloured stuffs of Cambay and unravel them, and again weave the threads with their white thread and in this manner they make coloured stuffs, by means of which they get much gold.

Kingdom of Benamatapa (Muninumutapa)

On entering within this country of Sofala, there is the kingdom of Benamatapa, which is very large and peopled by Gentiles, whom the Moors call Cafers. These are brown men, who go bare, but covered from the waist downwards with coloured stuffs, or skins of wild animals; and the persons most in honour among them wear some of the tails of the skin behind them, which go trailing on the ground for state and show, and they make bounds and movements of their bodies, by which they make these tails wag on either side of them. They carry swords in scabbards of wood bound with gold or other metals, and they wear them on the left hand side as we do, in sashes of coloured stuffs, which they make for this purpose with four or five knots, and their tassels hanging down, like gentlemen; and in their hands aza-gayes, and others carry bows and arrows; it must be mentioned that the bows are of middle size, and the iron points of the arrows are very large. They are men of war and some of them are merchants: their women go naked as long as they are girls, only covering their middles with cotton cloths, and when they are married and have children, they wear other cloths over their breasts.

Zinbaoch (Zimbabwe)

Leaving Sofala for the interior of the country, there is a large town of Gentiles, which is called Zimbaoch; and it has houses of wood and straw in which town the King of Benamatapa frequently dwells, and from there to the city of Benanatap there are six days journey, and the road goes from Sofala, inland, towards the Cape of Good Hope. And in the said Benamatapa, which is a very large town the king is used to make his longest residence and it is thence that the merchants bring to Sofala the gold which they sell to the Moors without weighing it, for coloured stuffs and beads of Cambay, which are much used and valued amongst them; and the people of this city of Benamatapa say that this gold comes from still further of towards the Cape of Good Hope. From another kingdom subject to this king of

Benamatapa, who is a great lord, and holds many other kings as his subjects, and many other lands, which extend far inland, both towards the Cape of Good Hope and towards Mozambich. And in this town he is each day served with large presents, which the kings and lords, his subjects, send to him; and when they bring them, they carry them bareheaded through all the city, until they arrive at the palace, from whence the king sees them come from a window, and he orders them to be taken up from there, and the bearers do not see him, but only hear his words and afterwards, he bids them call the persons who have brought these presents, and to dismisses them. This king constantly takes with him into the field a captain, whom they call Sono, with a great quantity of men-at-arms, and amongst them they bring six thousand women, who also bear arms and fight. With these forces he goes about subduing and pacifying whatever kings rise up or desire to revolt. The said king of Benamatapa sends, each year, many honourable persons throughout his kingdoms to all the towns and lordships, to give them new regulations, so that all may do them obeisance, which is in this manner: each one of the envoy comes to a town, and bids the people extinguish all the fires that there are in it; and after they have been put out, all the inhabitants go to this man who has been sent as commissary, to get fresh fire from him in sign of subjection and obedience, and whoever should not do this is held as a rebel and the king immediately sends the number of people that are necessary to destroy him, and these pass through all the towns at: their expense their rations are meat, rice, and oil of sesame.

Source: Duarte Barbosa, *A Description of the Coasts of East Africa and Malabar in the Beginning of the Sixteenth Century,* translated by Henry E. J. Stanley (London: Hakluyt Society, 1866), 4–8.

FATHER JEROME LOBO

Portuguese Missionaries in Ethiopia, 1645

Father Jerome Lobo (1593–1678) was among the eight Jesuit priests recruited to go to Ethiopia for evangelism. He had previously spent a year in India, where he completed studies in divinity. In this account, he details the constant strife between the mission and hostile Ethiopia leaders.

I continued two years at my residence in Tigre (in northern Ethiopia), entirely taken up with the duties of the mission, preaching, confessing, baptizing, and enjoying a longer quiet and repose than I had even done since I left Portugal. During this time one of our fathers, being always sick, and of a constitution which the air of Abyssinia was very hurtful to, obtained a permission from our superiors to return to the Indies. I was willing to accompany him through part of his way, and went with him over a desert, at no great distance from my residence, where I found many trees loaded with a king of fruit, called by the natives, Anchoy, about the bigness of an apricot, and very yellow, which is much eaten without any ill effect.

I therefore made no scruple of gathering and eating it, without knowing that the inhabitants always peeled it, the rind between a violent purgative, so that eating the fruit and skin together, I fell into such a disorder as almost brought me to my end. The ordinary dose is six of these rinds, and I had devoured twenty.

I removed from thence to Debaroa, fifty-four miles nearer the sea, and crossed in my way the desert of the province of Saraoe. The country is fruitful, pleasant, and populous. There are greater numbers of Moors in these parts than in any other province of Abyssinia; and the Abyssins of this country are not much better than the Moors.

I was at Debaroa when the persecution was first set on foot against the Catholics. Sultan Sequed, who had been so great a favourer of us, was grown old, and his spirit and authority decreased with his strength. His son, who was arrived at manhood, being weary of waiting so long for the crown he was to inherit, took occasion to blame his father's conduct, and found some reason for censuring all his actions; he even proceeded so far as to give orders sometimes contrary to the emperor's. He had embraced the Catholic religion, rather through complaisance than conviction or in-clination; and many of the Abyssins, who had done the same, waited only for an opportunity of making public profession of the ancient erroneous opinions, and of re-uniting themselves to the church of Alexandria. So artfully can this people dis-semble their sentiments, that we had not been able hitherto to distinguish our real from our pretended favourers; but as soon as this prince began to give evident tokens of his hatred, even in the life-time of the emperor, we saw all the courtiers and gov-ernors, who had treated us with such a shew of friendship, declare against us, and persecute us as disturbers of the public tranquility; who had come into Ethiopia with no other intention than to abolish the ancient laws and customs of the country, to sow divisions between father and son, and preach up a revolution.

After having borne all sorts of affronts and ill-treatments, we retired to our house at Fremona, in the midst of our countrymen, who had been settling round about us a long time, imagining we should be more secure there, and that, at least during the life of the emperor, they would not come to extremities or proceed to open force. I laid some stress upon the kindness which the viceroy of Tigre had shown to us, and in particular to me; but was soon convinced that those hopes has no real foundation, for he was one of the most violent of our prosecutors. He seized upon all our lands, and advancing with his troops to Fremona, blocked up the town. The army had not been stationed there long before they committed all sorts of dis-orders; but that one day a Portuguese, provoked beyond his temper at the insolence of some them, went out with his four sons, and wounding several of them, forced the rest back to their camp.

We thought we had good reason to apprehend an attack; their troops were in-creasing, our town was surrounded, and on the point of being forced. Our Portuguese therefore thought, that without staying till the last extremities, they might lawfully repel one violence by another; and sallying out, to the number of fifty, wounded about threescore of the Abyssins, and had put them to the sword, but that they feared it might bring too great an odium upon our cause. The Portuguese were some of them wounded, but happily none died on either side.

Though the times were by no means favourable to us, every one blamed the conduct of the viceroy; and those who did not commend our action, made the necessity we were reduced to of self-defence an excuse for it. The viceroy's principal design was to get my person into his possession, imagining, that if I was once in his power, all the Portuguese would pay him a blind obedience. Having been unsuccessful in his attempt by open force, he made use of the arts of negotiation, but with an event not more to his satisfaction. This viceroy being recalled, a son-in-law of the emperor succeeded, who treated us even worse than his predecessor had done.

When he entered upon his command, he loaded us with kindness, giving us so many assurances of his protection, that, while the emperor lived, we thought him one of our friends; but no sooner was our protector dead, than this man pulled off his mask; and quitting all shame, let us see that neither the fear of God nor any other consideration was capable of restraining him, when we were to be distressed. The persecution then becoming general, there was no longer any place of security for us in Abyssinia, where we were looked upon by all as the authors of all the civil commotions; and many councils were held to determine in what manner they should dispose of us. Several were of opinion, that the best way would be kill us all at once, and affirmed, that no other means were left of re-establishing order and tranquility in the kingdom.

Source: Father Jerome Lobo, *A Voyage to Abyssinia,* translated by Samuel Johnson (London: A. Bettesworth and C. Hitch, 1735), 125–131.

OLFERT DAPPER

Christianity in the Congo, 1686

Olfert Dapper (1636–1689), a Dutch geographer, wrote some of the most authoritative accounts of the Congo in the 17th century. This narrative on the introduction of Christianity in the Congo sheds light on global cultural and religious exchange and international relations.

Before the Portuguese entered the land of Congo, the inhabitants were extremely idolatrous, and each one fabricated a god to his own fancy. The Congolese adored dragons, serpents of a prodigious girth, billygoats, imagining that the honors they accorded them would stop them from doing harm. Birds, grass, trees, even the skins of animals filled with straw were the object of their cult. Their religious ceremonies consisted of genuflections and prostrations. They covered their heads with dust and offered to the idols whatever was most previous to them. Finally, about two centuries ago, Christianity (or at least a semblance of the Christian religion) was introduced into the kingdom.

In the year 1484 Dom Joao II, the Portuguese king who sponsored the discoveries of the coasts of Africa and the route to India, had a fleet equipped under the leadership of Diogo Cao, who, having arrived at the mouth of the Zaire (Congo) and having learned from the signs made by the few Negroes whom he met on the coast that there was a powerful king in the interior, sent some of his people to him. But seeing that they did not come back, he took with him four Congolese who seemed intelligent and promised to bring them back in fifteen moons. The King of Portugal looked kindly upon these foreigners, and having had them taught the language and religion, he sent them back with presents under the same pilot. When he was once again anchored at the mouth of the Zaire, Diogo Cao sent one of these Negroes to the King of Congo to beg him to send back his Portuguese to him because he had brought back the Congolese, as he had promised.

During their stay in that land, the Portuguese had so put themselves in the good graces of the Count of Soyo, the uncle of the king, and had impressed him with such a great horror of idolatry and such a vivid interest in our mysteries that the prince went to find his nephew, the king, and strongly encouraged him to abandon pagan superstitions and to embrace Christianity. Because the king was half convinced, he asked Diogo to bring Cacuta, one of the four Negroes who had been with him in Portugal, so that, acting as his ambassador, Cacuta would ask King Dom Joao for priests to instruct his people. Cacuta learned Portuguese and Christianity so well that he was baptized with his followers. He left King Joao, after having received a thousand signs of friendship, and brought back with him priests, images, crosses, and other church ornaments, whose novelty was received by the Negroes with great admiration and pleasure.

The first to receive baptism in the country were Count of Soyo and his son, who were baptized on Christmas Day of the year 1491. The count was given the name Emmanuel and his son was named Anthony. The king, his wife, and the younger of their children did the same and took the names of the House of Portugal. Thus, the kin was named Joao, the Queen Eleonor, and their son Affonso. A great many people of both sexes followed the example of their princes, and since then the Portuguese have expended much effort to banish pagan idolatry among these people. That is why they established several posts for schoolmasters who would teach reading, writing, and the principles of religion and that is why they support many Portuguese and mulatto priests who celebrate the mysteries according to the ceremonies in the Latin Church. But even though the majority of these Negroes outwardly profess to be Christians, the greater number are still idolatrous in their hearts and secretly worship false gods, tigers, leopards, and wolves, imagining that in this way they will escape feeling the effects of their fury. They are straightforward hypocrites who act like Christians only in the presence of Europeans and who have more respect for their kings than they do for the true God. Those who live around the churches and under the gaze of the Portuguese have their marriages blessed by the priest, but they are not willing to go very far to seek this benediction; furthermore, even those who receive it did not in the least admit to the condition under which it is given and they take as many concubines as they can feed.

The Negroes of Soyo are Christians of the same strength; they all have two strings in their bow—the Catholic religion and paganism, and when the saints do not answer their prayers, they invoke the fetishes. Yet to see them all covered with crosses and rosaries one would take them for sanctimonious people. Many churches and many Negro and mulatto priests are found in their province. When the Court of Soyo goes to mass, he dresses himself superbly and wears golden chains and collars of coral. He marches pompously to the sound of drums and horns, surrounded by guards among whom there are five or six musketeers who fire from time to time and others who carry flags and are followed by a great crowd of people.

Between 1644 and 1647, at the request of the King of Congo, the People sent a mission of Capuchins from Sicily and Cabis to that country. As the Capuchins entered Soyo, the court kept a few of them, and the others spread throughout the kingdom of Congo. The Negroes of the province of Oando (Luanda) are good Christians, according to what they say; at least great care is taken to make good Catholics of them. There are churches, Negro schoolmasters, and priest who baptize and say mass.

Source: Olfert Dapper, *Description de l'Afrique,* translated by Nell Elizabeth Painter and Robert O. Collins (Amsterdam: Wolfgan, Weesekerge, Boom, and Van Someren, 1868), 355–358.

AYUBA SULEIMAN DIALLO
Return to Africa, 1734

Ayuba Suleiman Diallo of Bondu, known to Europeans as Job Ben Solomon, was captured during a commercial venture to Gambia in 1731 and sold to the Atlantic slave trade. He was enslaved in Maryland, where he worked on a tobacco plantation. Diallo was rescued during an attempted escape from slavery by Thomas Bluett and presented to the British court in England. Diallo was later allowed to return to his home in Africa. His account of his adventures was first published in 1734 and was reprinted many times in English and French.

The next day (8 August 1734) about noon came up the *Dolphin* snow, which saluted the fort with nine guns, and had the same number returned; after which came on shore the captain, four writers, one apprentice to the Company, and one black man, by name Job Ben Solomon, a Pholey (Pulo) of Bundo in Foota, who in the year 1731, as he was traveling in Jagra (Jarra), and driving his herds of cattle across the countries, was robbed and carried to Joar, where he was sold to Captain Pyke, commander of the ship *Arabella,* who was then trading there. By him he was carried to Maryland, and sold to a planter, with whom Job lived about a twelve month without being once beat by his master; at the end of which time he had the good fortune to have a letter of his own writing in the Arabic tongue conveyed to England. This letter coming to the hand of Mr. Oglethorpe, he sent the same to Oxford to be translated; which, when done, gave him so much satisfaction, and so good an opinion of the man, that he directly order'd him to be bought from his master, he soon after setting out for Georgia. Before he returned from thence, Job came to England; where being brought to the acquaintance of the learned Sir Hans Sloane, he was by him found a perfect master of the Arabic tongue, by translating several manuscripts and inscriptions upon metals: he was by him recommended to his Grace the Duke of Montague, who being pleased with the sweetness of humour, and mildness of temper, as well as genius and capacity of the man, introduced him to court, where he was graciously received by the Royal Family, and most of the nobility, from whom he received distinguishing marks of favour. After he had continued in England about fourteen months, he wanted much to return to his native country, which is Bundo (a place about a week's travel over land from the Royal African Company's factory at Joar, on the River Gambia) of which place his father was High-Priest, and to whom he sent letters from England. Upon setting out from England he received a good many noble presents from her most Gracious Majesty Queen Caroline, his Highness the Duke of Pembroke, several ladies of quality, Mr. (Samuel) Holden, and the Royal African Company, who have ordered their agents to show him the greatest respect.

Job Ben Solomon having a mind to go up to Cower to talk with some of his countrymen, went along with me. In the evening we weighed anchor, saluting the fort with five guns, which returned the same number. On the 26th (of August 1734) we arrived at the Creek of Damasensa, and having some old acquaintances at the town of Danasensa, Job and I went up to the yawl; in the way, going up a very narrow place for about half a mile, we saw several monkeys of a beautiful blue and red, which the natives tell me never set their feet on the ground, but live entirely amongst the trees, leaping from one to another at so great distances, as any one, where they not to see it, would think improbable.

In the evening, as my friend Job and I were sitting under a great tree at Damasensa, there came by us six or seven of the very people who robbed and made a slave of Job, about thirty miles from hence, about three years ago; Job, tho' a very even tempered man at other times, could not contain himself when he saw them, but fell into a most terrible passion, and was for killing them with his broad sword and pistols, which he always took care to have about him. I had much ado to dissuade him from falling upon the six men; but at last, by representing to him the ill consequences that would infallibly attend such a rash action, and the impossibility of mine or his own escaping alive, if he should attempt it, I made him lay aside the thoughts of it, and persuaded him to sit down and pretend not to know them, but ask them questions about himself; which he accordingly did, and they answered nothing but the truth. At last he asked them how the king their master did; they told him he was dead, and by further enquiry we found, that amongst the goods for which he sold Job to Captain Pyke there was a pistol, which the king used commonly to wear slung about his neck with a string; and as they never carry arms without being loaded, one day this accidentally went off, and the ball's lodging in his throat, he died presently. At the closing of his story Job was so very much transported that he immediately fell on his knees, and returned thanks to Mahomet for making this man die by the very goods for which he sold him into slavery; and then turning to me, he said, "Mr. Moore, you see now God Almighty was displeased at this man's making me a slave, and yet I ought to forgive him says he, because had I not been sold, I should neither have known anything of the English tongue, nor have had any of the fine, useful and valuable things I now carry over, nor have known that in the world there is such as place as England, not such noble good and generous people as Queen Caroline, Prince William, and Duke of Montague, the Earl of Pembroke, Mr. Holden, Mr. Oglethorpe, and the Royal Africa Company."

On the 1st of September we arrived at Joar, the freshes being very strong against us. I immediately took an inventory of the company's effects, and gave receipts to Mr. Gill for the same. After which he unloaded the sloop, and then I sent her to Yanimarew (Niani Maro) for a load of corn for James Fort, where she stayed till the 25th, and then came back to Joar, during which time I made some trade with the merchants, though at a pretty high price.

Source: Francis Moore, *Travels into the Inland Parts of Africa* (London: Dr. Henry and R. Cave, St. John's Gate, 1738), 143–147. Reprinted in Philip D. Curtin, "Ayuba Suleiman Diallo," in *Africa Remembered: Narratives by West Africans From the Era of the Slave Trade,* edited by Philip D. Curtin (Prospect Heights: Waveland, 1967), 54–56.

JAMES BRUCE

Sheik Adlan and the Black Horse Calvary of Sennar, 1772

James Bruce (1730–1794) was appointed the British consul in Algiers. However, he committed many years to exploring the source of the Nile. Adlan later visited Ethiopia and the Funj kingdom of Sennar in Sudan. In this account, he detailed his fascination with the Black Horse Cavalry of Sheik Adlan of Sennar and other elements of royalty during his visit in 1772.

It was not till the 8th of May I had my audience of Shekh Adelan at Aira, which is three miles and a half from Sennaar; we walked out early in the morning, for the greatest part of the way along the side of the Nile, which had no beauty, being totally divested of trees, and the bottom foul and muddy, and the edges of the water, white with small concretions of calcareous earth, which with the bright sun upon them, dazzled and affected our eyes very much.

We then struck across a large sandy plain, without trees or bushes, and came to Adelan's habitation; two or three very considerable houses of one storey, occupied the middle of a large square, each of whose sides was at least half of an English mile. Instead of a wall to inclose this square, was a high fence or impalement of strong reeds, canes, or stalks of dora (I do not know which), in fascines strongly joined together by stakes and cords. On the outside of the gate, one each hand, were six houses of slighter construction than the rest; close upon the fence where sheds where the soldiers lay, the horses picqueted before them with their heads turned towards the sheds, and their food laid before them on the ground; above each soldier's sleeping-place, covered only on the top and open in the sides, were hung a lance, a small oval shield, and a large broad-sword. These, I understood, were chiefly quarters for couriers, who being Arabs, were not taken into the court or square, but shut out at night.

Within the gate was a number of horses, with the soldiers barracks behind them; they were all picqueted in ranks, their faces to their masters barracks. It was one of the finest sights I ever saw of the kind. They were all above sixteen hands high, of the breed of the old Saracen horses, all finely made, and as strong as our coach horses, but exceedingly nimble in their motion; rather thick and short in the forehand, but with the most beautify eyes, ears, and heads in the world; they were mostly black, some of them milk-white, foaled so, not white by age, with white eyes and white hoofs, not perhaps a great recommendation.

A steel of mail hung upon each man's quarters, opposite to his horse, and by it an antelope's skin, made soft like shamoy, with which it was covered from the dew of the night. A head-piece of copper, without crest or plumage, was suspended by a lace above the shirt of mail, and was the most picturesque part of the trophy. To these was added an enormous brand-sword, in a red leather scabbard; and upon the pummel hung two thick gloves, not divided into fingers as ours, but like hedgers gloves, their fingers is one poke. They told me, that within that inclosure at Aira, there was 400 horses, which, with the riders, and armour complete for each them, were all the property of Shekh Adelan, every horseman being his slave, and bought with his money. There were five or six (I know not which) of these squares or in-closures, none of them half a mile from the other, which contained the king's horses, slaves, and servants. Whether they were all in as good order as Adelan's I cannot say, for I did not go further; but no body of horse could ever be more magnificently diposed under the direction of my Christian power.

Adelan was then sitting upon a piece of the trunk of a palm tree, in the front of one of these divisions of his horses, which he seemed to be contemplating with pleasure; a number of black people, his own servants and friends, were standing around him. He had on a long drab coloured camblet gown, lined with yellow sat-tin, and camlet cap like a head-piece, with two short points that covered his ears. This, it seems, was his dress when he rose early in the morning to visit his horses, which he never neglected. The Shekh was a man above six feet high, and rather corpulent, had a heavy walk, seemingly more from affection of grandeur, than want of agility. He was about sixty, of the colour and features of an Arab, and not of a Negro, but had rather more beard than falls to the lot of people in this country; large piercing eyes, and a determined, though at the same time, a very pleasing countenance. Upon my coming near him, he got up; "You that are a horseman," says he without any salutation, "what would your king of Habesh give for these horses?" "What king," answered I, in the same tone, "would not give any price for such horses, if he knew their value?" "Well," replied he, in a lower voice, to the people about him, "if we are forced to go to Habesh, as Baady was, we will carry our horses along with us." I understood by this he alluded to the issue of his approaching quarrel with the king.

We then went into a large salon, hung round with mirrors and scarlet damask; in one of the longest sides, were two large sofas covered with crimson and yellow damask, and large cushions of cloth of gold, like to the king's. He now pulled off his camlet gown and cap, and remained in a crimson sattin coat reaching down below his knees, which lapped over at the breast, and was girt round his waist with a scarf or sash in which he had stuck a short dagger in an ivory sheath, mounted with gold; and one of the largest and most beautiful amethysts, upon his finger that ever I saw, mounted plain, without any diamonds, and a small gold ear-ring in one of his ears.

Source: James Bruce, *Travels to Discover the Source of the Nile, 1768–73* (Edinburgh, UK: Archibald Constable and Co. and Manner and Miller, 1813), 359–365.

OLAUDAH EQUIANO

The Interesting Narrative of the Life of Olaudah Equiano, 1789

Olaudah Equiano (ca. 1745–1797), also known as Gustavus Vassa, was kidnapped in an area now in modern-day southwestern Nigeria at the age of 11 and sold first into domestic slavery within his community and later to the Americas. In the United States he worked with many masters, received his freedom, and learned to read and write. Equiano would later become an abolitionist, fighting to end human cargo and servitude. Equiano's autobiography, The Interesting Narrative of the Life of Olaudah Equiano, *first published in 1789, played a significant role in the antislavery movement in Great Britain and the United States.*

I hope the reader will not think I have trespassed on his patience in introducing myself to him with some account of the manner and customs of my country. They had been implanted in me with great care, and made an impression on my mind, which time would not erase, and which all the adversity and variety of fortune I have since experienced served only to river and record: for, whether the love of one's country be real or imaginary, or a lesson of reason, or an instinct of nature, I still look back with pleasure on the first scenes of my life, though that pleasure has been for the most part mingled with sorrow.

I have already acquainted the reader with the time and place of my birth. My father, besides many slaves, had a numerous family, of which seven lived to grow up, including myself and a sister, who was the only daughter. As I was the youngest of the sons, I became, of course, the greatest favourite with my mother and was always with her; and she used to take particular pain to form my mind. I was trained up from my earliest years in the arts of agriculture and war; my daily exercise was shooting and throwing javelins, and my mother adorned me with emblems, after the manner of our greatest warriors. In this way I grew up till I was turned the age of eleven when an end was put to my happiness in the following manner. Generally, when the grown people in the neigbourhood were gone far in the fields to labour, the children assembled together in some of the neigbours' premises to play; and commonly some of us used to get up a tree to look out for any assailant, or kidnapper that might come upon us; for they sometimes took these opportunities of our parents' absence, to attack and carry off as many as they could seize. One day, as I was watching at the top of a tree in our yard, I saw one of these people come into the yard of our next neigbour but one, to kidnap, there being many stout young people in it. Immediately, on this, I gave the alarm of the rogue, and he was surrounded by the stoutest of them, who entangled him with cords, so that he could not escape till some of the grown people came and secured him. But, alas! Ere long it was my fate to be thus attacked, and to be carried off, when none of the grown people were nigh. One day, when all our people gone out to their works as usual, and only I and my dear sister were left to mind the house, two men and a woman got over our walls, and in a moment seized us both; and, without giving us time to cry out, or make resistance, they stopped our mouths, tied our hands, and ran off with us into the nearest wood: and continued to carry us as far as they could, till night came on, when we reached a small house, where the robbers halted for refreshment, and spent the night. We were then unbound, but were unable to take any food; and being quite overpowered by fatigue and grief, our only relief was some slumber, which allayed our misfortune for a short time. The next morning we left the house and continued travelling all the day. For a long time we had kept the woods, and but at last we came into a road which I believed I knew. I had now some hopes of being delivered; for we had advanced but a little way before I discovered some people at a distance, on which I began to cry out for their assistance; but my cries had no other effect than to make them tie me faster, and stop my mouth, and then they put me into a large stack. They also stopped my sister's mouth, and tied her hands; and in this manner we proceeded till we were out of the sight of these people.

When we went to rest the following night they offered us some victuals; but we refused them; and the only comfort we had was in being in one another's arms all that night, and bathing each other with our tears. But, alas! We were soon deprived of even the smallest comfort of weeping together. The next day proved a day of greater sorrow then I had yet experienced; for my sister and I were then separated, while we lay clasped in each other's arms. It was in vain that we besought them not to part us; she was torn from me, and immediately carried away, while I was left in a state of distraction not to be described. I cried and grieved continually; and for several days did not eat anything but what they forced into my mouth. At length, after many days travelling, during which I had often changed masters, I got into the hands of a chieftain, in a very pleasant country. This man had two wives and some children, and they all used me extremely well, and did all they could to comfort me; particularly the first wife, who was something like my mother. Although I was a great many days journey from my father's house, yet these people spoke exactly the same language with us. This first master of mine, as I may call him, was a smith, and my principal employment was working his bellows, which was same kind as I had seen in my vicinity. They were in some respect not unlike the stoves here in gentlemen's kitchens; and were covered over with leather; and in the middle of that leather a stick was fixed, and a person stood up and worked it, in the same manner as is done to pump water out of cask with hand-pump. I believe it was gold he worked, for it was of a lovely bright yellow colour, and was worn by the women in their wrists and ankles. I was there I suppose about a month, and they at last used to trust me some little distance from the house. This liberty I used in embracing every opportunity to inquire the way to my own home: and I also sometimes, for the same purpose, went with the maidens, in the cool of the evenings, to bring pitchers of water from the springs for the use of the house.

Source: Olaudah Equiano, *The Interesting Narrative of the Life of Olaudah Equiano, or Gustavus Vassa, the African, Written by Himself* (London: Printed for the Author, 1794), 30–34.

DIXON DENHAM

Tripoli to Mourzuk, 1822

Dixon Denham was a member (with Hugh Clapperton and Walter Oudney) of a British expedition to Bornu in 1821. Denham died in 1828 while serving as the British administrator of Sierra Leone.

Previous to any knowledge I had received of the intentions of His Majesty's government to follow up the mission of Mr. Richie and Captain Lyon, I had volunteered my services to Lord Bathurst to proceed to Timbucktoo, by nearly the same route which Major Laing is now pursuing. I learnt in reply, that an expedition had been planned, and that Doctor Oudney and Lieutenant Clapperton, both of the navy, were appointed; and with these gentlemen, by the kindness of Lord Bathurst, I was, at my request, associated. My companions left London before me; but, as soon as ready, I lost no time in proceeding in the packet to, where I found that they had left the island for Tripoli nearly a month before. By the kindness of Admiral Sir Graham Moore, Sir Manley Power, Sir Richard Plasket, and Captain Woolley, commissioner of the dock-yard, all my wants were amply supplied; and judging that the assistance of a shipwright or carpenter might prove of essential use, and being allowed by my instructions to engage any one, at a reasonable salary, who might choose to volunteer to accompany the mission, William Hillman, shipwright, a man of excellent character, immediately offered his services, on an agreement that he should receive 120/. a year so long as he should continue to be employed.

I embarked in the Express schooner, which the admiral lent me for the purpose, and, on the 18th November, after three days' sail, arrived at Tripoli, and found my two companions at the house of Mr. Consul Warrington, anxiously expecting my arrival. Of this gentleman it is not too much to say, that by his cheerful and good humoured disposition, his zeal, perseverance, and extraordinary good management, we owe, in a great degree, that influence which England possess with this government far beyond that of any other of the Barbary powers. The English name, in fact, is of such importance in Tripoli, that there is scarcely a point to carry, or a dispute to settle, in which the bashaw does not request the interference of the

British Consul; and to him, indeed, is, in a great degree, owing the origin and success of the late mission. He stated broadly to the government at home, that the road from Tripoli to Bornou was as open as that London to Edinburgh; which, with a small allowance for Oriental hyperbole, was found to be true—witness the journey of my lamented friend Toole, and also of Mr. Tywhitt, the latter laden with valuable presents.

But this is not all: the British flag has a peculiar power of protection, and the roof of the English consul always affords a sanctuary to the perpetrator of any crime, not even exception murder; and scarcely a day passes that some persecuted Jew or unhappy slave, to escape the bastinado, does not rush into the court-yard of the British consulate for protection. A circumstance occurred in returning from one of our excursions, which shows in what high estimation the English character is held in Tripoli. A poor wretch, who, for some trifling offence, was sentenced to five hundred bastinadoes, having, while on his way to receive the sentence of the law, contrived a slip from the custody of his guards, fortunately met with the child and servant of Doctor Dickson, a most respectable and intelligent English physician practicing in Tripoli: the condemned wretch, with wonderful presence of mind snatched up the child in his arms, and halted boldly before her pursuers. The talisman was sufficiently powerful: the emblem of innocence befriended the guilty, and the culprit walked on uninterrupted, triumphantly claiming the protection of the British flag.

But the following proves still more strongly to what extent the influence of the British flag might be carried. Since the reduction of the refractory Arabs to submission, no chief had received such repeated marks of kindness and attention from the bashaw as sheikh Belgassam be Khalifa, head of the powerful ethnic group of ElGibel. At the particular request of the former, sheikh Khalifa had quitted his tents and flocks, resided in the city, and was high in his prince's confidence—fatal pre-eminence in Barbary states!—and had been presented, but a few months before with one of the most beautiful gardens in the Minshea. Returning from the castle after an evening of music and dancing in the bashaw's private apartments, Belgassam kissed the hand that had signed his death-warrant, and took his leave. At his own door a pistol-shot wounded him in the arm, and on entering the skiffs, or passage, a second entered his body. The old sheikh, after his slave had fastened the door, staggered on his carpet, and then, in the arms of his wife, proclaimed his assassin to be his own nephew, sheikh Mahmoud Belgassam Wilde Sowdoweah. The work being however, but half done, others rushed in, and seven stabs put an end to his suffering, notwithstanding the screams of his wife, who received two wounds herself, in endeavouring to save her husband.

The poor old man was almost instantly buried, and the three persons who had undertaken the murder fled to the British consulate for protection. Early the next morning, however, the consul dispatched his dragoman to give the bashaw notice, "that the murderers of Khalifa would find no protection under the flag of England." The bashaw said, "he was shocked at the murder, and regretted the assassins having taken refuge in the consulate, as it was a sanctuary he could not violate, particularly as he understood they meant to resist, and were not armed." Our consul replied, "that the bashaw was at liberty to send any force he pleased, and use any means be thought best, to drag them from beneath a banner that never was disgraced by giving protection to assassins." The minister also came and expressed the bashaw's delicacy; and it was evident he did not expect such would be the conduct of the consul: he was, however, peremptory, and the beshaw dared not seem to favour such an act of villany. It was sunset before he decided on taking them away, when about sixteen of the chosen people of the castle entered the consulate, and the wretches, although provided with arms, which they loaded.

Source: Dixon Denham, Hugh Clapperton, and Walter Oudney, *Narrative of Travel and Discoveries in Northern and Central Africa in the Years 1822, 1823, and 1824,* Vol. 1 (London: John Murray, 1828), 1–5.

HENRY FRANCIS FYNN
Shaka, 1830

Henry Francis Fynn was the leader of an expedition of the Farewell Trading Company to open up the eastern coast of Africa in 1824. He first arrived in South Africa in 1818. His account is among the earliest written record of Nguni history and culture. Fynn met with Shaka and traded with him and Dingane, his successor until 1834. Fynn would later serve as magistrate and a respected authority on African affairs in the British colony of Natal.

I may at once state that the distance from the port of Shaka's residence was 200 miles. Our progress was exceedingly slow[,] each day's journey being arranged by Mbikwana (Shaka's uncle). We afterwards found out that he had not taken us by a direct route, but to kraals of minor chiefs and some of the barracks of Shaka's regiments. Cattle-slaughtering occurred sometimes twice and thrice a day. Numbers of Zulus joined our column in order to relieve Mbikwana's people of their burdens. We were struck with astonishment at the order and discipline maintained in the country through which we travelled. The regimental kraals, especially the upper parts thereof, also the kraals of chiefs, showed that cleanliness was a prevailing custom and this not only inside their huts but outside, for there were considerable spaces where neither dirt nor ashes were to be seen. Frequently on the journey we saw largely parties seated with grotesquely dressed men apparently lecturing in their midst, and on several occasions saw individuals seized and carried off and instantly put to death. The grotesque characters we learned were "witch finders" whilst those singled out and put to death were said to be "evil doers."

Messengers passed three or four times a day between Shala and Mbikwana, the former enquiring about our progress and doubtless directing how we should proceed so as to fall in with his own preparations for our reception. We had thus dallied 13 days on the road in travelling 200 miles, when the locality of Shaka's residence was pointed out to us about 15 miles off. While encamped that night we saw much commotion going on in our neighoorhood. Troops of cattle were being driven in advance; regiments were passing near by and on distant hills, interspersed with regiments of girls, decorated in beads and brass with regimental uniformity, carrying on their heads large pitchers of native beer, milk, and cooked food. The approaching scene we anticipated witnessing cheered us considerably that evening. Farewell and Petersen expressed extreme affection and attachment for one another, with mutual apologies for past small differences.

It was not until ten o'clock the following morning that a proposal was made about advancing. In about two hours we arrived at a ridge from which we beheld an extensive and very picturesque basin before us, with a river running through it, called the Umfolozi. While in this position, messengers went backwards and forwards between Mbikwana and Shaka. At length one came and desired Mr. Farewell and myself to advance, leaving Mr. Peterson and our servants and native followers, who were carrying Shaka's present, at the euphorbia tree. Mbikwana and about 20 of his followers accompanied us.

On entering the great cattle kraal we found drawn up within it about 80,000 natives in their war attire. Mbikwana requested me to gallop within the circle, and immediately on my starting to do so one general shout broke forth from the whole mass, all pointing at me with their sticks. I was asked to gallop round the circle two or three times in the midst of tremendous shouting of the words, "*Ujojo wokhalo!*" (the sharp or active finch of the ridge). Mr. Farewell and Iwere then led by Mbikwana to the head of the kraal, where the masses of the people were considerably denser than elsewhere. The whole force remained stationary, as, indeed, it had been since the commencement of the reception.

Mbikwana, standing in our midst, addressed some unseen individuals in a long speech, in the course of which we were frequently called upon by him to answer "*Yebo,*" that is to affirm as being true all he was saying, though perfectly ignorantly of what was being said. While the speech was being made I caught sight of an individual in the background whom I concluded to be Shaka, and turning to Farewell, pointed out and said: "Farewell, there is Shaka." This was sufficiently audible for him to hear and perceive that I had recognized him. He immediately held up his hand, and shaking his finger at me approvingly. Farewell, being near-sighted and using an eye-glass, could not distinguish him.

Elephant tusks were then brought forward. One was laid before Farewell and another before me. Shaka then raised the stick in his hand and after striking with it right and left, the whole mass broke from their position and formed up into regiments. Portions of each of these rushed to the rover and the surrounding hills, while the remainder, forming themselves into a circle[,] commenced dancing with Shaka in their midst. It was a most exciting scene, surprising to us, who could not have imagined that a nation termed "savages" could be so disciplined and kept in order. Regiments of girls headed by officers of their own sex, then entered the centre of the arena to the number of 8,000–10,000, each holding a slight staff in her hand. They joined in the dance, which continued for about two hours.

Shaka now came towards us, evidently to seek our applause. (The following from Bird's *Annals of Natal,* contributed by the author, described the scene.) "The

King came up to us and told us not to be afraid of his people, who were now coming up to us in small divisions, each division driving cattle before it. The men were singing and dancing and whilst so doing advancing and receding even as one sees the surf do on a seashore. The whole country, as far as our sight could reach, was covered with numbers of people and droves of cattle. The cattle [had] been assorted according to their colour. . . . After exhibiting their cattle for two hours, they drew together in a circle, and sang and danced to their war song. Then the people returned to the cattle, again exhibiting them as before, and, at intervals, dancing and singing. The women now entered the kraal, each having a long thin stick in the right hand, and moving it in time to the song. They had not been dancing many minutes, when they had to make way for the ladies of the seraglio (harem), besides about 150 others, who were called sisters."

Source: Henry Francis Fynn, *Diaries,* edited by James Stuart and Daniel McKinnon Malcolm (Pietermaritzburg: Shuter and Shooter, 1950), 70–80.

RICHARD LANDER

Religion, Law, and Government: From Badagry to Soccatoo (Sokoto), 1830

Richard Lander was assistant to the Scottish explorer Hugh Clapperton during the expedition of West Africa in 1825. Clapperton died in Sokoto in 1827, thus leaving Lander as the only member of the expedition who returned to Britain in 1828. Accompanied by his brother John, Lander returned to West Africa in 1830, landing first at Badagry, and explored the Benue River and the Niger Delta.

The religion of the natives from Badagry to Soccato (Sokoto) is either Mohammedism or Paganism; or as it frequently appeared to us, a mixture of both, so nicely blended, as to make it impossible to ascertain with accuracy which belief had the ascendancy. Idols, or figures of birds, beasts, and reptiles, are worshipped, in Badagry, Jannah, and Yaribas exclusively, while in the kingdoms of Borghoo, Nyffe, and Houssa, Islamism prevails in a greater or less degree.

The professors of the former faith have a vague and indistinct notion of one great Being reigning above the skies, and is infinitely superior to every other in the nature of his attributes, and the extent of his power and influence. To this unknown God they pay divine adoration, through the medium of insignificant and inanimate objects, by the offering up of sacrifices to the latter, under the belief that the Great Spirit exits at so immeasurable a distance from them, and his time is so much employed in other and more important matters, that he cannot listen to the prayers of every individual. In consequence of this he appoints innumerable subordinate agents and machines, who aid and assist them, and minister to the affairs of mankind. They believe also in the existence of a powerful malevolent Spirit, who endeavours to counteract the good deeds of the Most High by every means, and is the author of all the mischief that annoys them. The people stand in the greatest dread of the power and machinations of this terrible demon, and strive to avert his wrath, and conciliate his favour, by ablations of dogs, sheep, and in many cases, of human beings. Fetish-huts are the temples of their worship, which are regarded with superstitious awe by rich and poor; and are each furnished with one or more priests, who alone are acquainted with the mysteries of their religion. Some of the people are very sincere in their devotional exercise, which are energetic and simple; whilst many pay little respect to the exterior forms of worship, openly ridiculing those who profess a greater share of sanctity than themselves; and, whenever they are unsuccessful in their pursuits and enterprises, even belabour their household gods without mercy. They entertain also an idea that the soul hovers round the scenes it had known in the body, for an indefinite length of time; but that it is ultimately conducted to a place of happiness or misery; a kind of haven for the peaceable, and hell of the turbulent, according to the deeds it has suggested in this life, and there to remain everlastingly. Both Mohammedan and Pagan attach miraculous qualities to fetishes or charm, which to them are an affectual panoply against every danger; sometimes a chief or a great man is actually covered with them from head to foot, and in this state considers himself as secure as Achilles in his armour. I have often been urged to discharge a pistol loaded with ball, at the breast of an individual this supernaturally defended, but it is unnecessary to say that I never risked the men's lives at the expense of their ignorance and credulity, having endeavoured in every instance, although unsuccessfully, to persuade them out of their superstitious prejudices by less dangerous experiments. The native appear to have no gloomy foreboding as the hour of death approaches; nor do they, as I have often been given to understand, anticipate dissolution with any symptoms of fear or alarm.

Those who profess the Mohammedan religion amongst the negroes are as ignorant and superstitious as their idolatrous brethren; nor does it appear that their having adopted a new creed has either improved their manners, or battered their state and condition in life. On the contrary, I have generally found the followers of the Prophet to be less hospitable to strangers, less kin to each other, and infinitely more mischievous and wicked than the heathen portions of the community, whom they, whimsically enough, affect to despise as rude barbarians, although their claim to superior intelligence are grounded simply on the oral communication of the principles of the Koran, received from time to time from the wandering Moors and Arabs; or from traditional legends of their country. The artful Arabian, however, withholds from them a full half of the little he himself may be acquainted with, taking care to teach them no more than is absolutely necessary to promote his own views, and enlarge his own interests. The Mohammedan negroes go through their ablutions regularly, and when water is not to be obtained, make use of sand, as the Koran enjoins. The Tuaricks, or "Berebers" (Children of the Desert), adopt the latter method on all occasions, the trouble of applying water, even when they have abundance within their reach, being too irksome and unpleasant to them.

The Falatahs, who profess Islamism, understand and make use of a few Arabic praters, but the negro that can utter so long a sentences as "*La illah el Allah Rasoul Allahi*" (There is but one God, and Mohammed is his prophet), is styled *mallam*, or learned, and is regarded with looks of respect and reverence by his less intelligent countrymen. These mallams are scattered in great numbers over the country, and procure an easy and respected subsistence by making fetishes, or writing charms on bits of wood, which are washed off carefully into a bason, and drunk with avidity by the credulous multitude, who consider the dirty water used in the operation as a panacea for every disease and affliction. As the office of mallam, which answers to that of priest in Catholic countries, is one of great sanctity as well as considerable emolument's, every one burns with impatience to get initiated into its sacred mysteries, and enjoy a like comfortable and indolent life as the mallams themselves; for a learned man never toils or spins, but is bountifully fed, and pampered in luxury by his lay countrymen. Every caravan is furnished with one or more of these corpulent drones, who loll at their case, while their employers are at the same time, perhaps, actually killing themselves with over-exertion.

Source: Richard Lander, *Records of Captain Clapperton's Last Expedition to Africa,* 2 vols. (London: Henry Colburn and Richard Bentley, 1830), 1:270–275.

SAMUEL AJAYI CROWTHER

The Capture and Sale of Ajayi to Slavery, 1837

Samuel Ajayi Crowther (ca. 1809–1891), a Yoruba born in the town of Osogun, was the first African bishop of the Anglican Church. His narrative (a letter to Reverend William Jowett, the secretary of the Church Missionary Society) detailed how his town was raided and how he was enslaved at the age of 12 or 13. Crowther was fortunate that the Portuguese ship on which he was traveling to the Western Hemisphere was intercepted by the British antislavery force. He was resettled in Freetown, Sierra Leone, where he started a life journey that would later make him the first black Anglican bishop.

Rev. and Dear Sir,

As I think it will be interesting to you to know something of the conduct of Providence in my being brought to this Colony, where I have the happiness to enjoy the privilege of the Gospel, I give you a short account of it; hoping I may be excused if I should prove rather tedious in some particulars.

I suppose some time about the commencement of the year 1821, I was in my native country, enjoying the comforts of father and mother and the affectionate love of brothers and sisters. From this period I must date the unhappy, but which I am now taught, in other respects, call blessed day, which I shall never forget in my life. I call it unhappy day because it was the day in which I was violently turned out of my father's house, and separated from relations; and in which I was made to experience what is called to be in slavery—with regard to its being called blessed, it being the day which Providence had marked out for me to set out on my journey from the land of heathenism, superstition, and vice, to a place where His Gospel is preached.

For some years, war had been carried on in my Eyo (Oyo) Country, which was always attended with much devastation and bloodshed; the women, such men as had surrendered or were caught, with the children, were taken captives. The enemies who carried on these wars were principally the Oyo Mahomedans, with whom my country abounds—with the Foulahs (Fulbe), and such foreign slaves had escaped from their owners, joined together, making a formidable force of about 20,000, who annoyed the whole country. They had no other employment but selling slaves to the Spaniards and Portuguese on the coast.

The morning in which my town, Ocho-gu (Osogun), shared the same fate which many other had experienced, was fair and delightful; and most of the inhabitants were engaged in their respective occupations. We were preparing breakfast without any apprehension, when about 9 o'clock A.M., a rumour was spread in the town, that the enemies had approached with intentions of hostility. It was not long after when they had almost surrounded the town, to prevent any escape of the inhabitants; the town being rudely fortified with a wooden fence, about four miles in circumference, containing about 12,000 inhabitants not being duly prepared, some not being at home; those who were having about six gates to defend, as well as many weak places about the fence to guard against, and, to say in a few words, the men being surprised, and therefore confounded—the enemies entered the town after about three hours' resistance. Here a most sorrowful scene imaginable was to be witnessed!—women, some with three, four, or six children clinging to their arms, with the infants on their backs, and such baggage as they could carry on their heads, running as fast as they could through prickly shrubs, which hooking their bliss and other loads, drew them down from the heads of the bearers. While they found it impossible to go along with their loads, they endeavoured only to save themselves and their children: even this was impracticable with those who had many children to care for. While they were endeavouring to disentangle themselves from the ropy shrubs, they were overtaken and caught by the enemies with a noose of rope thrown over the neck of every individual, to be led in the manner of goats tied together, under the drove of one man.

In many cases a family was violently divided between three or four enemies, who each led his away, to see one another no more. Your humble servant was thus caught—with his mother, two sisters, one an infant about ten months old, and a cousin—while endeavouring to escape in the manner above described. My load consisted in nothing else than my bow, and five arrows in the quiver; the bow I had lost in the shrub, while I was extricating myself, before I could think of making any use of it against my enemies. The last view I had of my father was when he came from the fight, to give us the signal to flee: he entered into our house, which was burnt some time back for some offence given by my father's adopted son. Hence I never saw him more.—Here I must take thy leave, unhappy, comfortless father!—I learned, some time afterward, that he was killed in another battle.

Our conquerors were Oyo Mahomedans, who led us away through the town. On our way, we met a man sadly wounded on the head, struggling between life and death. Before we got half way through the town, some Foulah (Fulbe), among the enemies themselves, hostilely separated my cousin! His mother was living in another village.

The town on fire—the houses being built with mud, some about twelve feet from the ground with high roofs, in square forms, of different dimensions and spacious areas: several of these belonged to one man, adjoined to, with passages communicating with each other. The flame was very high. We were led by my grandfather's house, already desolate; and in a few minutes after, left the town to the mercy of the flame, never to enter or see it any more. Farewell, place of my birth, the play-ground of my childhood, and the place which I thought would be the repository of my mortal body in its old age! We were now out of Osogun, going into a town called Isehi (Iseyin), the rendez-vous of the enemies, about twenty miles from our town. On the way we saw our grandmother at a distance, with about three or four of my other cousins taken with her, for a few minutes: she was missed through the crowd, to see her no more.

Source: *The Journal of Rev. James Frederick Schon and Mr. Samuel Crowther* (London: Hatchard and Son, 1842), 10–12.

HEINRICH BARTH

Al-Hajj Bashir and Kukawa, 1852

Heinrich Barth, a German, was one of the most respected 19th-century European explorers of Africa. A member of the British expedition to Sudan in 1850, Barth along with his colleagues crossed the Sahara and visited Kano, Katsina, and Kukawa, the capital of Bornu built by Shaykh al-Kanami in 1814 and destroyed by the sultan of Wadai in 1846. Barth also explored Lake Chad and the Benue River.

I have peculiar reason to thank providence for having averted the storm which was gathering over his head during my stay in Bornu, for my intimacy with him (al-Hajj Bashir) might very easily have involved me also in the calamities, which be-fell him. However, I repeat that altogether, he was a most excellent kind, liberal, and just man, and might have done much good to the country if he had been less selfish and more active. He was incapable, indeed, of executing by himself any act of severity, such as the unsettled state of a semi-barbarous kingdom may at times be necessary; and being conscious of his own mildness, he left all those matters to a man named Lamino, to whom I gave the title of "the shameless left hand of the vizier," and whom I shall have frequent occasion to mention.

I pressed upon the viziers the necessity of defending the northern frontier of Bornu against the Tawarck (Tuareg) by more effectual measures than had been then adopted, and this retrieving, for cultivation and the peaceable abode of his fellow subjects, the fine borders of the Komidugu, and restoring security to the road to Fezzan. Just about this time the Tawarek has made another expedition into the border districts on a large scale, so that Kashella Balal, the first of the war chiefs, was obliged to march against them; and the road to Kano which I, with my usual good luck, had passed unmolested, had become unsafe that a numerous cara-van was plundered, and a well-known Arab merchant, the Sherif el Ghali, killed.

I remonstrated with him on the shamefully-neglected state of the shores of the lake, which contained the finest pasture grounds, and might yield an immense quantity of rice and cotton. He entered with spirit into all my proposals, but in a short time all was forgotten. He listened with delight to what little historical knowledge I had of these countries, and inquired particularly whether Kanem had really been in former times a mighty kingdom, or whether it would be worth retaking. It was in consequence of these conversations that he began to take an interest in the former history of the country, and that the historical records of Edris Alawoma (Idris Alawma) came to light; but he would not allow me to take them into my hands, and I could only read over his shoulders. He was a very religious man; and though he admired Europeans very much on account of their greater accomplishments, he was shocked to think that they drank intoxicating liquors. However, I tried to console him by telling him that, although the Europeans were also very partial to the fair sex, yet they did not indulge in this luxury on so large scale as he did, and that therefore he ought to allow them some other little pleasure.

He was very well aware of the misery connected with the slave-trade; for, on his pilgrimage to Mekka, in the mountainous region between Fezzan and Ben-Ghazi, he had lost, in one night, forty of his slaves by the extreme cold, and he swore that he would never take slaves for sale if he were to travel again. But it was more difficult to make him sensible of the horrors of slave-hunting, although, when accompanying him on the expedition to Musgu, I and Mr. Overweg urged this subject with more success, as the further progress of my narrative will show. He was very desirous to open a commerce with the English, although he looked with extreme suspicion upon the form of articles in which the treaty was proposed to be drawn up; but he wished to forbid to Christians the sale of two things, viz, spirituous liquors, and Bibles. He did not object to Bibles being brought into the country, and even given as presents, but he would not allow of their being sold. . . .

Having now a horse whereon to mount, I rode every day, either into the eastern town to pay a visit to the sheikh or to the vizier, or roving around the whole circuit of the capital, and peeping into the varied scenes which the life of the people exhibited. The precincts of the town, with its suburbs, are just as interesting, as its neighborhood (especially during the months that precede the rainy season) is monotonous and tiresome in the extreme. Certainly the arrangement of the capital contributes a great deal to the variety of the picture which it forms, laid out as it is, in two distinct towns, each surrounded with its wall, the one occupied chiefly by the rich and wealthy, containing very large establishments, which the other, with the exception of the principal thoroughfare, which traverses the town from west to east, consists of rather crowded dwellings, with narrow, winding lanes. These two distinct towns are separated by a space about half a mile broad, itself thickly inhabited on both sides of a wide, open road, which forms the connection between them, but laid out less regularly, and presenting to the eye a most interesting medley of large clay buildings and small thatched huts, of massive clay walls surrounding immense yards, and light fences of reeds in a more or less advanced state of decay, and with a variety of color, according to their age, from the brightest yellow down to the deepest black. All around these two towns there are small villages or clusters of huts, and large detached farms surrounded with clay walls, low enough to allow a glimpse from horseback over the thatched huts which they inclose.

In this labyrinth of dwellings a man, interested in the many forms which human life presents, may rove about at any time of the day with the certainty of never failing amusement, although the life of the Kanuri people passes rather monotonously along, with the exception of some occasionally feasting. During the hot hours, indeed, the town and its precincts became torpid, except on market-days, when the market place itself, at least, and the road leading to it from the western gate, are most animated just at that time. For, singular, as it is, in kukawa, as well as almost all over this part of Negroland, the great markets do not begin to be well attended till the heat of the day grows intense; and it is curious to observe what a difference prevails in this, as well as in other respects, between these countries and Yoruba, where almost all the markets are held in the cool of the evening.

Source: Heinrich Barth, *Travels and Discoveries in North and Central Africa from the Journal of an Expedition Undertaken under the Auspices of H.B.M.'s Government in the Years 1849–1855* (Philadelphia: J. W. Bradley, 1859), 181–189.

ANN MARTIN HINDERER
Progress of Work, 1853

Ann Hinderer was among the few European women travelers and missionaries in 19th-century Africa. Born in Norfolk in 1827, she was the English wife of David Hinderer, a German missionary of the Church Missionary Society who was stationed in Ibadan in 1853. David opened a school for children as part of the broader Christian missionary work. In this portion of her diary and account of life in Ibadan, Ann detailed the reaction of the locals to their newly built home and its amenities.

Ibadan, May 14th [1854]: Yesterday I reached my loved Ibadan home amidst a hearty greeting from the dear boys. Laniyono, who was the most sorrowful when I left, gave a shriek of delight, and sprang into my arms, with his legs, round my waist, hanging there to his heart's content, shouting and making the oddest remarks you ever heard; that I was never to go away again, seemed to be a certainty to his mind. But a tinge of bitterness is generally mixed with every cup, so I found here. Two of my boys had been taken away by their parents in my absence: Adelotan is not allowed to appear anywhere, but Abudu came at once to see me. I put my hand on his shoulder, and he burst into a flood of tears. "O Iya, it is not me, it is not me, it is my father who has done it." Poor child! I could only soothe and calm him, and bid him be patient. I believe he will soon get leave from his father to come back.

Our new house, after all the toil in building it promises to possess all the comforts we could expect or desire in this country; it is water-tight! Has a good sized sitting and bed-room, white-washed walls, and a good iron roof; comfortable piazzas, and all very airy, and as cool as anything can be in Africa, which was my principal desire. It is wonderful what my dear husband has achieved in my absence, and now he rejoiced to have his wife in it, and so does she to be there. We pray that a rich blessing may be given us with it, and that though we have the comfort of dwelling, we may never forget that this is not our home, but a tent pitched for the day.

May 17th—Bale, the head chief, paid us a special visit to-day. He came in great state, with drums and various strange instruments of music, with his host of attendants, singing men and singing women. He marveled greatly at our house and could not imagine how it was made. He was quite alarmed to think of mounting the steps; but with my husband pulling, and other pushing, we got him up. I stood at the top to receive him, in his mass of silks and velvets; he very graciously took my hand, and we walked into the room, at the sight of which he gave a great shout and wondered; he then took a fancy to the sofa, and sat there. We admitted upstairs his wives, his eldest son, and a few of his great people, and then we obliged to move away the steps, or the house, strong as it is, must have broken down with the mass of people. We gave him, and those in the room with him, a little refreshment. English bread, biscuits, and a few raisins. They looked at the bedroom, and all the things in both rooms. Bale was extremely amused to see himself in the looking-glass. I took the women by themselves; the washing-stand attracted their attention, so I washed my hands to show them the use of it. My soap was wonderful; and that I wiped my hands after I had washed them, was a thing unheard of. But they took it into their heads to follow my example, and all the hands must touch the soap, and go into the water, and there was a fine splashing, and a pretty towel, for the indigo dye comes off their clothes so very much, that I believe the towel will be blue and white forever. At last we got into a state of composure again, and all being quiet, Mr. Hinderer made a little speech, telling Bale how glad we were to see him, why we built the house, and what brought us to his country.

May 22—A woman of about fifty years of age came to me. I noticed her in church, two or three Sundays before I went away, and again she was there yester-day. She brought with her a fowl, and corn to feed it with, and yams; she put them before me as a present, and said, "Iya, all my life I have served the devil; he has been my god; but he never gave me peace in my heart. My husband was stolen away by war, the devil did not help me; my children all died, the devil could not help me; but since you white people have come, I have heard the words of the Great God, which we never heard before, and they are sweet to me. I want to hear more, and to walk in the right road, for it has been a wrong road, for it has been a wrong road all my life." She has thrown her husband's images into the water. After our last words, "God bless you, and give you peace in your heart!" she uttered a most fervent and hearty "Amen." As it is the constant practice to take fowls, cow-ries, and other offerings to their gods, I thought it necessary to tell her we did not desire she should bring a "full hand" to us; she said she knew it, but begged we would accept her little present, to make her happy. I had a little chintz bag hanging up, with not a handful of cowries in it; she would not have had cowries as a pay-ment on any account, but the bag she could not refuse; such a possession she never thought to have, and she went off with it greatly delighted.

"Now dear friends, farewell; remember us in our work, our weakness and infirmities, bodily and mental, and may all your love, sympathy, and prayers be returned in tenfold measure in blessings on yourselves."

Source: Richard A. Hone, ed., *Seventeen Years in the Yoruba Country: Memorials of Anna Hinderer Gathered from Her Journals and Letters* (London: Seeley, Jackson and Halliday, 1883), 99–106.

MARY KINGSLEY
West and East Africa, 1893

Mary Kingsley made two trips to Africa, in 1893 and 1895. But unlike many travelers before and after her who were mostly interested in political matters and relations between European powers and African kings, Kingsley did trade with African communities in order to learn about local customs and cultures. Her writings are a useful addition to the scholarship on the ethnography of Africa in the 19th and 20th centuries.

On my return to Talagouga, I find both my good friends sick with fever—M. Forget very indeed. Providentially the *Eclaireur* came up the river, with the Doctor Administrator on board, and he came ashore and prescribed and in a few days M. Forget was better. I say good-bye to Talagouga with much regret, and go on board the *Eclaireur,* when she returns from Njole, with all my bottles and belongings. On board I find no other passenger; the captain's English has widened out considerably; and he is as pleasant, cheery, and spoiling for a fight as ever; but he has a preoccupied manner, and a most peculiar set of new habits, which I find are shared by the engineer. Both of them make rapid dashes to the rail, and nervously scanned the river for a minute and then return to some occupation, only to dash from it to the rail again. During breakfast their conduct is nerve-shaking.

Hastily taking a few mouthfuls, the captain drops his knife and fork and simply hurls his seamanlike form through the nearest door out on to the deck. In another minute he is back again, and with just a shake of his head to the engineer, continues his meal. The engineer shortly afterwards flies from his seat, and being far thinner than the captain, goes through his nearest door with even greater rapidity; returns, and shakes his head at the captain, and continues his meal. Excitement of this kind is infectious, and I also wonder whether I ought not to show a sympathetic friendliness by flying from my seat and hurling myself on to the deck through my nearest door, too. But although there are plenty of doors, as four enter the saloon from the deck, I do not see my way to doing this performance aimlessly, and what in this world they are both after I cannot think. So I confine myself to woman's true sphere and assist in a humble way by catching the wine and Vichy water bottles, glasses, and plates of food, which at every performance are jeopardized by the members of the nobler sex starting off with a considerable quantity of the ample table cloth wrapped round their legs. At last I can stand it no longer, so ask the captain point-blank what is the matter. "Nothing," says he, bounding out of his chair and flying out of his doorway; but on his return he tells me he has got a bet on of two bottles of champagne with Woermann's agent for Njole, as to who shall reach Lembarene first, and the German agent had started off some time before the *Eclaireur* in his little steam launch.

During the afternoon we run smoothly along; the free pulsations of the engines telling what a very different thing coming down the Ogowe is to going up against its terrific current. Every now and again we stop to pick up cargo, or discharge over-carried cargo, and the captain's mind becomes lulled by getting no news of the Woermann's launch having passed down. He communicates this to the engineer; it is impossible she could have passed the *Eclaireur* since they started, therefore she must be somewhere behind at a subfactory, "*N' est-ce pas?*" "*Oui, Oui, certainement,*" says the engineer. The engineer is, by these considerations, also lulled, and feels he may do something else but scan the river *à la* sister Ann. What that something is puzzles me; it evidently requires secrecy, and he shrinks from detection. First he looks down one side of the deck, no one there; good so far. I then see he has put his head through one of the saloon potholes; no one there; he hesitates a few seconds until I begin to wonder whether his head will suddenly appear through port; but he regards this as an unnecessary precaution, and I hear him enter his cabin which abuts on mine and there is silence for some minutes. Writing home to his mother, think I, as I go on putting a new braid round the bottom of a worn skirt. Almost immediately after follows the sound of a little click from the next cabin, and then apparently one of the denizens of the infernal regions has got its tail smashed in a door and the heavy hot afternoon air is reft by an inchoate howl of agony. I drop my needlework and take to the deck; but it is after all only that shy retiring young man practicing secretly on his clarionet.

The captain is drowsily looking down the river. But repose is not long allowed to that active spirit; he sees something in the water—what? "*Hippopotame,*" he ejaculates. Now both he and the engineer frequently do this thing, and then fly off to their guns—bang, bang, finish; but this time he does not dash for his gun, nor does the engineer, who flies out of his cabin at the sound of the war shout. "*Hippopotame.*" In vain I look across the broad river with its stretches of yellow sandbanks, where the "*hippopotame*" should be, but I can see nothing but four black stumps sticking up in the water away to the right. Meanwhile the captain and the engineer are flying about getting off a crew of blacks into the canoe we are towing alongside. This being done the captain explains to me that on the voyage up "the engineer had fired at, and hit a hippopotamus, and without doubt this was its body floating." We are now close enough even for me to recognize the four stumps as the deceased legs, and soon the canoe is alongside them and makes fast to one, and then starts to paddle back, hippo and all, to the *Eclaireur.* But no such thing; let them paddle and shout as hard as they like, the hippo's weight simply anchors them. The *Eclaireur* by now has dropped down the river past them, and has to sweep round and run back.

Source: Mary Kingsley, *Travels in West Africa* (London: Macmillan, 1897), 101–123.

MARY HALL

Usumbora to Kanyinya, 1905–1906

*Mary Hall was among the few European women travelers of Africa before the out-
break of World War I in 1914. She made two visits, first in 1904 to Southern Africa
and another in 1905–1906 to East Africa. Her account touched on relations with
African interpreters and carriers, natural environment, and friendly reception from
locals.*

My caravan, numbering forty-two, got into line towards noon on October 9th. After
some kindly words of encouragement and good wishes from the German officers,
I was carried off in my machila (hammock), catching a last glimpse of my hospitable friends and hosts waving farewells from the little outlook at the angle of the
Boma wall. The excitement of the start was enhanced by the thunder rumbling
in the distance and the black clouds which looked ready to drench us at any
moment.

The porters were followed for some distance by their relatives and friends, some
of them, as a last little attention to their chums, carrying the machila and loads for a
time, until I wondered whether, or not, the whole village was coming with me. But
the degrees they dwindled away, and a certain account of quiet ensued.

We made across country to the hills, which we began to ascend, and in about
three hours pitched camp for the night. Round about my tent every four or five men
built for themselves a charming little circular hut of interlaced grasses and reeds,
thickly thatched with banana leaves. I expressed my regret to Mike (one of the interpreters) that it was too late to take a photograph, but he told me that it was of no
consequence as they would build similar huts every day. My other men had never
put up any kind of shelter, but always lay in the open, round the fires.

Towards evening I strolled to a small hill close by, whence I obtained a perfect
view of the lake beneath, and the valley left by its receding waters. It was a glorious
view, and I turned from it regretfully, thinking it was the last I should see of
Tanganyinka, but in this I was mistaken, as the following day I got several beautiful
vistas as we ascended the heights.

When I returned to camp I found the men were busy doing up my bundles of
salt, to prevent them getting wet. They are very ingenious and handy when they
like. They had cut the dry stem of a banana plant and split it open, placing the
bundle in the centre; then they drew up the strips of think bark round it, and tied the
whole together with strong fibre. It was a most satisfactory covering, and would
resist any moisture.

I went to bed fully imbued with the idea that I should wake in the morning to
find most of the men had deserted. Maffi also seemed suspicious of things in general, and neither of us slept very soundly. However, daylight revealed the full com-
plement of porters, and I felt happier. The sun was overcast, but that kept the
temperature cooler. These carriers had never seen a machila before, so were quite
new to the work; consequently they went very slowly, and instead of my being in

advance of the loads, as I had always been across the Tanganyinka Plateau, we all kept together.

Later on, when we were doubtful as to the route, and might easily have gone astray if separated, it proved to be the best possible arrangement. One of the askari walked in front of the procession and one on the rear. The road as far as it reaches—about five to six hours' journey from the lake—is excellent, and broad enough for any army of soldiers to march along comfortably, eight or nine abreast.

We travelled uphill all day, looking down upon banana groves and well-tended gardens in the valleys beneath us. The produce of these gardens is taken to the noisy market at Usumbora. About nine o'clock we came to the end of the engineered road. Hundreds of natives were at work on it with quaint little short-handled hoes, breaking up the earth and collecting it in small baskets to be distributed where needed for levelling purposes. The soil is of a bright red colour and forms a delightful contrast to the vivid green of the hills around.

While I was enjoying the prospect the porters had put down their loads, and most of them having found acquaintances among the road-makers, were telling them of the hopes and fears they entertained as to the hundred and one things which might happen before they met again, and of the wonders of the new calico and drapery they would being back in triumph. I think the fact of their being members of a party to take a European women so far, made them, in the eyes of their companions, men to be looked up to.

We continued our way along a very narrow track, which was very much more to my taste than the high-road we had just quitted. We had not gone far when the daily thunderstorm, which we had eluded the morning before, burst upon us, and in a moment we were in the midst of torrential rain. It was a funny, albeit mournful, sight to see the men, like drowned rats, literally drenched to the skin, which is about all they had on. I was fairly well protected in my machila, but rugs and pillows would not be kept within bounds and soon became very wet. As at night they formed part of my bedding. I was filled with unpleasant anticipations of an uncomfortable night with a severe cold to follow.

The tent was already pitched when I arrived in camp, but everything was wet and uncomfortable, so we set to work and dried what we could at the fires the men had made, and I luckily thought of my hot-water bottle, which was filled and used like a warming-pan to air my bed. About midnight I awoke to find another heavy storm in progress, but I was then safely under cover, and hugging the clothes about me, soon fell asleep again.

After a storm everything is wet and more difficult to pack, and in consequence it was nearly seven next morning before we were on our way again. This was not so serious as it would have been a few days before: ever since we left Usumbora we had been steadily rising until we were now nearly on the top of the plateau, where the temperature was considerably lower, and there was not the same necessity to get to camp early, as even at mid-day it was not too hot.

Source: Mary Hall, *A Woman's Trek from the Cape to Cairo* (London: Methuen, 1907), 106–131.

Further Reading

Abimbola, Wande. *Sixteen Great Poems of Ifa.* Paris: UNESCO, 1975.

Abubakar, Sa'ad. *The Lāmībe of Fombina: A Political History of Adamawa, 1809–1901.* Zaria: Ahmadu Bello University Press, 1977.

Abubakar, Sa'ad. "Queen Amina of Zaria." In *Nigerian Women in Historical Perspective,* edited by Bolanle Awe, 13–23. Lagos: Sankore, 1992.

Abun-Nasr, Jamil M. *A History of the Maghrib in the Islam Period.* Cambridge: Cambridge University Press, 1987.

Adams, William Y. *Nubia: Corridor to Africa.* Princeton, NJ: Princeton University Press, 1977.

Adediran, Biodun. *The Frontier States of Western Yorubaland, 1600–1889.* Ibadan: IFRA, 1994.

Adekunle, Julius. "Education." In *Africa,* Vol. 2, *African Cultures and Societies before 1885,* edited by Toyin Falola, 59–72. Durham, NC: Carolina Academic Press, 2000.

Adeleye, R. A. *Power and Diplomacy in Northern Nigeria, 1804–1906: The Sokoto Caliphate and Its Enemies.* Ibadan: Oxford University Press, 1971.

Aderinto, Saheed. "Crime and Punishment in Africa." In *Encyclopedia of Society and Culture in the Ancient World,* Vol. 1, edited by Peter Bogucki, 296–297. New York: Facts on File, 2008.

Aderinto, Saheed. "European Invasion and African Resistance." In *Africa and the Wider World,* edited by Hakeem Ibikunle Tijani, Tiffany Jones, and Raphael Njoku, 247–261. Boston: Pearson, 2010.

Aderinto, Saheed. *Guns and Society in Colonial Nigeria: Firearms, Culture, and Public Order.* Bloomington: Indiana University Press, 2018.

Aderinto, Saheed. "'Ijebu a b'eyan . . . ?' [Ijebu or a Human Being . . . ?]: Nineteenth Century Origin of Discrimination against Ijebu Strangers in Colonial Ibadan, Nigeria." In *Minorities and the State in Africa,* edited by Chima J. Korieh and Michael Mbanaso, 143–168. Amherst: Cambria, 2010.

Aderinto, Saheed. "Law and Legal Codes in Africa." In *Encyclopedia of Society and Culture in the Ancient World,* Vol. 4, edited by Peter Bogucki, 621–622. New York: Facts on File, 2008.

Aderinto, Saheed. *When Sex Threatened the State: Illicit Sexuality, Nationalism, and Politics in Colonial Nigeria, 1900–1958.* Urbana: University of Illinois Press, 2015.

Agiri, B. A. "A Reconsideration of the Chronology of Ogbomoso History before the Colonial Period." *Odu* 15 (1977): 19–29.

Agiri, B. A. "When Was Ogbomoso Founded?" *Transafrican Journal of History* 5(1) (1976): 32–51.

Ajayi, J. F. A. *Christian Missions in Nigeria, 1841–1891: The Making of a New Elite.* Evanston, IL: Northwestern University Press, 1965.

Ajayi, J. F. A. "Colonialism: An Episode in African History." In *Colonialism in Africa, 1870–1960,* Vol. 1. edited by L. H. Gann and Peter Duignan, 497–509. Cambridge: Cambridge University Press, 1969.

Akinjogbin, A. I. *Dahomey and Its Neighbors, 1708–1818.* Cambridge: Cambridge University Press, 1967.

Akinjogbin, A. I., ed. *The Cradle of a Race: Ile-Ife from the Beginning to 1980.* Port Harcourt, Nigeria: Sunray Publications, 1992.

Atanda, J. A. *The New Oyo Empire: Indirect Rule and Change in Western Nigeria, 1894–1934.* London: Longman, 1973.

Awe, Bolanle. "The Iyalode in the Traditional Yoruba Political System." In *Sexual Stratification: A Cross Cultural View,* edited by Alice Schlegel, 144–160. New York: Columbia University Press, 1977.

Awolalu, J. Omosade, and P. Adelumo Dopamu. *West African Traditional Religion.* Ibadan: Onibonoje, 1979.

Ayele, Bekerie. *Ethiopic, an African Writing System: Its History and Principles.* Lawrenceville, NJ: Red Sea, 1997.

Balogun, Ismail. *The Life and Works of Uthman dan Fodio.* Sokoto: Islamic Publication Bureau, 1975.

Barry, Boubacar. *Senegambia and the African Slave Trade.* New York: Cambridge University Press, 1998.

Bascom, William. *Ifa Divination: Communication between Gods and the Men in West Africa.* Bloomington: Indiana University Press, 1991.

Bay, Edna G. *Wives of the Leopard: Gender, Politics, and Culture in the Kingdom of Dahomey.* Charlottesville: University of Virginia Press, 1998.

Beach, D. N. *The Shona and Their Neighbours.* Oxford, UK: Blackwell, 1994.

Berman, Edward H. *African Reactions to Missionary Education.* New York: Teachers College Press, 1975.

Birmingham, David. *Trade and Conflict in Angola: The Mbundu and Their Neighbours under the Influence of the Portuguese, 1483–1790.* Oxford, UK: Clarendon, 1966.

Bobboyi, Hamid. *Adamawa Emirate 1901–1965: A Documentary Source Book.* Abuja, Nigeria: Centre for Regional Integration, 2009.

Bonnet, Charles, and Dominique Valbelle. *The Nubian Pharaohs: Black Kings on the Nile.* New York: American University in Cairo Press, 2007.

Bovill, E. W. *The Golden Trade of the Moors.* London: Oxford University Press, 1958.

Brett, Michael, and Elizabeth Fentress. *The Berbers.* Oxford, UK: Blackwell, 1997.

Bulimo, Shadrack Amakoye. *Luyia Nation: Origins, Clans and Taboos.* Bloomington, IN: Trafford Publishing, 2013.

Burstein, Stanley. *Ancient Civilizations: Kush and Axum.* Princeton, NJ: Markus Publishers, 1998.

Chilver, E. M., and P. M. Kaberry. *Traditional Bamenda: The Pre-Colonial History and Ethnography of the Bamenda Grassfields.* Buea, Cameroon: National Government Publication, 1967.

Chittick, H. Neville. *Kilwa: An Islamic Trading City on the East African Coast.* Nairobi, Kenya: British Institute in Eastern Africa, 1974.

Cohen, David W. *The Historical Tradition of Busoga: Mukama and Kintu.* Oxford, UK: Clarendon, 1972.

Connah, Graham. *African Civilizations: An Archaeological Perspective.* 2nd ed. Cambridge: Cambridge University Press, 2001.

Connah, Graham. *Forgotten Africa: An Introduction to Its Archaeology.* London: Routledge, 2004.

Curtin, Philip. *The Image of Africa: British Ideas and Action, 1780–1850.* Madison: University of Wisconsin Press, 1964.

Davidson, Basil. *Africa in History: Themes and Outlines.* New York: Touchstone Books, 1966.

Davidson, Basil. *African Kingdoms.* New York: Time-Life Books, 1966.

Denzer, LaRay. "The Iyalode in Ibadan Politics and Society: A Preliminary Study." In *Ibadan: An Historical, Cultural, and Socio-Economic Study of an African City,* edited by G. O. Ogunremi, 201–234. Lagos: Cargo Press and Oluyole Club, 2000.

Diop, Cheikh Anta. *The African Origins of Civilization: Myth or Reality.* Translated by Mercer Cook. New York: Lawrence Hill, 1974.

Edgerton, Robert B. *The Fall of the Asante Empire: The Hundred-Year War for Africa's Gold Coast.* New York: Free Press, 1995.

Egharevba, J. U. *A Short History of Benin.* Ibadan: Ibadan University Press, 1968.

El Hour, Rachid. "The Andalusian Qadi in the Almoraivd Period: Political and Judicial Authority." *Studia Islamica,* no. 90 (2000): 67–83.

Fajana, Adewunmi. *Education in Nigeria, 1842–1939: An Historical Analysis.* London: Longman, 1978.

Fallers, Lloyd A. *Bantu Bureaucracy: A Century of Political Evolution among the Basoga of Uganda.* Chicago: University of Chicago Press, 1965.

Falola, Toyin. *Key Events in African History: A Reference Guide.* Westport, CT: Greenwood Press, 2002.

Falola, Toyin, ed. *Africa,* Vol. 1, *African History before 1885.* Durham, NC: Carolina Academic Press, 2000.

Falola, Toyin, ed. *Africa,* Vol. 2, *African Cultures and Societies before 1885.* Durham, NC: Carolina Academic Press, 2000.

Falola, Toyin, and Saheed Aderinto. *Nigeria, Nationalism, and Writing History.* Rochester, NY: University of Rochester Press, 2010.

Fentress, Elizabeth W. B. *Numidia and the Roman Army: Social, Military and Economic Aspects of the Frontier Zone.* Oxford, UK: BAR, 1979.

Fletcher, Madeleine. "The Almohad Tawhid: Theology Which Relies on Logic." *Numen* 38(1) (June 1991): 110–127.

Gomez, Michael A. *Pragmatisms in the Age of Jihad: The Precolonial State of Bundu.* Cambridge: Cambridge University Press, 1992.

Griaule, Marcel. *Conversations with Ogotemmeli: An Introduction to Dogon Religious Ideas.* London: Oxford University Press, 1965.

Grzymski, K. A. "Recent Research at the Palaces and Temples of Meroe: A Contribution to the Study of Meroitic Civilization." In *Between the Cataracts, Part I,* edited by W. Godlewski and A. Lajtar, 227–238. Warsaw: Wydawnictwa Uniwersytetu Warszawskiego, 2008.

Hamilton, Carolyn. *Terrific Majesty: The Powers of Shaka Zulu and the Limits of Historical Invention.* Cambridge, MA: Harvard University Press, 1998.

Harris, Joseph E. *Africans and Their History.* New York: Penguin, 1987.

Henze, Paul B. *Layers of Time: A History of Ethiopia.* New York: Palgrave Macmillan, 2004.

Heywood, Linda M., and John K. Thornton. *Central Africans, Atlantic Creoles, and the Foundation of the Americas, 1585–1660.* Cambridge: Cambridge University Press, 2007.

Hiribarren, Vincent. *A History of Borno: Trans-Saharan African Empire to Failing Nigerian State.* London: Hurst and Oxford University Press, 2017.

Holt, Peter Malcolm, ed. *The Sudan of the Three Niles: The Funj Chronicle.* Boston: Brill, 1999.

Horton, Mark, and John Middleton. *The Swahili: The Social Landscape of a Mercantile Society.* Oxford, UK: Blackwell, 2000.

Huffman, T. N. "Mapungubwe and Great Zimbabwe: The Origin and Spread of Social Complexity in Southern Africa." *Journal of Anthropological Archaeology* 28(1) (2009): 37–54.

Idowu, E. Bolaji. *Olodumare: God in Yoruba Belief.* London: Longman, 1962.

Isaacman, Allen F. *Mozambique: The Africanization of a European Institution; The Zambesi Prazos, 1750–1902.* Madison: University of Wisconsin Press, 1972.

Jackson, John G. *African Civilization.* New York: University Books, 1970.

Jackson, Robert B. *At Empire's Edge: Exploring Rome's Egyptian Frontier.* New Haven, CT: Yale University Press, 2002.

Jemkur, J. F. *Aspects of the Nok Culture.* Zaria: Ahmadu Bello University Press, 1992.

Johnson, Samuel. *The History of the Yorubas: From the Earliest Times to the Beginning of the British Protectorate.* 1921; reprint, London: Routledge/Kegan Paul, 1966.

Karugire, Samwiri R. *A History of the Kingdom of Nkore in Western Uganda to 1896.* Kampala, Uganda: Fountain Publishers, 2008.

Kirk-Greene, Anthony. *Adamawa, Past and Present: An Historical Approach to the Development of a Northern Cameroons Province.* Oxford: Oxford University Press, 1958.

Kopytoff, Jean H. *Preface to Modern Nigeria: The "Sierra Leonians" in Yoruba, 1830–1890.* Madison: University of Wisconsin Press, 1965.

Kyles, Perry. "The African Origin of Humanity." In *Africa and the Wider World,* edited by Hakeem Ibikunle Tijani, Raphael Chijioke Njoku, and Tiffany Fawn Jones, 28–40. New York: Learning Solutions, 2010.

Lancel, Serge. *Carthage: A History.* Oxford, UK: Blackwell, 1995.

Last, D. M. *The Sokoto Caliphate.* New York: Humanities Press, 1967.

Law, Robin. *Ouidah: The Social History of a West African Slaving Port, 1727–1892.* Athens: Ohio University Press, 2004.

Law, Robin. *The Oyo Empire, c. 1600–c. 1836: A West African Imperialism in the Era of the Atlantic Slave Trade.* Oxford, UK: Clarendon, 1977.

Law, Robin. *The Slave Coast of West Africa, 1550–1750: The Impact of the Atlantic Slave Trade on an African Society.* Oxford, UK: Clarendon, 1991.

Mack, Beverly B., and Jean Boyd. *One Woman's Jihad: Nana Asma'u, Scholar and Scribe.* Bloomington: Indiana University Press, 2000.

Mair, Lucy. *African Kingdoms.* Oxford, UK: Clarendon, 1977.

Mann, Kristin. *Slavery and the Birth of an African City: Lagos, 1760–1900.* Bloomington: Indiana University Press, 2007.

Masonen, P. *The Negroland Revisited: Discovery and Invention of Sudanese Middle Ages.* Helsinki: Finnish Academy of Science and Letters, 2000.

Mazrui, Ali. *The Africans: A Triple Heritage.* Boston: Little, Brown, 1986.

McCaskie, T. C. "Denkyira in the Making of Asante, 1660–1720." *Journal of African History* 48(1) (2007): 1–25.

Miller, Joseph C. *Kings and Kinsmen: Early Mbundu States in Angola.* London: Oxford University Press, 1976.

Moon, Karen. *Kilwa Kisiwani: Ancient Port City of the East African Coast.* Dar es Salaam: Tanzania Printers, Ministry of Natural Resources and Tourism, Tanzania, 2005.

Mulira, J. G. "A History of the Mahi Peoples from 1774 to 1920." PhD dissertation, UCLA, 1984.

Munro-Hay, S. C. *Aksum: An African Civilisation of Late Antiquity.* Edinburgh, UK: Edinburgh University Press, 1991.

Naylor, Phillip C. *North Africa: A History from Antiquity to the Present.* Austin: University of Texas Press, 2009.

Newitt, Malyn D. D. "The Early History of the Maravi." *Journal of African History* 23(2) (1982): 145–162.

Niane, D. T. *Sundiata: An Epic of Old Mali.* Translated by G. D. Pickett. London: Longman, 1965.

Nurse, Derek, and Thomas Spear. *The Swahili: Reconstructing the History and Language of an African Society, 800–1500.* Philadelphia: University of Pennsylvania Press, 1985.

O'Connor, Kathleen. "Talking to Gods: Divination Systems." In *Africa,* Vol. 2, *African Cultures and Societies before 1885,* edited by Toyin Falola, 95–105. Durham, NC: Carolina Academic Press, 2000.

O'Fahey, R. S. *The Darfur Sultanate: A History.* New York: Columbia University Press, 2008.

Olajubu, Oyeronke. *Women in the Yoruba Religious Sphere.* Albany: State University of New York Press, 2003.

Oliver, Roland, and Anthony Atmore. *Medieval Africa, 1250–1800.* Cambridge: Cambridge University Press, 2001.

Oloruntimehin, B. O. *The Segu Tukulor Empire.* London: Longman, 1972.

Onwukwe, S. O. *Rise and Fall of the Arochukwu Empire, 1400–1902.* Enugu, Nigeria: Fourth Dimension Publishing, 1995.

Osborn, Emily Lynn. *Our New Husbands Are Here: Households, Gender, and Politics in a West African State from the Slave Trade to Colonial Rule.* Athens: Ohio University Press, 2011.

Phiri, Kings M. "Northern Zambezia: From 1500 to 1800." *Society of Malawi Journal* 32(1) (1979): 6–22.

Phiri, Kings M. "Pre-Colonial States of Central Malawi: Towards a Reconstruction of Their History." *Society of Malawi Journal* 41(1) (1988): 1–29.

Pikirayi, Innocent. *The Zimbabwe Culture: Origins and Decline in Southern Zambezian States.* Walnut Creek, CA: AltaMira, 2001.

Reid, R. *Political Power in Pre-Colonial Buganda: Economy, Society and Welfare in the Nineteenth Century*. Oxford, UK: James Currey, 2002.

Robinson, David. *Chiefs and Clerics: Abdul Bokan Kan and Futa Toro, 1853–1891*. London: Oxford University Press, 1975.

Roller, Duane W. *The World of Juba II and Kleopatra Selene: Royal Scholarship on Rome's African Frontier*. New York: Routledge, 2003.

Ross, David. "Robert Norris, Agaja, and the Dahomean Conquest of Allada and Whydah." *History in Africa* 16 (1989): 311–324.

Ruffini, Giovanni R. *Medieval Nubia: A Social and Economic History*. New York: Oxford University Press, 2012.

Ryder, A. F. C. *Benin and the Europeans, 1485–1897*. London: Longman, 1977.

Scanlon, David D., ed. *Church, State, and Education in Africa*. New York: Teachers College Press, 1966.

Schoffeleers, J. Matthew. "The Zimba and the Lundu State in the Late Sixteenth and Early Seventeenth Century." *Journal of African History* 28(3) (1987): 337–355.

Shillington, Kevin. *History of Africa*. New York: Palgrave Macmillan, 2005.

Smaldone, Joseph P. *Warfare in the Sokoto Caliphate: Historical and Sociological Perspectives*. Cambridge: Cambridge University Press, 1977.

Smith, Robert S. *Kingdoms of the Yoruba*. London: Methuen, 1969.

Strouhal, Eugen. *Life in Ancient Egypt*. Norman: University of Oklahoma Press, 1989.

Thompson, Leonard. *Survival in Two Worlds: Moshoeshoe of Lesotho, 1786–1870*. New York: Oxford University Press, 1976.

Thornton, K. John. *The Kingdom of Kongo: Civil War and Transition 1641–1718*. Madison: University of Wisconsin Press, 1983.

Tishken, Joel. "Indigenous Religions." In *Africa*, Vol. 2, *African Cultures and Societies before 1885*, edited by Toyin Falola, 73–94. Durham, NC: Carolina Academic Press, 2000.

Ukwedeh, J. N. *History of Igala Kingdom, 1534–1854*. Zaria: Ahmadu Bello University Press, 2003.

Vansina, J. *The Children of Woot: A History of the Kuba Peoples*. Madison: University of Wisconsin Press, 1978.

Vansina, J. *Kingdoms of the Savanna: A History of Central African States until European Occupation*. Madison: University of Wisconsin Press, 1968.

Vansina, J. *Oral Tradition as History*. London: James Currey, 1985.

Webster, J. B. *The African Churches among the Yoruba, 1888–1922*. London: Clarendon, 1964.

Welsby, Derek. *The Kingdom of Kush: The Napatan and Meroitic Empires.* Princeton, NJ: Markus Wiener, 1998.

Welsby, Derek. *The Medieval Kingdoms of Nubia: Pagans, Christians and Muslims in the Middle Nile.* London: British Museum, 2002.

Wilks, Ivor. *Asante in the Nineteenth Century: The Structure and Evolution of a Political Order.* Cambridge University Press, 1975.

Wilks, Ivor. *Forests of Gold: Essays on the Akan and the Kingdom of Asante.* Athens: Ohio University Press, 1993.

About the Editor and the Contributors

Editor

Saheed Aderinto is an associate professor of history at Western Carolina University. He has authored or edited six books, including *When Sex Threatened the State: Illicit Sexuality, Nationalism, and Politics in Colonial Nigeria, 1900–1958* (University of Illinois Press, 2015). In addition, his works have appeared in leading Africanist and specialist journals such as the *Canadian Journal of African Studies,* the *Journal of the History of Sexuality,* the *Journal of Colonialism and Colonial History, History in Africa: A Journal of Method, Frontiers: A Journal of Women's Studies, Africa: The Journal of the International African Institute,* the *Journal of Social History,* and the *Journal of the History of Childhood and Youth,* among others.

Contributors

Kabir Abdulkareem is a PhD candidate in history at the University of KwaZulu–Natal, South Africa. His article on the impact of Islam in precolonial West Africa has appeared in the *Journal of the Students' Historical Society of Nigeria.*

Lady Jane Acquah is a doctoral candidate at the University of Texas at Austin. Her research interests are Islamic developments in Ghana, West Africa, and Africa; gender issues in the Muslim world; and African American Islam. Acquah has published book reviews, encyclopedia entries, and a book chapter on African history, cultures, Islam, and colonialism.

Peter Damilola Adegoke is a research associate and digital technologies specialist at the African Leadership Centre, King's College London. He was a visiting research fellow in the Department of Political Science and Public Administration, University of Buea, Cameroon, where he taught foreign policy analysis and Africa in international relations. Adegoke coauthored the essay "Actor-Network Theory" in A. O. Olutayo and O. and Akanle, eds., *Sociological Theory for African Students* (2013).

Odunyemi Oluseyi Agbelusi is a recent masters graduate in conservation studies from the University College London in Qatar (UCL Qatar) and holds a BA in archaeology from the University of Ibadan, Nigeria. His research interests include historical archaeology, archaeological pedagogy, cultural heritage law, and conservation of archaeological materials, sites, and monuments. Agbelusi has published in a number of international journals such as *Anistoriton,* the *West African Journal of Archaeology, Dig It,* and *Archaeologies.*

Tosin Akinjobi-Babatunde teaches European history, diplomatic and consular law, and international relations and diplomacy at Elizade University, Nigeria. Her articles have appeared in such journals as the *African Security Review.*

Shina Alimi teaches history at Obafemi Awolowo University, Nigeria, where he obtained his BA, MPhil, and PhD in history. He has participated in different conferences and published in various reputable journals. Alimi's articles include "The Nigerian Press and Challenges of Private Newspaper Ownership: A Study of the Nigerian Tribune," *Journal of African Media Studies* 4(3) (2012).

Cyrelene Amoah-Boampong is a lecturer of history at the University of Ghana. She teaches courses on African history, historical methodology, the black diaspora, and gender studies. Amoah-Boampong has published a book chapter on women during the Nkrumah era and articles in such journals as *History in Action* and the *Legon Journal of International Affairs and Diplomacy.*

Nana-Akua Amponsah has a PhD in African history and currently teaches African and global history at the University of North Carolina–Wilmington. Her books include *Women's Roles in Sub-Saharan Africa* and *Women, Gender and Sexualities in Africa.* Amponsah's current book project, titled *The Reproductive Body and Biomedical Politics in British West Africa,* examines the introduction and implications of Western biomedical practices on African reproductive practices in colonial British West Africa.

Morenikeji Asaaju is an assistant lecturer in the Department of History at Obafemi Awolowo University, Ile-Ife, Nigeria, where she teaches courses in African history and world history. Asaaju is also a doctoral student at the Bayreuth International Graduate School of African Studies, University of Bayreuth, Germany. Her research interests are women, gender, contemporary, and social history.

Tokunbo A. Ayoola teaches African history, African diaspora history, and global history and politics at Elizade University, Nigeria. His scholarly writings have appeared in edited volumes and international journals, including the *West African Review,* the *Journal of Retracing Africa,* the *Lagos Historical Review,* the *Business History Review, Lagos Notes and Records, Ofo: Journal of Transatlantic Studies,* and the *Journal of History and Diplomatic Studies,* among others.

Abidemi Babatunde Babalola received his PhD from Rice University, Texas. He is the 2016–2017 McMillan-Stewart Fellow at the W. E. B. Du Bois Institute, Hutchins

Center for African and African American Research, Harvard University. Babalola is an African archaeologist and has conducted archaeological investigations in Nigeria, Tanzania, and the United States. His areas of interest include early technologies and technological change, urbanism, African arts, Atlantic Africa, African and African diaspora studies, and cultural heritage. Babalola's works have appeared or are forthcoming in specialist journals such as *Antiquity,* the *Journal of African Archaeology,* and the *Journal of Archaeological Science.* He is currently completing a book manuscript titled *Craft Production in Early West Africa: Archaeological and Historical Perspectives on Glass Making in Ile-Ife, Nigeria, 1000–1500 CE.*

Waseem-Ahmed Bin-Kasim is a PhD history candidate at Washington University in St. Louis. His PhD dissertation focuses on sanitary segregation in colonial Accra and Nairobi. Bin-Kasim is currently developing a course on cities in 20th-century Africa.

Anna Lucille Boozer is an assistant professor of Roman Mediterranean archaeology and ancient history at Baruch College, City University of New York. At Baruch, she teaches courses in ancient Egypt and Nubia, the Roman Empire, global ancient empires, and ancient world history. Boozer's monograph *A Late Romano-Egyptian House in the Dakhla Oasis: Amheida House B2* (2015) offers a material ethnography of a Romano-Egyptian house and a comprehensive analysis of the objects, texts, and organic materials that were found within it. Her articles have appeared in such journals as the *American Journal of Archaeology,* The *Journal of Mediterranean Archaeology,* and *Ancient West & East.*

Gérard L. Chouin is an associate professor of African history at the College of William & Mary, where he teaches and researches medieval to modern histories of Africa. He also is the founder and codirector of the Ife-Sungbo Archaeological Project. Chouin's last book focused on 17th-century Atlantic Africa. He is also the author of a number of book chapters and articles on West Africa published in edited volumes and international journals, including the *Journal of African History, History in Africa, Afriques, Afrique contemporaine* and *Afrique, Archéologie et Arts.*

Dawne Y. Curry is an associate professor of history and ethnic studies at the University of Nebraska, where she teaches courses in African history, oral history, and African studies. Her book *Apartheid on a Black Isle: Removal and Resistance in Alexandra, South Africa,* was published by Palgrave Macmillan in 2012, and her articles have appeared in *Safundi: A Journal of South African and American Studies* and the *International Journal of Interdisciplinary Social Sciences.*

Adrian M. Deese is a PhD candidate in divinity at the University of Cambridge, where he studies world Christianity and precolonial Yoruba Christian literature. He is writing a dissertation on Christian writers from Abeokuta that examines how they negotiated the town's dynamic monarchical politics. Deese is interested in the relationship of religion and kingship in West Africa. At Cornell University, he wrote a thesis titled "Making Sense of the Past: Ajayi KọláwọlẹAjíṣafẹ and the (Re)-Making of Modern Abeokuta (Nigeria)" (2013).

Alioune Dème received his PhD in anthropology from Rice University. He is currently an assistant professor of archaeology in the Department of History, Cheikh Anta Diop University. Dème teaches courses in African history, African archaeology, and global comparative archaeology. His article titled "Excavations at Walalde: New Light on the Settlement of the Middle Senegal Valley by Iron-Using Peoples," coauthored with Susan McIntosh, appeared in the *Journal of African Archaeology.*

Carla De Ycaza is an adjunct assistant professor at New York University, where she teaches courses on African civil wars, transitional justice, international criminal law, genocide, torture, human rights, and international relations. She has published in *Ufahamu: A Journal of African Studies,* the *Human Rights Review, Societies without Borders,* the *International Studies Review,* the *African Journal of Conflict Resolution,* and the *New York International Law Review.*

Jacob Durieux is a researcher at the Autonomous Laboratory of Anthropology and Archaeology in Paris, where he works on the history of Northwest Africa. He has been lecturing in various international academic institutions and in the general public in art and social centers. Durieux has published articles on the Maghrib.

Damilola D. Fagite teaches courses in East, Central, and North African history at Obafemi Awolowo University, Nigeria. Her research interests include medical and health history and colonial history. She is currently completing her dissertation on medical policies and the management of the smallpox epidemic in southwestern Nigeria.

Marcus Filippello is an assistant professor of history at the University of Wisconsin–Milwaukee, where he teaches African, world, and environmental history. His first book, *The Nature of the Path: Reading a West African Road,* is forthcoming in 2017.

Ola-Oluwa A. Folami is a faculty member in the Department of History and International Relations at Cuttington University, Liberia. Folami is also a doctorate student in the Department of Public Management and Economics, Durban University of Technology, Durban, South Africa. His areas of specialization include diplomatic and strategic studies as well as African history. He is a coauthor *African History and Civilisation from the Earliest Times Up to 1800.*

Kathryn L. Green completed BA degrees in history and French at the University of California–Davis and MA and a PhD degree in African history from Indiana University. She has taught in various universities in the United States and is currently an associate professor of history at Mississippi Valley State University. Green has published on precolonial, colonial, and post-European colonial periods of African history and currently works on both African and African American history on subjects of slavery, mass incarceration, and colonial policies impacting ethnic identities and government.

Maryalice Guilford is a historian, an independent scholar, and trustee at the Women's Institute for African Rural Development. She has taught courses in American, African American, world, the developing world, Western civilization, and women's history. Her research focuses on rural development policy in sub-Saharan West Africa.

Emilie Guitard defended her PhD thesis, titled "'The Great Chief Must Be Like the Great Trash Pile': Waste Management and Power Relations in the Cities of Garoua and Maroua (Cameroon)," in December 2014 at the University of Paris Ouest–Nanterre La Defense. She is also a researcher at IFRA Nigeria, where she is studying the relationship between urban African societies and their environments. Her articles have appeared in such journals as *Politique Africaine, Ethnologie Francaise Mouvements, Anthropology News,* and soon the *Journal of Material Culture and Techniques et Culture.*

Vincent Hiribarren is a lecturer in modern African history at King's College–London, where he teaches courses in African and world history. He is the author of *A History of Borno: Trans-Saharan African Empire to Failing Nigerian State* (Hurst and Oxford University Press, 2017).

Abdulai Iddrisu is an associate professor at St. Olaf Collge, where he teaches African history, Muslim societies, and women in Africa. His publications have appeared in various journals including *Africa Development,* the *Canadian Journal of African Studies, Islam Et Societés Au Du Sahara,* the *Journal of Muslim Minority Affairs,* and the *Journal for Islamic Studies* among others.

Mufutau Oluwasegun Jimoh is a lecturer of history at Federal University Birnin–Kebbi in Nigeria, where he teaches courses in African history, Nigerian history, and disease in Nigerian history. His previous books include *The Balogun in Yoruba Land: The Changing Fortunes of a Military Institution* (2016) and *A History of Lagos State* (2015). His articles have appeared in such journals as the *Journal of Asian and African Studies, African Notes,* and the *Lagos Historical Review.*

Henry Kam Kah is an associate professor of history at the University of Buea, Cameroon, where he teaches courses on Cameroon, African, and gender history. He is the author of *The Sacred Forest: Gender and Matriliny in Laimbwe History c. 1750–2001,* and several articles published in such journals as *Afrika Zamani,* the *African Studies Quarterly,* the *Conflict Studies Quarterly, African Development,* the *Ghana Social Science Journal,* and the *Lagos Historical Review.*

Daniel Kahozi completed his PhD in comparative literature in 2016 from the University of Texas at Austin, where he taught French for four years. His work focuses on the representation of war trauma in African literature, music, and films. Dr. Kahozi is currently working on his first book proposal.

Sara Katz is a PhD candidate at the University of Michigan, where she is writing her dissertation, "Pilgrims, Prestige and Politics: The Development of the Hajj from Southwest Nigeria, 1914–2000."

Michael Kpughe Lang teaches history at the Higher Teacher Training College, University of Bamenda. His articles covering themes such as missiology, church governance, corruption, religious diversity, ecumenism, etc., have featured in such journals as the *Lagos Historical Review,* the *Ibadan Journal of Gender Studies, DANUBIUS, Rural Theology,* the *Nigerian Journal of the Humanities,* and *Transformation: An International Journal of Holistic Mission Studies,* among others.

Olisa Godson Muojama is an assistant professor of history at the University of Ibadan, Nigeria, where he teaches courses in African history, development studies, political economy, and political ideas. He is the author of a forthcoming book, *Nigerian Cocoa Industry and International Economy in the 1930s: A World-Systems Approach.* Muojama's articles have appeared in the *Journal of the Historical Society of Nigeria* and the *International Journal of Arts and Humanities.*

Monsuru Muritala teaches African history at the University of Ibadan, Nigeria. He has published in local and internationally journals. Muritala is a 2015 Post-Doctoral Cadbury Fellow of African Studies at the Department of African Studies and Anthropology, University of Birmingham, Birmingham, United Kingdom.

Walter Gam Nkwi is a lecturer of history at the University of Buea, where he teaches courses on Cameroon, Africa, and world history. His books include *Voicing the Voiceless: Towards Closing Gaps in Cameroon History, c. 1958–2009* (2010), *Sons and Daughters of the Soil: Land and Boundary Conflicts in Bamenda Grassfields, Cameroon, c. 1955–2005* (2011), *Kfaang and Its Technologies: Towards a Social History of Mobility in Kom, Cameroon, 1928–1998* (2011), and *University Crisis and Student Protests in Africa: The 2005–2006 University Students Strike in Cameroon* (2012), among others. Nkwi's articles have appeared in such journals as *African Study Monographs,* the *Lagos Historical Review,* the *Conflict Study Quarterly,* and the *International Review of Social History.*

Artur Obluski is the director of the Research Center in Cairo, Polish Centre of Mediterranean Archaeology, University of Warsaw, and research associate at the Oriental Institute, University of Chicago. He has been studying African civilizations since 1996 and has published several articles and a book on the state formation of Nubian kingdoms. Recently Obluski has been involved in several projects focused on Christian monasticism in the Nile Valley and excavating a medieval Christian monastery of al-Ghazali in Sudan.

Hannington Ochwada received his PhD from Indiana University, Bloomington. He teaches African history at University of Kansas.

David M. M. Riep is assistant professor of art history at Colorado State University and associate curator of African art at the Gregory Allicar Museum of Art. He specializes in the arts of Africa and teaches courses on global art history and museum studies while also producing documentary films on South Sotho arts and culture. Riep is currently working on a chapter for a volume on South African ceramics and has published articles in *African Arts* magazine, *Southern African Humanities,* and the *Journal of African Cinemas,* and on the website Art and Life in Africa.

Marsha R. Robinson is a visiting assistant professor of world history at Miami University. Her interest in African history began when she was a student at the School of Foreign Service at Georgetown University. While working on her master's degree at Central Connecticut State University, she learned more about American commerce with some African nations that did not involve the sale of humans. At Ohio State University, Robinson focused on African history and culture in the Department of African American and African Studies before undertaking her doctoral program in women's history with a global perspective. Her scholarship explores the frontier between matriarchal and patriarchal societies, with research conducted in Morocco, Senegal, Nigeria, and England. Robinson is the author of *Matriarchy, Patriarchy, and Imperial Security in Africa: Explaining Riots in Europe and Violence in Africa* (Lexington, 2012) and several book chapters and articles and is the editor of several volumes.

Giovanni R. Ruffini is a professor of history and classical studies at Fairfield University, Connecticut, where he teaches classes on Greek, Roman, and ancient African civilization. His books include *Medieval Nubia: A Social and Economic History* (2012) and *The Bishop, the Eparch, and the King: Old Nubian Texts from Qasr Ibrim IV* (2014).

Andrea Felber Seligman is an assistant professor of African history at City College of New York, where she teaches courses on African history and the use of nondocumentary sources. She is presently working on a book manuscript titled *Crafting New Economies: Inland Trade in Central East Africa, ca. 1st–17th Centuries.* Seligman has recently published articles in the *International Journal of African Historical Studies* and *History in Africa.*

Aidan Stonehouse taught African history at Leeds University before joining the third sector to take up directorship of a charity working with survivors of genocide. His articles have appeared in the *Journal of Eastern African Studies.*

Aribidesi Usman is an associate professor of anthropology at Arizona State University, where he teaches courses in archaeology, anthropology, African art, and the African diaspora. His previous books include *State-Periphery Relations and Sociopolitical Development in Igbominaland, North-Central Yoruba, Nigeria* (2001); as editor, *Movements, Borders, and Identities in Africa* (2008); and *The Yoruba Frontier* (2012). Usman's articles have appeared in various journals such as the *Journal of African Archaeology,* the *African Archaeological Review,* the *West African Journal of Archaeology,* and the *Journal of Anthropological Archaeology.*

Sarah E. Watkins is a junior fellow at the Center for Historical Research at Ohio State University. She earned her PhD in history and feminist studies from the University of California, Santa Barbara, in 2014. Watkins is currently working on a manuscript titled *Mistress of the Drum: The Practice of Power in Rwanda, 1795–1962.*

Stephanie Zehnle is an assistant professor of history at the University of Duisburg–Essen in Germany, where she teaches courses in African history, colonial history, and the history of Islam. Her monograph titled *A Geography of Jihad,* about the Sokoto jihad in precolonial central Sahel, will be published in 2017. Zehnle's articles have appeared in such journals as *Critical African Studies* and *Islamic Africa.*

Index

Main entries indicated in **bold**.

Abbadid dynasty, 10
Abbadid Empire, 12–13
Abdullah, 30
Abeokuta, 53
Abiodun, 246
Abomey Plateau, 53, 187
Achimota School, 83
Action Group of Nigeria, 119, 231, 245
Adae, 112
Adama, Modibbo, 1
Adamawa, **1–3**
  Bata, 1
  British, 2
  Chamba, 1
  Chekke, 1
  colonial, 2
  Fali, 1
  French, 2
  Fulani, 1–2
  Germans, 2
  Gude, 1
  Gudur, 1
  Islam, 1–2
  Kilba, 1
  Margi, 1
  Mbere region, 2
  Mbororo, 2
  Mbum, 1
  Ngaoundéré, 1
  Tikar ethnic groups, 1
  traditional religions, 2
  Yola, 1–2
Adamawa Plateau, 33
Adandozan, 188
Adeboa, Nana Ayekraa, 60
Adeniyi, Sunday, 237
Adesanya, Oba, 76

Adesowon, Alara, 76
Adeyemi, Adeniran II, 245
Adherbal, 229
Adingra, Kofi, 112
Afnu, Dala, 58
Afo-a-Kom, 151
Afonja, Are Ona Kakanfo, 246
Afonso, Mani-Kongo I, 158–159
Africa, general
  ancient period, xxvii
  archaeological discoveries, xv
  colonial period, xxix–xxx
  colonialism, xxii
  deracialization of civilization, xv
  education, indigenous, xxii–xxiii
  gender roles, traditional, xxii
  knowledge systems, xv
  mischaracterization of, xiv–xvii
  origin stories, xix
  politics, xxiv
  postcolonial period, xxx–xxxi
  precolonial period, xviii–xix, xxvii
  social, political, and religious institutions
    and thought in, xviii
  state and empire building in, xiv–xviii
  timeline, xxvii–xxxi
Africa Oil and Nuts Company, 75
African Union, 12
Africanus, Leo, 87
Afrikaner Nationalist Party, 176
Agaja, 53–55
Agana-Poje, 117
Aganmede, Oba, 240
Agaw Zagwe dynasty, 6
Agbadjigbetos, 54–55
Agbaja, 76
Agbala, 226

Agbogungboro, Ogedengbe, 128
Agemo masquerade, 240
Aggrey, Kwegyir, 199
Aggrey Memorial College, 21
Agona State, 60
Agyeman, Kwadwo, 112
Ahmad, Shehu, 269
Ahmadu Bello University, 136
Ahmose I, 73
Ahoua, 235
Ain Farah, 58
Airo, Oba, 238
Aiye, Oduduwa Olofin, 127
Aja, 55
    Allada, 28
    Hwala, 28
    Setto, 28
    Tori, 28
Ajagbo, 231
Ajagungbade III, Oba Jimoh Oladunni
    Oyewumi, 231
Ajaka, Owa Ajibogun, 127
Akaba, 54
Akagera National Park, 249
Akan, 23, 59, 60, 83–85, 110, 112, 154,
    198, 231
Akatamanso War, 25
Aké: The Years of Childhood, 67
Akeh, 151
Akinkunmi, Taiwo, 113
Akinsanya, Oba, 121
Akinsemoyin, Eleko, 28
Akintola, Samuel Ladoke, 231, 233
Ako-Agbo, 68
Aksum, **2–7**, 79, 208, 211
    Aksum (city of), 3, 6
    archeological studies, 3–4, 6
    Bega, 4
    Christianity, 3–6
    coinage, 5
    Islam, 3, 6
    languages, 3, 5–6
    obelisks, 5
    oral tradition, 4
    origins, 3
    Roman Empire, 3, 5–6
    Sabaeans, 3
    trade, 3, 5
Akuapem, 85

Akuma, 22
Akwesidae Kesse, 26
Akyem, 24
Aladaxonu dynasty, 53
Alafèka, 235
Al-Amin, Muhammad, 30–31
Alawoma, Idris, 30, 316
Al-Azahar University, 88
Al-Bakri, 100–101, 192–193, 263
Al-Daj, Ahmad, 57
Alfa, Almamy Karamoka, 93
Al-Fazari, 99
Alfonso, 11
Alfonso VI, 14
Al-Ghazali, 10
Algeria, 206, 228
Algiers, 50, 87, 30
Al-Hasan, Ali bin, 143
Al-Hasan, Mawlay, 89–90
Al-Houari, Zeineb bint Ishaq al-Nefzaoui,
    13–14
Ali, Abul-Hassan, 206
Ali, Sonni, 260, 288
Al-Idrisi, 101–102
Al-Kabir, Sidiyya, 97
Allada, **7–9**, 53, 55
    decline, 55
    Dutch, 8
    end of, 8–9
    landscape, 7
    Offra, 7
    oral traditions, 7–8
    origins, 7
    population, 8
    Portuguese, 8
    slave trade, 7–9
    trade, 8
    warfare, 8
Allah, Idris ibn Abd Allah, 87
Allah, Idris II, 88
Al-Madusi, 99
Al-Mansur, 11
Al-Mansur, Abu Yusuf Yaqub, 11–12
Al-Ma'qur, Ahmad, 57
Almohad, **9–12**, 205–206
    Aghmet, 10
    Christianity, 9
    Fez, 11–12, 14
    Islam, 9–10

Marrakesh, 9–12, 14, 206
  origins, 9
  Rabat, 11–12
  revolution, 11
  Sali, 11
  Seville, 11–12
  Tinmel, 10–11
  Tlemcen, 11
Almoravid, **12–15**, 205, 264
  Christianity, 14–15
  colonial structure, 14
  economy, 14–15
  military, 14
  origins, 12–13
  slave trade, 13
  Spain, 14
  trade, 12–13
Al-Mu'min, Abd, 11
Alodia (Alwa), **15–17**, 63, 220
  archeological studies, 15–16
  Christianity, 16–17
  decline, 16
  Islam, 16
  origins, 15–16
  rulers, 16
  Soba, 15–16
Aloma, Mai Idris, xviii
Alooma, Idris, 38
Al-Siddiq, Abu Bakr, 111
Al-Wathiq, Idriss II, 12
Al-Yaqubi, 15
Al-Zubayr, Rabih, 32
Al-Zuhri, 101
Ama-Mbala River Valley, 225
Amanishakheto, 208
Amanitore, 164
Amin, Idi, 20–21, 40, 47, 148
Amina, xviii
Amochje, Attah, 118
Amon, 74
Amon-Re, 74
Amono, Komfo, 198
Ampem, Wirempe, 60
Amun Temple, 209
Amusu, 253–254
Andalusia, 10
Anglican Missionary Society, 47
Anglo-Aro War, 22–23
Anglo-Boer Wars, 176

Anglo-Egba Treaty of 1893, 71
Anglo-Ibadan Treaty, 233
Anglo-Ijebu War, 121
Anglo-Zulu War, 289
Angoche, 204
Angola, 156, 186, 218
ANgoong, Mbul, 160
ANgoong, Shyaam aMbul, 160–161
Aniwura, Iyalode Afunsetan, xvii
Ankole (Nkore), **17–21**
  Bantu, 18–19
  British, 19–20
  cattle, 17
  Christianity, 20
  Chwezi, 18–19
  colonization, 19
  districts, 21
  Elder's Council, 21
  environmental concerns, 21
  Himas, 18–19
  Irus, 18–19
  Islam, 20
  Location, 17–18
  Luo Bitos, 18
  metalwork, 19
  mythology, 18
  natural resources, 17–19
  Nkore, 18–21
  oral tradition, 18
  trade, 18–20
  traditional religion, 19
Ankole Agreement, 19
Anlamani, 164
Anokye, Okomfo, 23–24
Antony, Mark, 229
Aphilas, 5
Aragon, 11
Arbousset, Thomas, 175
Ark of the Covenant, 3–4
Aro Confederation, 23
Arochukwu, **21–23**
  Akpa, 22
  Aro, 22–23
  Bende, 23
  Bonny markets, 23
  British, 22–23
  Ibibio, 21
  Igbo, 21
  location, 22

oracle, 23
slave trade, 23
trade, 23
Aromokoukomoulèkè, 236
Arusha Accords, 251
Asante (Ashanti), **23–26**, 59, 61–62, 85,
    110–111
    British, 24–25
    decline, 25
    exile of royals, 25
    Fante, 24–25
    government, 24–25
    Kumasi, 24
    natural resources, 26
    slave trade, 25
    trade, 24–25
    traditional religion, 26
    union, 23–24
Asantewaa, Yaa, 25
Ashwa, Sumyafa, 6
Asma'u, Nana, xxiii
Aspelta, 164
Assin, 24, 61
Atbara River, 15
Atlas Mountains, 10
Awolowo, Obafemi, 121
Ayegba, Atta, 117

Babessi, 149
Badagry, **27–29**, 53
    administrative districts, 29
    Aja, 28
    Awori, 27
    gender roles, 28
    location, 27–29
    Ogu, 27–28
    origin, 27
    slave trade, 27–29
Badagry Heritage Museum, 27
Bagauda, 134
Baguirmi, **29–32**, 107
    British, 32
    culture, 31
    French, 32
    Fula, 30
    government, 30
    history, 30
    Islam, 29–31
    Kanuri, 30

location, 29–30
Massenya, 30–31
metalworking, 31
Shuwa Arabs, 30
slave trade, 31
trade, 30
Baguirmi Protectorate, 32
Bagyendanwa, 19
Bahr al-Arab, 57
Baiso, 150
Bakr, Abu, 13–14
Bal, Sulayman, 97
Ballana, 221
Bambara, 192
Bamenda-Fundong, 152
Bamenda Grassfields, 149, 273–275
Bamum, **32–34**
    British, 34
    Foumban, 32, 34
    French, 34
    Germans, 34
    government, 33–34
    Islam, 34
    Samba Nguo, 33
    Tikar ethnic groups, 32–33
    topography, 33
    wars, 33
Bamwose, Cyprian, 44
Banems, xxiii
Banneker, Benjamin, 280
Bantu, 18–20, 44–45, 47, 217, 249–250
Bantu Homelands Citizenship Act,
    292
Banu Hillal, 57
Banu Marins, 12
Baptist Academy, 231
Barbosa, Duarte, 295–297
Barghwata Federation, 13
Barth, Heinrich, 31, 99, 242, 315–317
Bashong, 160–161
Basuto National Party, 176
Basutoland, 174–176
Bate society, xviii
Battle of Feyiase, 59, 61–62
Battle of Isandlwana, 292
Battle of Kansala, 133
Battle of Mhlatuze River, 290–291
Battle of Nsamankow, 25
Battle of Poredaka, 94

Battle of Talanson, 94
Bedini, Silvio, 280
Bedouins, 206
Begli, Abd al-Mahmud, 30
Bello, Muhammed, 242, 257–258, 269
Belly of the Rock (Batn el-Hajar), 220
Belo, 150
Benamatapa (Muninumutapa), 296–297
Benin (Republic of), 7, **35–37**, 128, 168,
    187, 234–235, 253
  Akure, 36, 126
  British, 35–36
  Cotonou, 7
  Edo, 35–36
  Ekiti, 36
  festivals, 37
  Godomey, 7
  government, 35
  Itsekiri, 36
  metalworking, 36
  Ogiso period, 35
  Portuguese, 36
  slave trade, 36
  trade, 36
  Ughoton, 36
  Urhobo, 36
Benue River Valley, 222
Ber, Sunni Ali, 266–267
Berbers, 49–50, 101, 137, 192, 206–207,
    228, 259–260, 265
  Alphabet, 250
  Masmuda, 10
  Tifinagh, 50
  Zenaga, 10
  Zenata, 205
Berger, Iris, 148
Berlin Museum, 74
Bernal, Martin, 72
Besse, Mbang Birni, 30
Beta Israel Jewish community, 3
Biko, Zum, 109
Binger, Louis, 153
Black Noba, 15
Blemmyan, 221
Boer Republic, 176
Boko Haram, 2, 39, 107, 136, 195
Bondu, Osei, 24
Bonnet, Charles, 141, 163
Bono State, 59

Bonsu, Mensa, 25
Book of Dali, 58
Book of Highways and Kingdoms, 100
Borbor Mfantse, 197
Borno (Kanem-Borno, Kanem-Bornu),
    xviii, 1–2, 30–32, **37–39**, 58, 109, 196,
    268, 307
  British, 38
  French, 38
  Germans, 38
  government, 38
  Independence, 38
  invasion, 37
  Islam, 38–39
  Kanembu, 37
  military, 38
  post-colonial, 39
  Sao, 38
  Sayfawa, 38
  size, 37
  slave trade, 39
  trade, 37–39
  Tueregs, 38
  Yobe, 39
Botswana, 199
Bouré, 94
Brahim, Thierno, 97
Bright of Benin, 28
British East Africa company, 46
British Museum, 208
British Slave Trade Act of 1807, 85
Bruce, James, 208, 303–305
Budge, Earnest Alfred Wallace, 208
Buganda, 18, **40–43**, 45, 147
  British, 42–43
  Buvuma Island, 40
  Christianity, 42–43
  colonial period, 40, 42–43
  economy, 41–43
  French, 42
  government, 40–43
  Islam, 42
  Kampala, 40
  location, 40
  natural resources, 40–41
  oral tradition, 41
  population, 40
  postcolonial, 40
  Sese Islands, 40

slave trade, 42
social structure, 42
trade, 42
traditional religion, 41
Buhaya, 18
Bum, 149
Bumba, xix
Bunyoro-Kitara, 18, 41, 45, 148
Burkina Faso, 24, 192, 241–244
Burundi, 250, 252
Genocide, 20, 251
Bushoong, xix
Busoga, **44–48**, 147
archeological studies, 45
Bagisu, 45
Bantu, 44–45, 47
British, 46–47
Budama, 44
Bugembe, 44
Bugiri, 47
Bugishu, 44
Bushmen, 45
Busiki, 47
Buswikara, 44
Christianity, 45
colonial, 46–47
constitution, 47
earliest inhabitants, 45
economy, 45
gender roles, 45
government, 45, 47
HIV/AIDS, 47
independence, 47
Iganga, 44–45, 47
Itesos, 45
Jinja, 45, 47
Kaliro, 45, 47
Kamuli, 45, 47
Langis, 45
Local Council Five, 47
Mayuge, 47
location, 44
natural resources, 44
population, 44, 47
topography, 44
trade, 45–46
traditional religion, 44
Busoga African Local Government, 46
Busoga Trust, 44

Buthelezi, Mangosuthu, 292
Byzantine Empire, 50, 221

Caesar, Julius, 229
Cailliaud, Frédéric, 208
Cameroon, 2, 30, 32, 34, 38–39, 109, 152, 197, 276,
Cão, Diogo, 157–158, 300
Cape Coast, 25
Cape Colony, 175
Cape of Good Hope, xv
Carter, Gilbert T., 129
Carthage, **49–51**, 229
archaeological studies, 50–51
Berbers, 49–50
Byrsa, 50
destruction of, 49–50
French, 50
Islam, 50
Phoenicians, 49–50
Romans, 49–50
trade, 50
Tunis, 49–50, 57
Umayyads, 49
Vandals, 49–50
Casalis, Eugene, 175
Casely-Hayford, Gus, 103
Catholic Mill Hill Fathers, 47
Cato the Younger, 229
Caton-Thompson, Gertrude, 106
Cele, Henry, 292
Chad (Republic of Chad), 30, 38, 57, 109
Chamba, 2
Chari River, 29–31, 107
Chidzonzi, Kalonga, 203
Chioko, Mambo, 213
Chittick, Neville, 146
Christian Reconquista, 12
Chukwu, 225–226
Church Missionary School, 231
Church Missionary Society, 116, 128–129, 313, 317
Clapperton, Hugh, 31, 307
Cleopatra, 229
Coexist, 249
Cold War, 219
Compagnie Francaise de la Côte d'Ivoire, 242
Compaoré, Blaise, 244

Congo Free State, 161–162, 184, 186
Congo River, 157
Constantine, 6
Constantinople, 6
Córdoba, 88–89
Côte d'Ivoire (Ivory Coast), 153, 155, 192
Cresques, Abraham, 189
Cross River, 22
Crowther, Samuel Ajayi, 313–315
Crusades, 10, 12, 15, 50, 90, 206
Cwezi-Kubandwa spirits, 147–148

D'Almeida, Francisco, 145–146
Dahomey, xvii–xviii, 7–8, 27–28, **53–57**,
    71, 169, 188
  Abomey, 53
  Agbadjigbetos, 54–55
  Amazons, 53
  economy, 55–56
  Ewe, 53
  Fon, 53
  French, 56
  gender roles, 54
  government, 54–55
  location, 53
  military campaigns, 53–55
  oral tradition, 55
  origins, 53
  slave trade, 55–56
  topography, 53
  Weme, 55
Daily Telegraph, 42
Daju dynasty, 57
Dakabere, Boa Amponsem, 60
Damascas, 9
Dan Fodio, Usman, xxiii, 1, 38, 138, 246,
    256–258
Dapper, Olfert, 299–301
Darfur, 32, **57–59**
  Berti, 57
  Birgid, 57
  Dajua, 57
  decline, 58
  economy, 58
  El Fashir, 59
  Furs, 57
  Islam, 57–58
  location, 57
  Meidob, 57

  slave trade, 58
  trade, 58
  Tungur, 57–58
  Uri, 58
  Zaghawa, 57
Daura, xviii
David, Nicholas, 195
Dawud, Askia, 267
De Bellefonds, Linant, 208
De Brazza, Pierre Savorgnan, 181
De Gama, Vasco, xv
De Gaulle, Charles, 112
De Mézières, Albert Bonnel, 99
Deffufa, 140–141
Delafosse, Maurice, 99–100
Delattre, Alfred-Louis, 50
Democratic Republic of Congo, 109, 147,
    156, 184–185, 252
Denham, Dixon, 307–309
Denkyira, 24, **59–62**
  Abankesieso, 60, 62
  Adanse Akorokyere, 60
  Adawufos, 59
  Agona clan, 60
  Akan, 59–60
  Bonatifi, 60
  decline, 62
  Dutch, 61
  economy, 60–61
  Elmina, 61
  English, 61
  gold, 61
  government, 60–61
  Jukwa, 62
  Kumase, 62
  location, 60
  military, 61
  oral tradition, 62
  origins, 59–60
  population, 60
  slave trade, 61
  trade, 61
  wars, 61
Diallo, Ayuba Suleiman, 301–303
Diamare Plain, 107–108
Dingane, 290, 309
Dingiswayo, 290
Diop, Cheikh Anta, 72
Diqn, Badi II Abu, 91

Divination practice, xxiii
Djibouti, 3
Djobdi, Ardo, 1
DoAklin, 8
Dodekaschoinos, 221
Dogon, xxiii
Doondari, xix
"Door of No Return, The," 279–280
Dorshit, Shau, 58
Dotawo, **63–65**
    archaeological studies, 63
    decline, 64
    government, 64
    Islam, 65
    trading, 64
Drama, Mamadu Lamin, 97
Dua, Kweku II, 25
Dunham, Dows, 209
Dunqas, Makk Amara, 91
Dunkwa-on-Offin, 62
Dutch West India Company, 8
Dzie-Nkwen, 150

East African Community, 252
Eastern Desert, 163
Ebuluejeonu, 117
Ebutu-Eje, 117
Ed-Dawla, Shams, 64
Edfu text, 72
Edna Bay, xviii
Edu, Shafi Lawal, 75
Egba (Abeokuta), **67–71**, 116
    Aké Township, 67
    British, 71
    Christianity, 68, 70–71
    economy, 67–68
    Egba Ake, 68, 70
    Egba Alake, 68
    Egba Aro, 69
    Egba Gbagura, 68, 114
    Egba Oke-Ona, 68
    Egba Olowu, 68, 70
    Ile-Ife, 68, 76
    Iwarefa Council, 69
    location, 67
    natural resources, 67
    Ode, 70
    Ogboni, 70
    origins, 68

Orile Ake, 68
Parakoyi, 70
population, 67
slave trade, 67–69
topography, 67
traditional religion, 68–69
Yoruba, 67–68
Egba Ologorun, 69
Egba United Board of Management, 71
Egungun masquerade, 114
Egypt, 39, 64–65, **71–75**, 139, 215
    Alexandria, 74
    Archaic period, 73
    artisanship, 73–74
    Assyrians, 74
    Aswan, 215, 221
    Cairo, 58, 88, 191
    Edfu, 72
    Eighteenth Dynasty, 73
    Fifth Dynasty, 163
    Fourth Dynasty, 73
    government, 74
    Hamites, 71–72
    Heliopolis, 74
    hieroglyphics, 74, 164
    Hyksos, 73–74, 141
    Kemet, 72
    Lower, 72, 74
    Middle Kingdom, 139, 162–163
    military, 73, 139
    Nubians, 74
    Old Kingdom, 73
    Persians, 74
    pyramids, 73
    religion, 74
    Romans, 74
    Second Intermediate Period, 139
    Sixth Dynasty, 73
    Theban House, 73
    Thebes, 141, 215, 221
    Third Dynasty, 73
    trade, 73
    Twenty-Fifth Dynasty, 141, 163, 216
    Upper, 72
    wars, 73, 141
Egyptian Air Force, 72
Ejiso, 25
Ekiti, 116, 126, 128
Ekitiparapo War, 128–129

El-Kanemi, Muhammad al-Amin, 37, 269
Endfield, Cy, 289
Endubis, 4–5
Epe, **75–78**, 238
 Awori, 76
 Eko Epe, 76
 government, 76–77
 Ijaw, 76
 Ijebu, 75–77, 126
 Isoko, 76
 Itshekiri, 76
 location, 75
 origin of, 76
 trade, 77
 Yoruba, 76
Epic of Sundiata, 193
Equiano, Olaudah, 305–307
Erediauwa, Omo N'Oba N'Edo Uku
  Akpolokpolo, 37
Eritrea, 3, 80
Eritrean Catholic Church, 3
Esigie, 35–36
Ethiopia, 3–4, **78–81**, 215, 297
 Aksum, 78
 Christianity, 81
 government, 80
 location, 78
 natural resources, 80
 obelisks, 5, 79
 Solomonic kings, 79
 10th century, 5
Ethiopian Catholic Church, 3
Ethiopian Orthodox Church, 3
Eweka, 35
Ewuare, Oba the Great, 35–36
Ezana, 4–6, 15

Fagg, Bernard, 222
Fante, 24, **83–87**
 Akan, 85
 Borbor Fante, 84
 Constitution, 85–87
 18th century, 84
 government, 84–87
 location, 3
 Mankessim, 84
 military, 85
 population, 84
 slave trade, 86–87

trade, 83
 wars, 85, 198
Fante-Asante wars, 198
Fante Confederacy/Confederation, 84–85,
  87, 198–199
Faras, 220
Fatamid Empire, 13
Federal University of Agriculture,
  Abeokuta, 71
Felipe, Mavura Mhande, 213
Fento', 274
Ferlini, Giuseppe, 208
Fez, **87–90**
 Andalus, 88
 Fez al-Bali, 88
 Islam, 89–90
 Kairouan, 88
 Maghrebi, 88
 natural resources, 88
 origins, 87
 White City, 89
Fleisher, Jeffrey, 143
Flower in the Gun Barrel, 249
Fofie, 112
Fombina, 1
Fouta Djallon Highlands, 92
Franco-Dahomean Wars, 56
Freeman, Thomas, 28
French, xviii, 9
French Congo, 181
French League of Nations, 2
Fulani, xix, 1–2, 69, 92–93, 109, 232–233,
  257
Funj (Sennar Sultanat), 17, **90–91**
 decline, 91
 government, 90–91
 location, 90
Futa Jallon, **92–95**
 Alfayas, 94
 economy, 94
 ecosystem, 92
 18th century, 93
 French, 94, 133
 Fulani, 92–93
 Fulbe, 92, 93, 95
 government, 94
 independence, 93
 Islam, 93–94
 location, 92, 94

origins, 91–92
Peuls, 94
social structure, 93–94
Soriyas, 94
trade, 93–95
Futa Toro, **96–98**, 147
Denyanke, 97
French, 97
Fulbe, 96
Islam, 96–97
natural resources, 96
population, 96
Fynn, Henry Francis, 309–311

Ga, 85–86
Gadarat, 4
Gala, 228
Gallus, Aelius, 210
Gambia, 192
Garstang, John, 209
Gayamusa, 134
Gbowèlé, 188
Geary, Christraud, 275
Geography, 4
Germano-Douala Treaty, 172
Gezira, 63
Gezo, 53, 188
Ghana, xxi, 10, 53, 83, **99–103**, 168, 193,
  263
archeological studies, 100–101
Asante, 23–24
Berbers, 101
Bono State, 59
Central Region, 197
Fante, 197
gold, 99
history, 99–101
Islam, 101–102
location, 99
natural resources, 100
population, 23, 84
trade, 101–102
Ghartey IV, 86
Gitar, 57
Glele, 53
Glover, John, 240–241
Gold Coast, 24, 59, 83, 85, 87, 241
Golden Stool, 24–25
Gorillas in the Mist, 249

Gosselin, Constant, 175
Gowon, Yakubu, 135
Grand Bara Desert, 3
Great Mosque of Kilwa, 145
Great Zimbabwe, **103–107**, 201, 212,
  296–297
abandonment, 106
archaeological studies, 106
great enclosure, 105
location, 103
origins, 104–105
Guiziga Bui Marva, **107–110**
contemporary, 107
Dogoys, 107
Fulani, 109
government, 108
Islam, 108–109
Kaliao, 109
Kitikil a Bui, 108–109
location, 107
Marva, 107–108
Masfaye, 107
paleo-Mofus, 107–108
Movos, 107
origins, 107
raids, 108
traditional religion, 108–109
Sao, 107
Gulf of Aden, 3
Gulf of Guinea, 60, 62
Gulf of Tunis, 49
Gummai, 31
Gwaranga, Abd al-Rahman, 32
Gyakari, Ntim, 59, 62
Gyaman, 24, **110–112**
Asante, 110–112
craftspeople, 111
economy, 111
festivals, 112
French, 111–112
government, 111
location, 110
slave trade, 111–112
social structure, 112
traditional religion, 112

Habyarimana, Juvenal, 251
Hadhramawt, 4
Hafsid dynasty, 50

Haley, Alex, 194
Hall, Mary, 321–322
Harvard University, 141
Hasdrubal, 228–229
Hausa, 1–2, 25, 30–31, 77, 109, 111,
    113, 128–129, 134–135, 233, 242,
    246
Hausaland, 26, 134, 136, 138, 257
Hawal River, 1
Hayford, Casely, 199
Herodotus, 72, 208
Hiempsa I, 229
Hillman, William, 307
Himyar, 4, 6
Hinderer, David, 317
Hinderer, Ann Martin, 317–319
History of Egypt, 72
History of the Patriarchs, 222
The History of the Yoruba, xxiii
Hochschild, Adam, 162
Hodgeson, Frederick, 25
Horton, James Africanus Beale, 85–87
Horus, 72
Hotel Rwanda, 249
Houndjroto, 188
Huffon, 278
Huraka, 76
Hutu Power, 251
Hyksos, 73–74, 141, 215

Ibadan, xvii, **113–116**
    British, 116
    colonial period, 114, 116
    economy, 113
    Eba Odan, 115
    Egba, 114
    festivals, 114
    Hausa, 113
    location, 113
    origins of, 114
    population, 113
    wars, 115–116
    Yoruba, 113–114
Ibadan-Ijaye War, 115
Ibadan School, 113
Ibn Ali, Abd al-Mu'min, 10
Ibn Battuta, 72, 124
Ibn Khaldun, 102
Ibn Rushd, 12

Ibn Selim, 16
Ibn Tachfin, Yusef, 14
Ibn Tufayl, 12
Ibn Tumart, Muhammad, 9–12
Ibn Umar, Yahya, 13–14
Ibn Yusuf, Ali, 11
Ibrim, Qasr, 63
Idia, 35
Idrissid dynasty, 10
Ifá, xxiii
Igala, **116–118**
    British, 118
    economy, 118
    government, 117
    kinship system, 117
    location, 116
    wars, 117
Igbo, xvi, 21–22, 85, 116, 224–225, 227
    Anioma, 227
    Asaba, 227
    Awka, 227
    Ezeagwu, 21–22
    Ibibio, 227
    Igala, 227
    Ijaw, 227
    modern, 227
    Nsukka, 227
    Onitsha, 227
Igbó Ilú, 235–236
Igboland, 22, 224–228
Igbomina, 126, 128
Igu Aro, 227–228
Igue, 37
Ihya 'Ulum al-Din, 10
Ijebu, xvii, 116, **118–121**
    British, 121
    colonialism, 121
    economy, 119
    festivals, 121
    government, 120
    Ilamuren society, 120
    natural resources, 119
    Odi society, 120–121
    origins, 118–119
    Osugbo society, 120
    Pampa society, 120
    social structure, 120
    Yoruba, 120
Ijebu-Ode, 76

Ijesa, 116, 125, 128
Ijesa Association, 129
Ijesa War, 233
Ijo, xix
Ikoku, Alvan, 21
Ile-Ife, 68, **121–126**, 127, 238,
    253–254
  archaeological studies, 123
  destruction, 125
  economy, 124–125
  festivals, 122
  government, 121, 124
  Ife Central, 121
  Ife East, 121
  Ife North, 121
  Ife South, 121
  location, 121
  metalwork, 124
  oral tradition, 123
  origins, 122–123
  population, 123, 125
  topography, 123
  trade, 124–125
  traditional religion, 122, 124
  Yoruba, 121–122
Ilesa, 125, **126–130**
  British, 128–129
  economy, 128
  Enu Owa, 127
  Enuwa, 127
  festivals, 126, 129
  Igadaye, 127
  Ilaje/Ipole Ijesa, 127
  Ilare, 127
  Ilemure/Ibokun, 127
  Ilowa, 127
  Islam, 129
  modern, 126
  name, 127
  19th century, 128
  oral tradition, 127
  population, 128
  slave trade, 128
  topography, 126–127
  towns and settlements, 127
  Yoruba, 126
Ilorin, 232
Ilunga, Chibunda, 184–185
Ilunga, Kalala, 182

Imasuen, Lancelot Oduwa, 35
Imo River, 23
Imperial East Africa Company, 42
In the Tall Grass, 249
Indian Ocean, 3
Inan, Abu, 206
Industrial Revolution, 67
Inkatha kaZulu, 292
Inobia, Agwu, 21
International Library of African Music,
    185
*Interesting Narrative of the Life of Olaudah
    Equiano, The*, 305–307
Invasion 1897, 35
Ishaq, Askia, 267
Isis, 74
Isona Ward, 129
Ivory Coast, 24
Iwude Ogun, 126, 129

Jabi, Labi ibn War, 264
Jaguna of Agbeyin, 71
Jata, Mari, 102
Jean, Wyclef, 249
Jebel Marra, 57
Jinabo I, 149–150
João I, 158
João II, 158, 299–300
Johnson, James, 129
Johnson, Samuel, xxiii, 119, 129
Jos Plateau, 222
Jowett, William, 313
Juba I, 229
Juba II, 229
Jugurtha, 229
Juju Music, 237

Kaabu, **131–133**
  history of, 132
  Kansala, 132
  military, 132
  oral tradition, 131
  origins, 131
  population, 133
Kabale, Ilunga, 183
KaDinuzulu, Magogo, 292
KaDinuzulu, Solomon, 292
Kaduna State, 139
Kagulu Hill, 45

Kairouan University, 88
Kaleb, 6
KaMpande, Cetshawayo, 291–292
Kan, Abdul Kader, 97
Kankan, Mansa, 190
Kano, **134–136**
   Christianity, 136
   climate, 134
   economy, 135
   festivals, 134
   Islam, 134–135
   Kano Walls, 134
   location, 134
   oral tradition, 134
   riots, 135–136
   trade, 135
Kante, Sumanguru, 190
Kanyinya, 321–322
Karagwe, 18
Karangaland, 204
Kasubi tombs, 41
Katanga region, 45
Katsina, **136–139**
   agriculture, 138–139
   economy, 138
   Fulani, 138
   Islam, 138
   location, 136
   origins, 137
   topography, 137
   trade, 138
Kayibanda, Gregoire, 251
Kebra Negast (Glory of Kings), 4
Kedjom Keku, 149
Keira dynasty, 58–59
Keita, Mansa Musa I. *See* Mansa Musa
Keita, Maghan I, 194
Keita, Suleiman, 194
Keita, Sundiata, 193–194
Kelsey, Francis W., 51
Kemsoe, 73
Kenya, 147, 252
Kerma, **139–142**, 215
   agriculture, 139
   archaeological studies, 139–141
   art, 140
   burials, 139–141
   Deffufa, 140–141
   economy, 139–140

Egyptianized, 141–142
   government, 140
   Hyksos, 141
   raids, 139
   traditional religion, 140
   wars, 141
Ketu, 68, 234
Keze, 276
Khalifa, Belgassam be, 308
Kiluanje, Ngola, 218
Kilwa Chronicle, 143
Kilwa Kisiwani, **142–146**
   archaeological studies, 142–143
   architecture, 143–145
   decline, 145–146
   economy, 145–146
   Husuni Kubwa, 144
   Islam, 146
   location, 142
   modern, 143
   oral tradition, 143–144
   Portuguese, 145–146
   social structure, 142
   Swahili, 142–143, 146
   trade, 143–144
   12th century, 143–144
Kilwa Masoko, 146
King Sunny Ade (Sunday Adeniyi), 237
King's College, London, 85
Kingsley, Mary, 319–320
Kintu, 41
Kiriji Wars, 128–129
Kitara, **147–149**
   Babito dynasty, 148
   Bacwezi dynasty, 147
   Batembuzi dynasty, 147
   Christianity, 147
   location, 147
   natural resources, 147
   origins, 148
   population, 147
   traditional religion, 147
   16th century, 147
Kitikil a Bui, 108–109
Kobo, Ousman Murzik, 288
Kokpon, 8
Kom, **149–153**
   Achaf clan, 150
   agriculture, 151

art, 151
British, 152
colonialism, 152
Din, 150–151
economy, 151
Ekwu clan, 150
Fulani, 150
Fuli, 150–151
Germans, 152
government, 149–152
industry, 151
Intinalah clan, 150
location, 149
19th century, 150
Nkwens, 150
oral tradition, 149
origins, 149
Kom Muni, 149
Kom-Wum Forest Reserve, 170
Komoé River, 154
Kong, **153–156**
agriculture, 154
Akans, 154–155
climate, 153–154
French, 156
Gar, 154
gold, 154
Islam, 154–156
Jula (Dyula), 153–155
Malinke, 155
oral tradition, 154–155
origins, 155
population, 153
Senoufo, 154
slave trade, 154–155
Sonongui, 153–155
topography, 154
Kong Mountains, 187
Kongo, **156–159**
Christianity, 158
Mbanza Kongo, 156–157
Mbanza Sonyo, 157
origins, 156
Portuguese, 156–157
provinces, 156
São Salvador, 159
Kor, 57
Kosoko, 28
Kotoko, 30

Koumbi Saleh, 99
Kouoka, 235
Kourita, 287
Koutoubia Mosque, 11
Kpingla, 188
Kuba, **159–162**
art, 161
Bashong, 160
destruction, 161–162
government, 160–161
location, 159–160
origins, 161
slave trade, 161
trade, 160
Zappo Zaps, 161–162
Kufuo, Nana, 62
Kuli, 108
Kumambong, 150
Kung, 31
Kursas, 15
Kush, 5, 139, **162–165**, 207, 215
archaeological studies, 163
Barya, 5
decline, 5–6
Egypt, 162–163, 164
first written reference, 162–163
gender roles, 164
government, 140, 164
Khasa, 5
Mangurto, 5
Nehesys, 163
Noba, 5
Rome, 164
writing system, 164
Kuta, Oba, 240
Kuti, Fela, 71
KwaZulu/Natal, 289

Ladeoko festival, 129
Lagos, xxi, 28, 67, 76, 121, **167–170**
agriculture, 169
Awori, 167
Benin, 168
British, 168–170
Broad Street, 168
Christianity, 28
climate, 167
colonization, 170
French, 168

Ojo, 27
Oko, 167–168
population, 170
Portuguese, 168
16th century, 168–169
slave trade, 169–1740
Spanish, 168
trade, 168, 170
Yoruba, 167
Lagelu, Jagun, 114–115
Lagos Island, 167
Lagos Lagoon, 75
Lagos Legislative Council, 21
Lagos Protectorate, 241
Laimbwe, **170–172**
British, 172
gender roles, 171–172
Germans, 172
location, 170
origins, 170–171
precolonial, 171
trade, 172
Lake Albert, 17
Lake Chad, 30, 37–38
Lake Kivu, 17
Lake Kyoga, 44
Lake Malawi, 202–204
Lake Tchad, 31
Lake Victoria, 21, 40, 42, 44–45
Lama Valley, 7, 234
Lamido of Banyo, 34
Lander, Richard, 311–313
Latoosa, Obadoke, 128
Lavigerie of Algiers, 50
Lawal, Muhammad, 1–2
League of Nations, 250
Leo X, xv
Leopold II, 161–162, 186
Lepsius, Karl Richard, 208
Lesko, Barbara S., 91
Lesotho, **172–177**
British, 175
contemporary, 173
government, 175–176
hydroelectric power, 174
location, 172–173
natural resources, 174
oral tradition, 173
Sotho, 173–174

Letsie III, 176
Leyo, 240
Liberia, 192
Libyan Desert, 57
Libya, 38
Likaylik, Abu, 91
Limpopo River, 199
Limpopo-Shashe Transfrontier
Conservation Area, 200
Lisabi, 69
Little Ardra, 8
Livy, 228–229
Liyen, Oba, 240
Loango, **177–181**
agriculture, 179
art, 178
avenue of mango trees, 177
Dutch, 178–180
Loango Bay, 179–180
Mayumba, 179–180
metalwork, 179
population movements, 178
Portuguese, 178–179
slave trade, 177, 180–181
social structure, 180–181
topography, 177–178
trade, 179
Vili class, 180
Lobo, Jerome, 297–299
Logon River, 12
Lokoja, 129
Lost Kingdoms of Africa, 103
Louis IX, 50
L'Overture, Toussain, 9
Luba, **181–184**, 202
Babudye, 183
decline, 181, 183–184
government, 183
location, 182
oral tradition, 181–182
origins, 181
slave trade, 183–184
Swahili, 184
trade, 183
traditional religion, 183
Twas, 182
Lugard, Frederick, 42, 129
Lugbesa, 76
Luju, Osemawe, 239–240

Lunda, **184–186**
  art, 186
  decline, 186
  economy, 185–186
  Gaaand, 184
  government, 185
  location, 184
  mining, 185
  oral tradition, 184–185
  origins, 184–185
  population, 185
Luyare, Oba, 240

Macauley, Herbert, 167
MacEachern, Scott, 196
Mafia Island, 142
Magaji, Ogundeyi, 71
Maghrib, 10, 205
Mahi, 53, **187–189**
  location, 187
  Sakpata, 188
  slave trade, 187–188
Maimonides, 12
Maitatsine, Mohammed Marwa, 136
Makeda (Queen of Sheba), 3–4, 6
Makuria, 15, 63, 220, 222
Malawi, 291
Mali, xx–xxi, 99, **189–191**, 288
  archeological studies, 189–190
  decline, 191, 259–260
  Gao, 190–191, 265, 267
  history, 99
  Islam, 190–191
  Jenne-Jeno, 189
  Madinka/Malinke, 190, 192
  Mossis, 191
  Niani, 190–191
  Tuaregs, 191
  Walata, 190, 265
Maliki, Almoravid, 10
Malinke, **192–195**
  Christianity, 194
  history, 192–193
  Islam, 193–194
  Mande, 193
  origins of, 193
  Sankore, 194
Mandara, 30, **195–197**
  British, 196–197

Dulo, 196
French, 196
Fulani, 196
Germans, 196
location, 195
metalwork, 196
19th century, 196
17th century, 196
16th century, 196
Mandara Mountains, 107, 109, 195
Manetho, 72
Mankessim, **197–199**
  agriculture, 197
  Asante, 198–199
  British, 198–199
  Etsii, 198
  Fante, 197–198
  festivals, 197
Mansa Musa, 189, 191, 193, 260,
  266–267
Mapungubwe, **199–202**
  archaeological studies of, 200–201
  art, 200
  gold, 201
  location, 199–200
  Original Gold Burial M1, A620, 201
  population, 200
  topography, 200
Mapungubwe Cultural Landscape, 200
Mapungubwe Hill, 200
Mapungubwe National Park, 200
Mapunzagutu, Dehwe, 213
Marabouts, 206
Maravi, **202–205**
  Banda, 202
  Batwa, 202
  government, 203
  Kalimanjira, 202
  Kalonga, 203
  Kaphwiti, 203
  Lolo, 203
  Lundu, 203
  Mankhamba, 202–203
  Manthimba, 203
  oral traditions, 202
  origins, 202–203
  Phiri clan, 203
  Portuguese, 203–204
  trade, 202–203

traditional religion, 202–204
Zambezi, 204
Zimba, 203
Margi, 30
Marinids, **205–207**
Christians, 207
collapse, 207
Islam, 205–206
New Fez, 206
wars, 206
Masinissa, 228–229
Mauch, Karl, 106
Mauritania, 96, 99, 192
Mbam, 150
Mbam River, 32–33
Mbandi, Ngola, 219
Mbengkas, 150
Mbesinaku, 151
Mbikwana, 309–310
Mbombouo, 34
Mbueni, 150
Meadows of Gold and Mines of Gems,
The, 99
Mecca, 39, 87, 191, 260
Medina, 58
Meffre, Philip Jose, 129
Mego, Ina, 254
Mejang, 150
Menelik I, 4, 79
Menes, 72–73
Mentuhotep II, 163
Merkurius, 222
Meröe, 3–4, 63, **207–212**
archaeological studies, 207–211
destruction, 211, 220–221
location, 207–208
natural resources, 208
pyramids, 208, 210,
Rome, 210–211
Temple M250, 209
trade, 208, 211
Metropolitan Museum of Art, 161
Micipsa, 229
Middle Congo, 181
Middle Senegal Valley, 263
Mills, John Evans Atta, 83
Mmen, 149
Mohlomi, 174
Mohlomi Memorial Lecture series, 173

Mongols, 90
Mono River, 8, 53
Moore, Graham, 307
Morija Arts and Cultural Festival, 173
Morija Museum and Archives, 173
Moroccan Army, 267
Morocco, 10, 87, 89, 206
Moshoeshoe, 174–176
Mosisili, Pakalitha, 176
Mount Elgon, 44–45
Mount Rwenzori, 17
Mousa Ali Mountains, 3
Mozambique, 212, 291
Mozambique Islands, 205
Mpologoma River, 44
Mpororo, 18
Msiri, 184
Mswati, 291
Mthethwa Confederacy, 290
Mubarak, Hosni, 72
Muhammad, Askia, 267, 288
Muhima, Nabongo, 271
Mukama, 44
Mukulu, Nkongolo, 181–182
Mulai Idris, 88
Muloki, Henry Wako, 47
Mumia, Peter, 273
Museum of Civilization, 112
Museveni, Yoweri, 20, 40, 47, 148,
251
Muslim Brotherhood, 72
Musu, Ola, 254
Mutapa, 204, **212–213**
Butwa, 213
Christianity, 212
gold, 212
location, 212
origins, 212
Portuguese, 212–213
Rozvis, 213
Shona, 212
trade, 212–213
Zvongombe, 212
Mutesa II, 43
Mutota, Nyatsimba, 212
Muzgu, 31
Muzura, 203–204
My Neighbor, My Killer, 249
Mzilikazi, 291

Naddi, Muhammad, 266
Nagoundere, 2
Nananom Mpow shrine, 84, 198
Nanda, 196
Nandi, 290
Nandong, 149
Napata, **215–217**
  architecture, 215–216
  Assyrians, 217
  Egyptian, 215–217
  Kushites, 215
  location, 215
Nar, Sinn, 91
National Council of Nigeria and the
  Cameroons, 121, 167, 245
National Union for Total Independence
  (UNITA), 219
National Museum (Khartoum), 209
National Resistance Army, 20, 40,
  47, 251
Native Affairs Bills, 292
Native Authorities, 152
Navarre, 11
Nayil, Dakin B., 91
Nchare, 33
Ndadaye, Melchior, 251
Ndi, John Fru, 34
Ndongo, **217–220**
  agriculture, 218
  government, 218
  location, 217–218
  Mbundus, 217
  Nationalist movements, 219
  Ngola dynasty, 218–219
  Portuguese, 218–219
  slave trade, 219
  topography, 217–218
Ndop Plain, 149
Nero, 211
Netya, Kweyu, 272–273
Netya, Osundwa, 272
Netya, Wabala, 272
Netya, Wamukoya, 272
New York Times, 162
Ngaoundere region, 33
Ngombe, Kumwimbe, 183
Niger Coast Protectorate, 36, 129
Niger Delta, xix
Niger Expedition, 118

Niger River, 265
Nigeria, xvi, xx, 2, 34, 37–38, 109, 113,
  127, 139, 237, 253
  Anambra State, 224
  British, 39, 129
  coup, 231
  Eastern Region, 23
  flag, 113
  government, 42
  Ibadan, 113–114, 121
  Ijo, xix
  Ilesa, 126
  Kaduna State, 222
  Lagos, 27, 39, 167
  Ogbomoso, 231
  Ogun State, 67
  Osun State, 121, 126
  slave trade, 27
  Western House of Assembly, 75
Nigerian Conservation Foundation, 75
Nigerian National Democratic Party
  (NNDC), 167, 231
Nigerian Union of Teachers, 21
Nigerian Youth Movement, 75, 121, 231
Nile River, 3, 5, 72, 91, 139, 215, 220
  Blue Nile, 15, 63, 90, 208, 217
  Victorian, 44
  White Nile, 15, 63, 90, 208, 217
Nile Valley, 15, 63, 65, 72–73, 90, 139, 163,
  220–221
Nimi, Lukeni Lua, 156–157
Njoya, Adamou Ndam, 34
Njoya, Ibrahim, 33
Njoya, Ibrahim Mbombo, 33–34
Nkisi N'Kondi/Mangaaka, 157
Nkusu, Mulumba, 161
Nkuwu, Nzinga, 158
Nkyiraas, 59–60
Nlado of Kemta, 71
Nnachi, Oke, 22
Nobadia, 63, **220–222**
  agriculture, 220
  Christianity, 221
  decline of, 221–222
  economy, 221
  Egyptians, 221
  origins, 221
  topography, 220
Nogbaisi, Oba Ovonramwen, 35

Nok, **222–224**
  archeological studies, 222–223
  climate, 222
  metalwork, 223
  pottery, 223–224
Nokoue lagoon, 7
Nouakchott, 99
Noun Department, 32, 34
Nri, **224–228**
  British, 225
  Christianity, 227
  economy, 225–226
  festivals, 227
  government, 225
  Igbo, 224–225, 227
  Nri clan, 225
  origins, 225
  population, 224
  precolonial, 224–225
  trade, 226
  traditional religion, 225–227
Nri Progress Union (NPU), 227
Nsamba, Jackson Kasozi, 147
Nso, 149
Ntaryamira, Cyprien, 251
Nubia, 15, 63, 72–73, 139, 220
  Abuja, 222
  archaeological studies, 63
  Egyptian occupation, 215–216
  gold mines, 73
  government, 64
  location, 215
  Lower, 63, 215
  Napata, 207, 217
  trade, 217
Numidia, **228–230**
  Berbers, 228
  location, 228
  Massylii, 228
  trade, 228
Nupe, 128
Nyamhandi, 213
Nzinga, 219
Nzinga, Afonso Mvemba a, 158

Obanita, 118–119
Obasanjo, Olusegun, 71, 224
Oboli, Onoja, 225
Obote, Milton, 20, 40, 47, 148, 251

Obrumankoma, 198
Odapagyan, 198
Odinani Museum, 227–228
Odu, 237
Odùduwà, 68, 238
Odumase, 62
Odutola, Adeola, 119, 121
Odwira, 26, 112
Oezalces, 228
Offin River, 60
Ofuten, 76
Ogbomoso, **231–234**
  army, 232
  British, 233
  Fulani, 232
  Islam, 233
  origins, 231–233
  Soun dynasty, 231–233
  Yoruba, 232
Ogboni Secret Society, 70
Ogedengbe, 128–129
Ogun, 122, 126
Ogunmola, Basorun, xxi
Ogunmude, 76
Ohori, **234–236**
  climate, 234–235
  Ohori-Ije, 234, 236
  oral tradition, 235–236
  origins, 235–236
  population, 234–236
  slave trade, 236
Ohunsile, 232
Ojude Oba, 121
Oke-Araromi, 123
Oke-Elerin, 232
Oke-Ijugbe, 123
Okemesi, 128
Oke M'ogun, 122
Oke-Obagbile, 123
Oke-Onigbin, 123
Oke-Ora, 123
Oke-Owu, 123
Oke-Pao, 123
Oko, 149
Okoliko, 117
Olofin, Oduduwa, 127
Olojo, 122
Olduvai Gorge, xv
Olowo, 118

Olu-Iwa, 119
Olubuse, Ooni Okunade Sijuwade II, 122
Olufowobi, 76
Olumo Rock, 67
Olympiodorus, 221
Omani Sultanate, 146
Omo Owa Obokun, 127
Omonide, 68
Ondo, 126, **236–241**
    British, 240–241
    festivals, 240
    gender roles, 239
    government, 237–240
    location, 237
    Oke Augwa quarter, 240
    Ondo City, 236–237
    origins, 236, 238
    Osemawe dynasty, 238–239
    population, 236–237
    social structure, 238–239
    traditional religion, 239–240
    Yoruba, 237–238
Onyeso, Eze Nri Ènweleána II Obidiegwu,
    224, 227
Oramfe, 239
Orange Free State, 175
Orange River Sovereignty, 175
Oraralada, Fabunmi, 128
Order of the Federal Republic of Nigeria,
    224
Ordinary Man, An, 249
Orile Egba, 68
Orun Oba Ado site, 123
Osanyin, 239
Osborn, Emily Lynn, xviii
Oshiomole, Adams, 37
Oshogbo, 126
Osim, 22
Osono, 198
Osun River, 126
Ouagadougou, **241–244**
    Christianity, 242
    Dagomba, 241
    French, 242–243
    location, 241
    Mossis, 241–242
    topography, 241–242
    traditional religion, 242
Ouali, 193

Oubri, 241
Oudney, Walter, 307
Ouémé River, 187, 253
Ouida, 187
Ousanas, 5
Owen Falls Dam, 46
Owena River, 126
Owo, 125
Owu War, 70
Oyo (Old Oyo), xvii, 7, 28, 53, 55, 68–69,
    113–115, 125, 128, 188, 231–232,
    239–240, **244–247**
    collapse, 233, 246–247
    crisis of 1954, 245
    economy, 246
    government, 245–246
    location, 244–245
    origins, 231
    slave trade, 246
    trade, 28
    traditional religion, 245
    Yoruba, 244
Oyan River, 253

Pacheco, Pereira, 124
Palace of Tunisian Presidents, 49
Panyin, Aha, 60
Panyin, Ahi, 60
Panyin, Annin, 60
Panyin, Mumunumfi, 60
Paris Evangelical Missionary Society, 175
Parti Démocratique de Guinée, 95
Periplus of the Erythaean Sea, 4
Petronius, Gaius, 210–211
Philips, Charles, 129
Piye, 163, 216
Plasket, Richard, 307
Pobé, 234
Poka, 76
*Political Economy of British Western
    Africa*, 86
Pompey, 229
Pongola River, 289
Popo, 53
Popular Liberation Movement of Angola
    (MPLA), 219
Porto Novo, 8, 169
Power, Manley, 307
Prempeh, Agyeman, 25

Prempeh, Asantehene Agyeman, 25
Prempeh, Otumfuo Baba I, 24
Presbyterian Church Bu, 172
Ptolemy, 4, 229
Pulaar, 34
Pupupu, 238–239

Qataban, 4
Qustul, 221

Rabah, 38–39
Rabis, War Jabi ibn, 263–264
Radio Television Libre Mille-Collines, 251
Ramepe, 76
Randall-MacIve, David, 106
Ransome-Kuti, Funmilayo, 71
Rassemblement Démocratique Africain, 95
Re, 74
Red Sea, 3–4, 6
Reisner, George, 141, 163, 209
Republic of Uganda, 17, 147
   independence, 20
   constitution, 20
Retief, Piet, 291
Rhodesia, 106, 186
Rice University, 143
Rift Valley, 17
Roger II of Sicily, 101
Roman Empire, 49–50, 228–229
   collapse of, 50
Roots, 194
Rosetta Stone, 74
Royal Niger Company, 118, 129
Royal Sound, 237
Ruanda-Urundi, 250
Ruhanga, 19
Rukidi, Isingoma Mpuga I, 148
Rumfa, Sarkin Mohammed, 134–135
Rwanda, 17–18, 147, **249–252**
   archaeological studies, 249–250
   Bantus, 249–250
   Belgians, 250–251
   Civil War, 251
   genocide, 20, 249, 251–252
   Germans, 250
   HIV/AIDS, 252
   Hutu, 250, 251
   independence, 250–251
   location, 249
   natural resources, 249
   refugees, 251–252
   social structure, 250
   Tutsi, 250–251
   Twas, 250
Rwanda Armed Forces (FAR), 251–252
Rwandese Patriotic Front (RPF), 251
Rx Bandits, 249

Sabé, **253–255**
   Amusus, 253
   government, 254
   location, 253
   origins, 254
   raids, 255
   trade, 253
Sadat, Anwar, 72
Sagbarafa, Oloja, 76
Sagranti War, 25
Saint-Domingue, 9
Saladin, 64
Sallah, 121
Sanda, Umaru, 2
Sango, 245
Sanhaja Confederation, 13
Sanje ya Kati, 142
Sankara, Thomas, 244
Sankore Mosque, 266
Sankre, 196
Sapara-Williams, Christopher Alexander, 129
Sarbah, Mensah, 199
Sasha River, 126
School of Oriental and African Studies, 83
Scipio, 228–229
Second Punic War, 228–229
Sefuwa, xviii
Sekenenre, 73
Seko, Mobutu Sese, 162
Sekyi, Kobina, 199
Selassie, Haile, 80
Select Committee report of 1865, 198,
Selene, Cleopatra, 229
Senegal, 96, 192, 279, 282–284
Senegal River, 96
Senufo, 156
Senzangakona, 290
Seychelles Islands, 24–25
Seyindemi, Sabinah Otobajo Odutola, 119

Seyindemi, Sanni Odutola, 119
Shaka, 289–292, 309–311
Shake Hands with the Devil, 249
Shambaa, **255–256**
    location, 255
    trade, 256
    Vugha, 255–256
Shashe River, 199
Shata, Mamman, 136
Sheppard, William Henry, 162
Shinnie, Peter, 15, 209
Shire River, 203
Shire Valley, 203
Shooting Dogs, 249
Shullukh, Badi IV Aba, 91
Sierra Leone, 24–25, 85, 192, 307, 313
Sighiri, Mogho Naba, 242
Sikaykain, Amara Abu, 91
Smuts, Jan, 292
Sobhuza, 291
Social Democratic Front, 34
Sofola, 295–296
Sokoto, **256–259**, 311–313
    agriculture, 256–257
    British, 258
    18th century, 257
    Islam, 258, 312–313
Sokoto Caliphate, xx, 1, 38–39, 256–258,
    269
Solomon, 4, 6
Somalia, 3, 72, 143
Sometimes in April, 249
Songhai, **259–261**, 287–288
    Berbers, 260
    camels, 259–260
    history, 99
    location, 259
    trade, 259–260
Songo Mnara, 142, 146
    archaeological studies, 143
Sophonisba, 229
Soso, 190
Soun, 232–233
Sound Vibration, 237
South Africa, 172–173, 175, 199, 291
Southern Nigeria Protectorate, 129
Sowdoweah, Belgassam Wilde, 308
Soyinka, Akinwande Oluwole "Wole, "
    67, 71

Stanley, Henry Morton, 42
Star Wars, 220
Sterner, Judy, 195
Strait of Gibraltar, 87
Sudan, 3, 17, 65, 124, 140, 215
    Khartoum, 207, 209, 215, 217
    North, 57, 139, 220
Sufism, 97
Suleyman, Mansa, 191
Sundiata, 190
Swaziland, 291
Syphax, 228–229

Tado, 7–8, 53
Taharka, 163
Taifa states, 13
Takkaze River, 15
Takrur, 96, **263–264**
    archaeological studies, 263–264
    dynasties, 264
    Islam, 263–264
    location, 263
    oral tradition, 264
Tamia, Ama, 111
Tanzania, 145–147, 252
    archeological studies, xv
    Dar es Salaam, 142
Tarikh al-fattash, 100
Tarikh al-Sudan, 99
Tchahounka, 188
Te-Agdanlin, 8
Tegbesu, 55
Temple of Horus, 72
Templier, Guillame, 242
Tenga, 242
Tenguella, Koly, 264
Thabane, Motsoahae Thomas, 173
Tibo, Kwadwo, 62
Timbo, 93
Timbuktu, xv, 31, 99–100, 190–191, 260,
    265–268
    archaeological studies, 265–266
    Berbers, 265
    gold, 266
    Islam, 266–267
    location, 265, 287
    Mossis, 266, 287–288
    population, 265
    scholars, 267–268

trade, 265–267
Tuaregs, 266
Tip, Tippu, 184
Togo, 24, 53, 187
Tomb of Askia the Great, 260–261
Török, László, 209
Torwa, 212
Toucouler, **268–270**
army, 269
Bandiaga, 270
Dinguiray, 269
French, 270
Islam, 268
location, 268
Nioro, 270
origins, 269
Toure, Ali Ibrahim "Farke, " 265
Toure, Almami Samore, 111
Toure, Samori, 155
Tracey, Hugh, 185
Treaties of 1885, 181
Treaty of Versailles, 250
Tripoli, 39
Tshumbeiseng, 274
Tuaregs, 10, 13
Tukela River, 289
Tukuu, 274
Tunisia, 11, 49, 88, 206, 228
Tunjur dynasty, 57–58
Tutu, Osei, 23–24, 59
Twifo, 61

Uganda, 40–42, 47, 252
Uganda Land Commission, 20
Uganda People's Congress, 20, 47
Uganda Protectorate, 19, 43, 46
Uganda Railway, 46
Ulikolasi, Oba, 238
Ulli, Mansa, 190
Umar, al-Hajj, 268–270
Umar, Seku, 97
Umar, Sheku, 97
Umayyad dynasty, 87, 89
UNESCO
List of World Heritage in Danger, 146
Salvage Campaigns, 211
World Heritage Sites, 49, 88, 103, 106, 146, 200, 211
Union Démocratique dur Cameroun, 34

Unity Movement, 9
United Nations
Assistance for Rwanda (UNAMIR), 251
International Criminal Tribunal for Rwanda, 252
Security Council, 252
University College, Ibadan, 67
University of Ghana, Legon, 83
University of Ibadan, 167
University of Michigan, Ann Arbor, 51
University of York, 143
Unveiling Modernity in 20th Century West African Islamic Reforms, 288
Upper Volta, 154–156, 241–244
Bobo Dioulasso, 155–156
Ouagadougou, 156, 193
Usmanu Danfodiyo University, 257
Usumbora, 321–322
Uyi Arere, 126, 129

Verunga Volcanoes National Park, 249
Victoria Island, 167
Vikings, 13
Volta River, 187
Voltaic Democratic Union-African Democratic Rally, 243

Wadai, 30–32
Wadi Halfa, 220
Wagadu, 102
Wali, Jankee, 133
Wandala Empire, 108
Wanga, **271–273**
Christianity, 273
civil war, 273
Ekhatola, 272
Jo-Ugenya, 272–273
location, 271
Maasai, 272
Mukulu, 273
19th century, 273
population, 272
slave trade, 273
War of Kirina, 190
Wari, Muhammadu, 137
Warrington, Consul, 307
Wasa Amenfi, 61–62
Watara, Seku, 155
Wattasids, 206

Wazeba, 5
Wegbaja, 54
Weh *fondom*, **273–277**
  Aghem, 275
  British, 276
  Chamba, 274
  Christianity, 277
  Germans, 273, 276
  Kuk, 275
  location, 273–272
  Menchum division, 277
  origins, 273
  precolonial, 275–276
  quarters, 275
  raids, 274
  topography, 274
  trade, 275–276
  traditional religion, 276
  Zhoa, 274
Welsby, Derek, 15–16
Weme River, 53
Whydah (Ouidah), 7–8, 55, **277–280**
  decline, 278
  government, 279
  location, 277
  origins, 277–278
  slave trade, 278–280
Willett, Frank, 123
Wingate, Reginal, 208
Winnam, 242
Wobgho, Naaba I, 288
Wobogo, Mogho Naba, 242
Wolof (Jolof, Wollof, Ouolof), **280–285**
  agriculture, 281–282
  British, 284
  French, 284
  government, 281, 283
  Islam, 283–284
  location, 280
  origins, 281
  Portuguese, 282–283
  slave trade, 282, 284
  topography, 280
  trade, 281
World War I, 34, 39, 90, 209, 321
World War II, 112, 152
Woyengi, xix
Wynne-Jones, Stephanie, 143

Yaa Asantewaa War, 25
Yadega, Naaba, 287
Yai, 254
Yaji, Sarkin, 135
Yatenga, **287–288**
  decline, 288
  French, 288
  Islam, 287–288
  location, 287
  origins, 287
  Mossi, 287
  trade, 287
  wars, 287–288
Yathar, Yusuf Asar, 6
Yemen, 3
Yemeogo, Maurice, 243
Yolomfaogoma, 287
Yoruba, xvii, xxi, xxiii, 8, 27–29, 35,
    36, 67–71, 76, 113–129, 167, 187,
    231–238, 240–242, 244–246,
    253–255, 317
  Akoko, 129
  Akure, 36
  cosmology, 68
  Ekiti, 129
  identification marks, 129
  Ifá, xxiii
  Igbomina, 129
  Ijebu, xvii, 129
  Owoh, 36
  Oyo, 129
  religion, xxiii
Yoruba Wars, 70, 115, 128, 169–170,
    240
Yorubaland, 55, 70, 115–117, 123, 125,
    169, 231–233, 237, 240
  British, 247
  Christianity, 28
Yuh, 151
Yusa, Sarkin, 134
Yusuf, Abu, 206

Zambia, 212, 291
Zanzibar, 146
Zazzau, xviii
Zenaga, 13
Zenata tribes, 13
Zimbabwe, 199, 201, 212

Zimui River, 256
Zou River, 53
Zulu, **289–293**
    British, 289, 292
    Isandhlwana, 289
    location, 289
    Mfecane, 289
    Ndebele, 291
    religion, xxiii
    Rorke's Drift, 289
    Zulu, 289, 292
Zwide, 290